Zits® en Concert

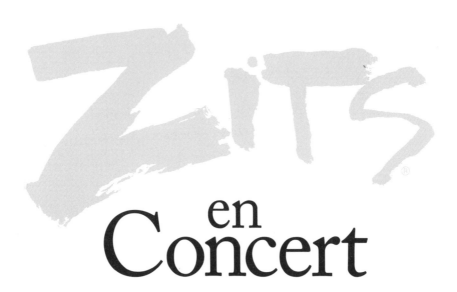

Also By Jerry Scott and Jim Borgman

Zits: Sketchbook 1
Growth Spurt: Zits Sketchbook 2
Don't Roll Your Eyes at Me, Young Man!: Zits Sketchbook 3
Are We an "Us"?: Zits Sketchbook 4
Zits Unzipped: Zits Sketchbook 5
Busted!: Zits Sketchbook 6
Road Trip: Zits Sketchbook 7
Teenage Tales: Zits Sketchbook No. 8
Thrashed: Zits Sketchbook No. 9
Pimp My Lunch: Zits Sketchbook No. 10
Are We Out of the Driveway Yet?: Zits Sketchbook No. 11
Rude, Crude, and Tattooed: Zits Sketchbook No. 12
Jeremy and Mom
Pierced
Lust and Other Uses for Spare Hormones
Jeremy & Dad
You're Making That Face Again
Drive!

Treasuries

Humongous Zits
Big Honkin' Zits
Zits: Supersized
Random Zits
Crack of Noon
Alternative Zits
My Bad
Sunday Brunch
Triple Shot, Double Pump, No Whip Zits

Gift Book

A Zits Guide to Living with Your Teenager

Zits®

en Concert

A ZITS® Treasury by Jerry Scott and Jim Borgman

Andrews McMeel
Publishing, LLC
Kansas City • Sydney • London

Zits® is syndicated internationally by King Features Syndicate, Inc.
For information, write King Features Syndicate, Inc.,
300 West Fifty-Seventh Street, New York, New York 10019.

Andrews McMeel Publishing, LLC
an Andrews McMeel Universal company
1130 Walnut Street, Kansas City, Missouri 64106
www.andrewsmcmeel.com

13 14 15 16 17 SDB 10 9 8 7 6 5 4 3 2 1

ISBN: 978-1-4494-3057-3

Library of Congress Control Number: 2013936559

ATTENTION: SCHOOLS AND BUSINESSES
Andrews McMeel books are available at quantity discounts with bulk purchase for educational,
business, or sales promotional use. For information, please e-mail the Andrews McMeel
Publishing Special Sales Department: specialsales@amuniversal.com

zitscomics.com • facebook.com/zitscomics • twitter.com/therealzits • rockgod99.tumblr.com

To Monkey Pants, for your under-the-covers flashlight-reading pleasure.
—JS

For Anna Banana and Sputnik, my unfiltered sunshine.
—JB

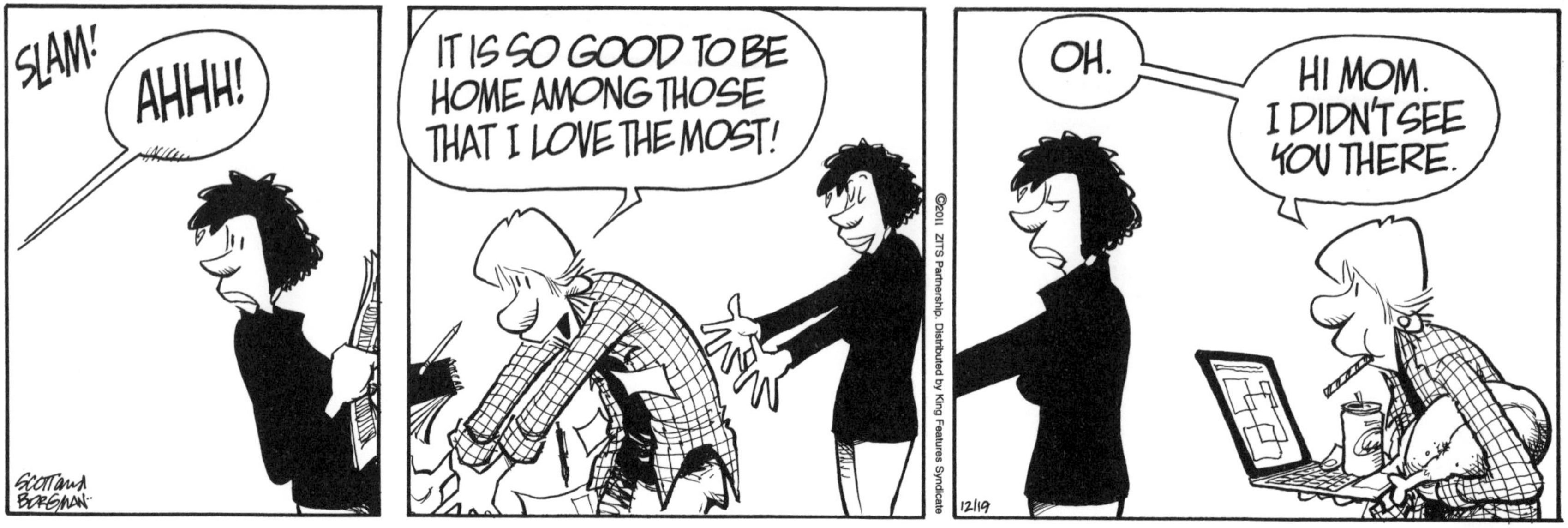
SLAM!
AHHH!
SCOTT and BORGMAN
IT IS SO GOOD TO BE HOME AMONG THOSE THAT I LOVE THE MOST!
©2011 ZITS Partnership. Distributed by King Features Syndicate
12/19
OH.
HI MOM. I DIDN'T SEE YOU THERE.

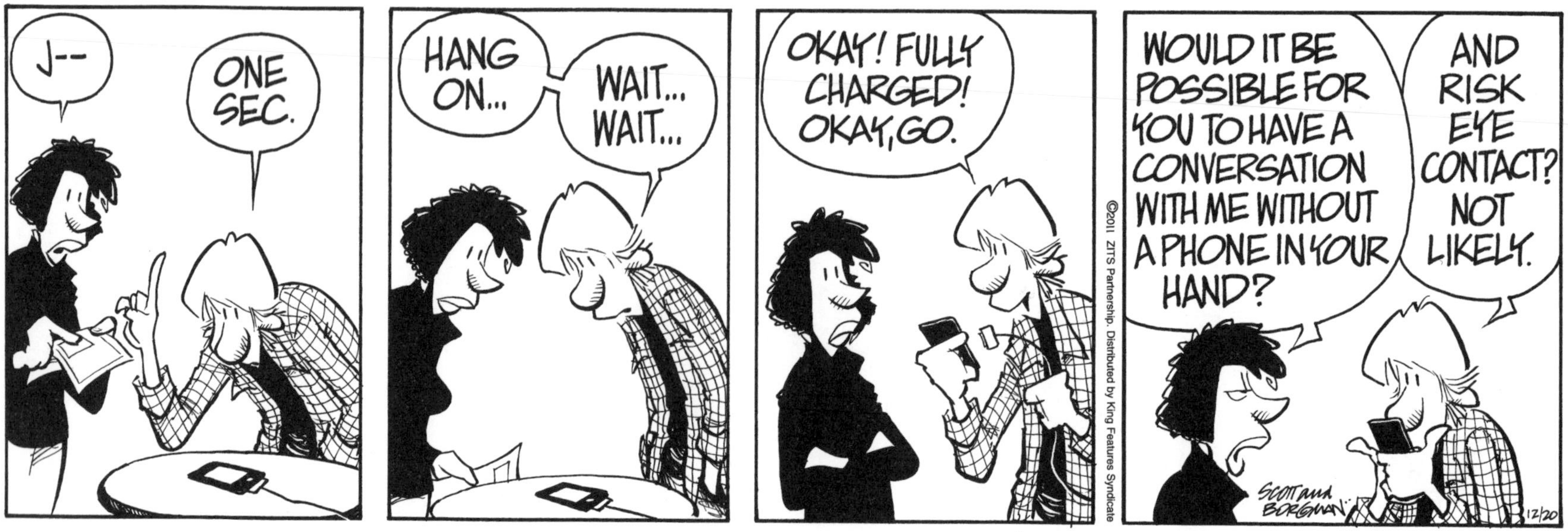
J--
ONE SEC.
HANG ON...
WAIT... WAIT...
OKAY! FULLY CHARGED! OKAY, GO.
©2011 ZITS Partnership. Distributed by King Features Syndicate
WOULD IT BE POSSIBLE FOR YOU TO HAVE A CONVERSATION WITH ME WITHOUT A PHONE IN YOUR HAND?
AND RISK EYE CONTACT? NOT LIKELY.
SCOTT and BORGMAN
12/20

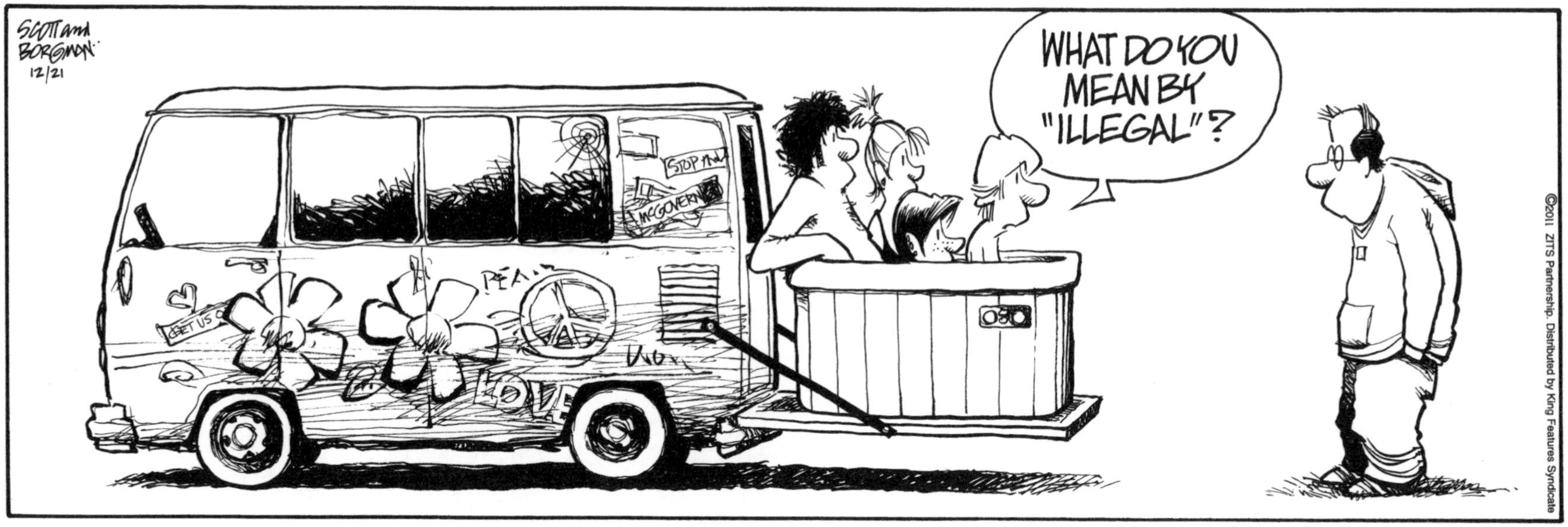
SCOTT and BORGMAN 12/21
WHAT DO YOU MEAN BY "ILLEGAL"?
©2011 ZITS Partnership. Distributed by King Features Syndicate

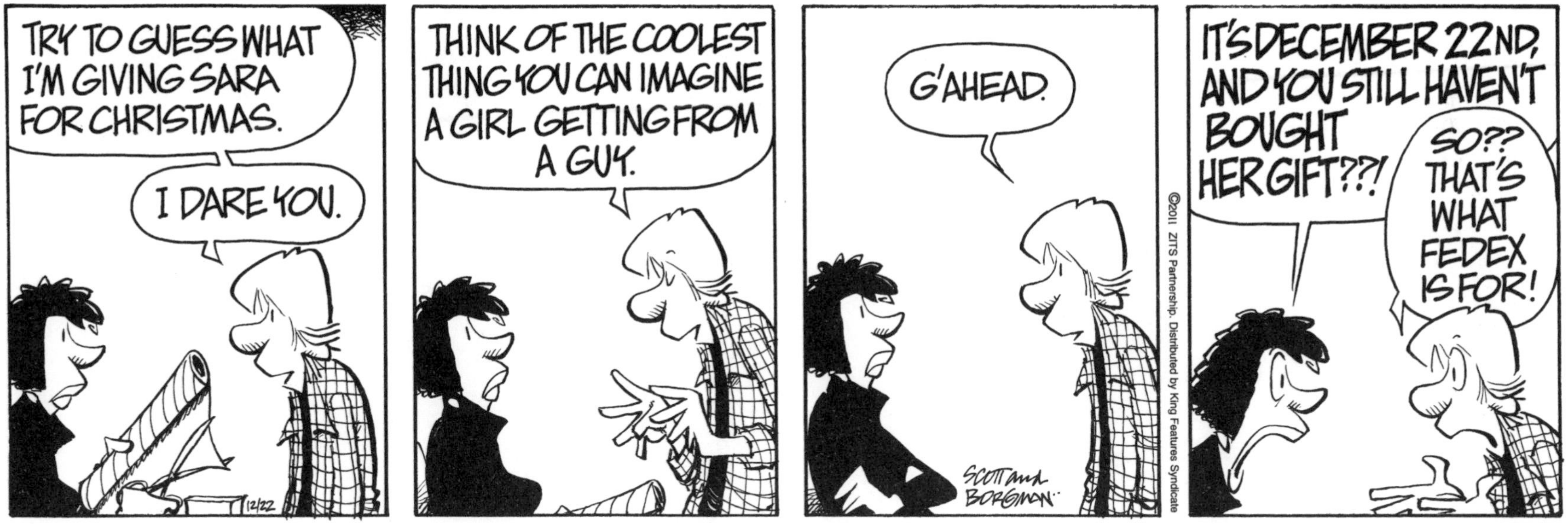
TRY TO GUESS WHAT I'M GIVING SARA FOR CHRISTMAS.
I DARE YOU.
12/22
THINK OF THE COOLEST THING YOU CAN IMAGINE A GIRL GETTING FROM A GUY.
G'AHEAD.
SCOTT and BORGMAN
©2011 ZITS Partnership. Distributed by King Features Syndicate
IT'S DECEMBER 22ND, AND YOU STILL HAVEN'T BOUGHT HER GIFT??!
SO?? THAT'S WHAT FEDEX IS FOR!

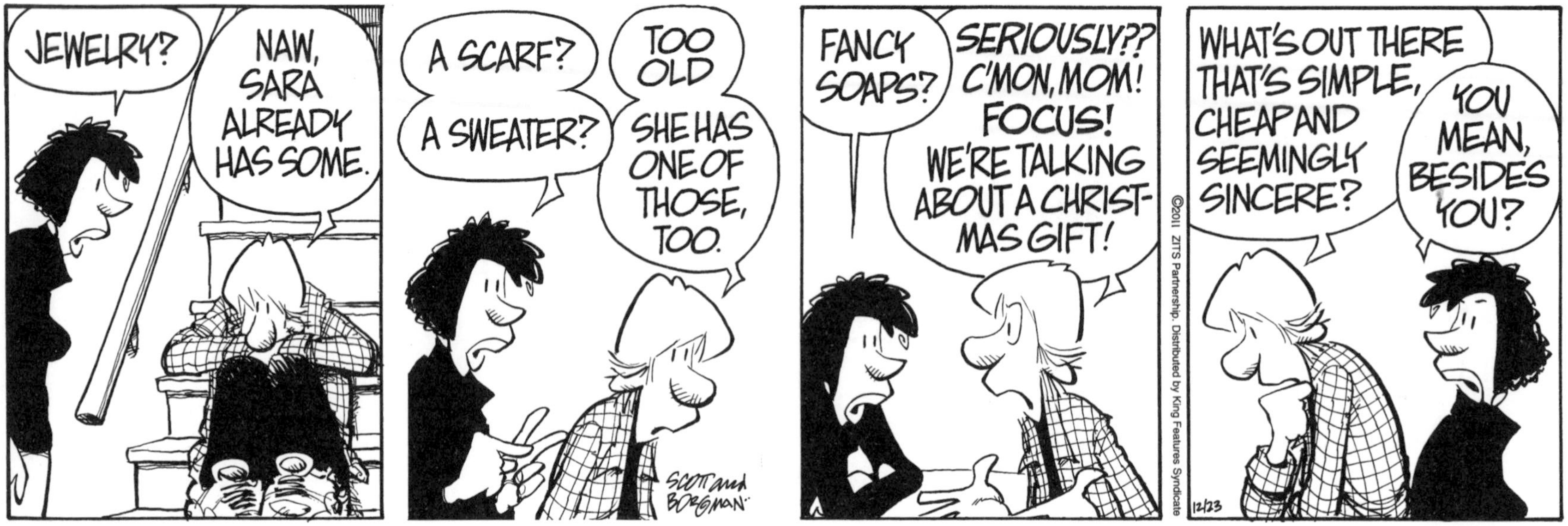
JEWELRY?
NAW, SARA ALREADY HAS SOME.
A SCARF?
A SWEATER?
TOO OLD
SHE HAS ONE OF THOSE, TOO.
FANCY SOAPS?
SERIOUSLY?? C'MON, MOM! FOCUS! WE'RE TALKING ABOUT A CHRIST-MAS GIFT!
WHAT'S OUT THERE THAT'S SIMPLE, CHEAP AND SEEMINGLY SINCERE?
YOU MEAN, BESIDES YOU?
SCOTT and BORGMAN
©2011 ZITS Partnership. Distributed by King Features Syndicate
12/23

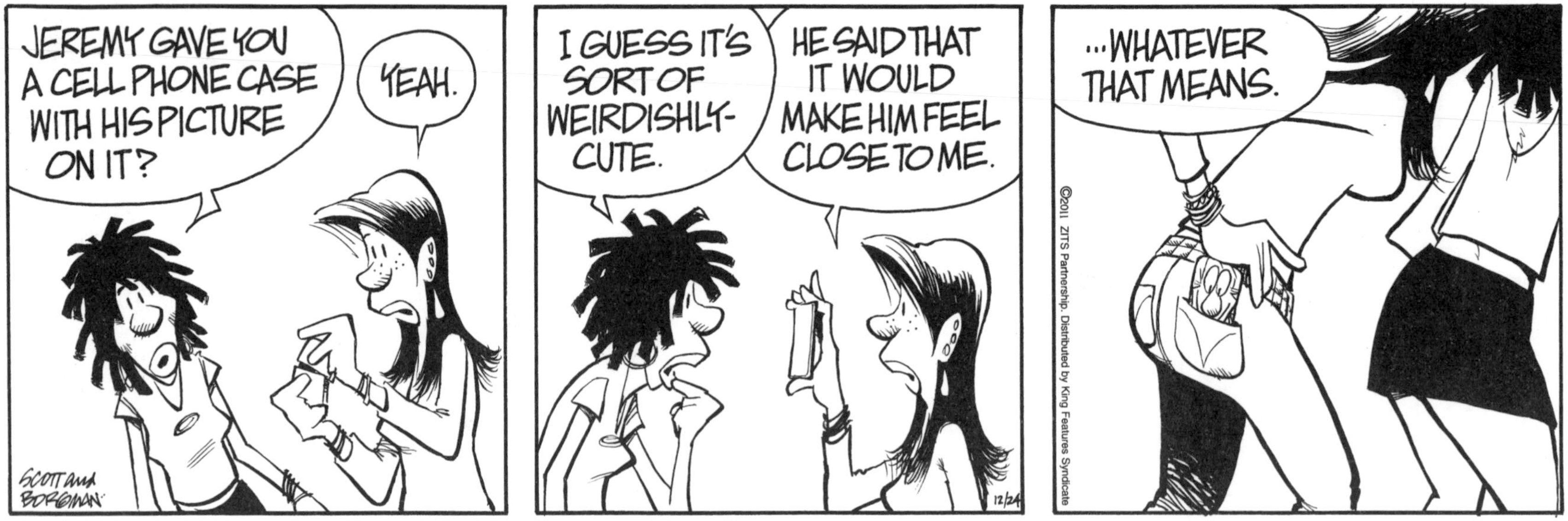
JEREMY GAVE YOU A CELL PHONE CASE WITH HIS PICTURE ON IT?
YEAH.
I GUESS IT'S SORT OF WEIRDISHLY-CUTE.
HE SAID THAT IT WOULD MAKE HIM FEEL CLOSE TO ME.
...WHATEVER THAT MEANS.
SCOTT and BORGMAN
12/24
©2011 ZITS Partnership. Distributed by King Features Syndicate

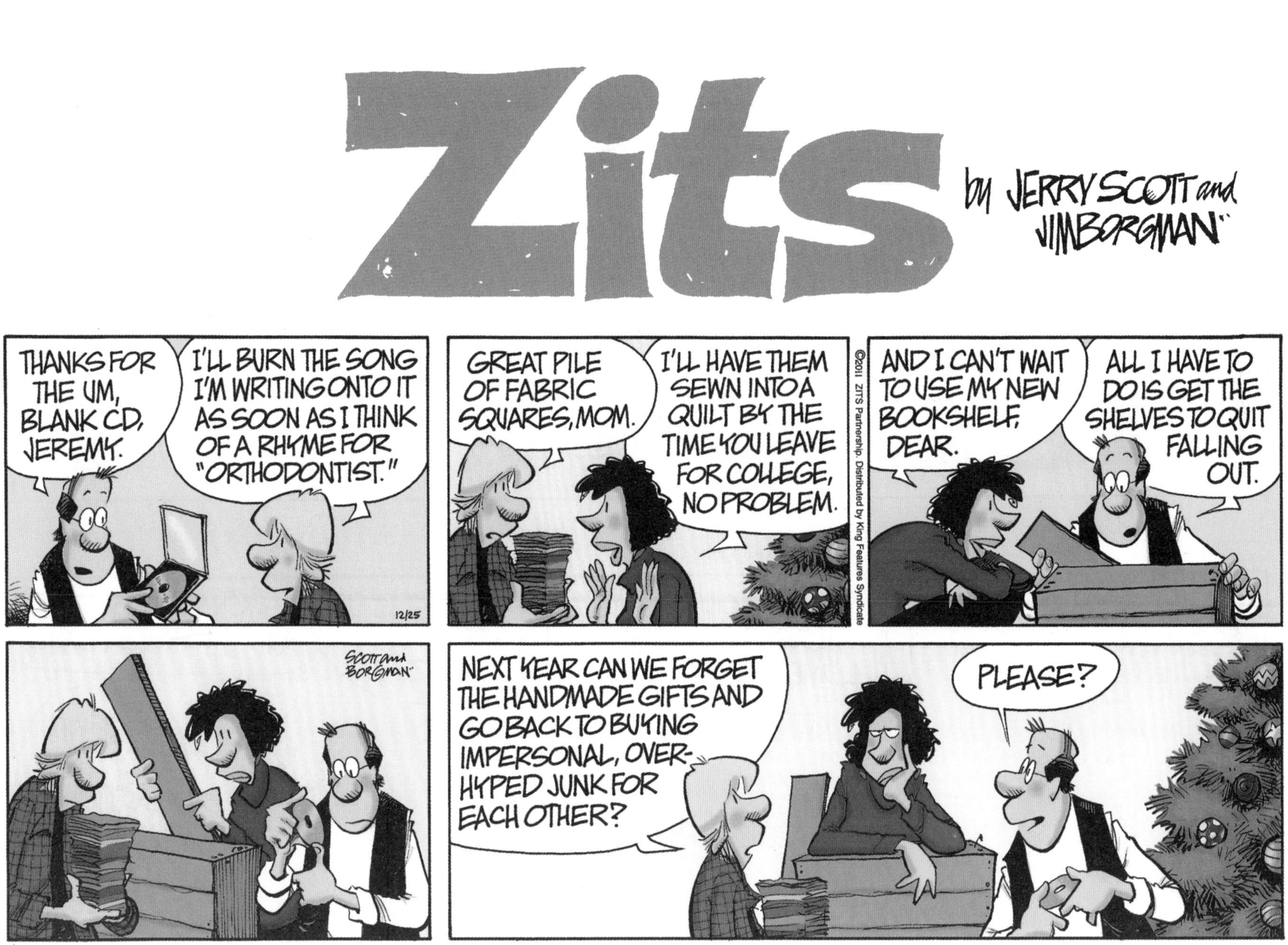
Zits
by JERRY SCOTT and JIM BORGMAN
THANKS FOR THE UM, BLANK CD, JEREMY.
I'LL BURN THE SONG I'M WRITING ONTO IT AS SOON AS I THINK OF A RHYME FOR "ORTHODONTIST."
12/25
GREAT PILE OF FABRIC SQUARES, MOM.
I'LL HAVE THEM SEWN INTO A QUILT BY THE TIME YOU LEAVE FOR COLLEGE, NO PROBLEM.
©2011 ZITS Partnership. Distributed by King Features Syndicate
AND I CAN'T WAIT TO USE MY NEW BOOKSHELF, DEAR.
ALL I HAVE TO DO IS GET THE SHELVES TO QUIT FALLING OUT.
SCOTT and BORGMAN
NEXT YEAR CAN WE FORGET THE HANDMADE GIFTS AND GO BACK TO BUYING IMPERSONAL, OVER-HYPED JUNK FOR EACH OTHER?
PLEASE?

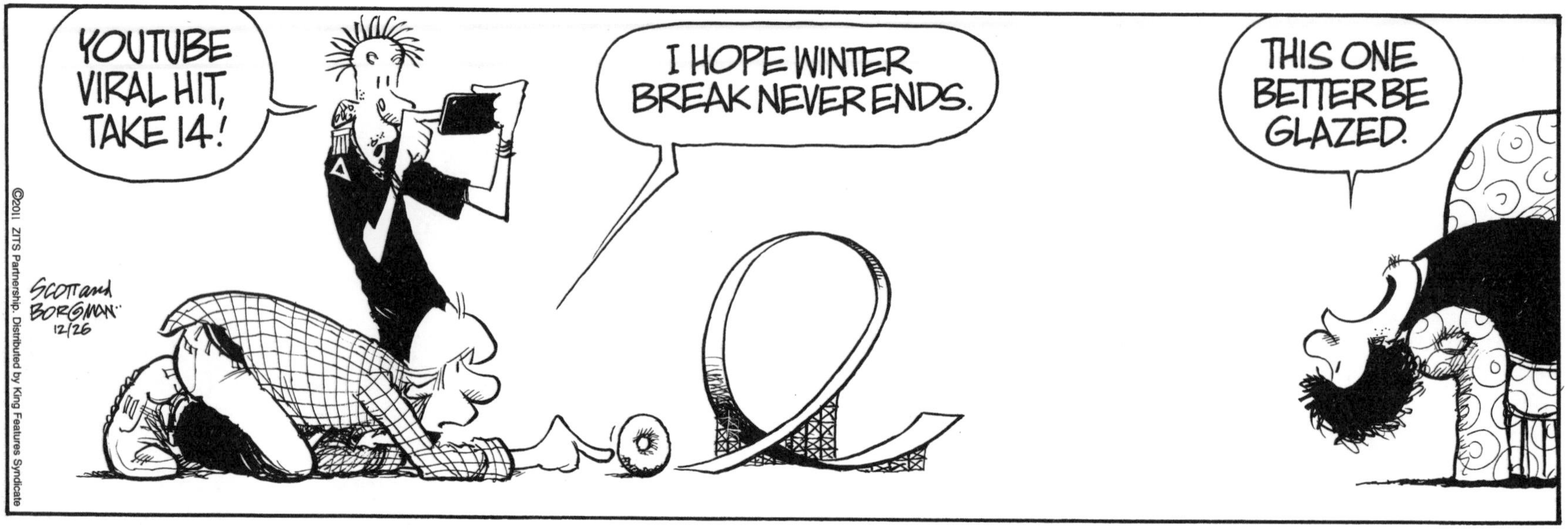
YOUTUBE VIRAL HIT, TAKE 14!
I HOPE WINTER BREAK NEVER ENDS.
THIS ONE BETTER BE GLAZED.
SCOTT and BORGMAN 12/26
©2011 ZITS Partnership. Distributed by King Features Syndicate

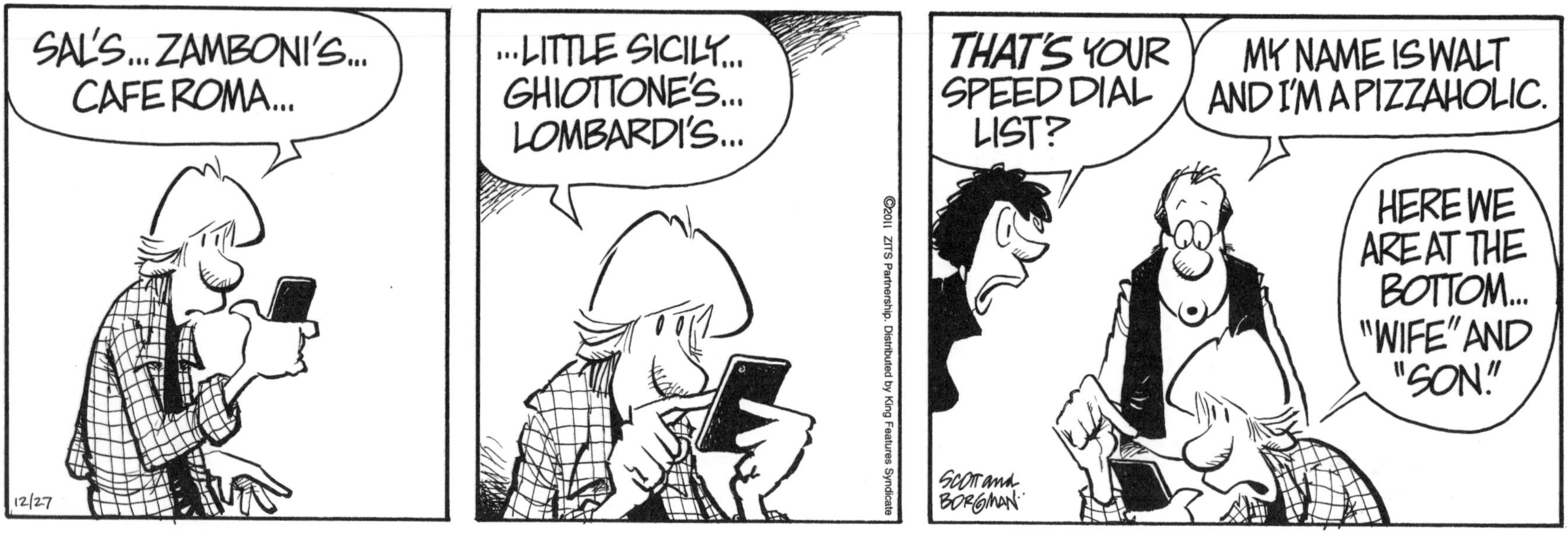
SAL'S... ZAMBONI'S... CAFE ROMA...
12/27
...LITTLE SICILY... GHIOTTONE'S... LOMBARDI'S...
©2011 ZITS Partnership. Distributed by King Features Syndicate
THAT'S YOUR SPEED DIAL LIST?
MY NAME IS WALT AND I'M A PIZZAHOLIC.
HERE WE ARE AT THE BOTTOM... "WIFE" AND "SON."
SCOTT and BORGMAN

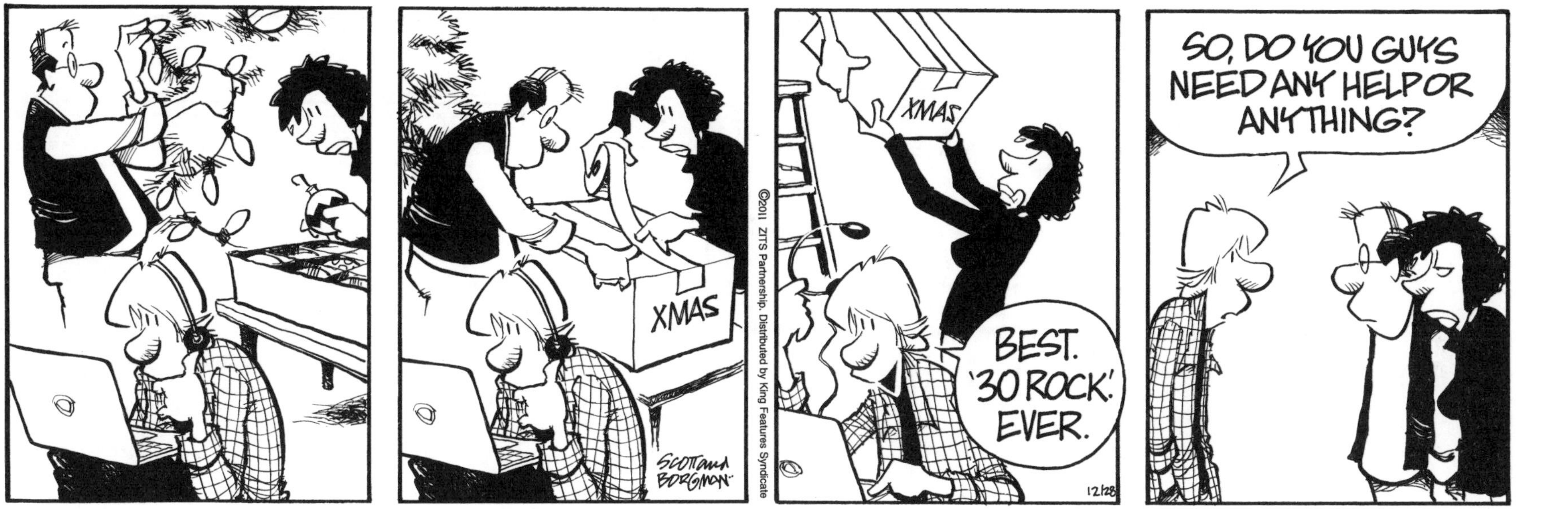
©2011 ZITS Partnership. Distributed by King Features Syndicate
XMAS
XMAS
SCOTT and BORGMAN
XMAS
BEST. '30 ROCK.' EVER.
12/28
SO, DO YOU GUYS NEED ANY HELP OR ANYTHING?

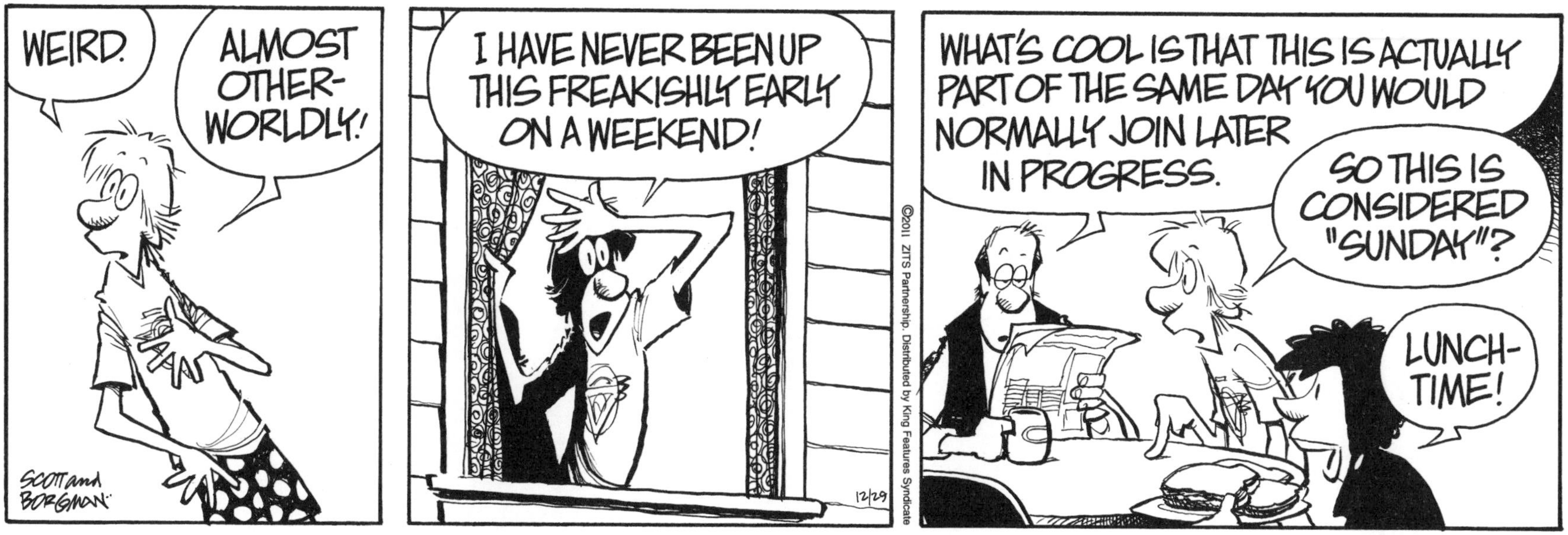
WEIRD.
ALMOST OTHER-WORLDLY!
SCOTT and BORGMAN
I HAVE NEVER BEEN UP THIS FREAKISHLY EARLY ON A WEEKEND!
12/29
©2011 ZITS Partnership. Distributed by King Features Syndicate
WHAT'S COOL IS THAT THIS IS ACTUALLY PART OF THE SAME DAY YOU WOULD NORMALLY JOIN LATER IN PROGRESS.
SO THIS IS CONSIDERED "SUNDAY"?
LUNCH-TIME!

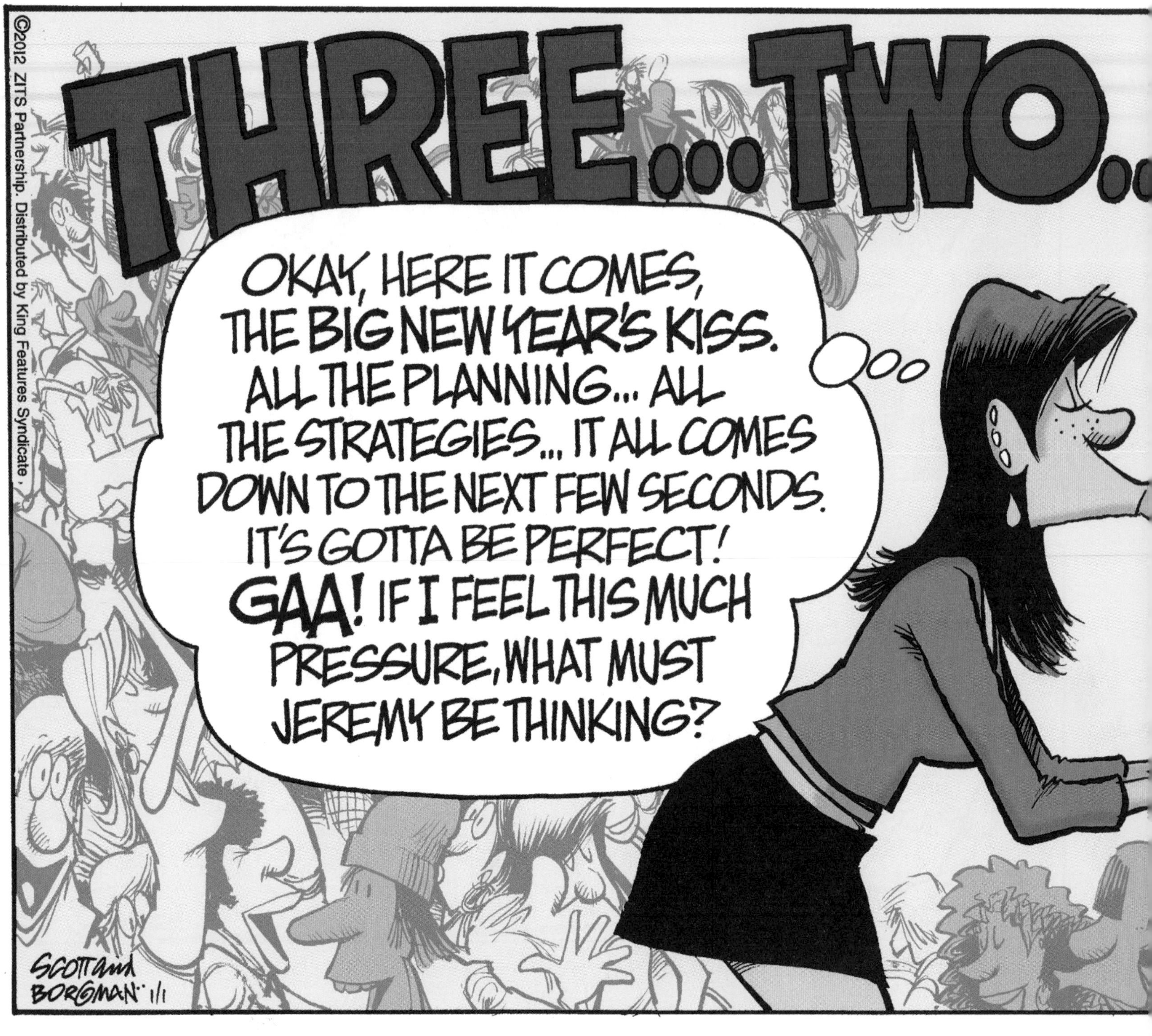
THREE... TWO...
OKAY, HERE IT COMES, THE BIG NEW YEAR'S KISS. ALL THE PLANNING... ALL THE STRATEGIES... IT ALL COMES DOWN TO THE NEXT FEW SECONDS. IT'S GOTTA BE PERFECT! GAA! IF I FEEL THIS MUCH PRESSURE, WHAT MUST JEREMY BE THINKING?
©2012 ZITS Partnership. Distributed by King Features Syndicate.
SCOTT and BORGMAN 1/1

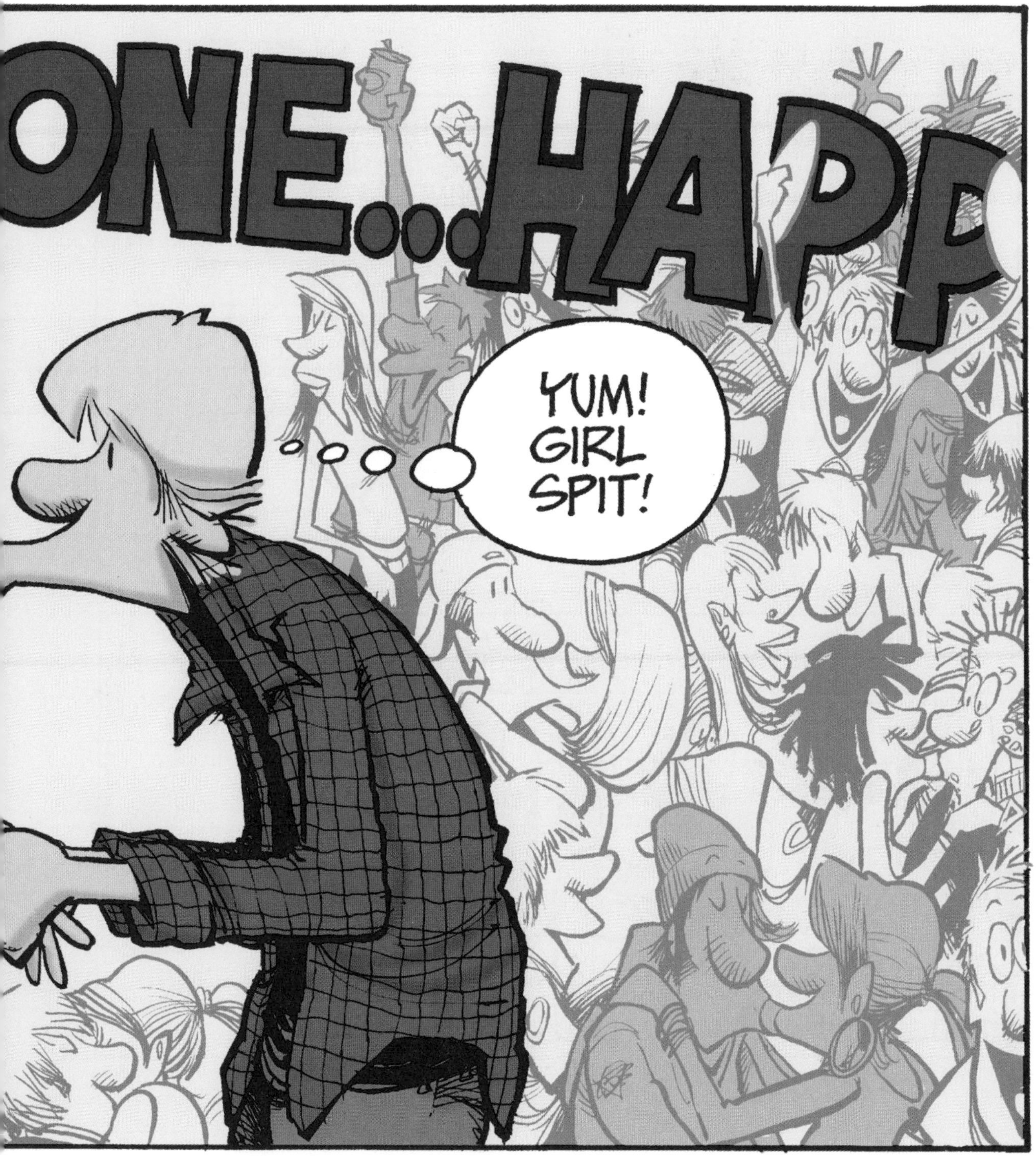
ONE...HAPP
YUM! GIRL SPIT!

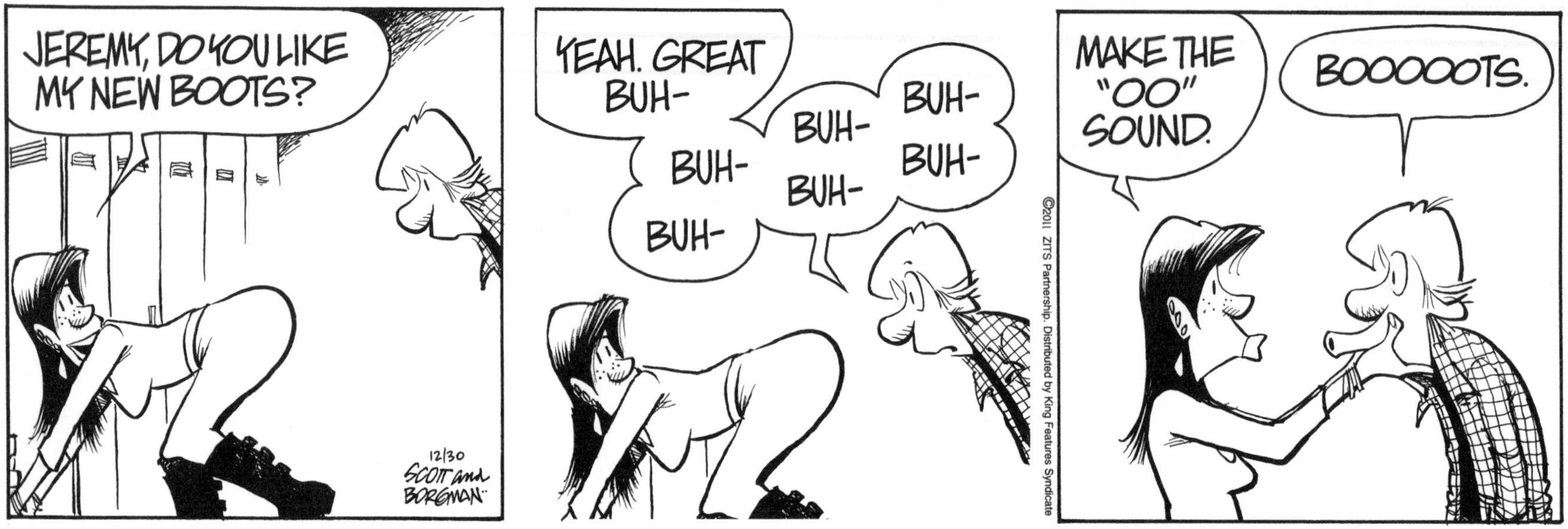
JEREMY, DO YOU LIKE MY NEW BOOTS?
12/30 SCOTT and BORGMAN
YEAH. GREAT BUH-
BUH-
BUH-
BUH-
BUH-
BUH-
BUH-
©2011 ZITS Partnership. Distributed by King Features Syndicate
MAKE THE "OO" SOUND.
BOOOOOOTS.

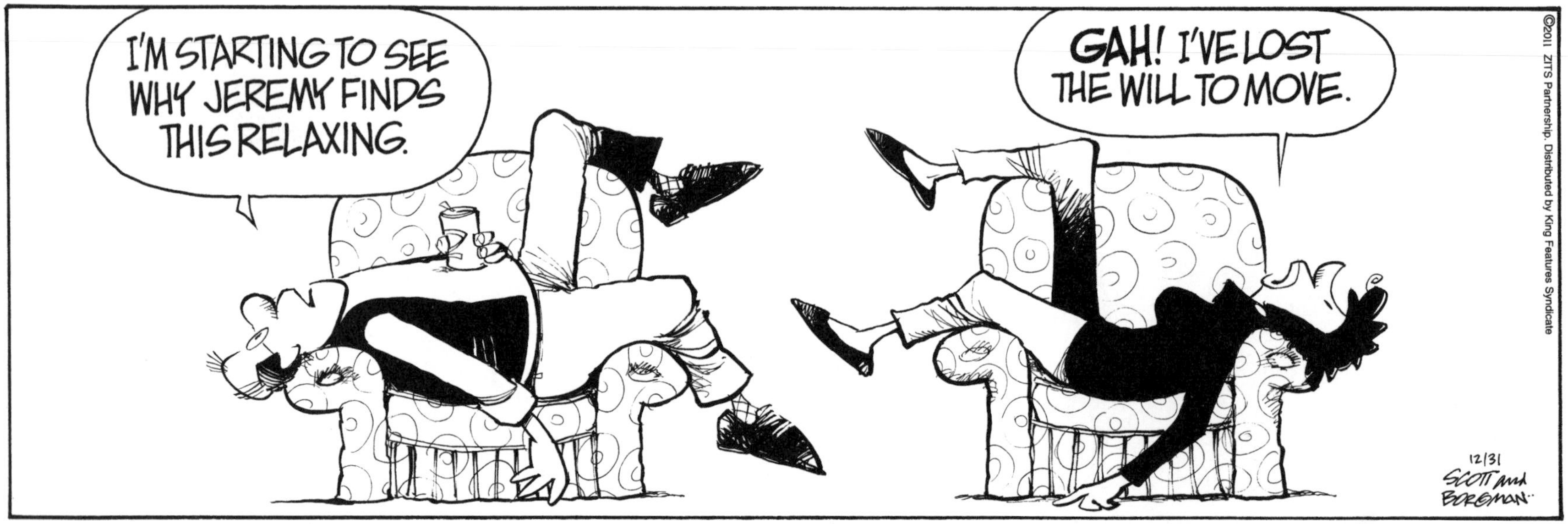
I'M STARTING TO SEE WHY JEREMY FINDS THIS RELAXING.
GAH! I'VE LOST THE WILL TO MOVE.
©2011 ZITS Partnership. Distributed by King Features Syndicate
12/31 SCOTT and BORGMAN

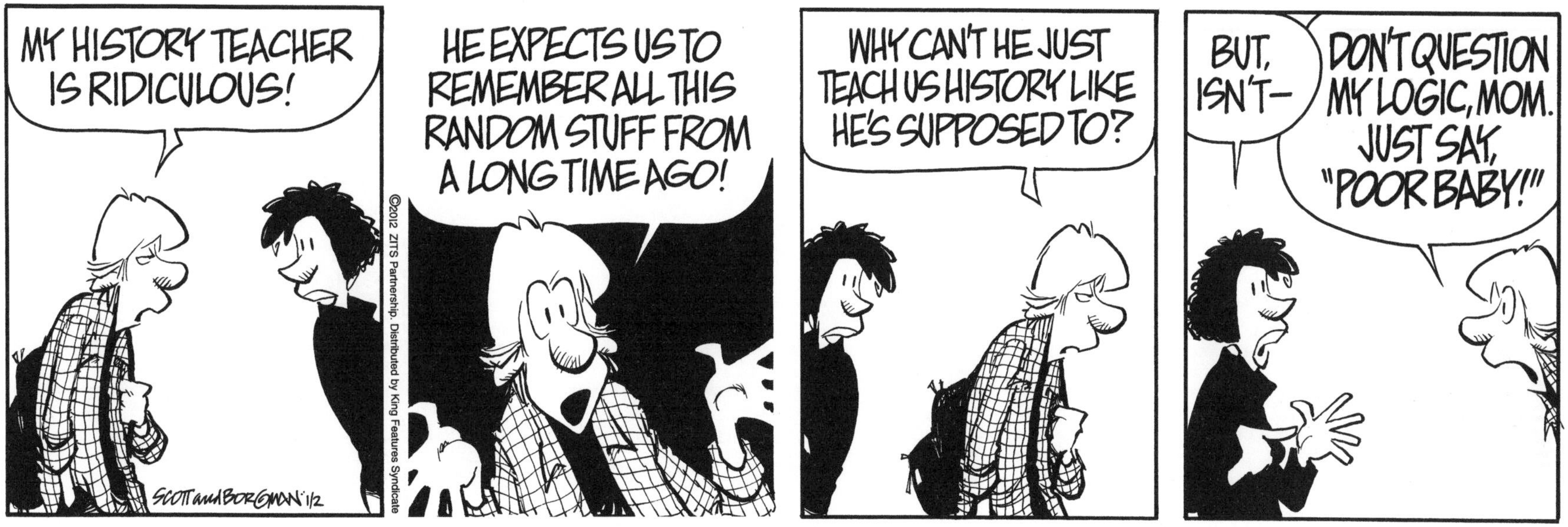
MY HISTORY TEACHER IS RIDICULOUS!
SCOTT and BORGMAN 1/2
©2012 ZITS Partnership. Distributed by King Features Syndicate
HE EXPECTS US TO REMEMBER ALL THIS RANDOM STUFF FROM A LONG TIME AGO!
WHY CAN'T HE JUST TEACH US HISTORY LIKE HE'S SUPPOSED TO?
BUT, ISN'T–
DON'T QUESTION MY LOGIC, MOM. JUST SAY, "POOR BABY!"

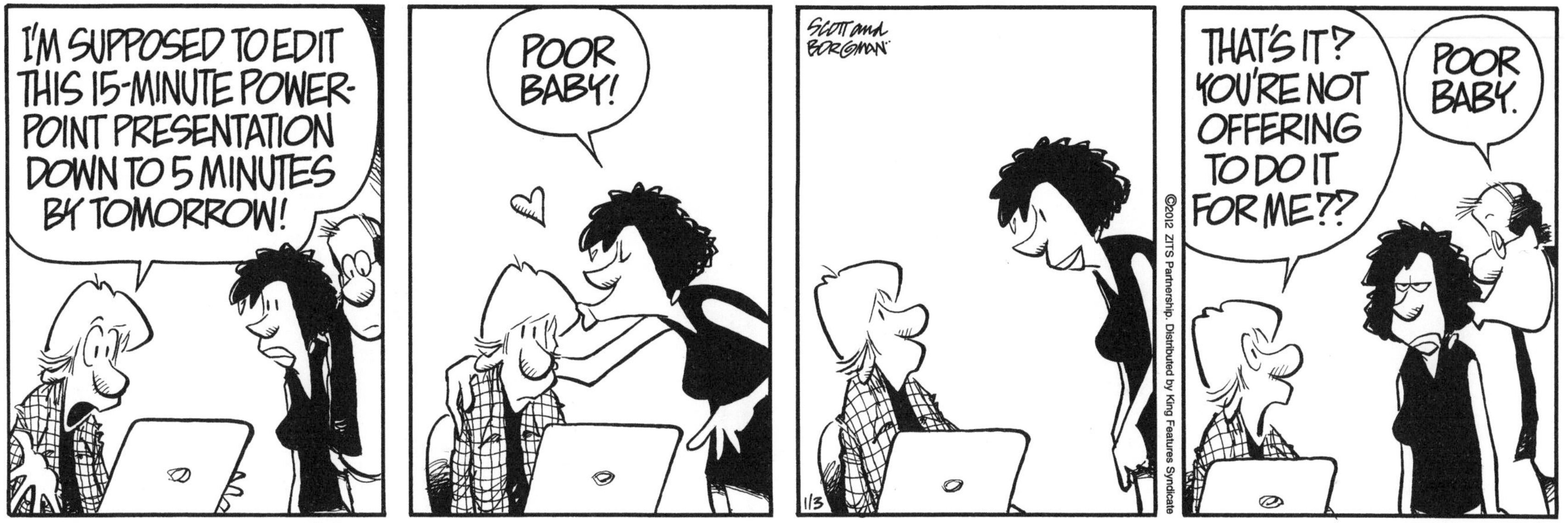
I'M SUPPOSED TO EDIT THIS 15-MINUTE POWER-POINT PRESENTATION DOWN TO 5 MINUTES BY TOMORROW!
POOR BABY!
SCOTT and BORGMAN
1/3
©2012 ZITS Partnership. Distributed by King Features Syndicate
THAT'S IT? YOU'RE NOT OFFERING TO DO IT FOR ME??
POOR BABY.

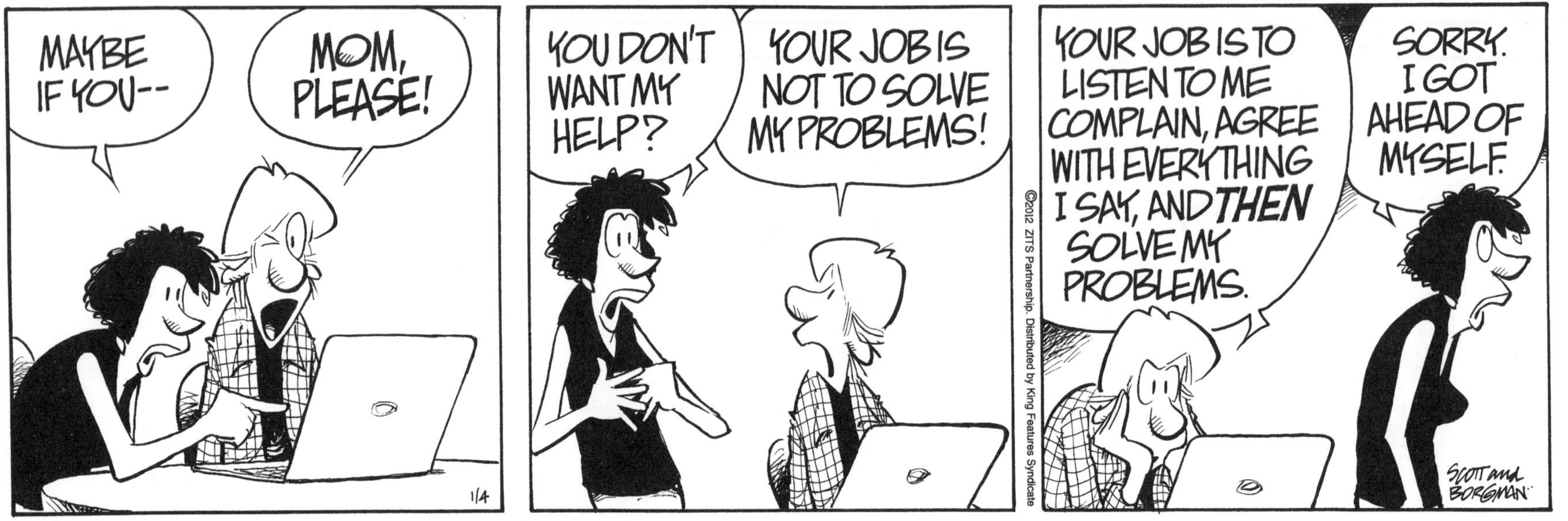
MAYBE IF YOU--
MOM, PLEASE!
1/4
YOU DON'T WANT MY HELP?
YOUR JOB IS NOT TO SOLVE MY PROBLEMS!
©2012 ZITS Partnership. Distributed by King Features Syndicate
YOUR JOB IS TO LISTEN TO ME COMPLAIN, AGREE WITH EVERYTHING I SAY, AND **THEN** SOLVE MY PROBLEMS.
SORRY. I GOT AHEAD OF MYSELF.
SCOTT and BORGMAN

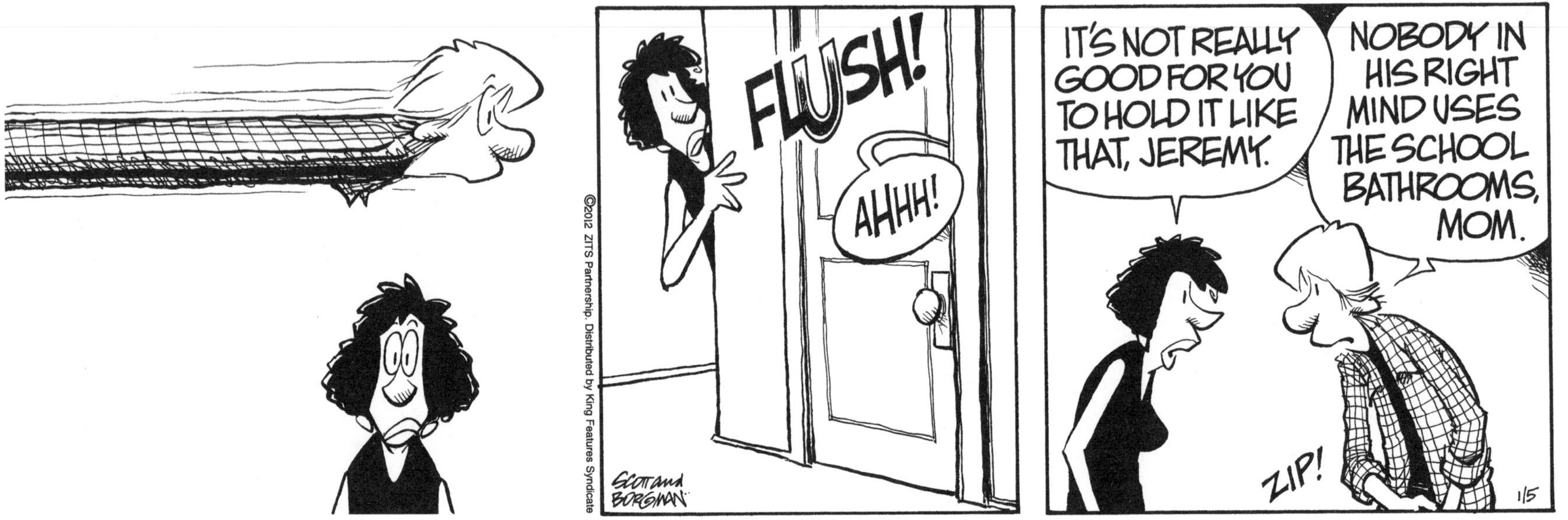
©2012 ZITS Partnership. Distributed by King Features Syndicate
FLUSH!
AHHH!
SCOTT and BORGMAN
IT'S NOT REALLY GOOD FOR YOU TO HOLD IT LIKE THAT, JEREMY.
NOBODY IN HIS RIGHT MIND USES THE SCHOOL BATHROOMS, MOM.
ZIP!
1/5

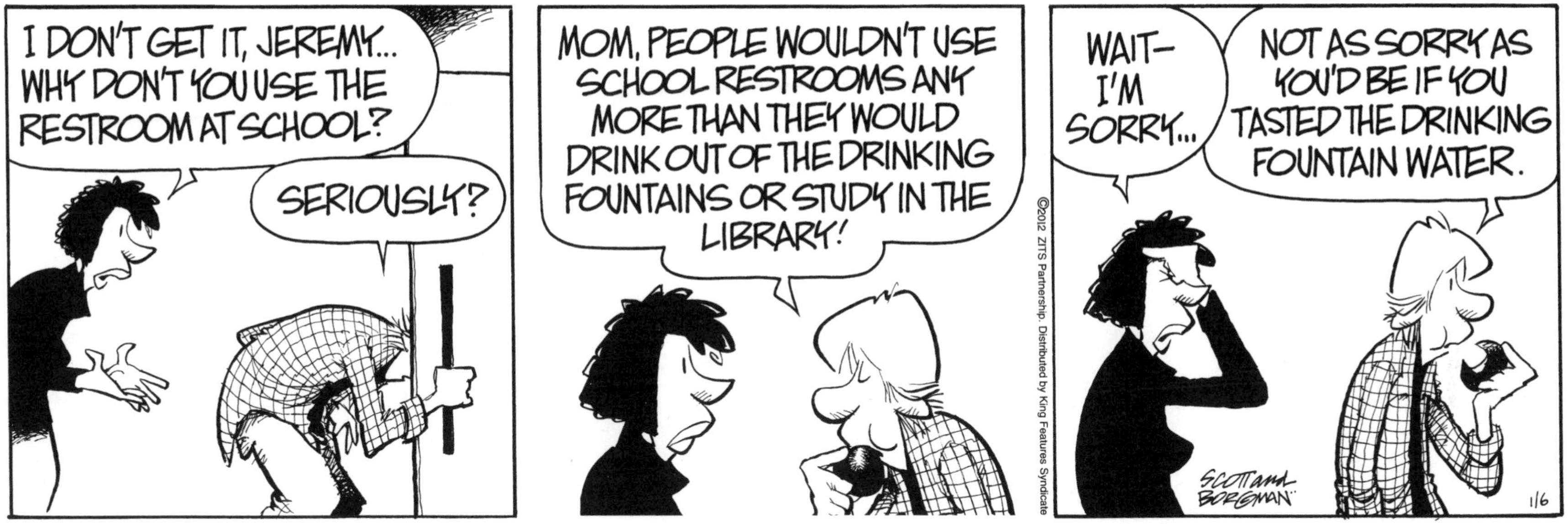
I DON'T GET IT, JEREMY... WHY DON'T YOU USE THE RESTROOM AT SCHOOL?
SERIOUSLY?
MOM, PEOPLE WOULDN'T USE SCHOOL RESTROOMS ANY MORE THAN THEY WOULD DRINK OUT OF THE DRINKING FOUNTAINS OR STUDY IN THE LIBRARY!
©2012 ZITS Partnership. Distributed by King Features Syndicate
WAIT– I'M SORRY...
NOT AS SORRY AS YOU'D BE IF YOU TASTED THE DRINKING FOUNTAIN WATER.
SCOTT AND BORGMAN
1/6

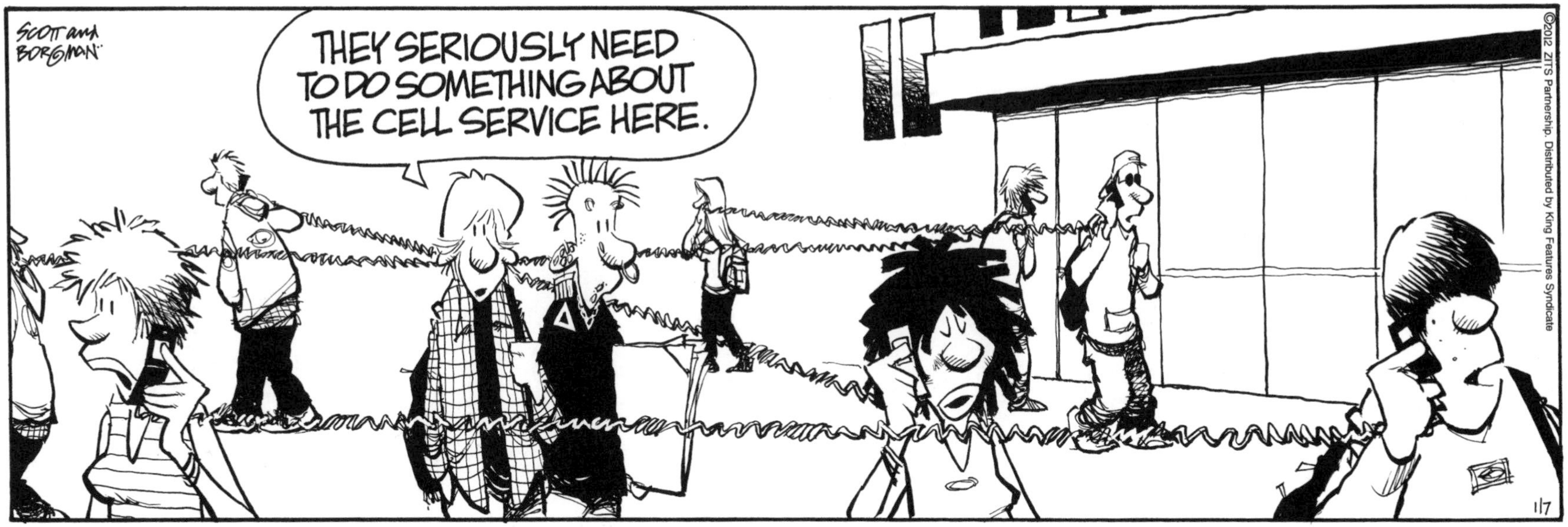
SCOTT AND BORGMAN
THEY SERIOUSLY NEED TO DO SOMETHING ABOUT THE CELL SERVICE HERE.
©2012 ZITS Partnership. Distributed by King Features Syndicate
1/7

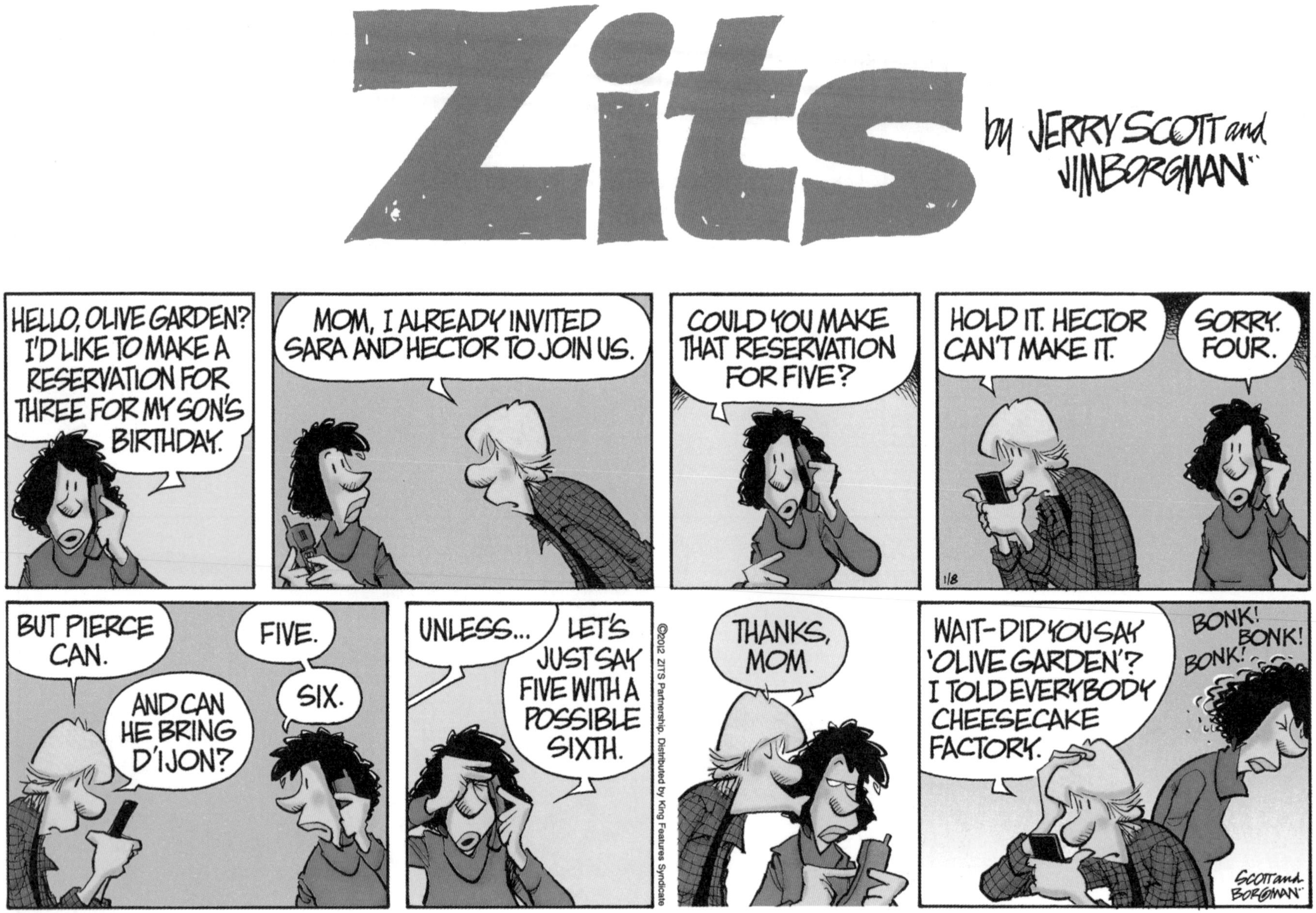
Zits
by JERRY SCOTT and JIM BORGMAN
HELLO, OLIVE GARDEN? I'D LIKE TO MAKE A RESERVATION FOR THREE FOR MY SON'S BIRTHDAY.
MOM, I ALREADY INVITED SARA AND HECTOR TO JOIN US.
COULD YOU MAKE THAT RESERVATION FOR FIVE?
HOLD IT. HECTOR CAN'T MAKE IT.
SORRY. FOUR.
1/18
BUT PIERCE CAN.
FIVE.
AND CAN HE BRING D'IJON?
SIX.
UNLESS...
LET'S JUST SAY FIVE WITH A POSSIBLE SIXTH.
THANKS, MOM.
WAIT-DID YOU SAY 'OLIVE GARDEN'? I TOLD EVERYBODY CHEESECAKE FACTORY.
BONK! BONK! BONK!
SCOTT and BORGMAN

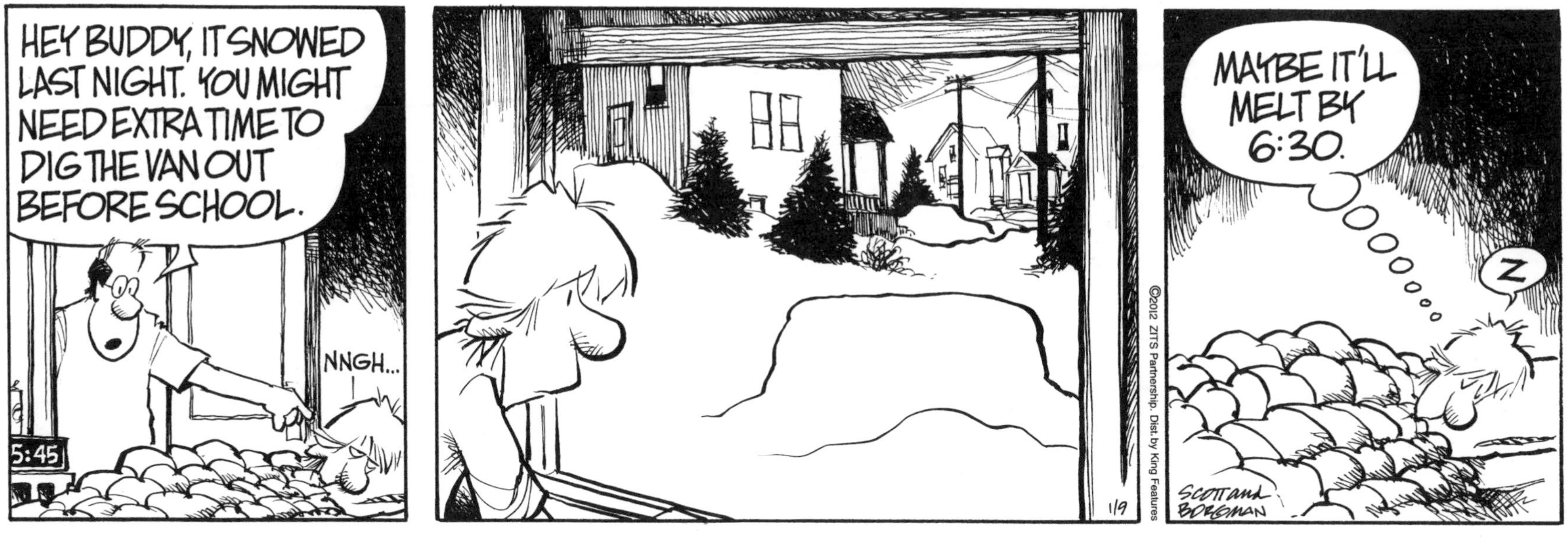
HEY BUDDY, IT SNOWED LAST NIGHT. YOU MIGHT NEED EXTRA TIME TO DIG THE VAN OUT BEFORE SCHOOL.
5:45
NNGH...
MAYBE IT'LL MELT BY 6:30.
Z
©2012 ZITS Partnership. Dist. by King Features
1/9
SCOTT AND BORGMAN

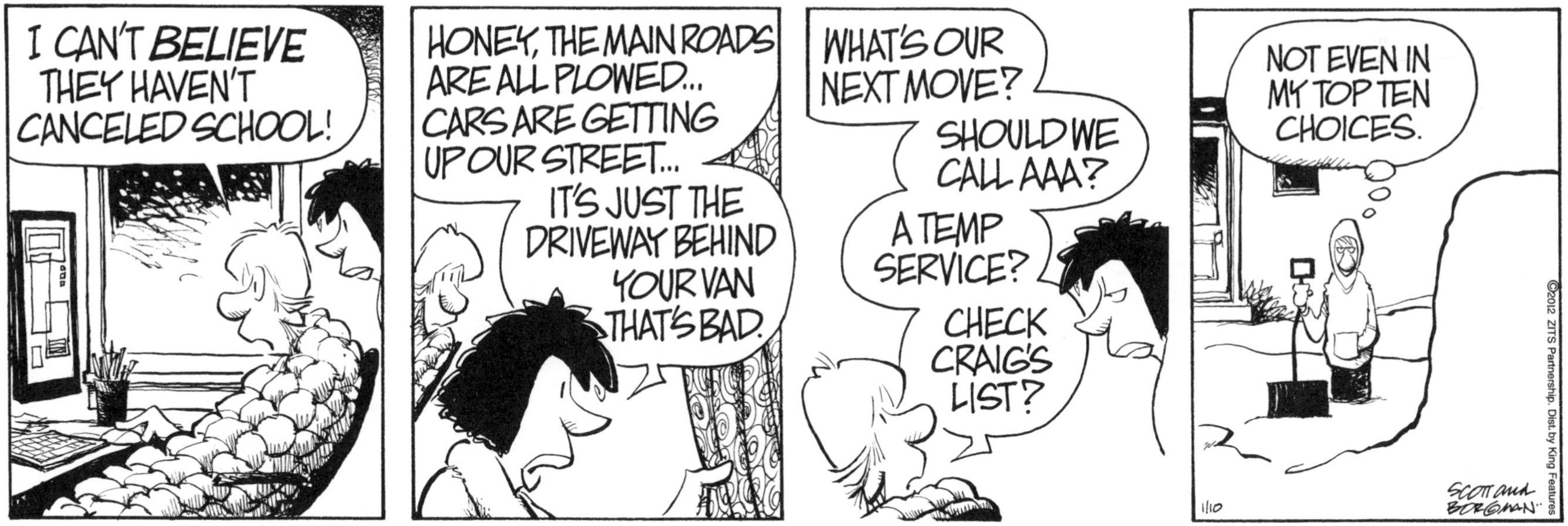
I CAN'T BELIEVE THEY HAVEN'T CANCELED SCHOOL!
HONEY, THE MAIN ROADS ARE ALL PLOWED... CARS ARE GETTING UP OUR STREET...
IT'S JUST THE DRIVEWAY BEHIND YOUR VAN THAT'S BAD.
WHAT'S OUR NEXT MOVE?
SHOULD WE CALL AAA?
A TEMP SERVICE?
CHECK CRAIG'S LIST?
NOT EVEN IN MY TOP TEN CHOICES.
1/10
©2012 ZITS Partnership. Dist. by King Features
SCOTT AND BORGMAN

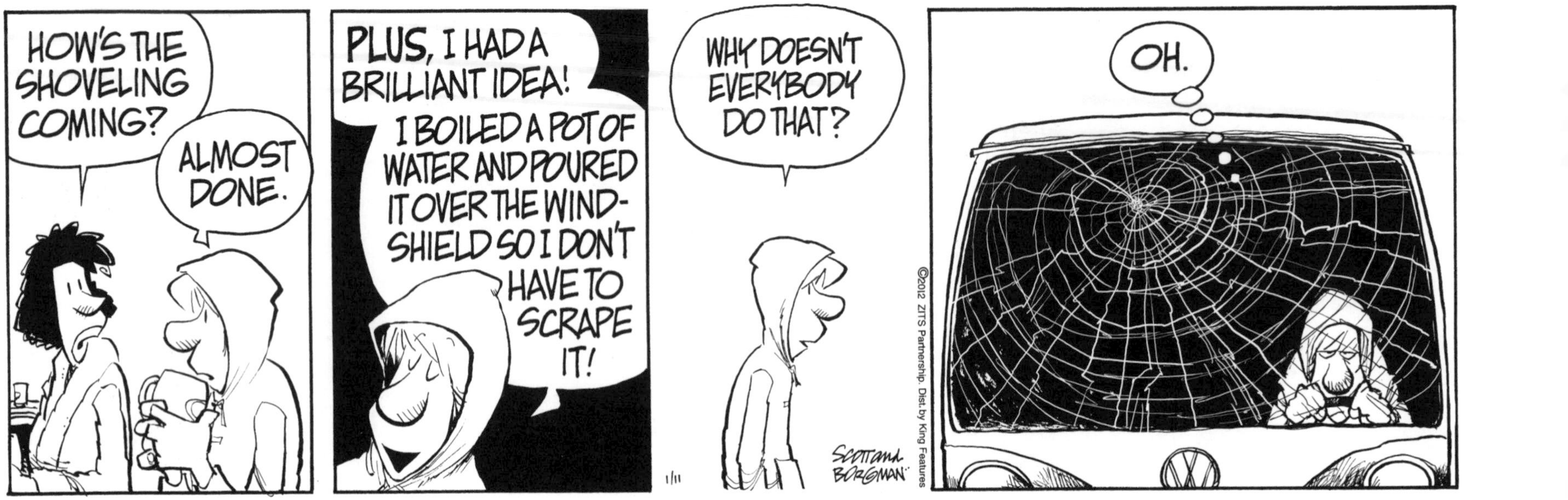
HOW'S THE SHOVELING COMING?
ALMOST DONE.
PLUS, I HAD A BRILLIANT IDEA!
I BOILED A POT OF WATER AND POURED IT OVER THE WIND-SHIELD SO I DON'T HAVE TO SCRAPE IT!
WHY DOESN'T EVERYBODY DO THAT?
1/11
SCOTT and BORGMAN
©2012 ZITS Partnership. Dist. by King Features
OH.

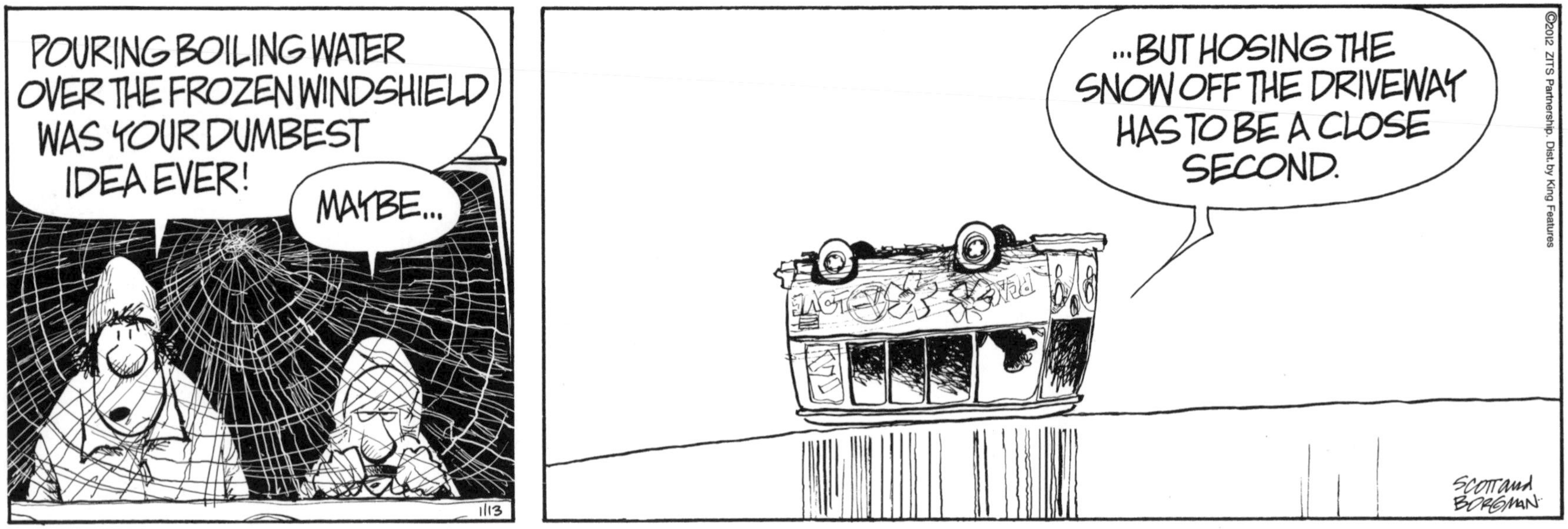
POURING BOILING WATER OVER THE FROZEN WINDSHIELD WAS YOUR DUMBEST IDEA EVER!
MAYBE...
1/13
...BUT HOSING THE SNOW OFF THE DRIVEWAY HAS TO BE A CLOSE SECOND.
SCOTT and BORGMAN
©2012 ZITS Partnership. Dist. by King Features

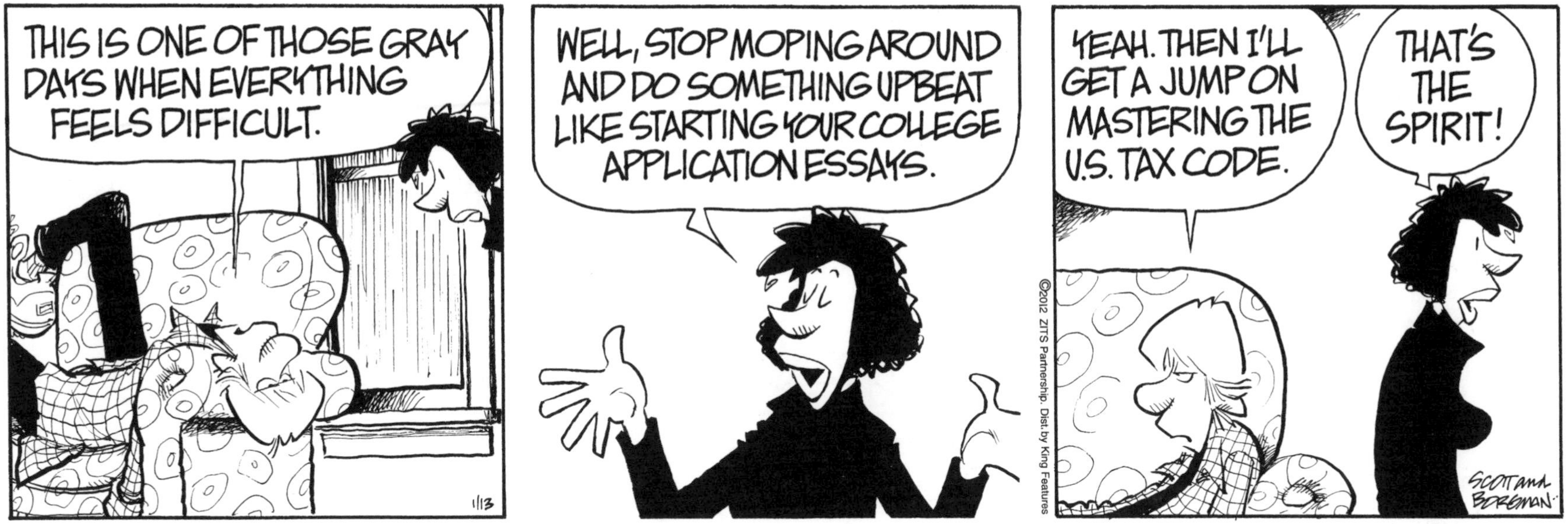
THIS IS ONE OF THOSE GRAY DAYS WHEN EVERYTHING FEELS DIFFICULT.
1/13
WELL, STOP MOPING AROUND AND DO SOMETHING UPBEAT LIKE STARTING YOUR COLLEGE APPLICATION ESSAYS.
©2012 ZITS Partnership. Dist. by King Features
YEAH. THEN I'LL GET A JUMP ON MASTERING THE U.S. TAX CODE.
THAT'S THE SPIRIT!
SCOTT AND BORGMAN

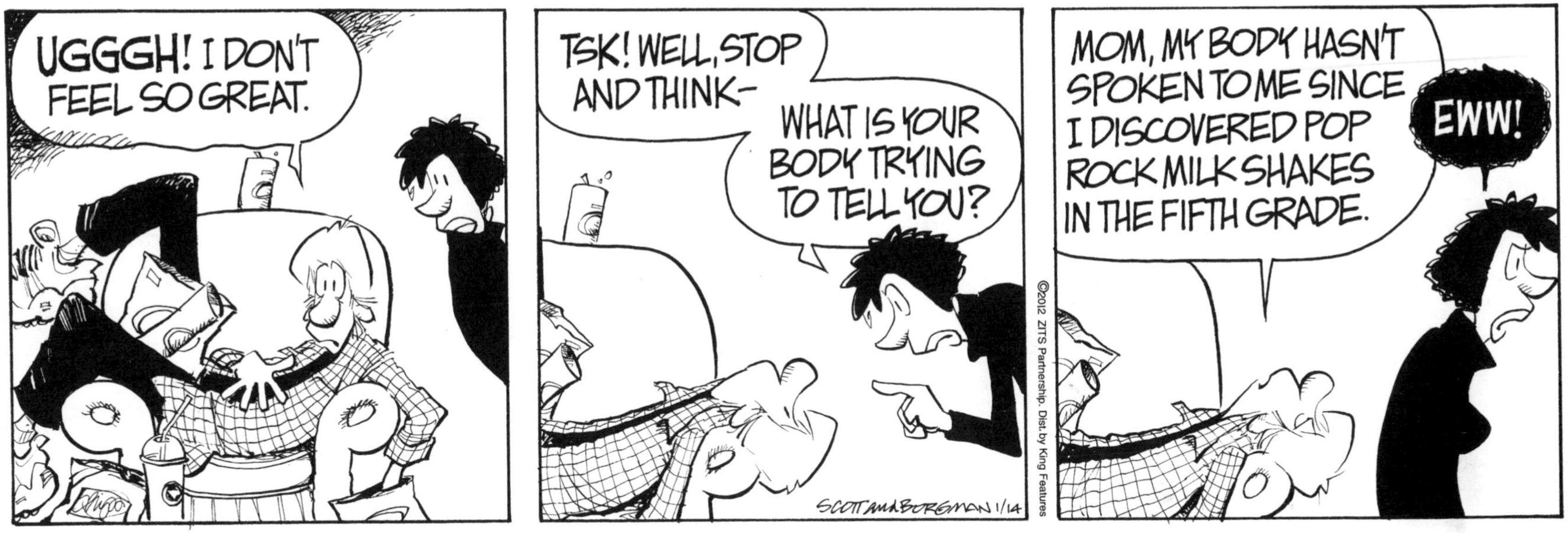
UGGGH! I DON'T FEEL SO GREAT.
TSK! WELL, STOP AND THINK–
WHAT IS YOUR BODY TRYING TO TELL YOU?
SCOTT AND BORGMAN 1/14
©2012 ZITS Partnership. Dist. by King Features
MOM, MY BODY HASN'T SPOKEN TO ME SINCE I DISCOVERED POP ROCK MILK SHAKES IN THE FIFTH GRADE.
EWW!

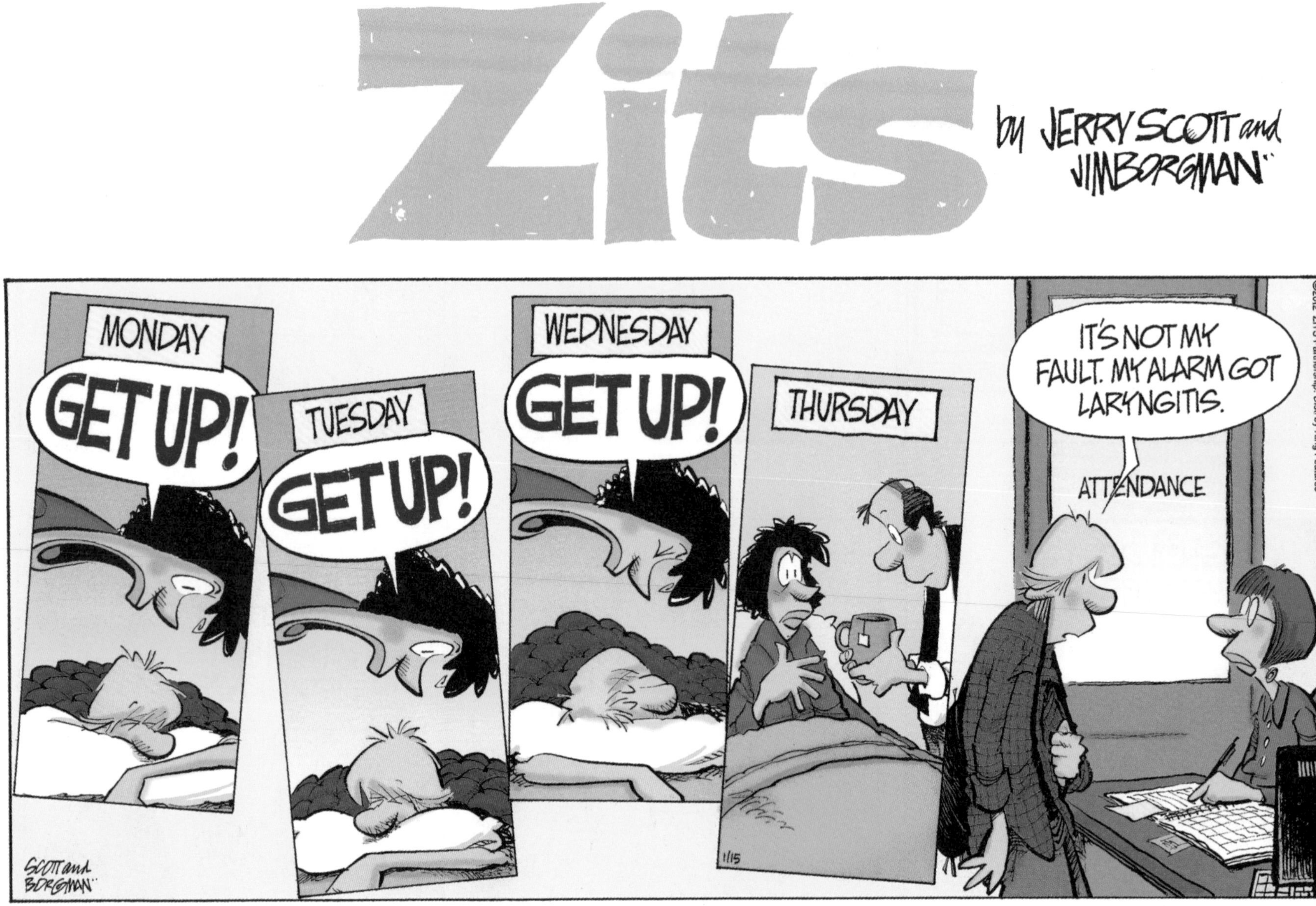
Zits
by JERRY SCOTT and JIM BORGMAN
MONDAY
GET UP!
TUESDAY
GET UP!
WEDNESDAY
GET UP!
THURSDAY
IT'S NOT MY FAULT. MY ALARM GOT LARYNGITIS.
ATTENDANCE
©2012 ZITS Partnership. Dist. by King Features
SCOTT and BORGMAN
1/15

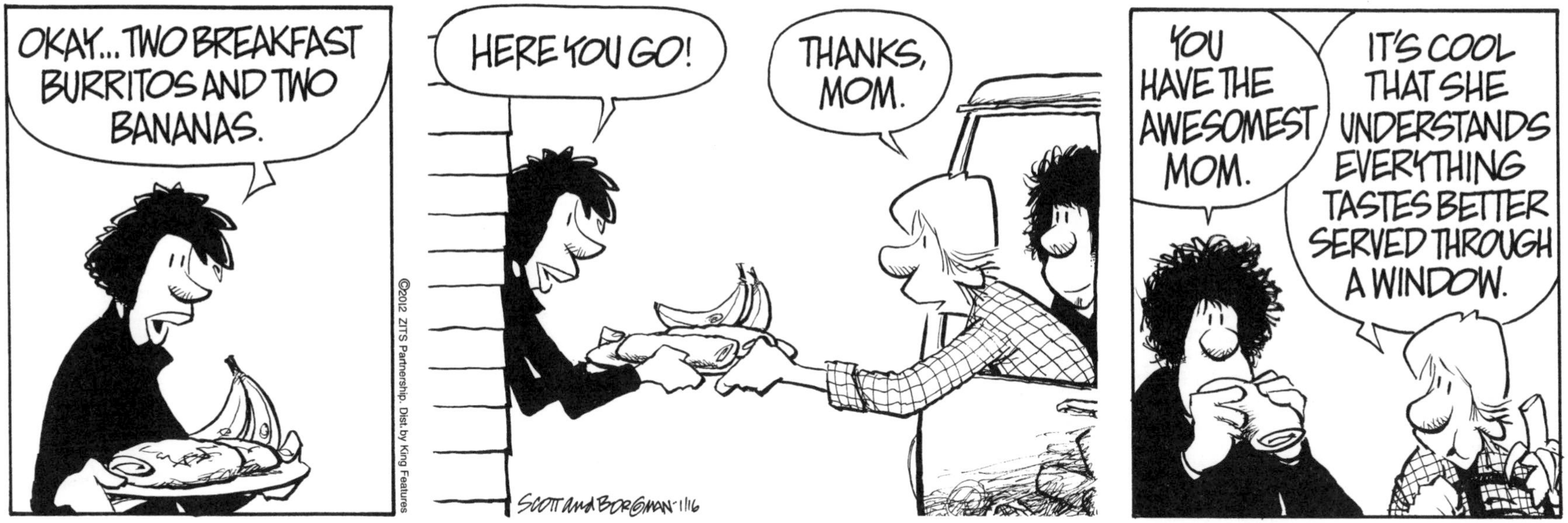
OKAY... TWO BREAKFAST BURRITOS AND TWO BANANAS.
HERE YOU GO!
THANKS, MOM.
YOU HAVE THE AWESOMEST MOM.
IT'S COOL THAT SHE UNDERSTANDS EVERYTHING TASTES BETTER SERVED THROUGH A WINDOW.
©2012 ZITS Partnership. Dist. by King Features
SCOTT and BORGMAN 1/16

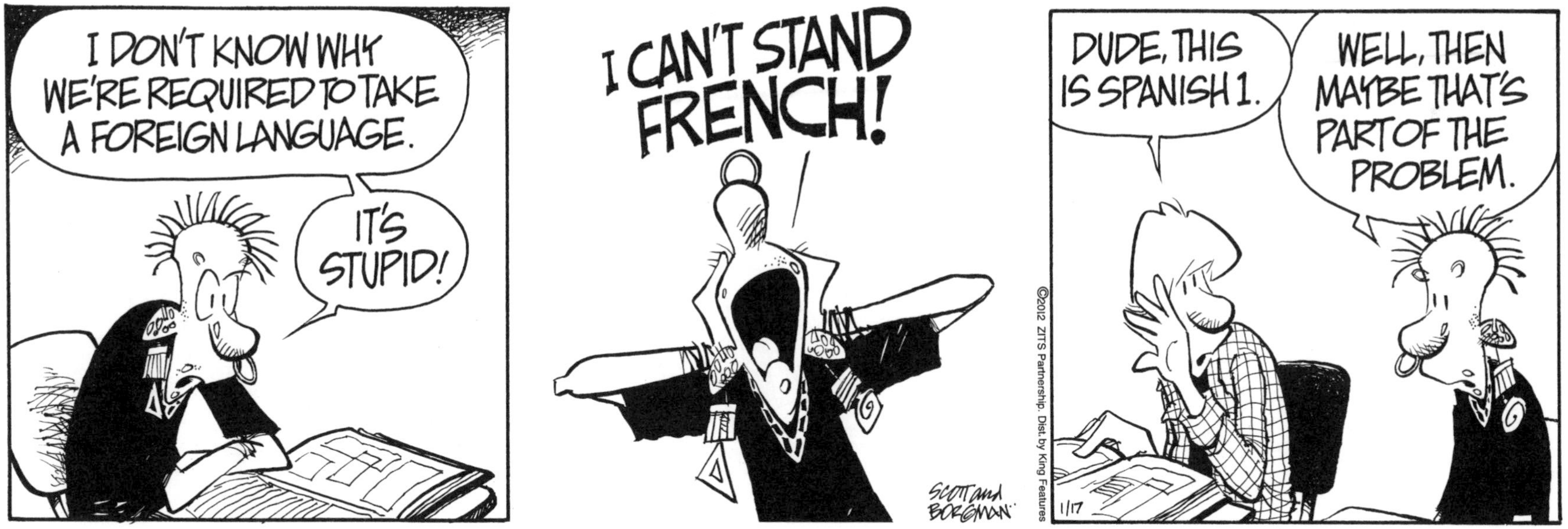
I DON'T KNOW WHY WE'RE REQUIRED TO TAKE A FOREIGN LANGUAGE.
IT'S STUPID!
I CAN'T STAND FRENCH!
DUDE, THIS IS SPANISH 1.
WELL, THEN MAYBE THAT'S PART OF THE PROBLEM.
©2012 ZITS Partnership. Dist. by King Features
SCOTT and BORGMAN
1/17

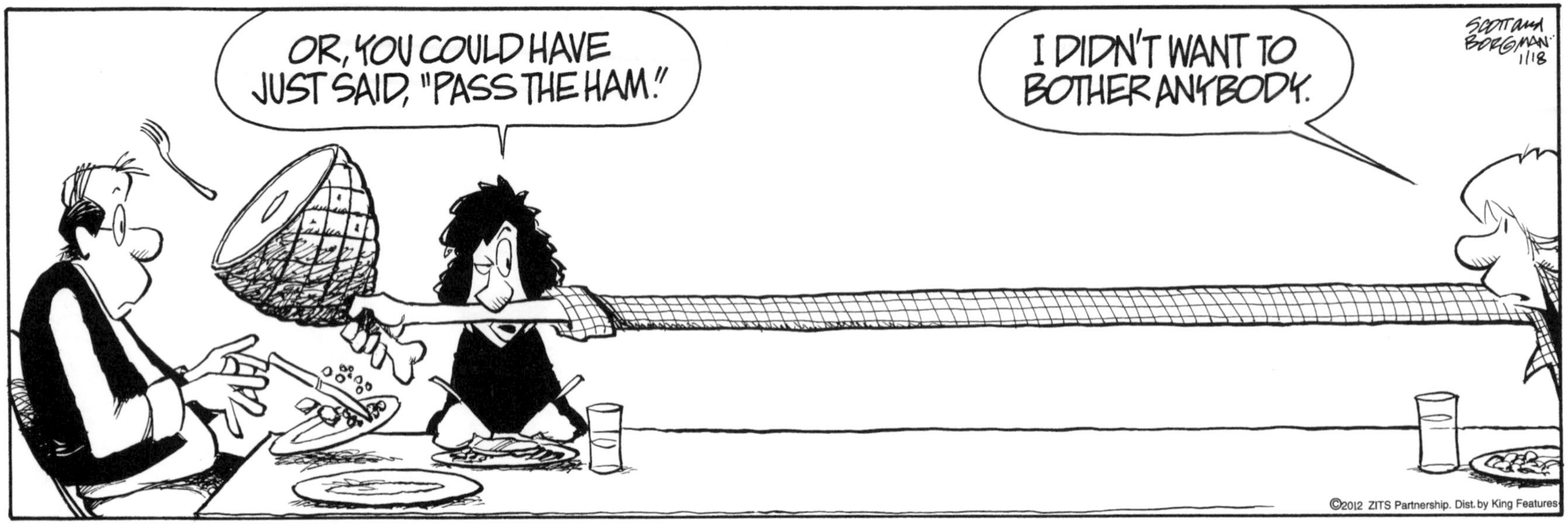
SCOTT and BORGMAN 1/18
OR, YOU COULD HAVE JUST SAID, "PASS THE HAM."
I DIDN'T WANT TO BOTHER ANYBODY.
©2012 ZITS Partnership. Dist. by King Features

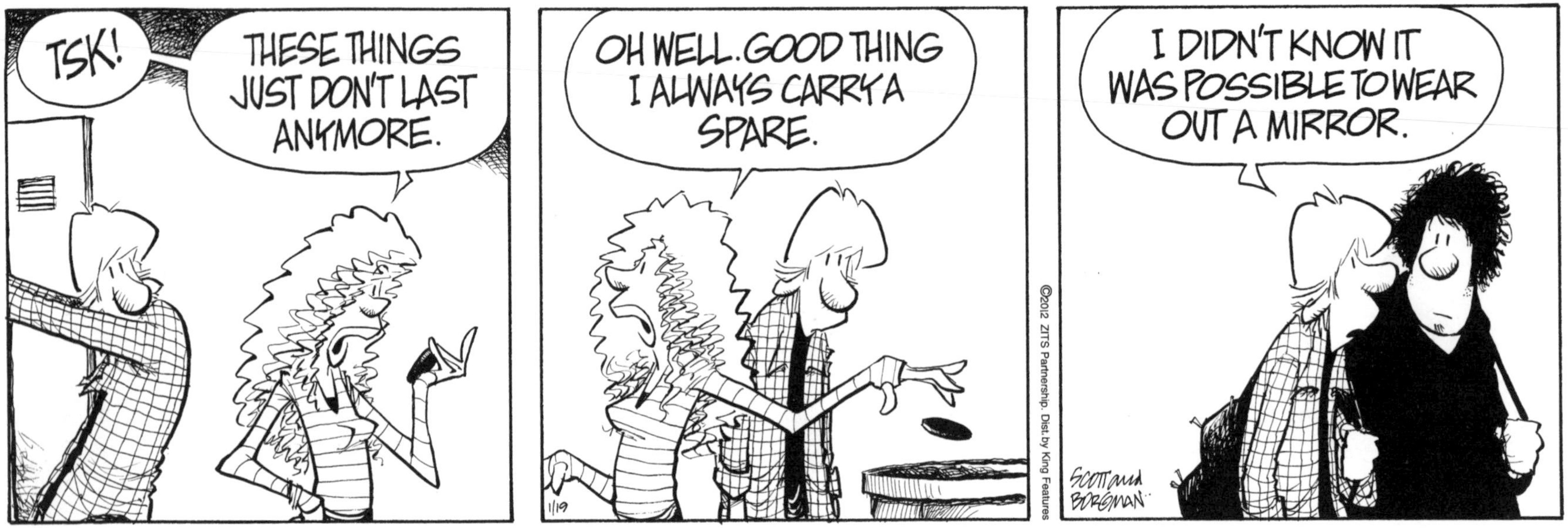
TSK!
THESE THINGS JUST DON'T LAST ANYMORE.
OH WELL. GOOD THING I ALWAYS CARRY A SPARE.
1/19
©2012 ZITS Partnership. Dist. by King Features
I DIDN'T KNOW IT WAS POSSIBLE TO WEAR OUT A MIRROR.
SCOTT and BORGMAN

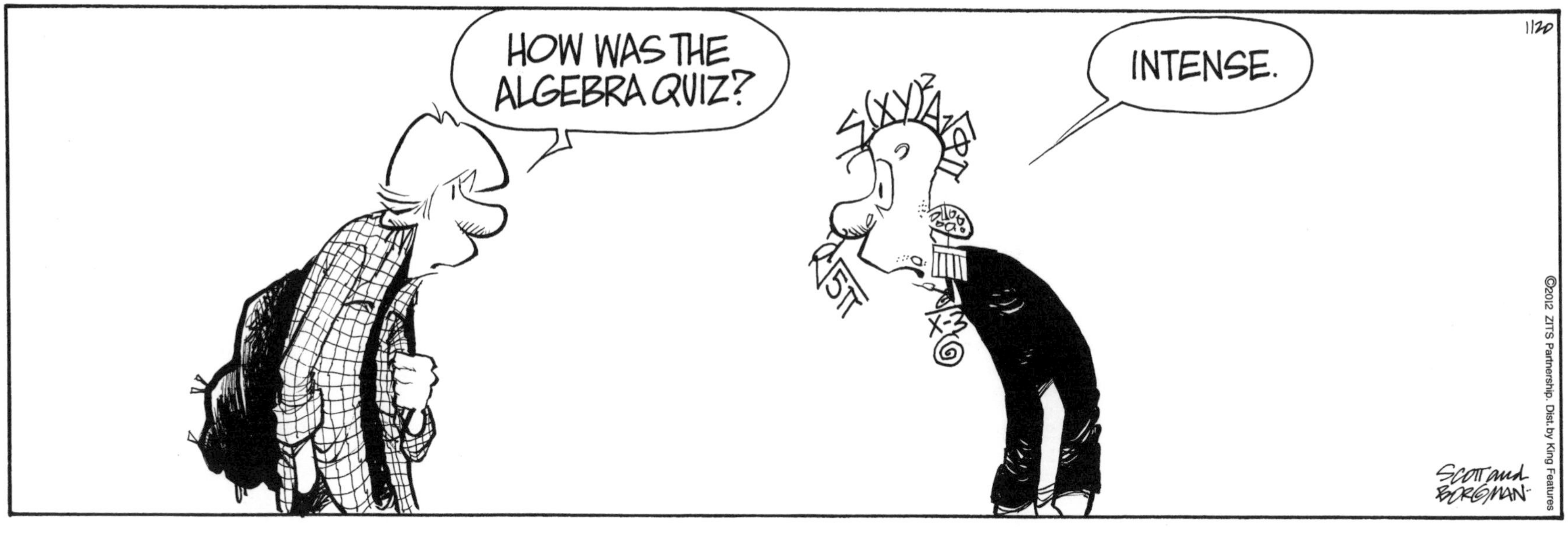
1/20
HOW WAS THE ALGEBRA QUIZ?
INTENSE.
©2012 ZITS Partnership. Dist. by King Features
SCOTT and BORGMAN

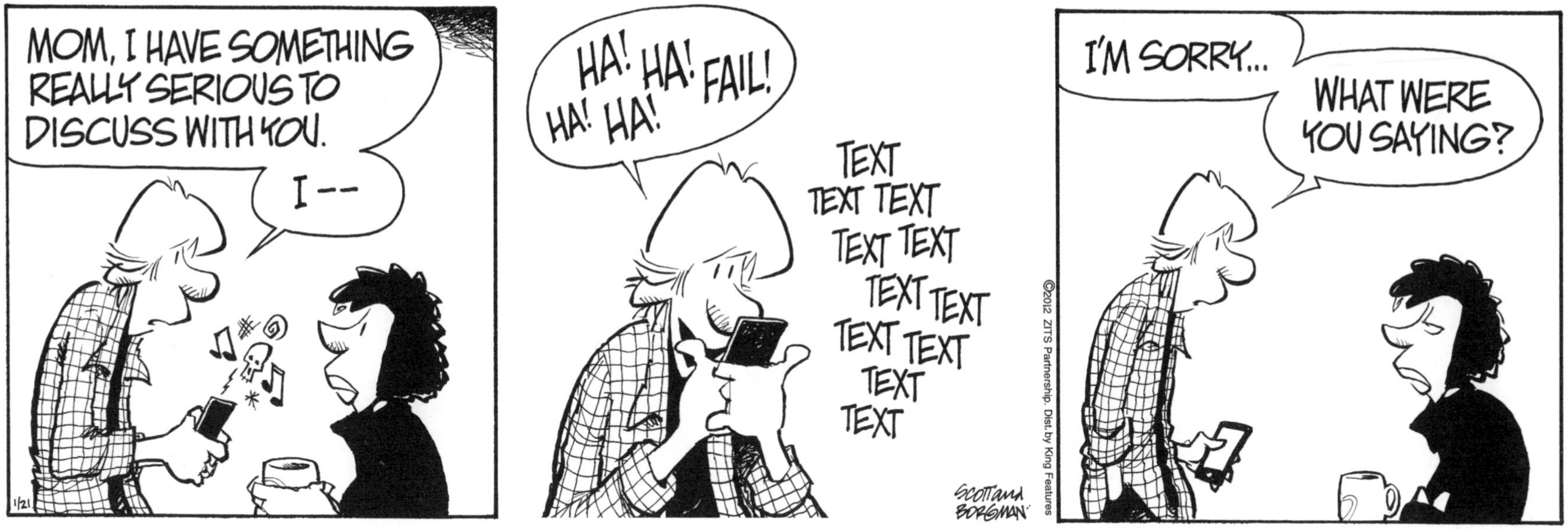
MOM, I HAVE SOMETHING REALLY SERIOUS TO DISCUSS WITH YOU.
I --
1/21
HA! HA! HA! HA! FAIL!
TEXT TEXT TEXT TEXT TEXT TEXT TEXT TEXT TEXT TEXT TEXT
©2012 ZITS Partnership. Dist. by King Features
SCOTT and BORGMAN
I'M SORRY...
WHAT WERE YOU SAYING?

Zits

by JERRY SCOTT and JIM BORGMAN

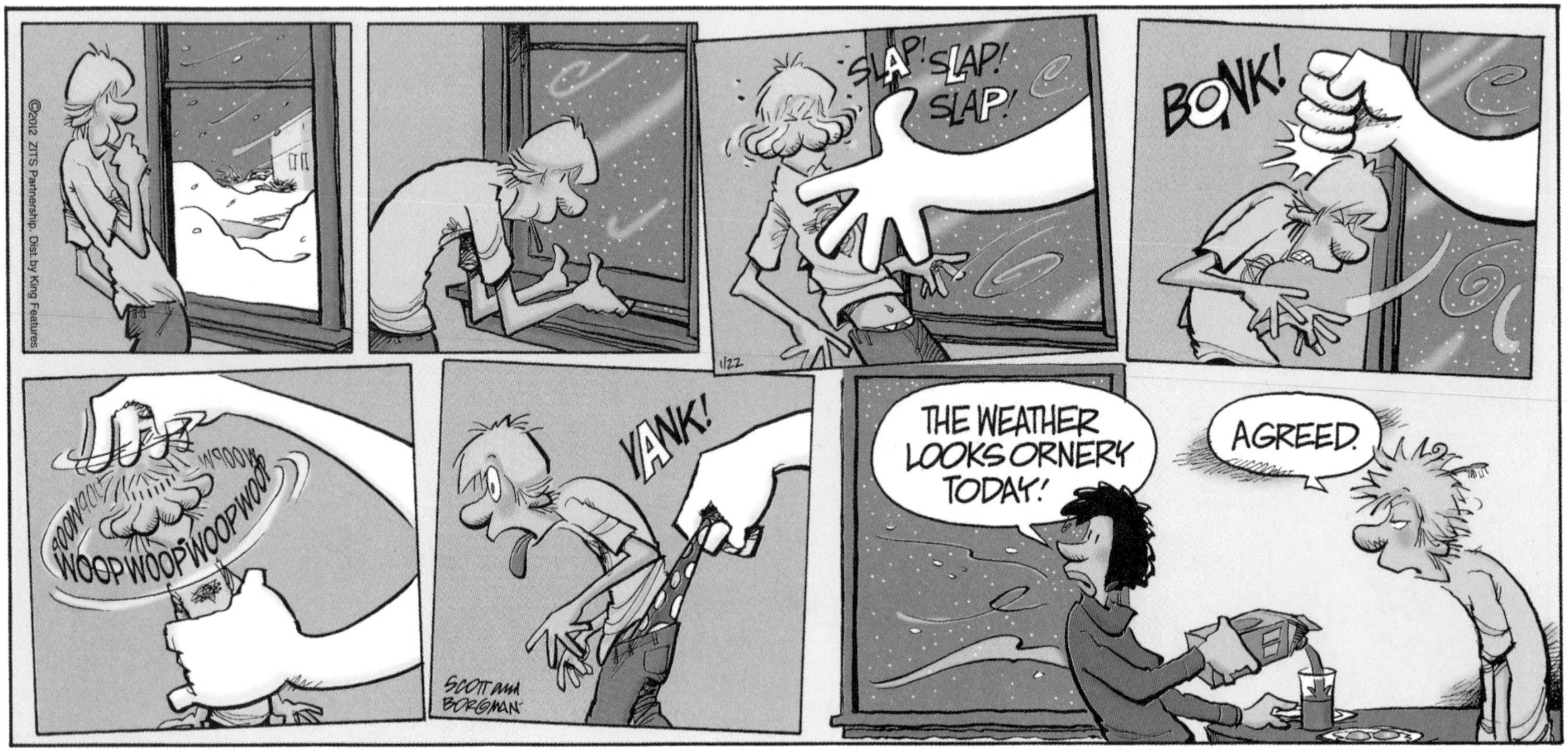
©2012 ZITS Partnership. Dist. by King Features
SLAP! SLAP! SLAP!
BONK!
WOOP WOOP WOOP WOOP
YANK!
SCOTT and BORGMAN
THE WEATHER LOOKS ORNERY TODAY!
AGREED.

WHAT'S THAT?
A STACK OF PAPER THAT SHOULD BE FULL OF WORDS.
WE WERE SUPPOSED TO KEEP A JOURNAL OF DAILY REFLECTIONS FOR ENGLISH CLASS, AND I KIND OF FORGOT.
SCOTT and BORGMAN 1/23
SINCE WHEN?
SEPTEMBER.
WHEN IS IT DUE?
TOMORROW.

YOU HAVE TO WRITE FIVE MONTHS OF DAILY REFLECTIONS IN ONE NIGHT??
RELAX, MOM.
THEY'RE JUST DAILY REFLECTIONS, IT'S NOT LIKE I HAVE TO PUT ANY THOUGHT INTO THEM.
RIGHT. YOU BLEW OFF "DAILY," WHY SWEAT "REFLECTIONS"?
WHAT WAS I NOT REALLY THINKING ABOUT ON SEPTEMBER FIRST?
SCOTT and BORGMAN
1/24

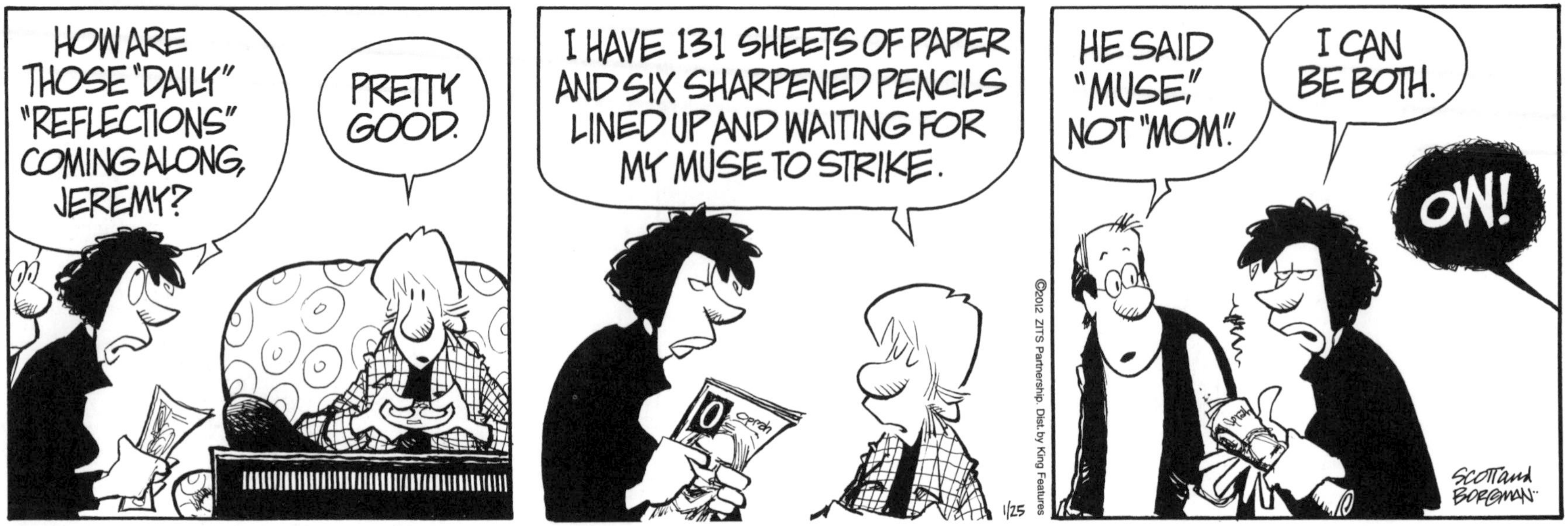
HOW ARE THOSE "DAILY" "REFLECTIONS" COMING ALONG, JEREMY?
PRETTY GOOD.
I HAVE 131 SHEETS OF PAPER AND SIX SHARPENED PENCILS LINED UP AND WAITING FOR MY MUSE TO STRIKE.
O Oprah
©2012 ZITS Partnership. Dist. by King Features
1/25
HE SAID "MUSE," NOT "MOM".
I CAN BE BOTH.
OW!
SCOTT and BORGMAN

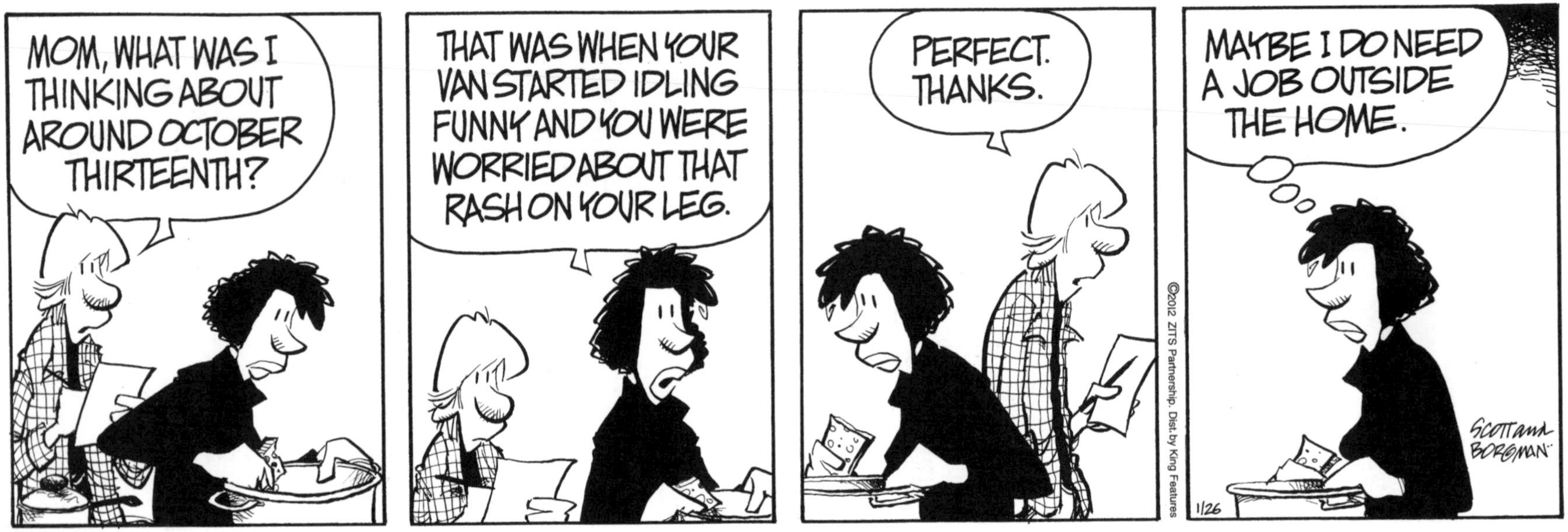
MOM, WHAT WAS I THINKING ABOUT AROUND OCTOBER THIRTEENTH?
THAT WAS WHEN YOUR VAN STARTED IDLING FUNNY AND YOU WERE WORRIED ABOUT THAT RASH ON YOUR LEG.
PERFECT. THANKS.
©2012 ZITS Partnership. Dist. by King Features
1/26
MAYBE I DO NEED A JOB OUTSIDE THE HOME.
SCOTT and BORGMAN

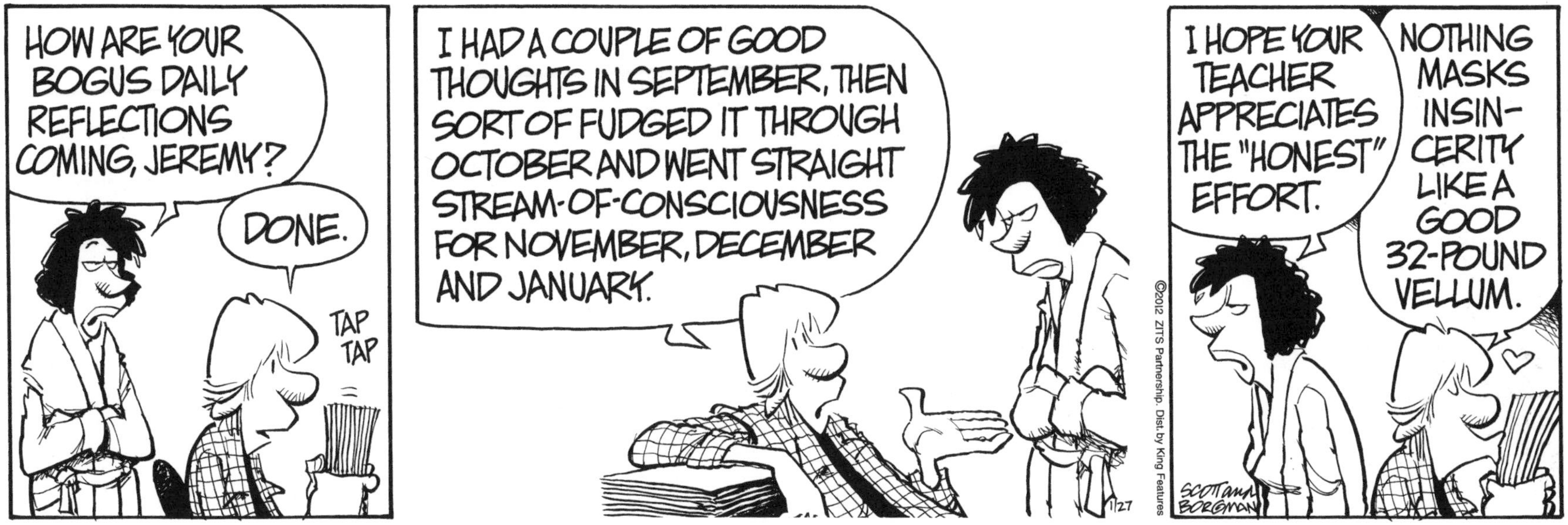
HOW ARE YOUR BOGUS DAILY REFLECTIONS COMING, JEREMY?
DONE.
TAP TAP
I HAD A COUPLE OF GOOD THOUGHTS IN SEPTEMBER, THEN SORT OF FUDGED IT THROUGH OCTOBER AND WENT STRAIGHT STREAM-OF-CONSCIOUSNESS FOR NOVEMBER, DECEMBER AND JANUARY.
1/27
©2012 ZITS Partnership. Dist. by King Features
I HOPE YOUR TEACHER APPRECIATES THE "HONEST" EFFORT.
NOTHING MASKS INSIN-CERITY LIKE A GOOD 32-POUND VELLUM.
SCOTT and BORGMAN

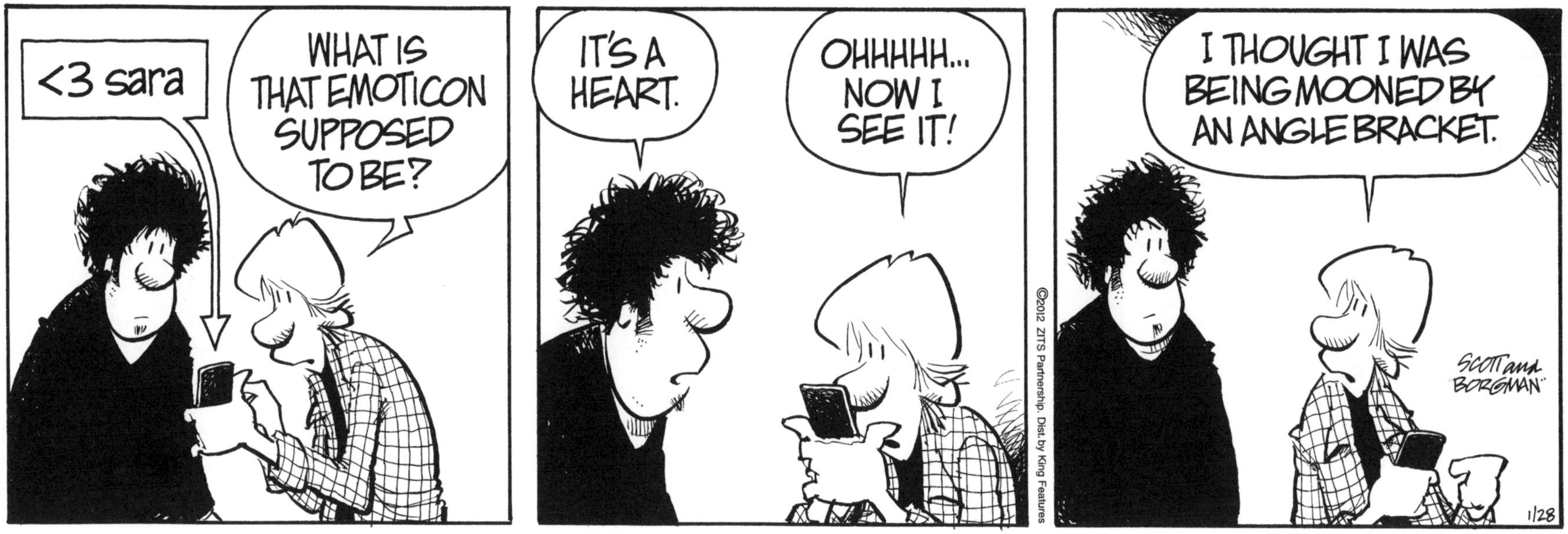
<3 sara
WHAT IS THAT EMOTICON SUPPOSED TO BE?
IT'S A HEART.
OHHHHH... NOW I SEE IT!
©2012 ZITS Partnership. Dist. by King Features
I THOUGHT I WAS BEING MOONED BY AN ANGLE BRACKET.
SCOTT and BORGMAN
1/28

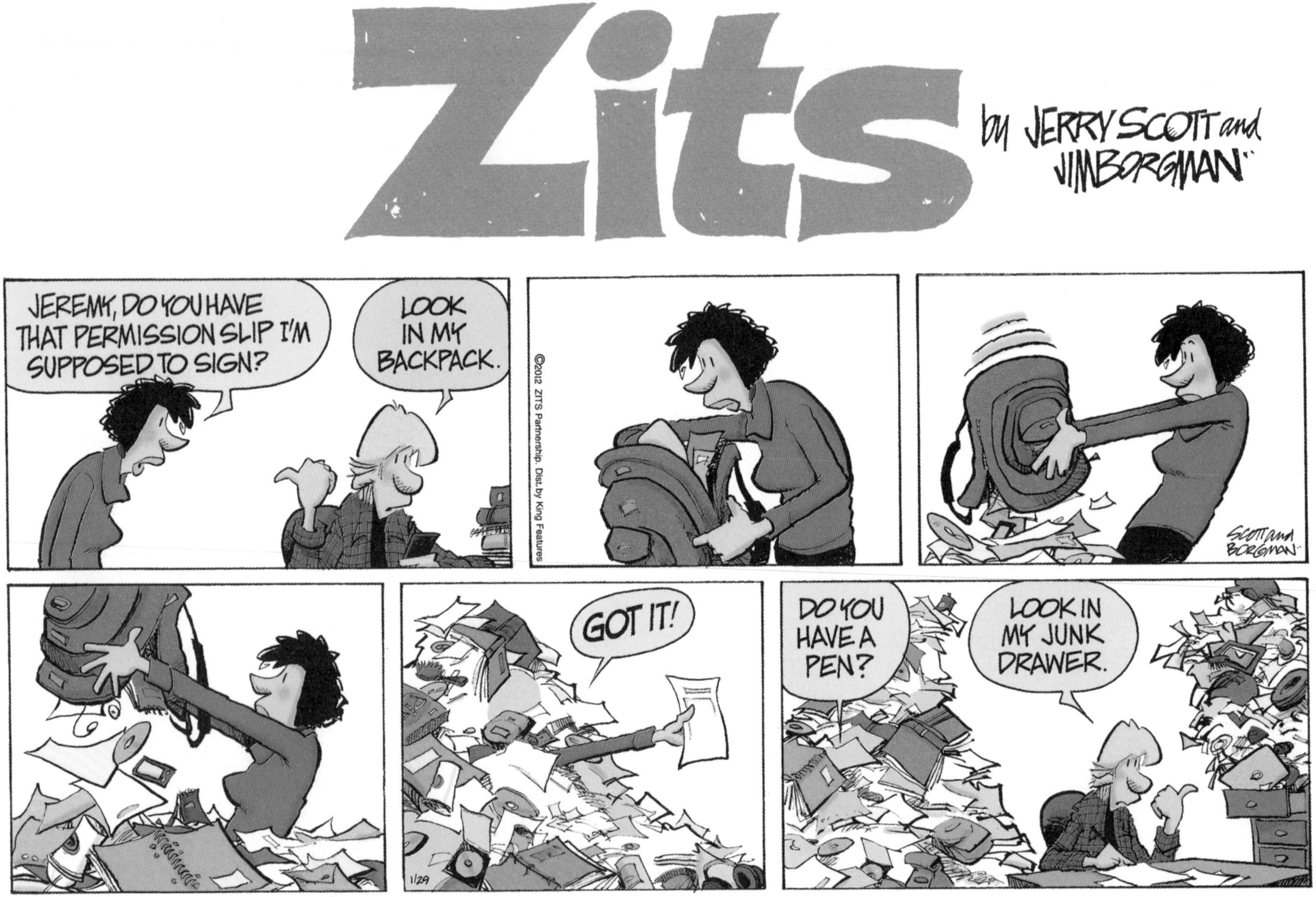
Zits
by JERRY SCOTT and JIM BORGMAN
JEREMY, DO YOU HAVE THAT PERMISSION SLIP I'M SUPPOSED TO SIGN?
LOOK IN MY BACKPACK.
©2012 ZITS Partnership. Dist. by King Features
SCOTT and BORGMAN
GOT IT!
1/29
DO YOU HAVE A PEN?
LOOK IN MY JUNK DRAWER.

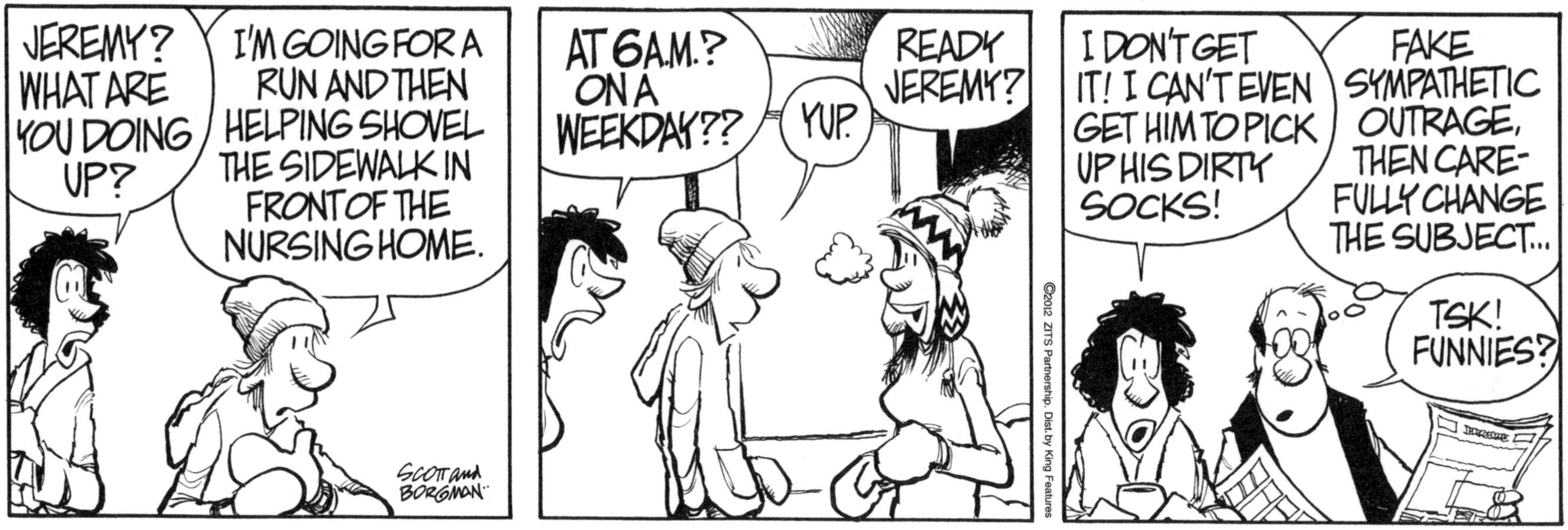
JEREMY? WHAT ARE YOU DOING UP?
I'M GOING FOR A RUN AND THEN HELPING SHOVEL THE SIDEWALK IN FRONT OF THE NURSING HOME.
SCOTT and BORGMAN
AT 6 A.M.? ON A WEEKDAY??
YUP.
READY JEREMY?
©2012 ZITS Partnership. Dist. by King Features
I DON'T GET IT! I CAN'T EVEN GET HIM TO PICK UP HIS DIRTY SOCKS!
FAKE SYMPATHETIC OUTRAGE, THEN CARE-FULLY CHANGE THE SUBJECT...
TSK! FUNNIES?

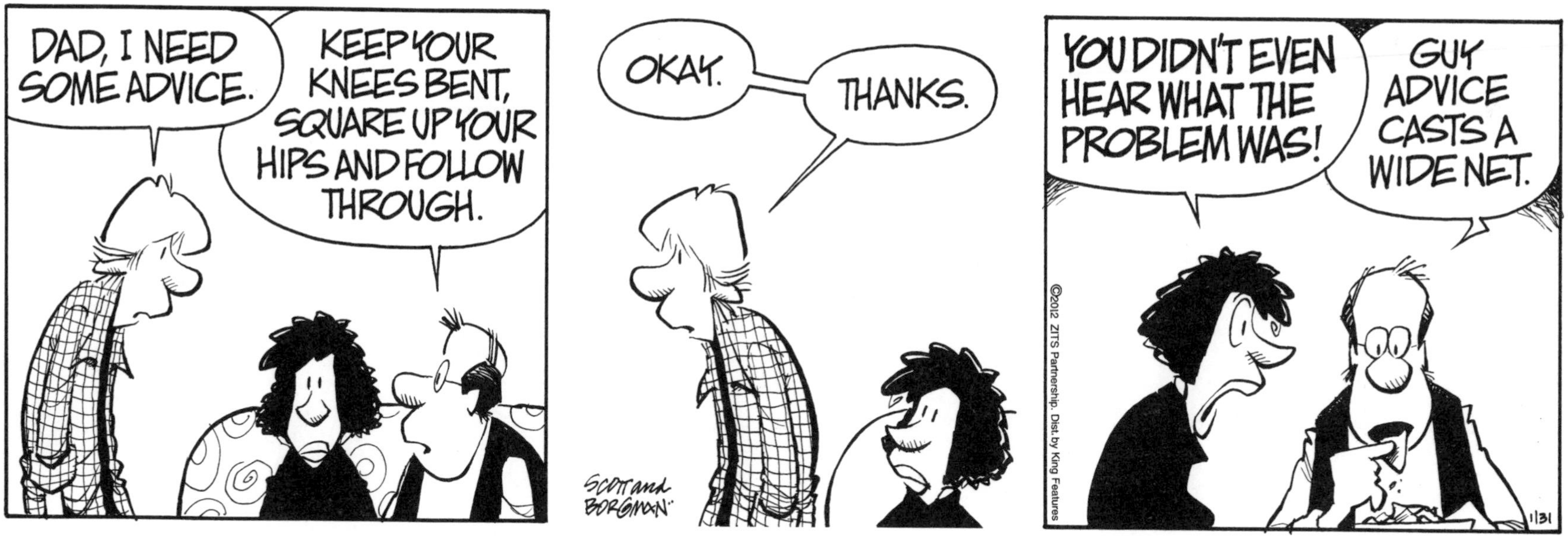
DAD, I NEED SOME ADVICE.
KEEP YOUR KNEES BENT, SQUARE UP YOUR HIPS AND FOLLOW THROUGH.
OKAY.
THANKS.
SCOTT and BORGMAN
©2012 ZITS Partnership. Dist. by King Features
YOU DIDN'T EVEN HEAR WHAT THE PROBLEM WAS!
GUY ADVICE CASTS A WIDE NET.
1/31

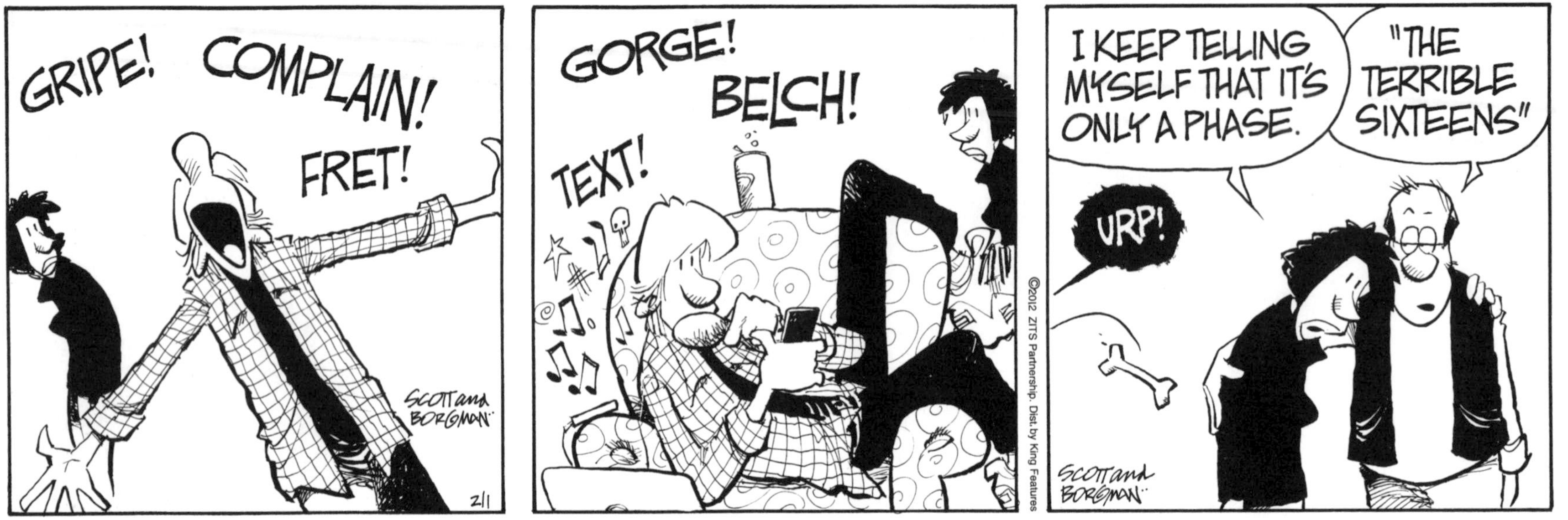
GRIPE!
COMPLAIN!
FRET!
SCOTT and BORGMAN
2/1
GORGE!
BELCH!
TEXT!
©2012 ZITS Partnership. Dist. by King Features
I KEEP TELLING MYSELF THAT IT'S ONLY A PHASE.
"THE TERRIBLE SIXTEENS"
URP!
SCOTT and BORGMAN

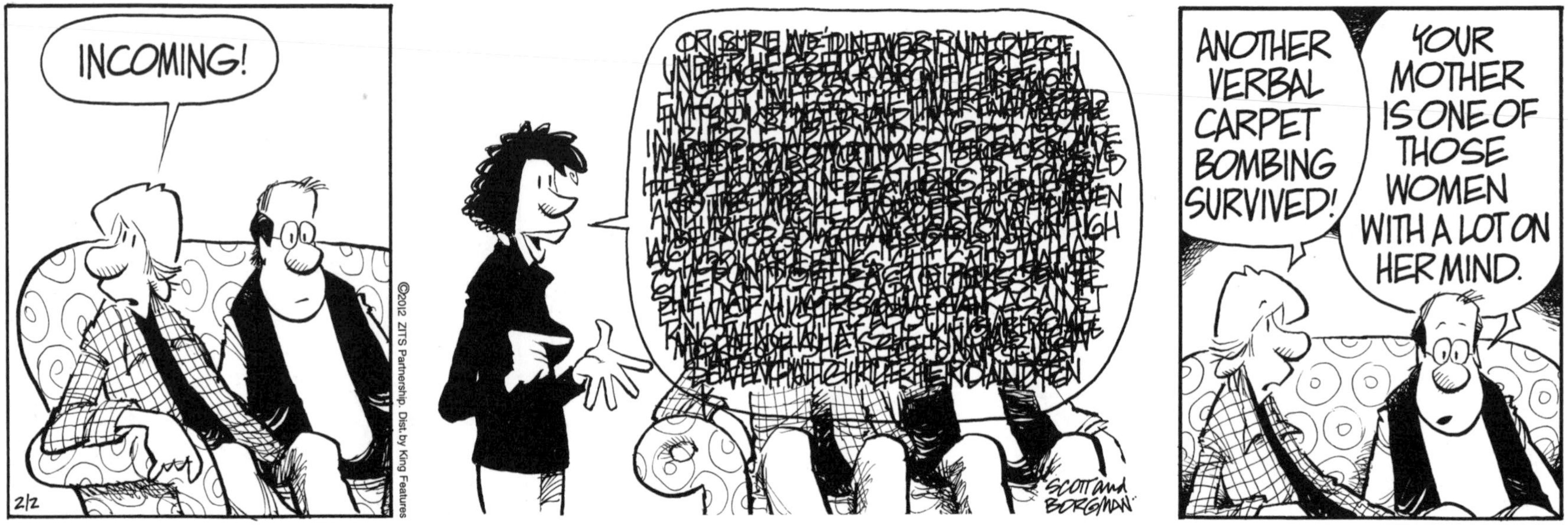
INCOMING!
2/2
©2012 ZITS Partnership. Dist. by King Features
SCOTT and BORGMAN
ANOTHER VERBAL CARPET BOMBING SURVIVED!
YOUR MOTHER IS ONE OF THOSE WOMEN WITH A LOT ON HER MIND.

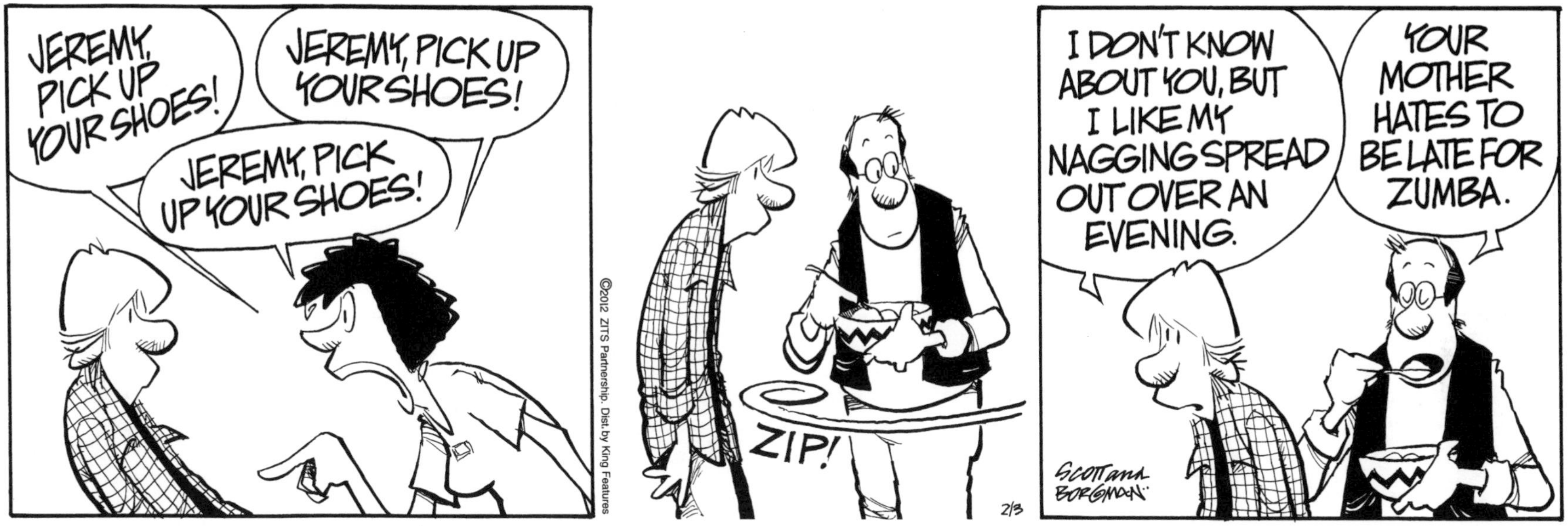
JEREMY, PICK UP YOUR SHOES!
JEREMY, PICK UP YOUR SHOES!
JEREMY, PICK UP YOUR SHOES!
©2012 ZITS Partnership. Dist. by King Features
ZIP!
2/3
I DON'T KNOW ABOUT YOU, BUT I LIKE MY NAGGING SPREAD OUT OVER AN EVENING.
YOUR MOTHER HATES TO BE LATE FOR ZUMBA.
SCOTT and BORGMAN

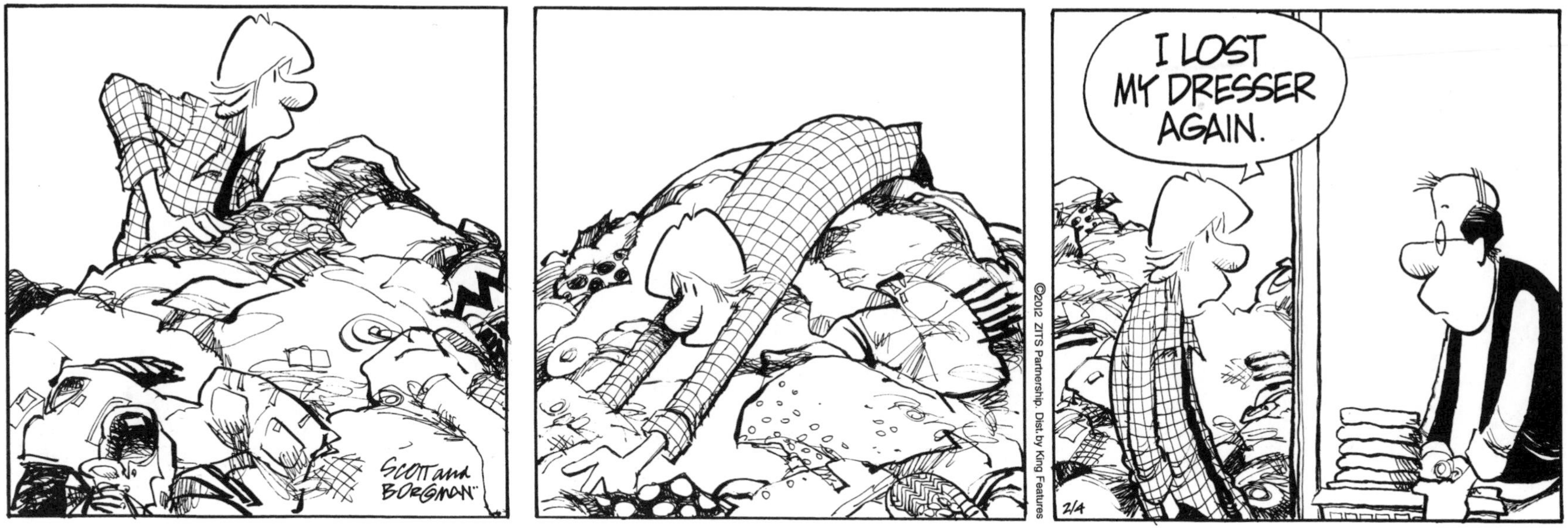
SCOTT and BORGMAN
©2012 ZITS Partnership. Dist. by King Features
2/4
I LOST MY DRESSER AGAIN.

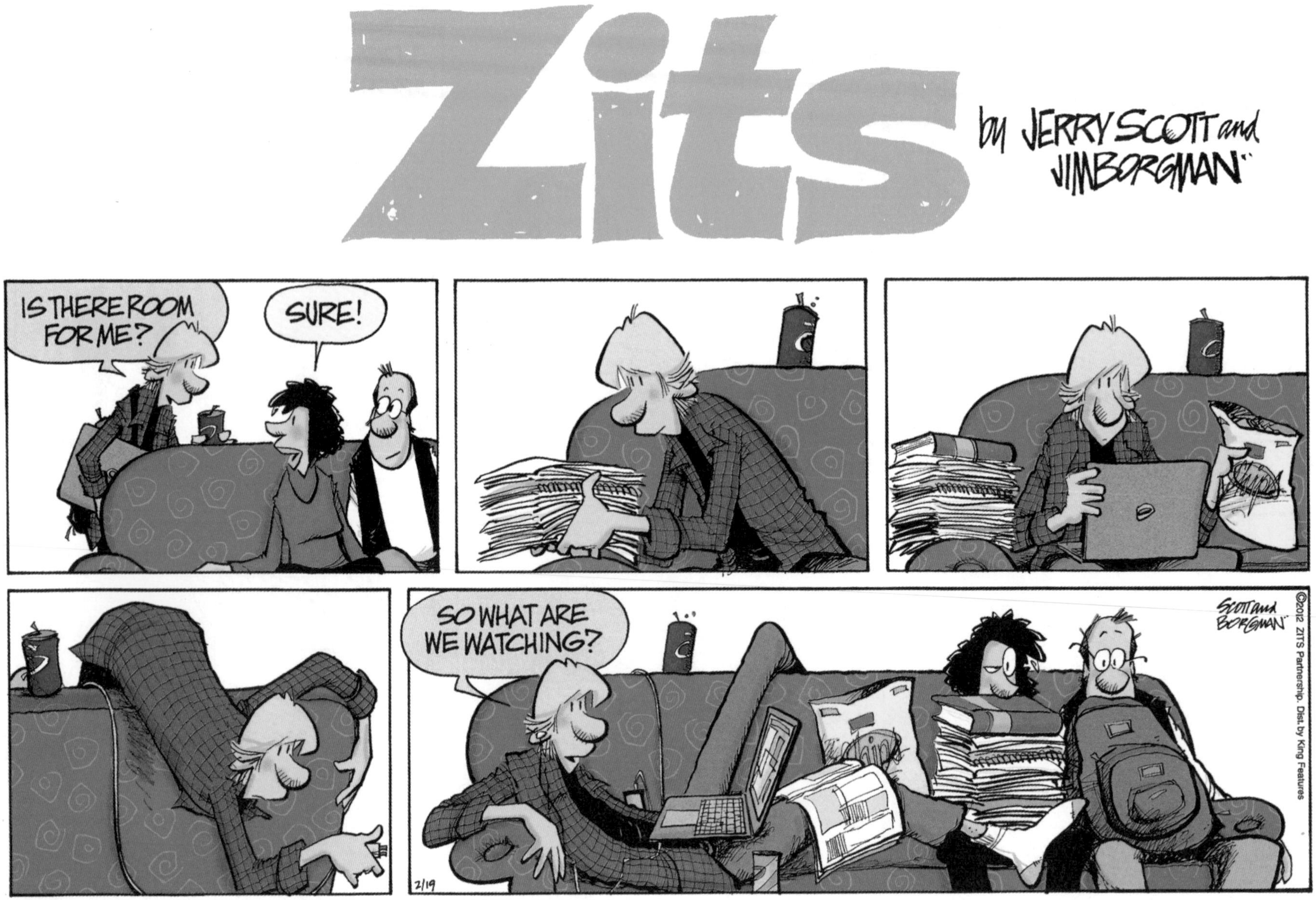
Zits
by JERRY SCOTT and JIM BORGMAN
IS THERE ROOM FOR ME?
SURE!
SO WHAT ARE WE WATCHING?
SCOTT and BORGMAN
©2012 ZITS Partnership. Dist. by King Features
2/19

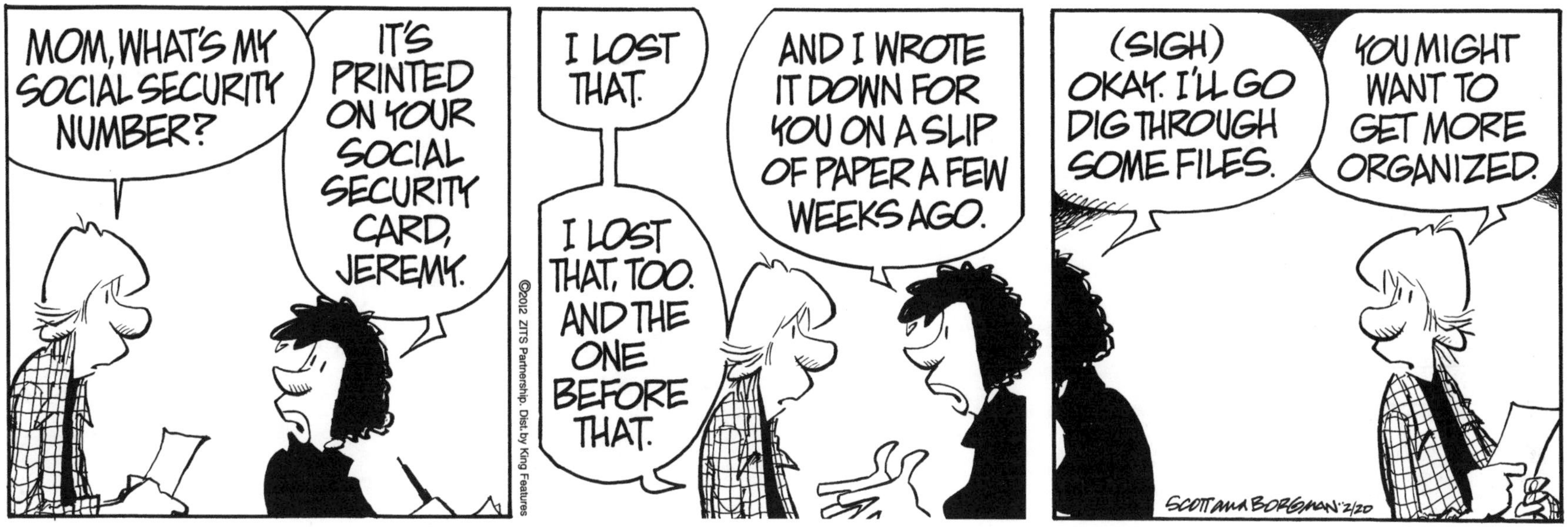
MOM, WHAT'S MY SOCIAL SECURITY NUMBER?
IT'S PRINTED ON YOUR SOCIAL SECURITY CARD, JEREMY.
I LOST THAT.
I LOST THAT, TOO. AND THE ONE BEFORE THAT.
AND I WROTE IT DOWN FOR YOU ON A SLIP OF PAPER A FEW WEEKS AGO.
(SIGH) OKAY. I'LL GO DIG THROUGH SOME FILES.
YOU MIGHT WANT TO GET MORE ORGANIZED.
©2012 ZITS Partnership. Dist. by King Features
SCOTT AND BORGMAN 2/20

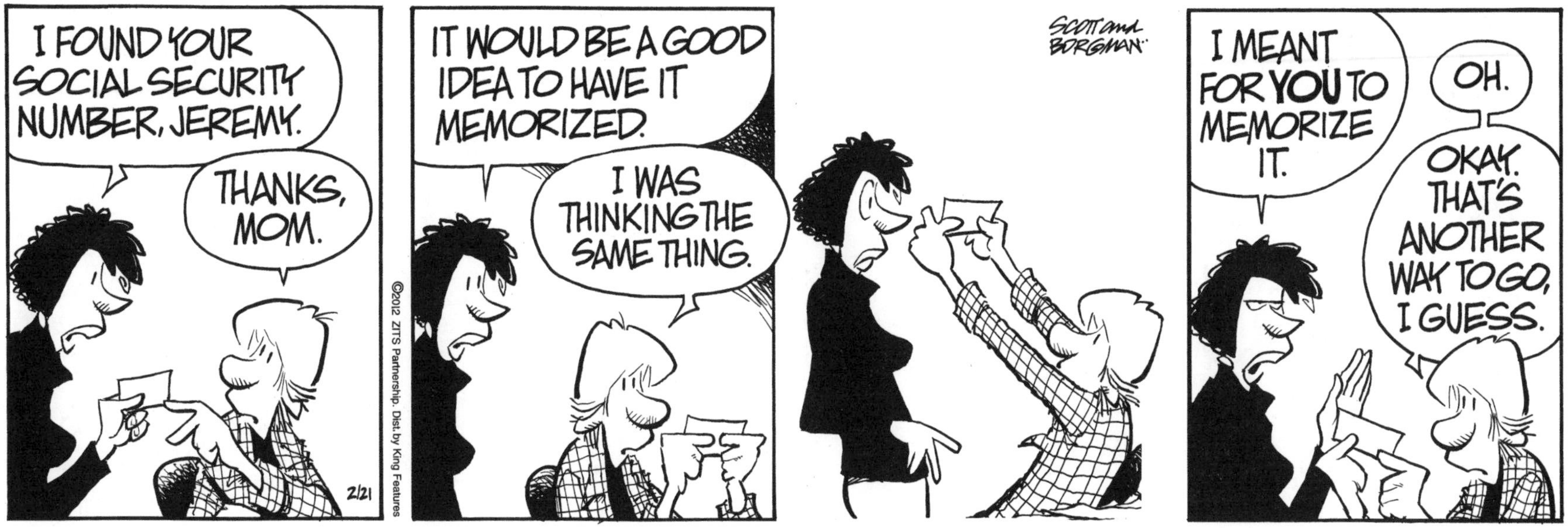
I FOUND YOUR SOCIAL SECURITY NUMBER, JEREMY.
THANKS, MOM.
IT WOULD BE A GOOD IDEA TO HAVE IT MEMORIZED.
I WAS THINKING THE SAME THING.
I MEANT FOR **YOU** TO MEMORIZE IT.
OH.
OKAY. THAT'S ANOTHER WAY TO GO, I GUESS.
©2012 ZITS Partnership. Dist. by King Features
2/21
SCOTT AND BORGMAN

DAD, CAN I DRIVE YOUR CAR?
WHY? IS THERE SOMETHING WRONG WITH THE VAN?
NO, I JUST THINK THAT IT'S GOOD FOR ME TO DRIVE A VARIETY OF VEHICLES TO KEEP MY SKILLS SHARP.
YOUR CAR HAS FEATURES THAT MINE DOESN'T, LIKE AN AUTOMATIC TRANSMISSION, CRUISE CONTROL, ABS...
...GAS.
HE'S ON TO US.
SCOTT and BORGMAN
2/22
©2012 ZITS Partnership. Dist. by King Features

WHO WANTS TO GO FOR A WALK?
WHO WANTS TO PLAY APPLES TO APPLES?
WHO WANTS TO SCRAPBOOK?
AS NATURE ABHORS A VACUUM, YOUR MOM ABHORS AN INACTIVE MALE.
ZUMBA, ANYONE?
SCOTT and BORGMAN
2/23
©2012 ZITS Partnership. Dist. by King Features

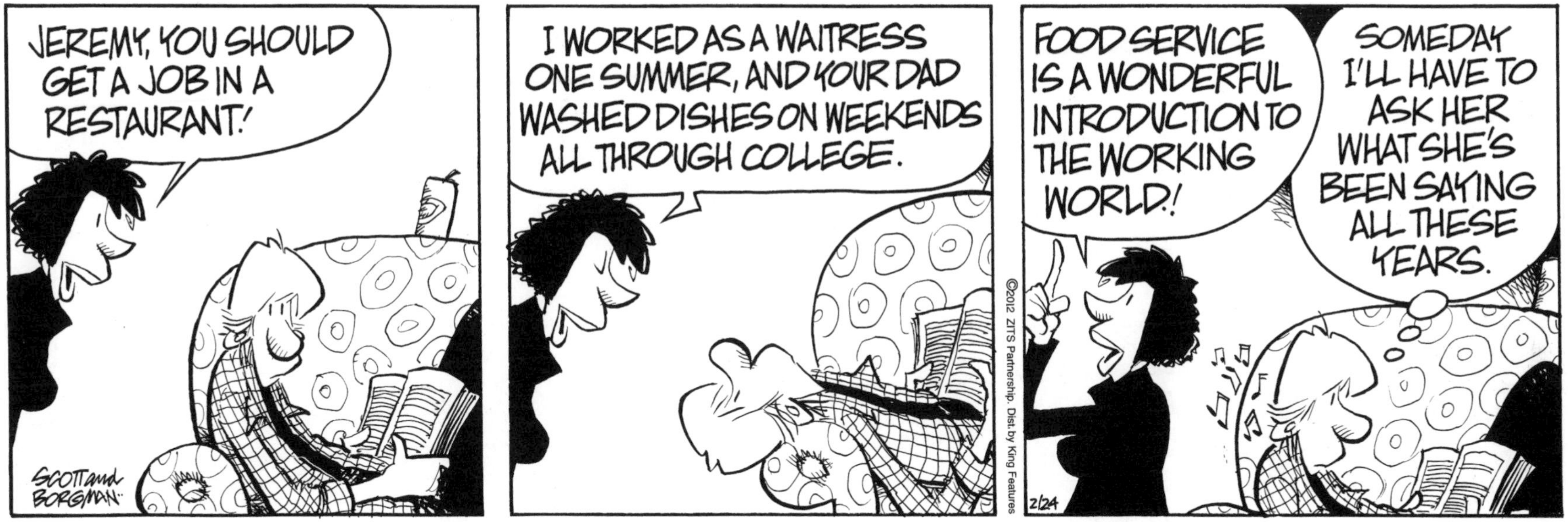
JEREMY, YOU SHOULD GET A JOB IN A RESTAURANT!
SCOTT and BORGMAN
I WORKED AS A WAITRESS ONE SUMMER, AND YOUR DAD WASHED DISHES ON WEEKENDS ALL THROUGH COLLEGE.
©2012 ZITS Partnership. Dist. by King Features
FOOD SERVICE IS A WONDERFUL INTRODUCTION TO THE WORKING WORLD!
SOMEDAY I'LL HAVE TO ASK HER WHAT SHE'S BEEN SAYING ALL THESE YEARS.
2/24

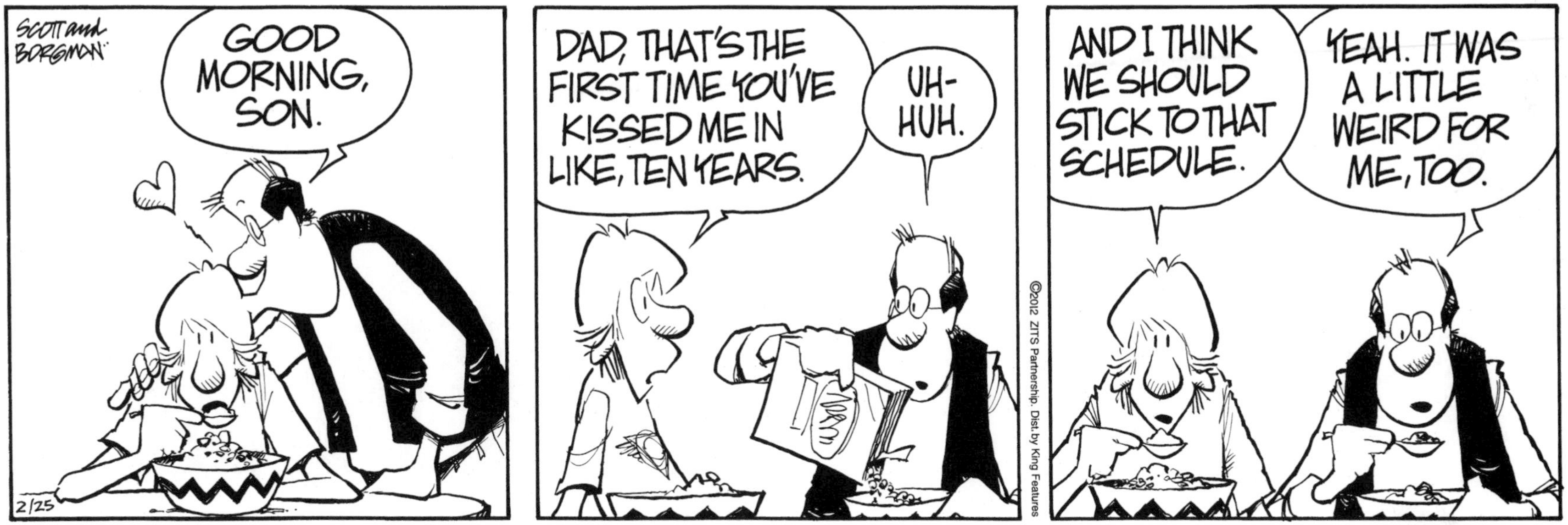
SCOTT and BORGMAN
GOOD MORNING, SON.
2/25
DAD, THAT'S THE FIRST TIME YOU'VE KISSED ME IN LIKE, TEN YEARS.
UH-HUH.
©2012 ZITS Partnership. Dist. by King Features
AND I THINK WE SHOULD STICK TO THAT SCHEDULE.
YEAH. IT WAS A LITTLE WEIRD FOR ME, TOO.

Zits

by JERRY SCOTT and JIM BORGMAN

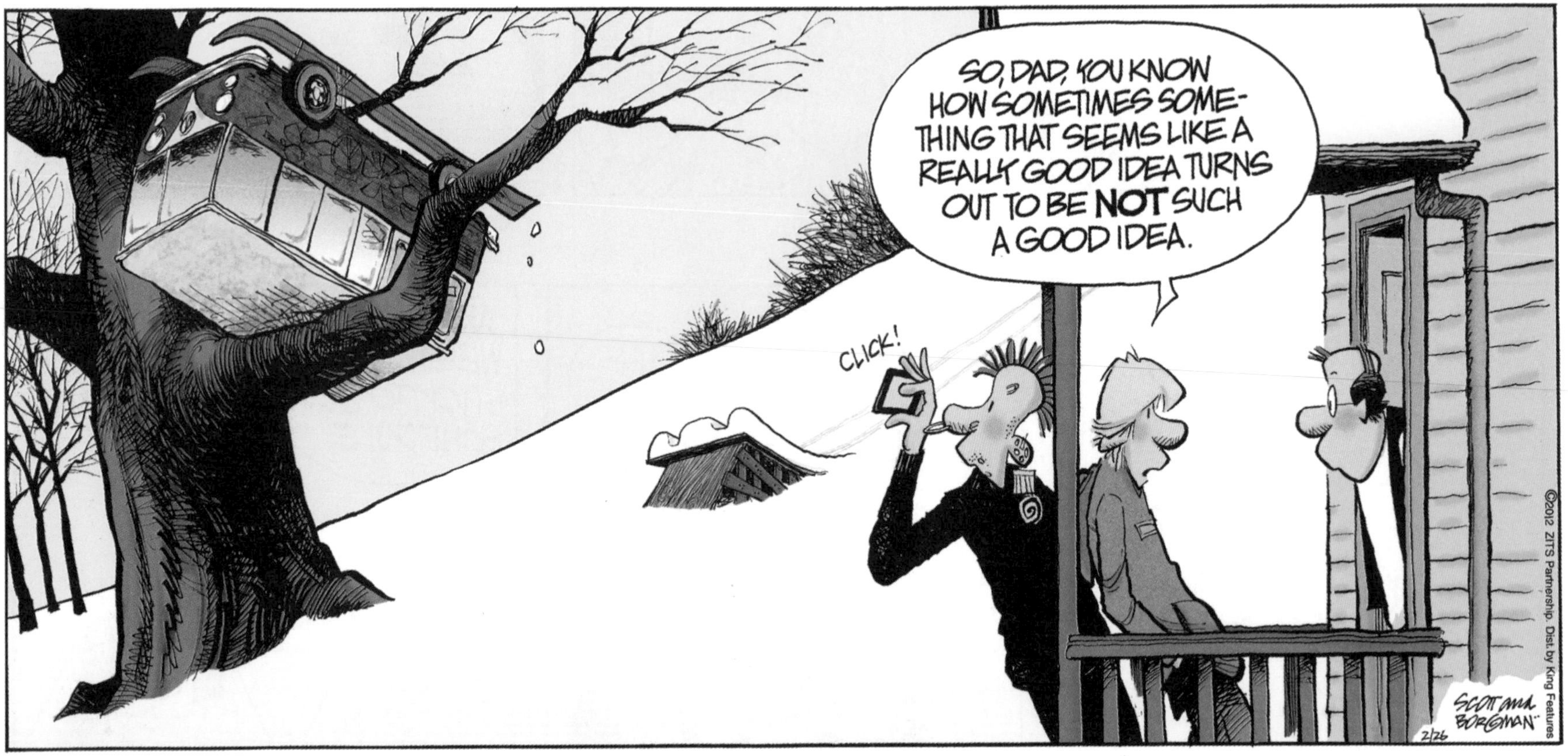
SO, DAD, YOU KNOW HOW SOMETIMES SOMETHING THAT SEEMS LIKE A REALLY GOOD IDEA TURNS OUT TO BE **NOT** SUCH A GOOD IDEA.
CLICK!
©2012 ZITS Partnership. Dist. by King Features
SCOTT and BORGMAN
2/26

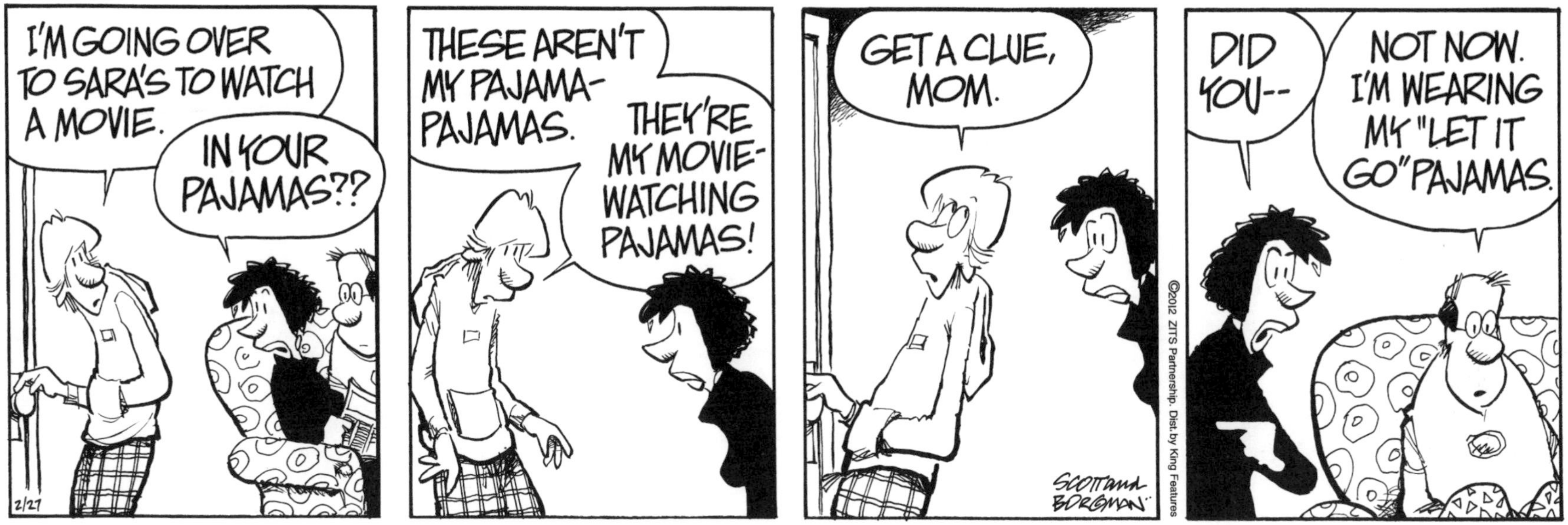
I'M GOING OVER TO SARA'S TO WATCH A MOVIE.
IN YOUR PAJAMAS??
THESE AREN'T MY PAJAMA-PAJAMAS.
THEY'RE MY MOVIE-WATCHING PAJAMAS!
GET A CLUE, MOM.
DID YOU--
NOT NOW. I'M WEARING MY "LET IT GO" PAJAMAS.
©2012 ZITS Partnership. Dist. by King Features
2/27

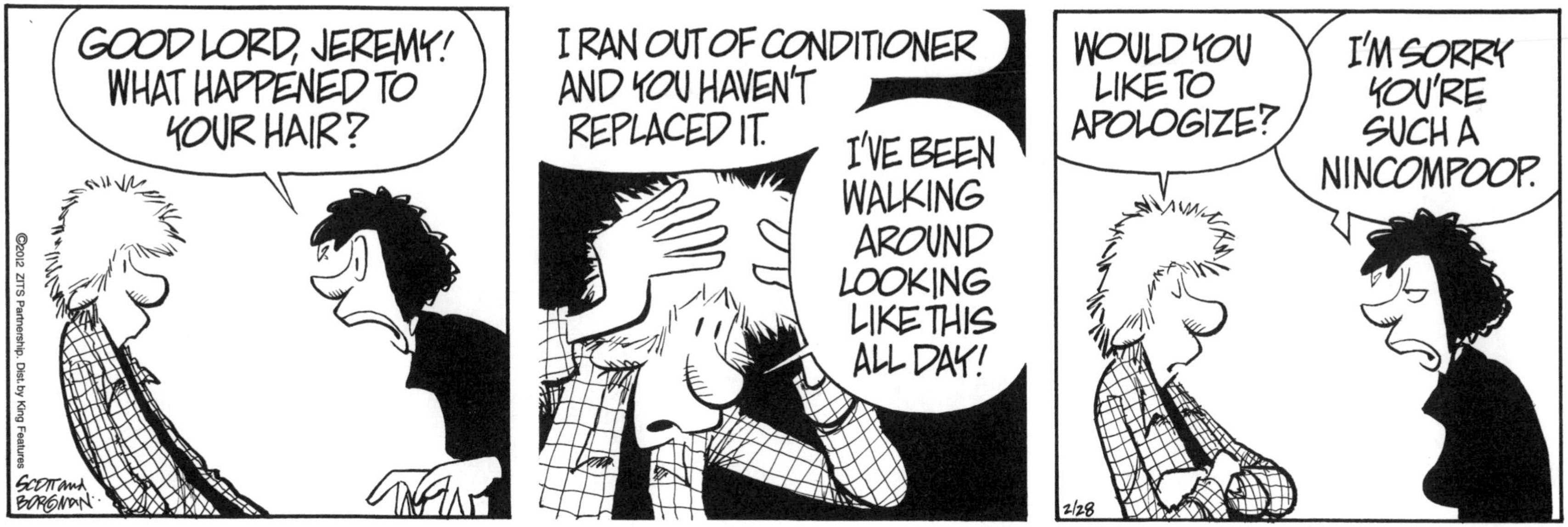
GOOD LORD, JEREMY! WHAT HAPPENED TO YOUR HAIR?
I RAN OUT OF CONDITIONER AND YOU HAVEN'T REPLACED IT.
I'VE BEEN WALKING AROUND LOOKING LIKE THIS ALL DAY!
WOULD YOU LIKE TO APOLOGIZE?
I'M SORRY YOU'RE SUCH A NINCOMPOOP.
©2012 ZITS Partnership. Dist. by King Features
2/28

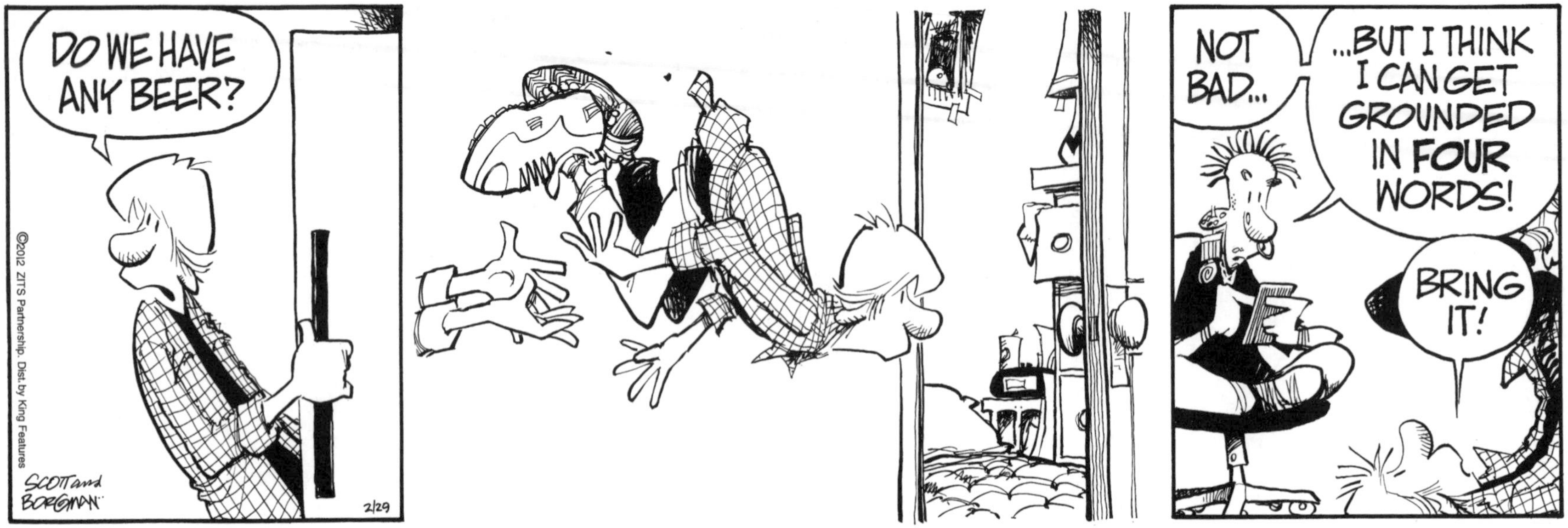
DO WE HAVE ANY BEER?
©2012 ZITS Partnership. Dist. by King Features
SCOTT and BORGMAN
2/29
NOT BAD...
...BUT I THINK I CAN GET GROUNDED IN FOUR WORDS!
BRING IT!

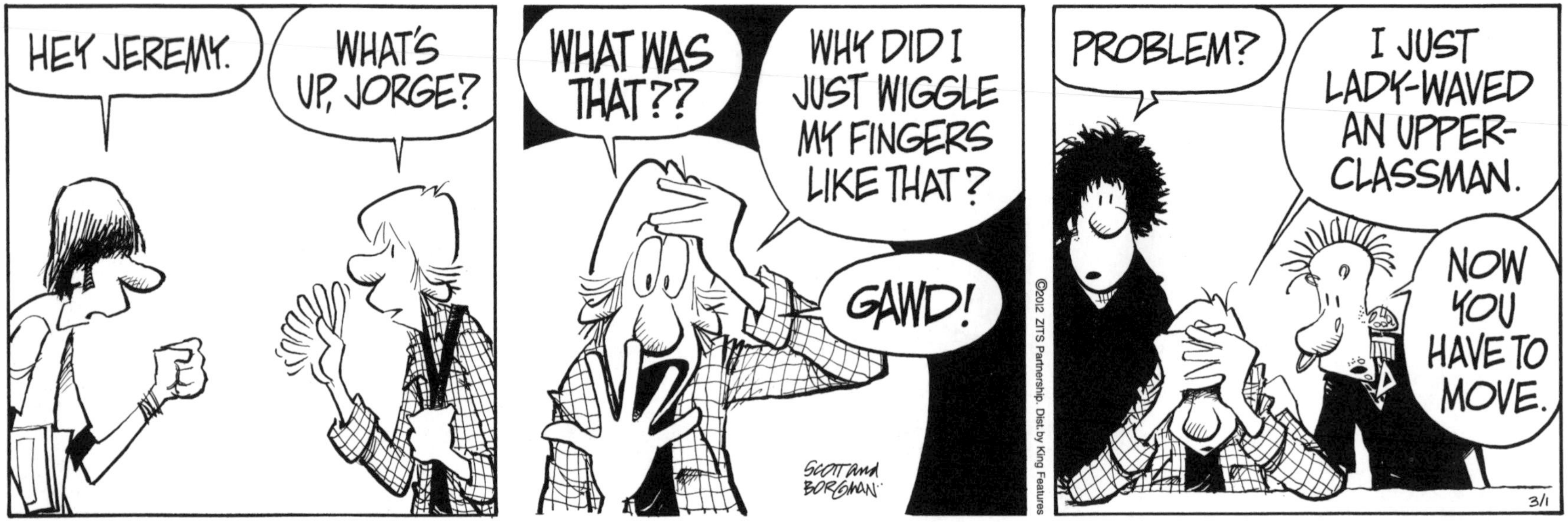
HEY JEREMY.
WHAT'S UP, JORGE?
WHAT WAS THAT??
WHY DID I JUST WIGGLE MY FINGERS LIKE THAT?
GAWD!
SCOTT and BORGMAN
©2012 ZITS Partnership. Dist. by King Features
PROBLEM?
I JUST LADY-WAVED AN UPPER-CLASSMAN.
NOW YOU HAVE TO MOVE.
3/1

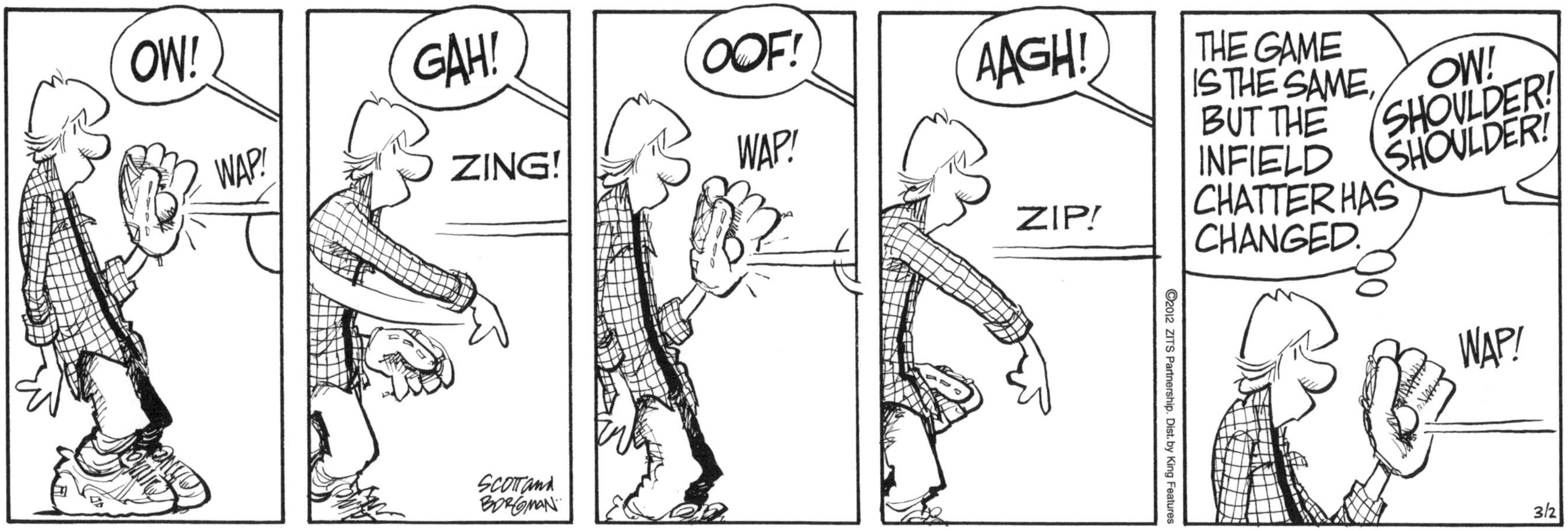
OW!
WAP!
GAH!
ZING!
SCOTT and BORGMAN
OOF!
WAP!
AAGH!
ZIP!
©2012 ZITS Partnership. Dist. by King Features
THE GAME IS THE SAME, BUT THE INFIELD CHATTER HAS CHANGED.
OW! SHOULDER! SHOULDER!
WAP!
3/2

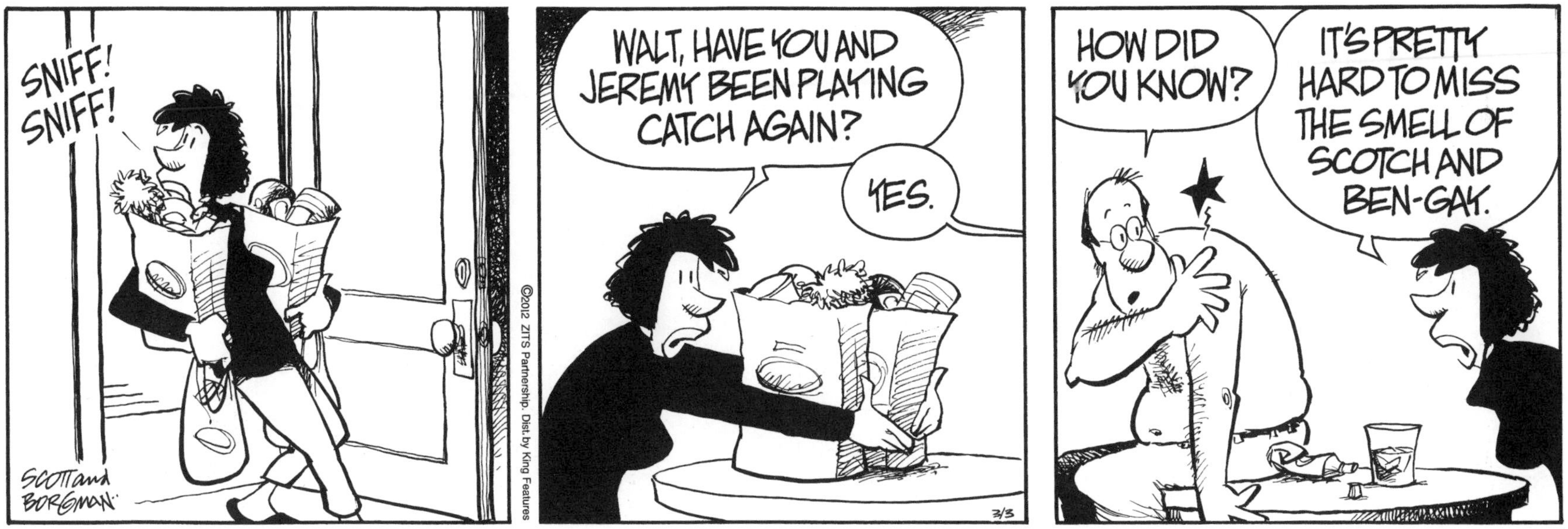
SNIFF! SNIFF!
SCOTT and BORGMAN
©2012 ZITS Partnership. Dist. by King Features
WALT, HAVE YOU AND JEREMY BEEN PLAYING CATCH AGAIN?
YES.
3/3
HOW DID YOU KNOW?
IT'S PRETTY HARD TO MISS THE SMELL OF SCOTCH AND BEN-GAY.

Zits

by JERRY SCOTT and JIM BORGMAN

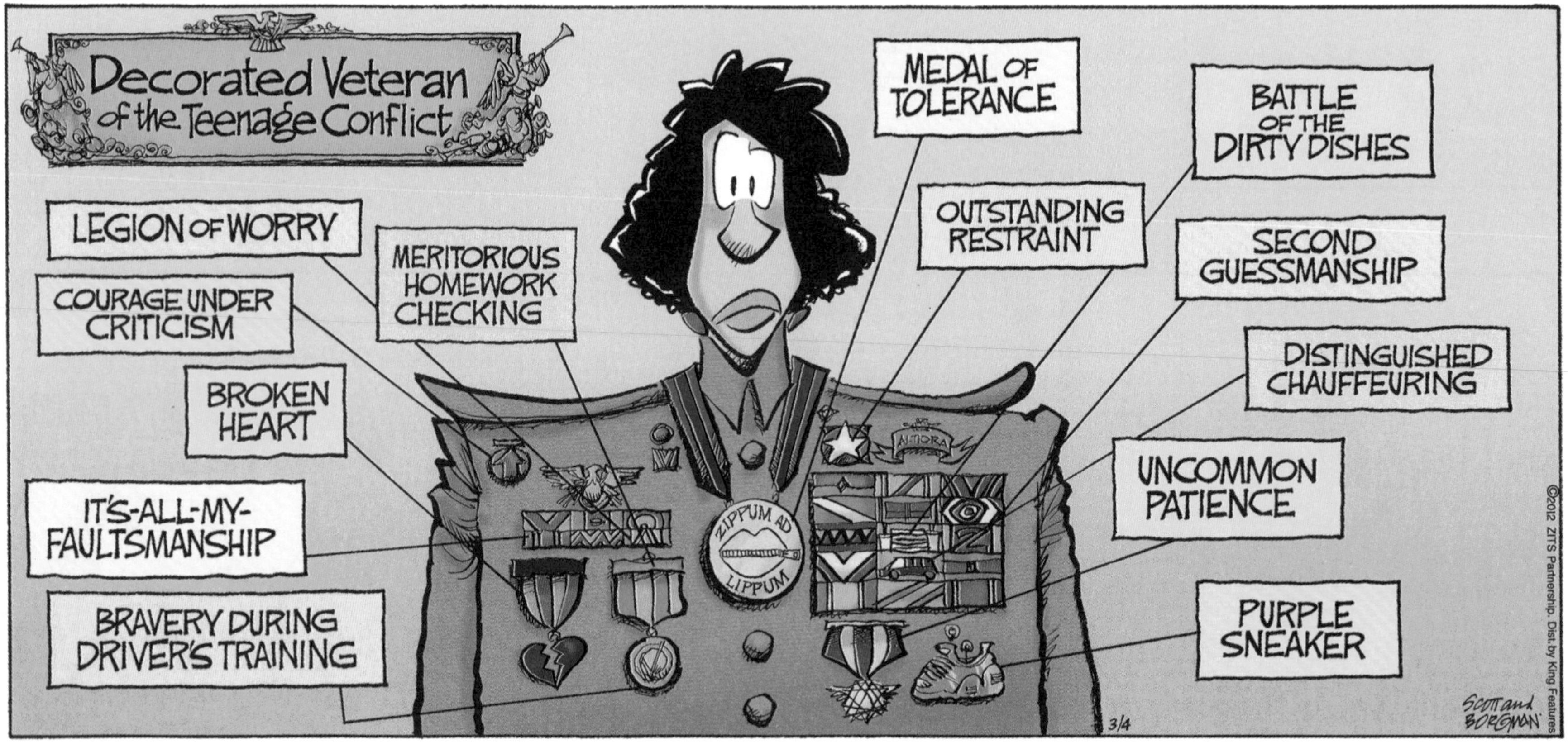
Decorated Veteran of the Teenage Conflict
LEGION OF WORRY
COURAGE UNDER CRITICISM
MERITORIOUS HOMEWORK CHECKING
BROKEN HEART
IT'S-ALL-MY-FAULTSMANSHIP
BRAVERY DURING DRIVER'S TRAINING
MEDAL OF TOLERANCE
BATTLE OF THE DIRTY DISHES
OUTSTANDING RESTRAINT
SECOND GUESSMANSHIP
DISTINGUISHED CHAUFFEURING
UNCOMMON PATIENCE
PURPLE SNEAKER
ZIPPUM AD LIPPUM
ALTIORA
3/4
SCOTT and BORGMAN
©2012 ZITS Partnership. Dist. by King Features

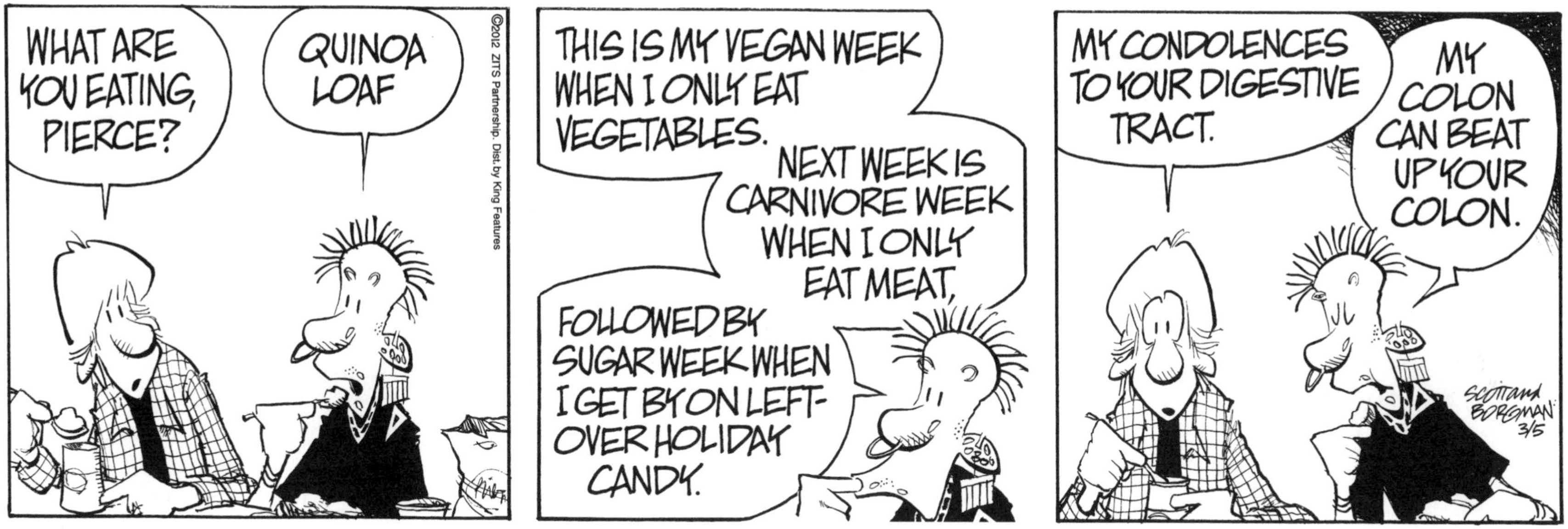
WHAT ARE YOU EATING, PIERCE?
QUINOA LOAF
©2012 ZITS Partnership. Dist. by King Features
THIS IS MY VEGAN WEEK WHEN I ONLY EAT VEGETABLES.
NEXT WEEK IS CARNIVORE WEEK WHEN I ONLY EAT MEAT,
FOLLOWED BY SUGAR WEEK WHEN I GET BY ON LEFT-OVER HOLIDAY CANDY.
MY CONDOLENCES TO YOUR DIGESTIVE TRACT.
MY COLON CAN BEAT UP YOUR COLON.
SCOTT and BORGMAN 3/5

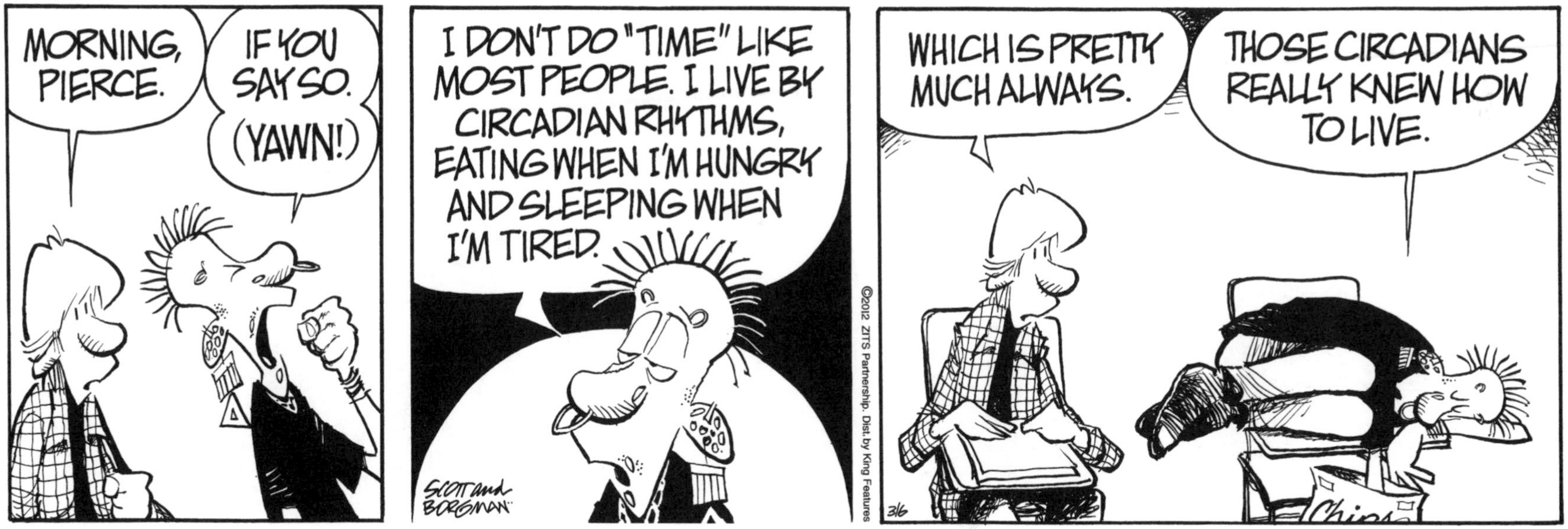
MORNING, PIERCE.
IF YOU SAY SO.
(YAWN!)
I DON'T DO "TIME" LIKE MOST PEOPLE. I LIVE BY CIRCADIAN RHYTHMS, EATING WHEN I'M HUNGRY AND SLEEPING WHEN I'M TIRED.
SCOTT and BORGMAN
©2012 ZITS Partnership. Dist. by King Features
WHICH IS PRETTY MUCH ALWAYS.
THOSE CIRCADIANS REALLY KNEW HOW TO LIVE.
3/6

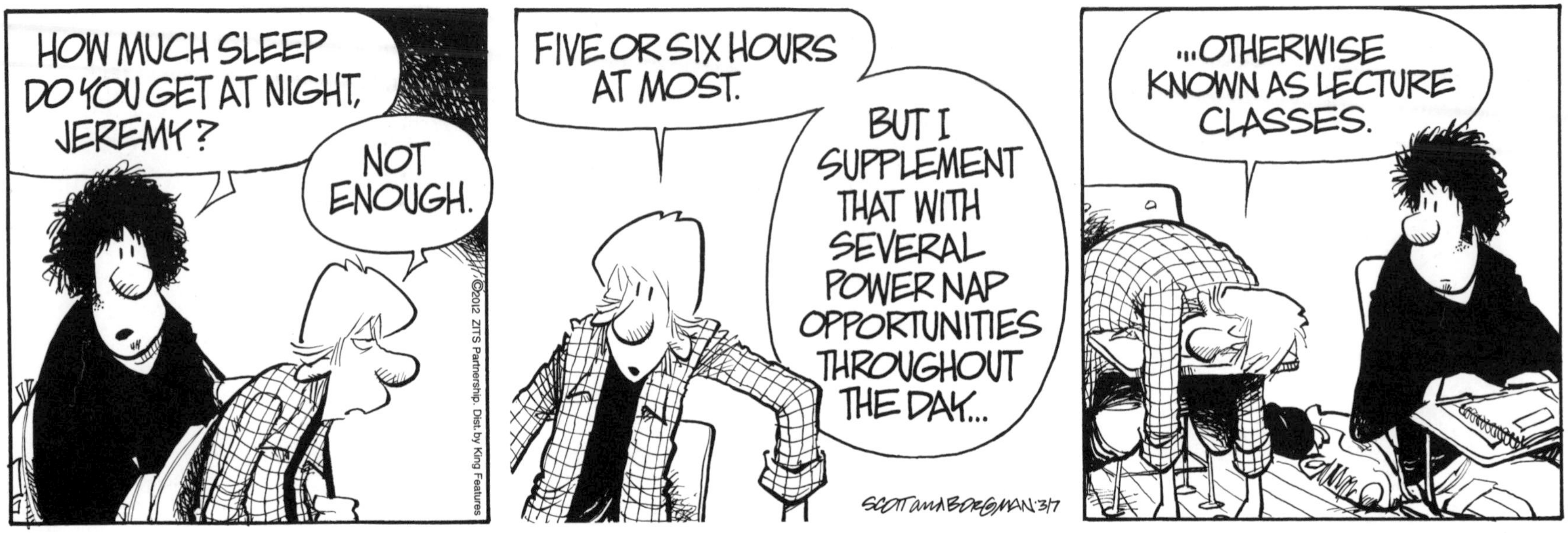
HOW MUCH SLEEP DO YOU GET AT NIGHT, JEREMY?
NOT ENOUGH.
FIVE OR SIX HOURS AT MOST.
BUT I SUPPLEMENT THAT WITH SEVERAL POWER NAP OPPORTUNITIES THROUGHOUT THE DAY...
...OTHERWISE KNOWN AS LECTURE CLASSES.
©2012 ZITS Partnership. Dist. by King Features
SCOTT and BORGMAN 3/7

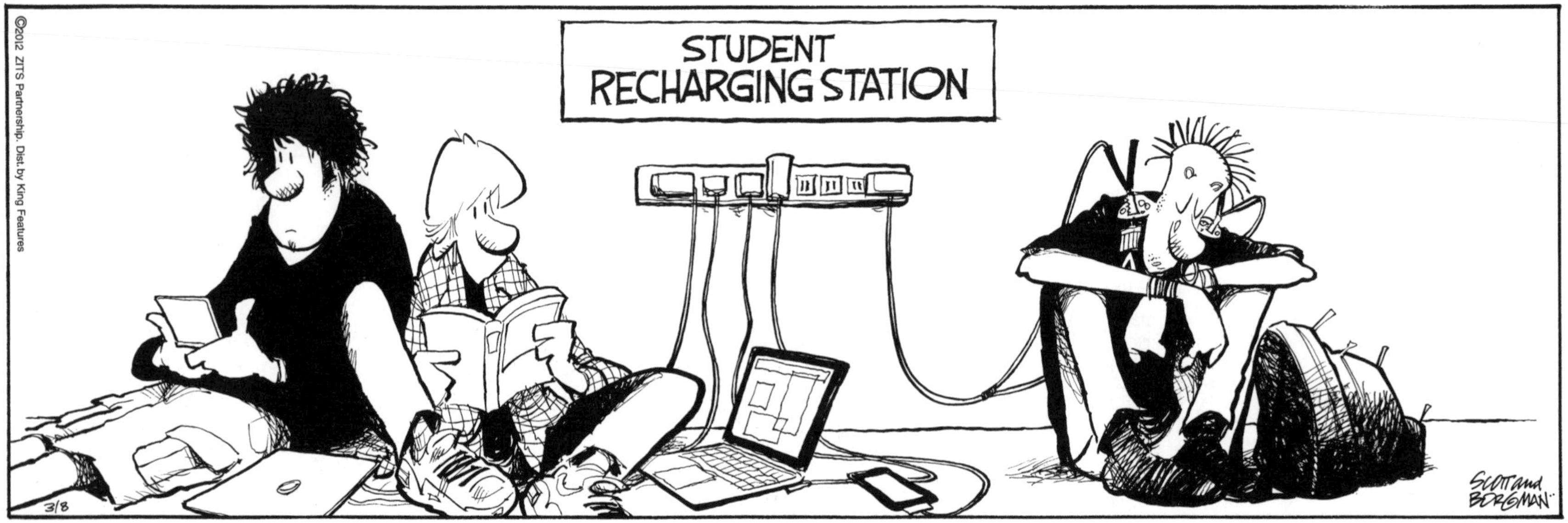
STUDENT RECHARGING STATION
©2012 ZITS Partnership. Dist. by King Features
3/8
SCOTT and BORGMAN

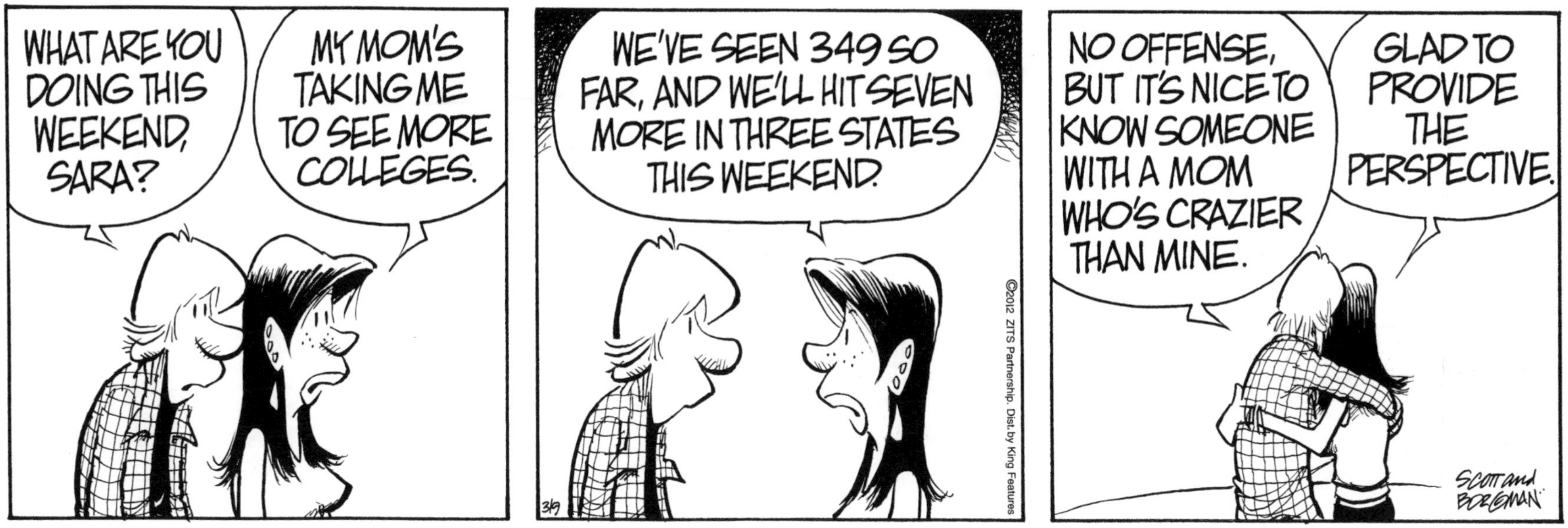
WHAT ARE YOU DOING THIS WEEKEND, SARA?
MY MOM'S TAKING ME TO SEE MORE COLLEGES.
WE'VE SEEN 349 SO FAR, AND WE'LL HIT SEVEN MORE IN THREE STATES THIS WEEKEND.
NO OFFENSE, BUT IT'S NICE TO KNOW SOMEONE WITH A MOM WHO'S CRAZIER THAN MINE.
GLAD TO PROVIDE THE PERSPECTIVE.
3/9
©2012 ZITS Partnership. Dist. by King Features
SCOTT and BORGMAN

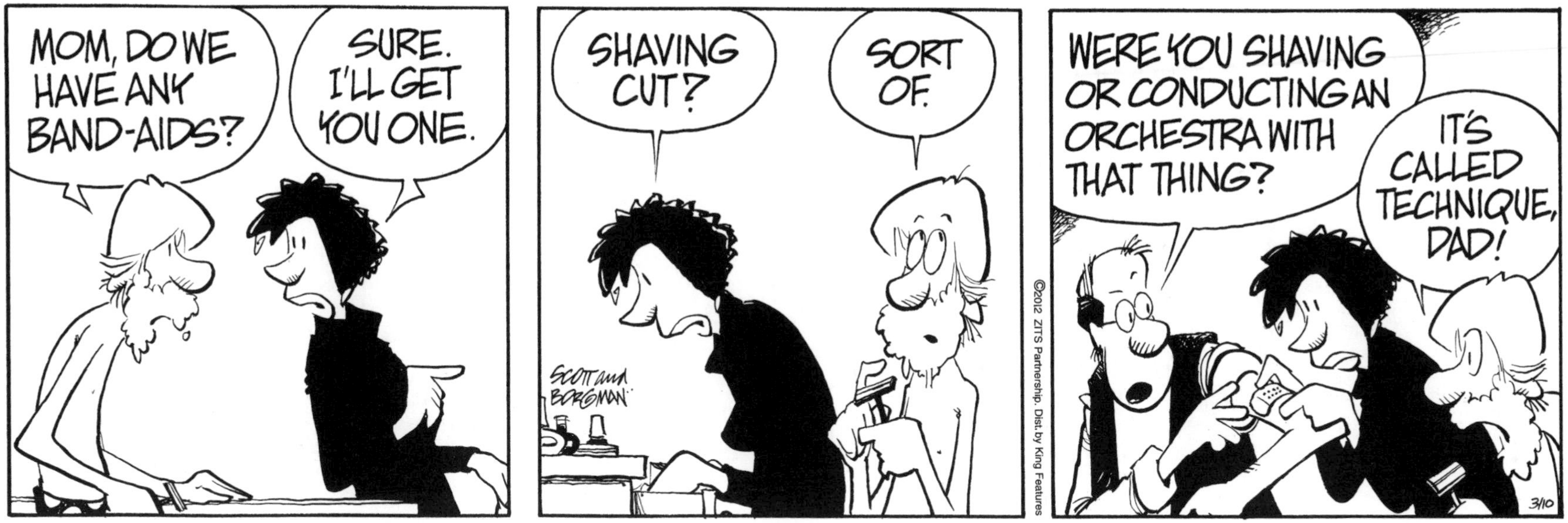
MOM, DO WE HAVE ANY BAND-AIDS?
SURE. I'LL GET YOU ONE.
SCOTT and BORGMAN
SHAVING CUT?
SORT OF.
©2012 ZITS Partnership. Dist. by King Features
WERE YOU SHAVING OR CONDUCTING AN ORCHESTRA WITH THAT THING?
IT'S CALLED TECHNIQUE, DAD!
3/10

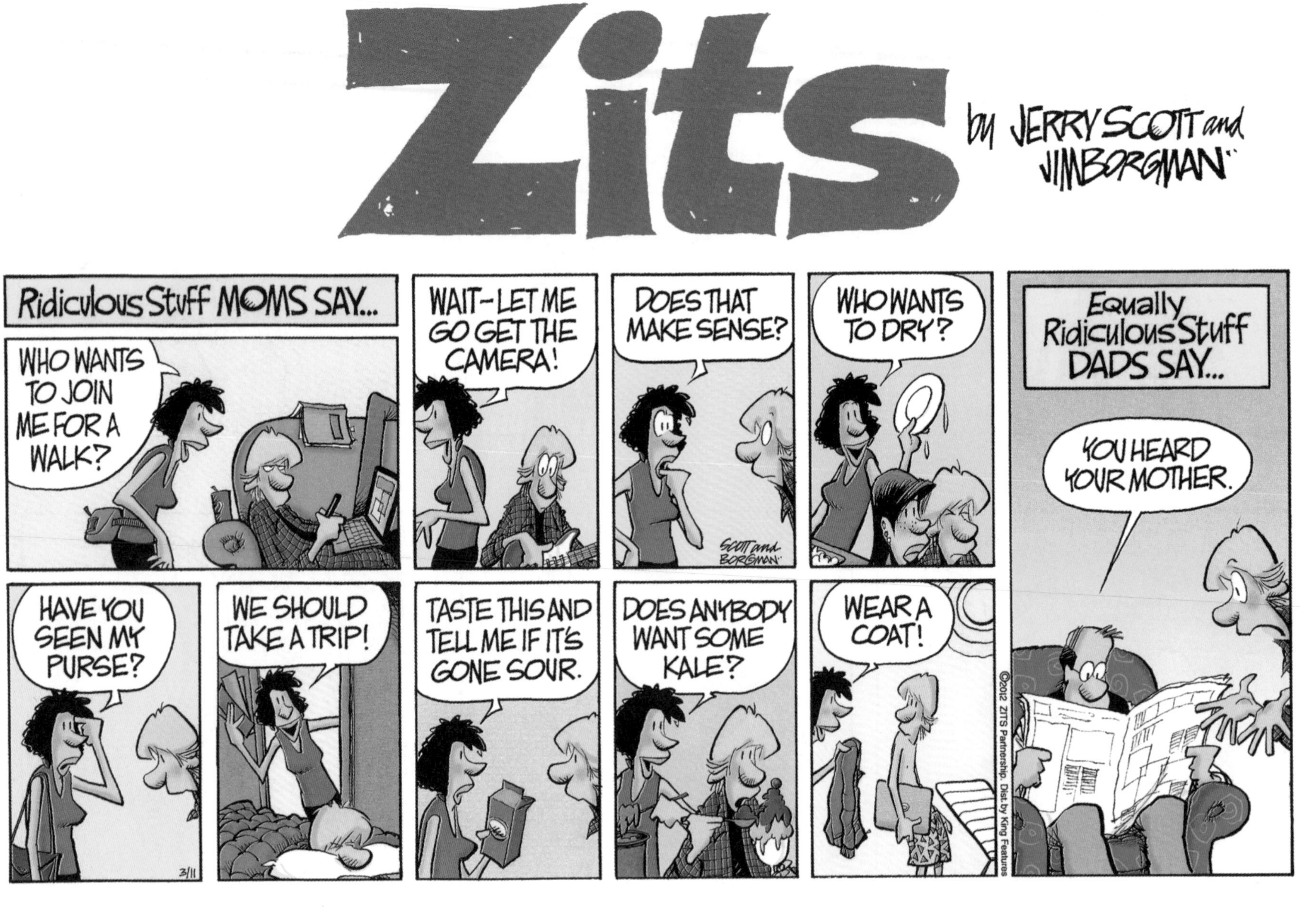
Zits
by JERRY SCOTT and JIM BORGMAN
Ridiculous Stuff MOMS SAY...
WHO WANTS TO JOIN ME FOR A WALK?
WAIT–LET ME GO GET THE CAMERA!
DOES THAT MAKE SENSE?
SCOTT and BORGMAN
WHO WANTS TO DRY?
HAVE YOU SEEN MY PURSE?
3/11
WE SHOULD TAKE A TRIP!
TASTE THIS AND TELL ME IF IT'S GONE SOUR.
DOES ANYBODY WANT SOME KALE?
WEAR A COAT!
©2012 ZITS Partnership. Dist. by King Features
Equally Ridiculous Stuff DADS SAY...
YOU HEARD YOUR MOTHER.

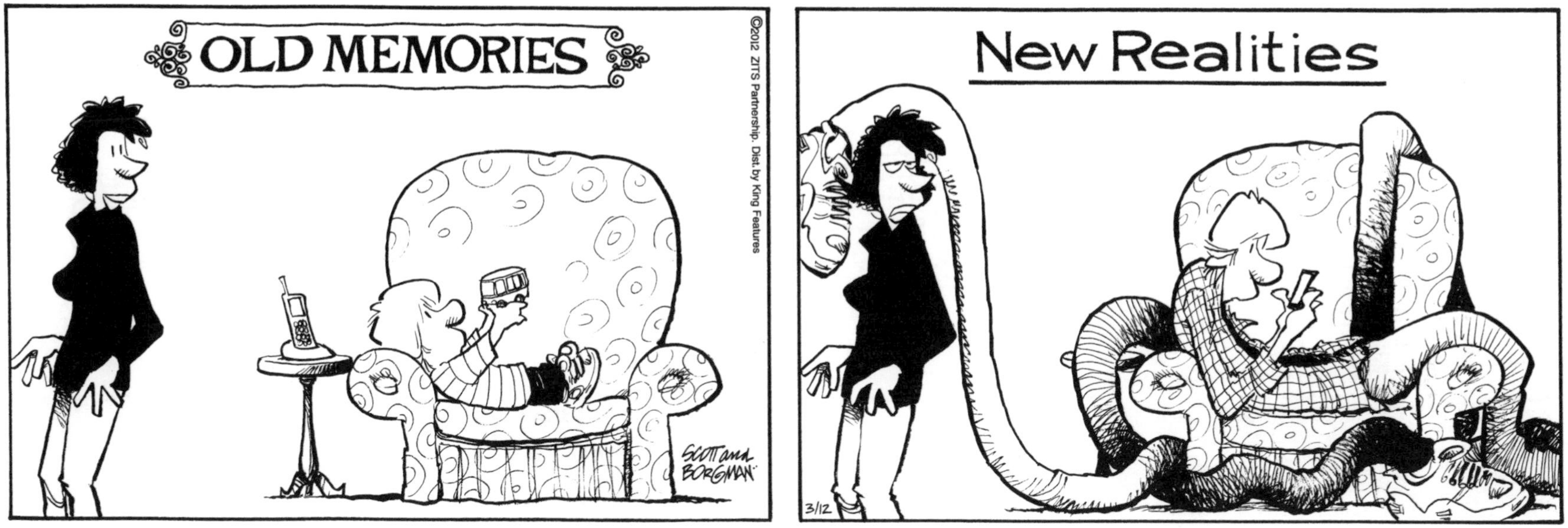
OLD MEMORIES
©2012 ZITS Partnership. Dist.by King Features
SCOTT and BORGMAN
New Realities
3/12

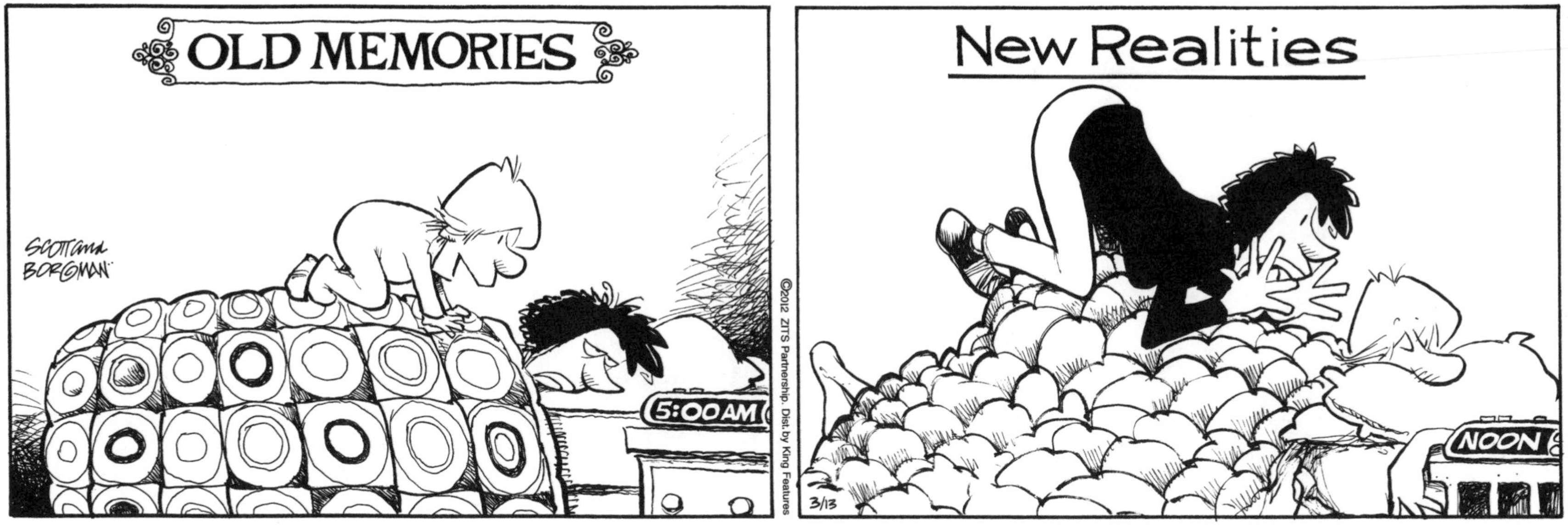
OLD MEMORIES
SCOTT and BORGMAN
5:00AM
©2012 ZITS Partnership. Dist.by King Features
New Realities
NOON
3/13

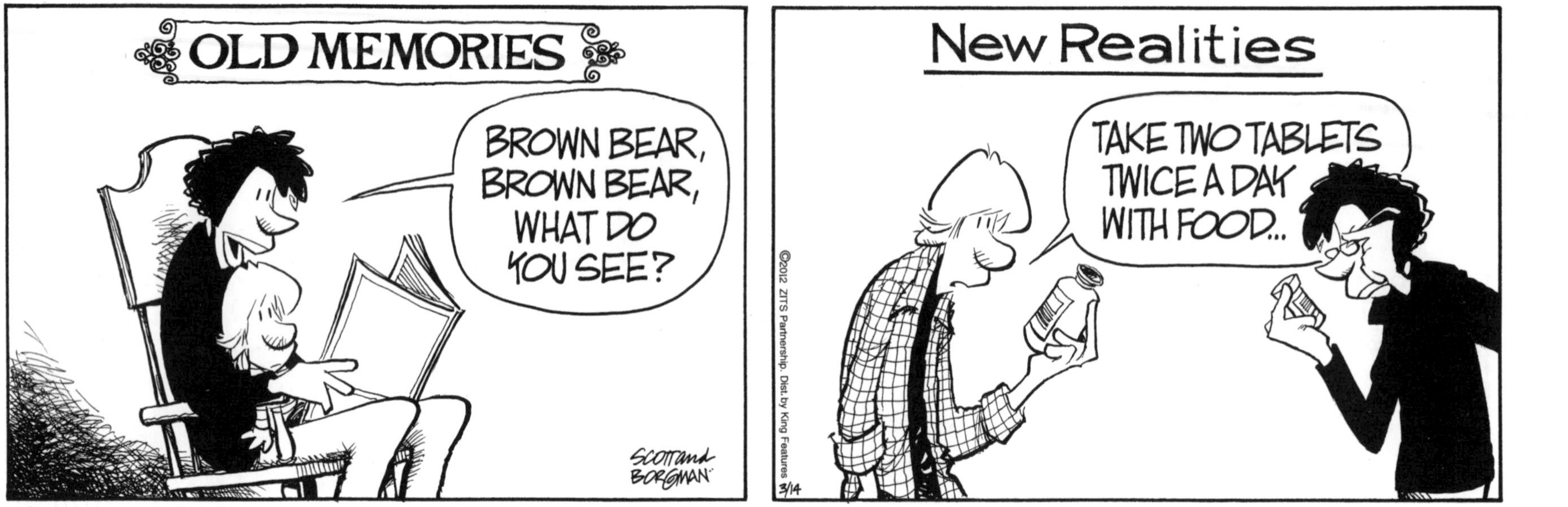
OLD MEMORIES
BROWN BEAR, BROWN BEAR, WHAT DO YOU SEE?
SCOTT and BORGMAN
New Realities
TAKE TWO TABLETS TWICE A DAY WITH FOOD...
©2012 ZITS Partnership. Dist. by King Features
3/14

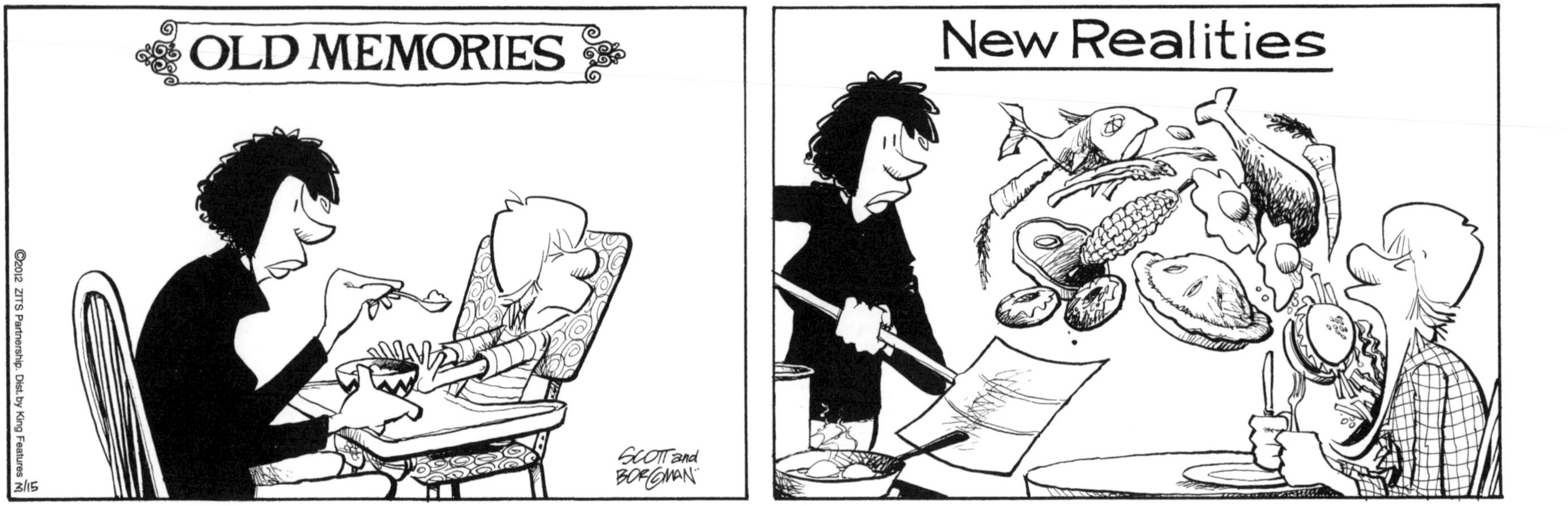
OLD MEMORIES
©2012 ZITS Partnership. Dist. by King Features
3/15
SCOTT and BORGMAN
New Realities

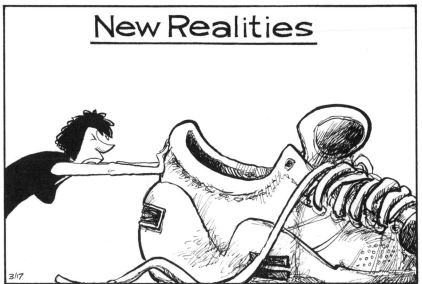

Zits

by JERRY SCOTT and JIM BORGMAN

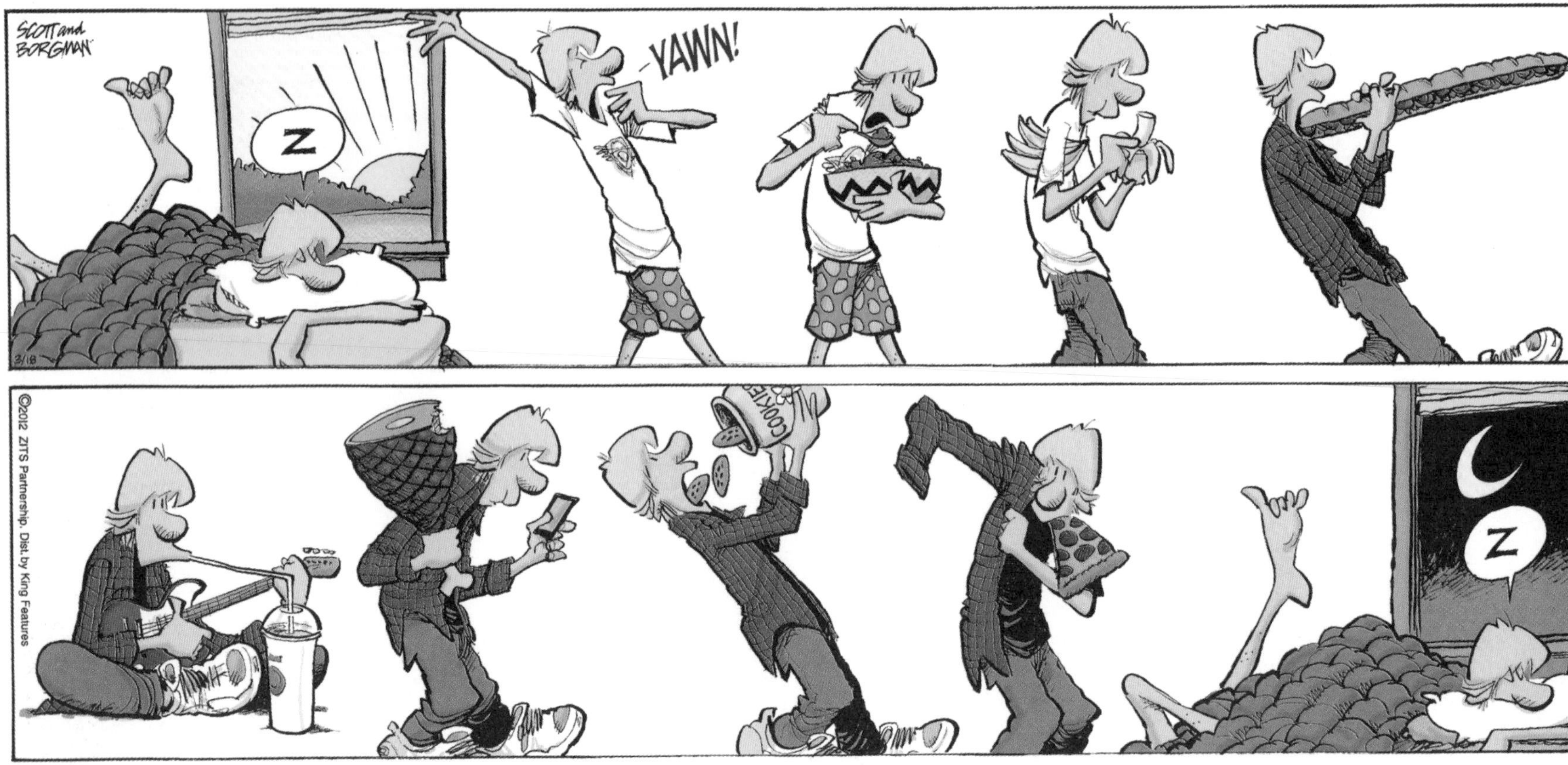
SCOTT and BORGMAN
Z
YAWN!
©2012 ZITS Partnership. Dist. by King Features
Z

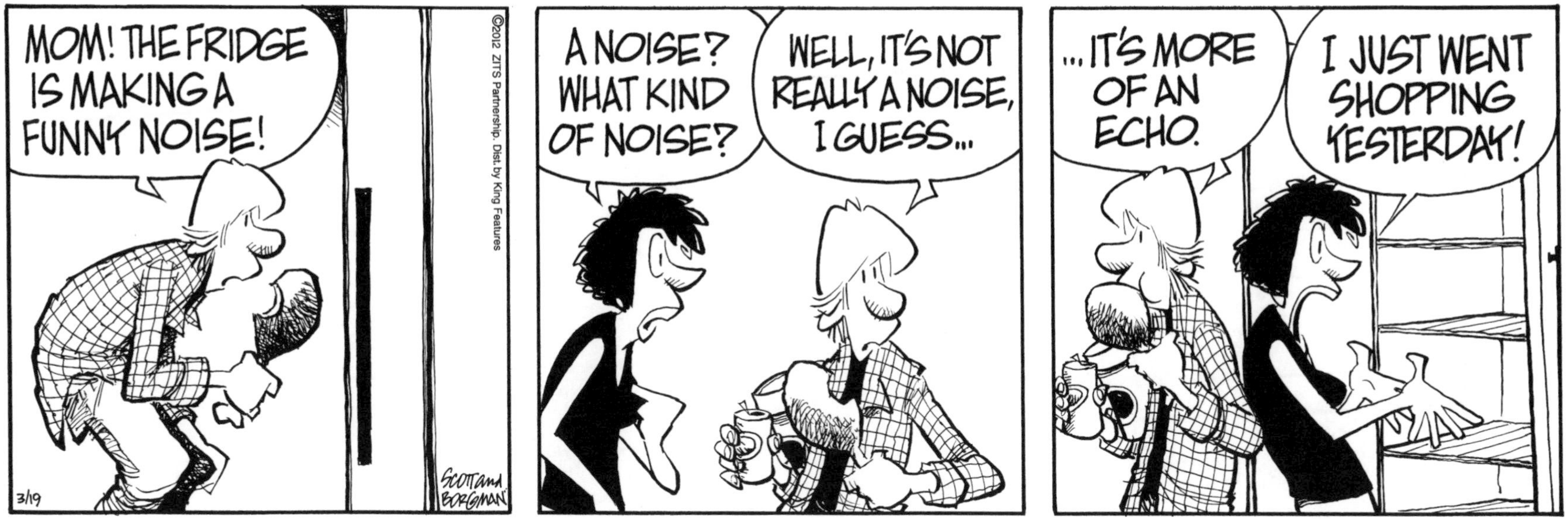
MOM! THE FRIDGE IS MAKING A FUNNY NOISE!
3/19
©2012 ZITS Partnership. Dist. by King Features
SCOTT and BORGMAN
A NOISE? WHAT KIND OF NOISE?
WELL, IT'S NOT REALLY A NOISE, I GUESS...
...IT'S MORE OF AN ECHO.
I JUST WENT SHOPPING YESTERDAY!

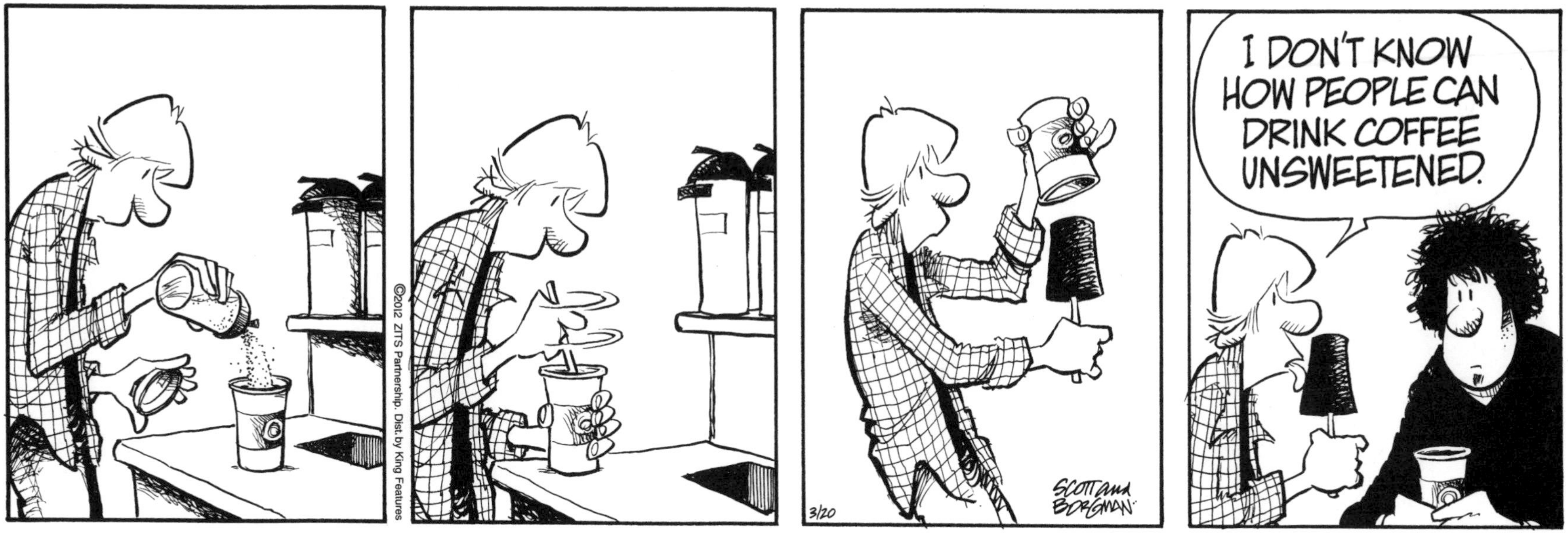
©2012 ZITS Partnership. Dist. by King Features
3/20
SCOTT and BORGMAN
I DON'T KNOW HOW PEOPLE CAN DRINK COFFEE UNSWEETENED.

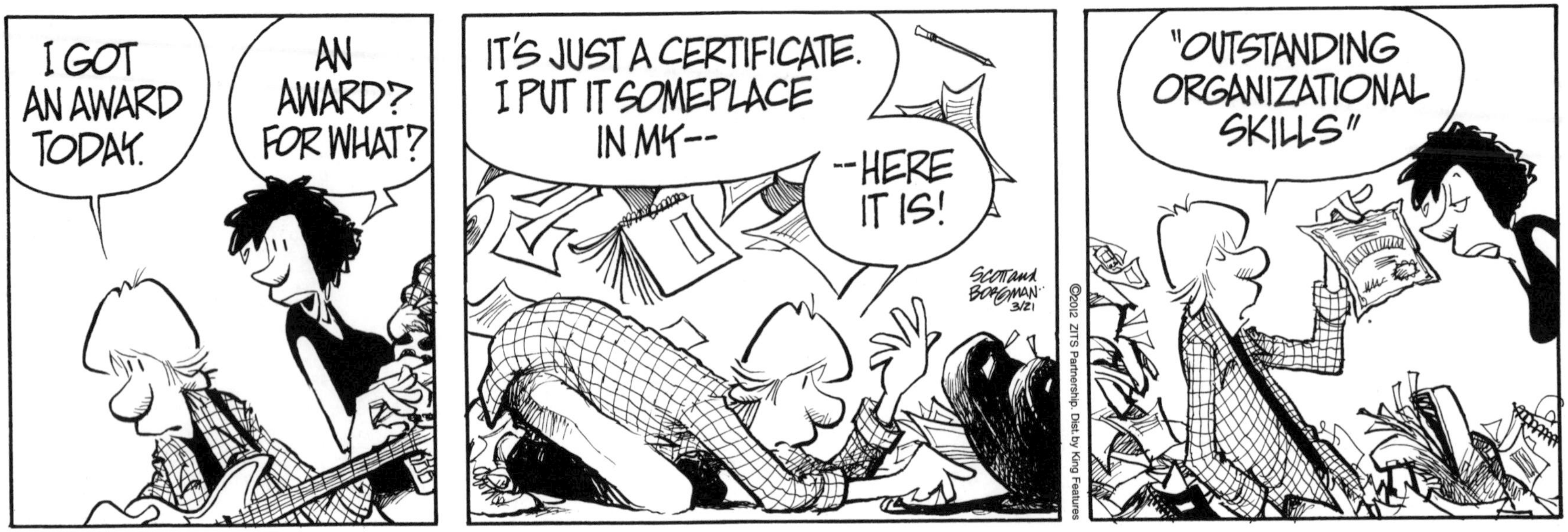
I GOT AN AWARD TODAY.
AN AWARD? FOR WHAT?
IT'S JUST A CERTIFICATE. I PUT IT SOMEPLACE IN MY--
--HERE IT IS!
SCOTT and BORGMAN 3/21
©2012 ZITS Partnership. Dist. by King Features
"OUTSTANDING ORGANIZATIONAL SKILLS"

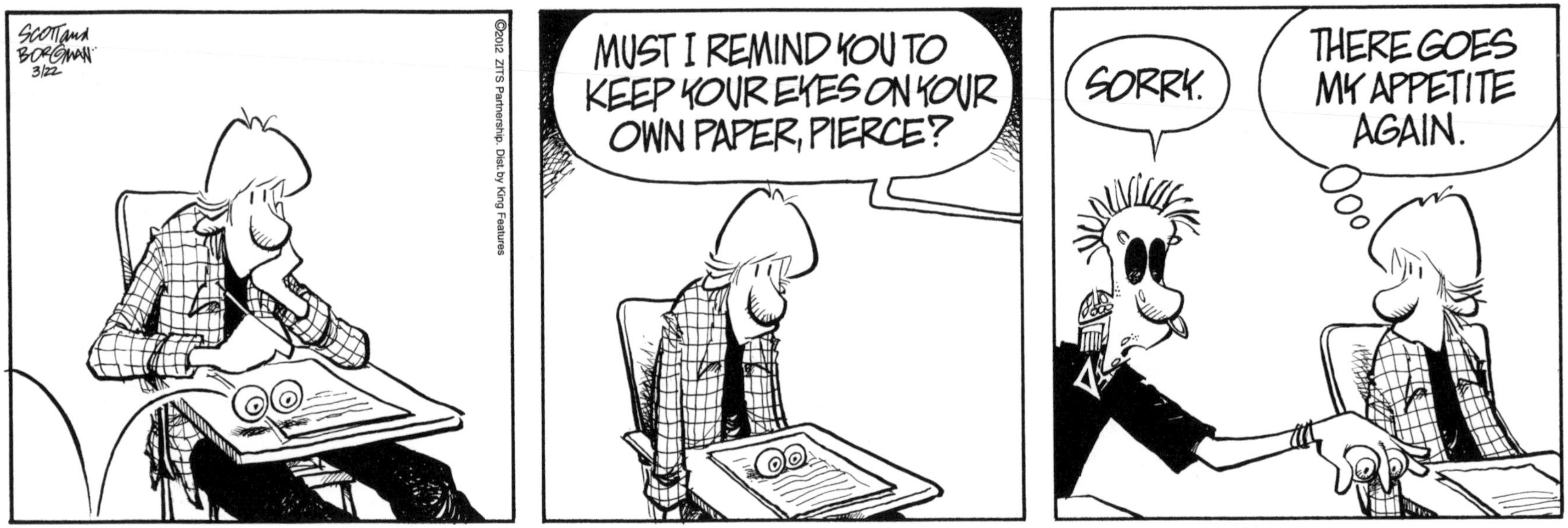
SCOTT and BORGMAN 3/22
©2012 ZITS Partnership. Dist. by King Features
MUST I REMIND YOU TO KEEP YOUR EYES ON YOUR OWN PAPER, PIERCE?
SORRY.
THERE GOES MY APPETITE AGAIN.

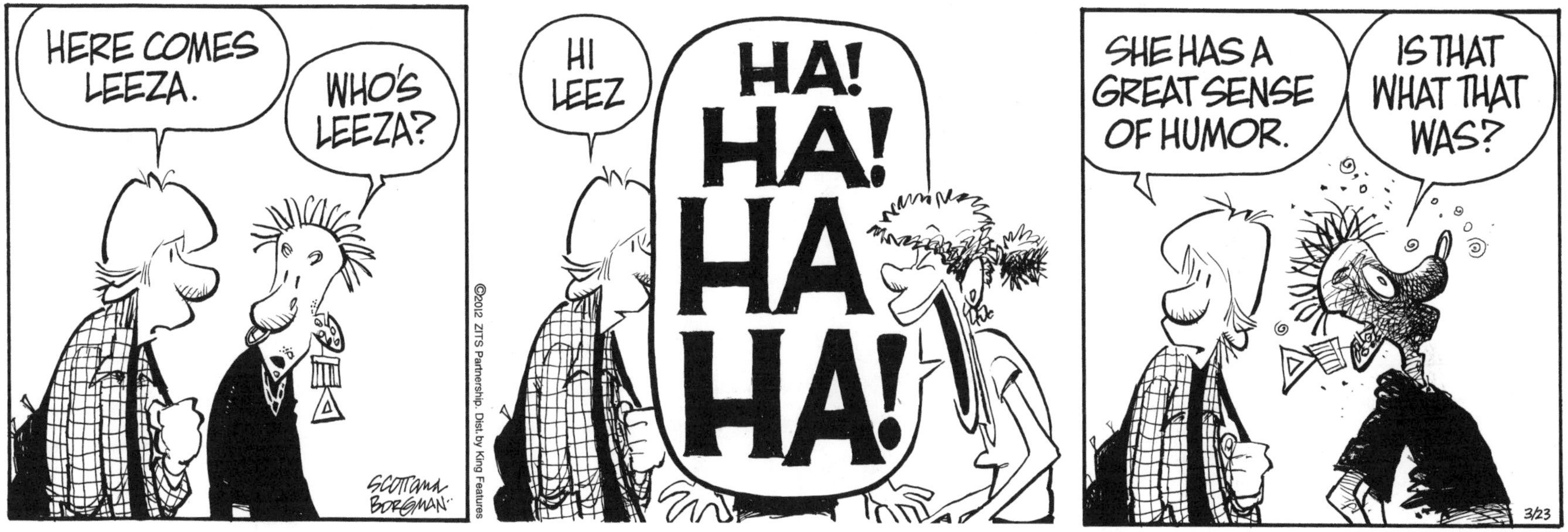
HERE COMES LEEZA.
WHO'S LEEZA?
SCOTT and BORGMAN
©2012 ZITS Partnership. Dist. by King Features
HI LEEZ
HA! HA! HA HA!
SHE HAS A GREAT SENSE OF HUMOR.
IS THAT WHAT THAT WAS?
3/23

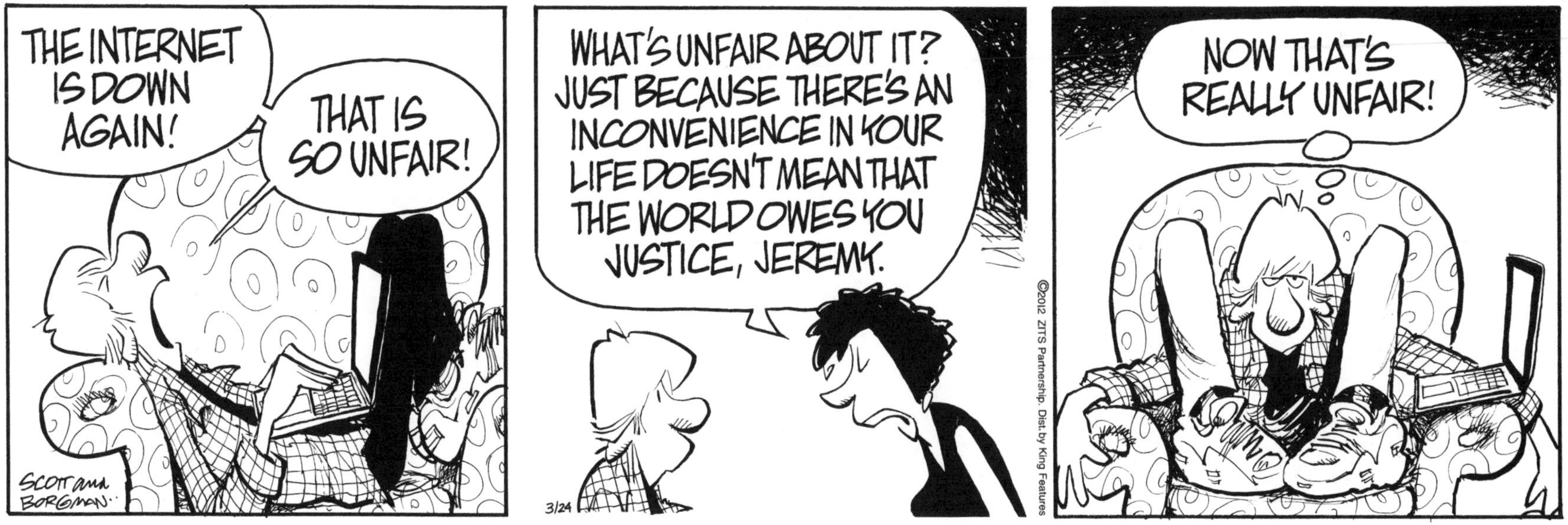
THE INTERNET IS DOWN AGAIN!
THAT IS SO UNFAIR!
SCOTT and BORGMAN
WHAT'S UNFAIR ABOUT IT? JUST BECAUSE THERE'S AN INCONVENIENCE IN YOUR LIFE DOESN'T MEAN THAT THE WORLD OWES YOU JUSTICE, JEREMY.
3/24
©2012 ZITS Partnership. Dist. by King Features
NOW THAT'S REALLY UNFAIR!

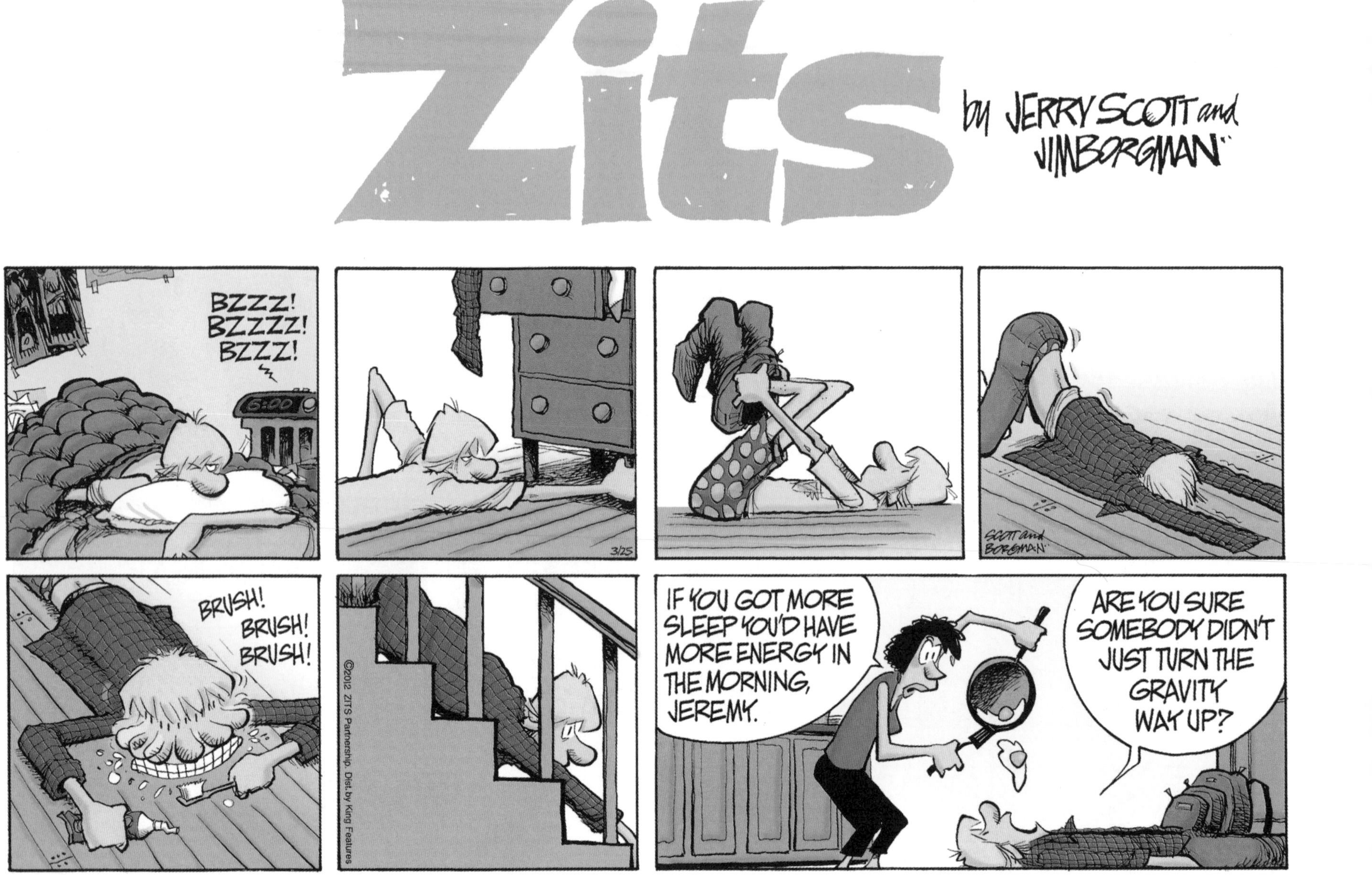
Zits
by JERRY SCOTT and JIM BORGMAN
BZZZ! BZZZZ! BZZZ!
6:00
3/25
SCOTT and BORGMAN
BRUSH! BRUSH! BRUSH!
©2012 ZITS Partnership. Dist. by King Features
IF YOU GOT MORE SLEEP YOU'D HAVE MORE ENERGY IN THE MORNING, JEREMY.
ARE YOU SURE SOMEBODY DIDN'T JUST TURN THE GRAVITY WAY UP?

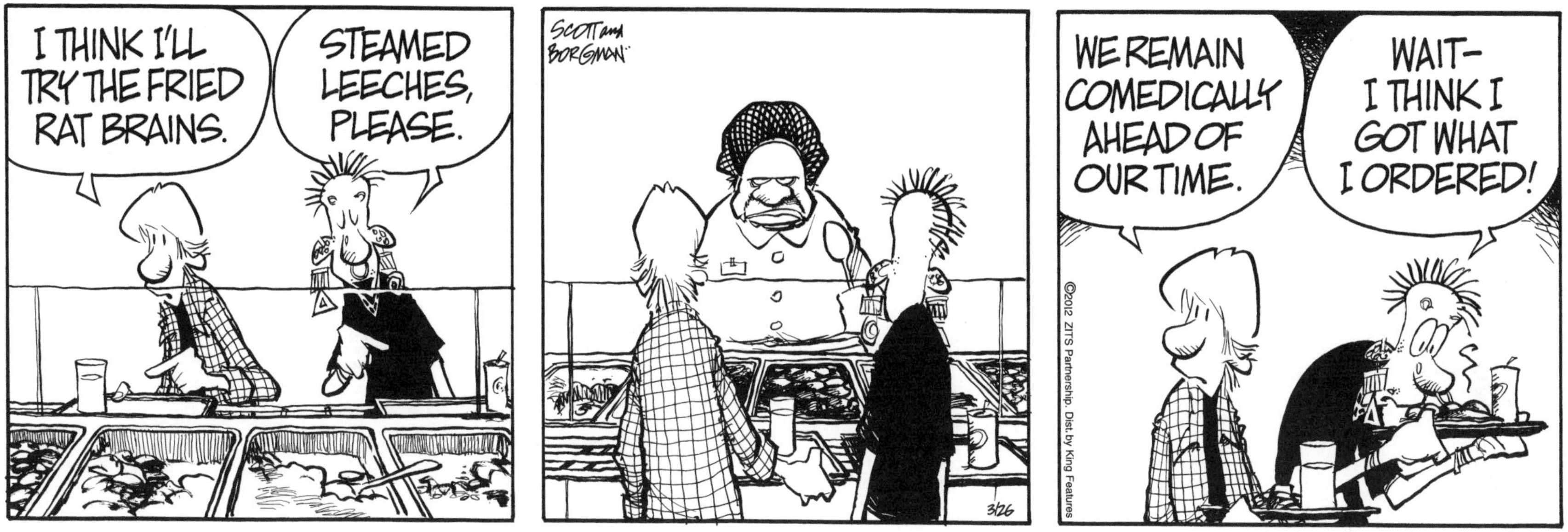
I THINK I'LL TRY THE FRIED RAT BRAINS.
STEAMED LEECHES, PLEASE.
SCOTT and BORGMAN
3/26
WE REMAIN COMEDICALLY AHEAD OF OUR TIME.
WAIT- I THINK I GOT WHAT I ORDERED!
©2012 ZITS Partnership. Dist. by King Features

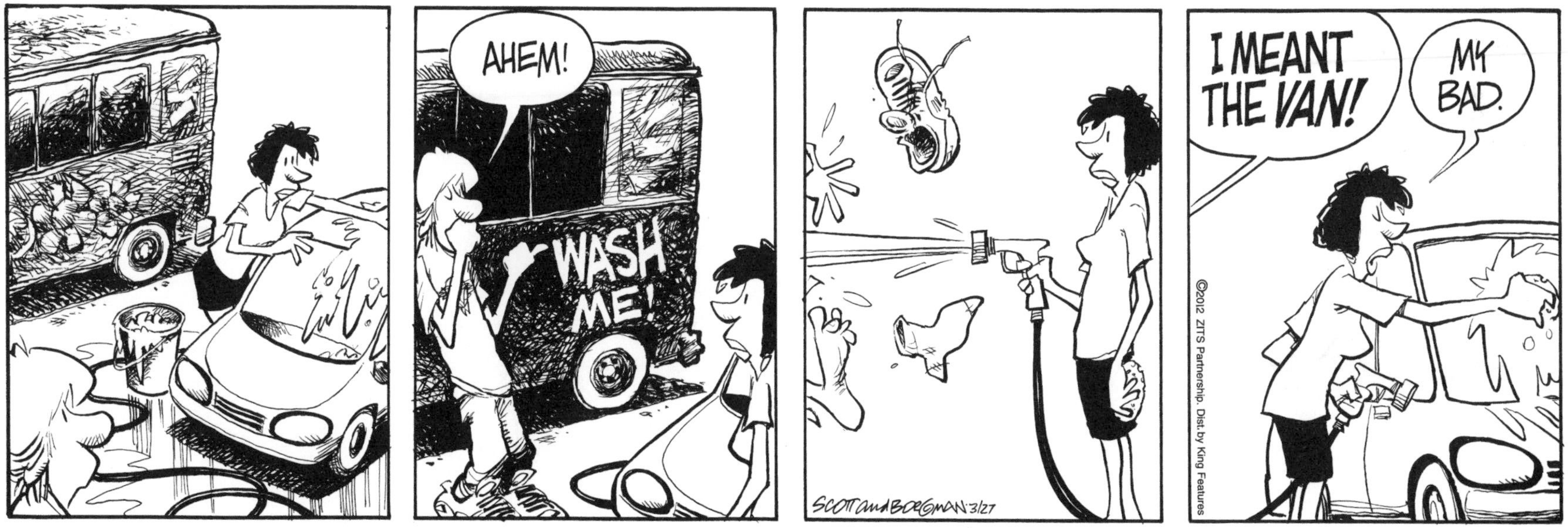
AHEM!
WASH ME!
SCOTT and BORGMAN 3/27
I MEANT THE VAN!
MY BAD.
©2012 ZITS Partnership. Dist. by King Features

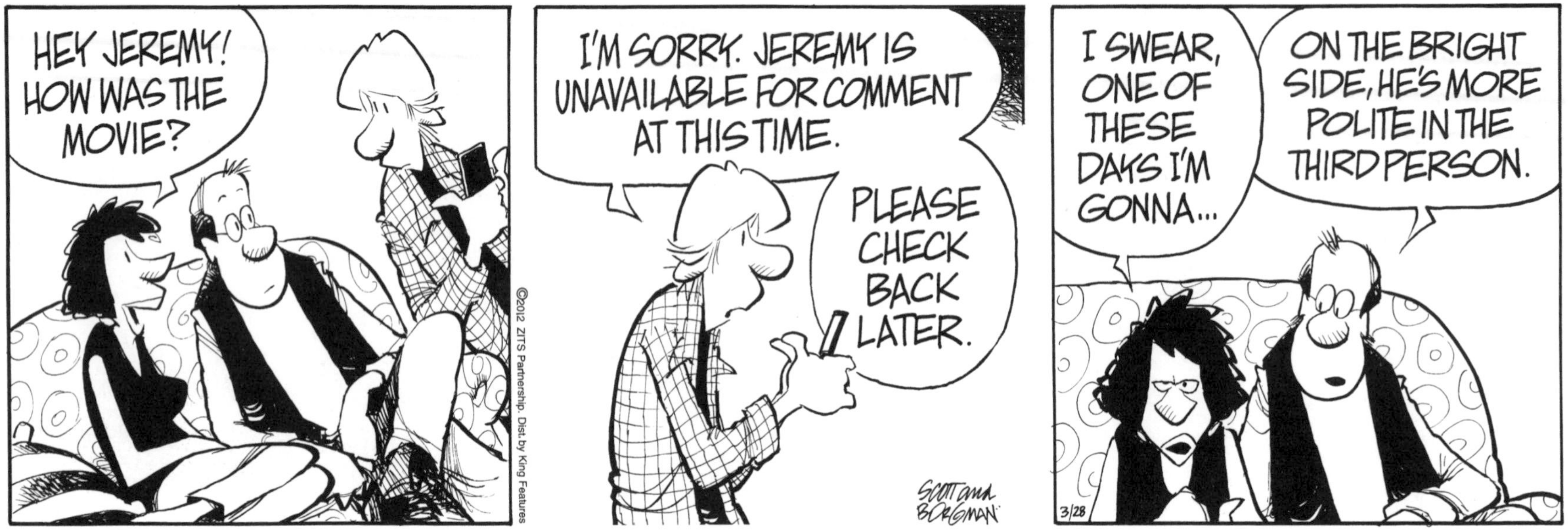
HEY JEREMY! HOW WAS THE MOVIE?
I'M SORRY. JEREMY IS UNAVAILABLE FOR COMMENT AT THIS TIME.
PLEASE CHECK BACK LATER.
I SWEAR, ONE OF THESE DAYS I'M GONNA...
ON THE BRIGHT SIDE, HE'S MORE POLITE IN THE THIRD PERSON.
©2012 ZITS Partnership. Dist. by King Features
SCOTT and BORGMAN
3/28

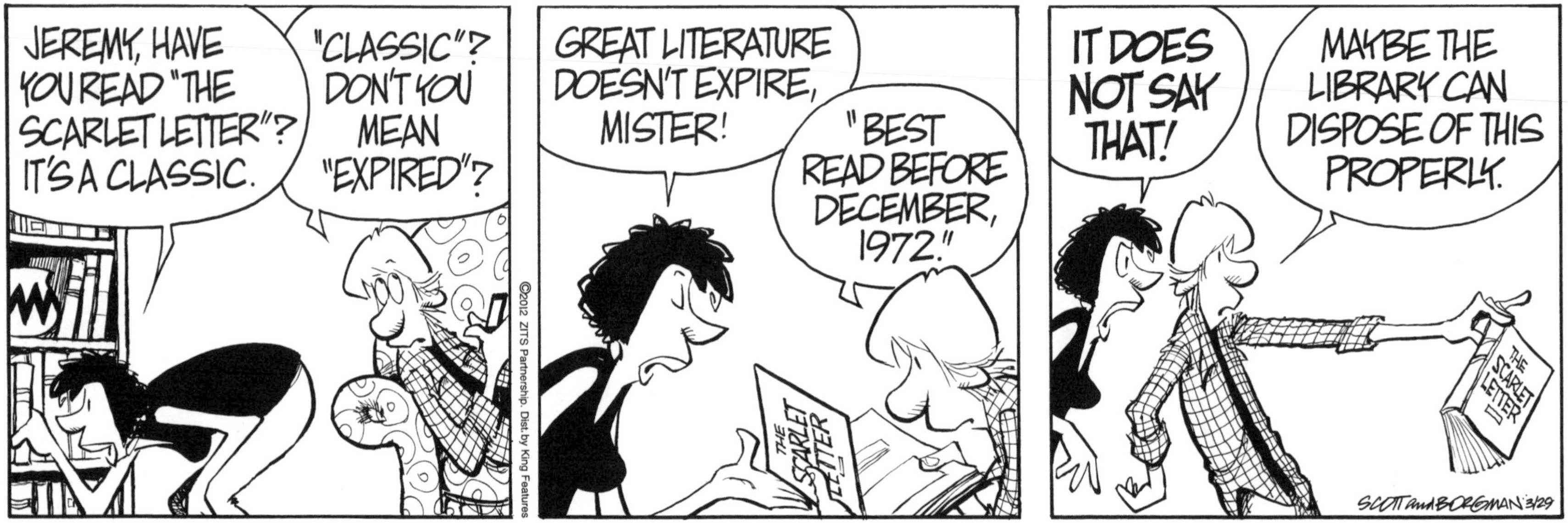
JEREMY, HAVE YOU READ "THE SCARLET LETTER"? IT'S A CLASSIC.
"CLASSIC"? DON'T YOU MEAN "EXPIRED"?
GREAT LITERATURE DOESN'T EXPIRE, MISTER!
"BEST READ BEFORE DECEMBER, 1972."
IT DOES NOT SAY THAT!
MAYBE THE LIBRARY CAN DISPOSE OF THIS PROPERLY.
THE SCARLET LETTER
©2012 ZITS Partnership. Dist. by King Features
SCOTT and BORGMAN 3/29

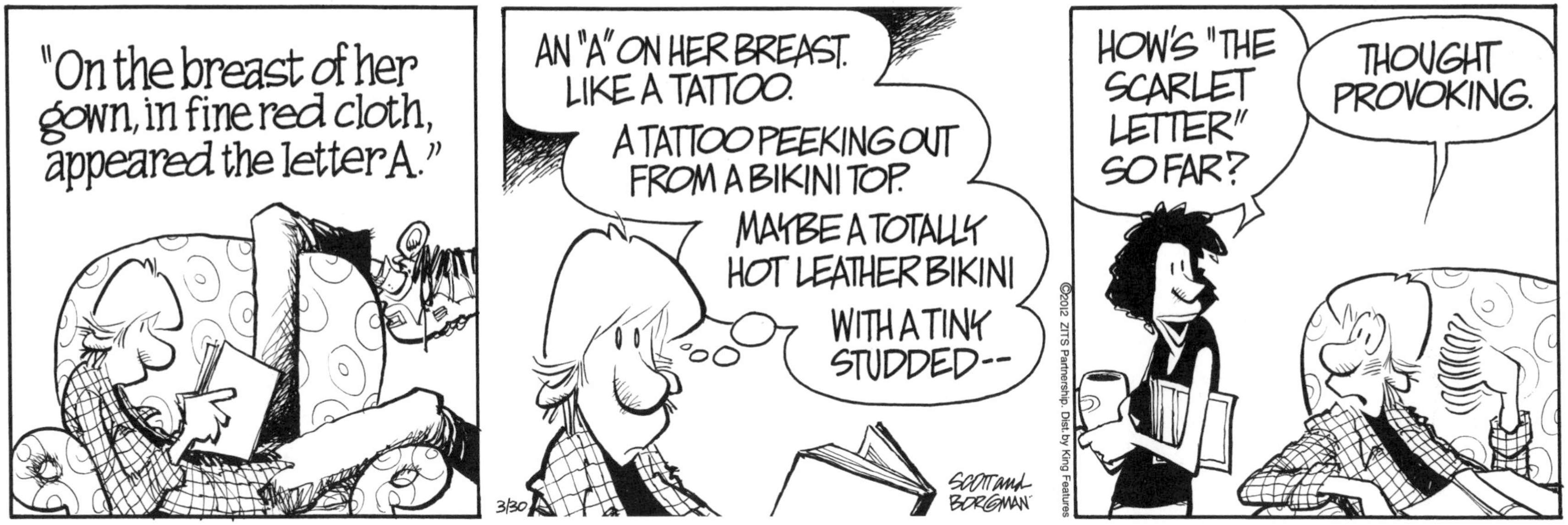
"On the breast of her gown, in fine red cloth, appeared the letter A."
AN "A" ON HER BREAST. LIKE A TATTOO.
A TATTOO PEEKING OUT FROM A BIKINI TOP.
MAYBE A TOTALLY HOT LEATHER BIKINI
WITH A TINY STUDDED--
3/30
SCOTT and BORGMAN
HOW'S "THE SCARLET LETTER" SO FAR?
THOUGHT PROVOKING.
©2012 ZITS Partnership. Dist. by King Features

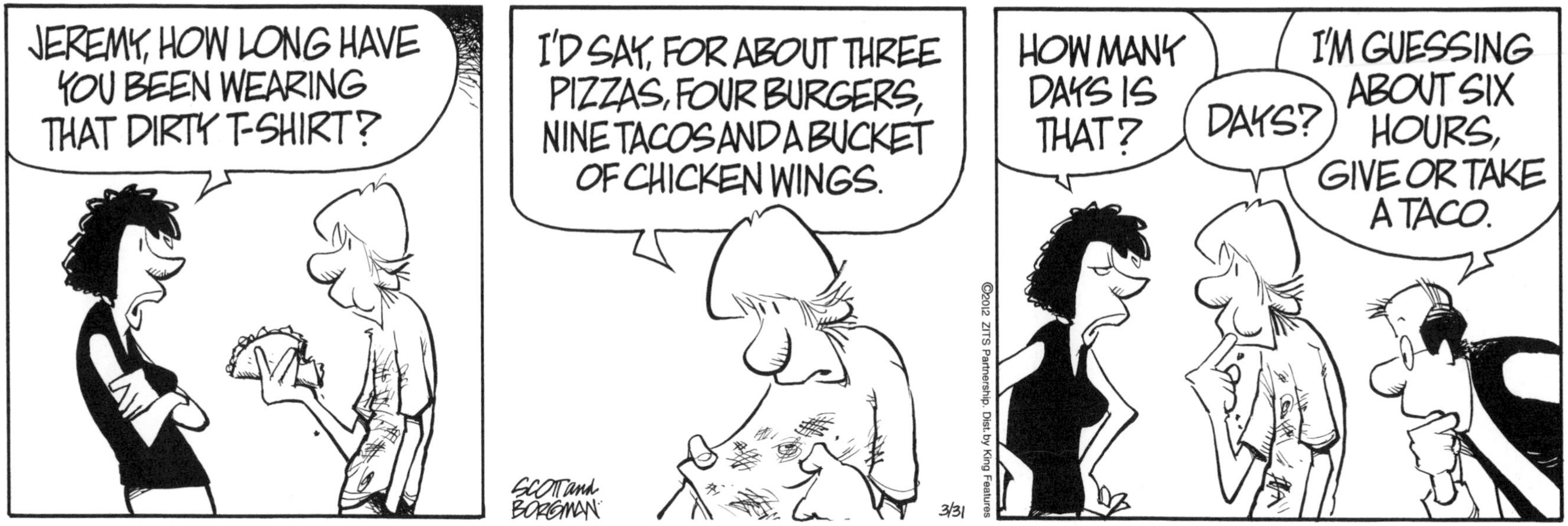
JEREMY, HOW LONG HAVE YOU BEEN WEARING THAT DIRTY T-SHIRT?
I'D SAY, FOR ABOUT THREE PIZZAS, FOUR BURGERS, NINE TACOS AND A BUCKET OF CHICKEN WINGS.
SCOTT and BORGMAN
3/31
©2012 ZITS Partnership. Dist. by King Features
HOW MANY DAYS IS THAT?
DAYS?
I'M GUESSING ABOUT SIX HOURS, GIVE OR TAKE A TACO.

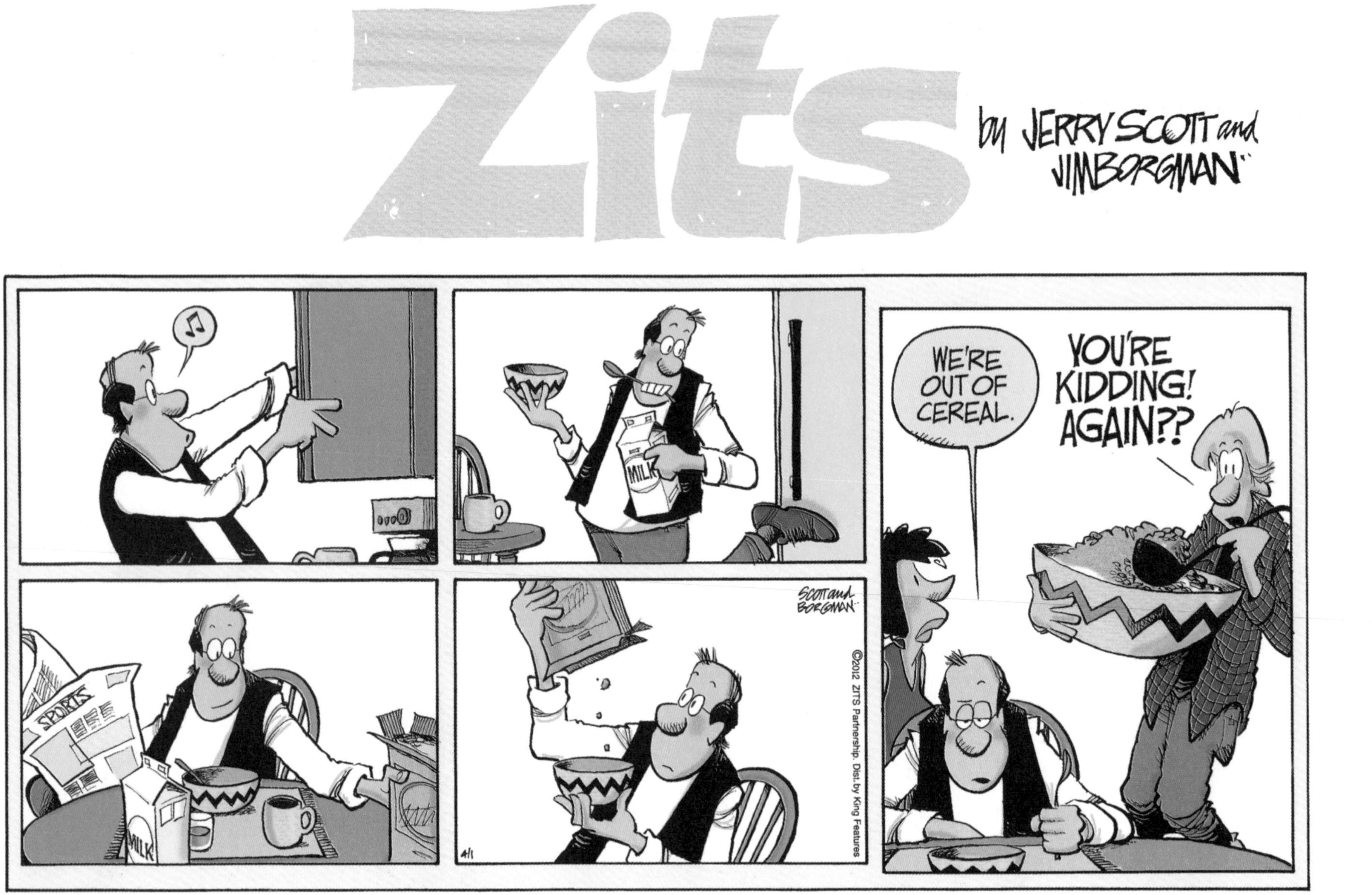
Zits
by JERRY SCOTT and JIM BORGMAN
MILK
SPORTS
MILK
SCOTT and BORGMAN
©2012 ZITS Partnership. Dist. by King Features
WE'RE OUT OF CEREAL.
YOU'RE KIDDING! AGAIN??

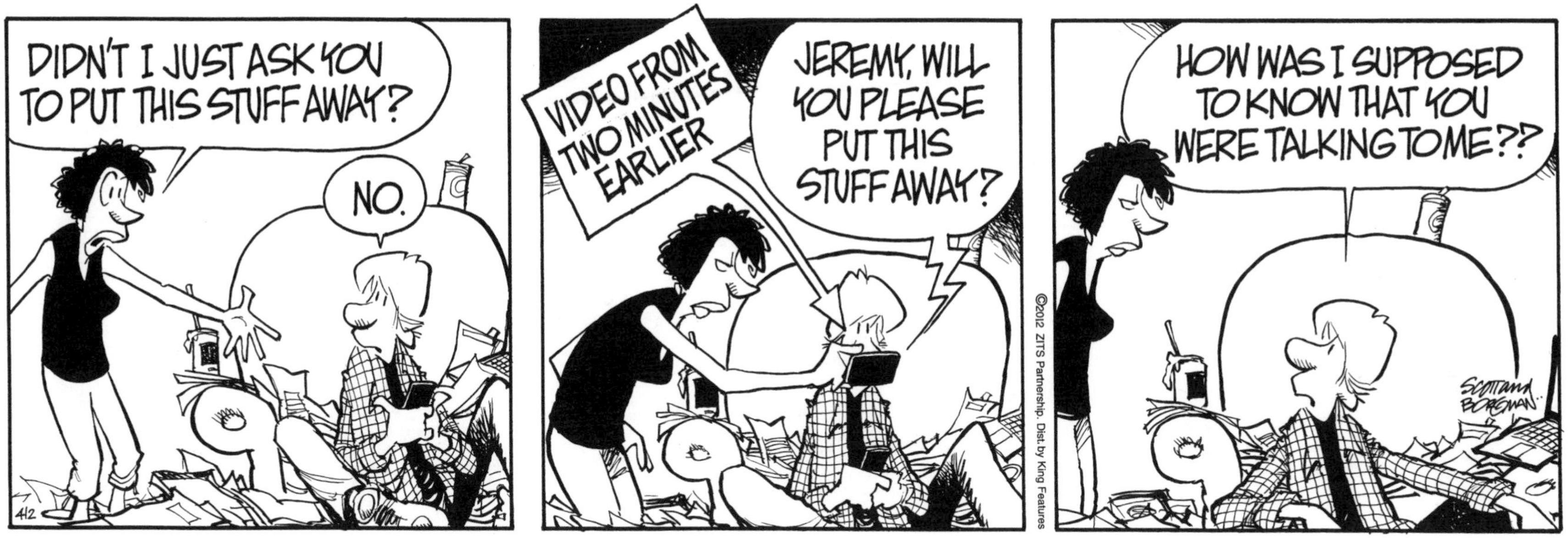
DIDN'T I JUST ASK YOU TO PUT THIS STUFF AWAY?
NO.
VIDEO FROM TWO MINUTES EARLIER
JEREMY, WILL YOU PLEASE PUT THIS STUFF AWAY?
HOW WAS I SUPPOSED TO KNOW THAT YOU WERE TALKING TO ME??
©2012 ZITS Partnership. Dist. by King Features

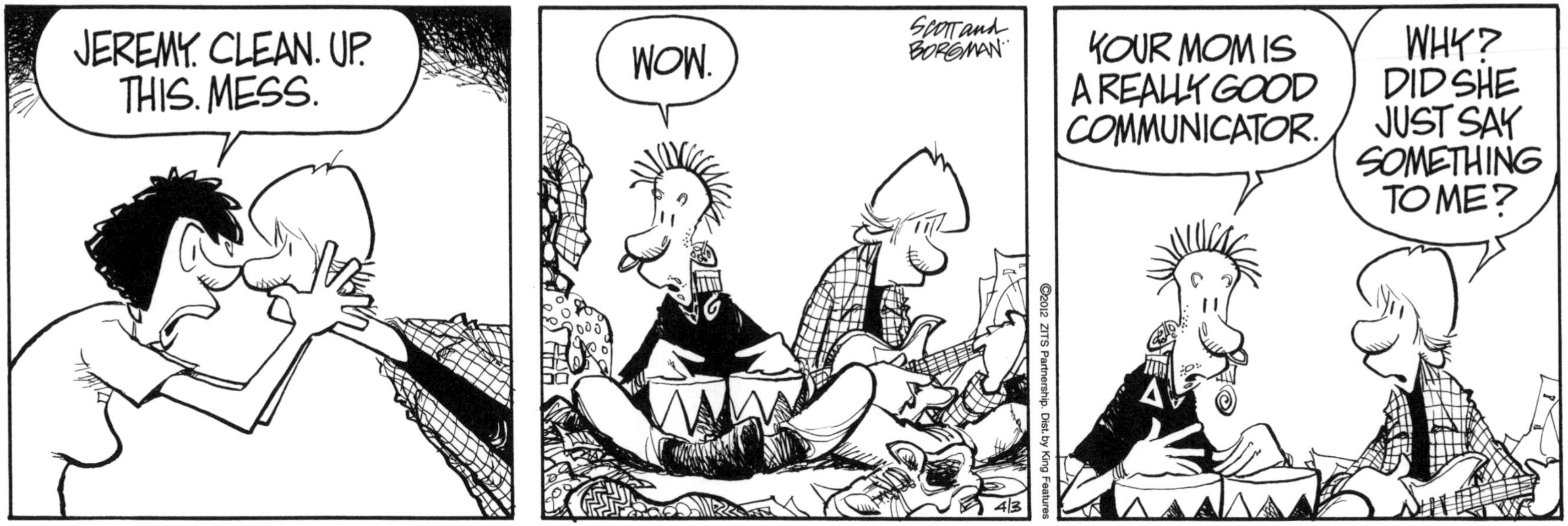
JEREMY. CLEAN. UP. THIS. MESS.
WOW.
YOUR MOM IS A REALLY GOOD COMMUNICATOR.
WHY? DID SHE JUST SAY SOMETHING TO ME?
©2012 ZITS Partnership. Dist. by King Features

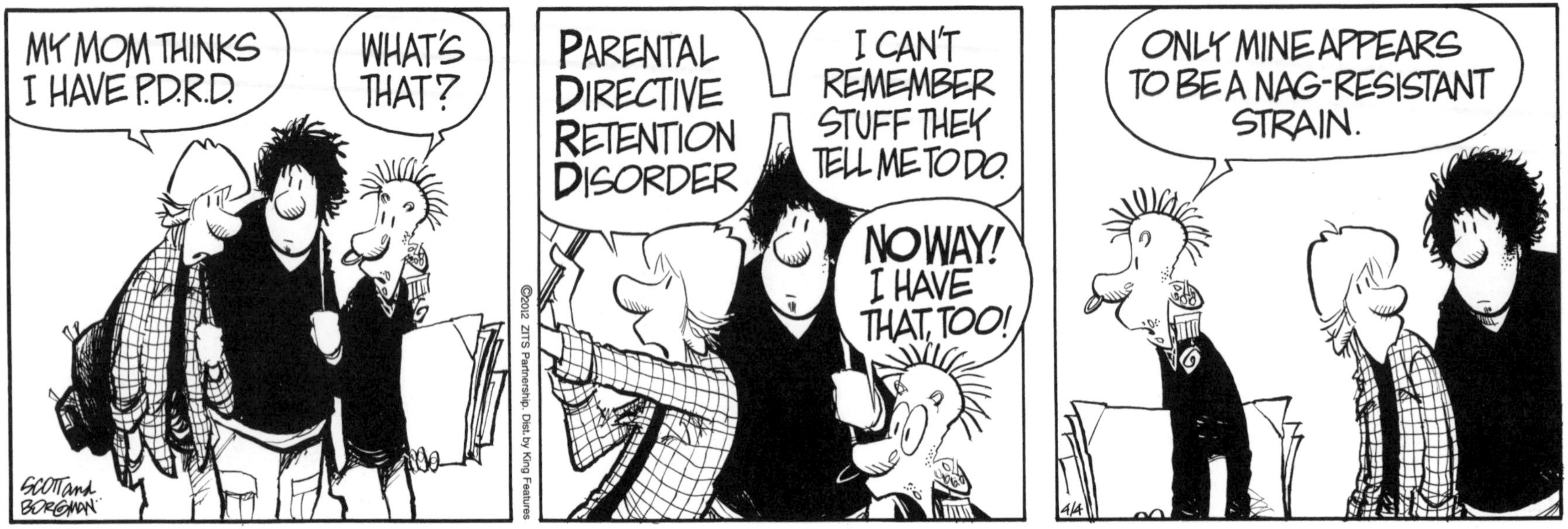
MY MOM THINKS I HAVE P.D.R.D.
WHAT'S THAT?
SCOTT and BORGMAN
PARENTAL DIRECTIVE RETENTION DISORDER
I CAN'T REMEMBER STUFF THEY TELL ME TO DO.
NO WAY! I HAVE THAT, TOO!
©2012 ZITS Partnership. Dist. by King Features
ONLY MINE APPEARS TO BE A NAG-RESISTANT STRAIN.
4/4

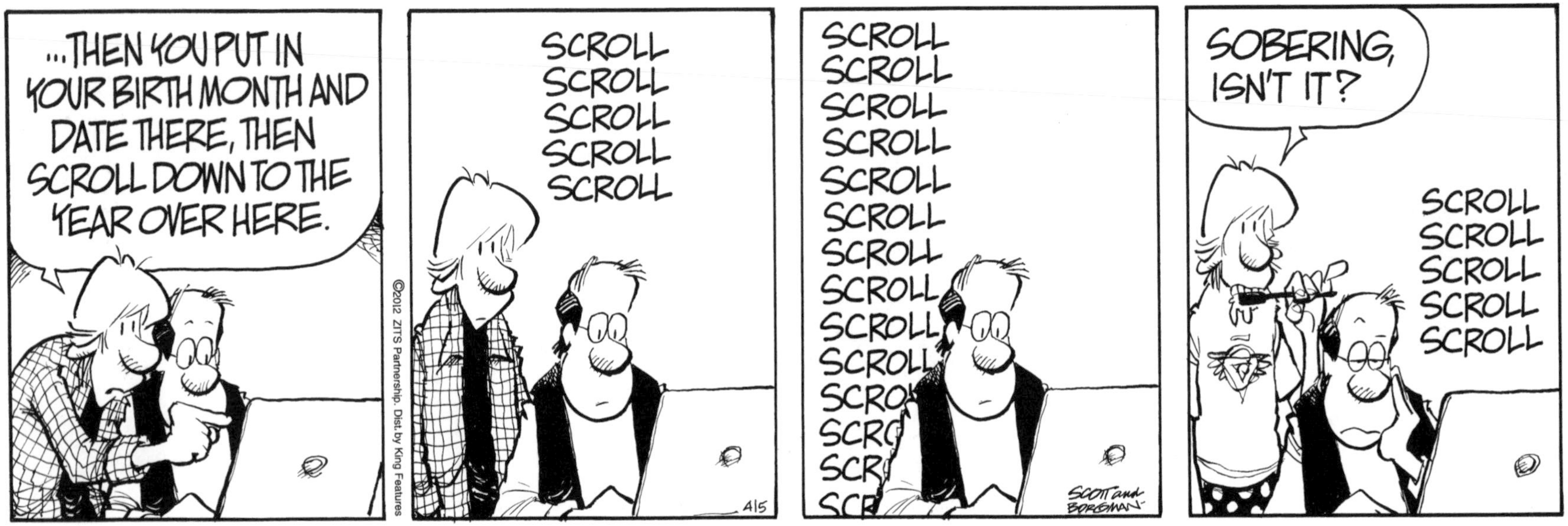
...THEN YOU PUT IN YOUR BIRTH MONTH AND DATE THERE, THEN SCROLL DOWN TO THE YEAR OVER HERE.
©2012 ZITS Partnership. Dist. by King Features
SCROLL
SCROLL
SCROLL
SCROLL
SCROLL
4/5
SCROLL
SCROLL
SCROLL
SCROLL
SCROLL
SCROLL
SCROLL
SCROLL
SCROLL
SCROLL
SCOTT and BORGMAN
SOBERING, ISN'T IT?
SCROLL
SCROLL
SCROLL
SCROLL
SCROLL

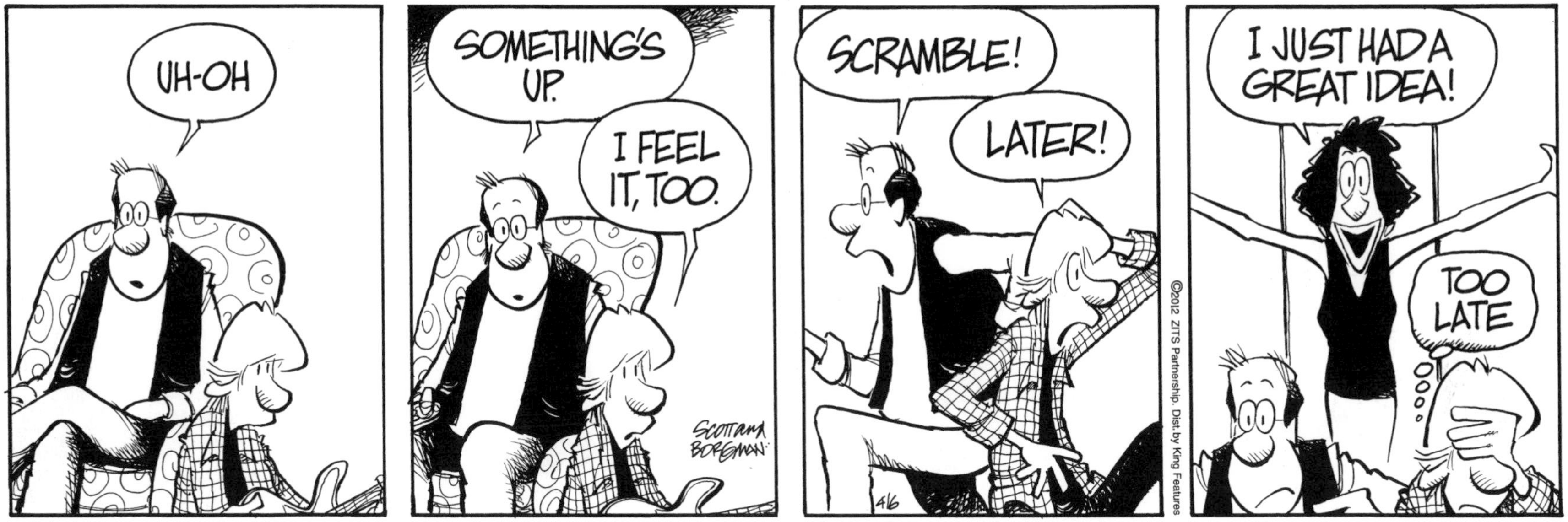
UH-OH
SOMETHING'S UP.
I FEEL IT, TOO.
SCRAMBLE!
LATER!
©2012 ZITS Partnership. Dist. by King Features
I JUST HAD A GREAT IDEA!
TOO LATE

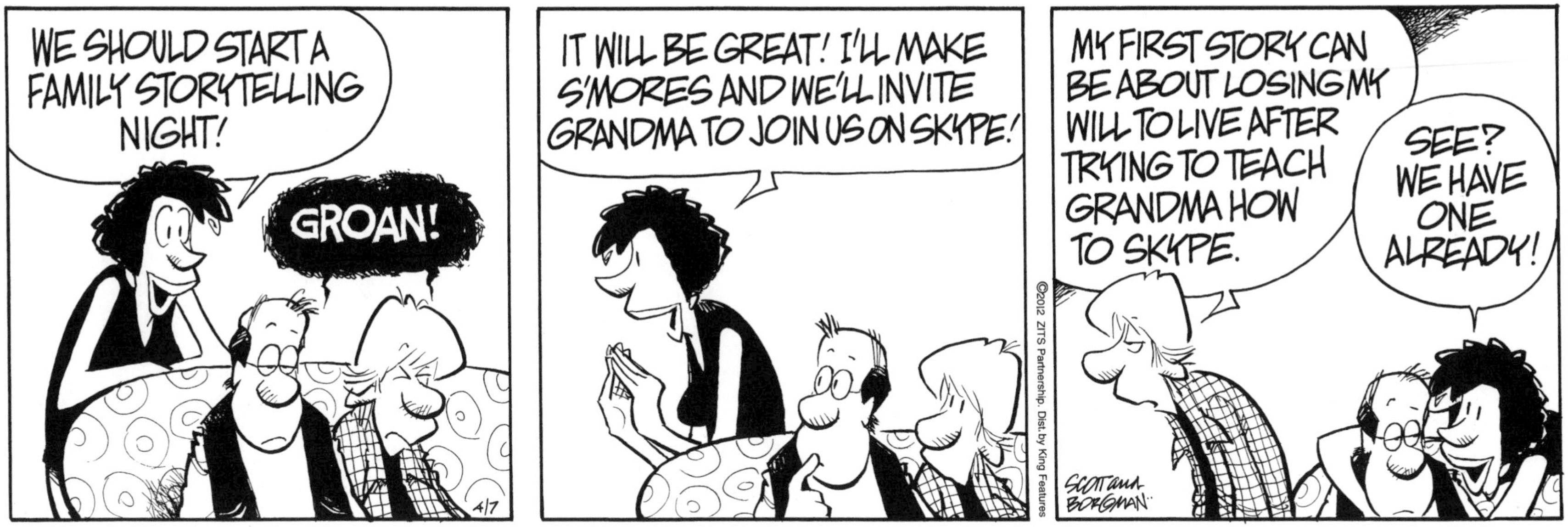
WE SHOULD START A FAMILY STORYTELLING NIGHT!
GROAN!
IT WILL BE GREAT! I'LL MAKE S'MORES AND WE'LL INVITE GRANDMA TO JOIN US ON SKYPE!
©2012 ZITS Partnership. Dist. by King Features
MY FIRST STORY CAN BE ABOUT LOSING MY WILL TO LIVE AFTER TRYING TO TEACH GRANDMA HOW TO SKYPE.
SEE? WE HAVE ONE ALREADY!

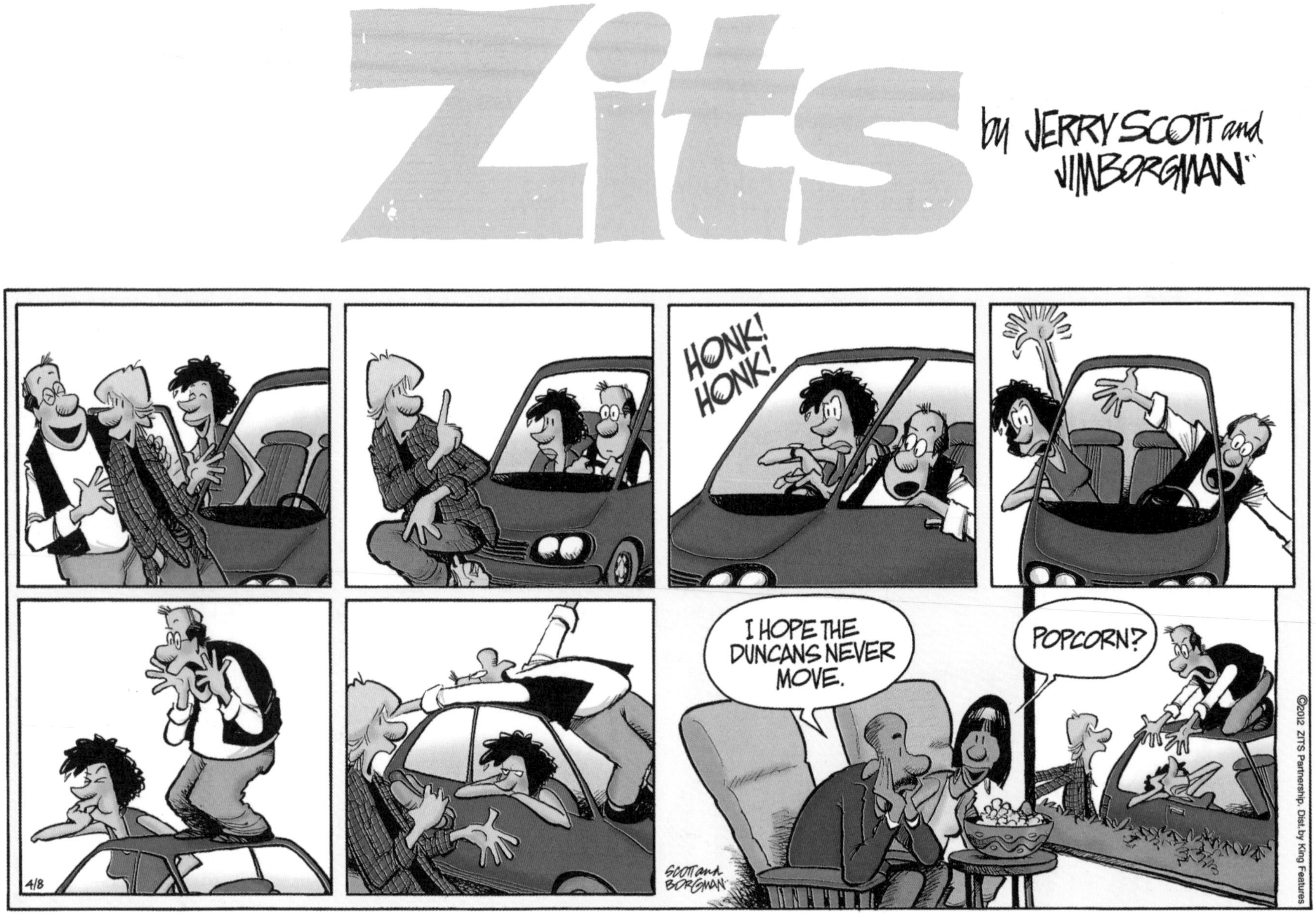
Zits
by JERRY SCOTT and JIM BORGMAN
HONK! HONK!
4/8
SCOTT and BORGMAN
I HOPE THE DUNCANS NEVER MOVE.
POPCORN?
©2012 ZITS Partnership. Dist. by King Features

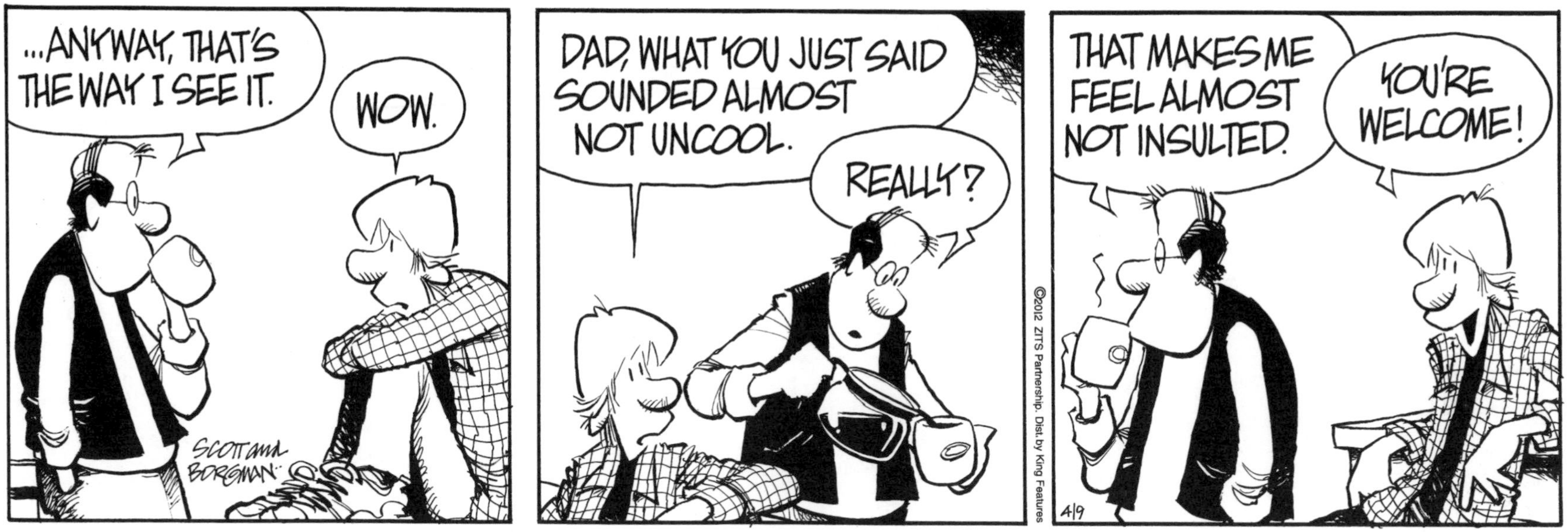
...ANYWAY, THAT'S THE WAY I SEE IT.
WOW.
SCOTT and BORGMAN
DAD, WHAT YOU JUST SAID SOUNDED ALMOST NOT UNCOOL.
REALLY?
©2012 ZITS Partnership. Dist. by King Features
4/9
THAT MAKES ME FEEL ALMOST NOT INSULTED.
YOU'RE WELCOME!

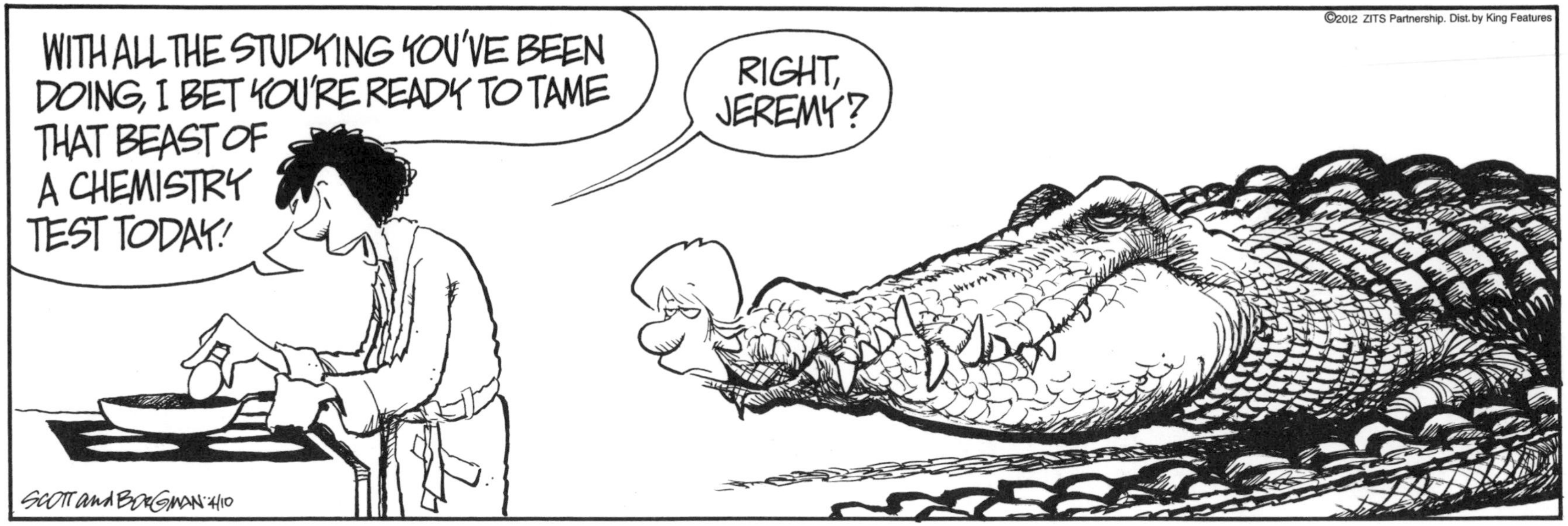
©2012 ZITS Partnership. Dist. by King Features
WITH ALL THE STUDYING YOU'VE BEEN DOING, I BET YOU'RE READY TO TAME THAT BEAST OF A CHEMISTRY TEST TODAY!
RIGHT, JEREMY?
SCOTT and BORGMAN 4/10

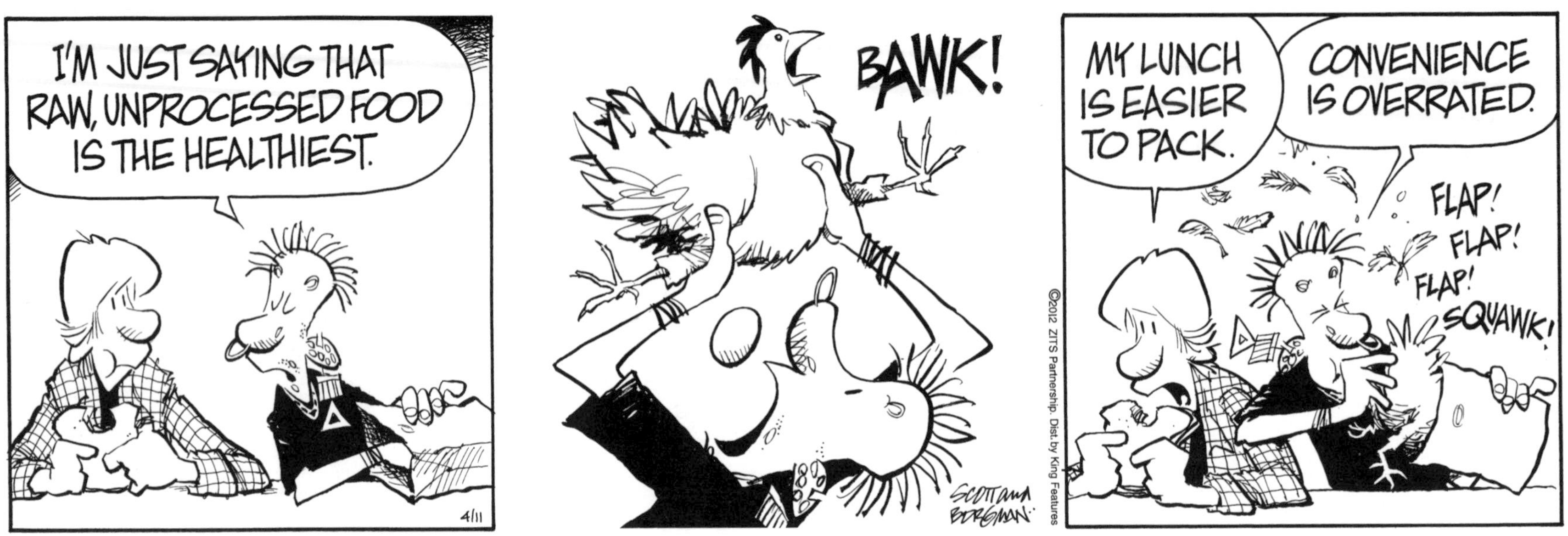
I'M JUST SAYING THAT RAW, UNPROCESSED FOOD IS THE HEALTHIEST.
4/11
BAWK!
SCOTT and BORGMAN
MY LUNCH IS EASIER TO PACK.
CONVENIENCE IS OVERRATED.
FLAP! FLAP! FLAP! SQUAWK!
©2012 ZITS Partnership. Dist. by King Features

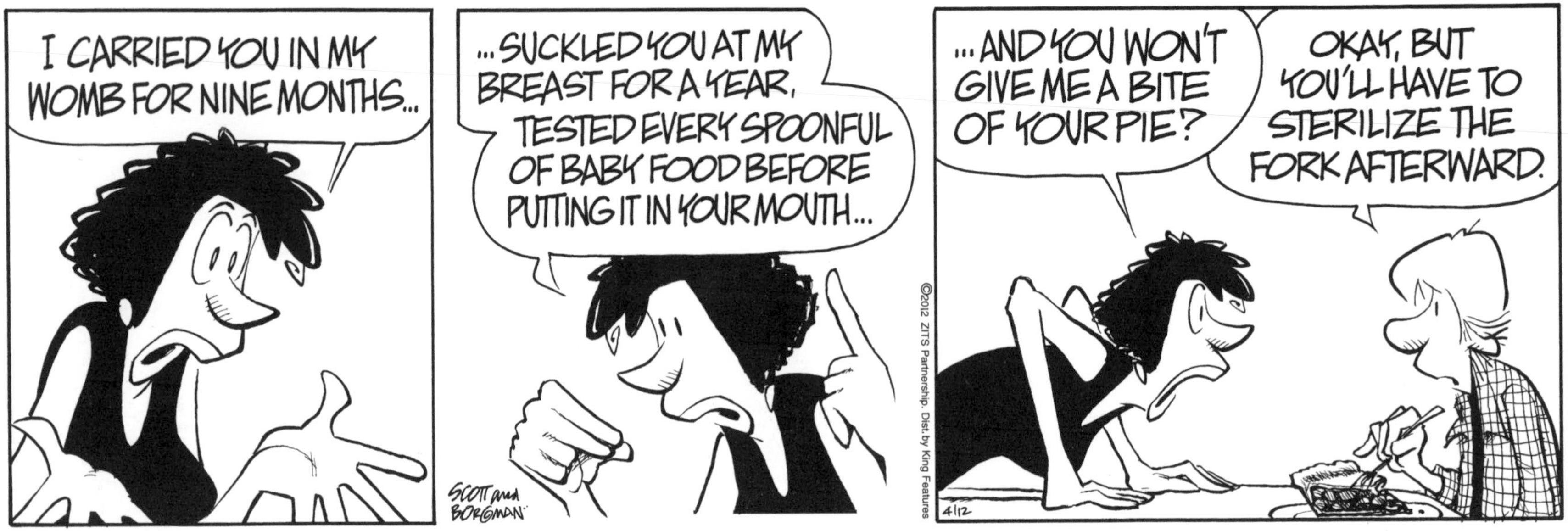
I CARRIED YOU IN MY WOMB FOR NINE MONTHS...
...SUCKLED YOU AT MY BREAST FOR A YEAR, TESTED EVERY SPOONFUL OF BABY FOOD BEFORE PUTTING IT IN YOUR MOUTH...
SCOTT and BORGMAN
...AND YOU WON'T GIVE ME A BITE OF YOUR PIE?
OKAY, BUT YOU'LL HAVE TO STERILIZE THE FORK AFTERWARD.
4/12
©2012 ZITS Partnership. Dist. by King Features

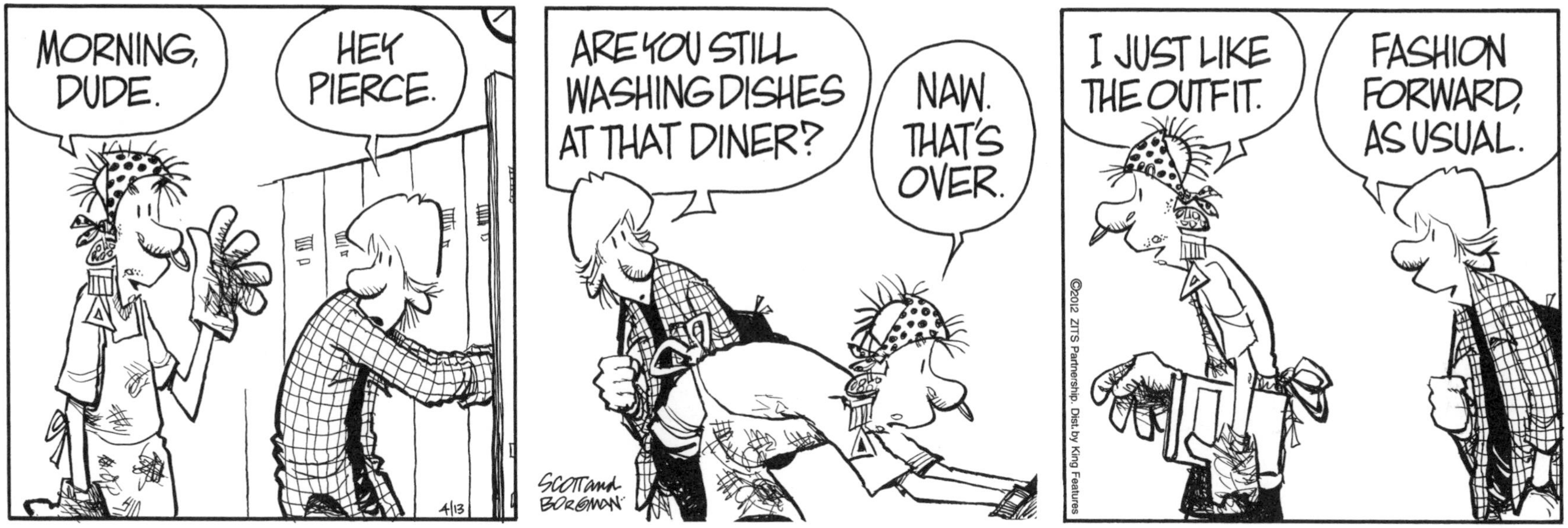
MORNING, DUDE.
HEY PIERCE.
ARE YOU STILL WASHING DISHES AT THAT DINER?
NAW. THAT'S OVER.
I JUST LIKE THE OUTFIT.
FASHION FORWARD, AS USUAL.
SCOTT and BORGMAN
©2012 ZITS Partnership. Dist. by King Features

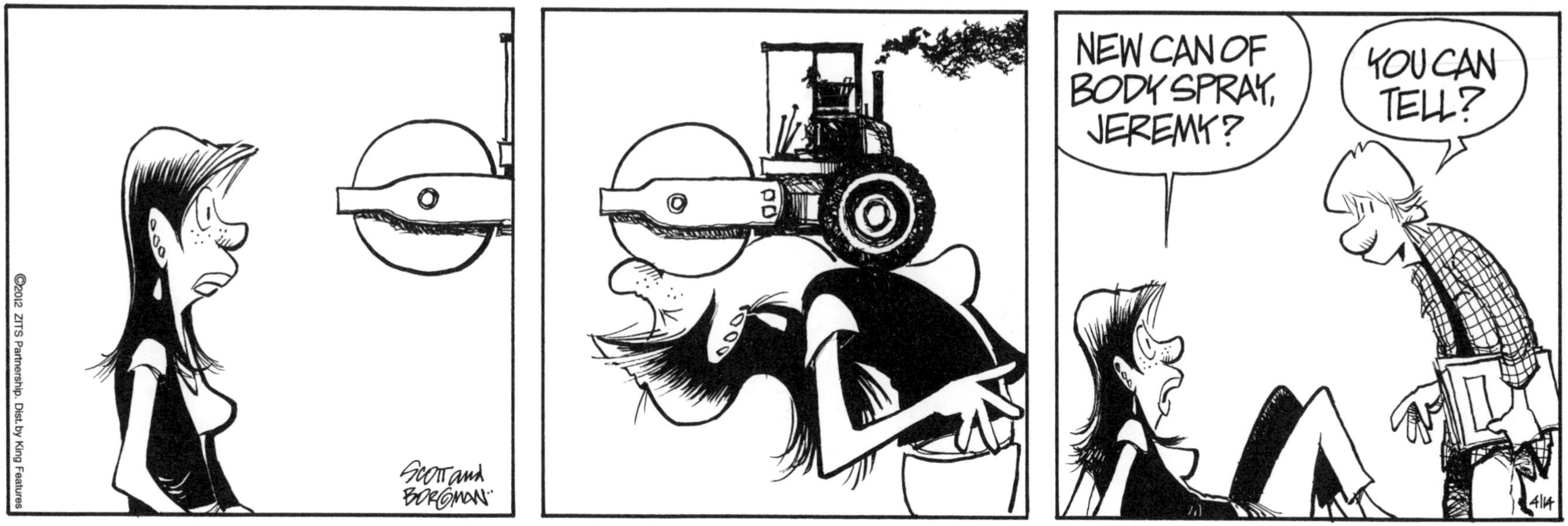
©2012 ZITS Partnership. Dist. by King Features
SCOTT and BORGMAN
NEW CAN OF BODY SPRAY, JEREMY?
YOU CAN TELL?

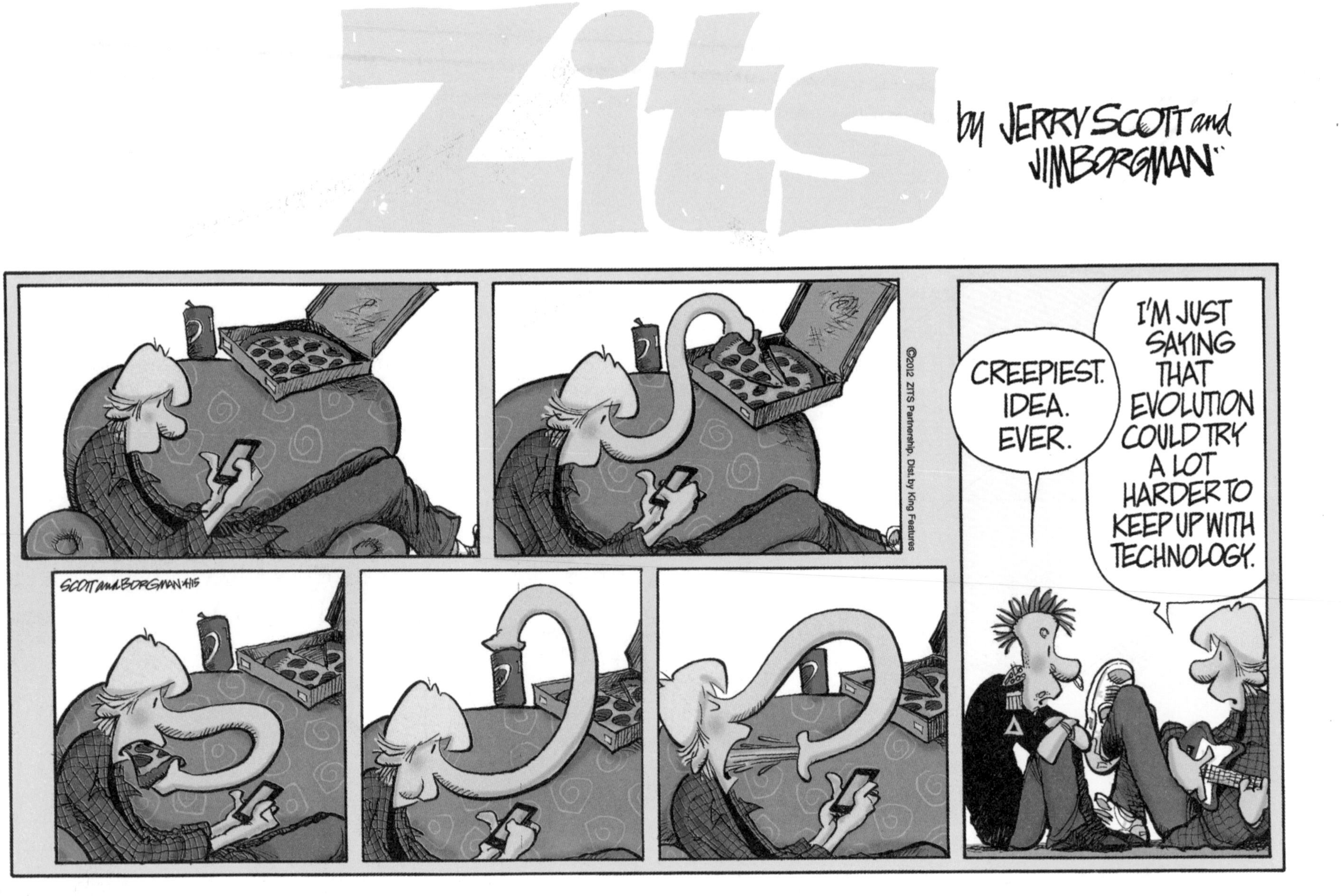
Zits
by JERRY SCOTT and JIM BORGMAN
©2012 ZITS Partnership. Dist. by King Features
CREEPIEST. IDEA. EVER.
I'M JUST SAYING THAT EVOLUTION COULD TRY A LOT HARDER TO KEEP UP WITH TECHNOLOGY.

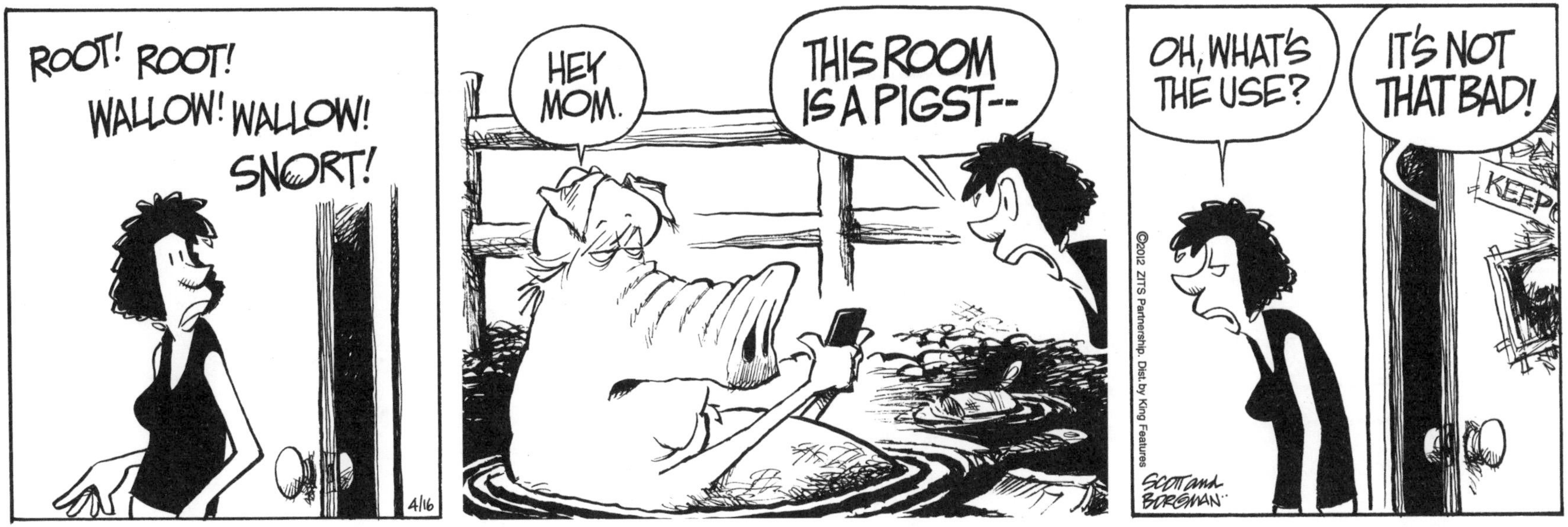
ROOT! ROOT!
WALLOW! WALLOW!
SNORT!
4/16
HEY MOM.
THIS ROOM IS A PIGST--
©2012 ZITS Partnership. Dist. by King Features
OH, WHAT'S THE USE?
IT'S NOT THAT BAD!
KEEP
SCOTT and BORGMAN

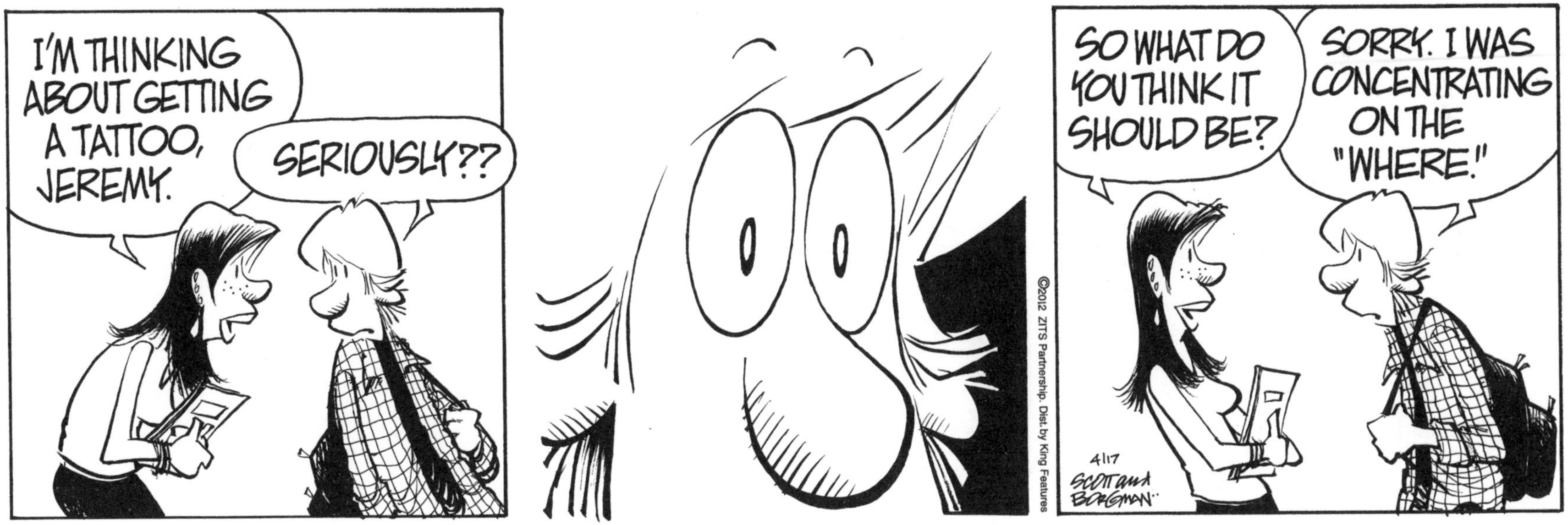
I'M THINKING ABOUT GETTING A TATTOO, JEREMY.
SERIOUSLY??
©2012 ZITS Partnership. Dist. by King Features
SO WHAT DO YOU THINK IT SHOULD BE?
SORRY. I WAS CONCENTRATING ON THE "WHERE."
4/17
SCOTT and BORGMAN

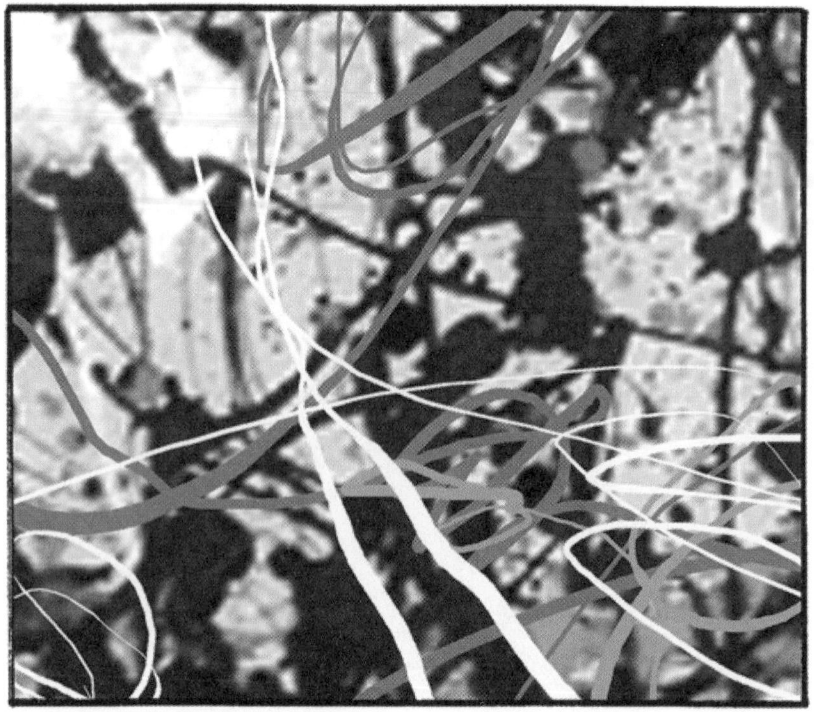
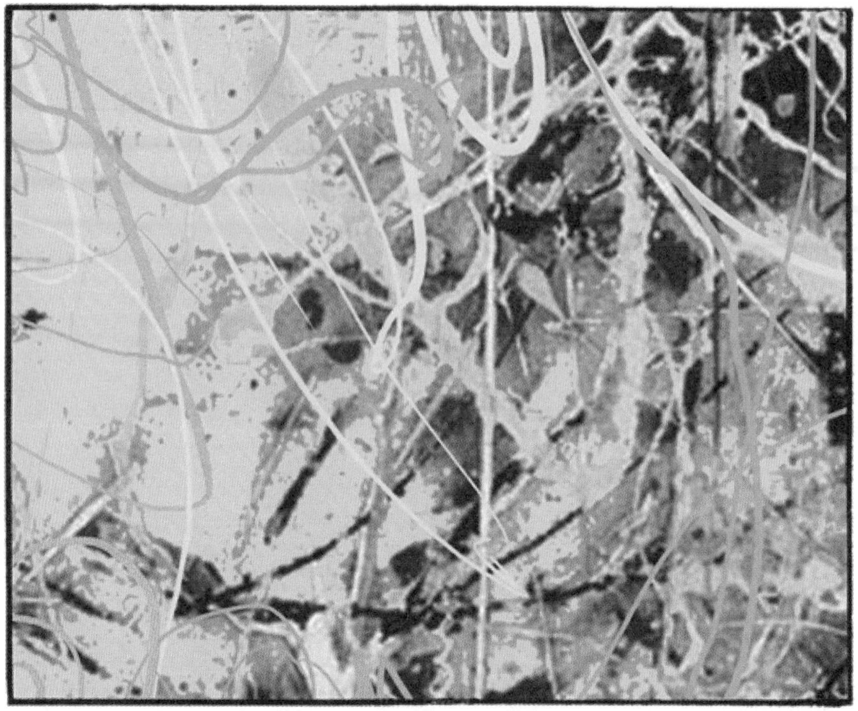
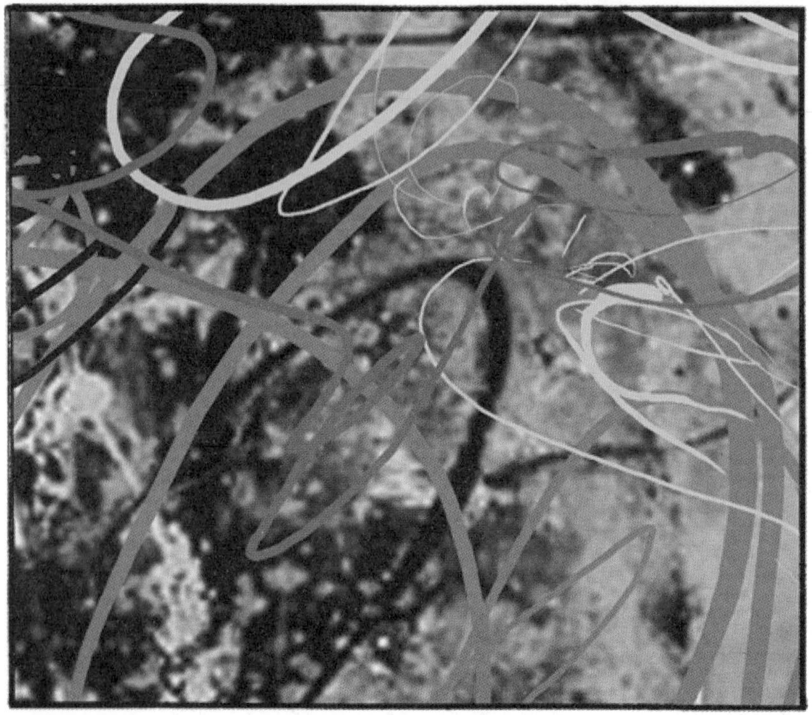
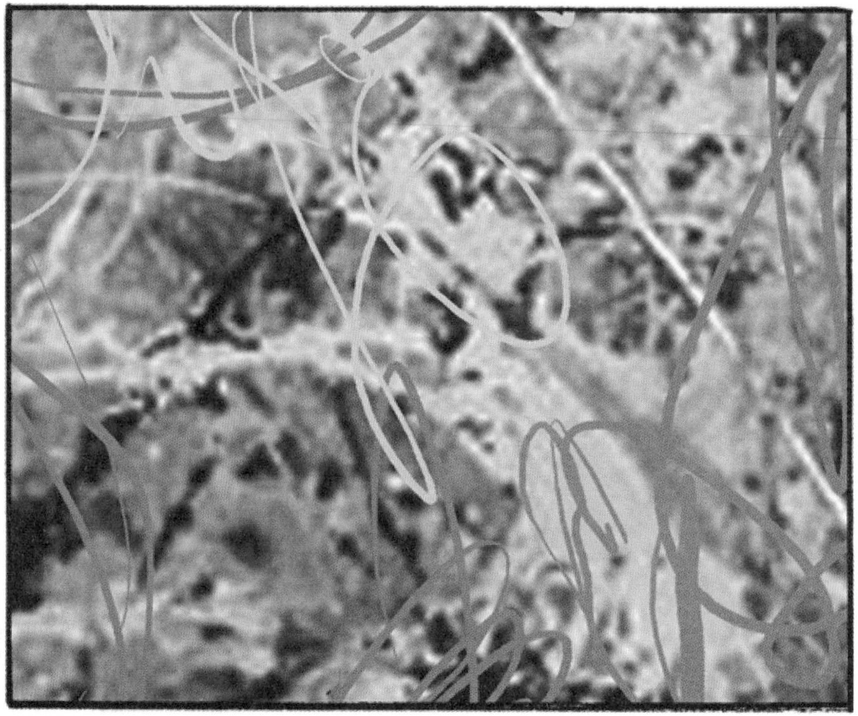

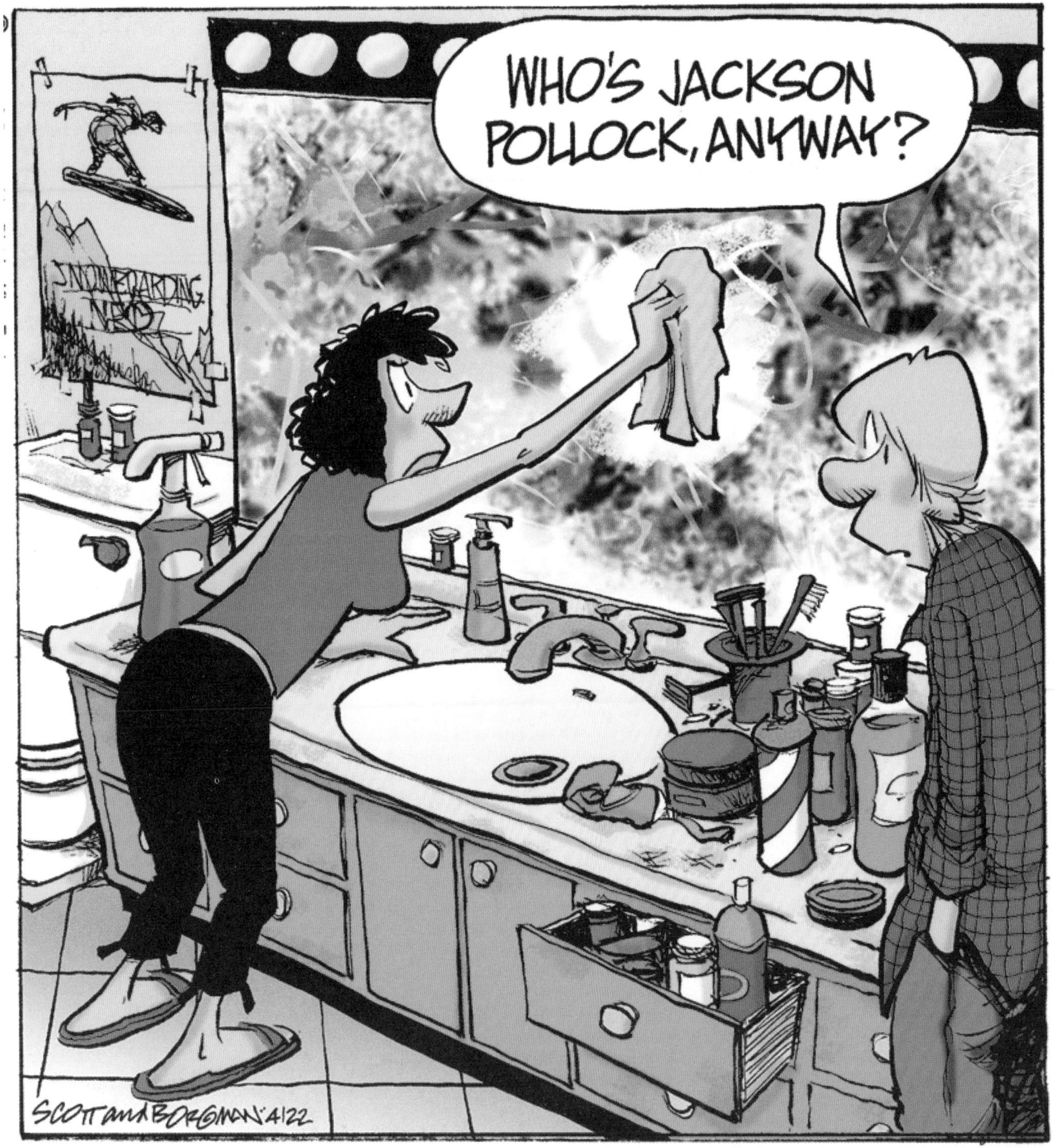
WHO'S JACKSON POLLOCK, ANYWAY?
SNOWBOARDING
SCOTT AND BORGMAN 4/22

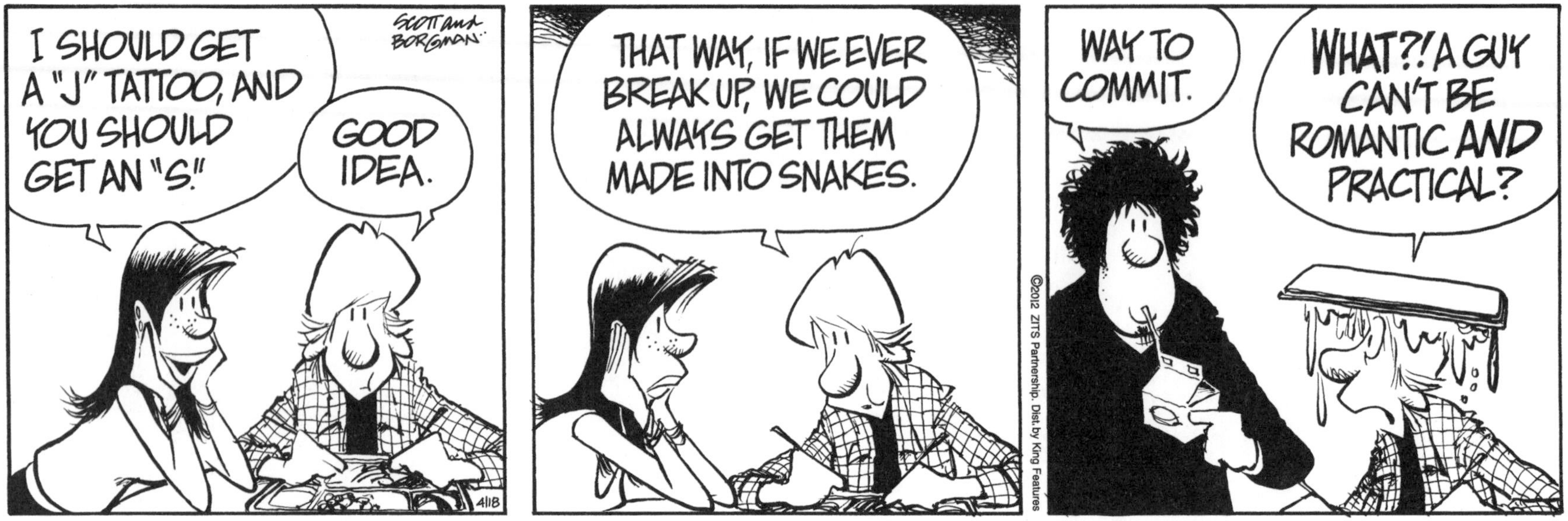
SCOTT and BORGMAN
I SHOULD GET A "J" TATTOO, AND YOU SHOULD GET AN "S."
GOOD IDEA.
4/18
THAT WAY, IF WE EVER BREAK UP, WE COULD ALWAYS GET THEM MADE INTO SNAKES.
©2012 ZITS Partnership. Dist. by King Features
WAY TO COMMIT.
WHAT?! A GUY CAN'T BE ROMANTIC AND PRACTICAL?

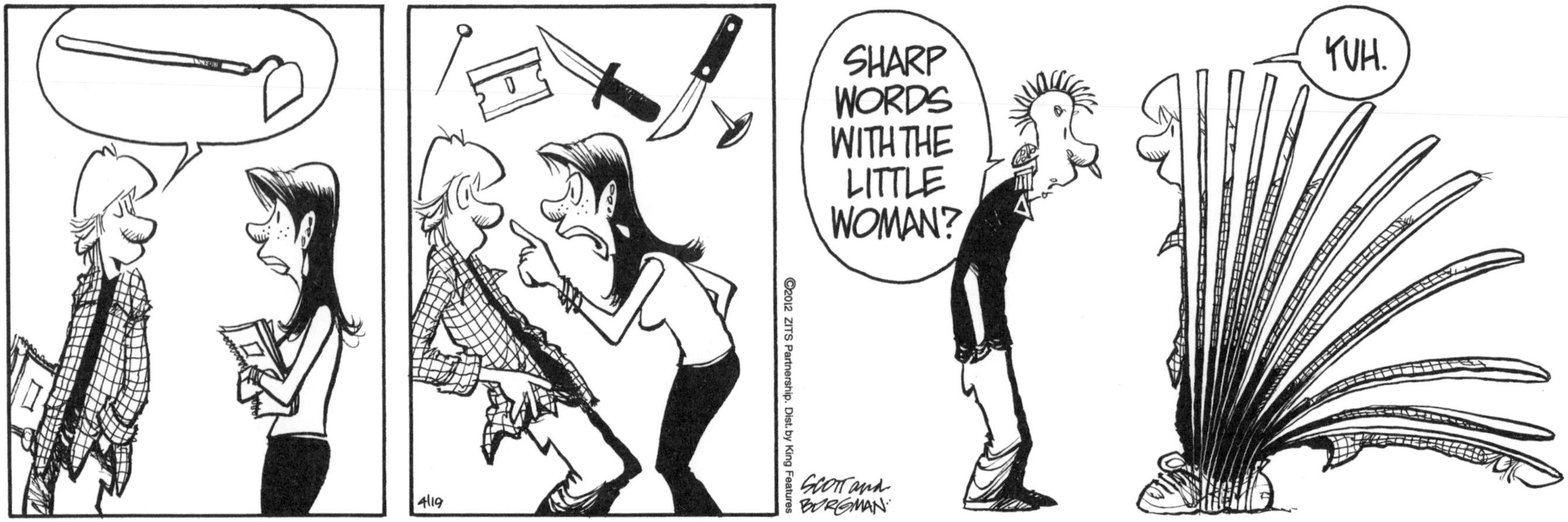
4/19
©2012 ZITS Partnership. Dist. by King Features
SCOTT and BORGMAN
SHARP WORDS WITH THE LITTLE WOMAN?
YUH.

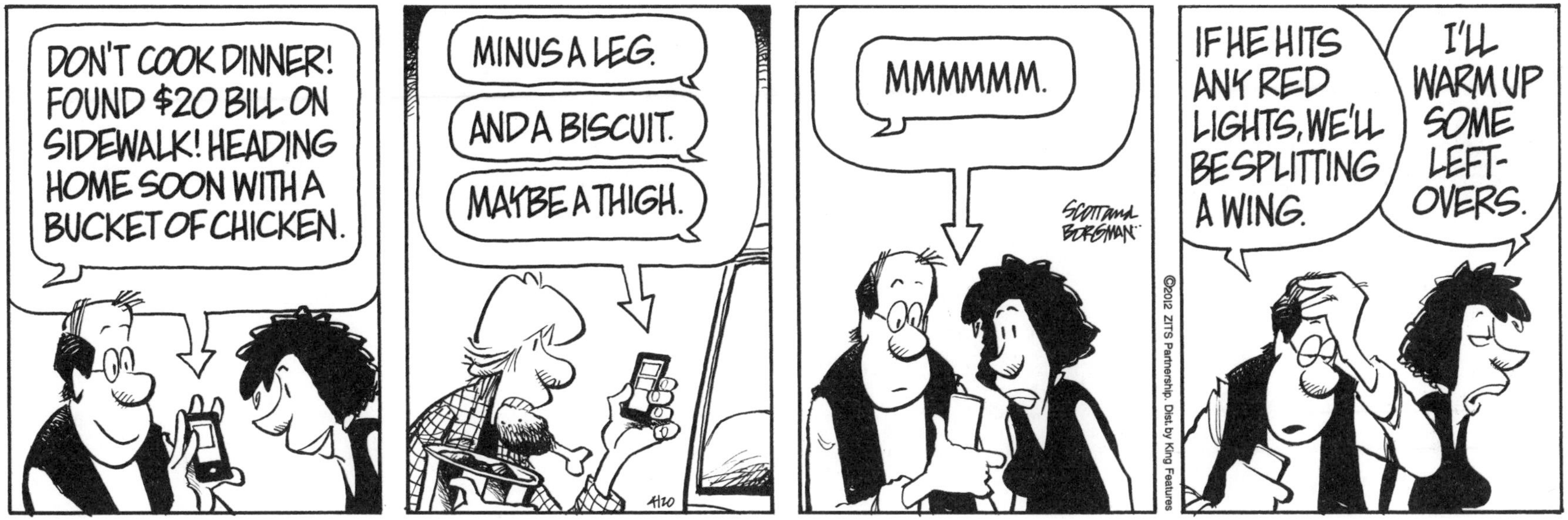
DON'T COOK DINNER! FOUND $20 BILL ON SIDEWALK! HEADING HOME SOON WITH A BUCKET OF CHICKEN.
MINUS A LEG.
AND A BISCUIT.
MAYBE A THIGH.
4/20
MMMMMM.
SCOTT and BORGMAN
©2012 ZITS Partnership. Dist. by King Features
IF HE HITS ANY RED LIGHTS, WE'LL BE SPLITTING A WING.
I'LL WARM UP SOME LEFT-OVERS.

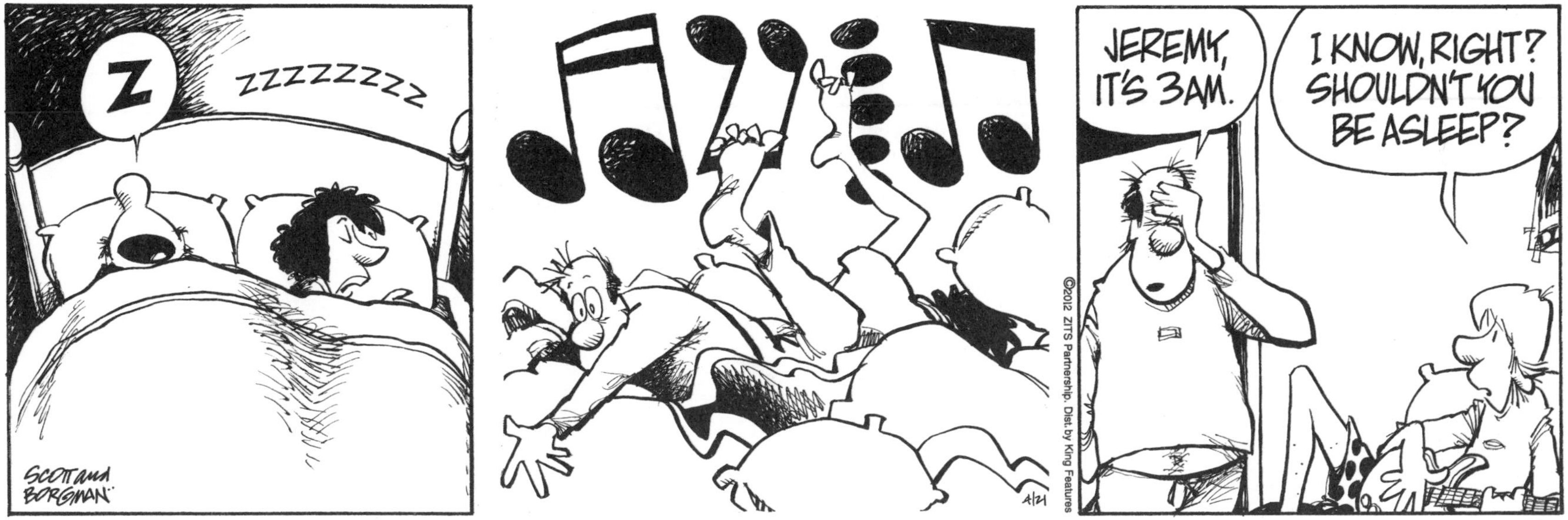
Z
ZZZZZZZZ
SCOTT and BORGMAN
4/21
©2012 ZITS Partnership. Dist. by King Features
JEREMY, IT'S 3AM.
I KNOW, RIGHT? SHOULDN'T YOU BE ASLEEP?

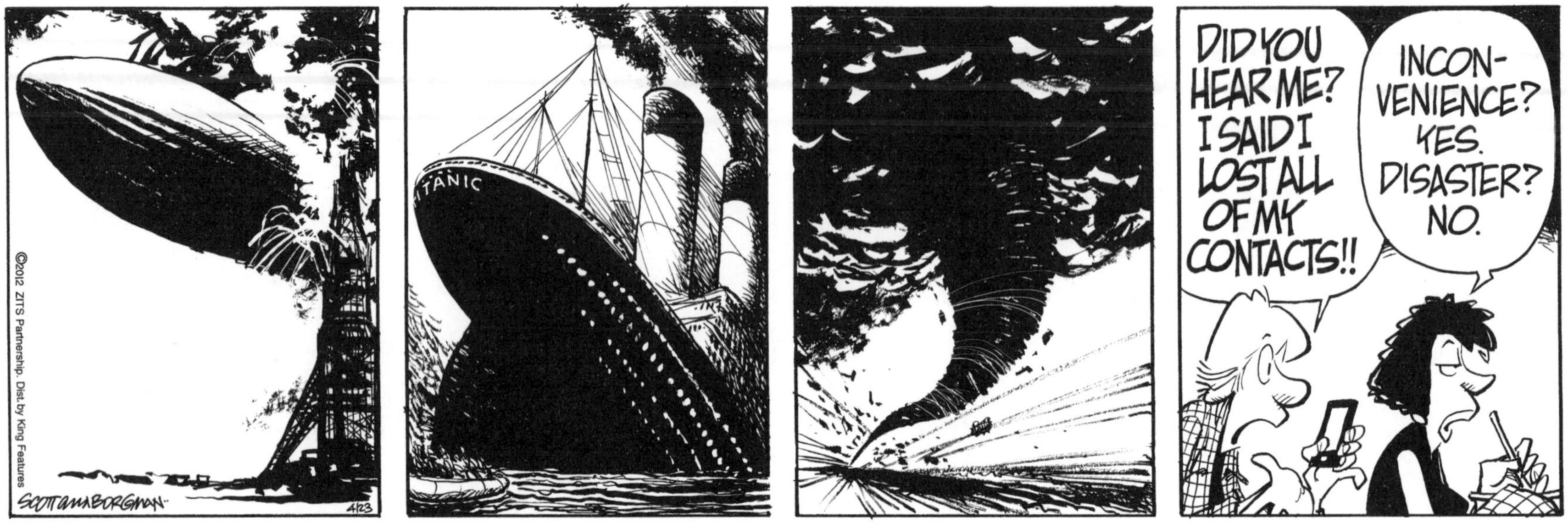
©2012 ZITS Partnership. Dist. by King Features
SCOTT and BORGMAN
4/23
TANIC
DID YOU HEAR ME? I SAID I LOST ALL OF MY CONTACTS!!
INCON- VENIENCE? YES. DISASTER? NO.

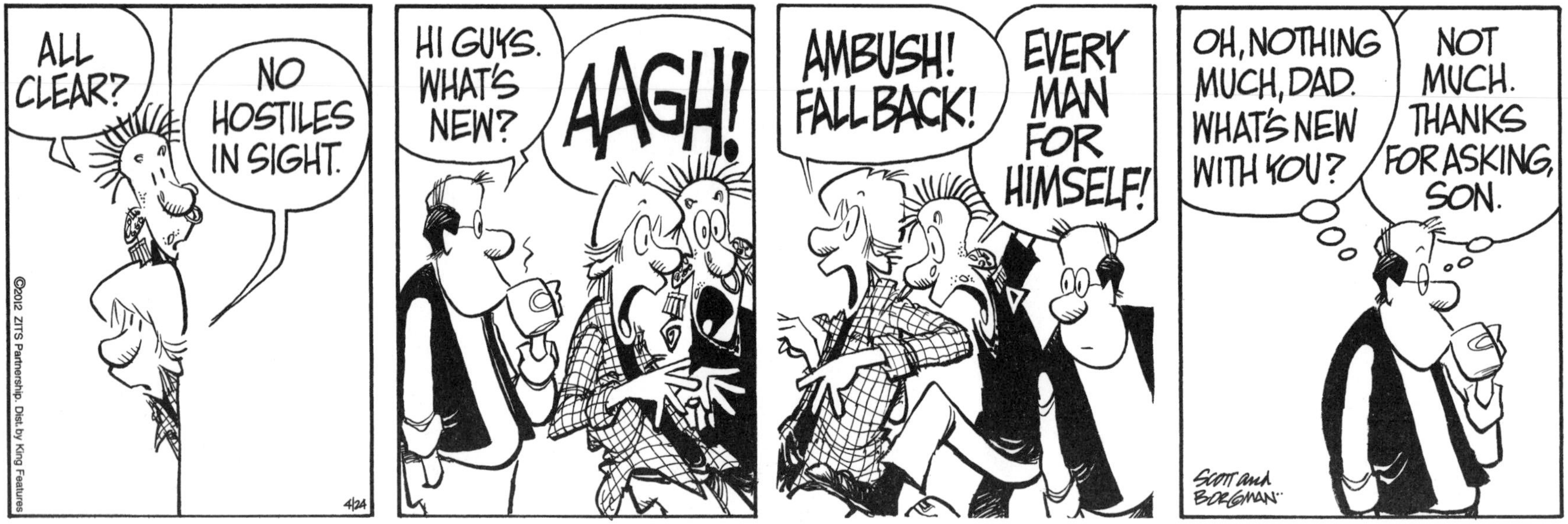
©2012 ZITS Partnership. Dist. by King Features
ALL CLEAR?
NO HOSTILES IN SIGHT.
4/24
HI GUYS. WHAT'S NEW?
AAGH!
AMBUSH! FALL BACK!
EVERY MAN FOR HIMSELF!
OH, NOTHING MUCH, DAD. WHAT'S NEW WITH YOU?
NOT MUCH. THANKS FOR ASKING, SON.
SCOTT and BORGMAN

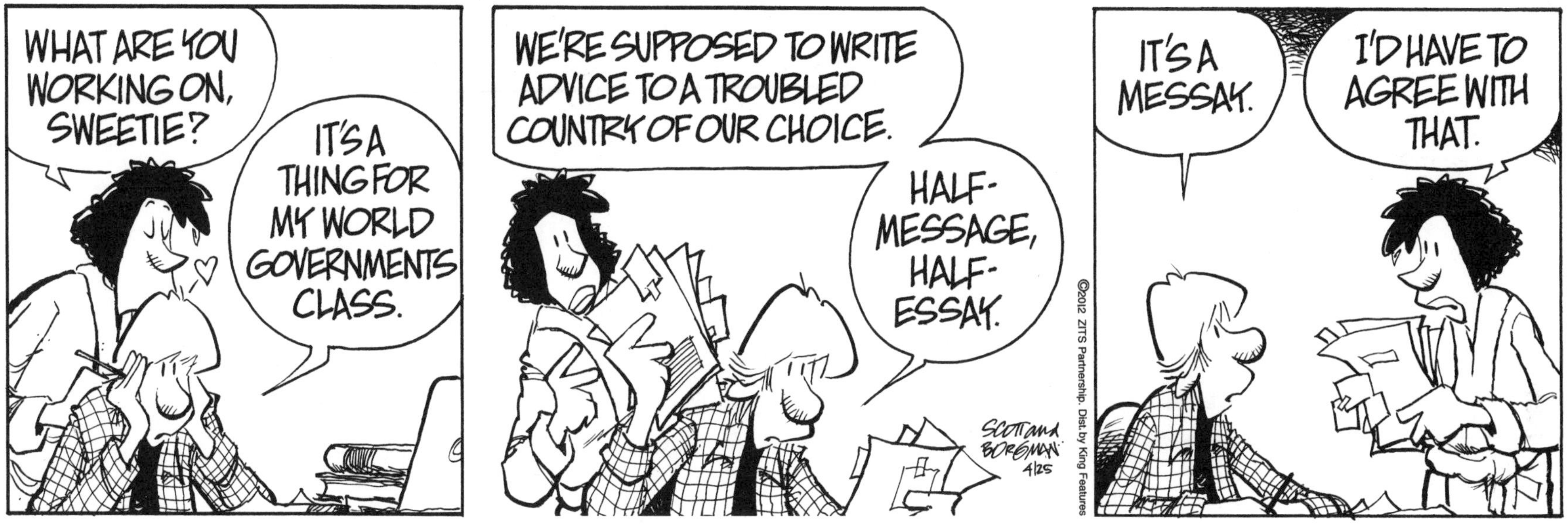
WHAT ARE YOU WORKING ON, SWEETIE?
IT'S A THING FOR MY WORLD GOVERNMENTS CLASS.
WE'RE SUPPOSED TO WRITE ADVICE TO A TROUBLED COUNTRY OF OUR CHOICE.
HALF-MESSAGE, HALF-ESSAY.
SCOTT and BORGMAN 4/25
©2012 ZITS Partnership. Dist. by King Features
IT'S A MESSAY.
I'D HAVE TO AGREE WITH THAT.

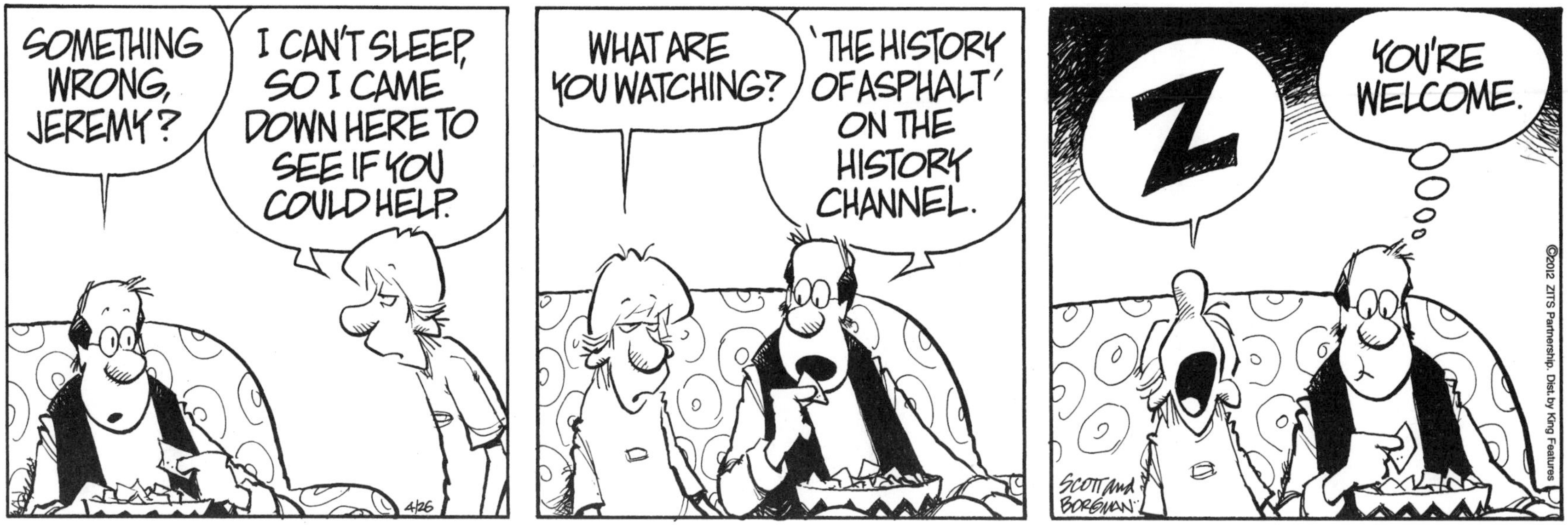
SOMETHING WRONG, JEREMY?
I CAN'T SLEEP, SO I CAME DOWN HERE TO SEE IF YOU COULD HELP.
4/26
WHAT ARE YOU WATCHING?
'THE HISTORY OF ASPHALT' ON THE HISTORY CHANNEL.
Z
YOU'RE WELCOME.
SCOTT and BORGMAN
©2012 ZITS Partnership. Dist. by King Features

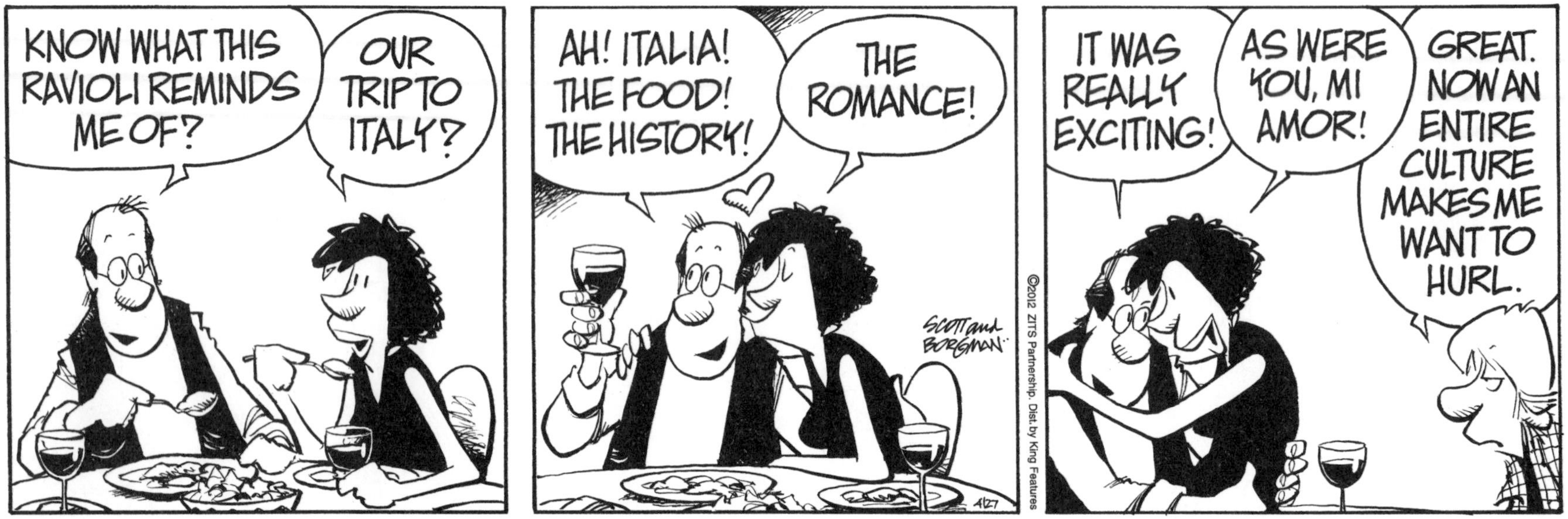
KNOW WHAT THIS RAVIOLI REMINDS ME OF?
OUR TRIP TO ITALY?
AH! ITALIA! THE FOOD! THE HISTORY!
THE ROMANCE!
IT WAS REALLY EXCITING!
AS WERE YOU, MI AMOR!
GREAT. NOW AN ENTIRE CULTURE MAKES ME WANT TO HURL.
SCOTT and BORGMAN
4/27
©2012 ZITS Partnership. Dist. by King Features

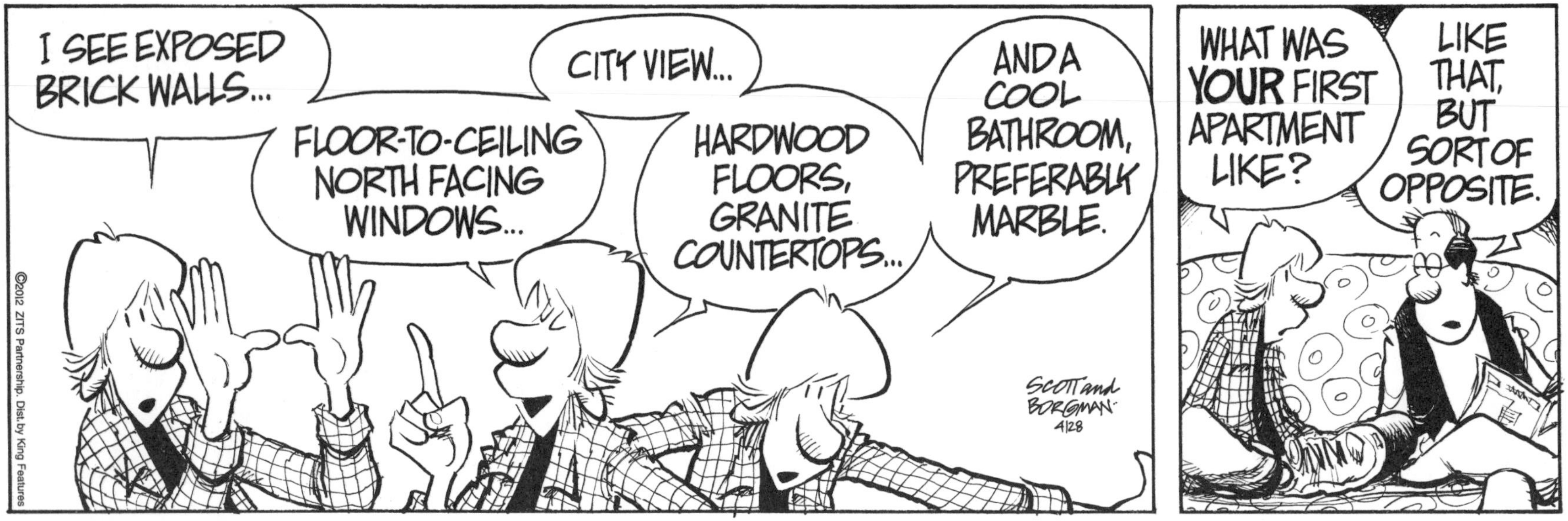
I SEE EXPOSED BRICK WALLS...
FLOOR-TO-CEILING NORTH FACING WINDOWS...
CITY VIEW...
HARDWOOD FLOORS, GRANITE COUNTERTOPS...
AND A COOL BATHROOM, PREFERABLY MARBLE.
WHAT WAS **YOUR** FIRST APARTMENT LIKE?
LIKE THAT, BUT SORT OF OPPOSITE.
SCOTT and BORGMAN
4/28
©2012 ZITS Partnership. Dist. by King Features

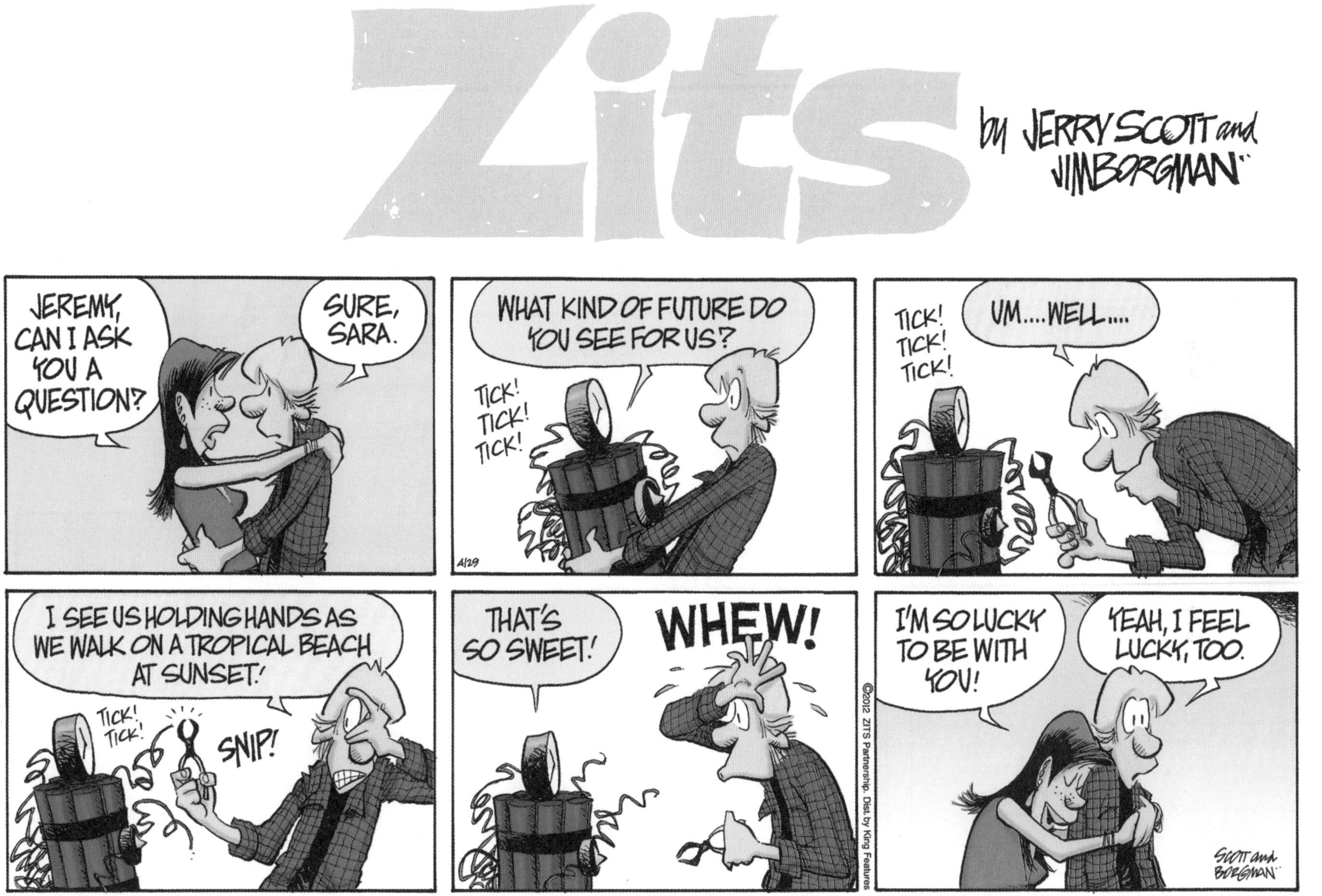
Zits
by JERRY SCOTT and JIM BORGMAN
JEREMY, CAN I ASK YOU A QUESTION?
SURE, SARA.
WHAT KIND OF FUTURE DO YOU SEE FOR US?
TICK! TICK! TICK!
4/29
TICK! TICK! TICK!
UM.....WELL....
I SEE US HOLDING HANDS AS WE WALK ON A TROPICAL BEACH AT SUNSET!
TICK! TICK!
SNIP!
THAT'S SO SWEET!
WHEW!
©2012 ZITS Partnership. Dist. by King Features
I'M SO LUCKY TO BE WITH YOU!
YEAH, I FEEL LUCKY, TOO.
SCOTT and BORGMAN

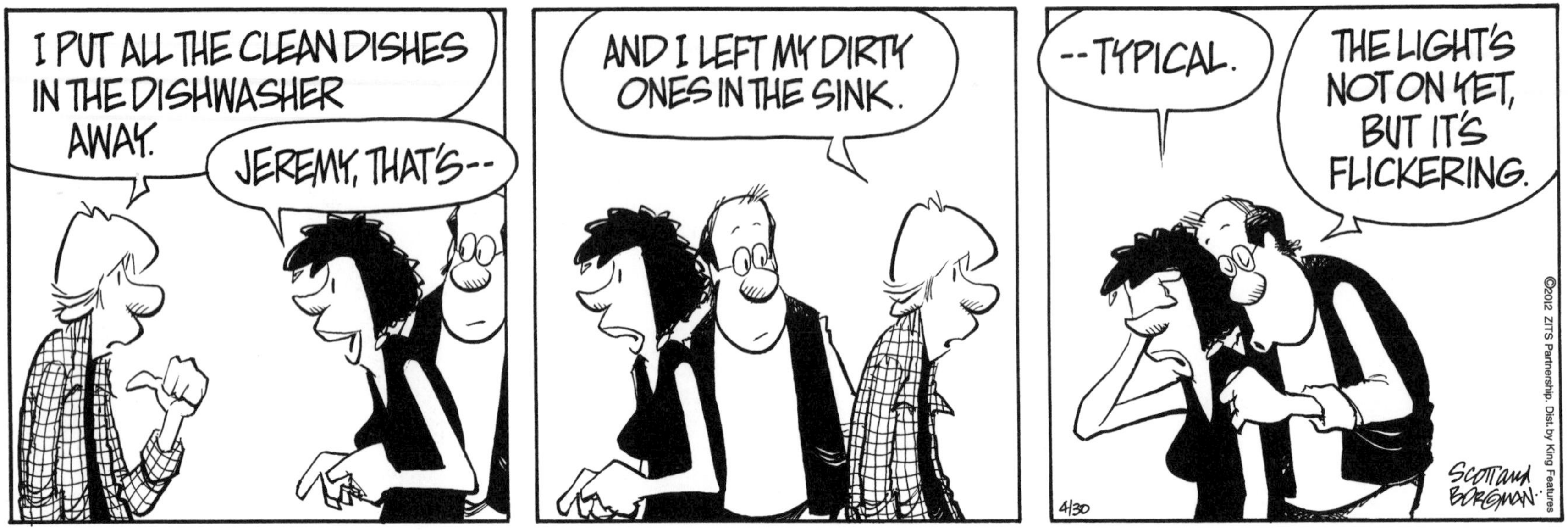
I PUT ALL THE CLEAN DISHES IN THE DISHWASHER AWAY.
JEREMY, THAT'S--
AND I LEFT MY DIRTY ONES IN THE SINK.
--TYPICAL.
THE LIGHT'S NOT ON YET, BUT IT'S FLICKERING.
4/30
SCOTT and BORGMAN
©2012 ZITS Partnership. Dist. by King Features

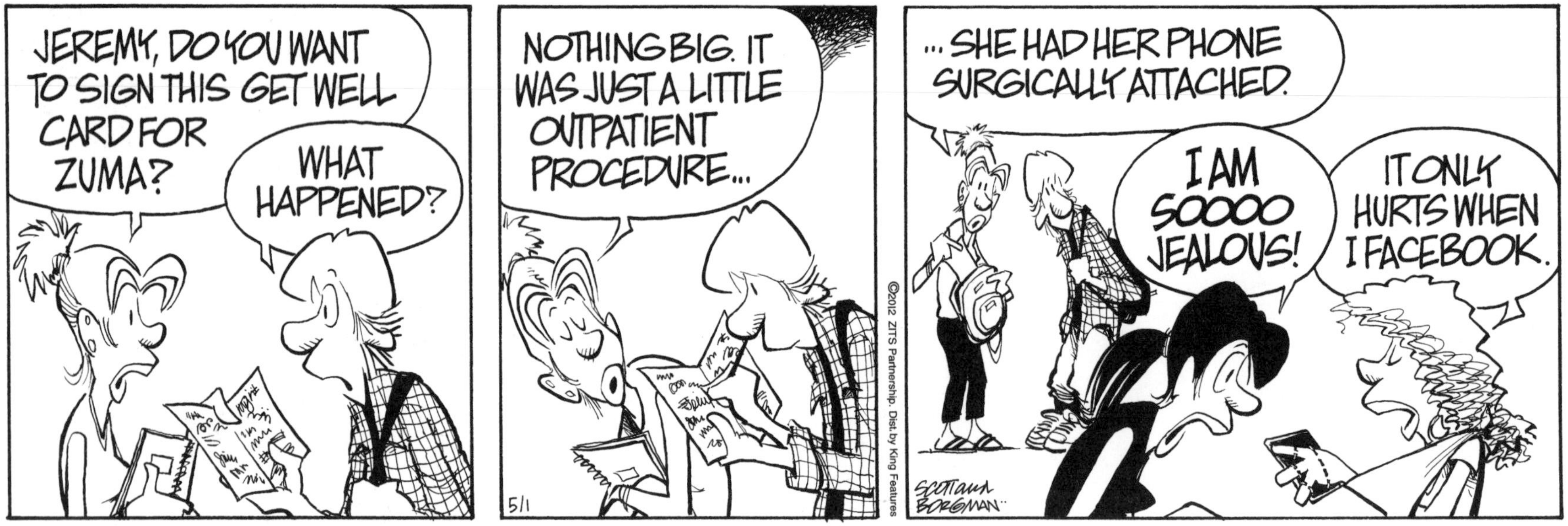
JEREMY, DO YOU WANT TO SIGN THIS GET WELL CARD FOR ZUMA?
WHAT HAPPENED?
NOTHING BIG. IT WAS JUST A LITTLE OUTPATIENT PROCEDURE...
...SHE HAD HER PHONE SURGICALLY ATTACHED.
I AM SOOOO JEALOUS!
IT ONLY HURTS WHEN I FACEBOOK.
5/1
SCOTT and BORGMAN
©2012 ZITS Partnership. Dist. by King Features

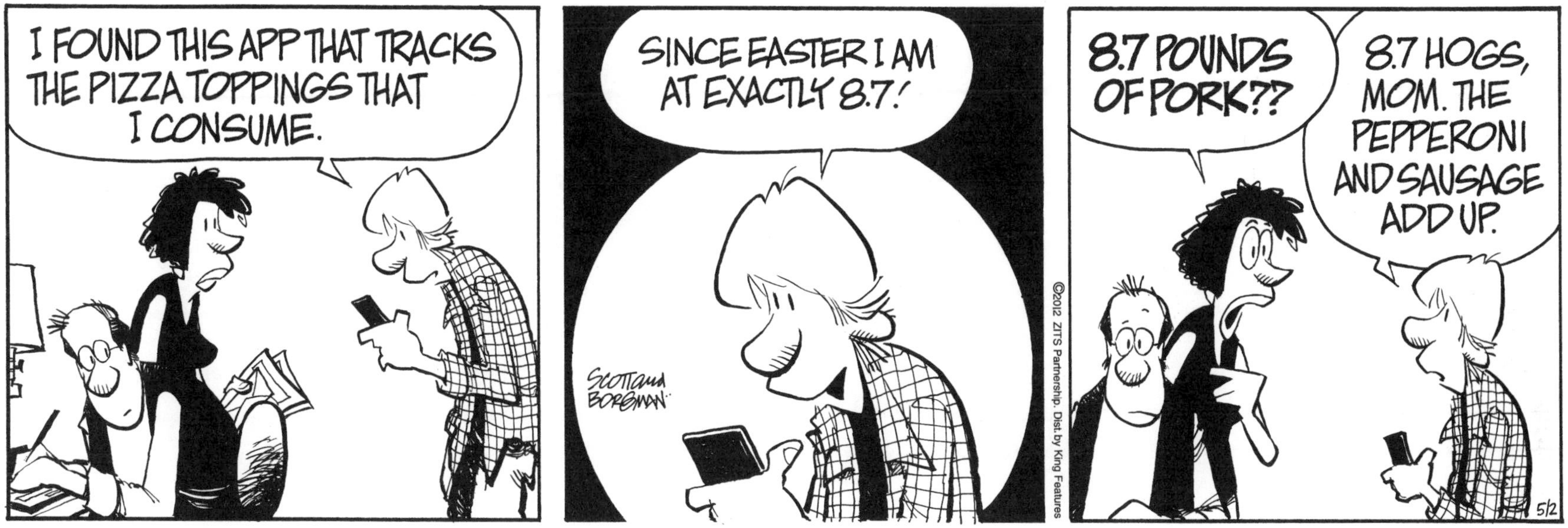
I FOUND THIS APP THAT TRACKS THE PIZZA TOPPINGS THAT I CONSUME.
SINCE EASTER I AM AT EXACTLY 8.7!
SCOTT AND BORGMAN
8.7 POUNDS OF PORK??
8.7 HOGS, MOM. THE PEPPERONI AND SAUSAGE ADD UP.
5/2
©2012 ZITS Partnership. Dist. by King Features

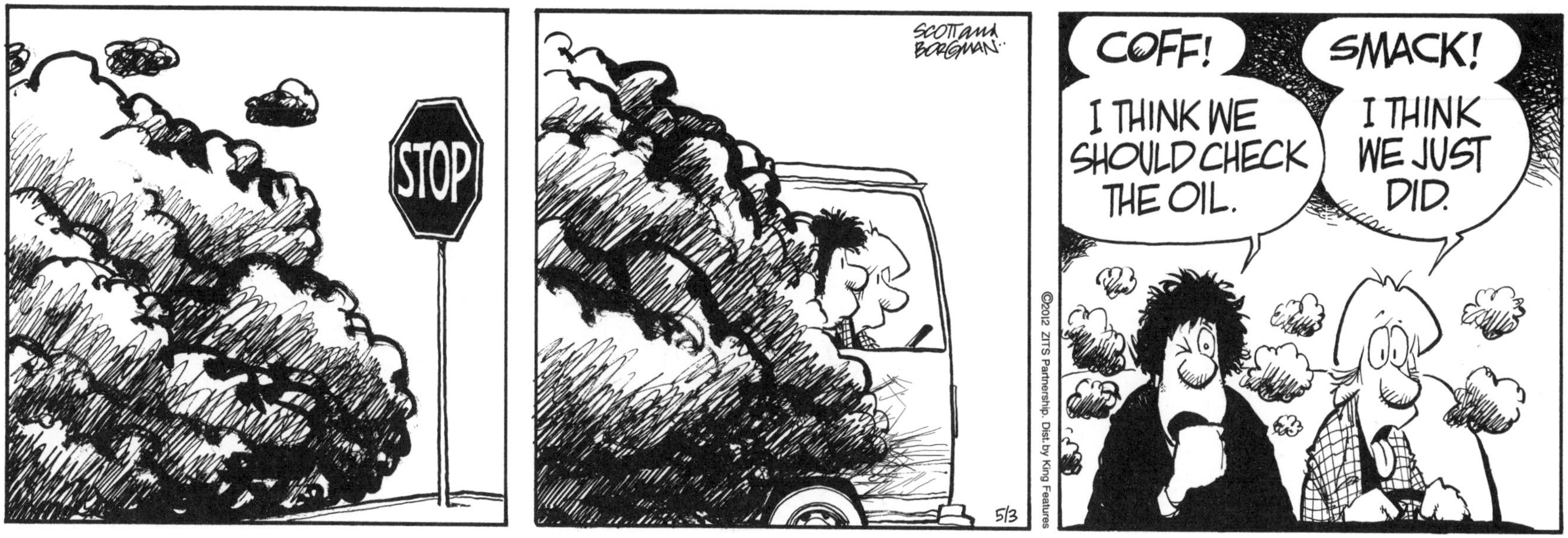
STOP
SCOTT AND BORGMAN
5/3
COFF!
I THINK WE SHOULD CHECK THE OIL.
SMACK!
I THINK WE JUST DID.
©2012 ZITS Partnership. Dist. by King Features

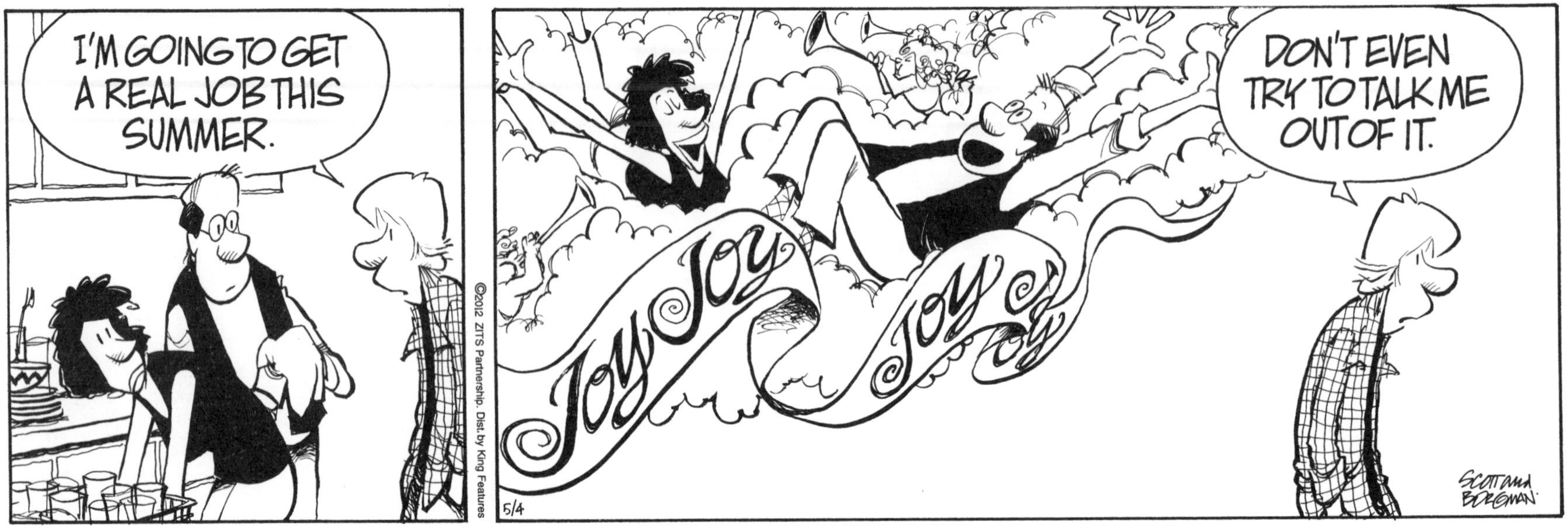

I'M GOING TO GET A REAL JOB THIS SUMMER.
©2012 ZITS Partnership. Dist. by King Features
JOY JOY JOY JOY
DON'T EVEN TRY TO TALK ME OUT OF IT.
5/4
SCOTT and BORGMAN

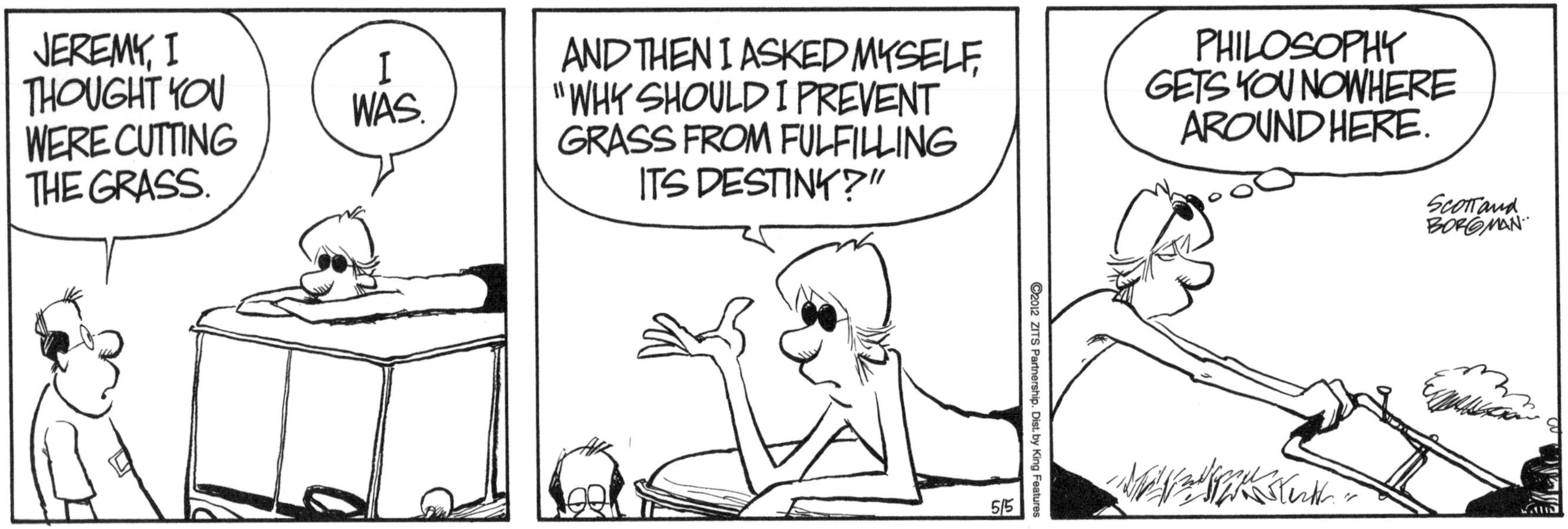

JEREMY, I THOUGHT YOU WERE CUTTING THE GRASS.
I WAS.
AND THEN I ASKED MYSELF, "WHY SHOULD I PREVENT GRASS FROM FULFILLING ITS DESTINY?"
5/5
©2012 ZITS Partnership. Dist. by King Features
PHILOSOPHY GETS YOU NOWHERE AROUND HERE.
SCOTT and BORGMAN

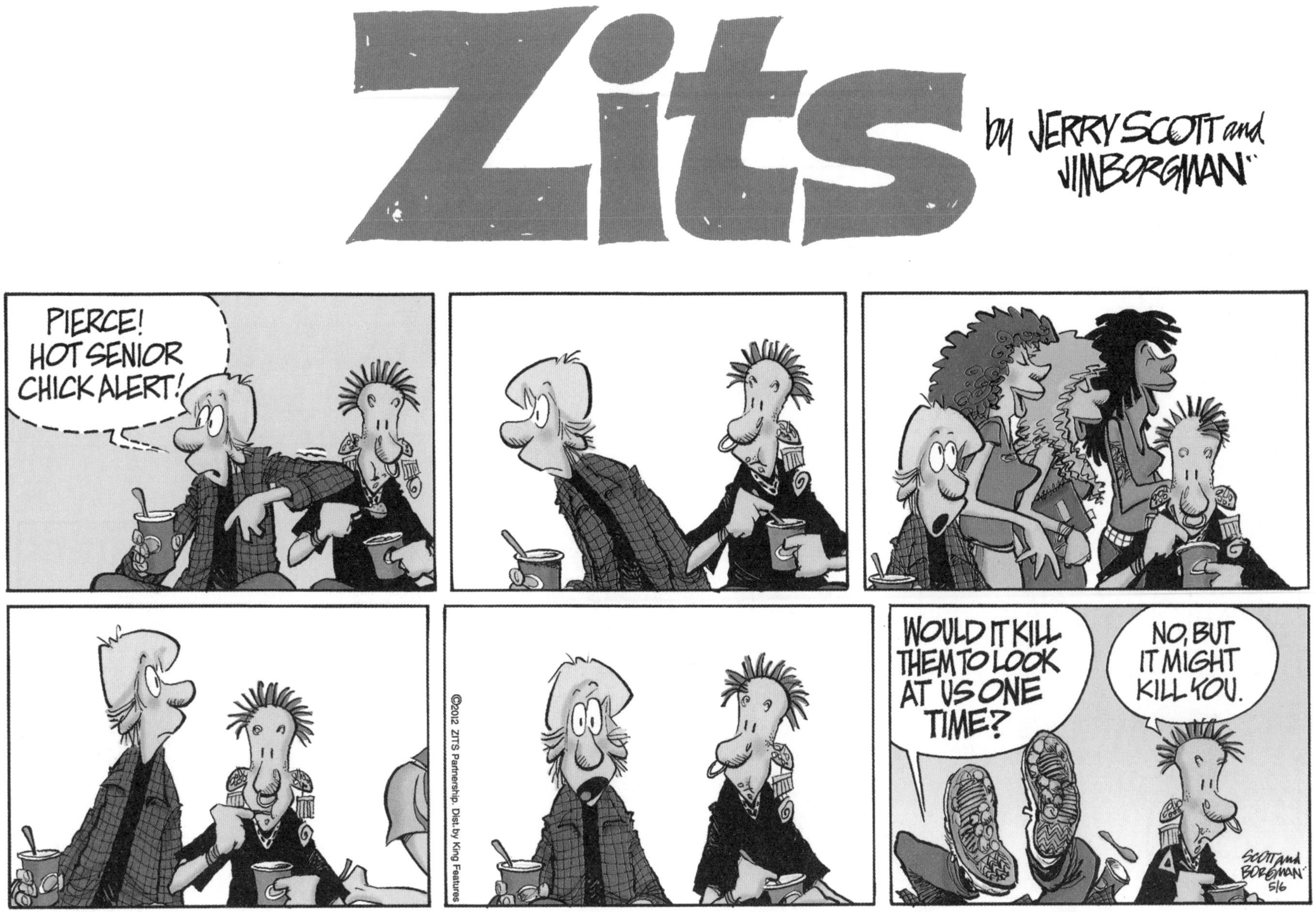
Zits
by JERRY SCOTT and JIM BORGMAN
PIERCE! HOT SENIOR CHICK ALERT!
©2012 ZITS Partnership. Dist. by King Features
WOULD IT KILL THEM TO LOOK AT US ONE TIME?
NO, BUT IT MIGHT KILL YOU.
SCOTT and BORGMAN 5/6

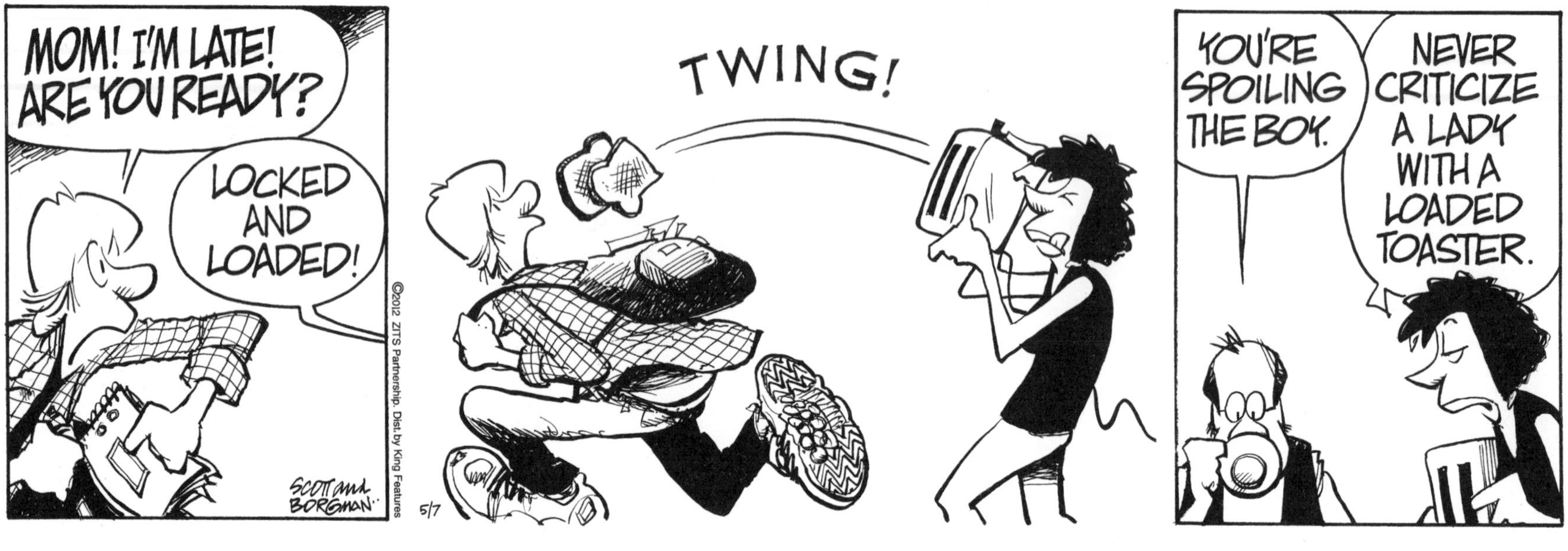
MOM! I'M LATE! ARE YOU READY?
LOCKED AND LOADED!
©2012 ZITS Partnership. Dist. by King Features
SCOTT and BORGMAN
5/7
TWING!
YOU'RE SPOILING THE BOY.
NEVER CRITICIZE A LADY WITH A LOADED TOASTER.

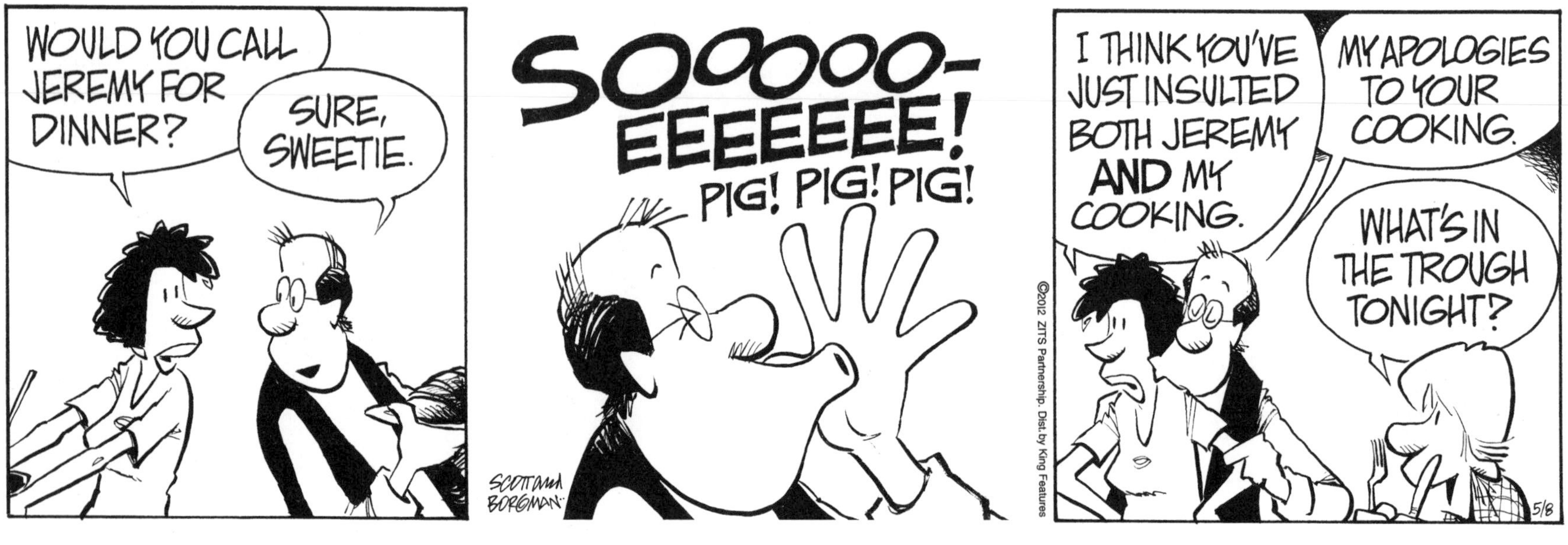
WOULD YOU CALL JEREMY FOR DINNER?
SURE, SWEETIE.
SOOOOO-EEEEEEE!
PIG! PIG! PIG!
SCOTT and BORGMAN
©2012 ZITS Partnership. Dist. by King Features
I THINK YOU'VE JUST INSULTED BOTH JEREMY AND MY COOKING.
MY APOLOGIES TO YOUR COOKING.
WHAT'S IN THE TROUGH TONIGHT?
5/8

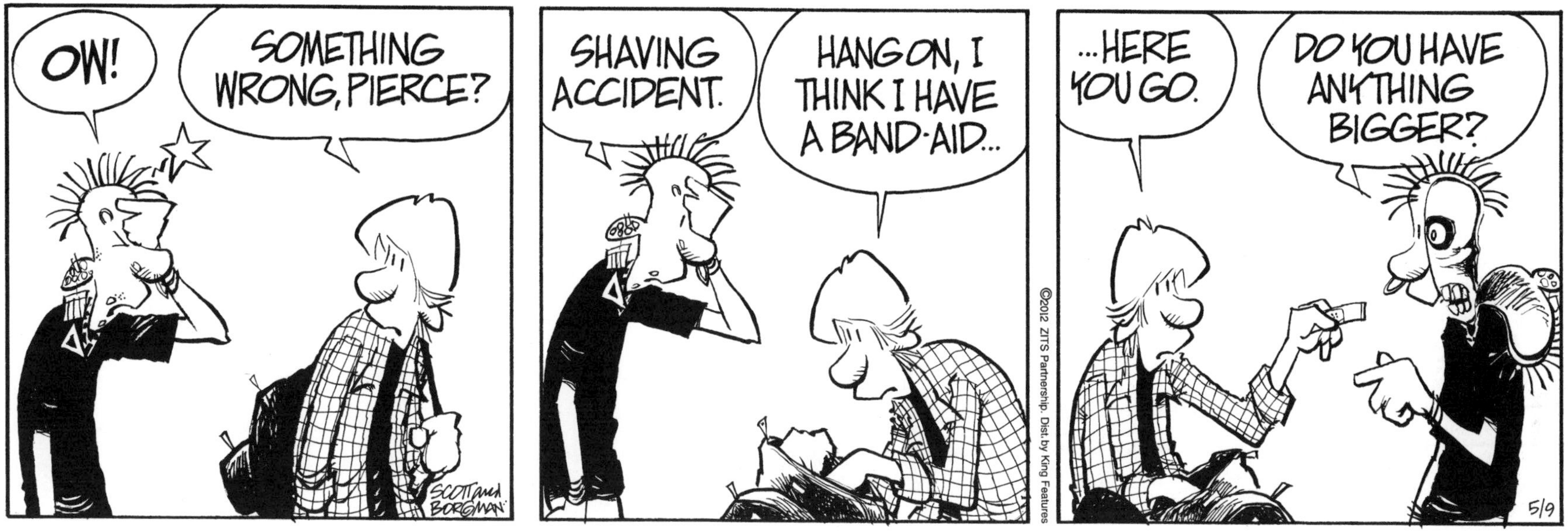
OW!
SOMETHING WRONG, PIERCE?
SHAVING ACCIDENT.
HANG ON, I THINK I HAVE A BAND-AID...
...HERE YOU GO.
DO YOU HAVE ANYTHING BIGGER?
SCOTT and BORGMAN
5/9
©2012 ZITS Partnership. Dist. by King Features

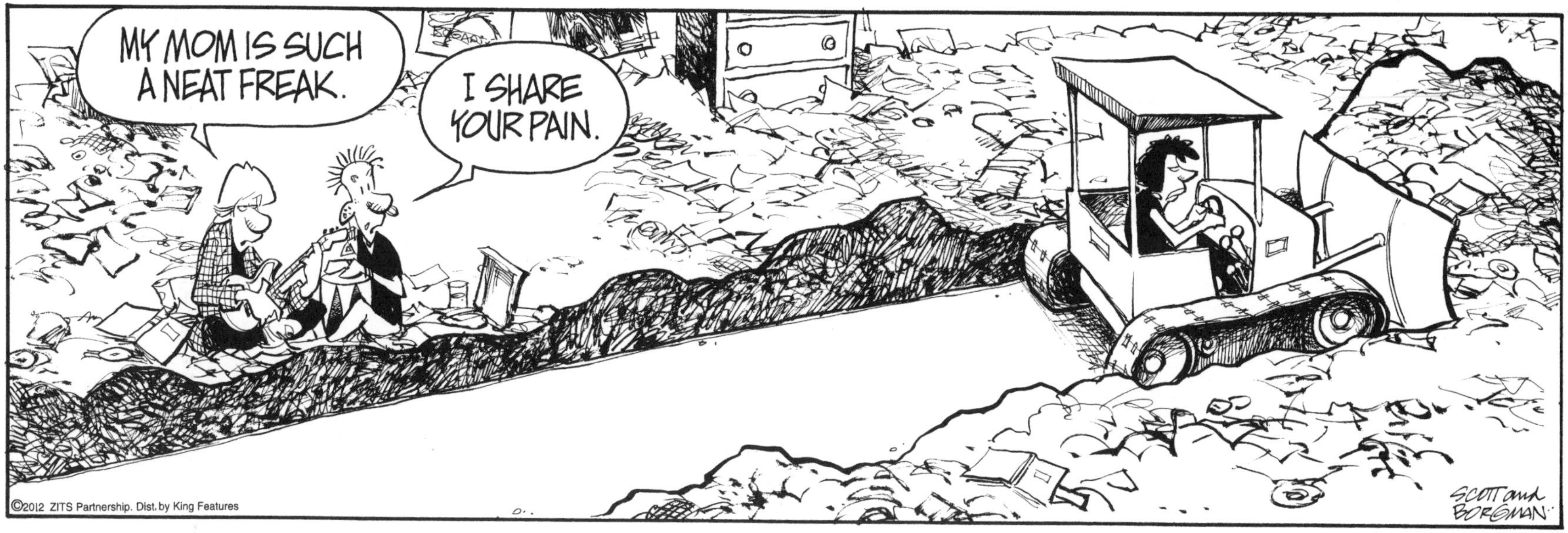
MY MOM IS SUCH A NEAT FREAK.
I SHARE YOUR PAIN.
©2012 ZITS Partnership. Dist. by King Features
SCOTT and BORGMAN

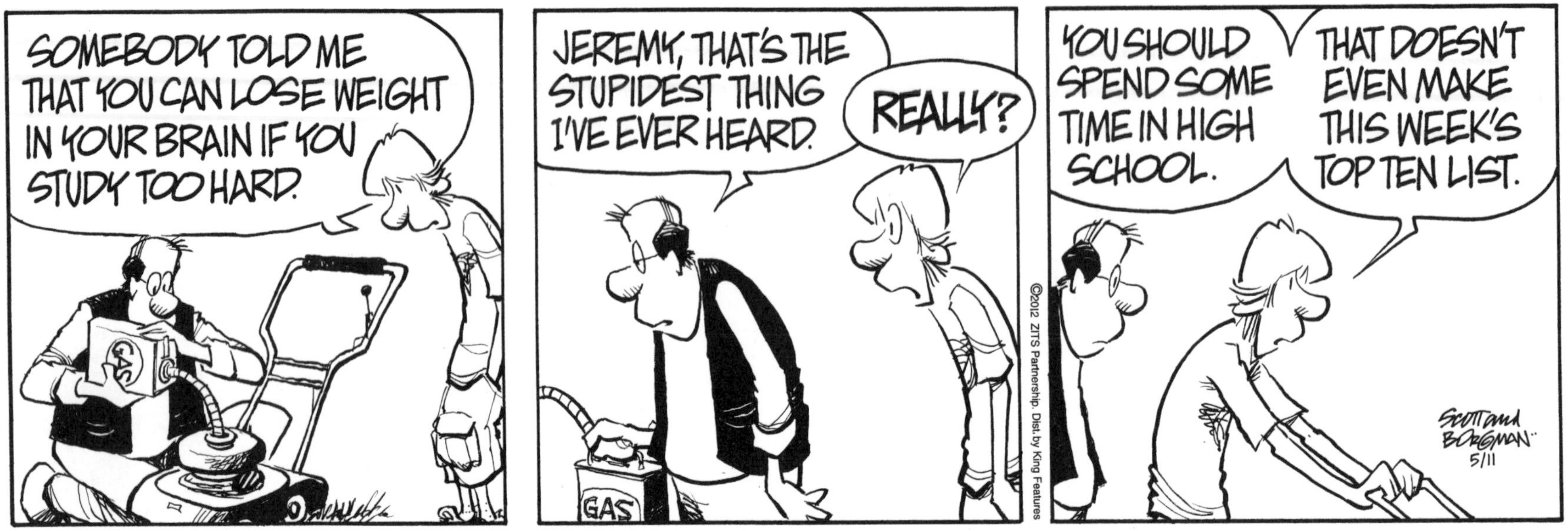
SOMEBODY TOLD ME THAT YOU CAN LOSE WEIGHT IN YOUR BRAIN IF YOU STUDY TOO HARD.
GAS
JEREMY, THAT'S THE STUPIDEST THING I'VE EVER HEARD.
REALLY?
GAS
©2012 ZITS Partnership. Dist. by King Features
YOU SHOULD SPEND SOME TIME IN HIGH SCHOOL.
THAT DOESN'T EVEN MAKE THIS WEEK'S TOP TEN LIST.
SCOTT and BORGMAN
5/11

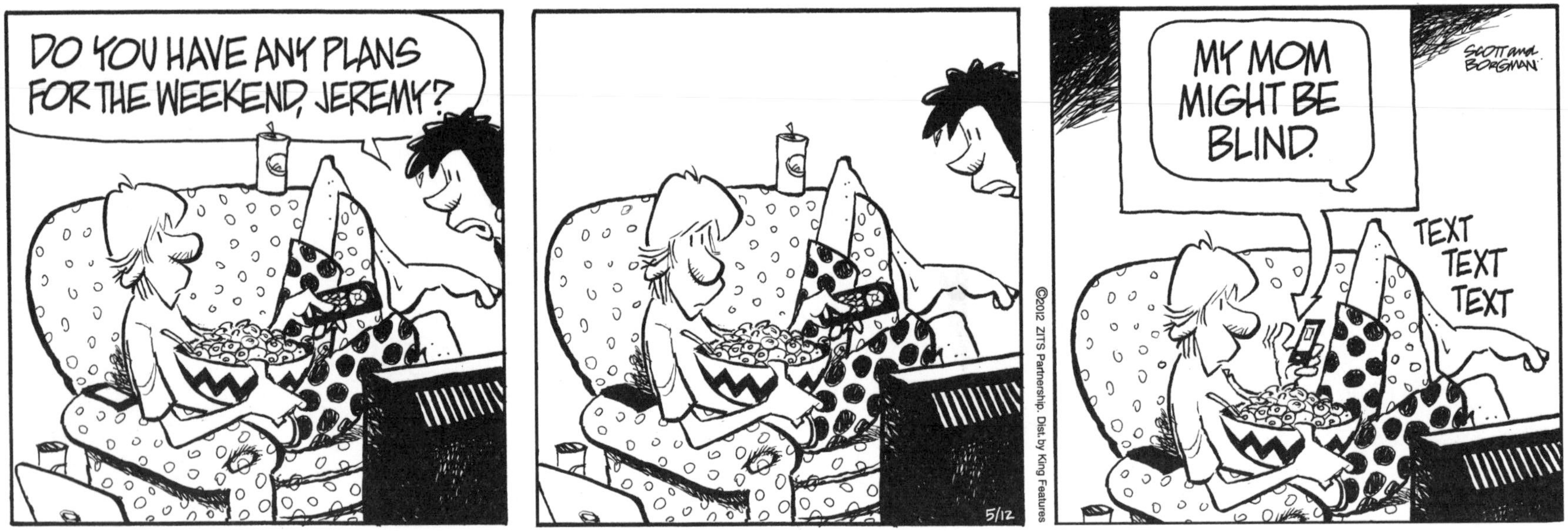
DO YOU HAVE ANY PLANS FOR THE WEEKEND, JEREMY?
5/12
©2012 ZITS Partnership. Dist. by King Features
SCOTT and BORGMAN
MY MOM MIGHT BE BLIND.
TEXT TEXT TEXT

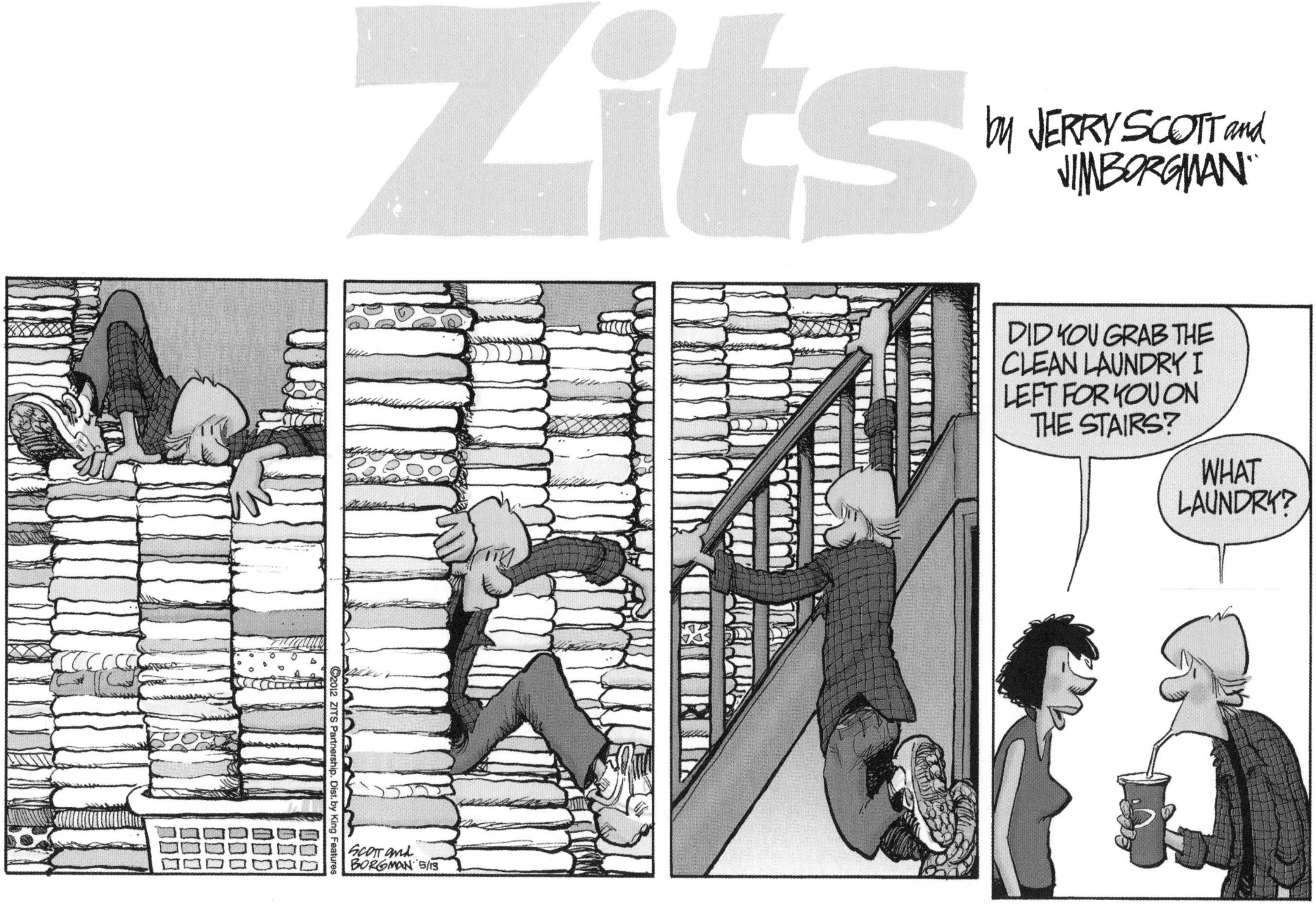
Zits
by JERRY SCOTT and JIMBORGMAN
©2012 ZITS Partnership. Dist. by King Features
SCOTT and BORGMAN 5/13
DID YOU GRAB THE CLEAN LAUNDRY I LEFT FOR YOU ON THE STAIRS?
WHAT LAUNDRY?

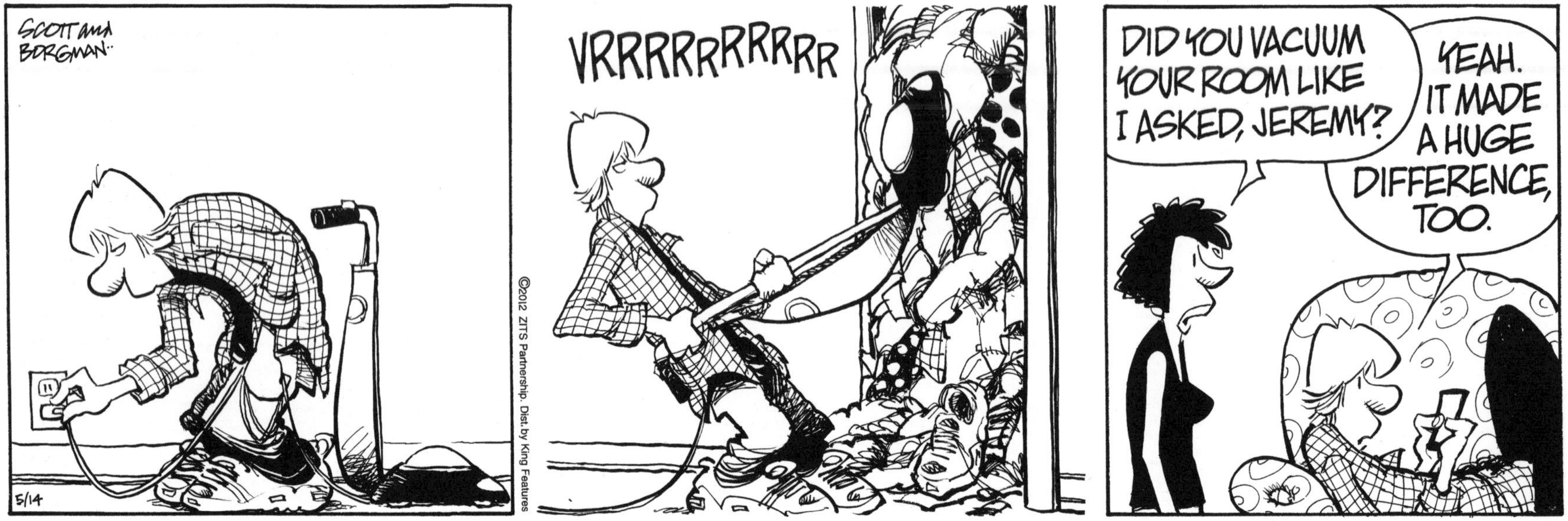
SCOTT AND BORGMAN
5/14
©2012 ZITS Partnership. Dist. by King Features
VRRRRRRRRRRR
DID YOU VACUUM YOUR ROOM LIKE I ASKED, JEREMY?
YEAH. IT MADE A HUGE DIFFERENCE, TOO.

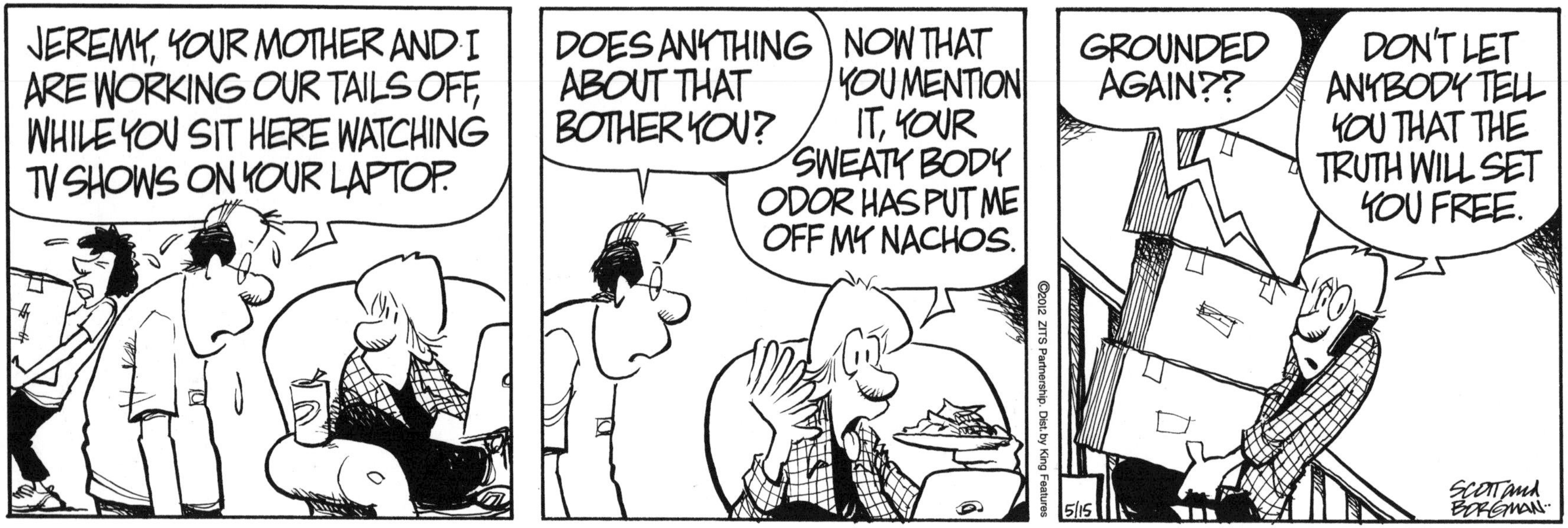
JEREMY, YOUR MOTHER AND I ARE WORKING OUR TAILS OFF, WHILE YOU SIT HERE WATCHING TV SHOWS ON YOUR LAPTOP.
DOES ANYTHING ABOUT THAT BOTHER YOU?
NOW THAT YOU MENTION IT, YOUR SWEATY BODY ODOR HAS PUT ME OFF MY NACHOS.
©2012 ZITS Partnership. Dist. by King Features
GROUNDED AGAIN??
DON'T LET ANYBODY TELL YOU THAT THE TRUTH WILL SET YOU FREE.
5/15
SCOTT AND BORGMAN

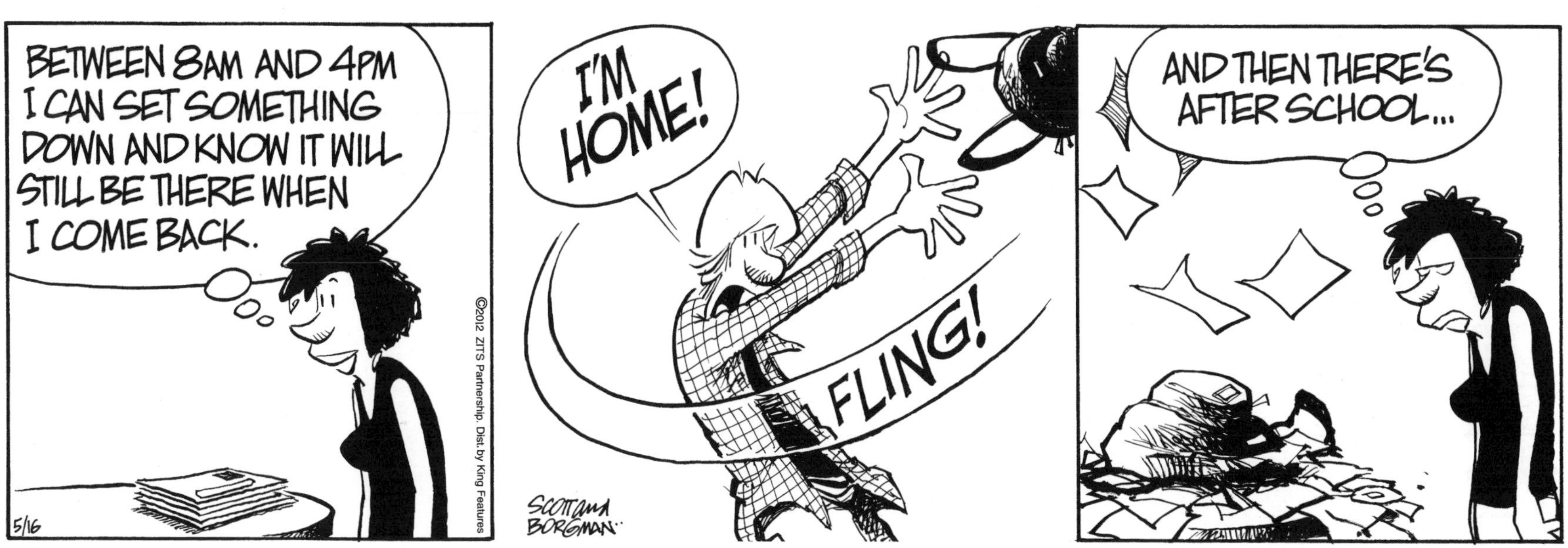
BETWEEN 8AM AND 4PM I CAN SET SOMETHING DOWN AND KNOW IT WILL STILL BE THERE WHEN I COME BACK.
5/16
©2012 ZITS Partnership. Dist.by King Features
I'M HOME!
FLING!
SCOTT and BORGMAN
AND THEN THERE'S AFTER SCHOOL...

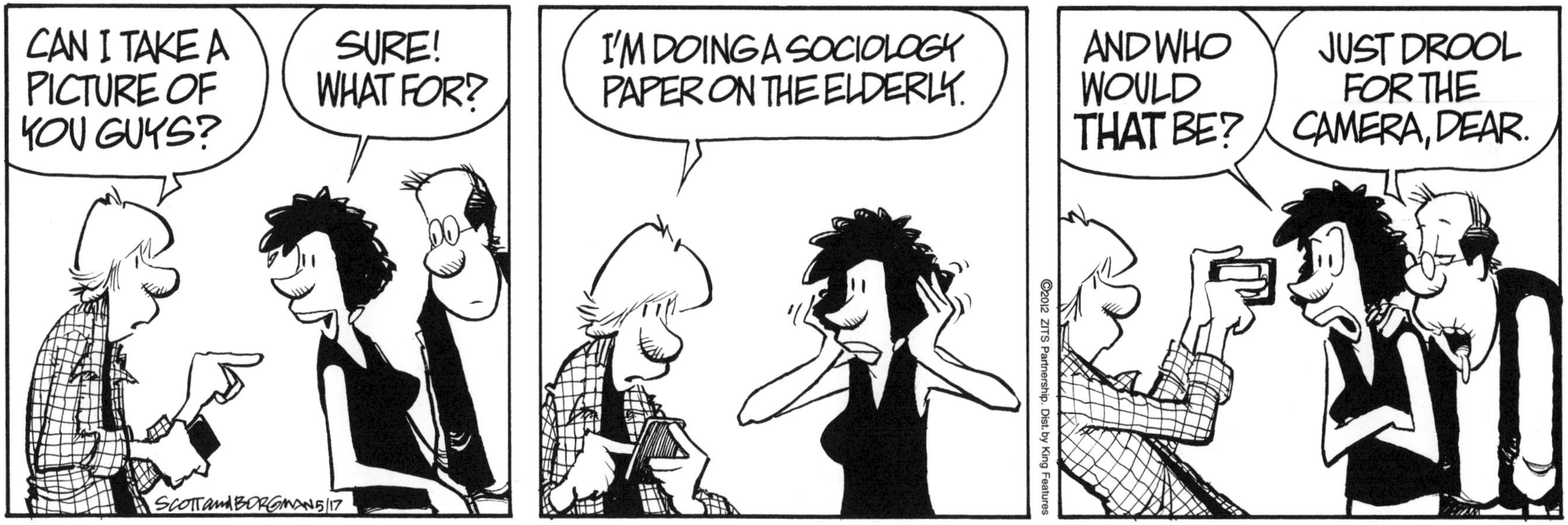
CAN I TAKE A PICTURE OF YOU GUYS?
SURE! WHAT FOR?
SCOTT and BORGMAN 5/17
I'M DOING A SOCIOLOGY PAPER ON THE ELDERLY.
©2012 ZITS Partnership. Dist.by King Features
AND WHO WOULD THAT BE?
JUST DROOL FOR THE CAMERA, DEAR.

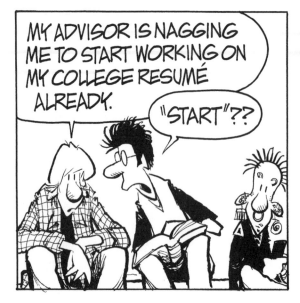

MY ADVISOR IS NAGGING ME TO START WORKING ON MY COLLEGE RESUMÉ ALREADY.
"START"??
JEREMY, IF YOU HAVEN'T DUG YOUR WELL IN AFRICA BY SOPHOMORE YEAR, DON'T EVEN BOTHER APPLYING.
WHY DOES EVERYBODY HAVE TO BE AN OVER-ACHIEVER?
HANG ON. I'M REORDERING RUBBER WRIST-BANDS FOR MY SRI LANKAN NON-PROFIT.
5/18
©2012 ZITS Partnership. Dist. by King Features
SCOTT and BORGMAN

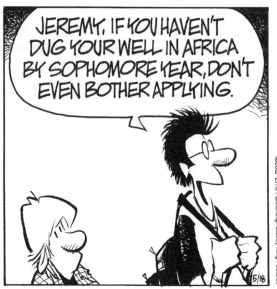

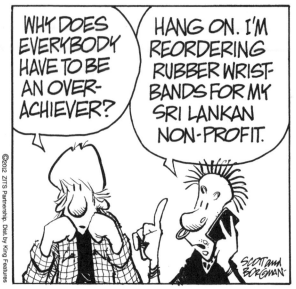

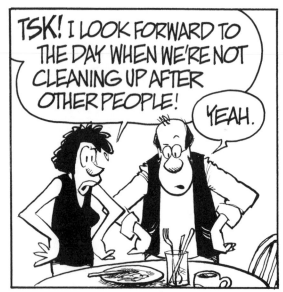

TSK! I LOOK FORWARD TO THE DAY WHEN WE'RE NOT CLEANING UP AFTER OTHER PEOPLE!
YEAH.
WAIT– I THINK THAT'S MY BREAKFAST PLATE.
AND YOUR COFFEE MUG.
OH.
SCOTT and BORGMAN
©2012 ZITS Partnership. Dist. by King Features
I'M **NOT** LOOKING FORWARD TO THE DAY WHEN WE CAN'T BLAME EVERYTHING ON THE TEENAGER.
LET'S STILL BE AN-NOYED WITH HIM, ANYWAY.
5/19

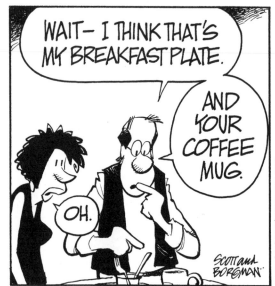

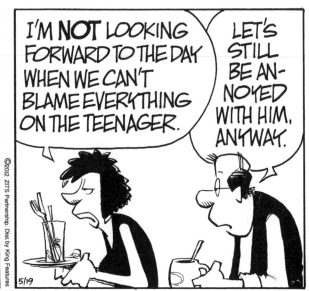

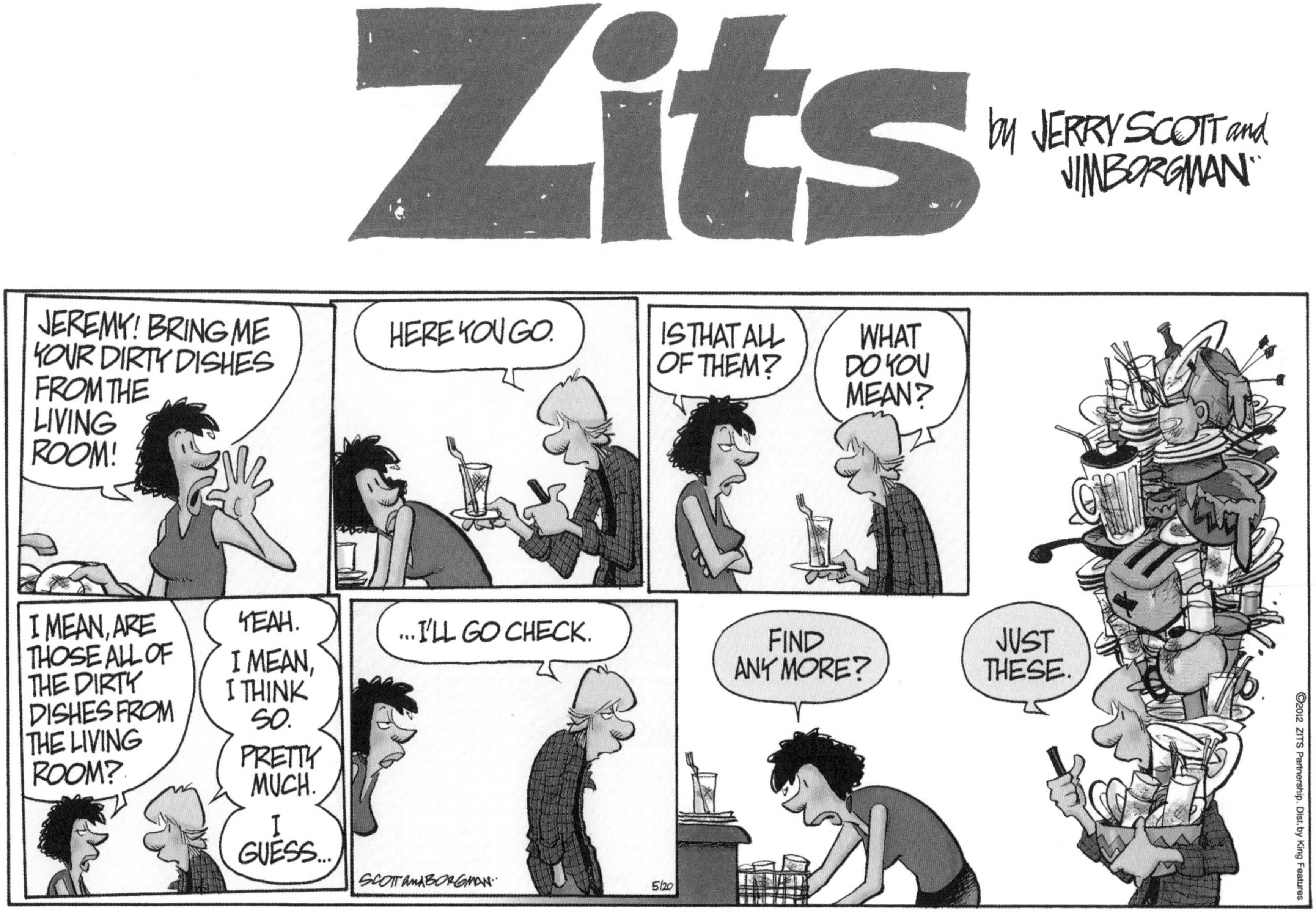
Zits
by JERRY SCOTT and JIM BORGMAN
JEREMY! BRING ME YOUR DIRTY DISHES FROM THE LIVING ROOM!
HERE YOU GO.
IS THAT ALL OF THEM?
WHAT DO YOU MEAN?
I MEAN, ARE THOSE ALL OF THE DIRTY DISHES FROM THE LIVING ROOM?
YEAH.
I MEAN, I THINK SO.
PRETTY MUCH.
I GUESS...
...I'LL GO CHECK.
FIND ANY MORE?
JUST THESE.
SCOTT and BORGMAN
5/20
©2012 ZITS Partnership. Dist. by King Features

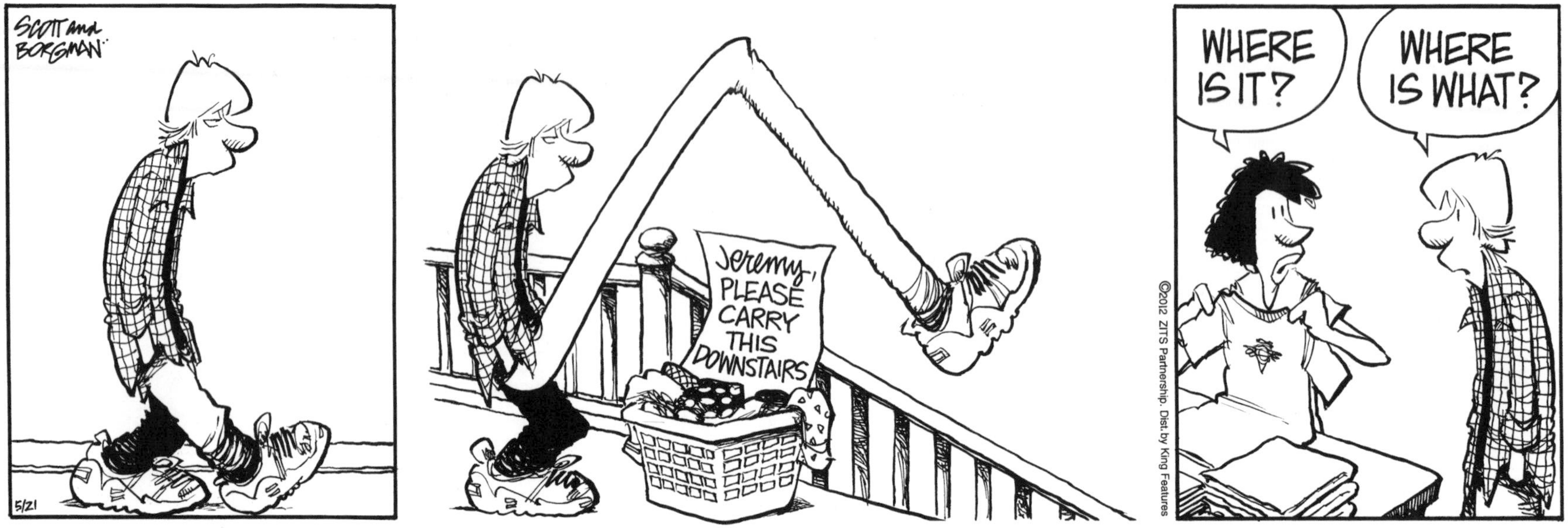
SCOTT and BORGMAN
5/21
Jeremy, PLEASE CARRY THIS DOWNSTAIRS
WHERE IS IT?
WHERE IS WHAT?
©2012 ZITS Partnership. Dist.by King Features

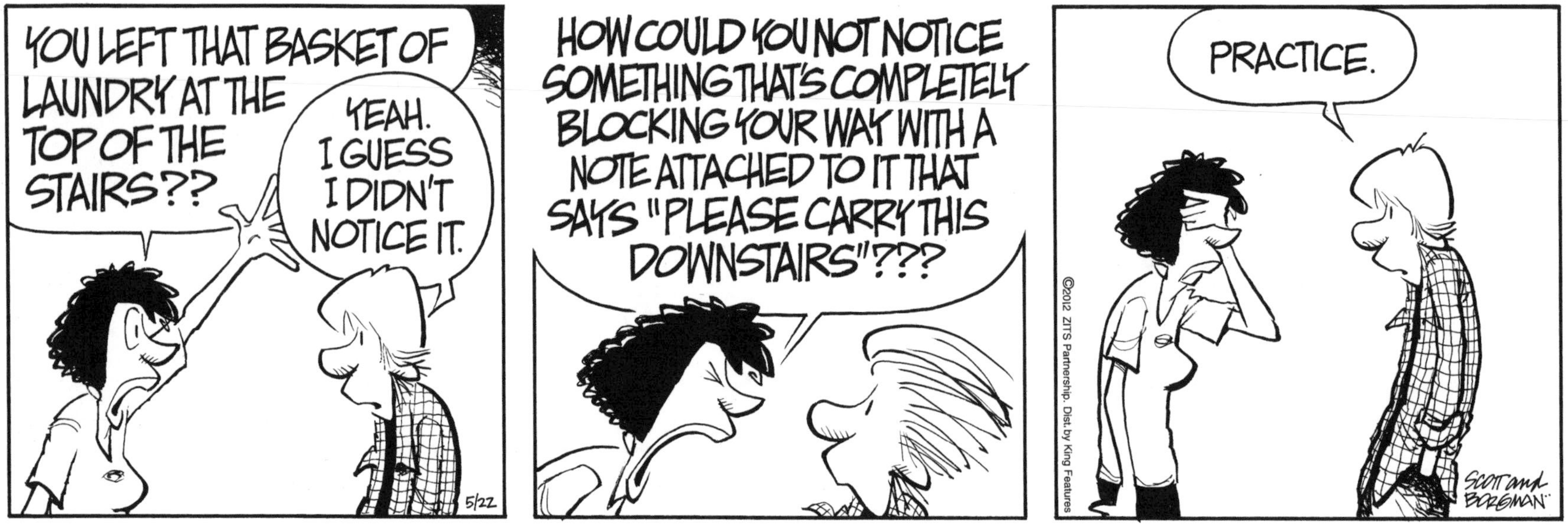
YOU LEFT THAT BASKET OF LAUNDRY AT THE TOP OF THE STAIRS??
YEAH. I GUESS I DIDN'T NOTICE IT.
5/22
HOW COULD YOU NOT NOTICE SOMETHING THAT'S COMPLETELY BLOCKING YOUR WAY WITH A NOTE ATTACHED TO IT THAT SAYS "PLEASE CARRY THIS DOWNSTAIRS"???
PRACTICE.
©2012 ZITS Partnership. Dist.by King Features
SCOTT and BORGMAN

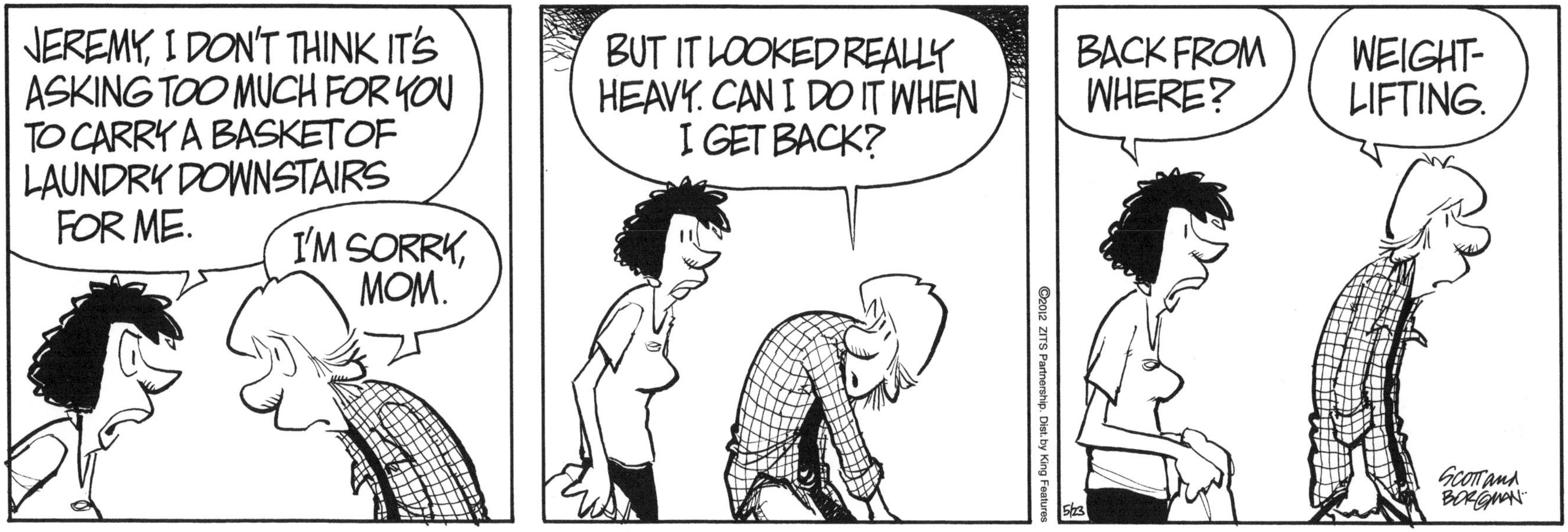
JEREMY, I DON'T THINK IT'S ASKING TOO MUCH FOR YOU TO CARRY A BASKET OF LAUNDRY DOWNSTAIRS FOR ME.
I'M SORRY, MOM.
BUT IT LOOKED REALLY HEAVY. CAN I DO IT WHEN I GET BACK?
©2012 ZITS Partnership. Dist. by King Features
5/23
BACK FROM WHERE?
WEIGHT-LIFTING.
SCOTT and BORGMAN

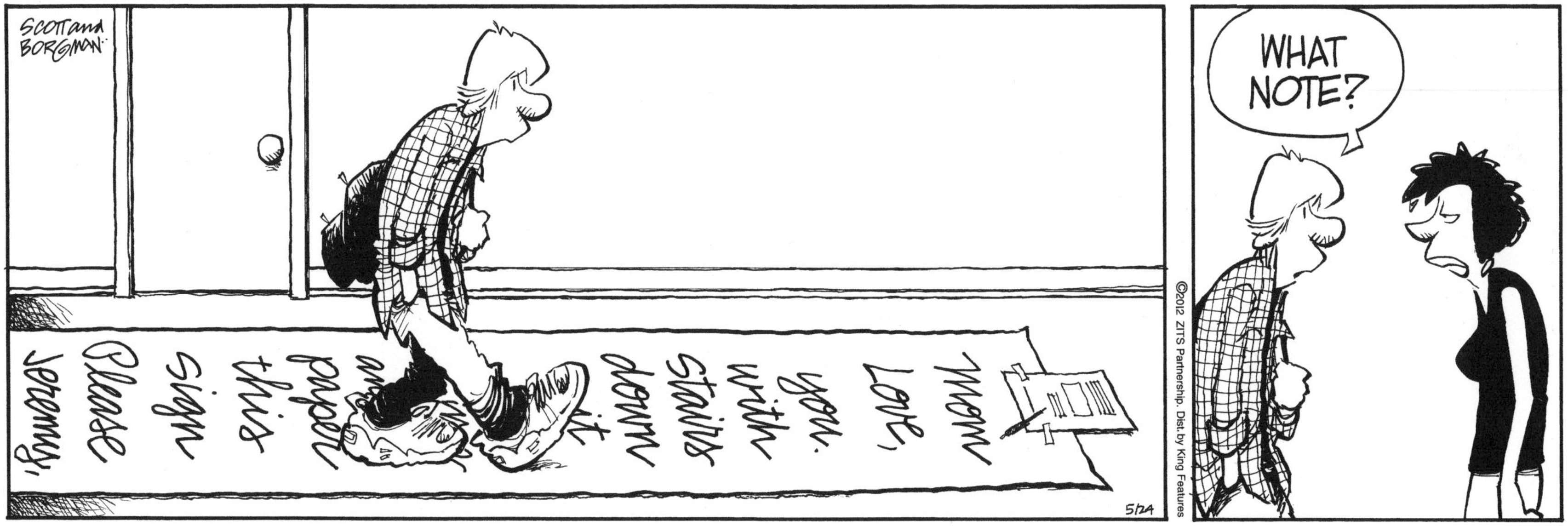
SCOTT and BORGMAN
Jeremy,
Please
sign
this
paper
down
stairs
with
you.
Love,
Mom
5/24
©2012 ZITS Partnership. Dist. by King Features
WHAT NOTE?

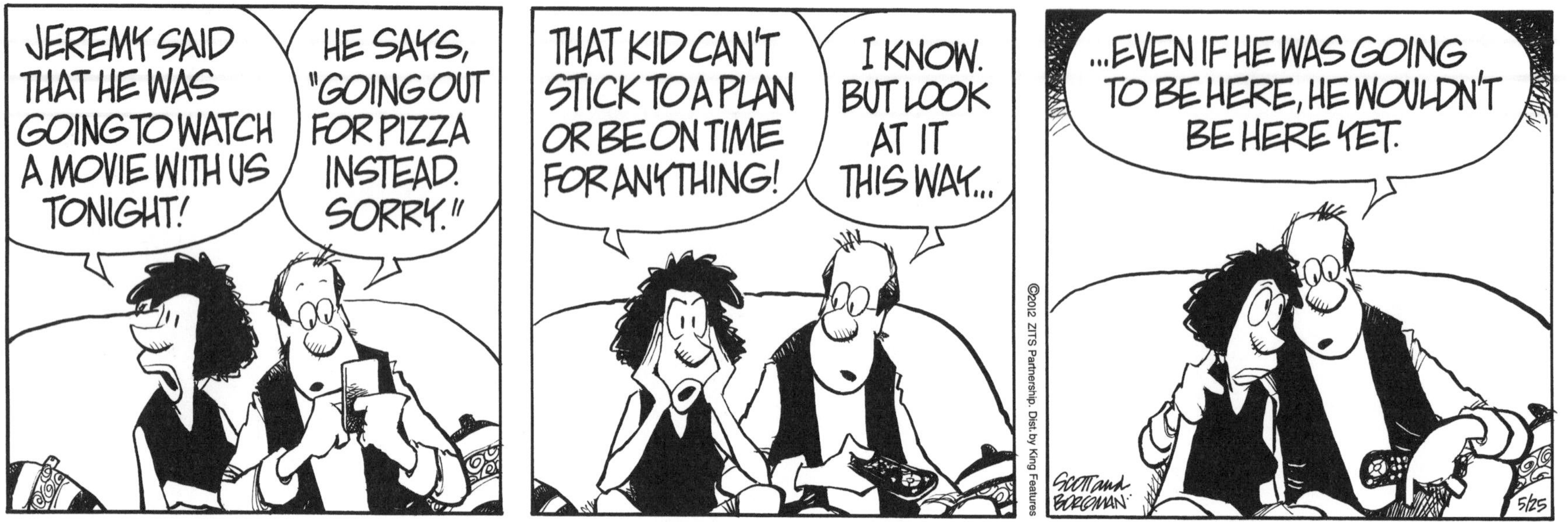
JEREMY SAID THAT HE WAS GOING TO WATCH A MOVIE WITH US TONIGHT!
HE SAYS, "GOING OUT FOR PIZZA INSTEAD. SORRY."
THAT KID CAN'T STICK TO A PLAN OR BE ON TIME FOR ANYTHING!
I KNOW. BUT LOOK AT IT THIS WAY...
...EVEN IF HE WAS GOING TO BE HERE, HE WOULDN'T BE HERE YET.
SCOTT and BORGMAN
5/25

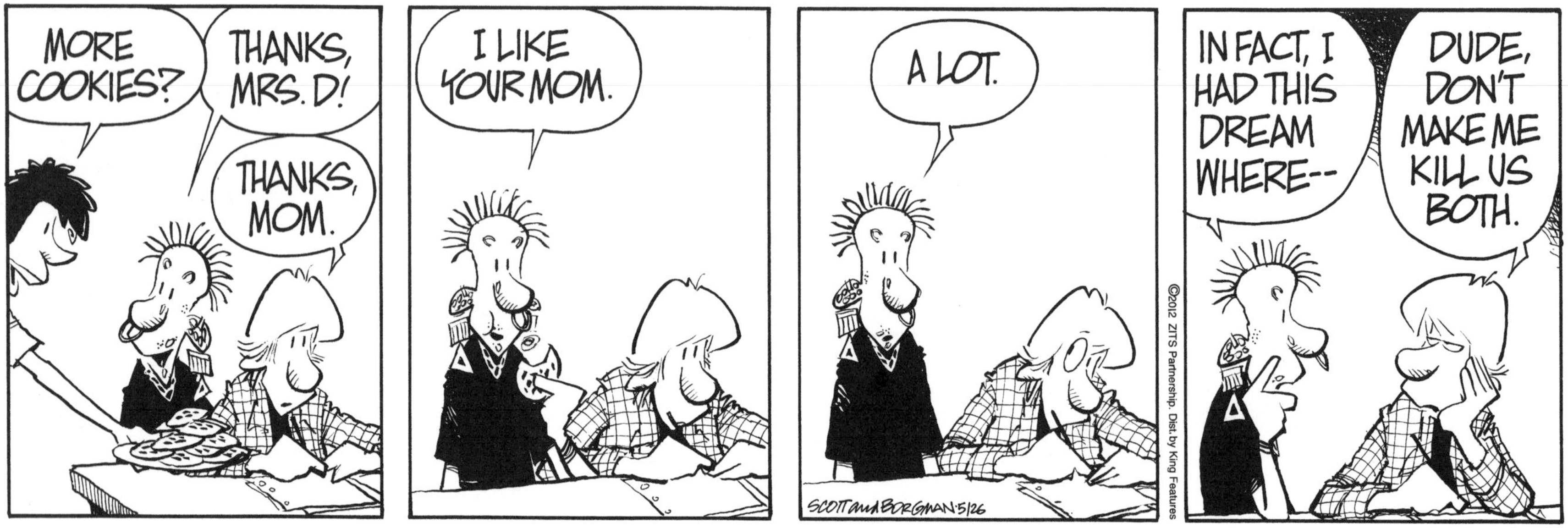
MORE COOKIES?
THANKS, MRS. D!
THANKS, MOM.
I LIKE YOUR MOM.
A LOT.
SCOTT and BORGMAN 5/26
IN FACT, I HAD THIS DREAM WHERE--
DUDE, DON'T MAKE ME KILL US BOTH.

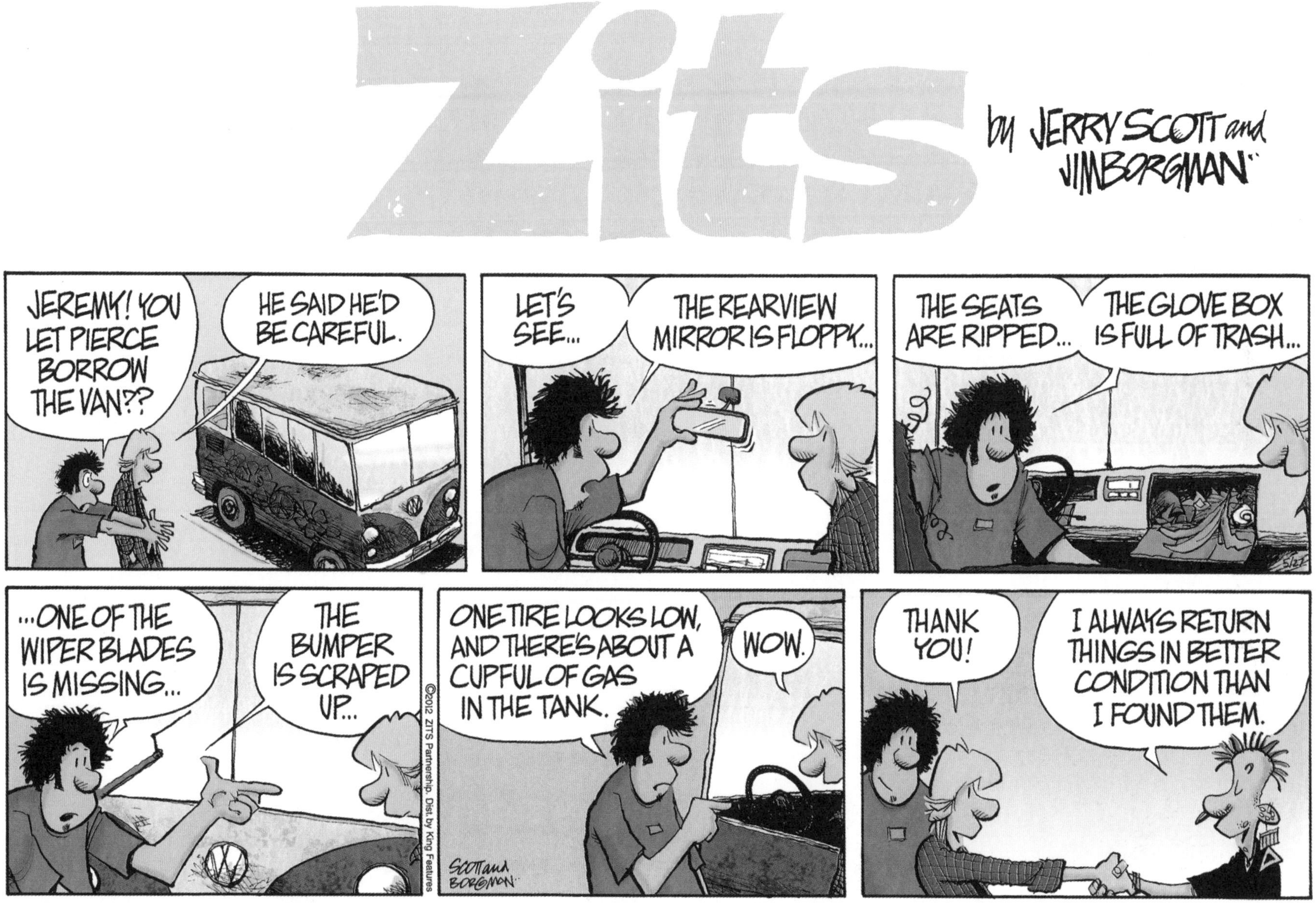
Zits
by JERRY SCOTT and JIM BORGMAN
JEREMY! YOU LET PIERCE BORROW THE VAN??
HE SAID HE'D BE CAREFUL.
LET'S SEE...
THE REARVIEW MIRROR IS FLOPPY...
THE SEATS ARE RIPPED...
THE GLOVE BOX IS FULL OF TRASH...
...ONE OF THE WIPER BLADES IS MISSING...
THE BUMPER IS SCRAPED UP...
©2012 ZITS Partnership. Dist. by King Features
ONE TIRE LOOKS LOW, AND THERE'S ABOUT A CUPFUL OF GAS IN THE TANK.
WOW.
SCOTT and BORGMAN
THANK YOU!
I ALWAYS RETURN THINGS IN BETTER CONDITION THAN I FOUND THEM.

YOU SURE LOOK RADIANT THIS MORNING, JEREMY!
I DO?
5/28
SCOTT and BORGMAN
THANKS FOR THE WARNING.
©2012 ZITS Partnership. Dist. by King Features

JEREMY, YOU SEEM RATHER DISCONSOLATE THIS MORNING.
VERY PERSPICACIOUS, DEAR.
SCOTT and BORGMAN
5/29
WOULD SOME BLUEBERRY PANCAKES MAKE YOU FEEL MORE SANGUINE?
THE GRANOLA IS AMBROSIAL!
©2012 ZITS Partnership. Dist. by King Features
IS HE COGITATING?
I'D SAY CHAFING.
THIS S.A.T. PREP IS GOING TO KILL ME.

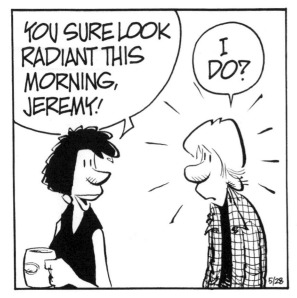

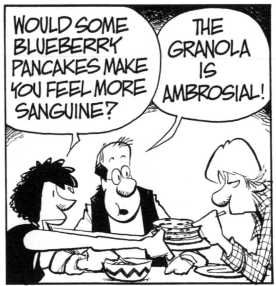

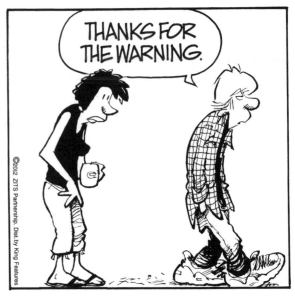

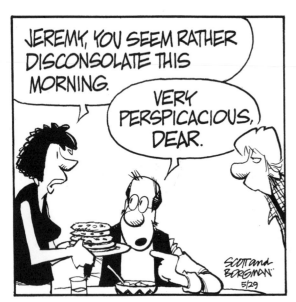

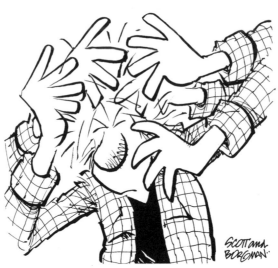

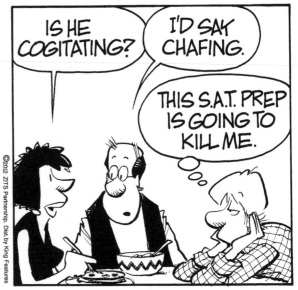

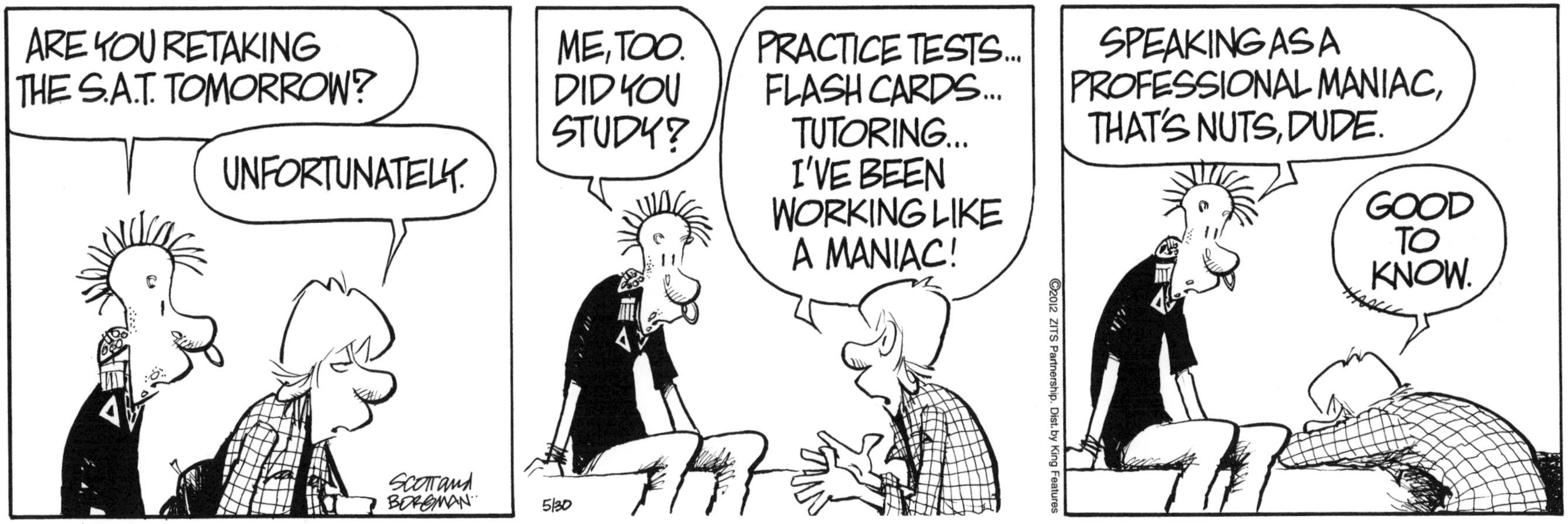
ARE YOU RETAKING THE S.A.T. TOMORROW?
UNFORTUNATELY.
SCOTT and BORGMAN
ME, TOO. DID YOU STUDY?
PRACTICE TESTS... FLASH CARDS... TUTORING... I'VE BEEN WORKING LIKE A MANIAC!
5/30
©2012 ZITS Partnership. Dist. by King Features
SPEAKING AS A PROFESSIONAL MANIAC, THAT'S NUTS, DUDE.
GOOD TO KNOW.

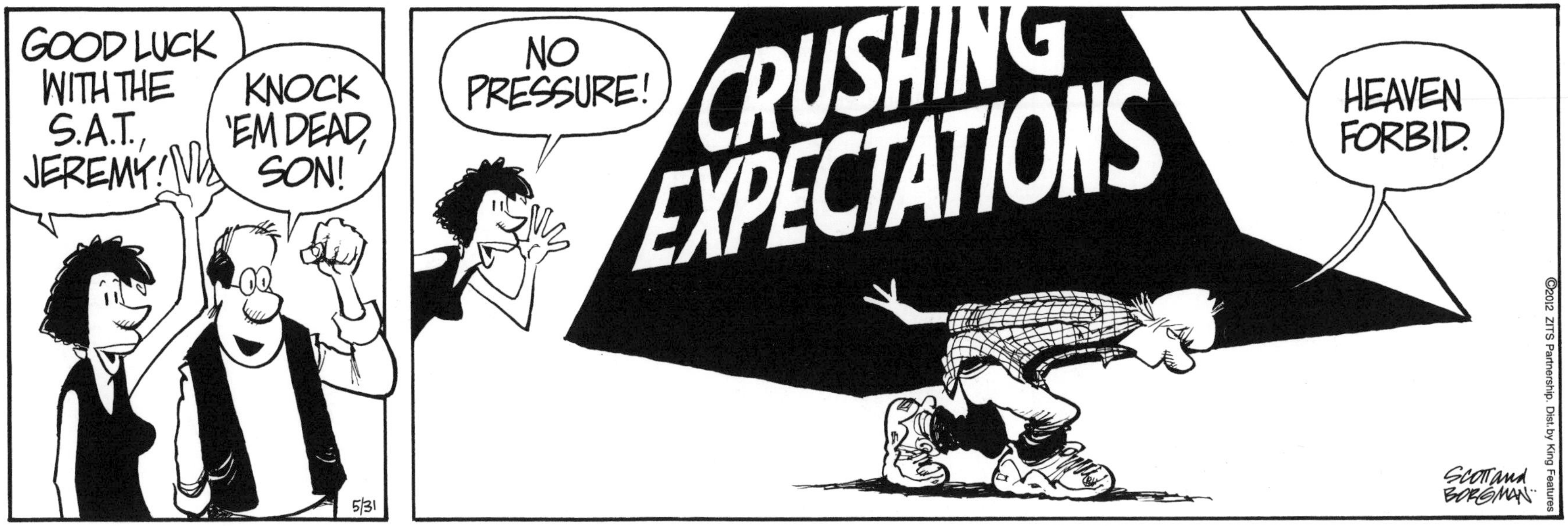
GOOD LUCK WITH THE S.A.T., JEREMY!
KNOCK 'EM DEAD, SON!
5/31
NO PRESSURE!
CRUSHING EXPECTATIONS
HEAVEN FORBID.
©2012 ZITS Partnership. Dist. by King Features
SCOTT and BORGMAN

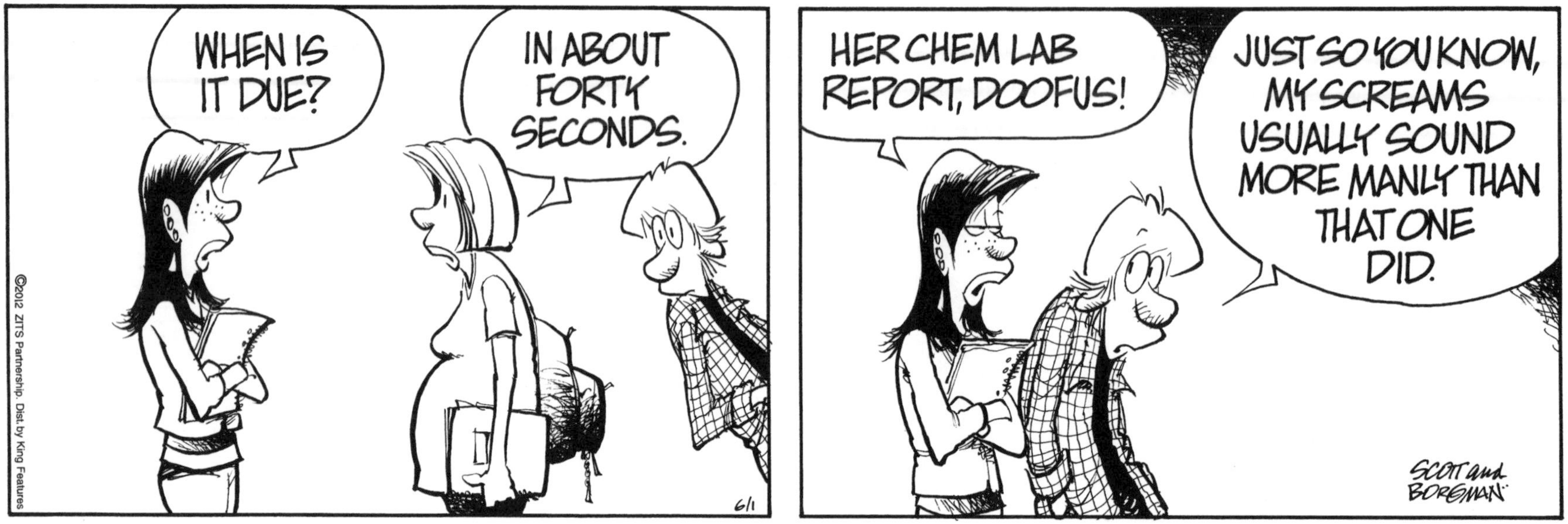
WHEN IS IT DUE?
IN ABOUT FORTY SECONDS.
HER CHEM LAB REPORT, DOOFUS!
JUST SO YOU KNOW, MY SCREAMS USUALLY SOUND MORE MANLY THAN THAT ONE DID.
©2012 ZITS Partnership. Dist. by King Features
6/1
SCOTT and BORGMAN

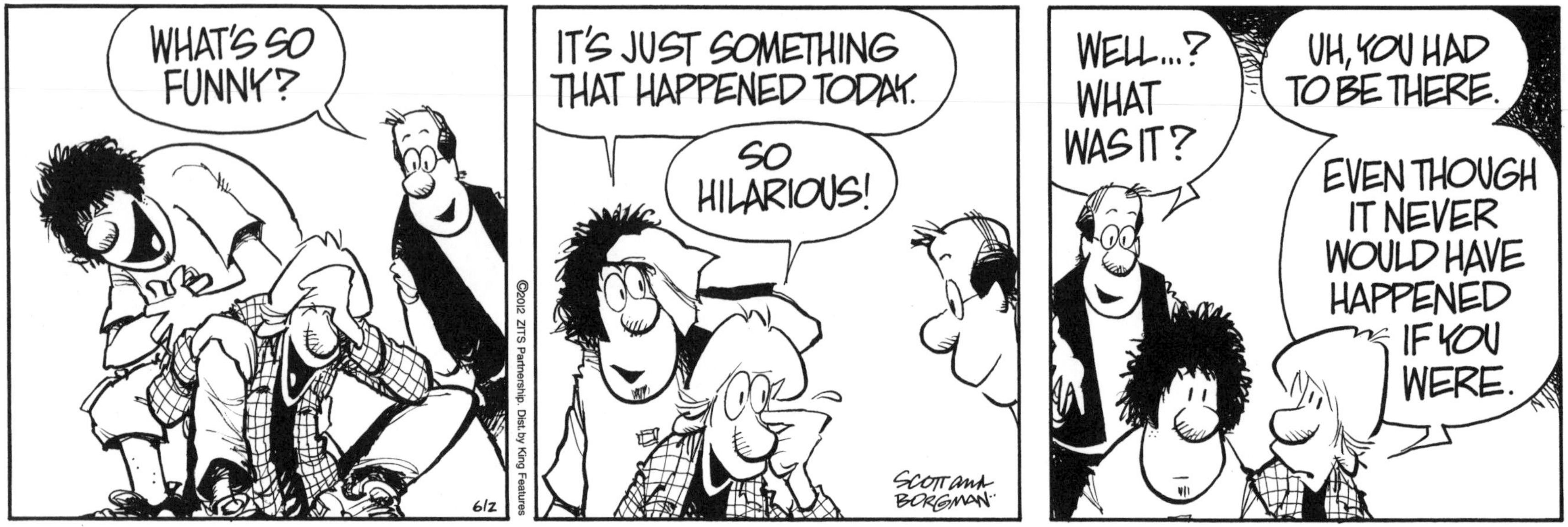
WHAT'S SO FUNNY?
6/2
©2012 ZITS Partnership. Dist. by King Features
IT'S JUST SOMETHING THAT HAPPENED TODAY.
SO HILARIOUS!
SCOTT and BORGMAN
WELL...? WHAT WAS IT?
UH, YOU HAD TO BE THERE.
EVEN THOUGH IT NEVER WOULD HAVE HAPPENED IF YOU WERE.

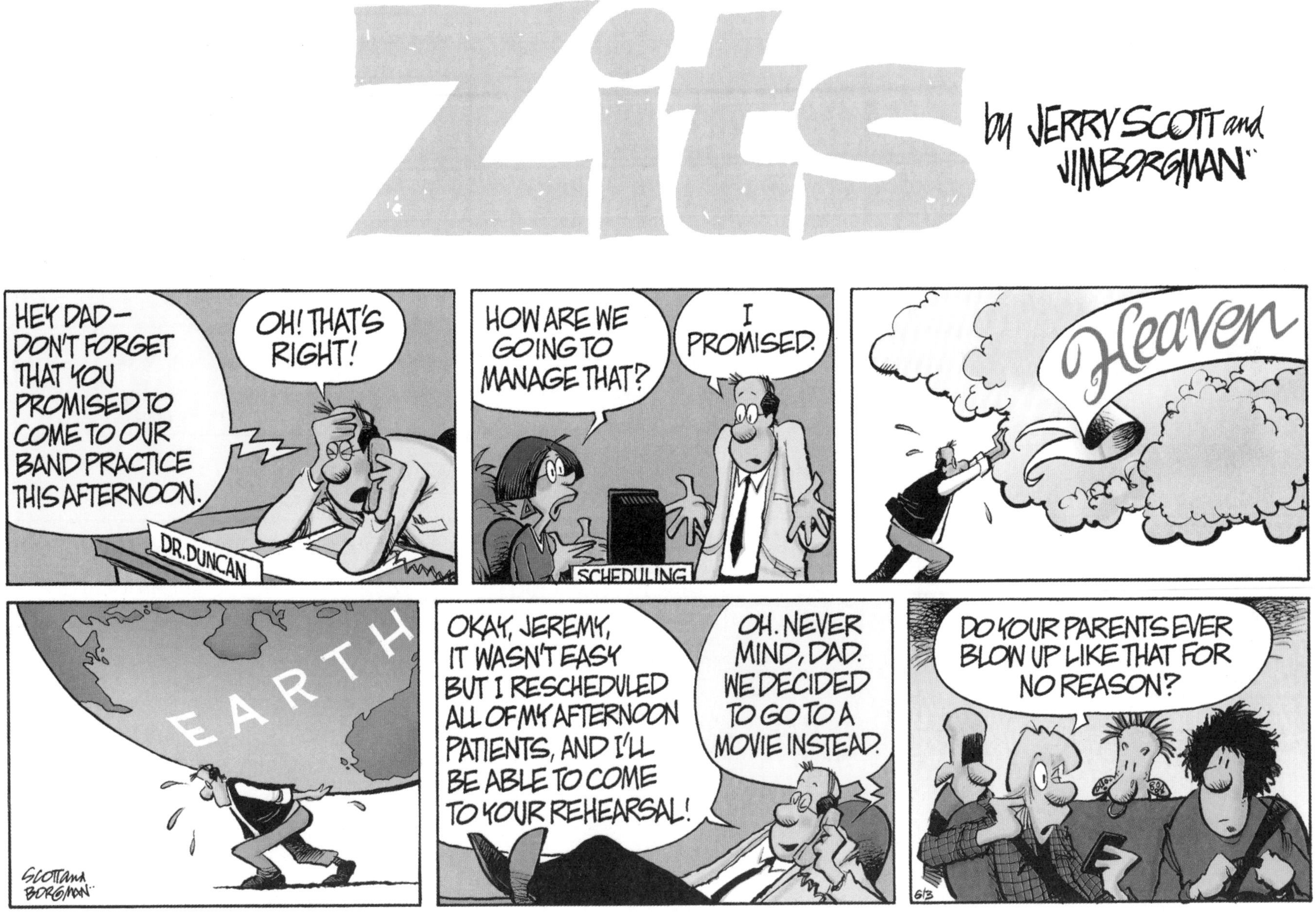
Zits
by JERRY SCOTT and JIM BORGMAN
HEY DAD— DON'T FORGET THAT YOU PROMISED TO COME TO OUR BAND PRACTICE THIS AFTERNOON.
OH! THAT'S RIGHT!
DR. DUNCAN
HOW ARE WE GOING TO MANAGE THAT?
I PROMISED.
SCHEDULING
Heaven
EARTH
OKAY, JEREMY, IT WASN'T EASY BUT I RESCHEDULED ALL OF MY AFTERNOON PATIENTS, AND I'LL BE ABLE TO COME TO YOUR REHEARSAL!
OH. NEVER MIND, DAD. WE DECIDED TO GO TO A MOVIE INSTEAD.
DO YOUR PARENTS EVER BLOW UP LIKE THAT FOR NO REASON?

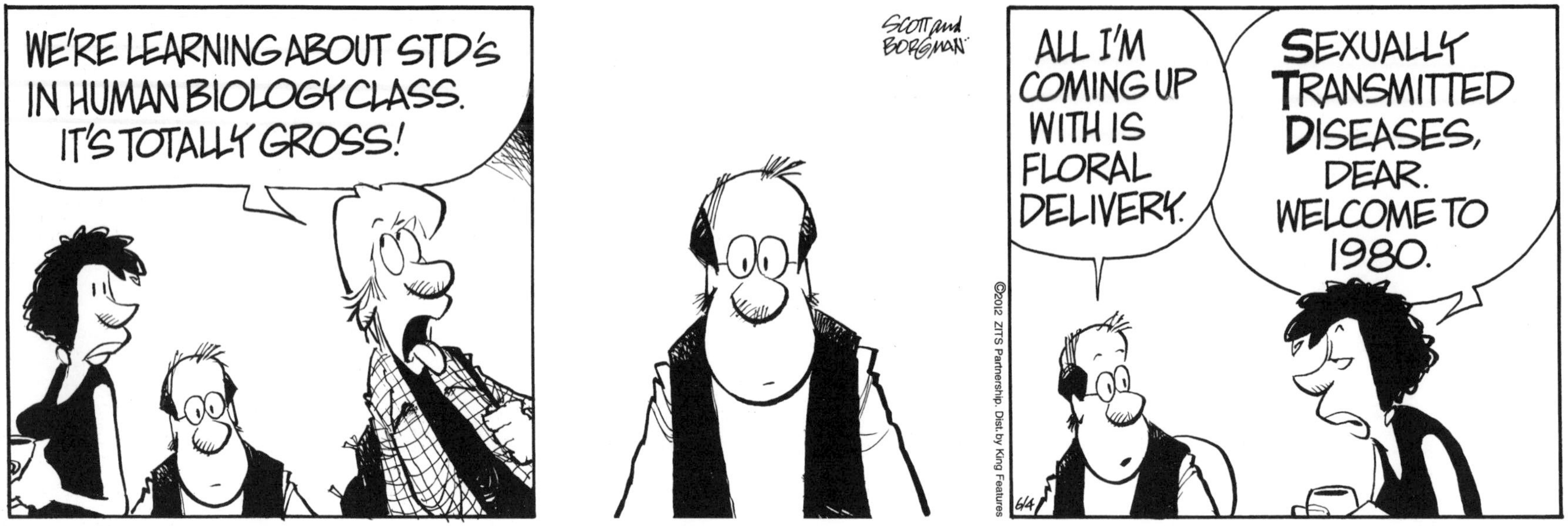
WE'RE LEARNING ABOUT STD'S IN HUMAN BIOLOGY CLASS. IT'S TOTALLY GROSS!
SCOTT and BORGMAN
ALL I'M COMING UP WITH IS FLORAL DELIVERY.
SEXUALLY TRANSMITTED DISEASES, DEAR. WELCOME TO 1980.
©2012 ZITS Partnership. Dist. by King Features
6/4

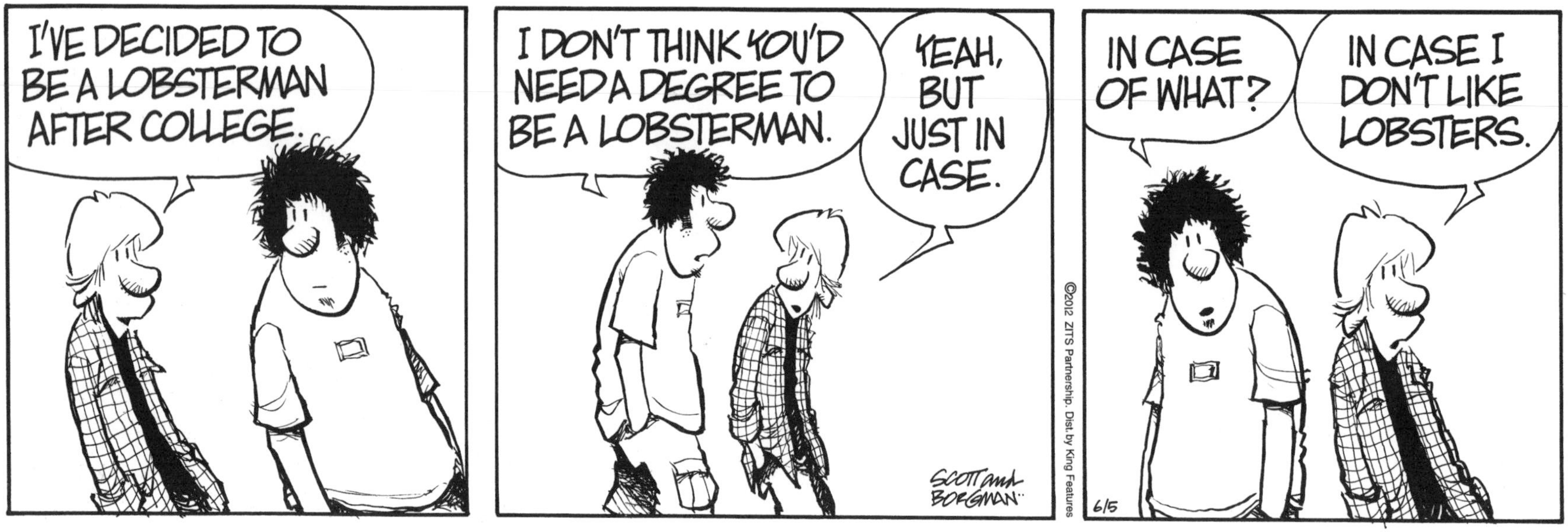
I'VE DECIDED TO BE A LOBSTERMAN AFTER COLLEGE.
I DON'T THINK YOU'D NEED A DEGREE TO BE A LOBSTERMAN.
YEAH, BUT JUST IN CASE.
SCOTT and BORGMAN
©2012 ZITS Partnership. Dist. by King Features
IN CASE OF WHAT?
IN CASE I DON'T LIKE LOBSTERS.
6/5

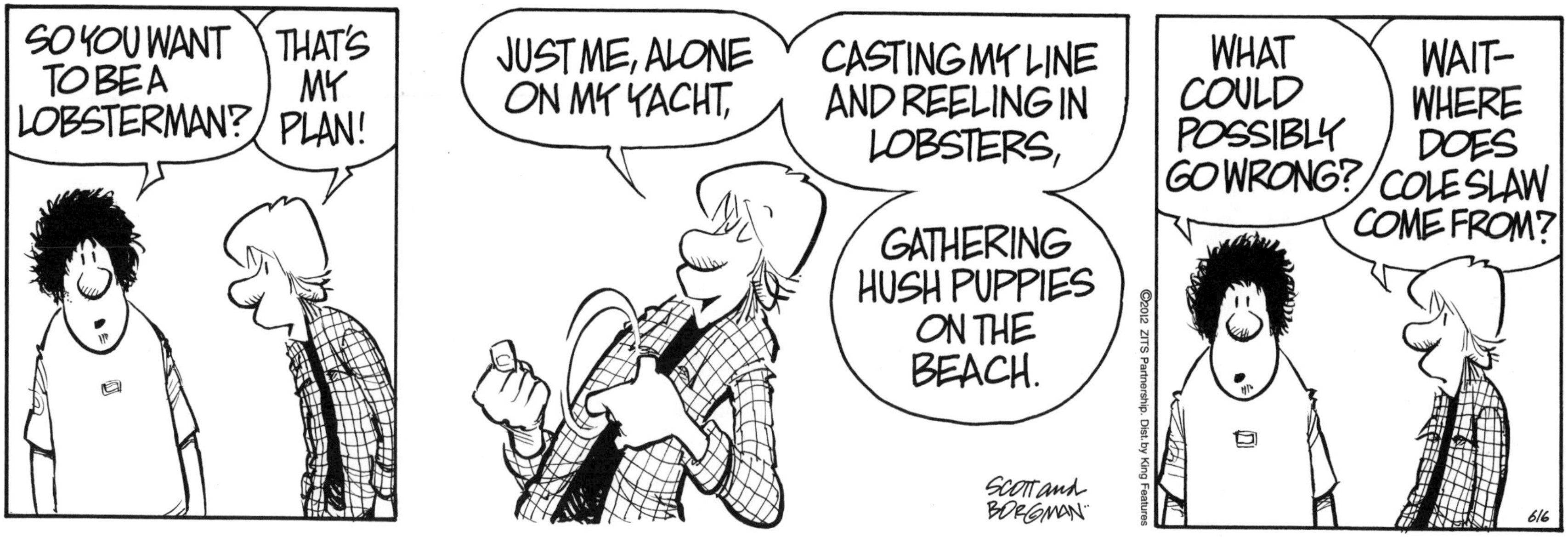
SO YOU WANT TO BE A LOBSTERMAN?
THAT'S MY PLAN!
JUST ME, ALONE ON MY YACHT,
CASTING MY LINE AND REELING IN LOBSTERS,
GATHERING HUSH PUPPIES ON THE BEACH.
WHAT COULD POSSIBLY GO WRONG?
WAIT- WHERE DOES COLE SLAW COME FROM?
SCOTT and BORGMAN
©2012 ZITS Partnership. Dist. by King Features
6/6

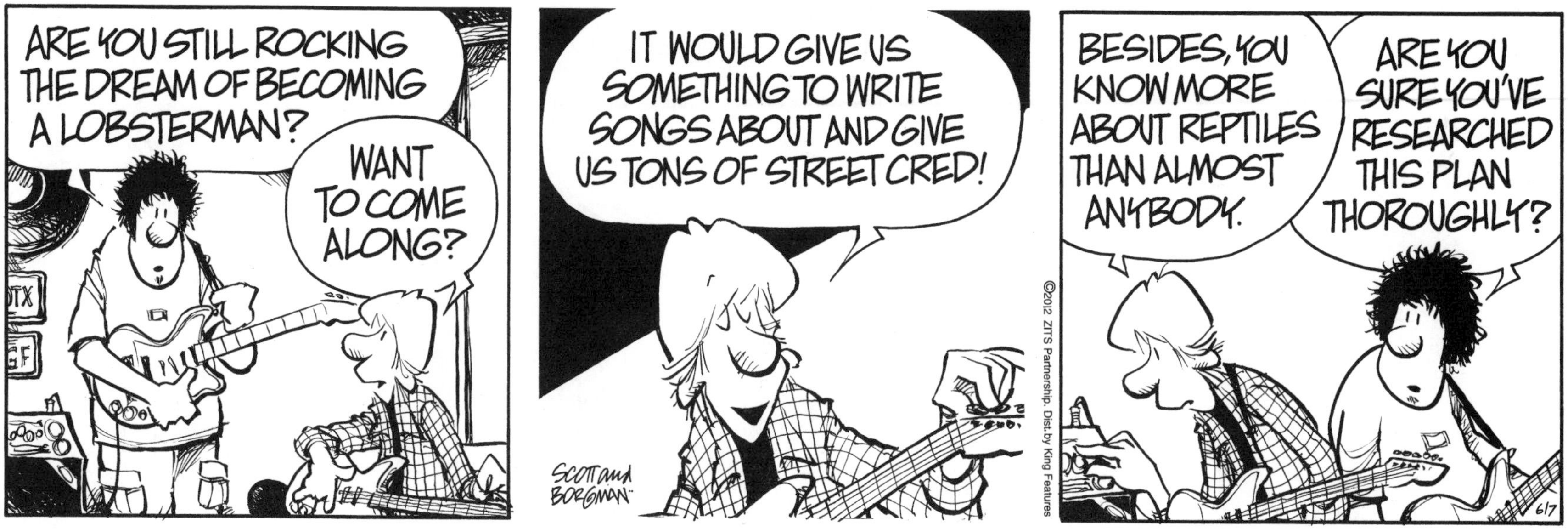
ARE YOU STILL ROCKING THE DREAM OF BECOMING A LOBSTERMAN?
WANT TO COME ALONG?
IT WOULD GIVE US SOMETHING TO WRITE SONGS ABOUT AND GIVE US TONS OF STREET CRED!
BESIDES, YOU KNOW MORE ABOUT REPTILES THAN ALMOST ANYBODY.
ARE YOU SURE YOU'VE RESEARCHED THIS PLAN THOROUGHLY?
SCOTT and BORGMAN
©2012 ZITS Partnership. Dist. by King Features
6/7

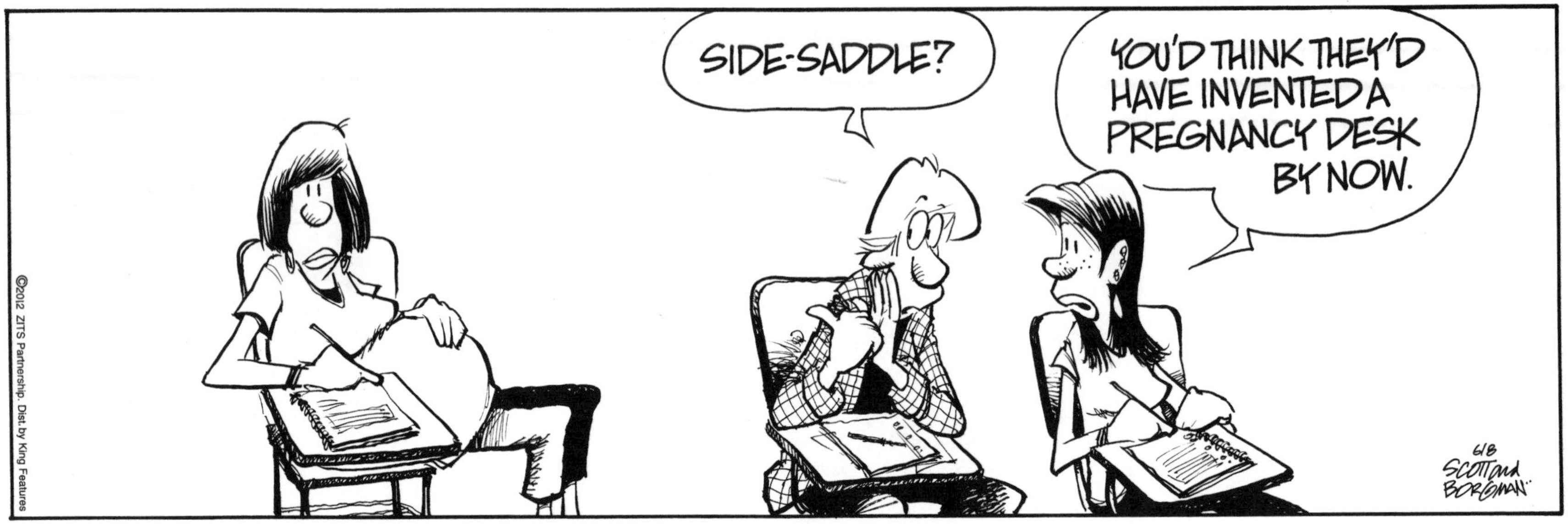
SIDE-SADDLE?
YOU'D THINK THEY'D HAVE INVENTED A PREGNANCY DESK BY NOW.
6/8
SCOTT and BORGMAN
©2012 ZITS Partnership. Dist. by King Features

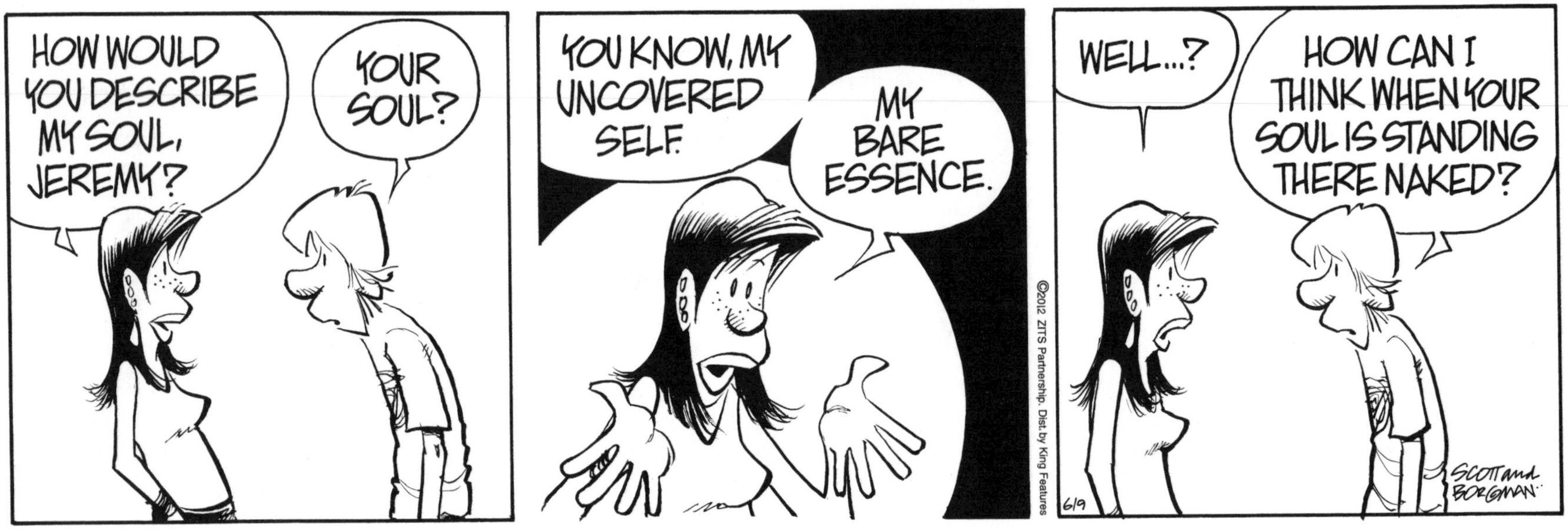
HOW WOULD YOU DESCRIBE MY SOUL, JEREMY?
YOUR SOUL?
YOU KNOW, MY UNCOVERED SELF.
MY BARE ESSENCE.
WELL...?
HOW CAN I THINK WHEN YOUR SOUL IS STANDING THERE NAKED?
6/9
SCOTT and BORGMAN
©2012 ZITS Partnership. Dist. by King Features

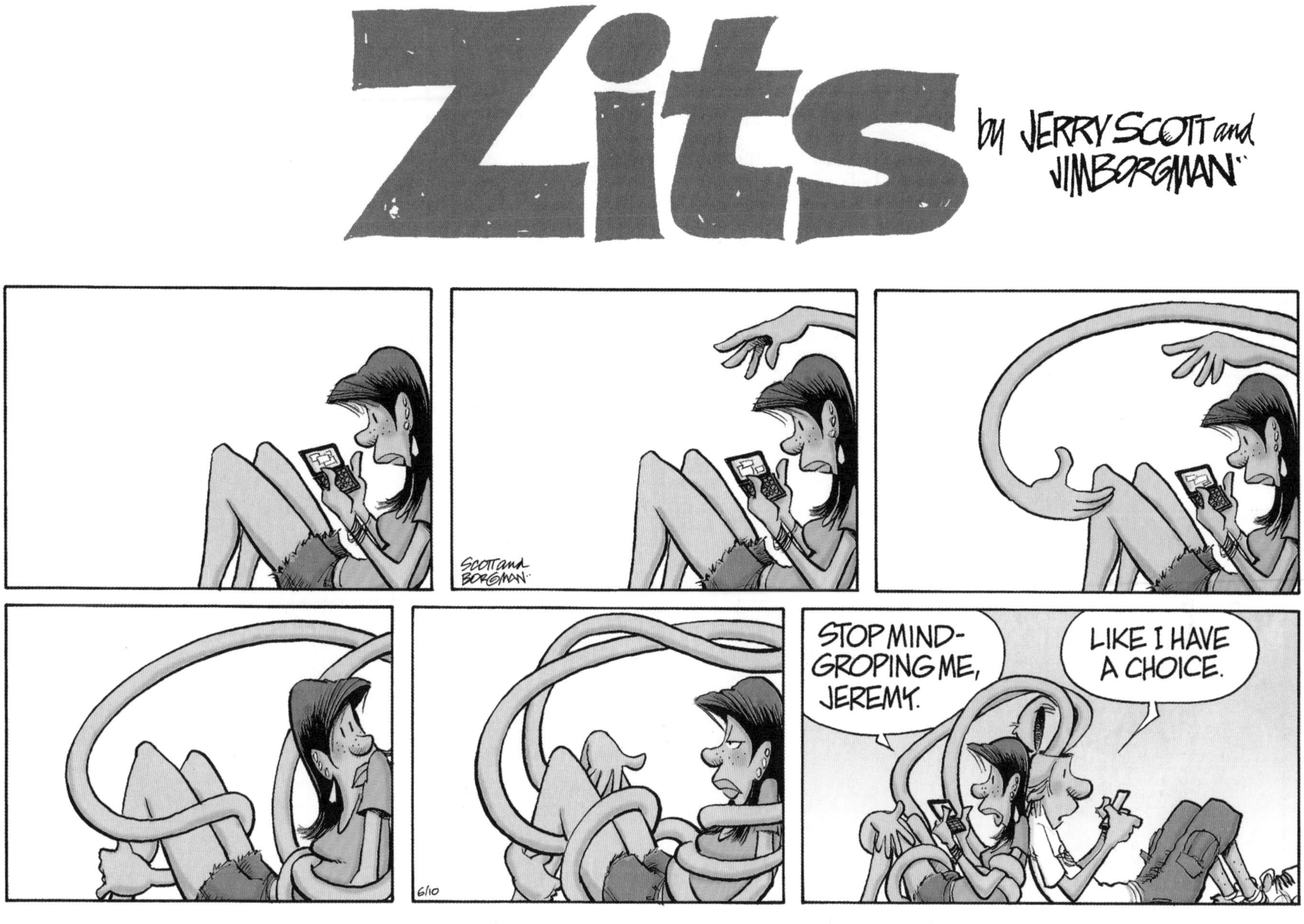
Zits
by JERRY SCOTT and JIM BORGMAN
SCOTT and BORGMAN
6/10
STOP MIND-GROPING ME, JEREMY.
LIKE I HAVE A CHOICE.

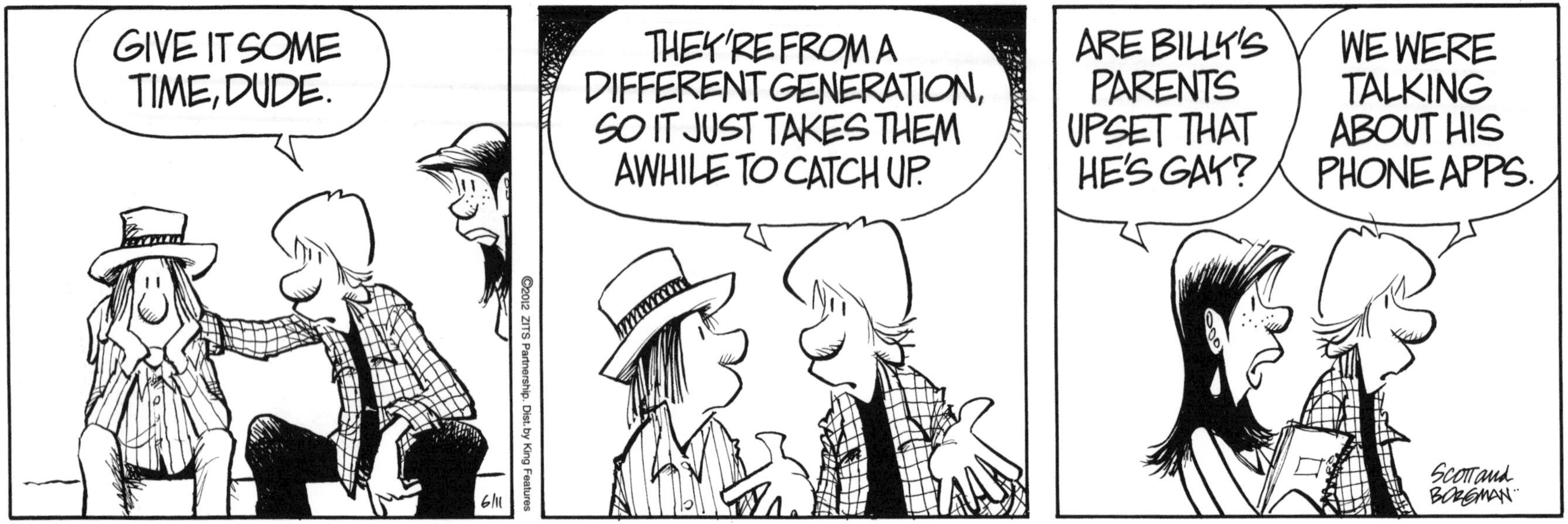
GIVE IT SOME TIME, DUDE.
6/11
©2012 ZITS Partnership. Dist. by King Features
THEY'RE FROM A DIFFERENT GENERATION, SO IT JUST TAKES THEM AWHILE TO CATCH UP.
ARE BILLY'S PARENTS UPSET THAT HE'S GAY?
WE WERE TALKING ABOUT HIS PHONE APPS.
SCOTT and BORGMAN

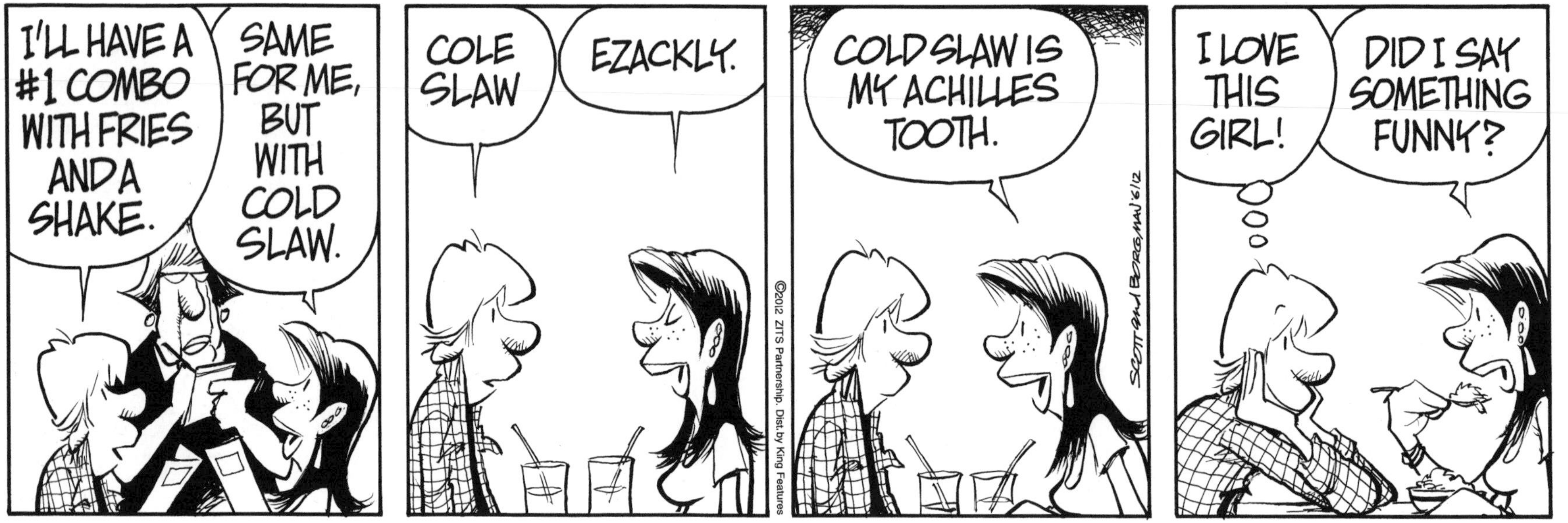
I'LL HAVE A #1 COMBO WITH FRIES AND A SHAKE.
SAME FOR ME, BUT WITH COLD SLAW.
COLE SLAW
EZACKLY.
©2012 ZITS Partnership. Dist. by King Features
COLD SLAW IS MY ACHILLES TOOTH.
SCOTT and BORGMAN 6/12
I LOVE THIS GIRL!
DID I SAY SOMETHING FUNNY?

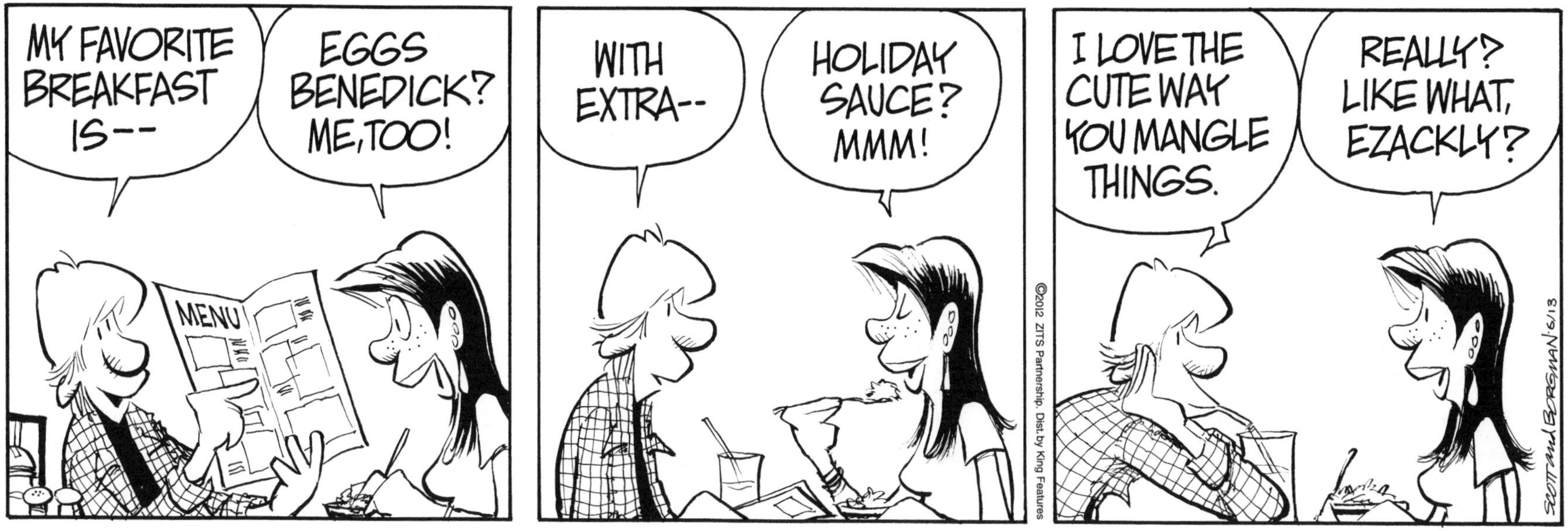
MY FAVORITE BREAKFAST IS--
EGGS BENEDICK? ME, TOO!
MENU
WITH EXTRA--
HOLIDAY SAUCE? MMM!
©2012 ZITS Partnership. Dist.by King Features
I LOVE THE CUTE WAY YOU MANGLE THINGS.
REALLY? LIKE WHAT, EZACKLY?
SCOTT and BORGMAN 6/13

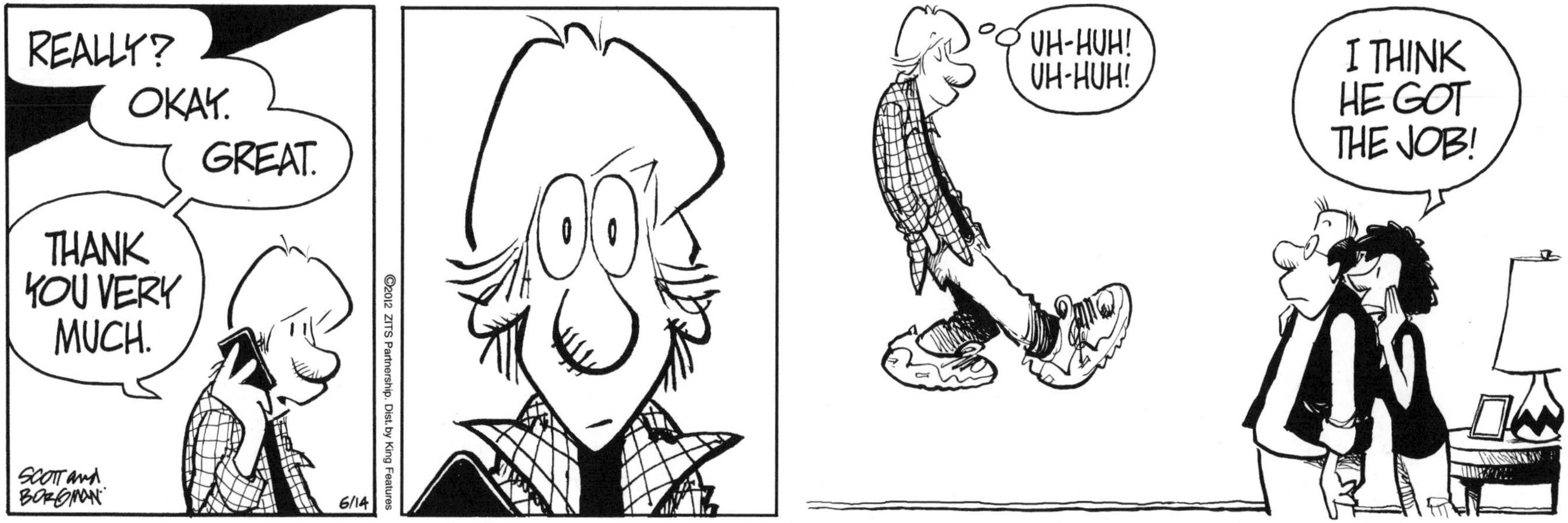
REALLY?
OKAY.
GREAT.
THANK YOU VERY MUCH.
SCOTT and BORGMAN 6/14
©2012 ZITS Partnership. Dist.by King Features
UH-HUH! UH-HUH!
I THINK HE GOT THE JOB!

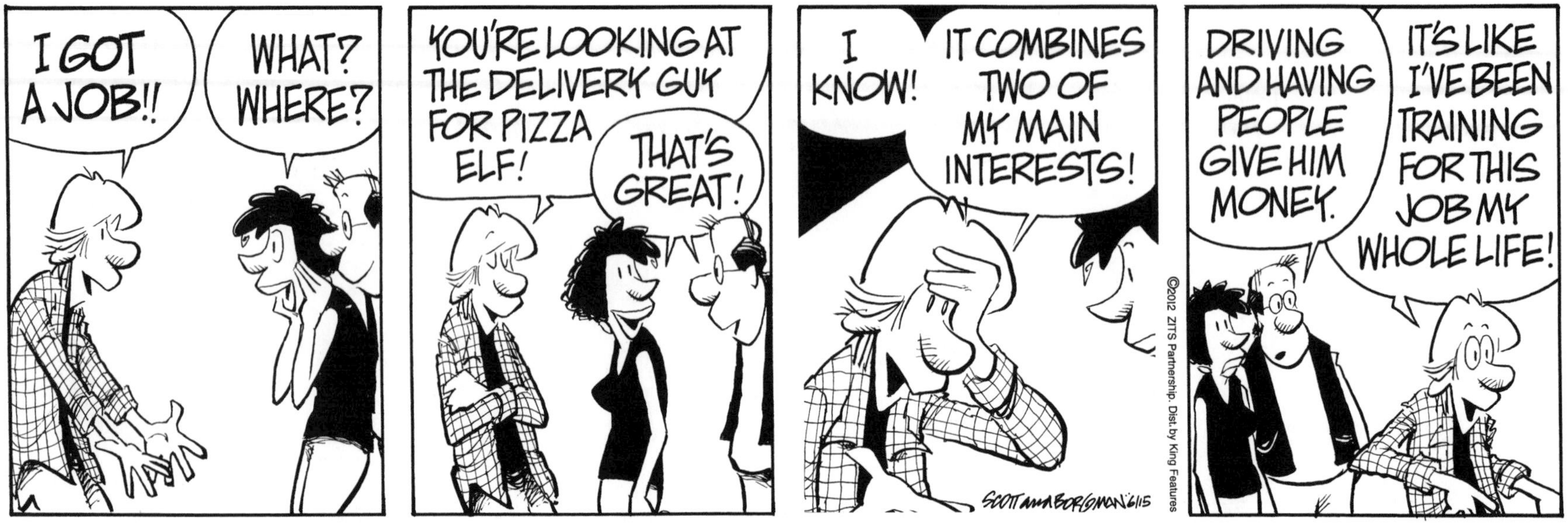
I GOT A JOB!!
WHAT? WHERE?
YOU'RE LOOKING AT THE DELIVERY GUY FOR PIZZA ELF!
THAT'S GREAT!
I KNOW!
IT COMBINES TWO OF MY MAIN INTERESTS!
SCOTT AND BORGMAN 6/15
©2012 ZITS Partnership. Dist. by King Features
DRIVING AND HAVING PEOPLE GIVE HIM MONEY.
IT'S LIKE I'VE BEEN TRAINING FOR THIS JOB MY WHOLE LIFE!

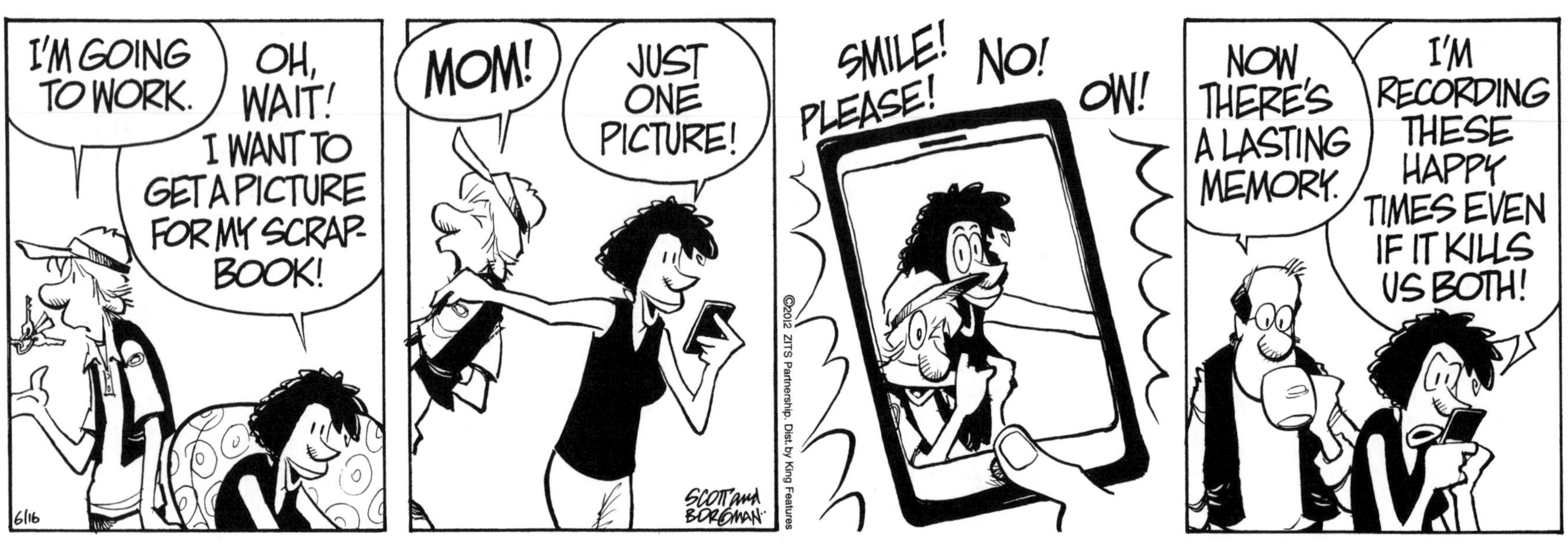
I'M GOING TO WORK.
OH, WAIT! I WANT TO GET A PICTURE FOR MY SCRAP-BOOK!
6/16
MOM!
JUST ONE PICTURE!
SCOTT AND BORGMAN
©2012 ZITS Partnership. Dist. by King Features
SMILE! PLEASE!
NO!
OW!
NOW THERE'S A LASTING MEMORY.
I'M RECORDING THESE HAPPY TIMES EVEN IF IT KILLS US BOTH!

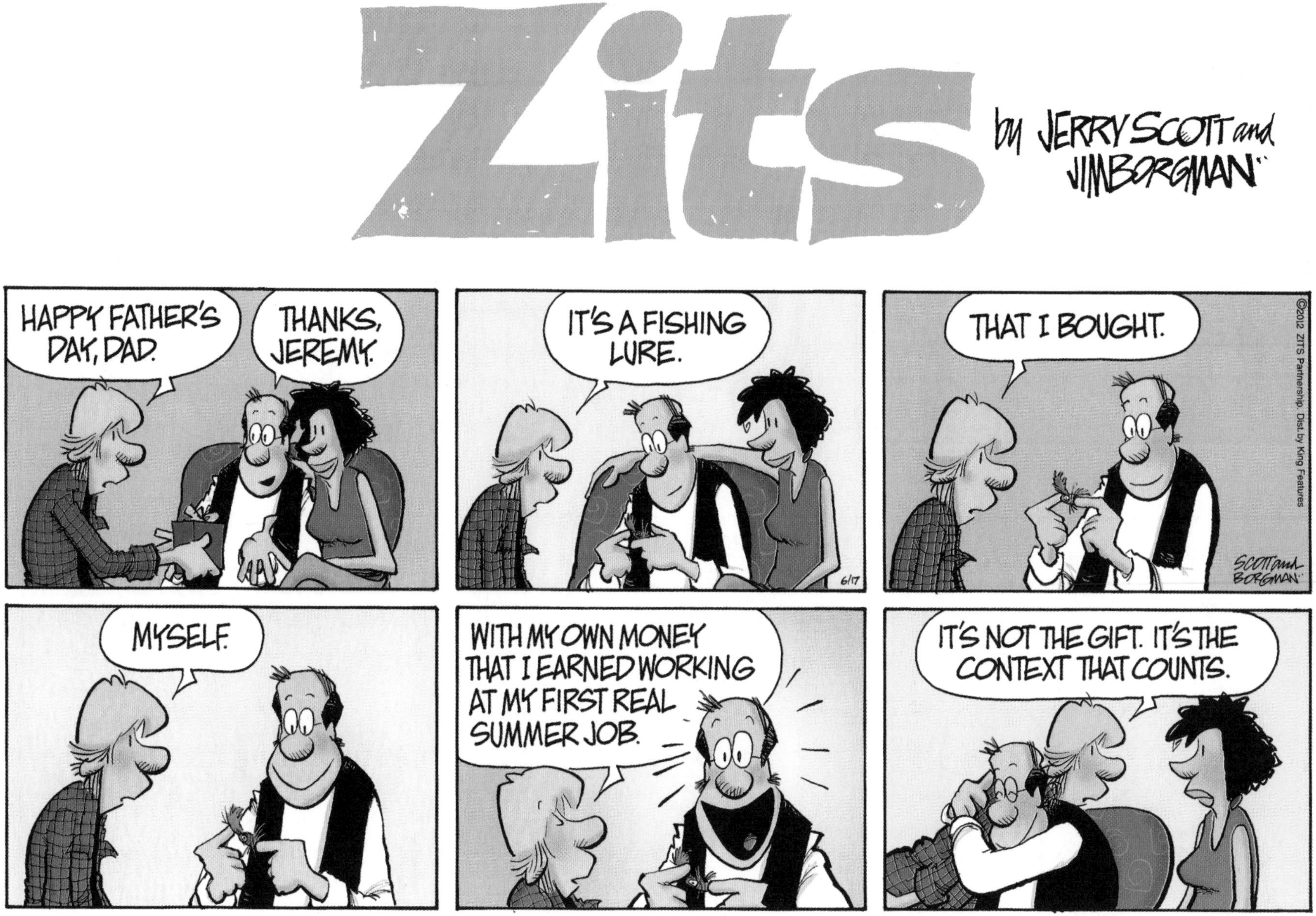
Zits
by JERRY SCOTT and JIM BORGMAN
HAPPY FATHER'S DAY, DAD.
THANKS, JEREMY.
IT'S A FISHING LURE.
THAT I BOUGHT.
©2012 ZITS Partnership. Dist. by King Features
SCOTT and BORGMAN
MYSELF.
WITH MY OWN MONEY THAT I EARNED WORKING AT MY FIRST REAL SUMMER JOB.
IT'S NOT THE GIFT. IT'S THE CONTEXT THAT COUNTS.

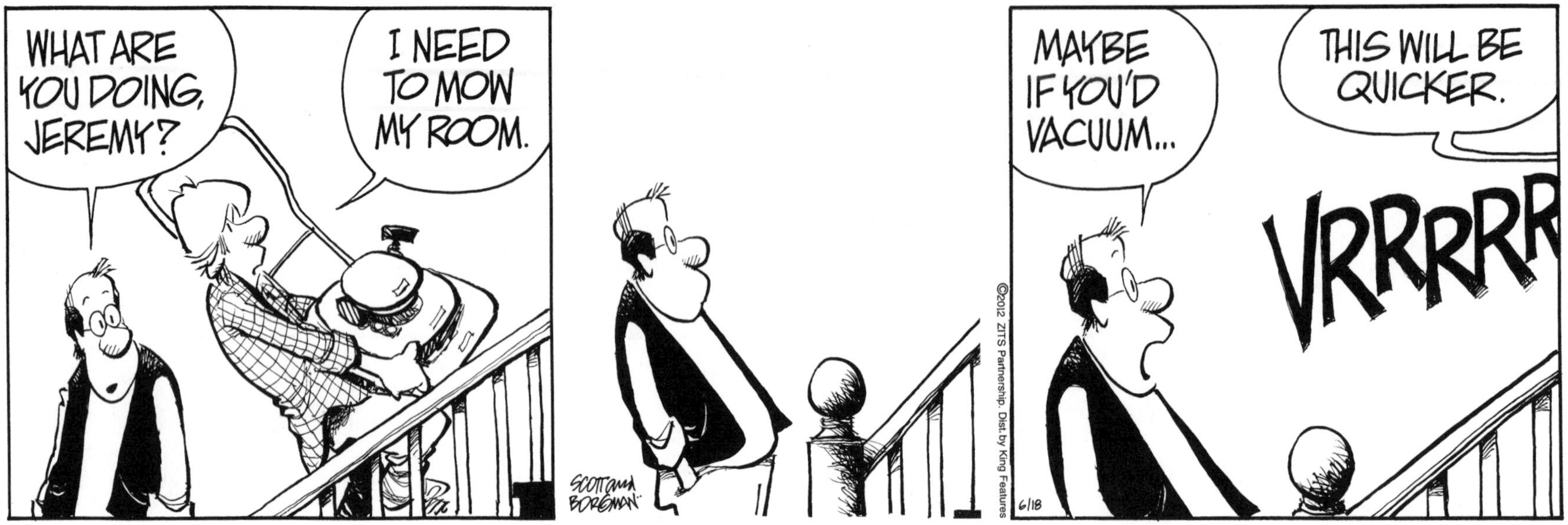
WHAT ARE YOU DOING, JEREMY?
I NEED TO MOW MY ROOM.
MAYBE IF YOU'D VACUUM...
THIS WILL BE QUICKER.
VRRRRR
SCOTT and BORGMAN
©2012 ZITS Partnership. Dist. by King Features
6/18

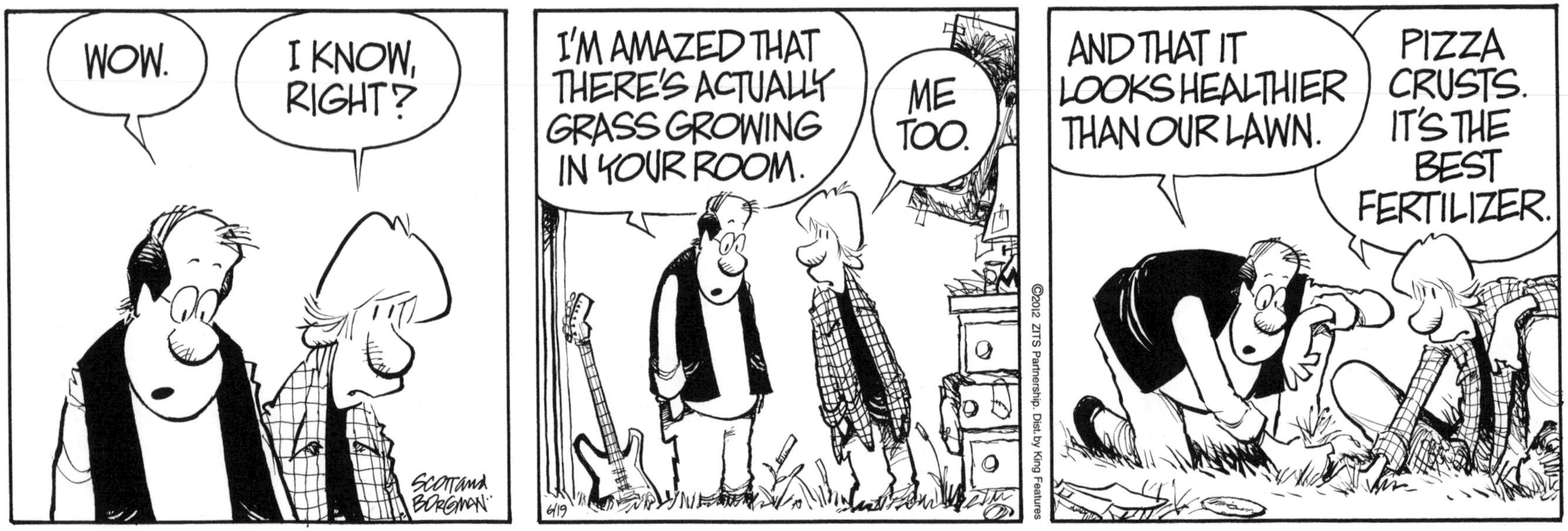
WOW.
I KNOW, RIGHT?
SCOTT and BORGMAN
I'M AMAZED THAT THERE'S ACTUALLY GRASS GROWING IN YOUR ROOM.
ME TOO.
6/19
AND THAT IT LOOKS HEALTHIER THAN OUR LAWN.
PIZZA CRUSTS. IT'S THE BEST FERTILIZER.
©2012 ZITS Partnership. Dist. by King Features

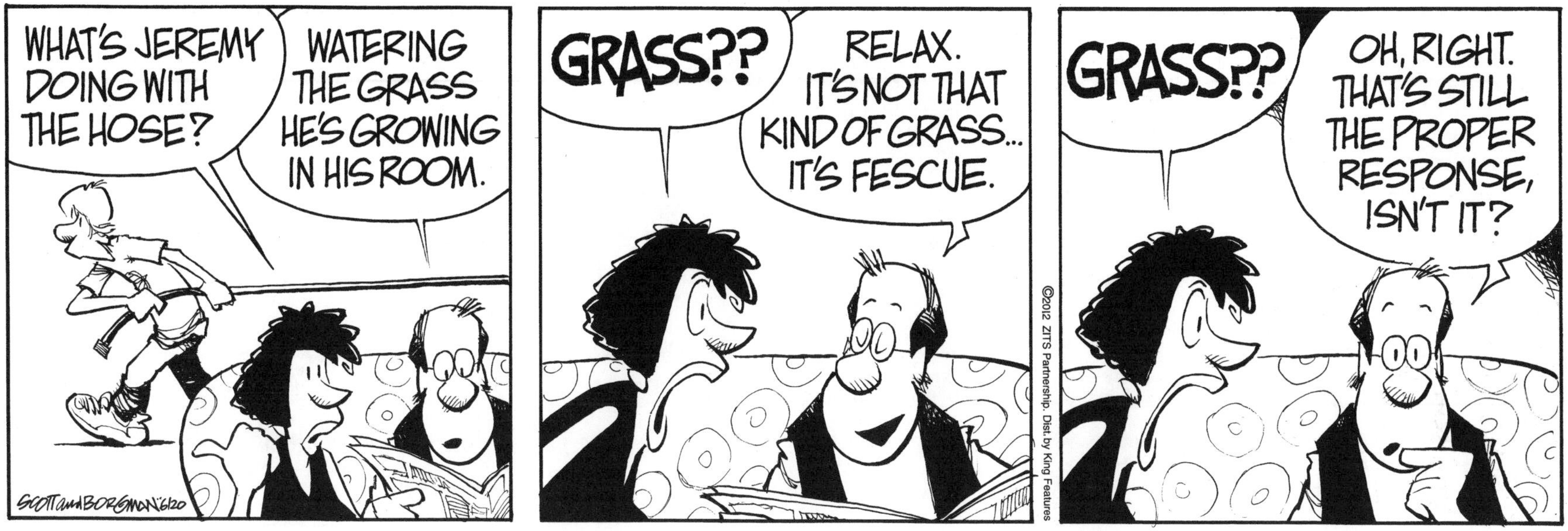
WHAT'S JEREMY DOING WITH THE HOSE?
WATERING THE GRASS HE'S GROWING IN HIS ROOM.
SCOTT and BORGMAN 6/20
GRASS??
RELAX. IT'S NOT THAT KIND OF GRASS... IT'S FESCUE.
©2012 ZITS Partnership. Dist. by King Features
GRASS??
OH, RIGHT. THAT'S STILL THE PROPER RESPONSE, ISN'T IT?

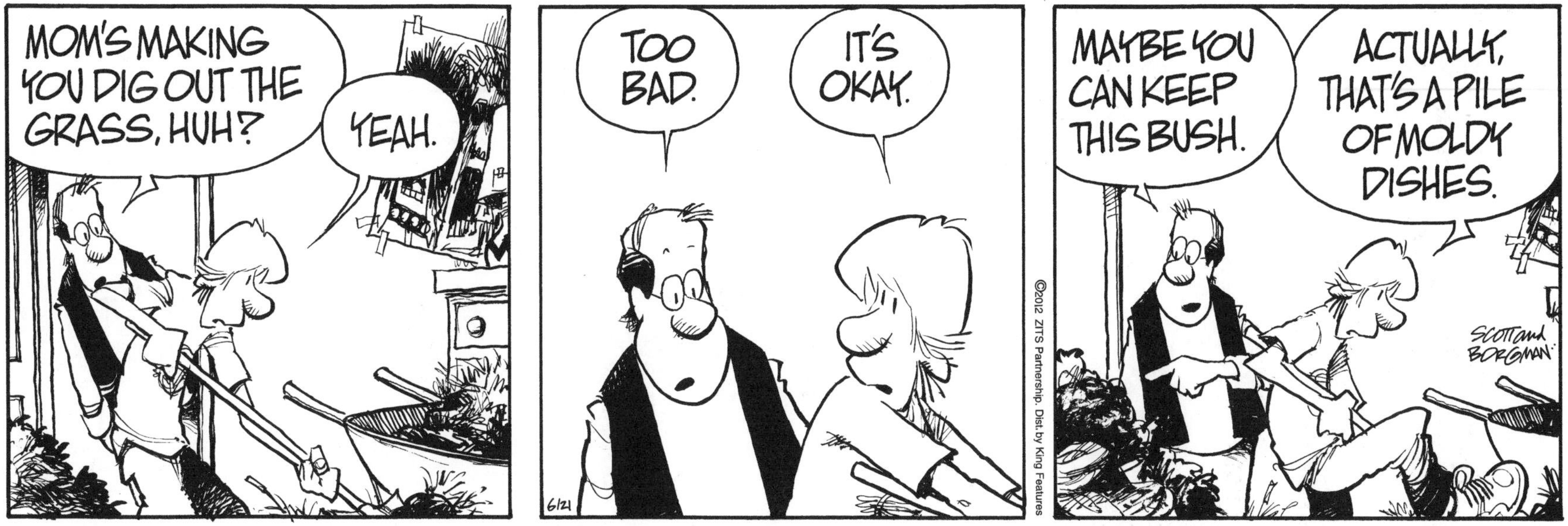
MOM'S MAKING YOU DIG OUT THE GRASS, HUH?
YEAH.
TOO BAD.
IT'S OKAY.
6/21
©2012 ZITS Partnership. Dist. by King Features
MAYBE YOU CAN KEEP THIS BUSH.
ACTUALLY, THAT'S A PILE OF MOLDY DISHES.
SCOTT and BORGMAN

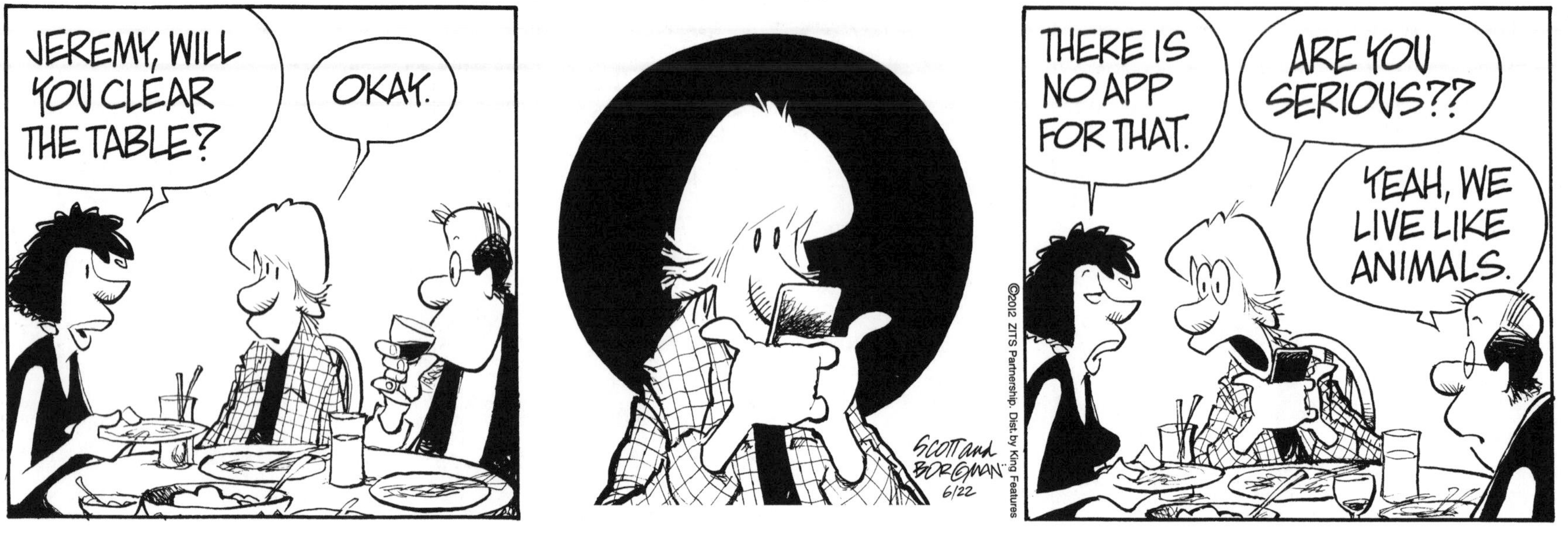
JEREMY, WILL YOU CLEAR THE TABLE?
OKAY.
THERE IS NO APP FOR THAT.
ARE YOU SERIOUS??
YEAH, WE LIVE LIKE ANIMALS.
SCOTT and BORGMAN 6/22
©2012 ZITS Partnership. Dist. by King Features

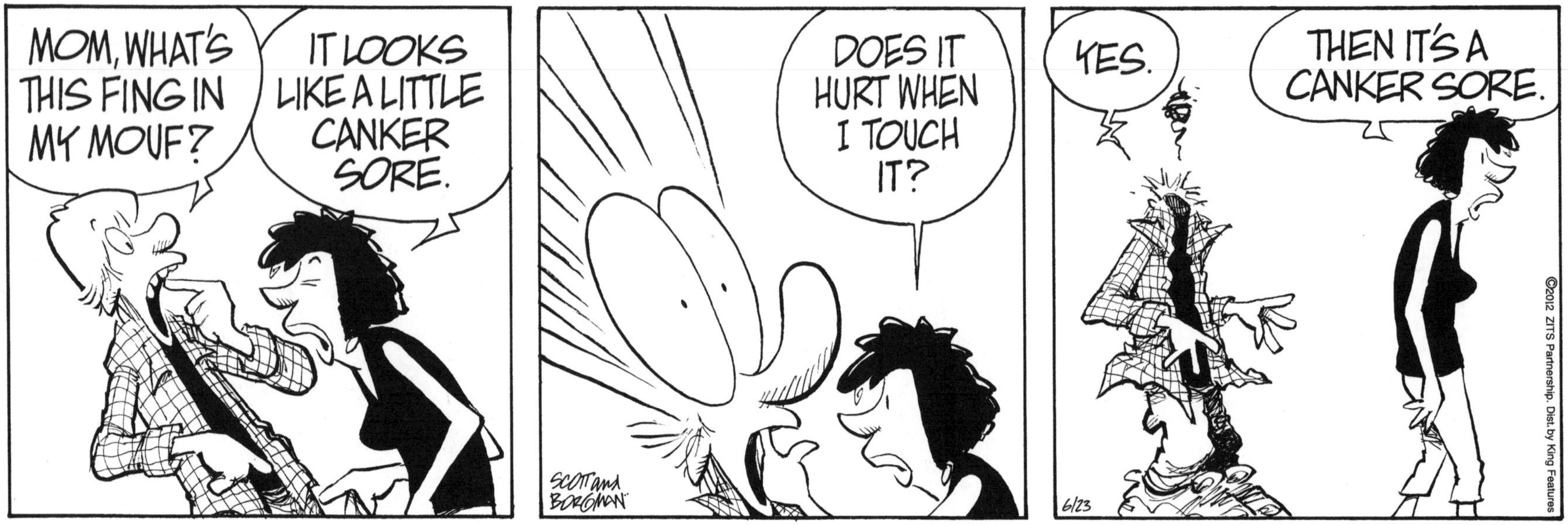
MOM, WHAT'S THIS FING IN MY MOUF?
IT LOOKS LIKE A LITTLE CANKER SORE.
DOES IT HURT WHEN I TOUCH IT?
YES.
THEN IT'S A CANKER SORE.
SCOTT and BORGMAN
6/23
©2012 ZITS Partnership. Dist. by King Features

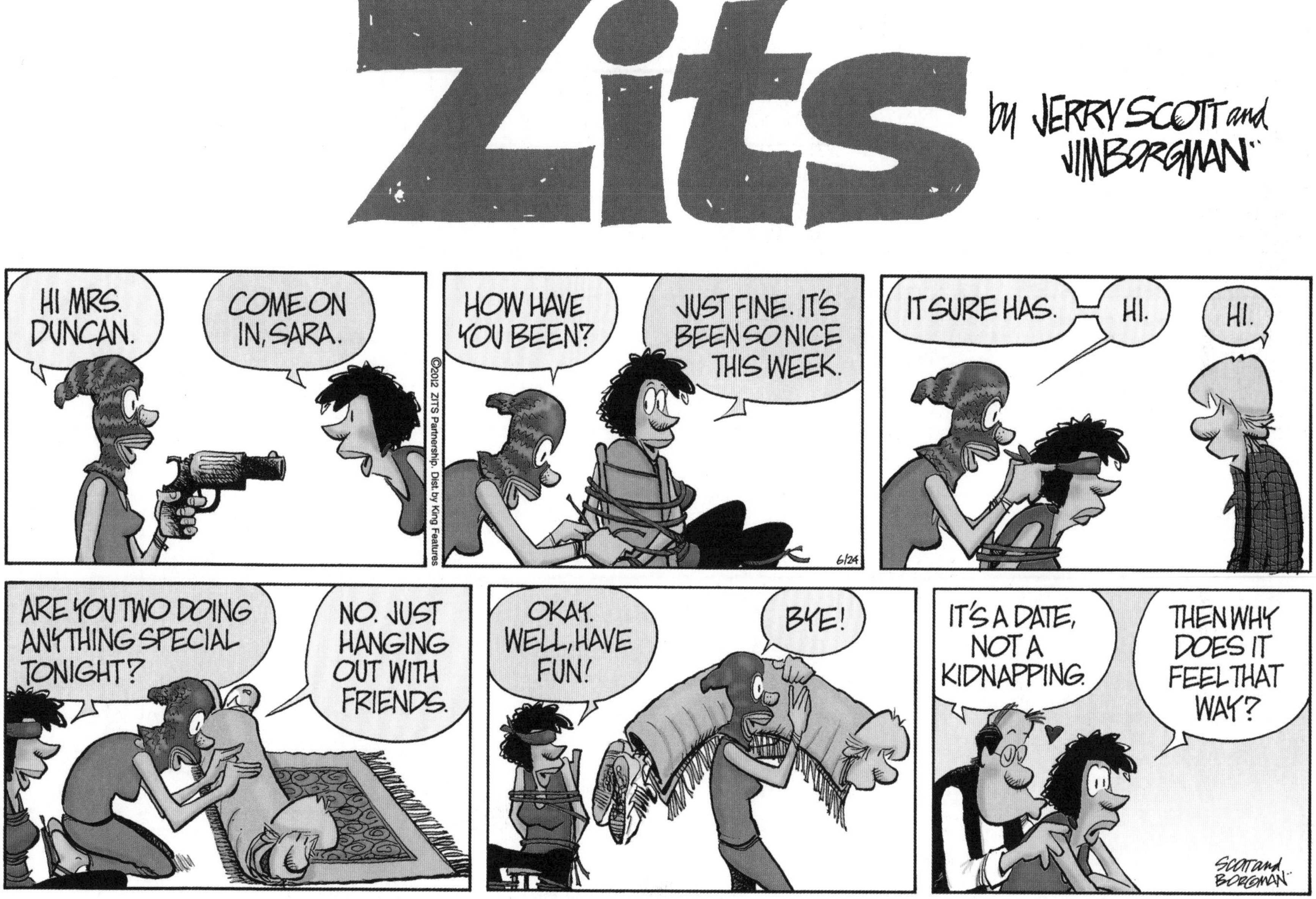
Zits
by JERRY SCOTT and JIM BORGMAN
HI MRS. DUNCAN.
COME ON IN, SARA.
©2012 ZITS Partnership. Dist. by King Features
HOW HAVE YOU BEEN?
JUST FINE. IT'S BEEN SO NICE THIS WEEK.
6/24
IT SURE HAS.
HI.
HI.
ARE YOU TWO DOING ANYTHING SPECIAL TONIGHT?
NO. JUST HANGING OUT WITH FRIENDS.
OKAY. WELL, HAVE FUN!
BYE!
IT'S A DATE, NOT A KIDNAPPING.
THEN WHY DOES IT FEEL THAT WAY?
SCOTT and BORGMAN

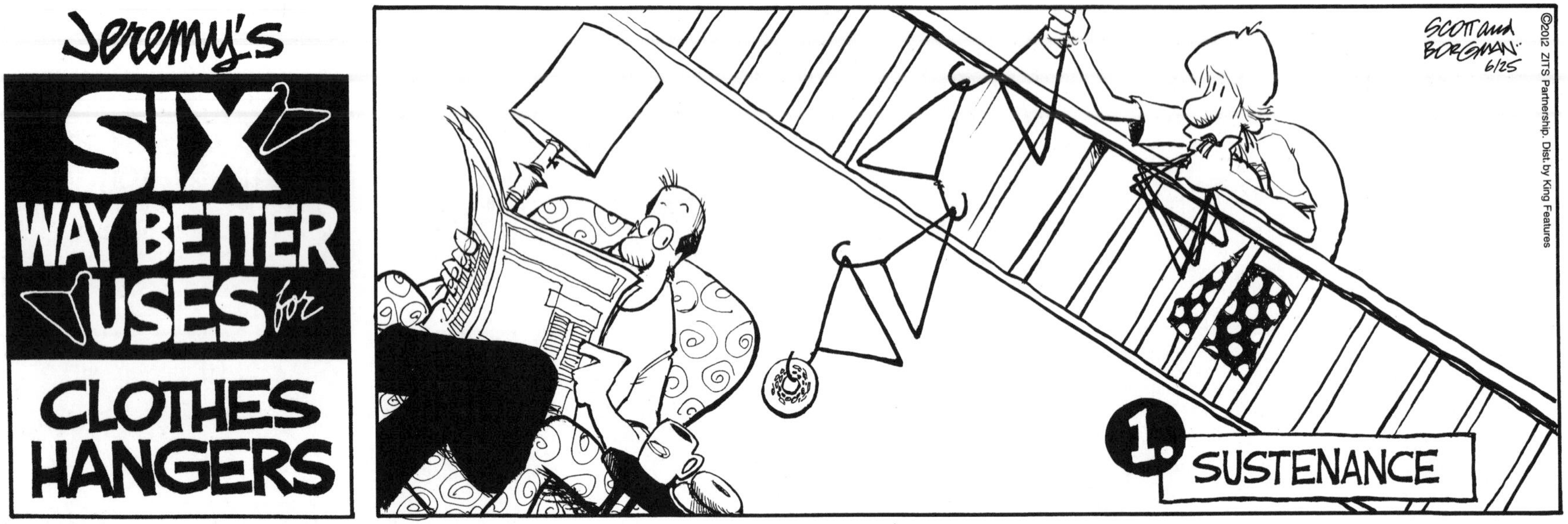
Jeremy's
SIX
WAY BETTER
USES for
CLOTHES
HANGERS
1. SUSTENANCE
SCOTT and BORGMAN 6/25
©2012 ZITS Partnership. Dist. by King Features

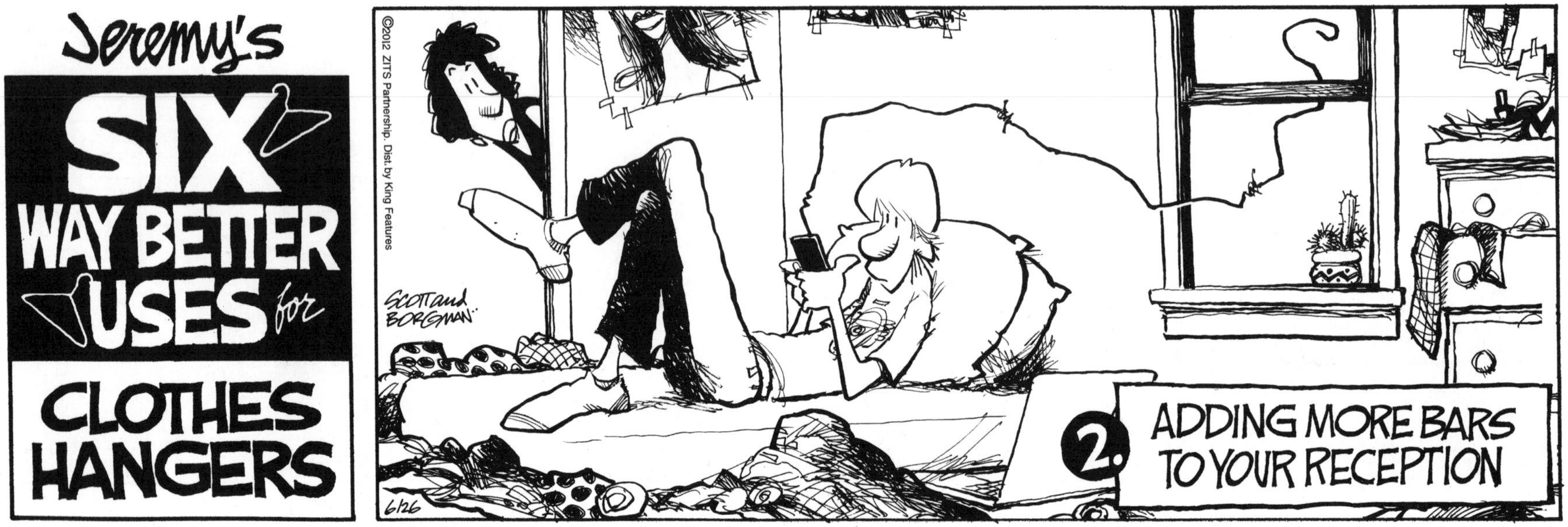
Jeremy's
SIX
WAY BETTER
USES for
CLOTHES
HANGERS
2. ADDING MORE BARS TO YOUR RECEPTION
SCOTT and BORGMAN 6/26
©2012 ZITS Partnership. Dist. by King Features

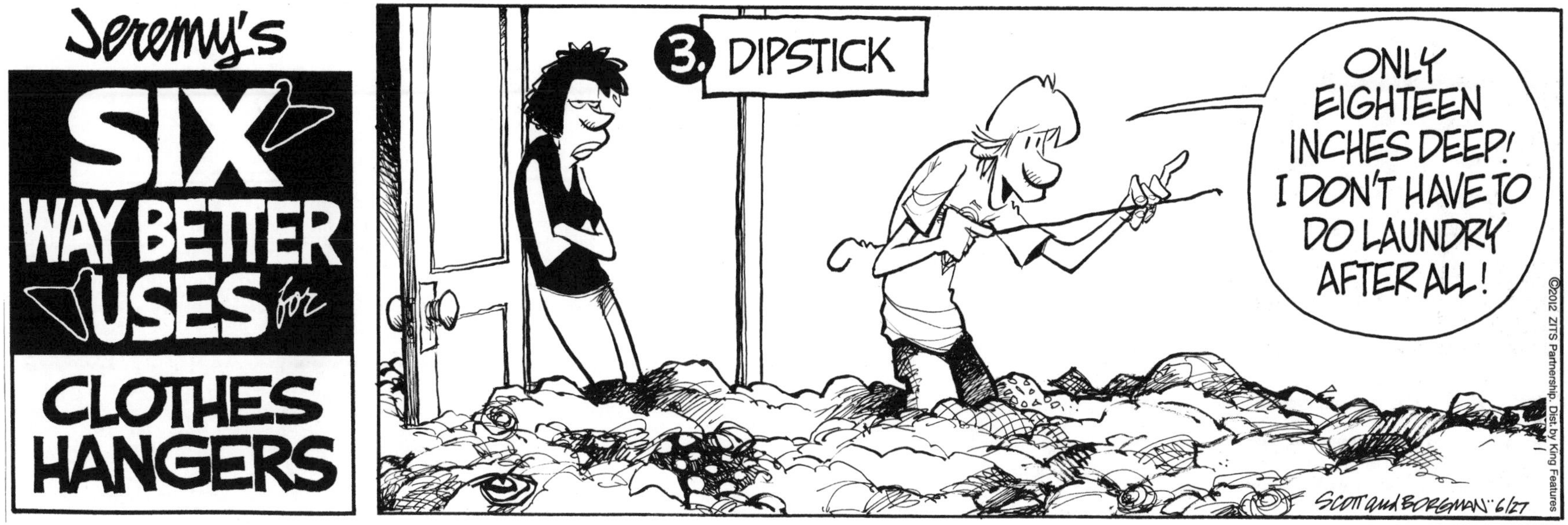
JEREMY'S
SIX WAY BETTER USES for
CLOTHES HANGERS
3. DIPSTICK
ONLY EIGHTEEN INCHES DEEP! I DON'T HAVE TO DO LAUNDRY AFTER ALL!
©2012 ZITS Partnership. Dist. by King Features
SCOTT and BORGMAN 6/27

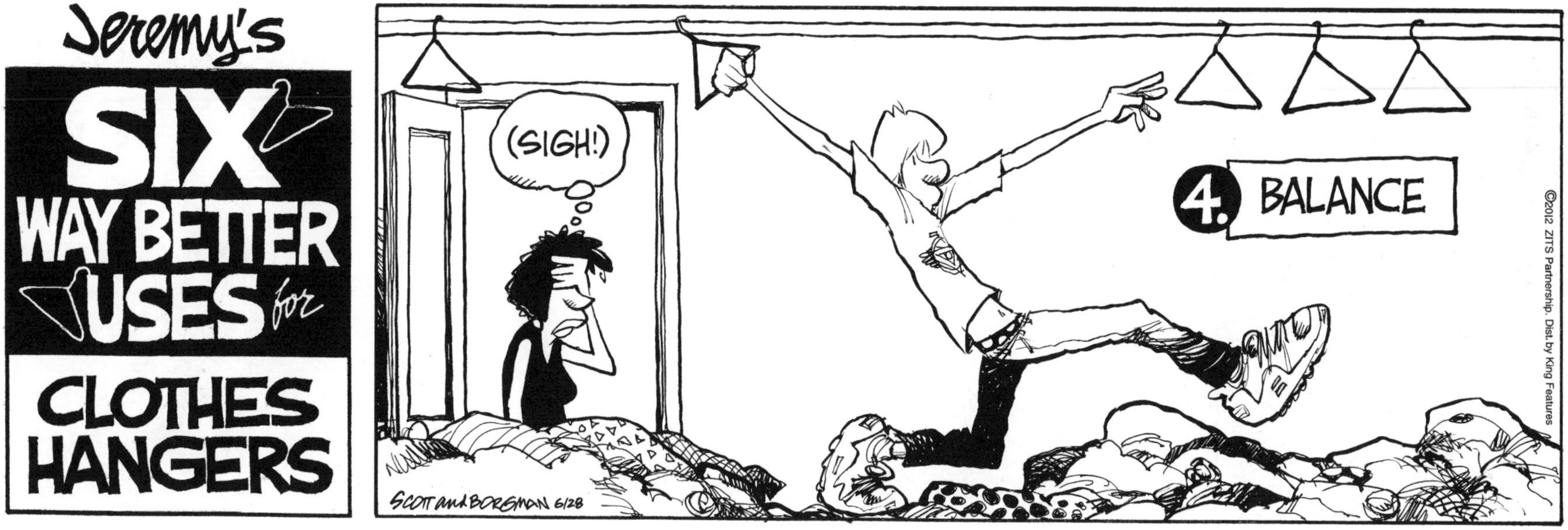
JEREMY'S
SIX WAY BETTER USES for
CLOTHES HANGERS
(SIGH!)
4. BALANCE
©2012 ZITS Partnership. Dist. by King Features
SCOTT and BORGMAN 6/28

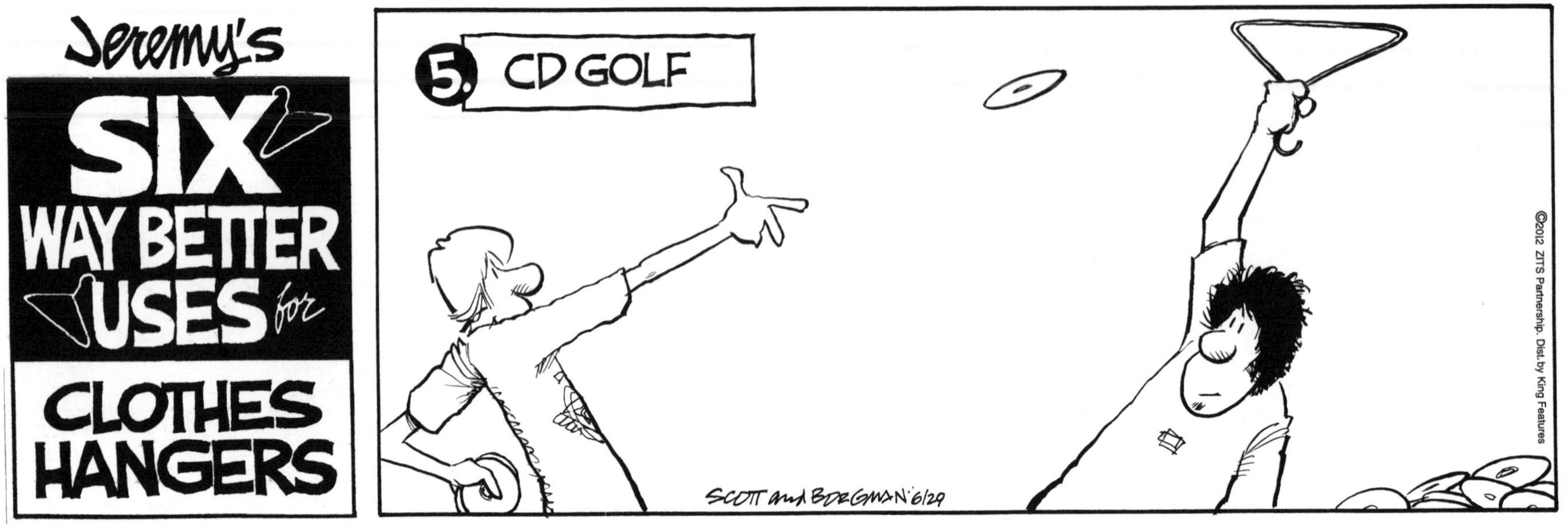
Jeremy's
SIX
WAY BETTER
USES for
CLOTHES
HANGERS
5. CD GOLF
SCOTT and BORGMAN 6/29
©2012 ZITS Partnership. Dist. by King Features

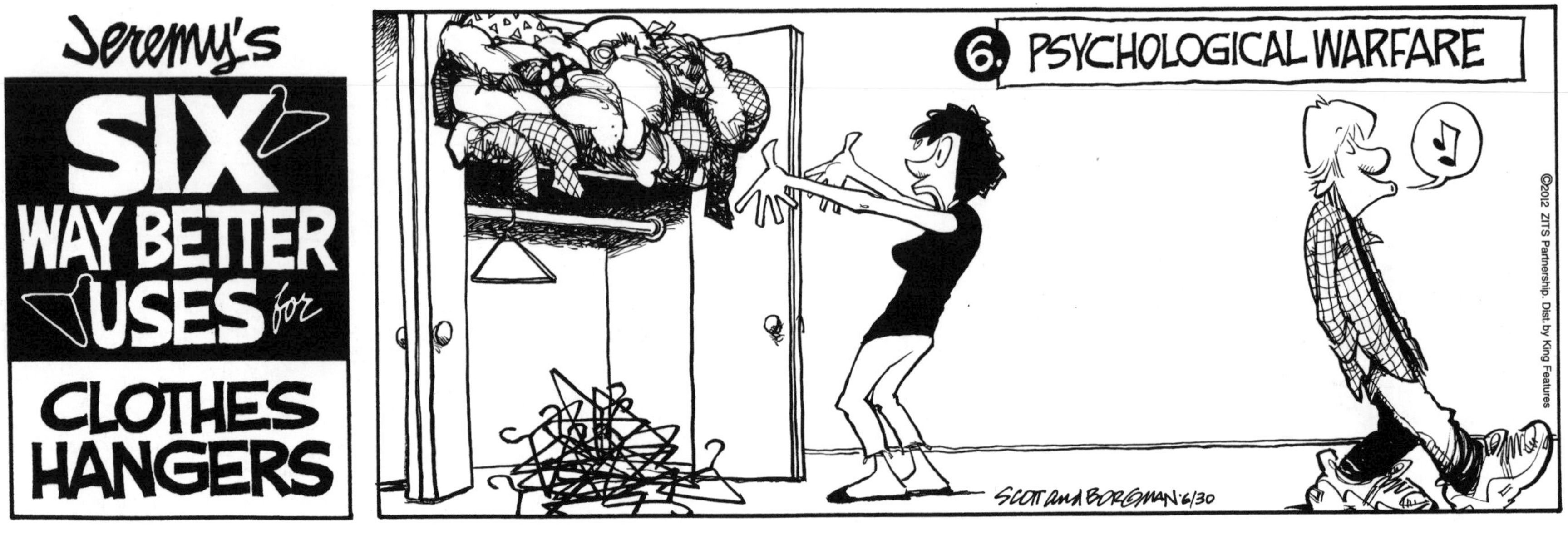
Jeremy's
SIX
WAY BETTER
USES for
CLOTHES
HANGERS
6. PSYCHOLOGICAL WARFARE
SCOTT and BORGMAN 6/30
©2012 ZITS Partnership. Dist. by King Features

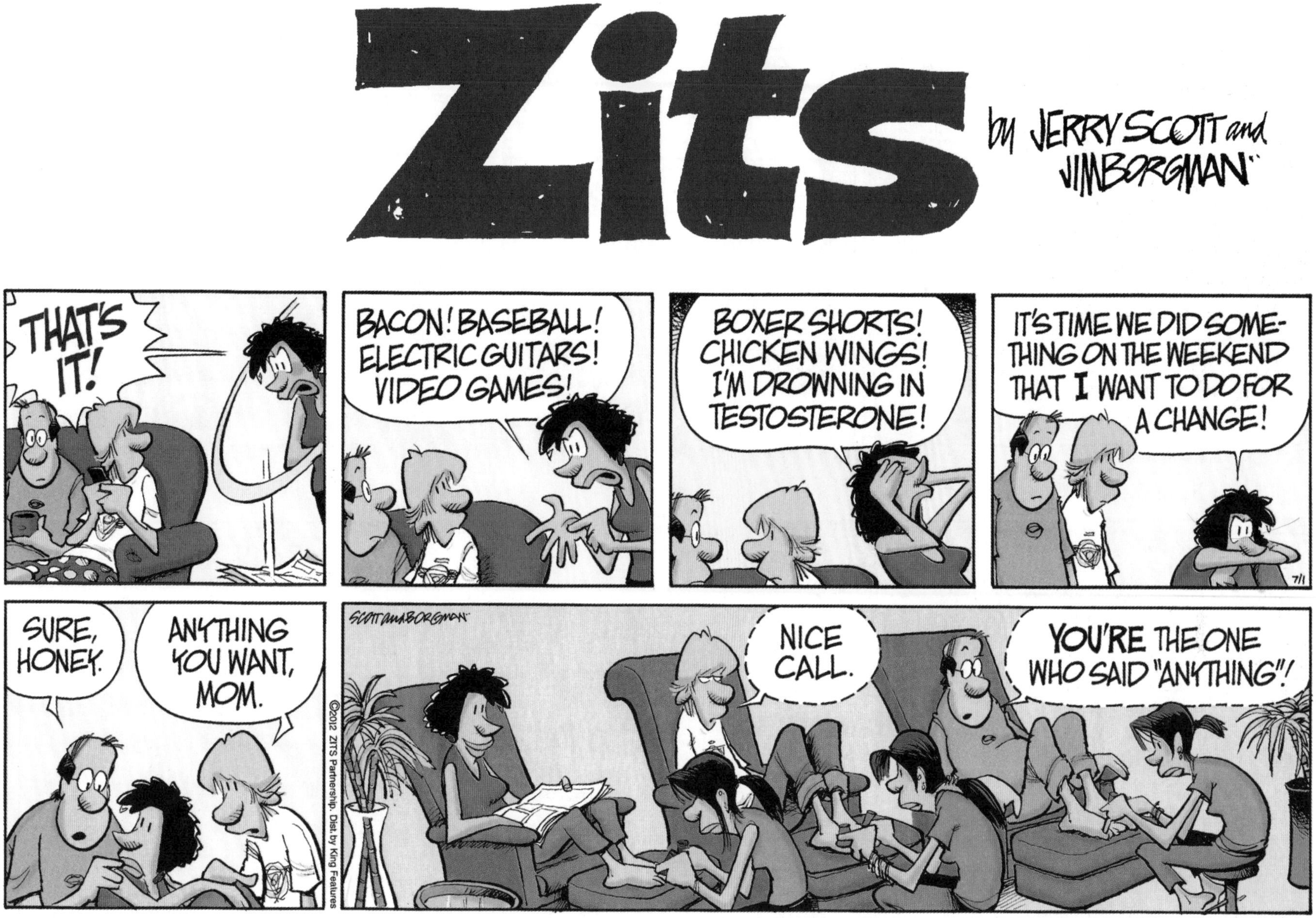
Zits
by JERRY SCOTT and JIM BORGMAN
THAT'S IT!
BACON! BASEBALL! ELECTRIC GUITARS! VIDEO GAMES!
BOXER SHORTS! CHICKEN WINGS! I'M DROWNING IN TESTOSTERONE!
IT'S TIME WE DID SOMETHING ON THE WEEKEND THAT I WANT TO DO FOR A CHANGE!
7/1
SURE, HONEY.
ANYTHING YOU WANT, MOM.
©2012 ZITS Partnership. Dist. by King Features
SCOTT and BORGMAN
NICE CALL.
YOU'RE THE ONE WHO SAID "ANYTHING"!

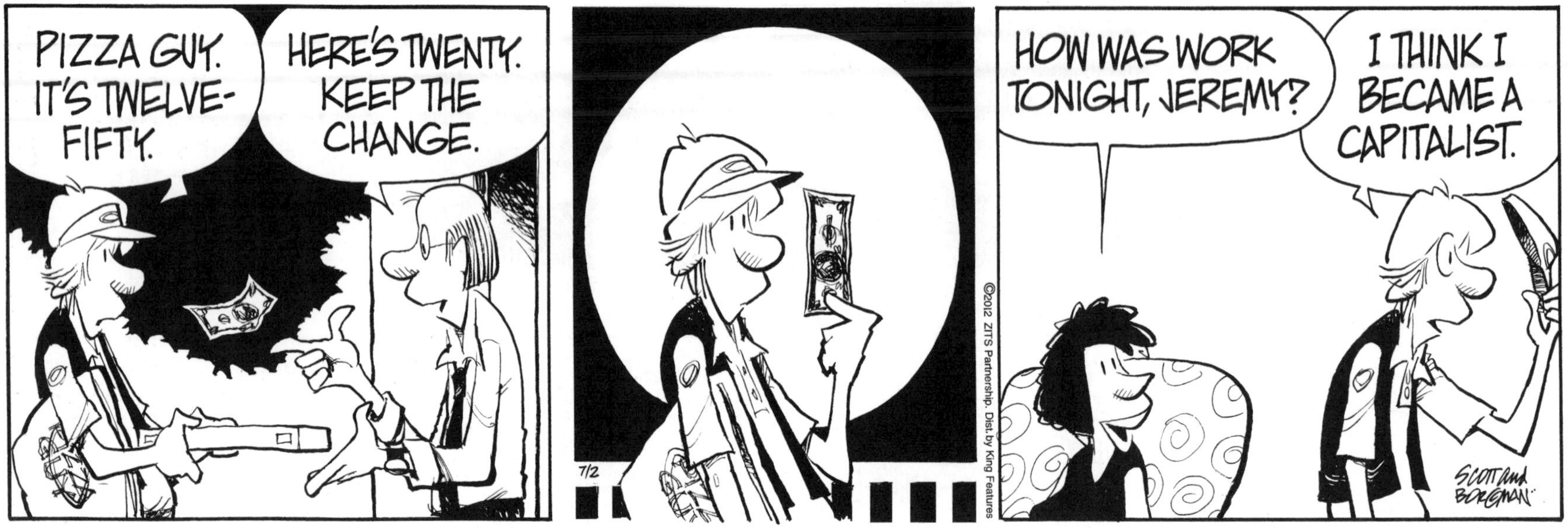
PIZZA GUY. IT'S TWELVE-FIFTY.
HERE'S TWENTY. KEEP THE CHANGE.
7/2
©2012 ZITS Partnership. Dist. by King Features
HOW WAS WORK TONIGHT, JEREMY?
I THINK I BECAME A CAPITALIST.
SCOTT and BORGMAN

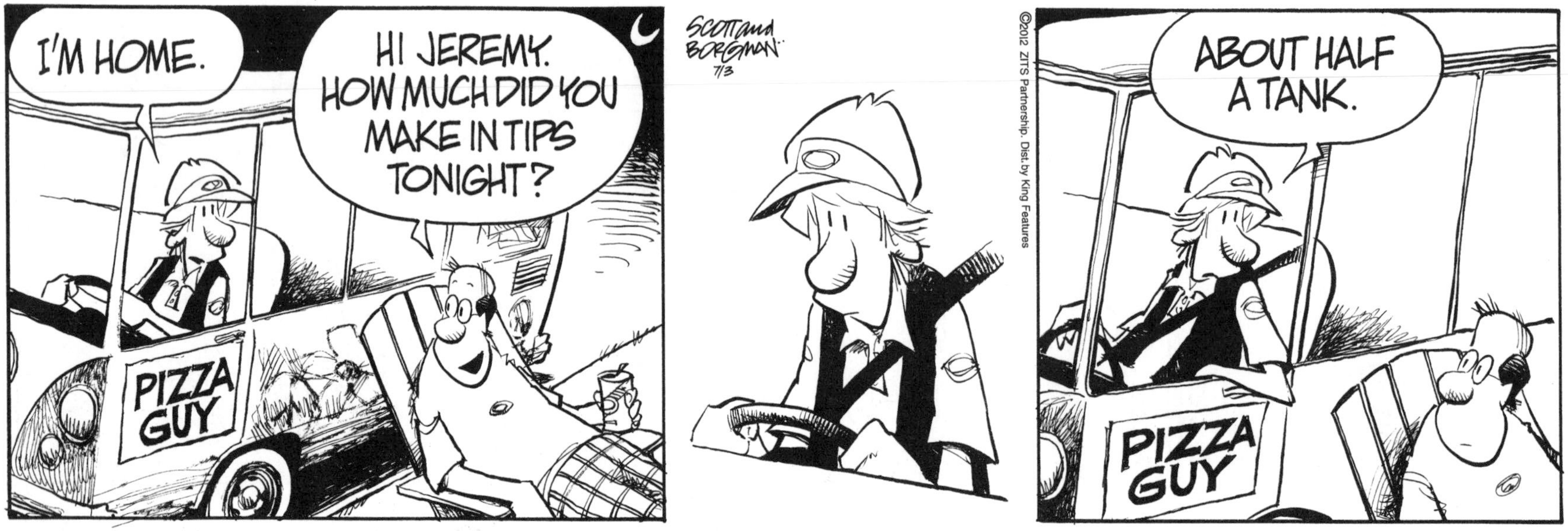
I'M HOME.
HI JEREMY. HOW MUCH DID YOU MAKE IN TIPS TONIGHT?
PIZZA GUY
SCOTT and BORGMAN
7/3
©2012 ZITS Partnership. Dist. by King Features
ABOUT HALF A TANK.
PIZZA GUY

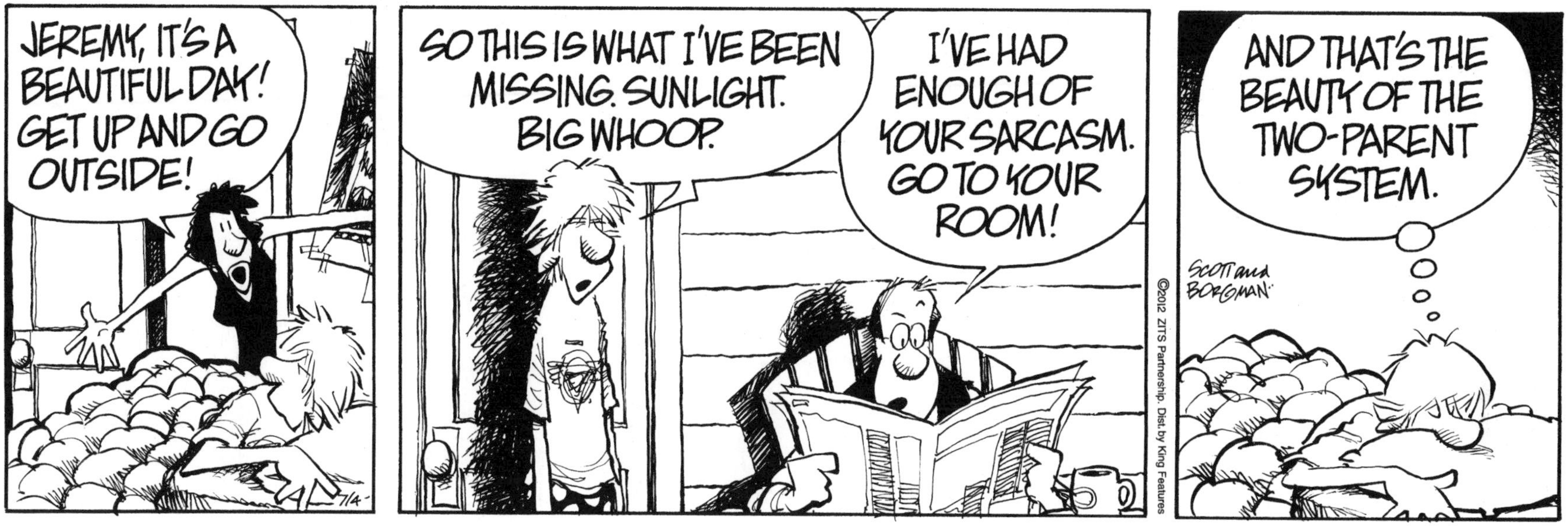
JEREMY, IT'S A BEAUTIFUL DAY! GET UP AND GO OUTSIDE!
SO THIS IS WHAT I'VE BEEN MISSING. SUNLIGHT. BIG WHOOP.
I'VE HAD ENOUGH OF YOUR SARCASM. GO TO YOUR ROOM!
AND THAT'S THE BEAUTY OF THE TWO-PARENT SYSTEM.
SCOTT and BORGMAN
©2012 ZITS Partnership. Dist. by King Features

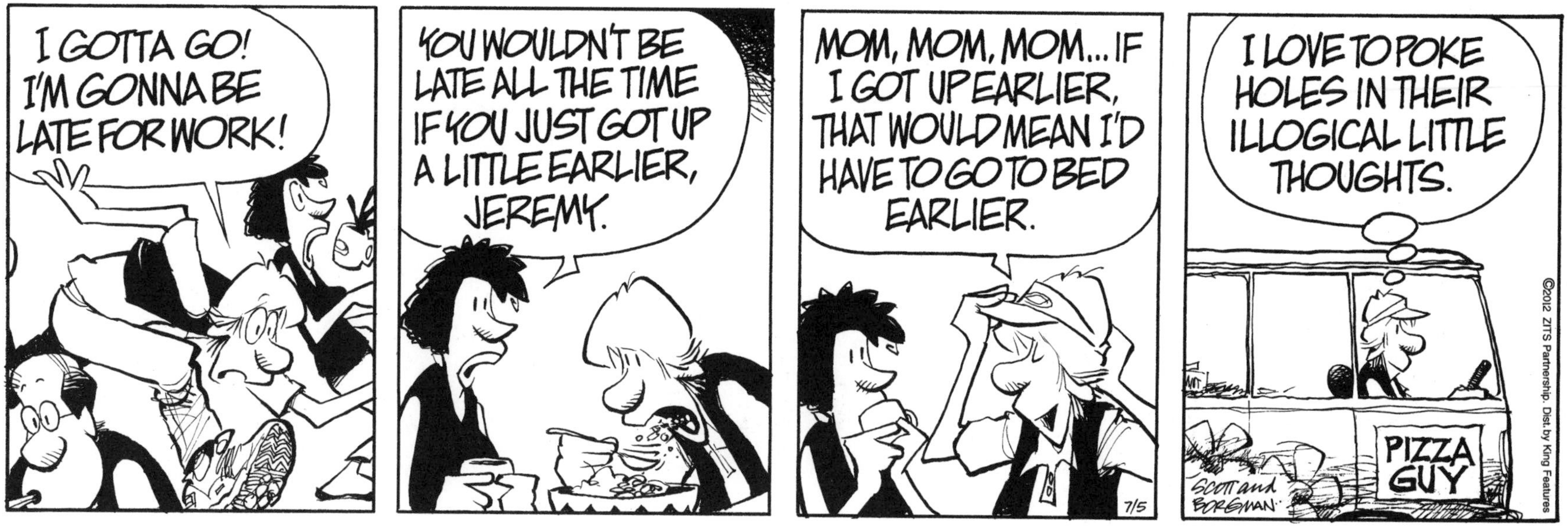
I GOTTA GO! I'M GONNA BE LATE FOR WORK!
YOU WOULDN'T BE LATE ALL THE TIME IF YOU JUST GOT UP A LITTLE EARLIER, JEREMY.
MOM, MOM, MOM... IF I GOT UP EARLIER, THAT WOULD MEAN I'D HAVE TO GO TO BED EARLIER.
I LOVE TO POKE HOLES IN THEIR ILLOGICAL LITTLE THOUGHTS.
PIZZA GUY
SCOTT and BORGMAN
©2012 ZITS Partnership. Dist. by King Features

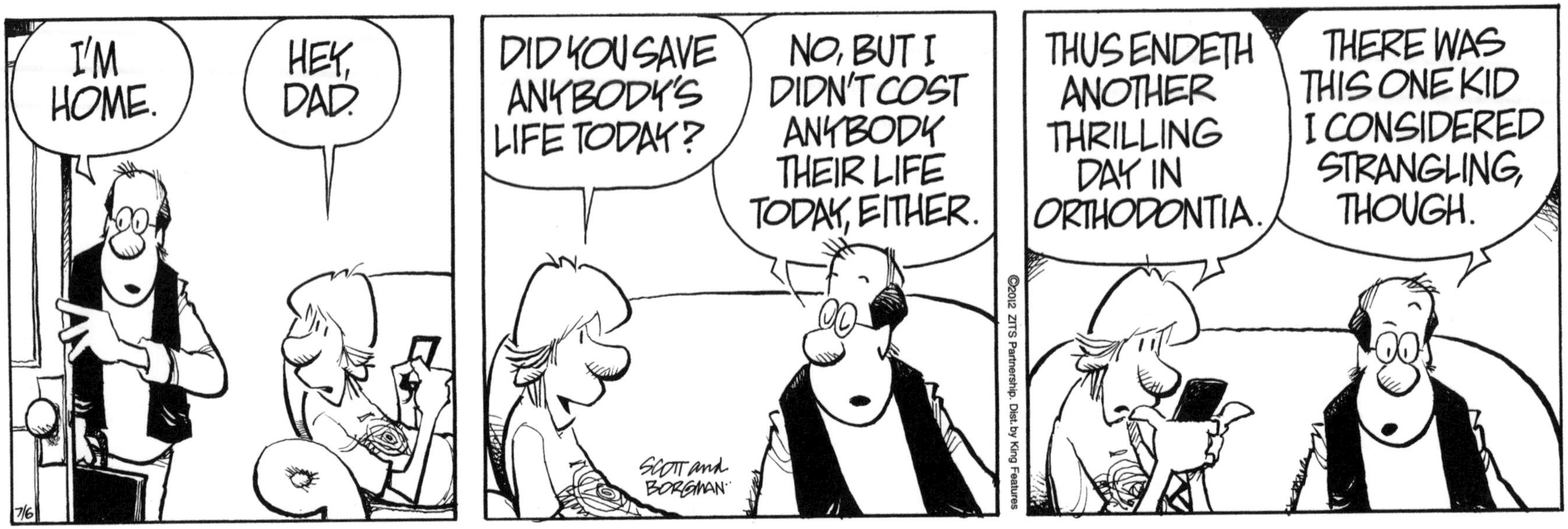
I'M HOME.
HEY, DAD.
DID YOU SAVE ANYBODY'S LIFE TODAY?
NO, BUT I DIDN'T COST ANYBODY THEIR LIFE TODAY, EITHER.
THUS ENDETH ANOTHER THRILLING DAY IN ORTHODONTIA.
THERE WAS THIS ONE KID I CONSIDERED STRANGLING, THOUGH.
7/6
SCOTT and BORGMAN
©2012 ZITS Partnership. Dist. by King Features

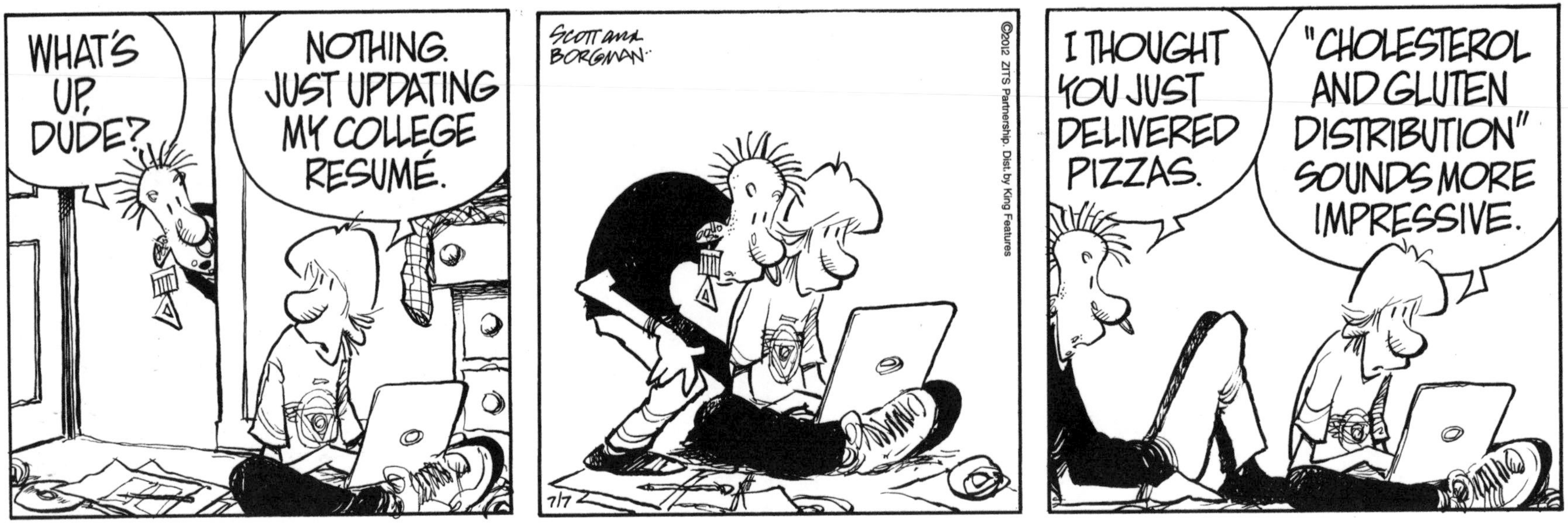
WHAT'S UP, DUDE?
NOTHING. JUST UPDATING MY COLLEGE RESUMÉ.
I THOUGHT YOU JUST DELIVERED PIZZAS.
"CHOLESTEROL AND GLUTEN DISTRIBUTION" SOUNDS MORE IMPRESSIVE.
SCOTT and BORGMAN
7/7
©2012 ZITS Partnership. Dist. by King Features

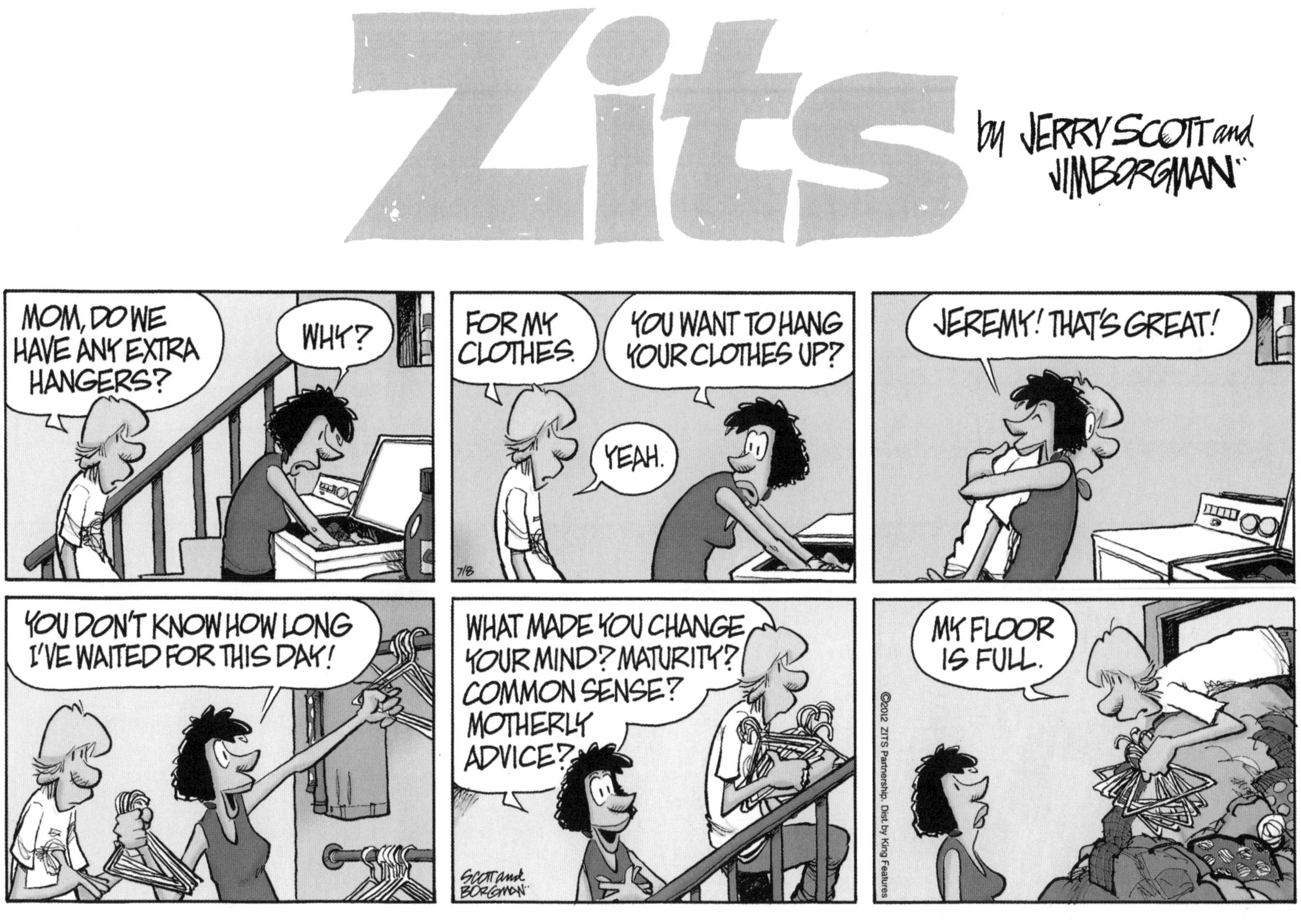
Zits
by JERRY SCOTT and JIM BORGMAN
MOM, DO WE HAVE ANY EXTRA HANGERS?
WHY?
FOR MY CLOTHES.
YOU WANT TO HANG YOUR CLOTHES UP?
YEAH.
JEREMY! THAT'S GREAT!
YOU DON'T KNOW HOW LONG I'VE WAITED FOR THIS DAY!
WHAT MADE YOU CHANGE YOUR MIND? MATURITY? COMMON SENSE? MOTHERLY ADVICE?
MY FLOOR IS FULL.
SCOTT and BORGMAN
©2012 ZITS Partnership. Dist. by King Features

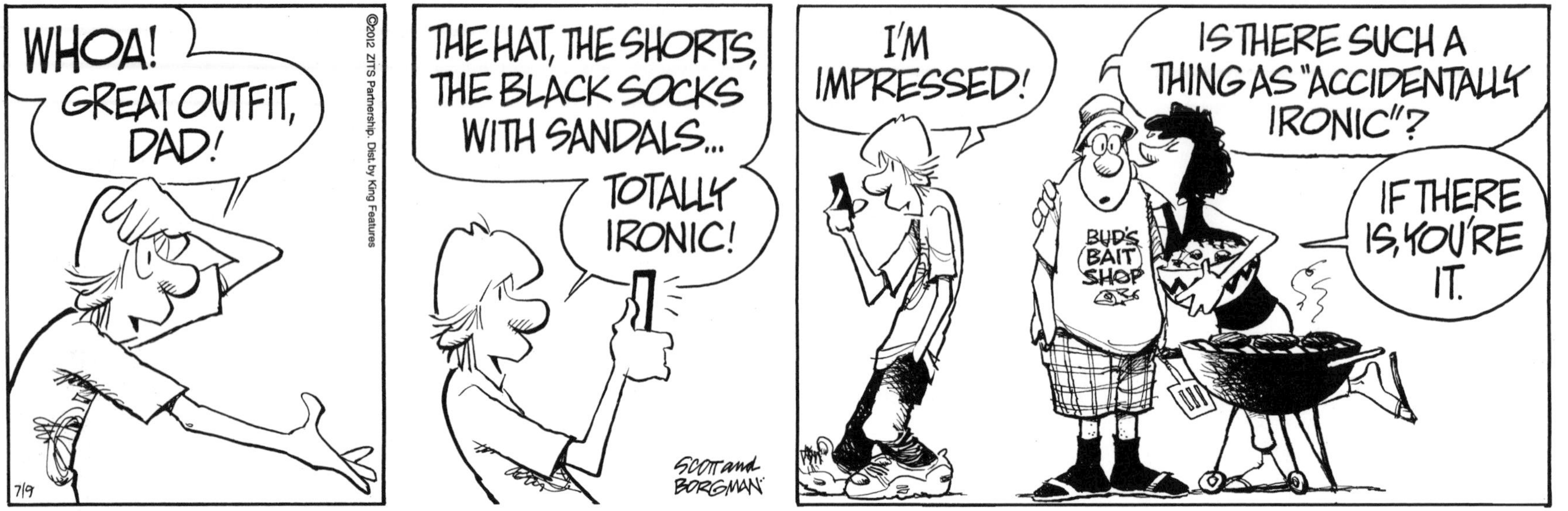
WHOA! GREAT OUTFIT, DAD!
©2012 ZITS Partnership. Dist. by King Features
THE HAT, THE SHORTS, THE BLACK SOCKS WITH SANDALS...
TOTALLY IRONIC!
SCOTT and BORGMAN
I'M IMPRESSED!
IS THERE SUCH A THING AS "ACCIDENTALLY IRONIC"?
BUD'S BAIT SHOP
IF THERE IS, YOU'RE IT.

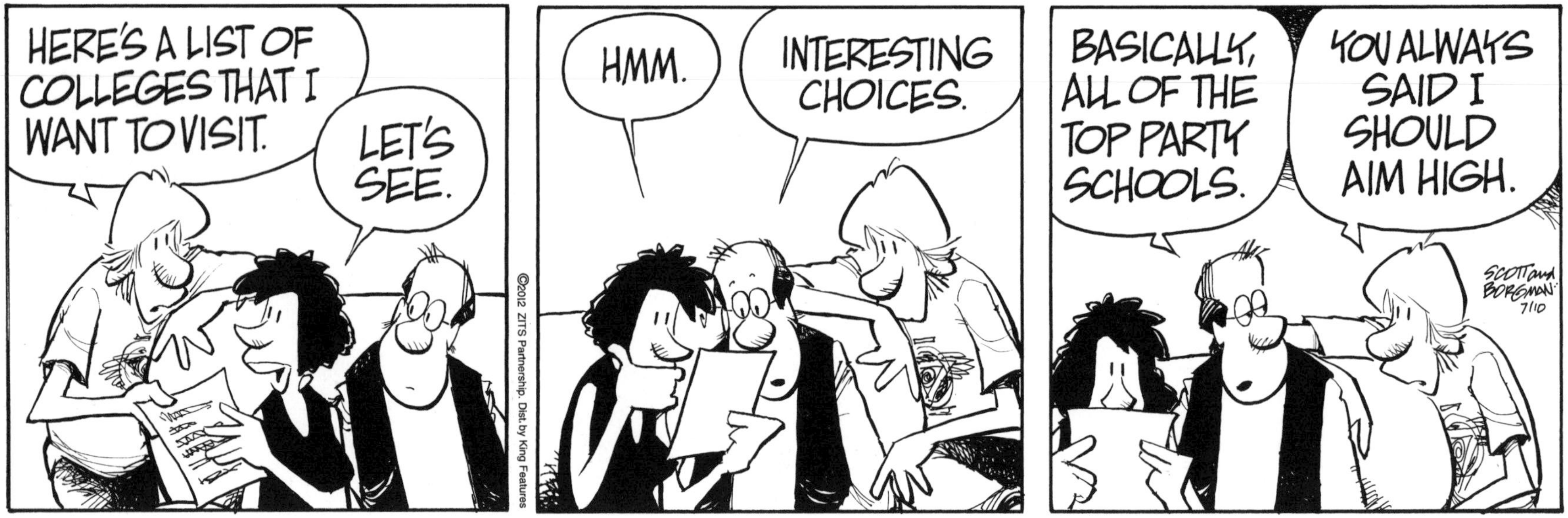
HERE'S A LIST OF COLLEGES THAT I WANT TO VISIT.
LET'S SEE.
©2012 ZITS Partnership. Dist. by King Features
HMM.
INTERESTING CHOICES.
BASICALLY, ALL OF THE TOP PARTY SCHOOLS.
YOU ALWAYS SAID I SHOULD AIM HIGH.
SCOTT and BORGMAN

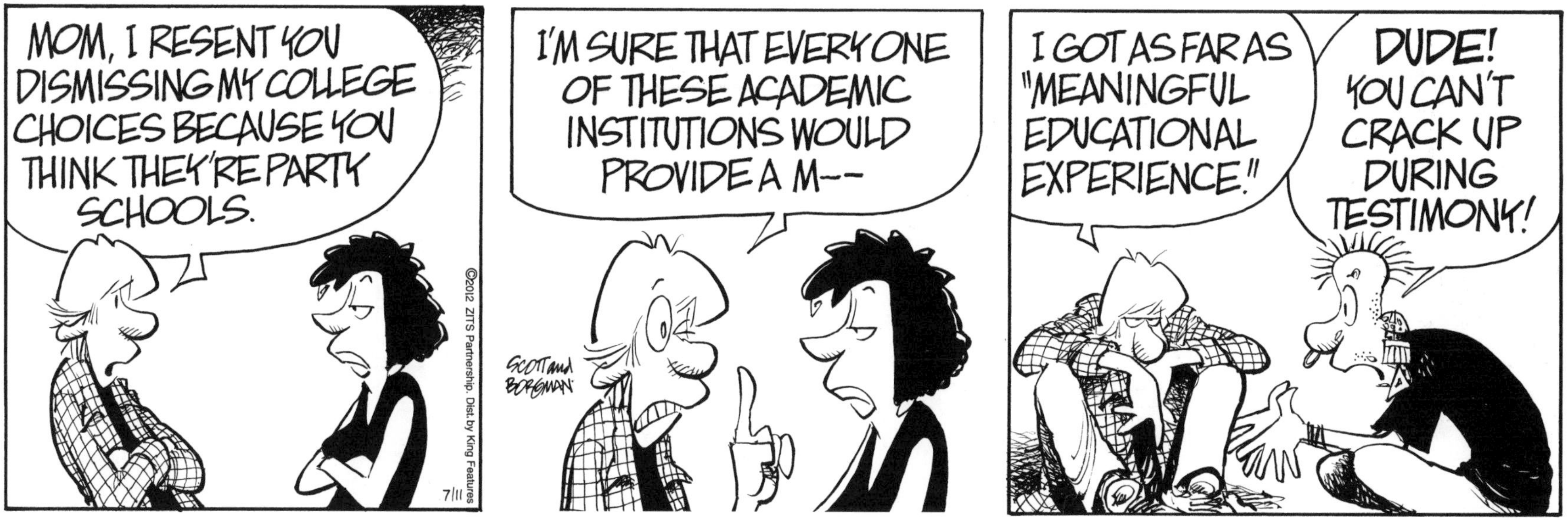
MOM, I RESENT YOU DISMISSING MY COLLEGE CHOICES BECAUSE YOU THINK THEY'RE PARTY SCHOOLS.
I'M SURE THAT EVERYONE OF THESE ACADEMIC INSTITUTIONS WOULD PROVIDE A M--
I GOT AS FAR AS "MEANINGFUL EDUCATIONAL EXPERIENCE."
DUDE! YOU CAN'T CRACK UP DURING TESTIMONY!
SCOTT and BORGMAN
©2012 ZITS Partnership. Dist. by King Features
7/11

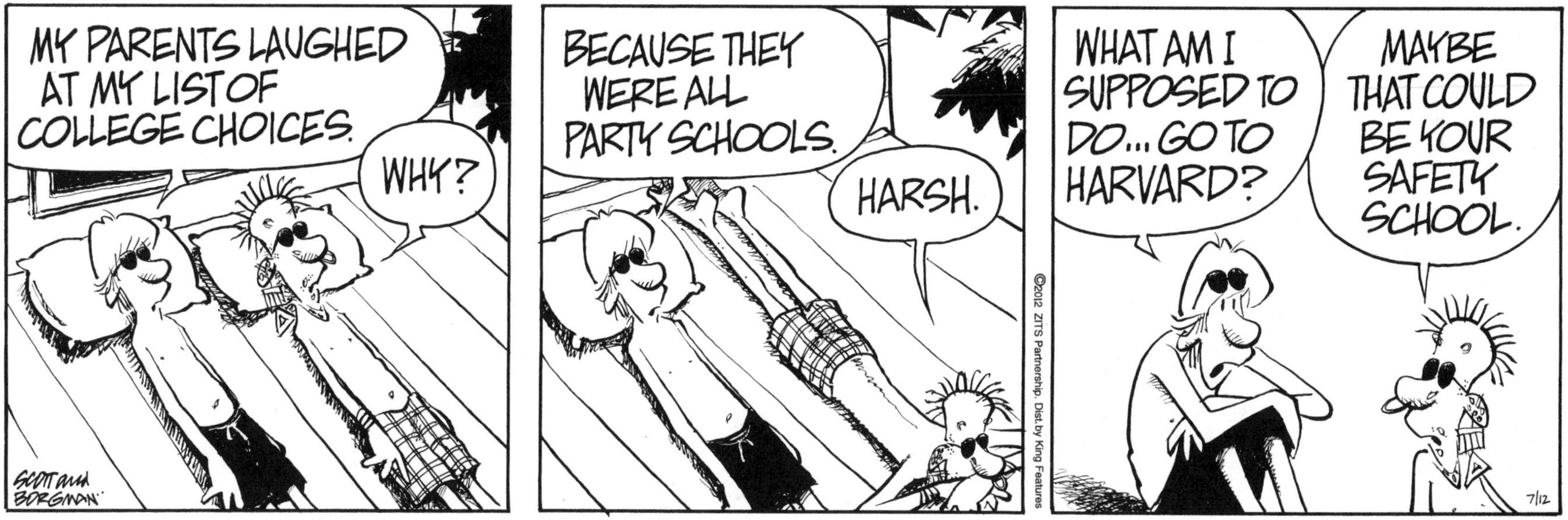
MY PARENTS LAUGHED AT MY LIST OF COLLEGE CHOICES.
WHY?
BECAUSE THEY WERE ALL PARTY SCHOOLS.
HARSH.
WHAT AM I SUPPOSED TO DO... GO TO HARVARD?
MAYBE THAT COULD BE YOUR SAFETY SCHOOL.
SCOTT and BORGMAN
©2012 ZITS Partnership. Dist. by King Features
7/12

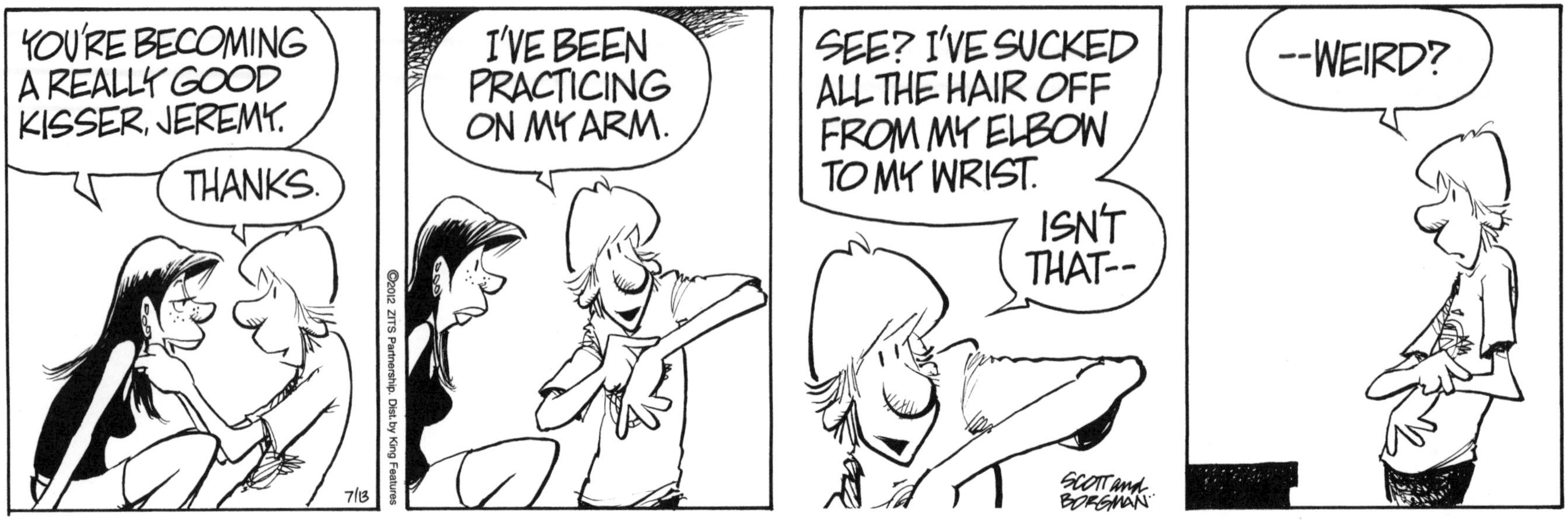
YOU'RE BECOMING A REALLY GOOD KISSER, JEREMY.
THANKS.
©2012 ZITS Partnership. Dist. by King Features
7/13
I'VE BEEN PRACTICING ON MY ARM.
SEE? I'VE SUCKED ALL THE HAIR OFF FROM MY ELBOW TO MY WRIST.
ISN'T THAT--
SCOTT and BORGMAN
--WEIRD?

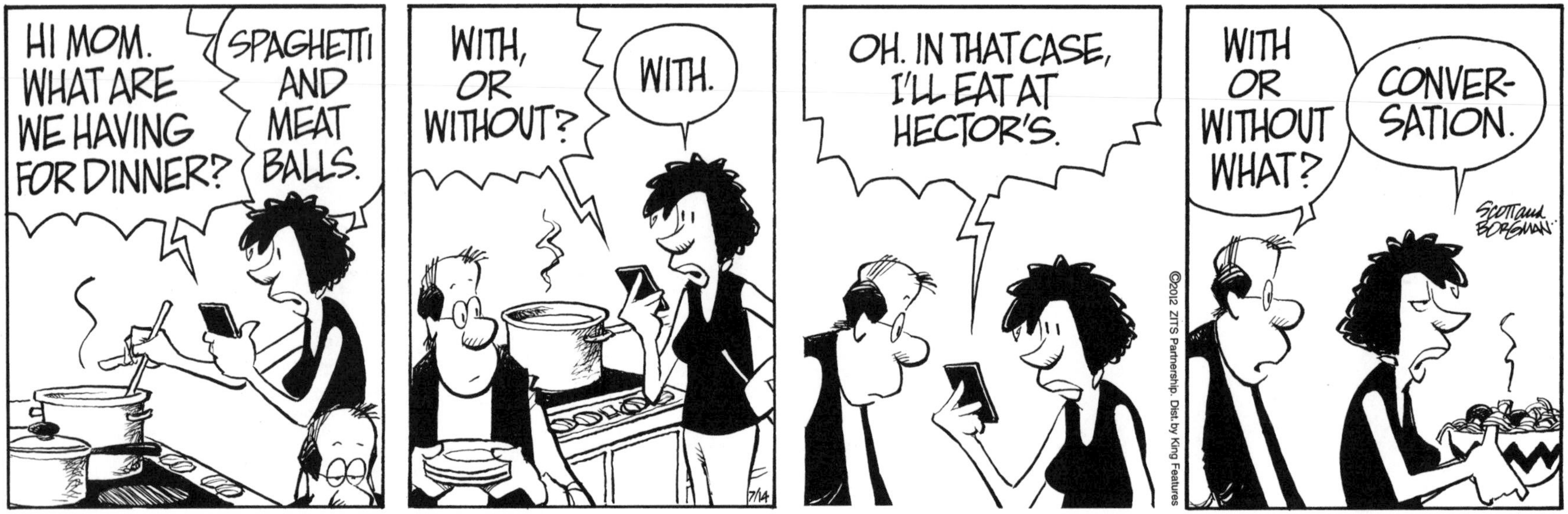
HI MOM. WHAT ARE WE HAVING FOR DINNER?
SPAGHETTI AND MEAT BALLS.
WITH, OR WITHOUT?
WITH.
7/14
OH. IN THAT CASE, I'LL EAT AT HECTOR'S.
©2012 ZITS Partnership. Dist. by King Features
WITH OR WITHOUT WHAT?
CONVER-SATION.
SCOTT and BORGMAN

Zits

by JERRY SCOTT and JIM BORGMAN

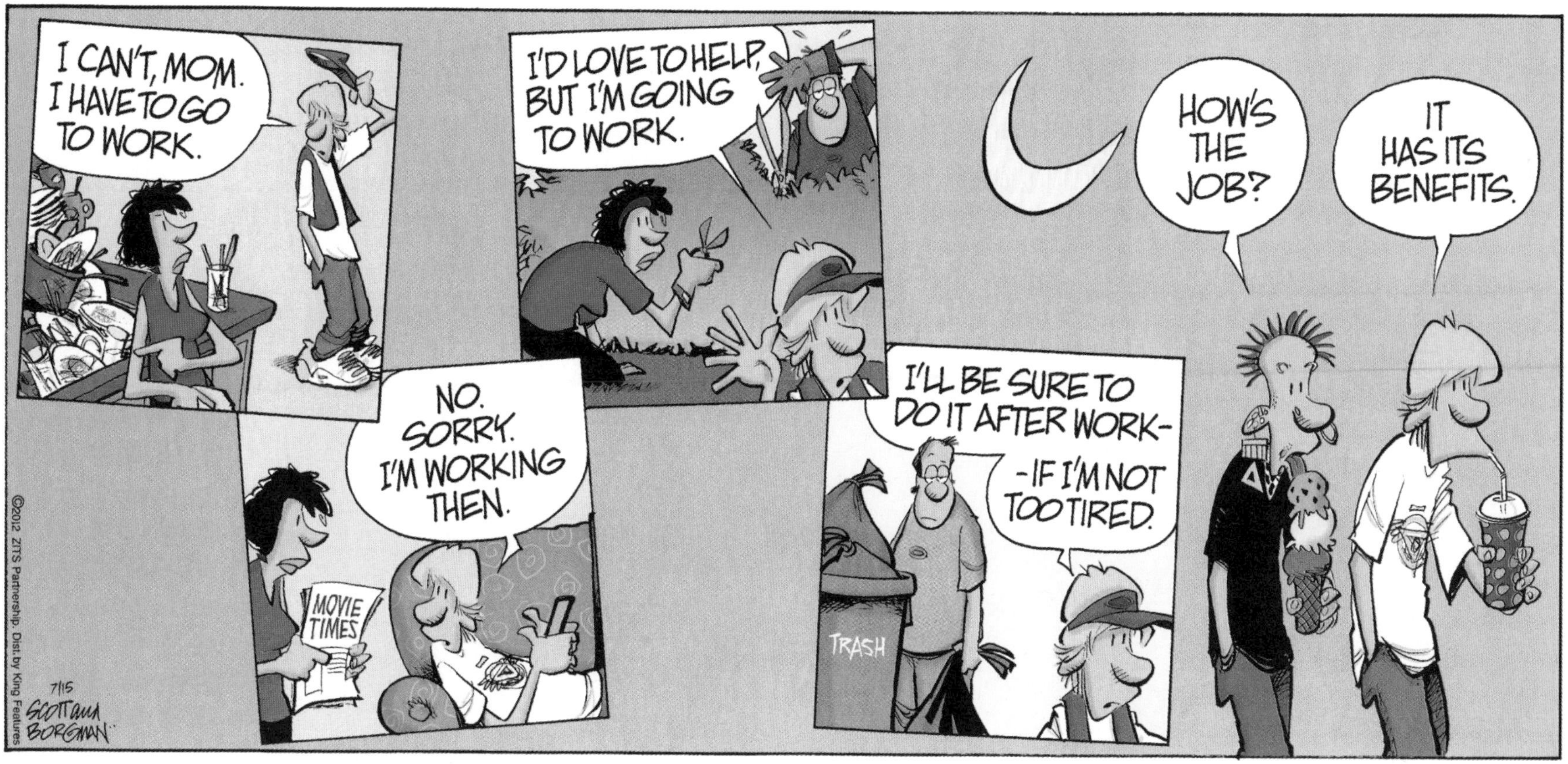
I CAN'T, MOM. I HAVE TO GO TO WORK.
I'D LOVE TO HELP, BUT I'M GOING TO WORK.
MOVIE TIMES
NO. SORRY. I'M WORKING THEN.
TRASH
I'LL BE SURE TO DO IT AFTER WORK-
-IF I'M NOT TOO TIRED.
HOW'S THE JOB?
IT HAS ITS BENEFITS.
©2012 ZITS Partnership. Dist. by King Features
7/15 SCOTT and BORGMAN

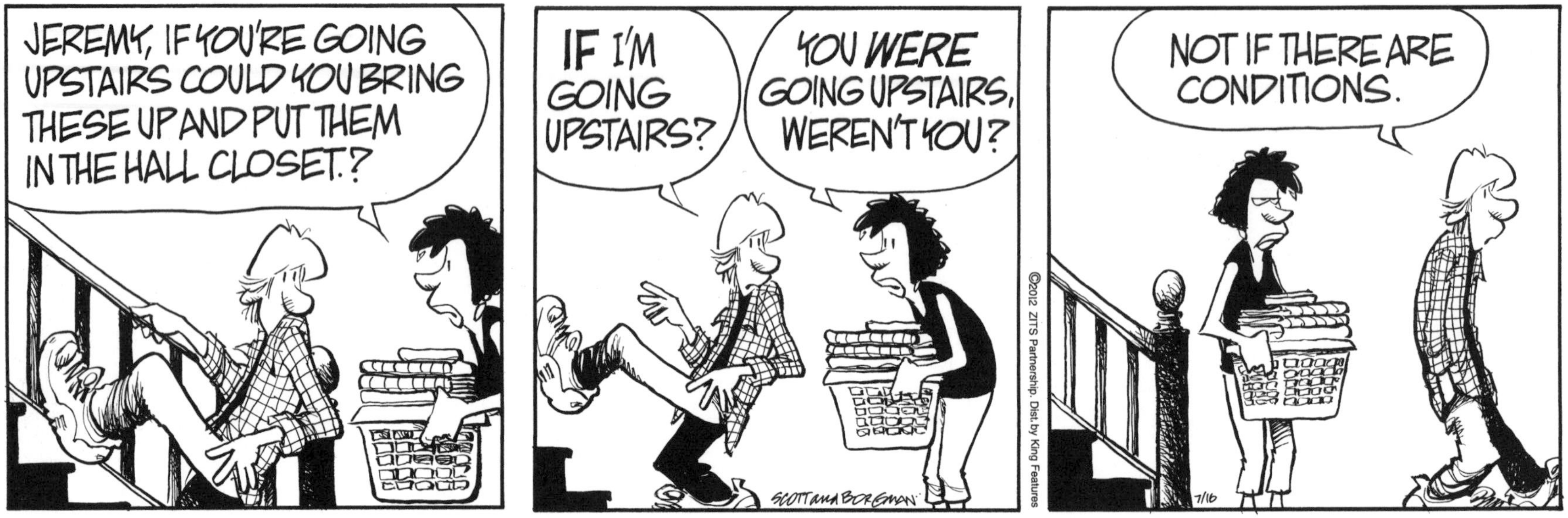
JEREMY, IF YOU'RE GOING UPSTAIRS COULD YOU BRING THESE UP AND PUT THEM IN THE HALL CLOSET.?
IF I'M GOING UPSTAIRS?
YOU WERE GOING UPSTAIRS, WEREN'T YOU?
NOT IF THERE ARE CONDITIONS.
SCOTT AND BORGMAN
©2012 ZITS Partnership. Dist. by King Features
7/16

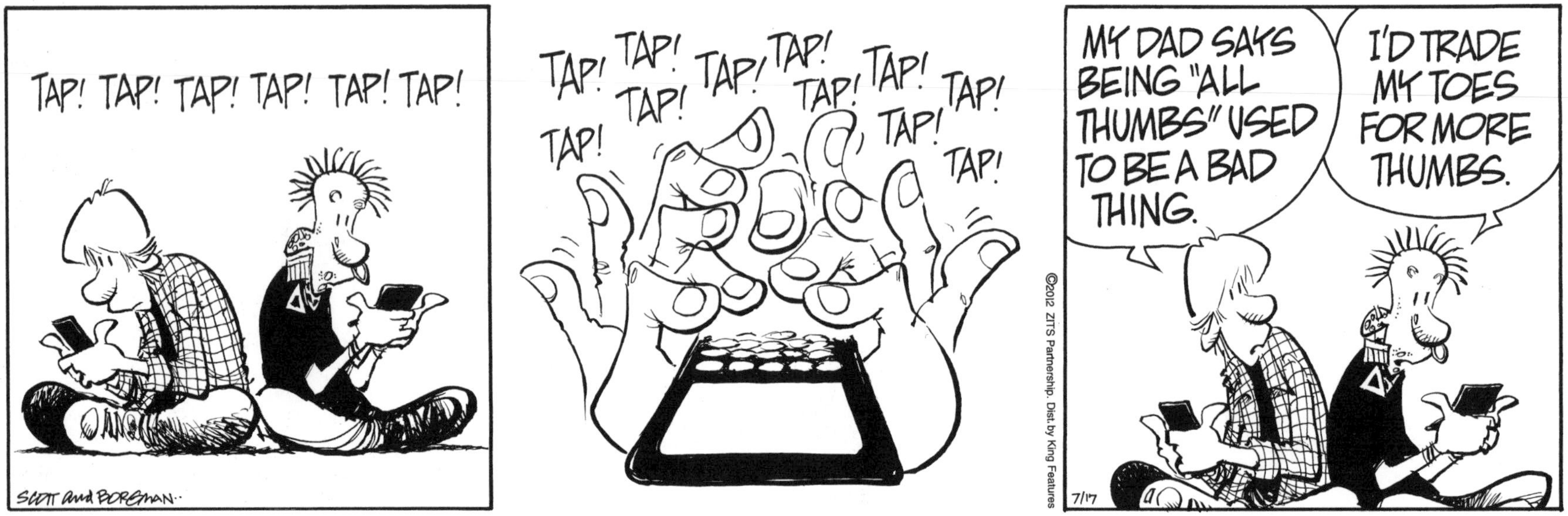
TAP! TAP! TAP! TAP! TAP! TAP!
SCOTT AND BORGMAN
TAP! TAP! TAP! TAP! TAP! TAP! TAP! TAP! TAP! TAP! TAP! TAP!
MY DAD SAYS BEING "ALL THUMBS" USED TO BE A BAD THING.
I'D TRADE MY TOES FOR MORE THUMBS.
©2012 ZITS Partnership. Dist. by King Features
7/17

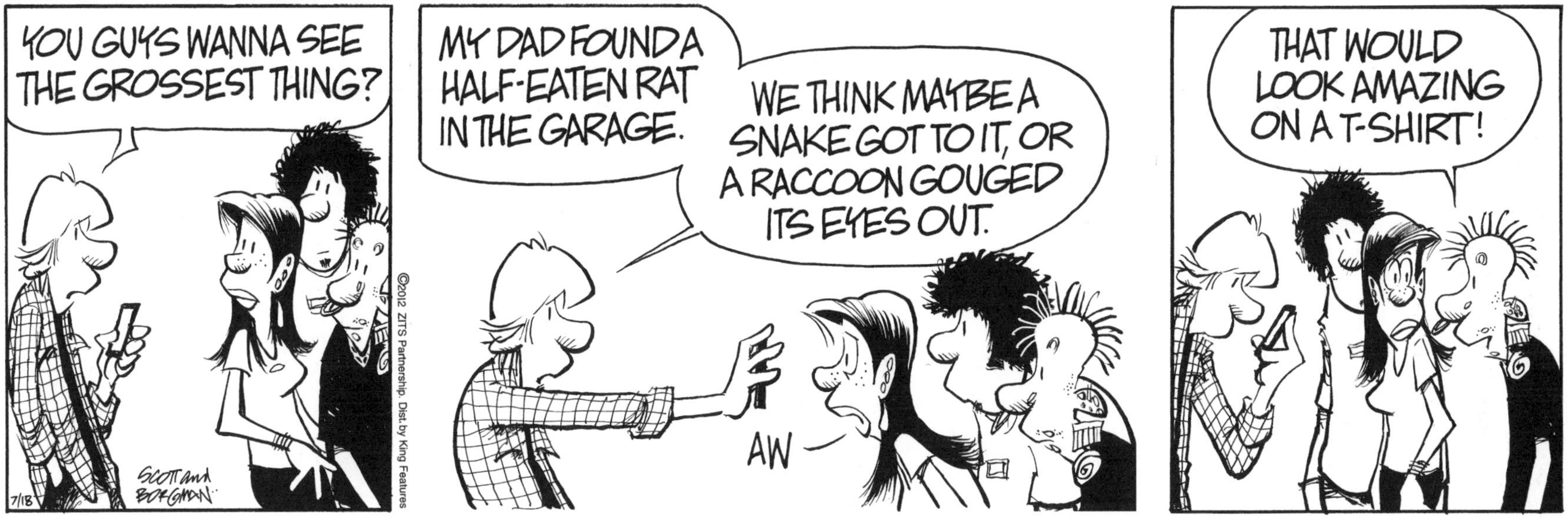
YOU GUYS WANNA SEE THE GROSSEST THING?
SCOTT and BORGMAN 7/18
©2012 ZITS Partnership. Dist. by King Features
MY DAD FOUND A HALF-EATEN RAT IN THE GARAGE.
WE THINK MAYBE A SNAKE GOT TO IT, OR A RACCOON GOUGED ITS EYES OUT.
AW
THAT WOULD LOOK AMAZING ON A T-SHIRT!

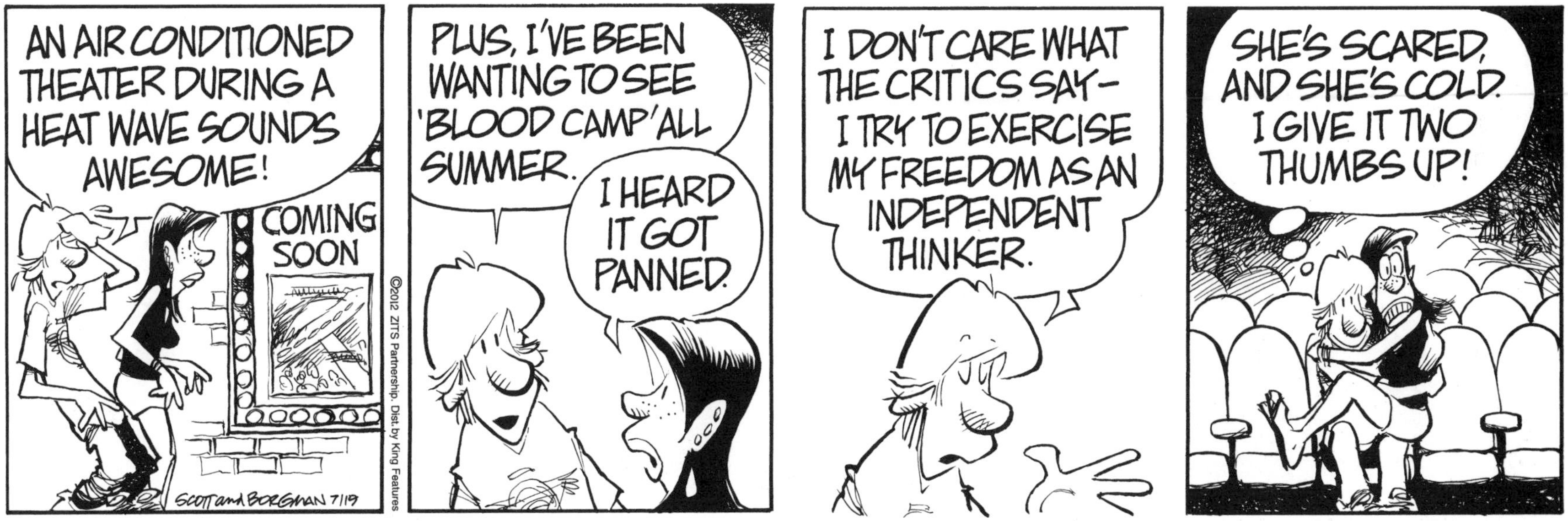
AN AIR CONDITIONED THEATER DURING A HEAT WAVE SOUNDS AWESOME!
COMING SOON
SCOTT and BORGMAN 7/19
©2012 ZITS Partnership. Dist. by King Features
PLUS, I'VE BEEN WANTING TO SEE 'BLOOD CAMP' ALL SUMMER.
I HEARD IT GOT PANNED.
I DON'T CARE WHAT THE CRITICS SAY- I TRY TO EXERCISE MY FREEDOM AS AN INDEPENDENT THINKER.
SHE'S SCARED, AND SHE'S COLD. I GIVE IT TWO THUMBS UP!

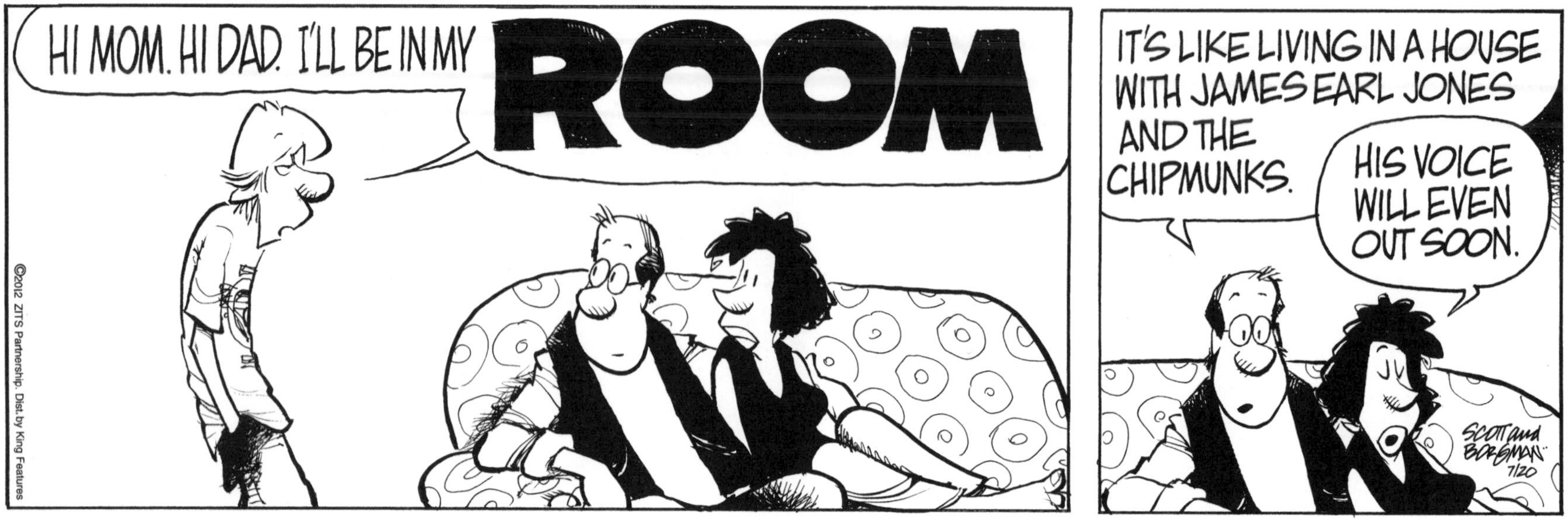
HI MOM. HI DAD. I'LL BE IN MY ROOM
IT'S LIKE LIVING IN A HOUSE WITH JAMES EARL JONES AND THE CHIPMUNKS.
HIS VOICE WILL EVEN OUT SOON.
©2012 ZITS Partnership. Dist. by King Features
SCOTT and BORGMAN 7/20

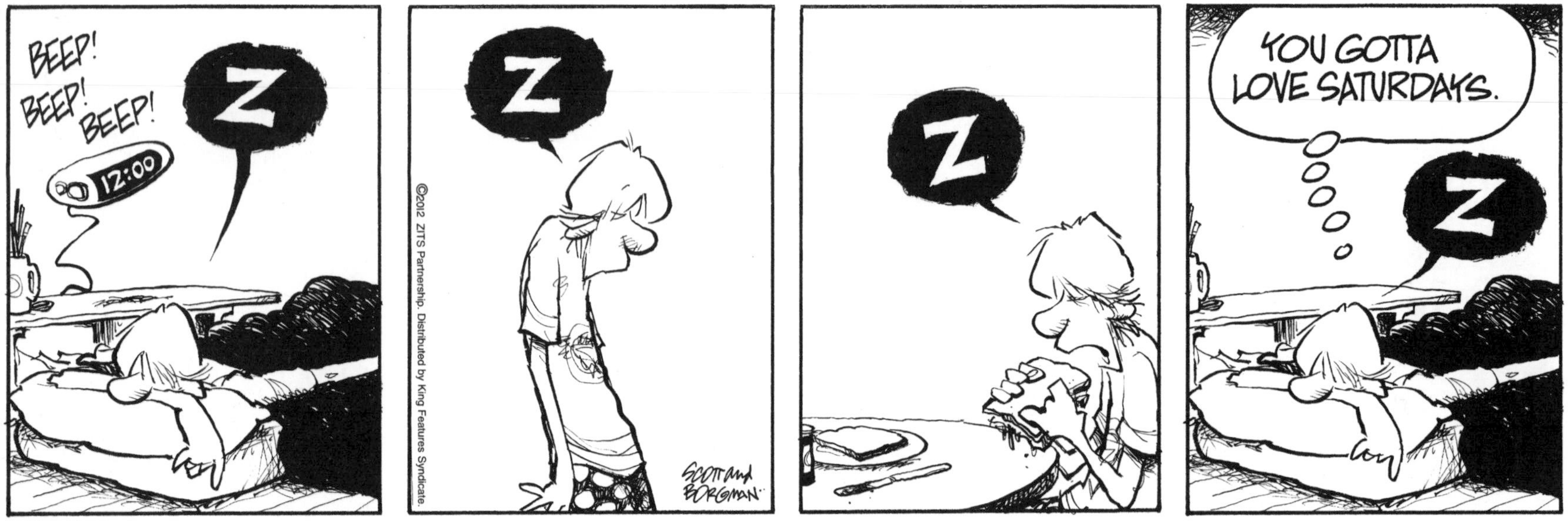
BEEP! BEEP! BEEP!
12:00
Z
Z
Z
YOU GOTTA LOVE SATURDAYS.
Z
©2012 ZITS Partnership. Distributed by King Features Syndicate.
SCOTT and BORGMAN

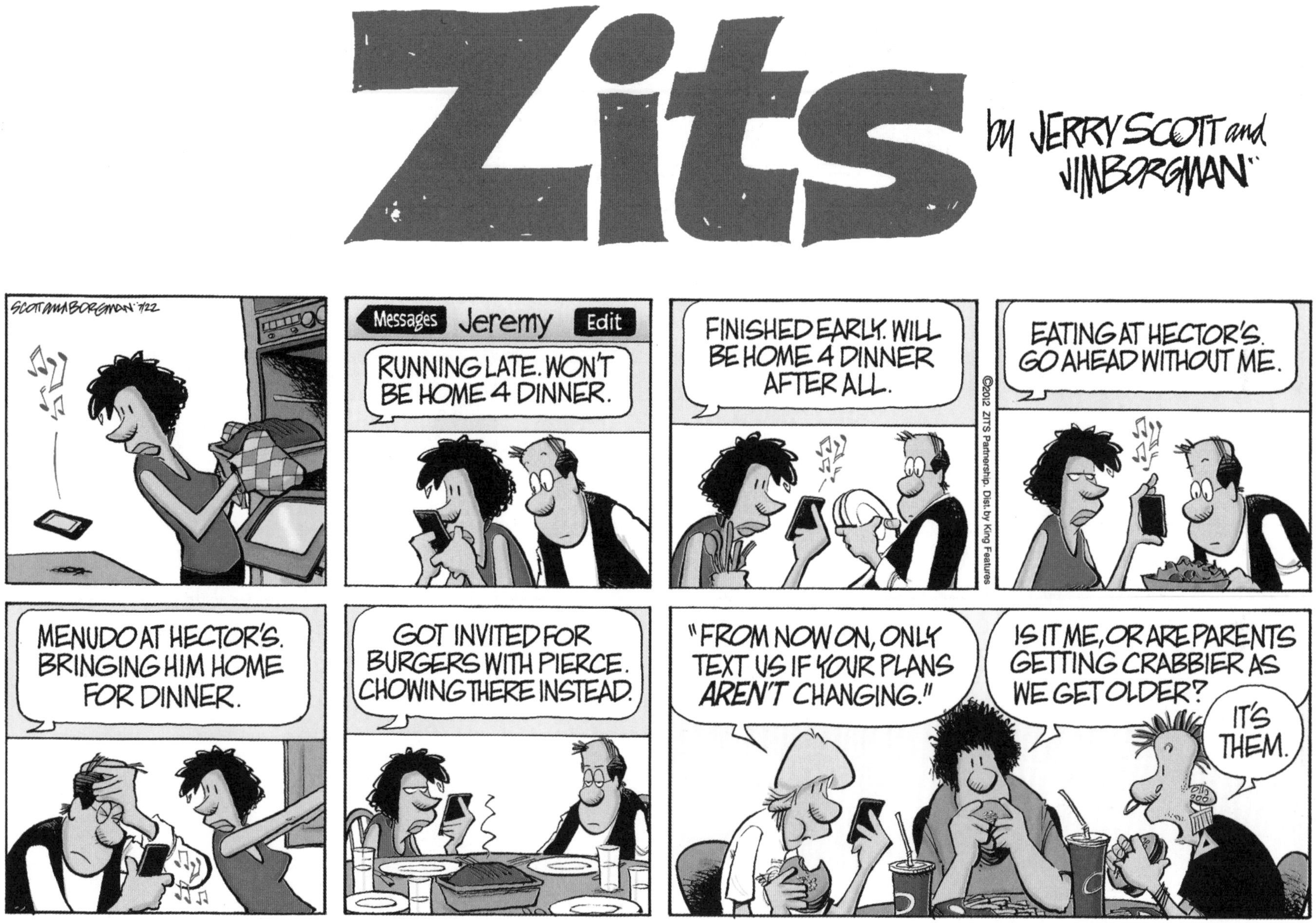
Zits
by JERRY SCOTT and JIMBORGMAN
SCOTT and BORGMAN 7/22
Messages Jeremy Edit
RUNNING LATE. WON'T BE HOME 4 DINNER.
FINISHED EARLY. WILL BE HOME 4 DINNER AFTER ALL.
©2012 ZITS Partnership. Dist. by King Features
EATING AT HECTOR'S. GO AHEAD WITHOUT ME.
MENUDO AT HECTOR'S. BRINGING HIM HOME FOR DINNER.
GOT INVITED FOR BURGERS WITH PIERCE. CHOWING THERE INSTEAD.
"FROM NOW ON, ONLY TEXT US IF YOUR PLANS *AREN'T* CHANGING."
IS IT ME, OR ARE PARENTS GETTING CRABBIER AS WE GET OLDER?
IT'S THEM.

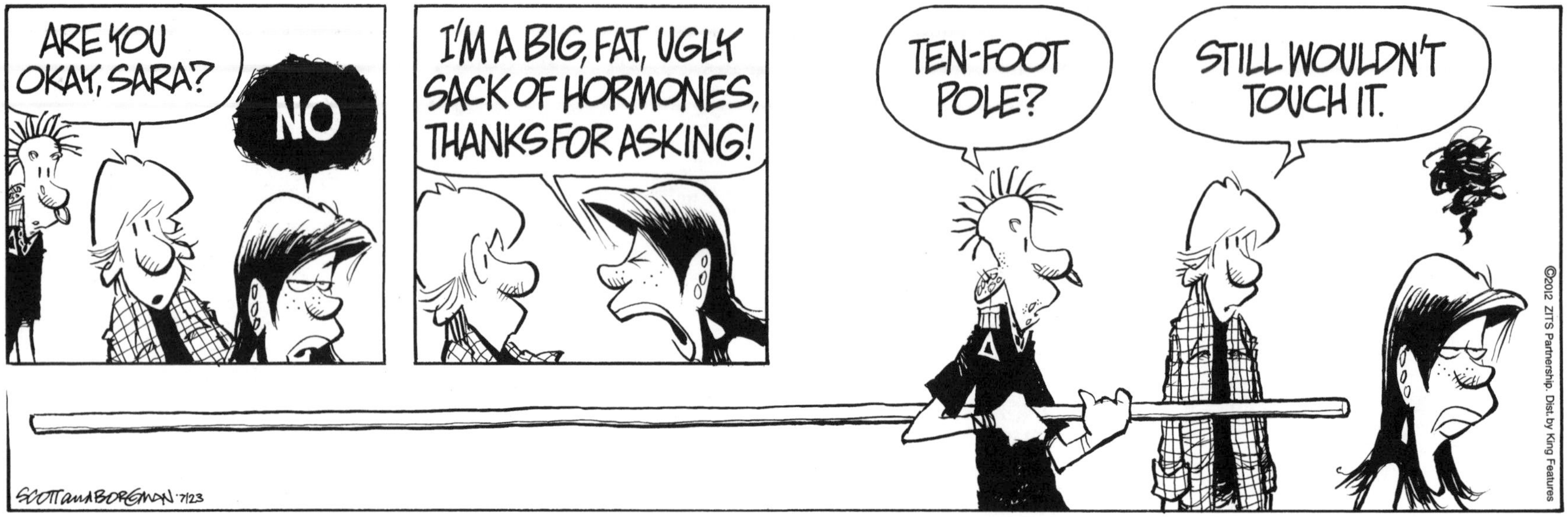
ARE YOU OKAY, SARA?
NO
I'M A BIG, FAT, UGLY SACK OF HORMONES, THANKS FOR ASKING!
TEN-FOOT POLE?
STILL WOULDN'T TOUCH IT.
SCOTT and BORGMAN 7/23
©2012 ZITS Partnership. Dist. by King Features

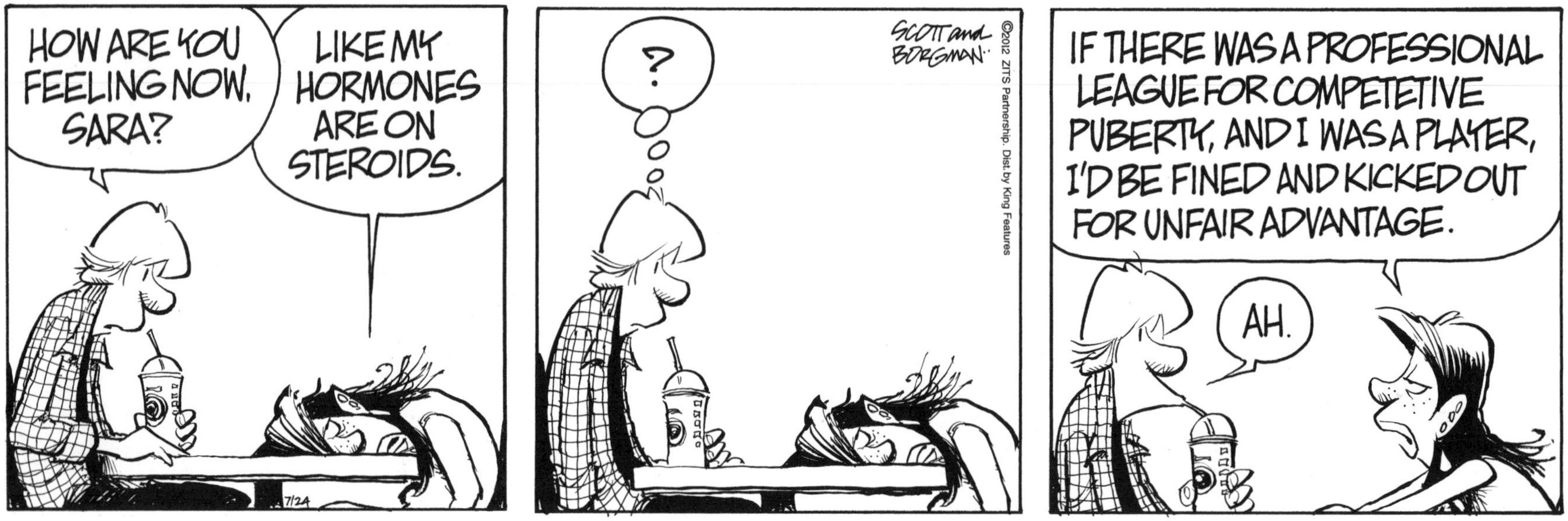
HOW ARE YOU FEELING NOW, SARA?
LIKE MY HORMONES ARE ON STEROIDS.
7/24
?
SCOTT and BORGMAN
©2012 ZITS Partnership. Dist. by King Features
IF THERE WAS A PROFESSIONAL LEAGUE FOR COMPETETIVE PUBERTY, AND I WAS A PLAYER, I'D BE FINED AND KICKED OUT FOR UNFAIR ADVANTAGE.
AH.

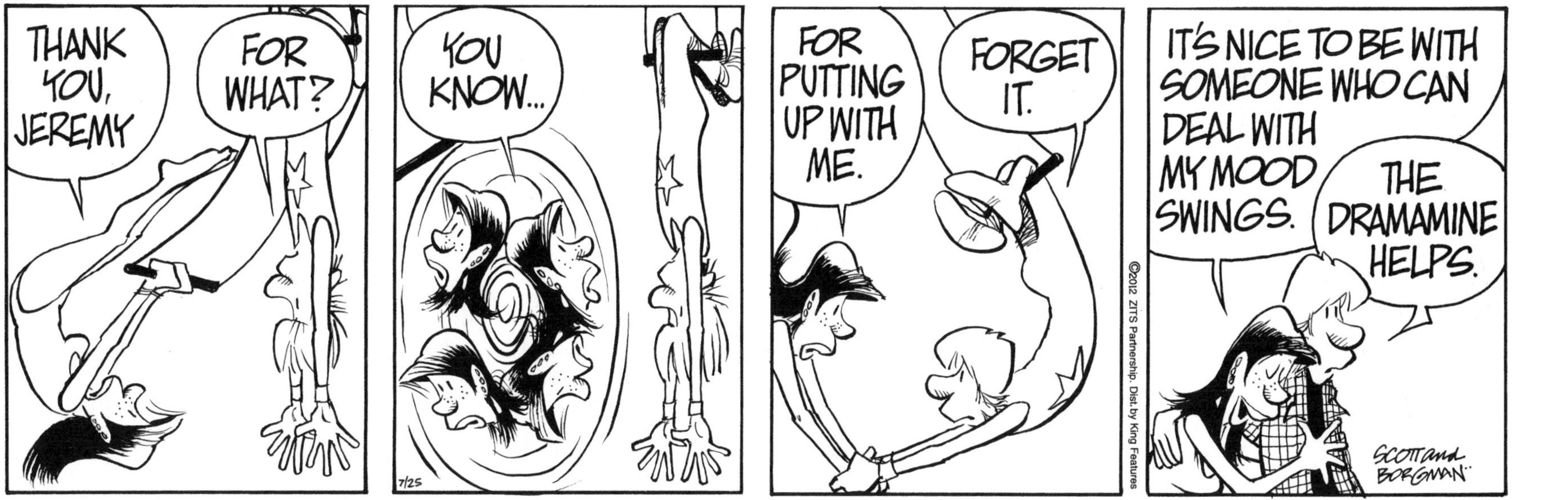
THANK YOU, JEREMY
FOR WHAT?
YOU KNOW...
FOR PUTTING UP WITH ME.
FORGET IT.
IT'S NICE TO BE WITH SOMEONE WHO CAN DEAL WITH MY MOOD SWINGS.
THE DRAMAMINE HELPS.
7/25
©2012 ZITS Partnership. Dist. by King Features
SCOTT and BORGMAN

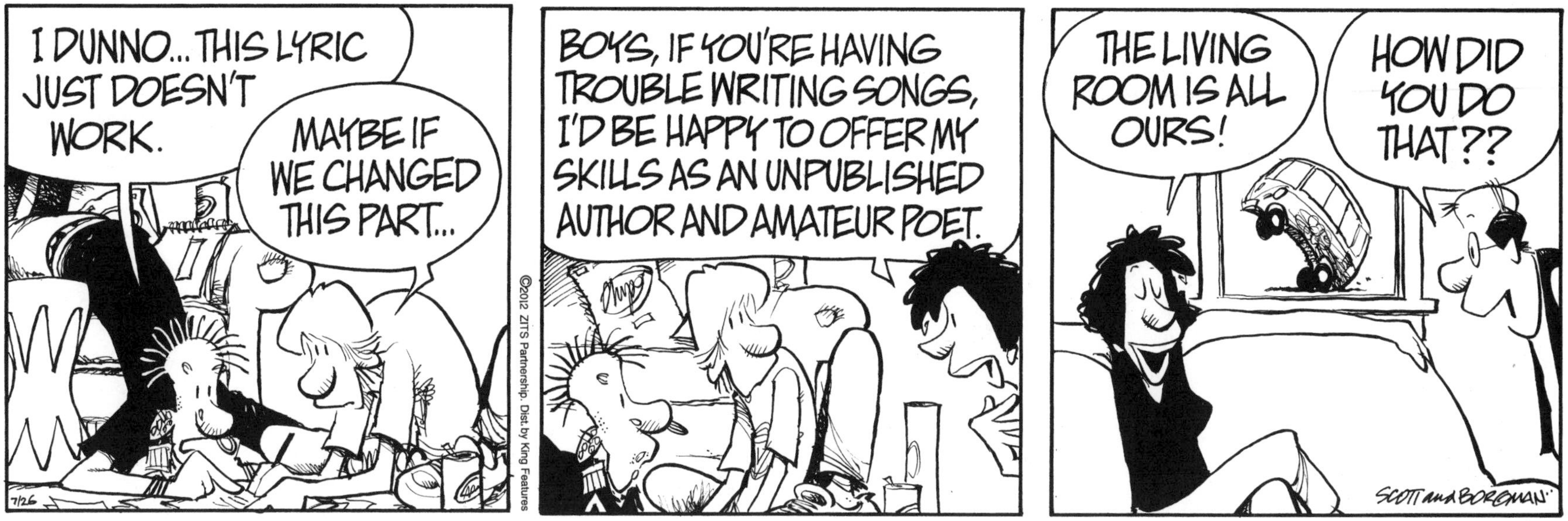
I DUNNO... THIS LYRIC JUST DOESN'T WORK.
MAYBE IF WE CHANGED THIS PART...
BOYS, IF YOU'RE HAVING TROUBLE WRITING SONGS, I'D BE HAPPY TO OFFER MY SKILLS AS AN UNPUBLISHED AUTHOR AND AMATEUR POET.
THE LIVING ROOM IS ALL OURS!
HOW DID YOU DO THAT??
7/26
©2012 ZITS Partnership. Dist. by King Features
SCOTT and BORGMAN

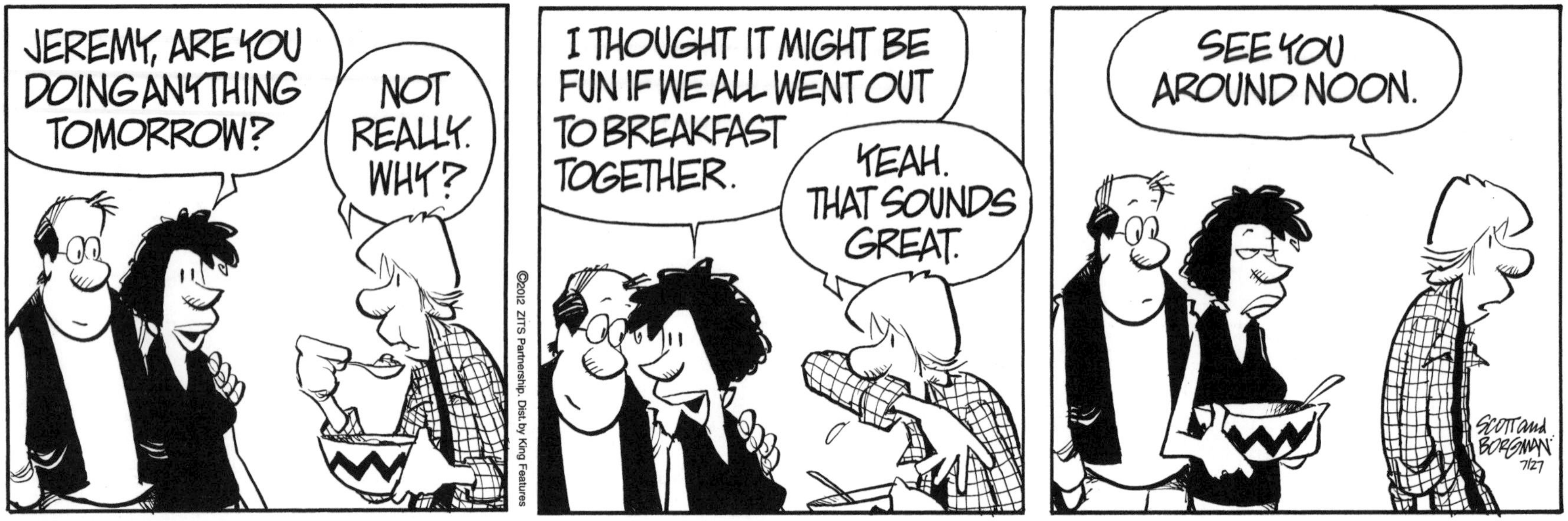
JEREMY, ARE YOU DOING ANYTHING TOMORROW?
NOT REALLY. WHY?
©2012 ZITS Partnership. Dist. by King Features
I THOUGHT IT MIGHT BE FUN IF WE ALL WENT OUT TO BREAKFAST TOGETHER.
YEAH. THAT SOUNDS GREAT.
SEE YOU AROUND NOON.
SCOTT and BORGMAN 7/27

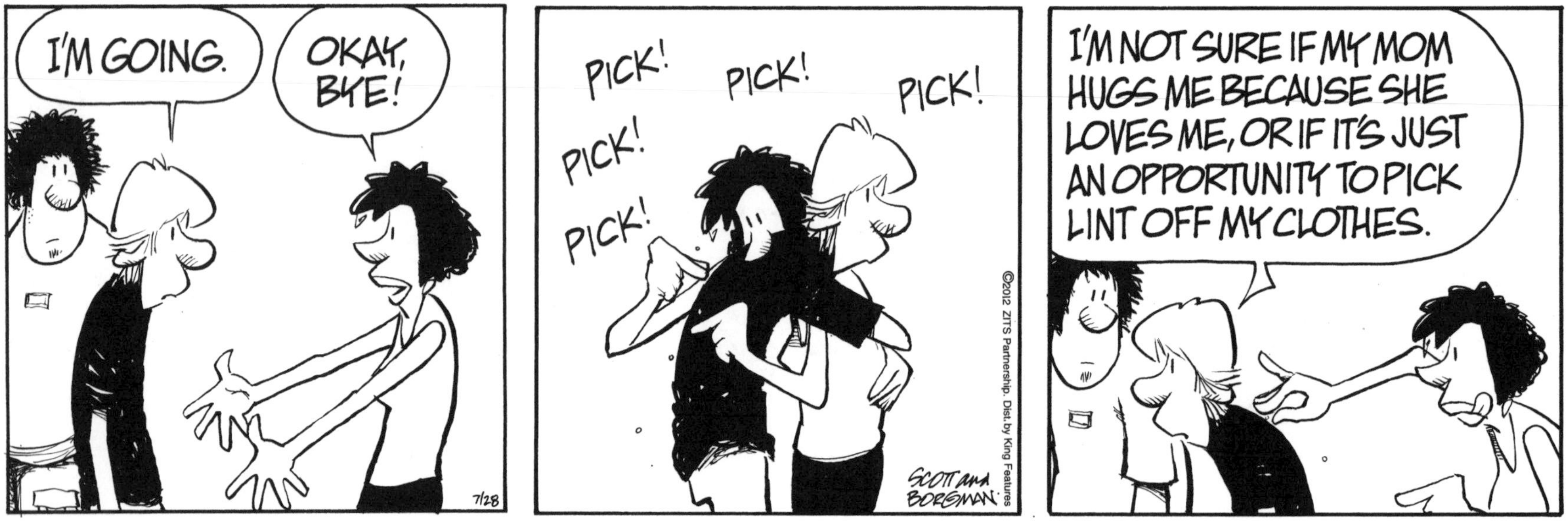
I'M GOING.
OKAY, BYE!
7/28
PICK!
PICK!
PICK!
PICK!
PICK!
©2012 ZITS Partnership. Dist. by King Features
SCOTT and BORGMAN
I'M NOT SURE IF MY MOM HUGS ME BECAUSE SHE LOVES ME, OR IF IT'S JUST AN OPPORTUNITY TO PICK LINT OFF MY CLOTHES.

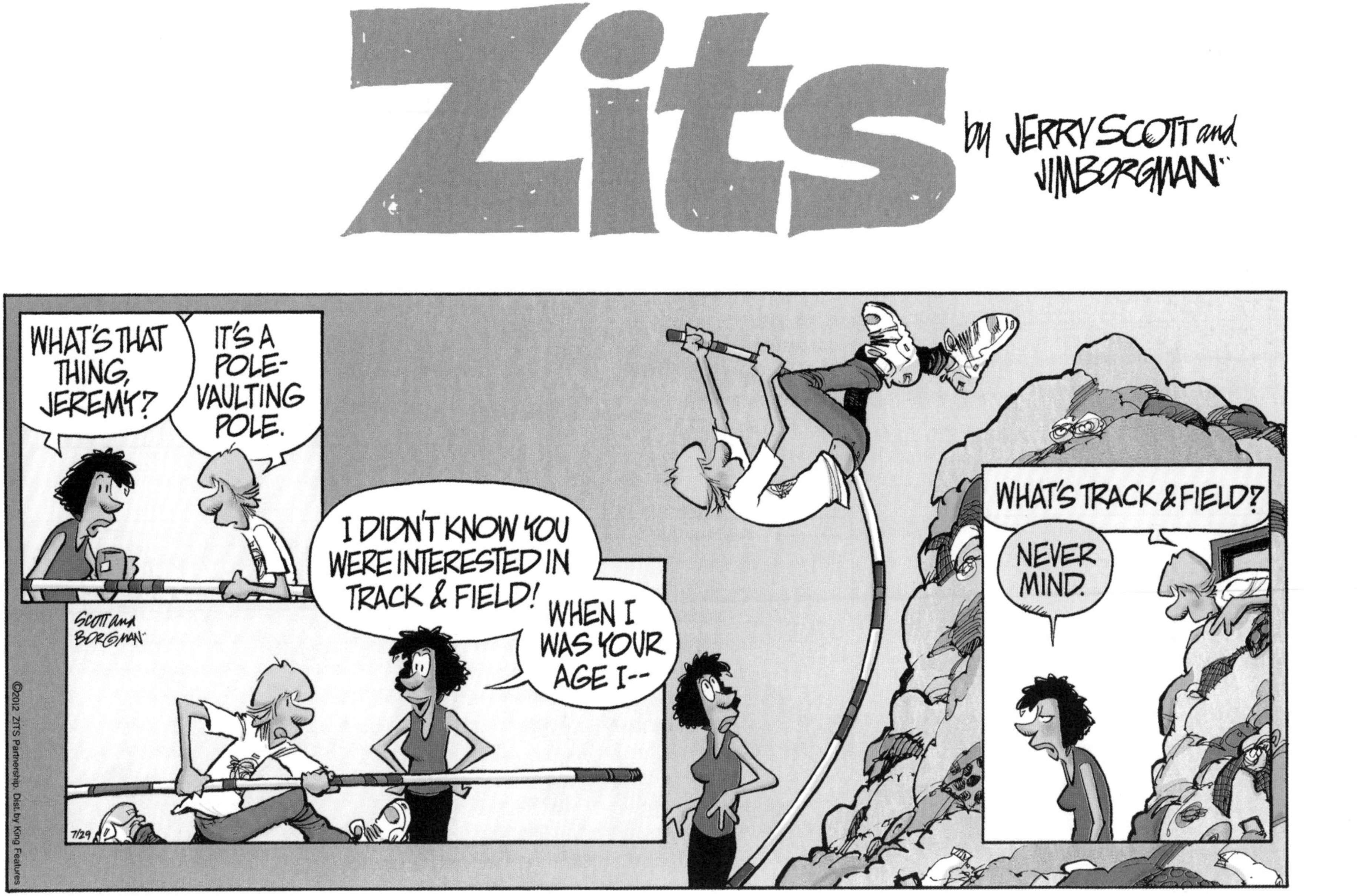

Zits
by JERRY SCOTT and JIM BORGMAN
WHAT'S THAT THING, JEREMY?
IT'S A POLE-VAULTING POLE.
I DIDN'T KNOW YOU WERE INTERESTED IN TRACK & FIELD!
WHEN I WAS YOUR AGE I--
WHAT'S TRACK & FIELD?
NEVER MIND.
SCOTT and BORGMAN
7/29
©2012 ZITS Partnership. Dist. by King Features

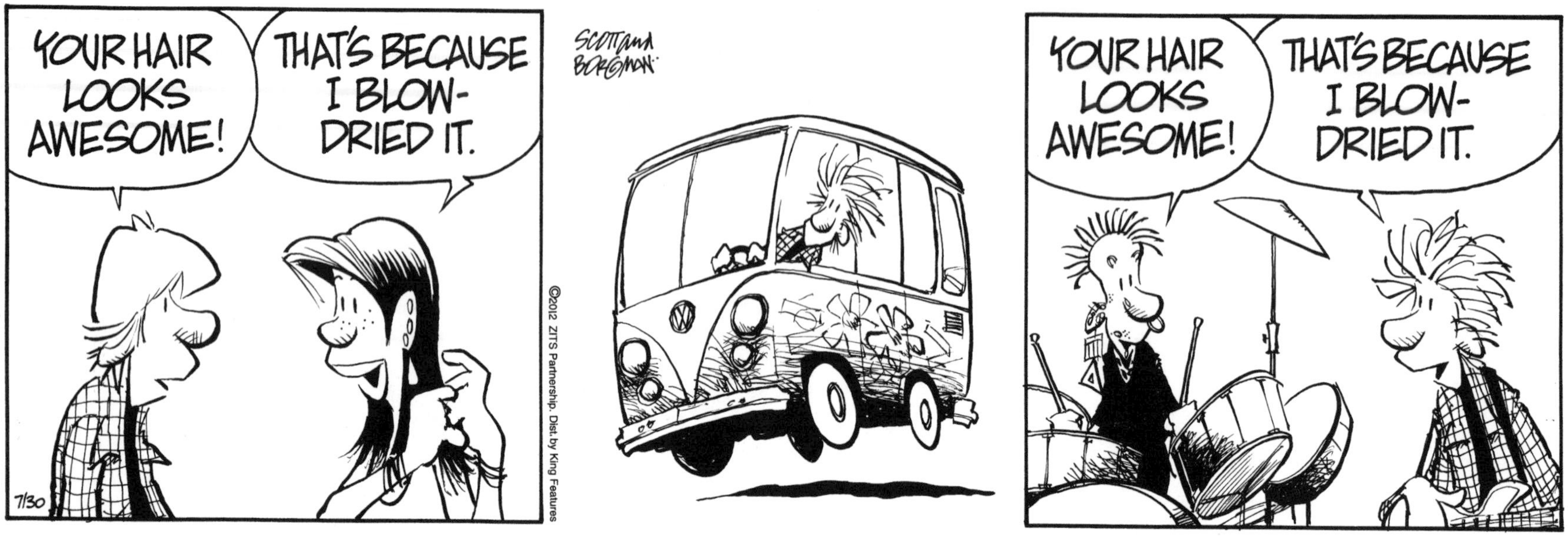
YOUR HAIR LOOKS AWESOME!
THAT'S BECAUSE I BLOW-DRIED IT.
7/30
©2012 ZITS Partnership. Dist. by King Features
SCOTT AND BORGMAN
YOUR HAIR LOOKS AWESOME!
THAT'S BECAUSE I BLOW-DRIED IT.

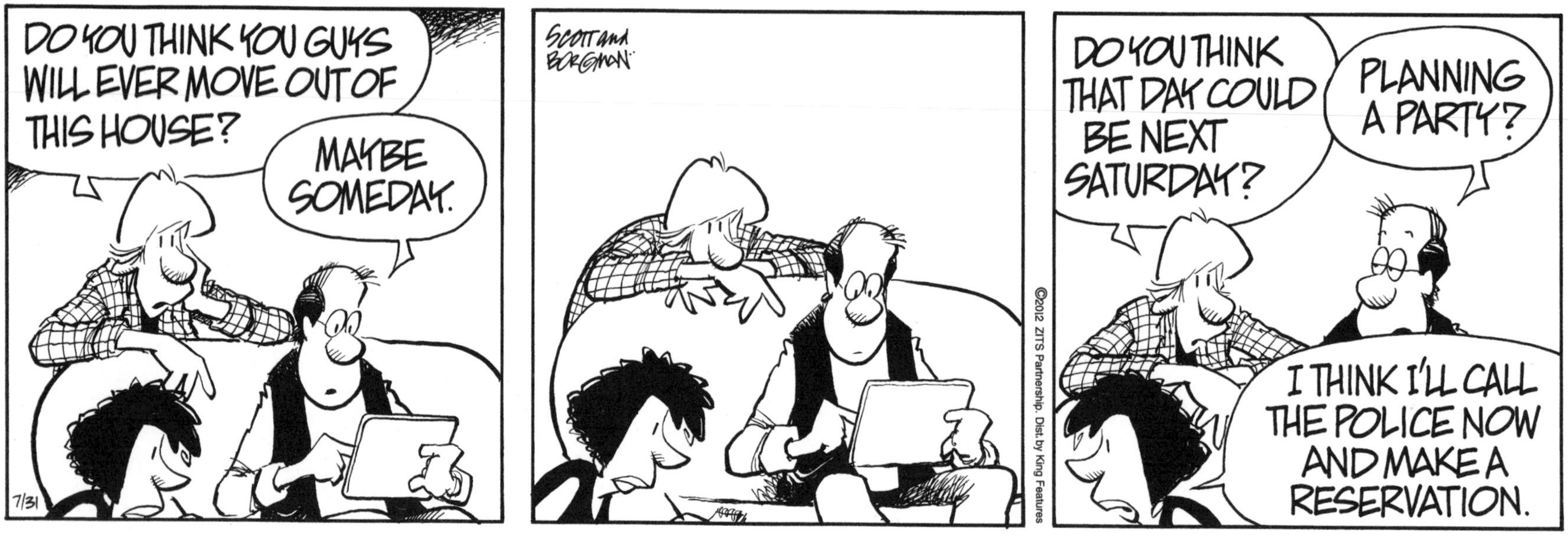
DO YOU THINK YOU GUYS WILL EVER MOVE OUT OF THIS HOUSE?
MAYBE SOMEDAY.
7/31
SCOTT AND BORGMAN
©2012 ZITS Partnership. Dist. by King Features
DO YOU THINK THAT DAY COULD BE NEXT SATURDAY?
PLANNING A PARTY?
I THINK I'LL CALL THE POLICE NOW AND MAKE A RESERVATION.

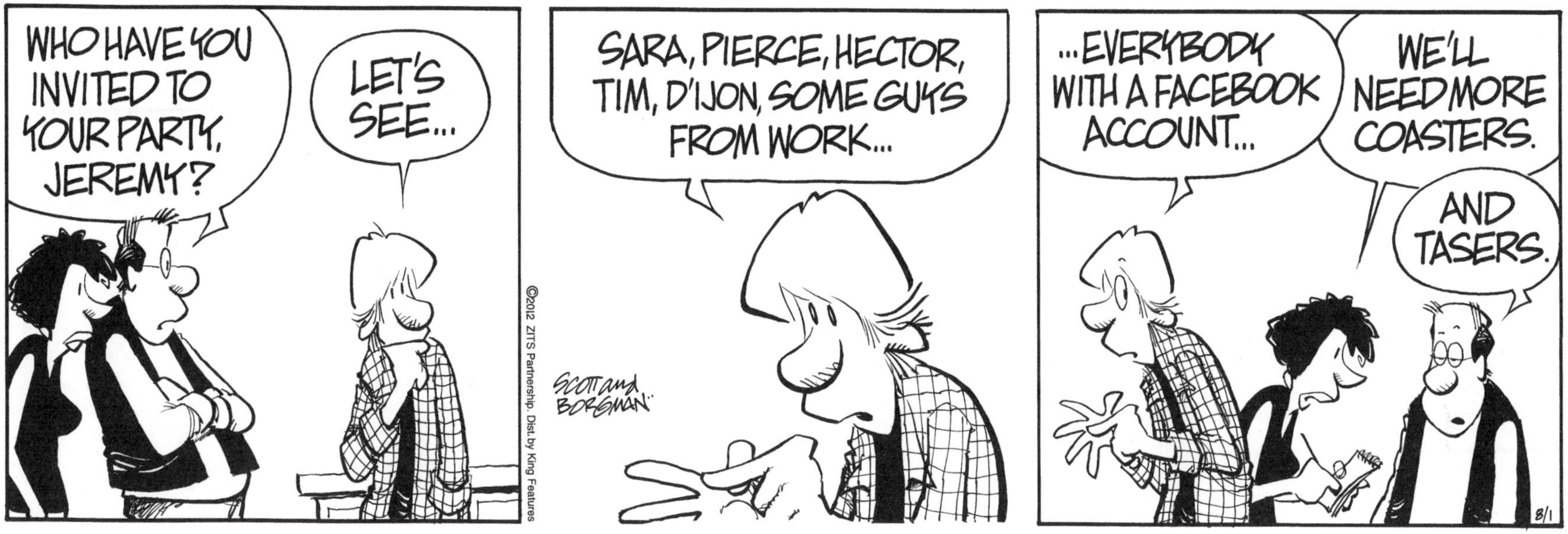
WHO HAVE YOU INVITED TO YOUR PARTY, JEREMY?
LET'S SEE...
SARA, PIERCE, HECTOR, TIM, D'IJON, SOME GUYS FROM WORK...
...EVERYBODY WITH A FACEBOOK ACCOUNT...
WE'LL NEED MORE COASTERS.
AND TASERS.
©2012 ZITS Partnership. Dist. by King Features
SCOTT and BORGMAN
8/1

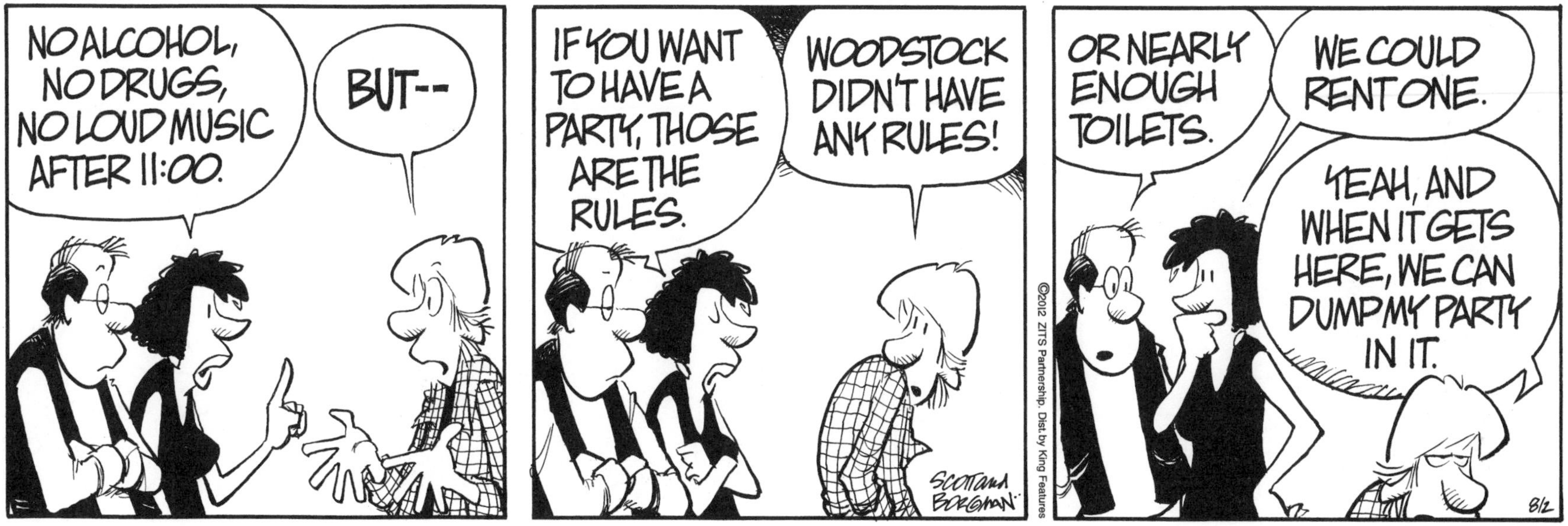
NO ALCOHOL, NO DRUGS, NO LOUD MUSIC AFTER 11:00.
BUT--
IF YOU WANT TO HAVE A PARTY, THOSE ARE THE RULES.
WOODSTOCK DIDN'T HAVE ANY RULES!
OR NEARLY ENOUGH TOILETS.
WE COULD RENT ONE.
YEAH, AND WHEN IT GETS HERE, WE CAN DUMP MY PARTY IN IT.
©2012 ZITS Partnership. Dist. by King Features
SCOTT and BORGMAN
8/2

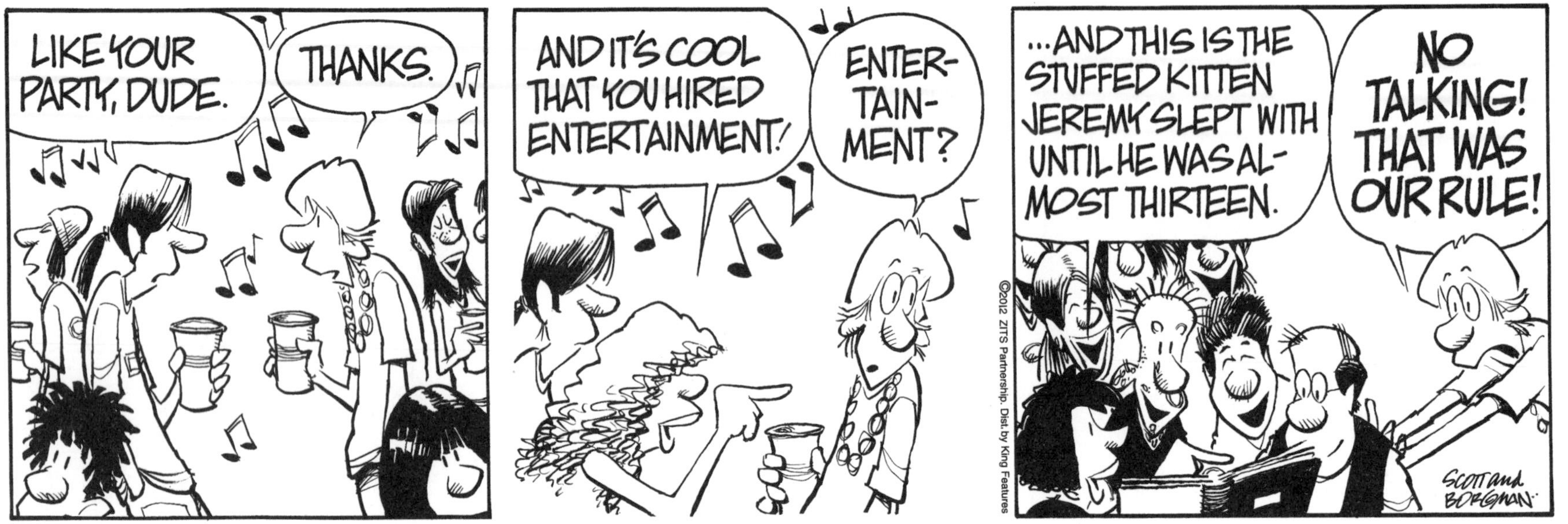
LIKE YOUR PARTY, DUDE.
THANKS.
AND IT'S COOL THAT YOU HIRED ENTERTAINMENT!
ENTER-TAIN-MENT?
...AND THIS IS THE STUFFED KITTEN JEREMY SLEPT WITH UNTIL HE WAS AL-MOST THIRTEEN.
NO TALKING! THAT WAS OUR RULE!
©2012 ZITS Partnership. Dist. by King Features
SCOTT AND BORGMAN

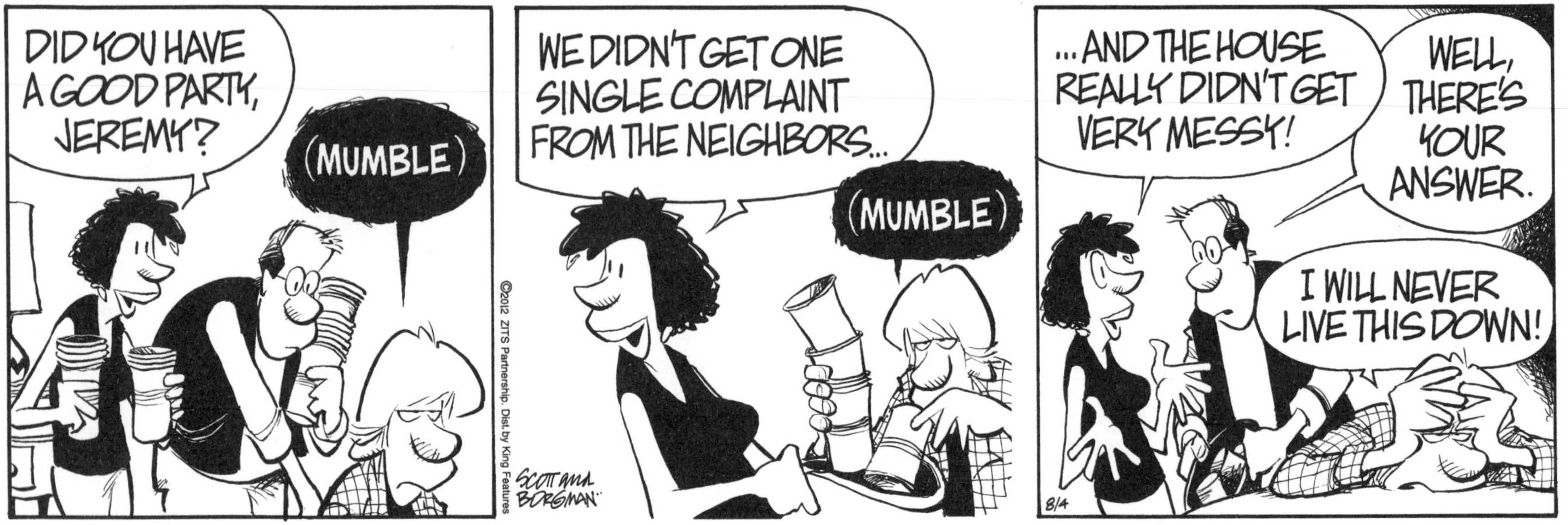
DID YOU HAVE A GOOD PARTY, JEREMY?
(MUMBLE)
WE DIDN'T GET ONE SINGLE COMPLAINT FROM THE NEIGHBORS...
(MUMBLE)
...AND THE HOUSE REALLY DIDN'T GET VERY MESSY!
WELL, THERE'S YOUR ANSWER.
I WILL NEVER LIVE THIS DOWN!
©2012 ZITS Partnership. Dist. by King Features
SCOTT AND BORGMAN
8/4

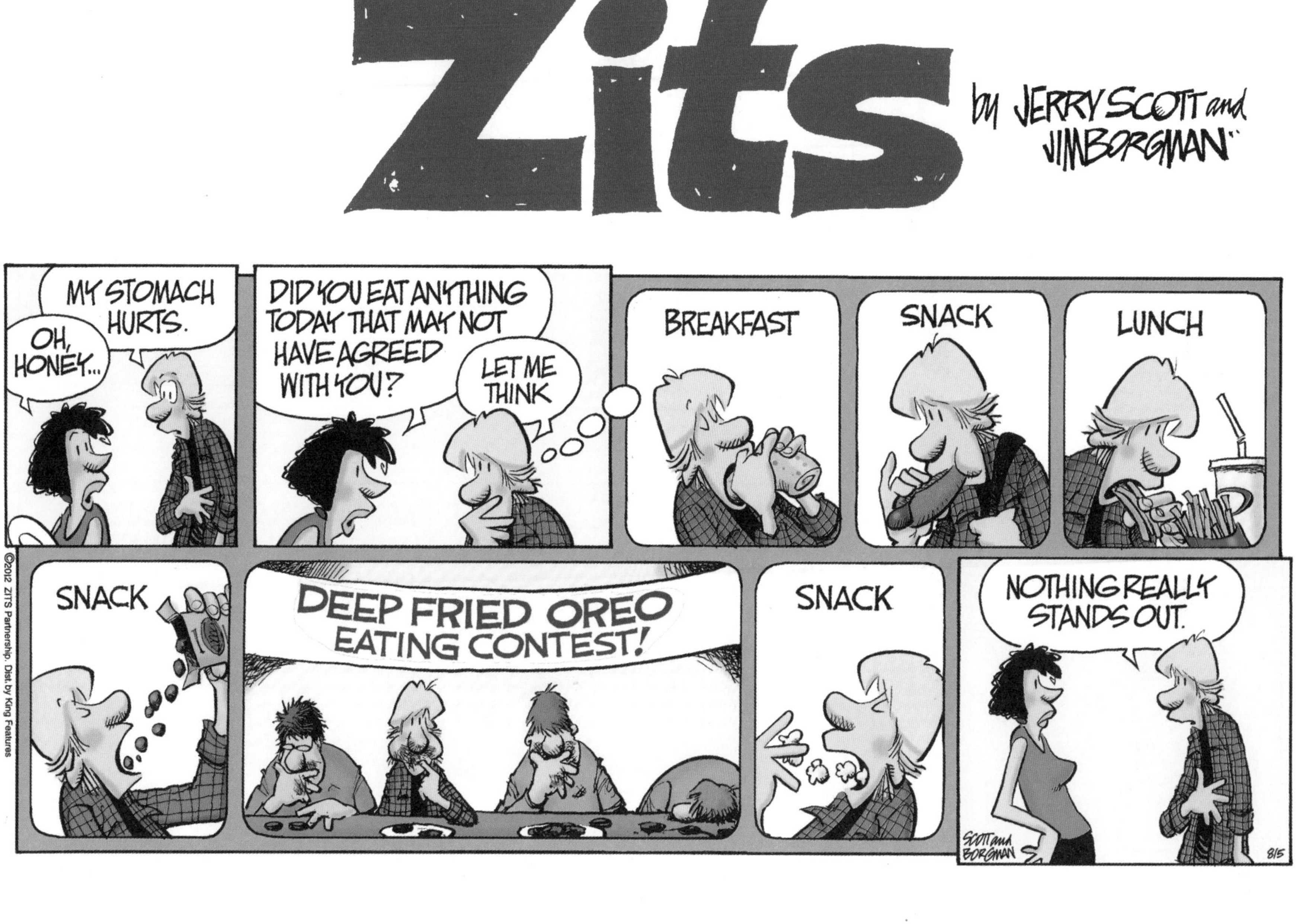
Zits
by JERRY SCOTT and JIM BORGMAN
MY STOMACH HURTS.
OH, HONEY...
DID YOU EAT ANYTHING TODAY THAT MAY NOT HAVE AGREED WITH YOU?
LET ME THINK
BREAKFAST
SNACK
LUNCH
SNACK
DEEP FRIED OREO EATING CONTEST!
SNACK
NOTHING REALLY STANDS OUT.
SCOTT and BORGMAN
8/15
©2012 ZITS Partnership. Dist. by King Features

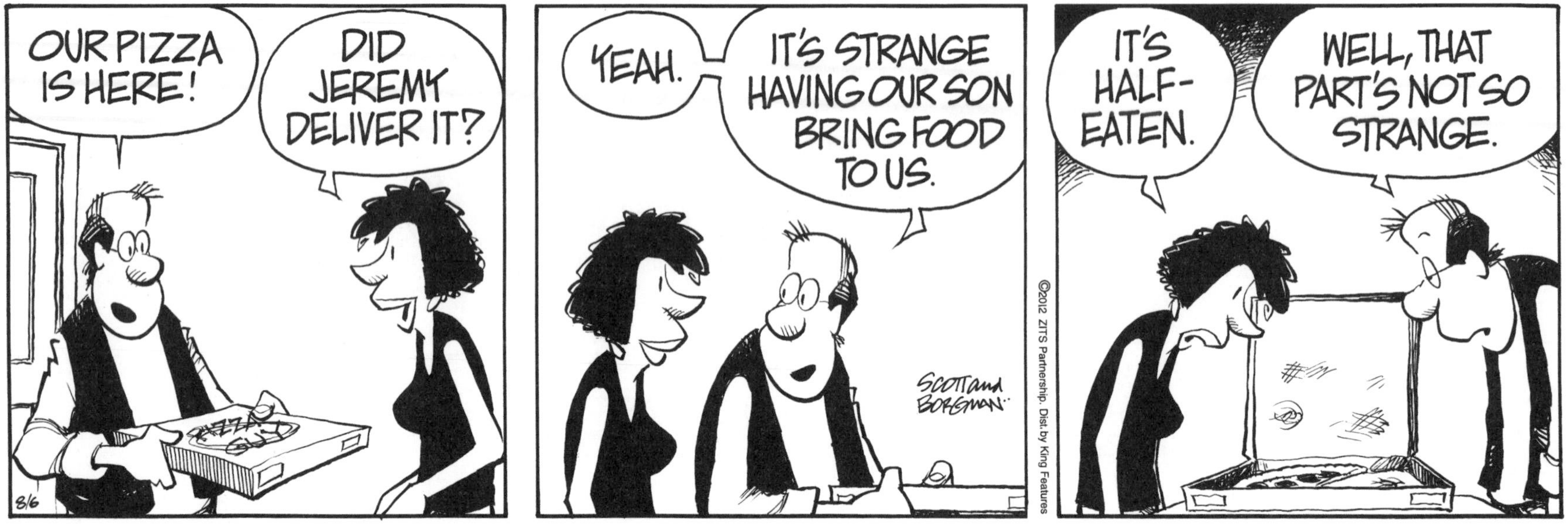
OUR PIZZA IS HERE!
DID JEREMY DELIVER IT?
8/6
YEAH.
IT'S STRANGE HAVING OUR SON BRING FOOD TO US.
SCOTT and BORGMAN
©2012 ZITS Partnership. Dist. by King Features
IT'S HALF-EATEN.
WELL, THAT PART'S NOT SO STRANGE.

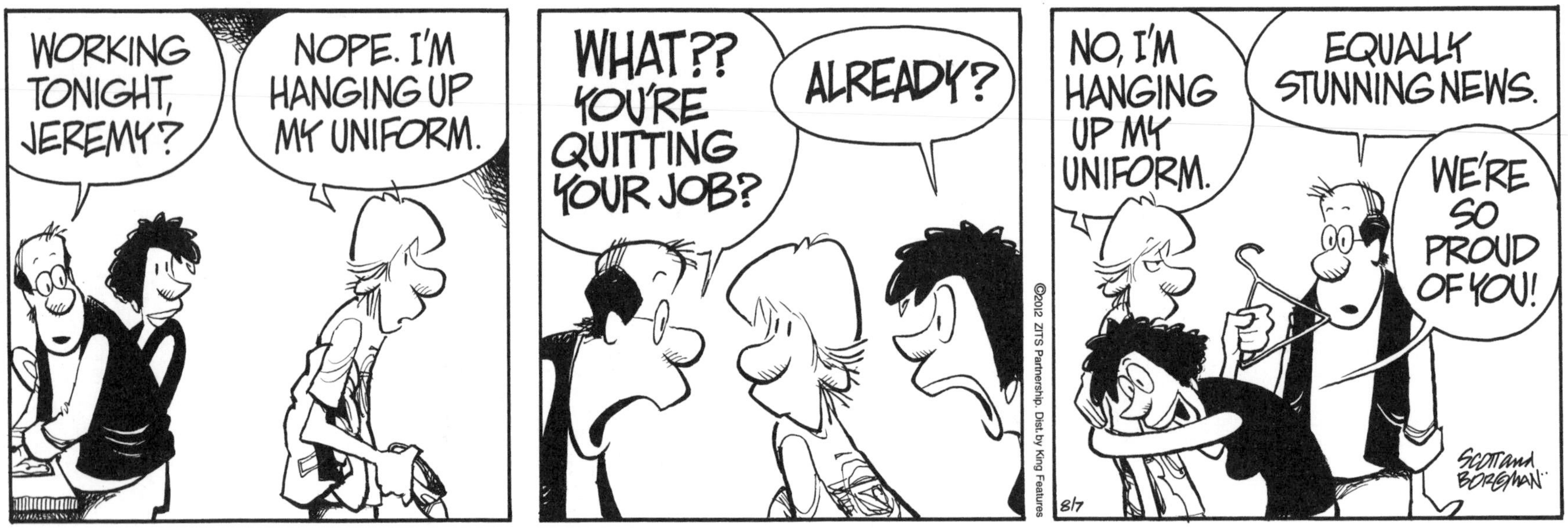
WORKING TONIGHT, JEREMY?
NOPE. I'M HANGING UP MY UNIFORM.
WHAT?? YOU'RE QUITTING YOUR JOB?
ALREADY?
©2012 ZITS Partnership. Dist. by King Features
NO, I'M HANGING UP MY UNIFORM.
EQUALLY STUNNING NEWS.
WE'RE SO PROUD OF YOU!
8/7
SCOTT and BORGMAN

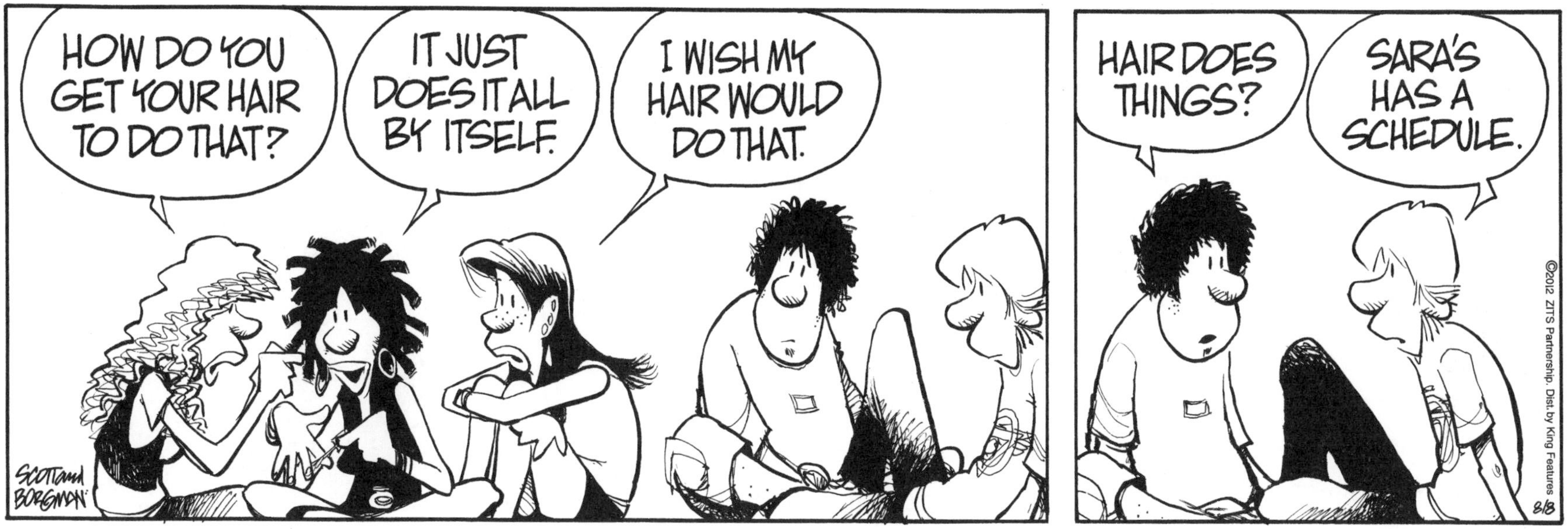
HOW DO YOU GET YOUR HAIR TO DO THAT?
IT JUST DOES IT ALL BY ITSELF.
I WISH MY HAIR WOULD DO THAT.
HAIR DOES THINGS?
SARA'S HAS A SCHEDULE.
SCOTT and BORGMAN
©2012 ZITS Partnership. Dist. by King Features
8/8

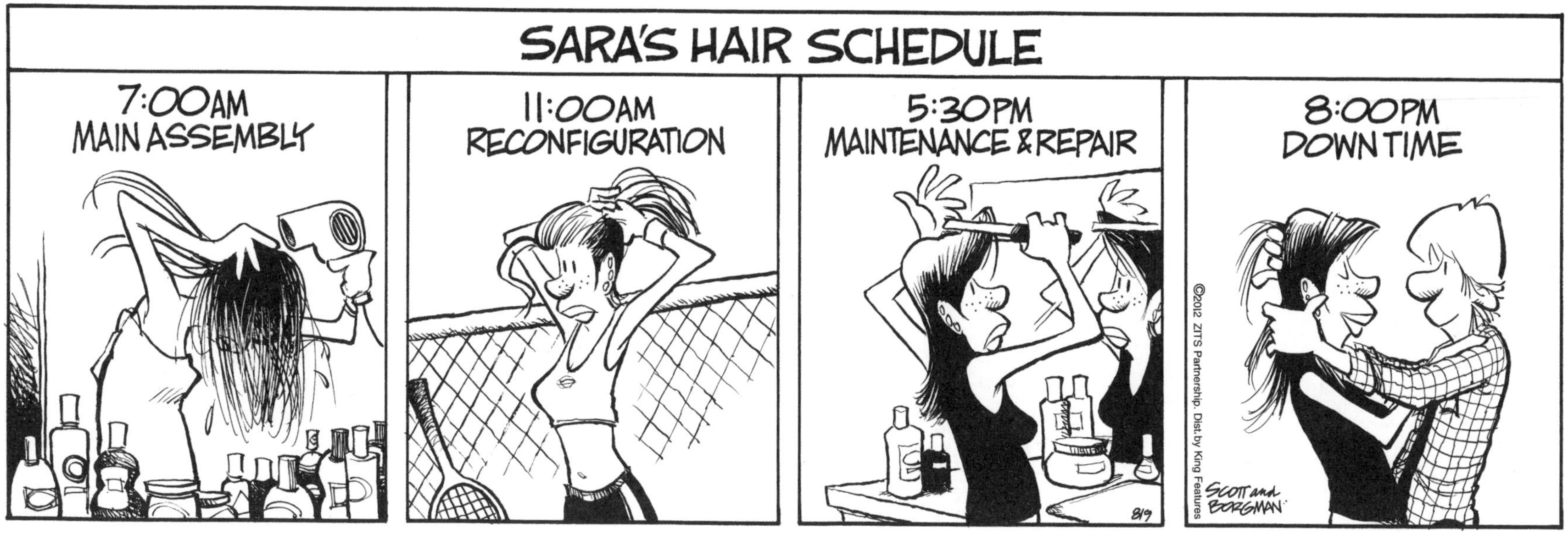
SARA'S HAIR SCHEDULE
7:00AM MAIN ASSEMBLY
11:00AM RECONFIGURATION
5:30PM MAINTENANCE & REPAIR
8:00PM DOWN TIME
8/9
©2012 ZITS Partnership. Dist. by King Features
SCOTT and BORGMAN

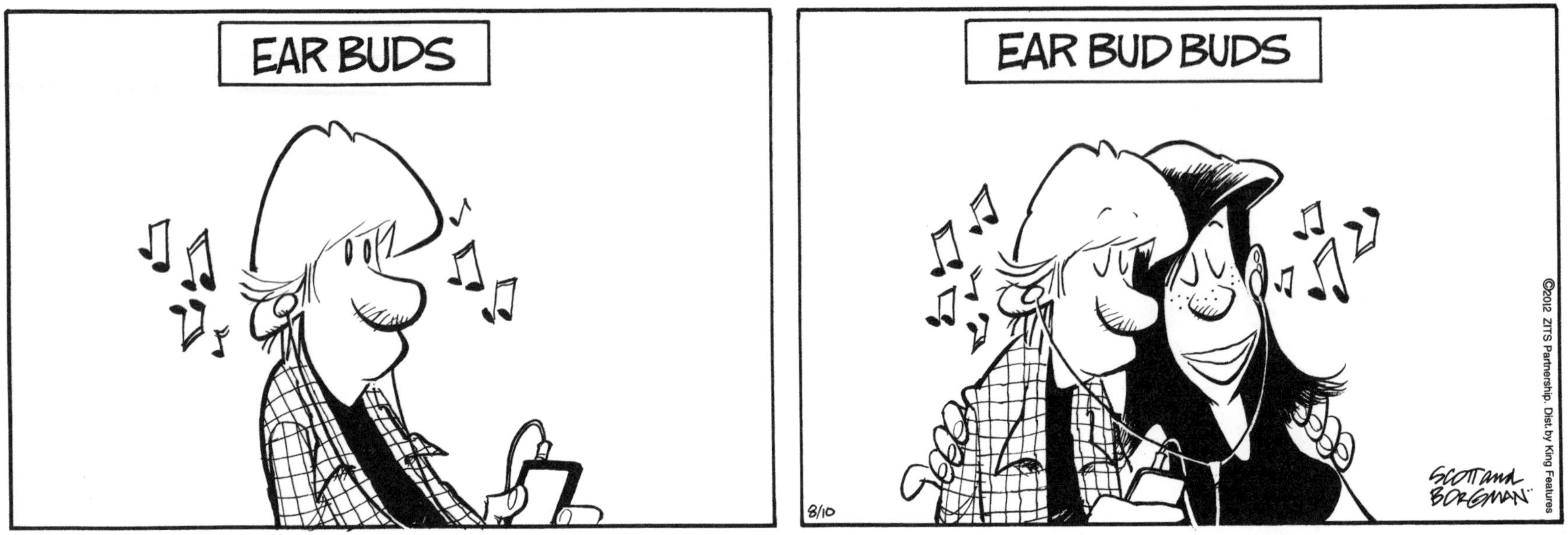
EAR BUDS
EAR BUD BUDS
8/10
SCOTT and BORGMAN
©2012 ZITS Partnership. Dist. by King Features

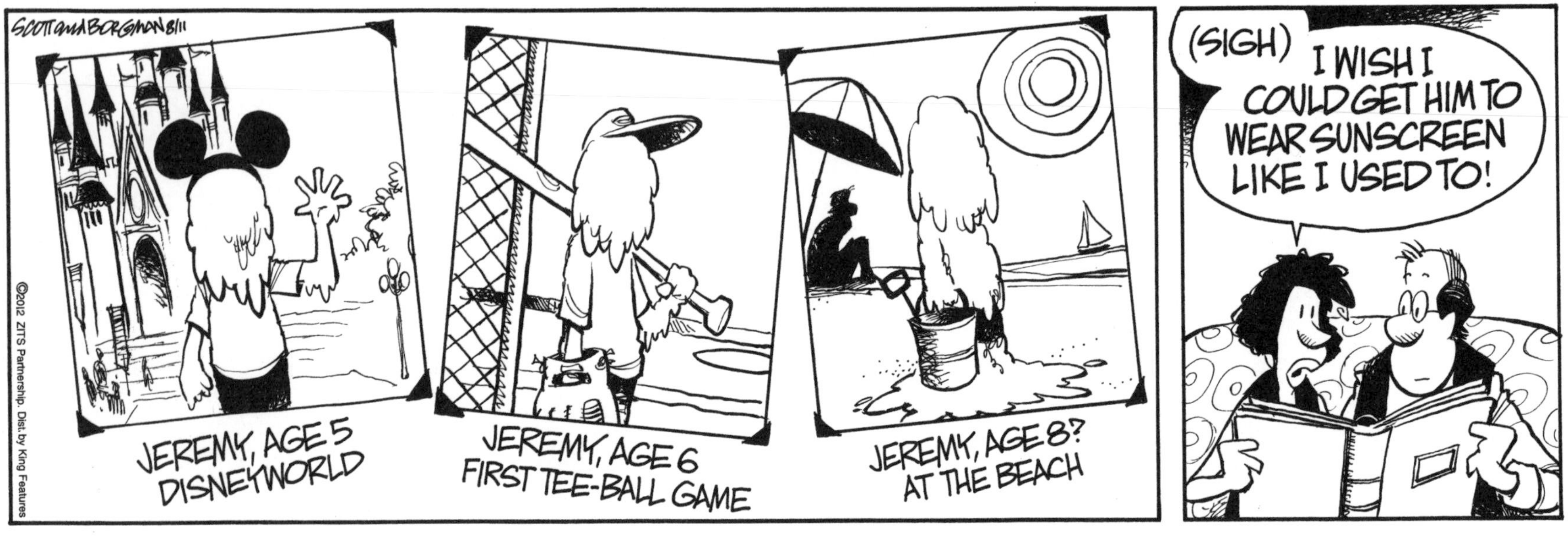
SCOTT and BORGMAN 8/11
JEREMY, AGE 5 DISNEYWORLD
JEREMY, AGE 6 FIRST TEE-BALL GAME
JEREMY, AGE 8? AT THE BEACH
(SIGH)
I WISH I COULD GET HIM TO WEAR SUNSCREEN LIKE I USED TO!
©2012 ZITS Partnership. Dist. by King Features

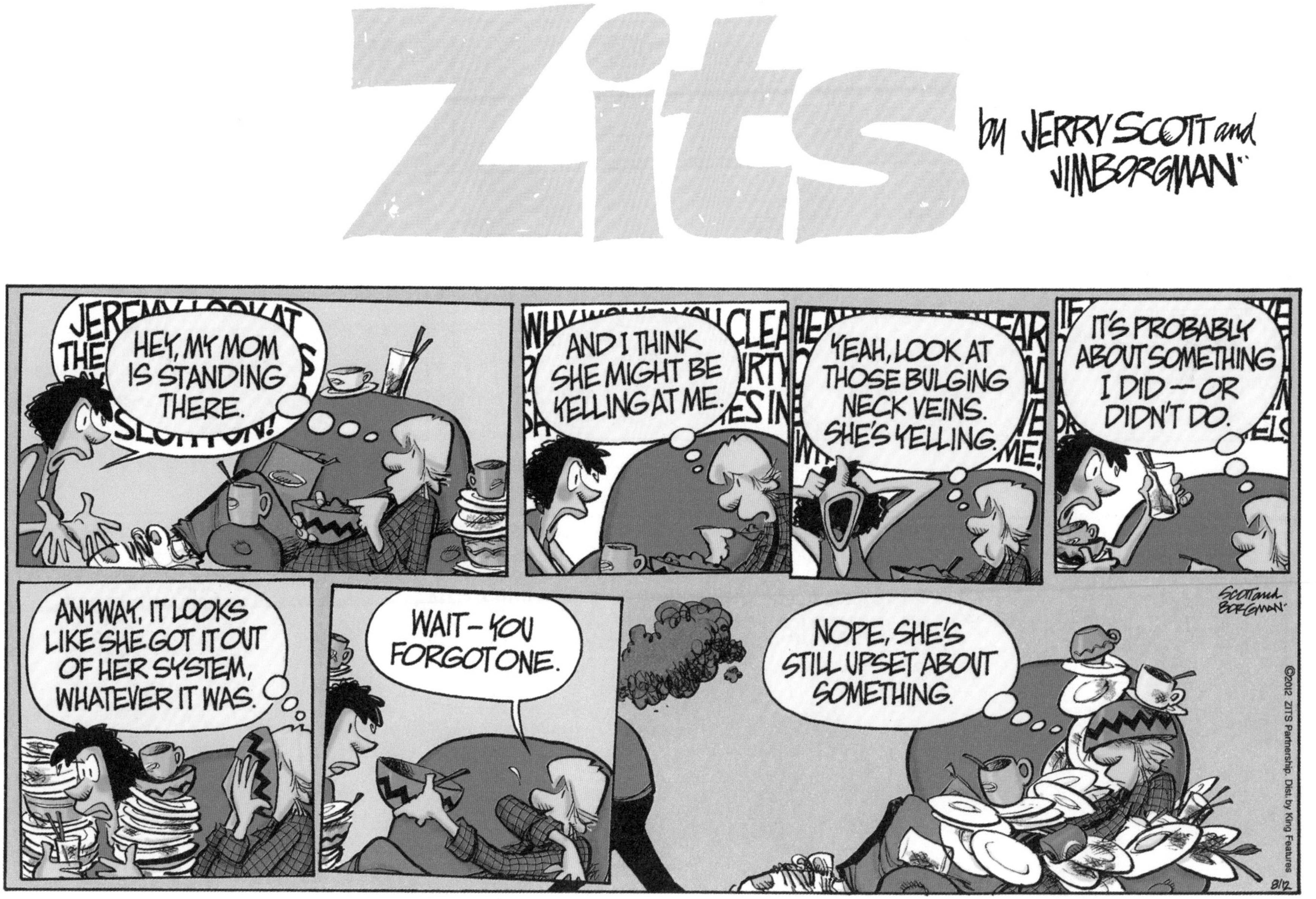
Zits
by JERRY SCOTT and JIM BORGMAN
HEY, MY MOM IS STANDING THERE.
AND I THINK SHE MIGHT BE YELLING AT ME.
YEAH, LOOK AT THOSE BULGING NECK VEINS. SHE'S YELLING.
IT'S PROBABLY ABOUT SOMETHING I DID -- OR DIDN'T DO.
ANYWAY, IT LOOKS LIKE SHE GOT IT OUT OF HER SYSTEM, WHATEVER IT WAS.
WAIT - YOU FORGOT ONE.
NOPE, SHE'S STILL UPSET ABOUT SOMETHING.
SCOTT and BORGMAN
©2012 ZITS Partnership. Dist. by King Features

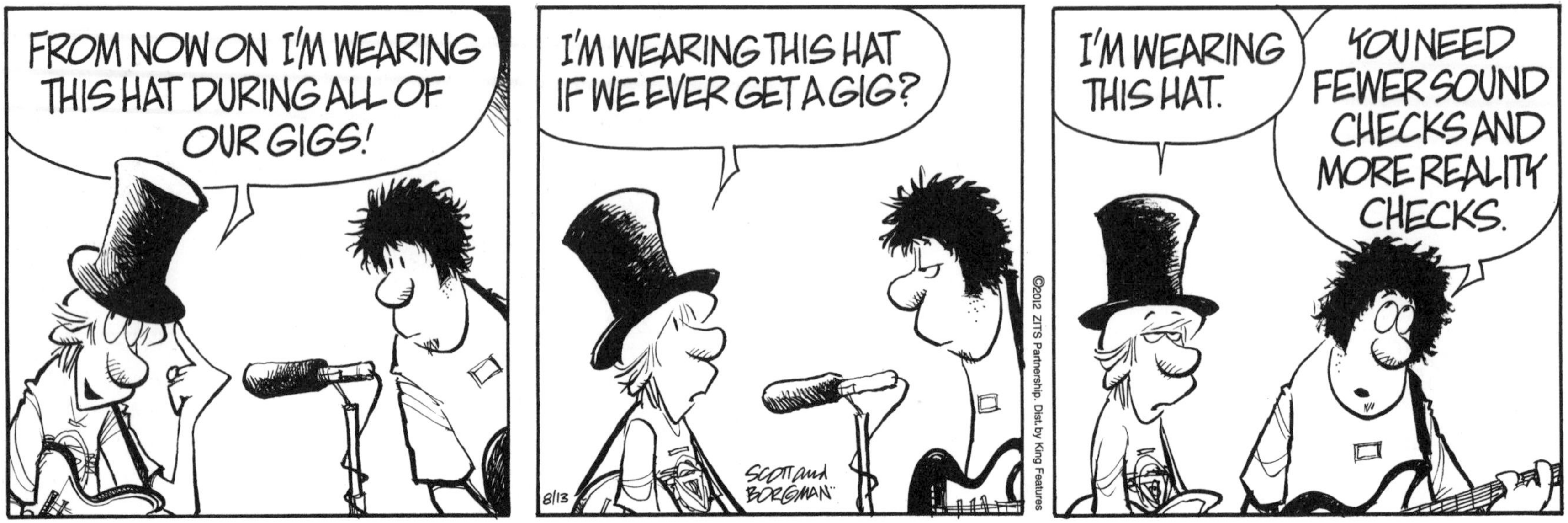
FROM NOW ON I'M WEARING THIS HAT DURING ALL OF OUR GIGS!
I'M WEARING THIS HAT IF WE EVER GET A GIG?
I'M WEARING THIS HAT.
YOU NEED FEWER SOUND CHECKS AND MORE REALITY CHECKS.
8/13
SCOTT and BORGMAN
©2012 ZITS Partnership. Dist. by King Features

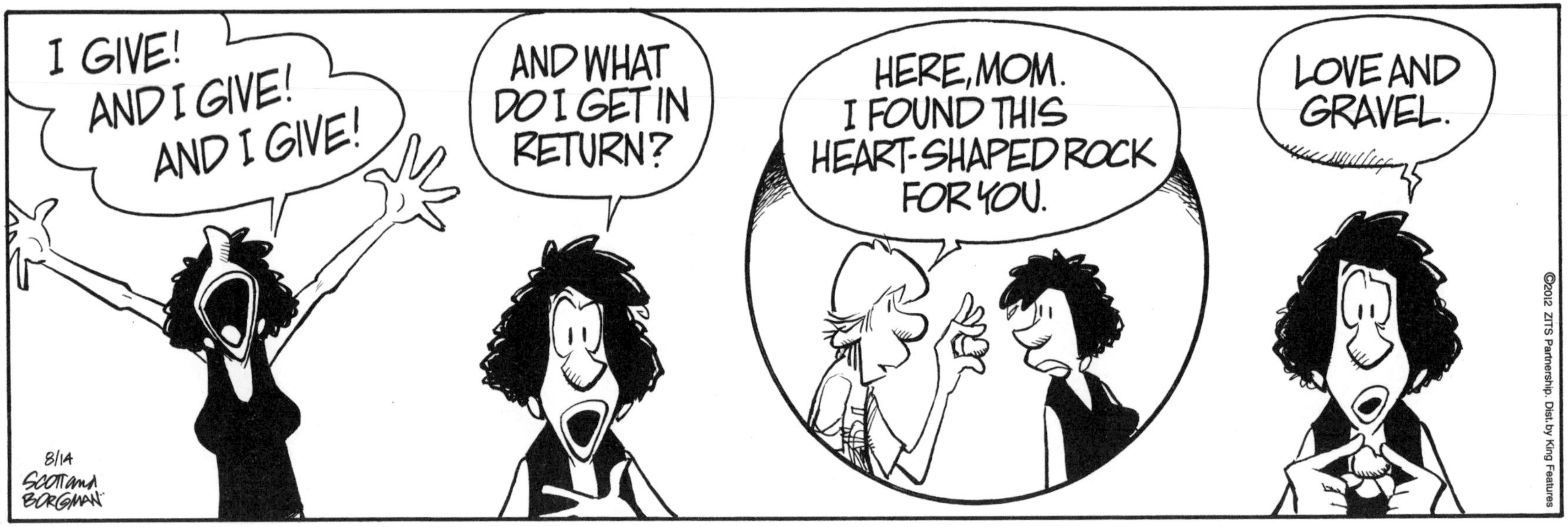
I GIVE! AND I GIVE! AND I GIVE!
AND WHAT DO I GET IN RETURN?
HERE, MOM. I FOUND THIS HEART-SHAPED ROCK FOR YOU.
LOVE AND GRAVEL.
8/14
SCOTT and BORGMAN
©2012 ZITS Partnership. Dist. by King Features

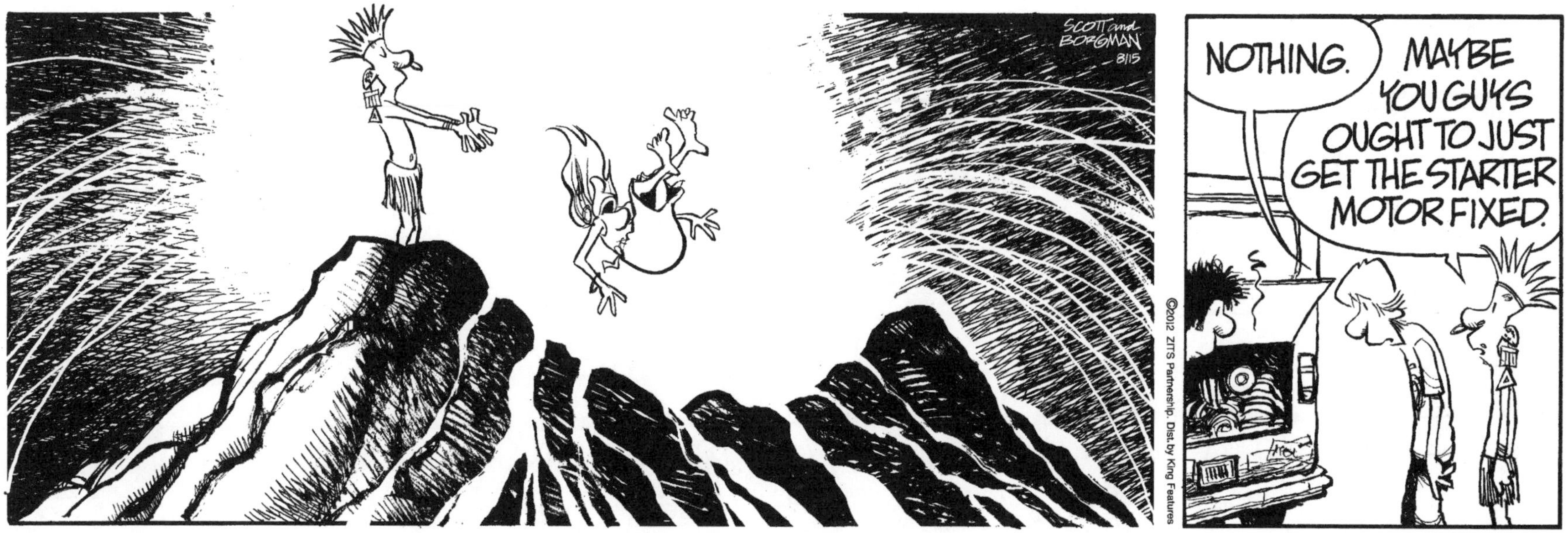
SCOTT and BORGMAN 8/15
NOTHING.
MAYBE YOU GUYS OUGHT TO JUST GET THE STARTER MOTOR FIXED.
©2012 ZITS Partnership. Dist.by King Features

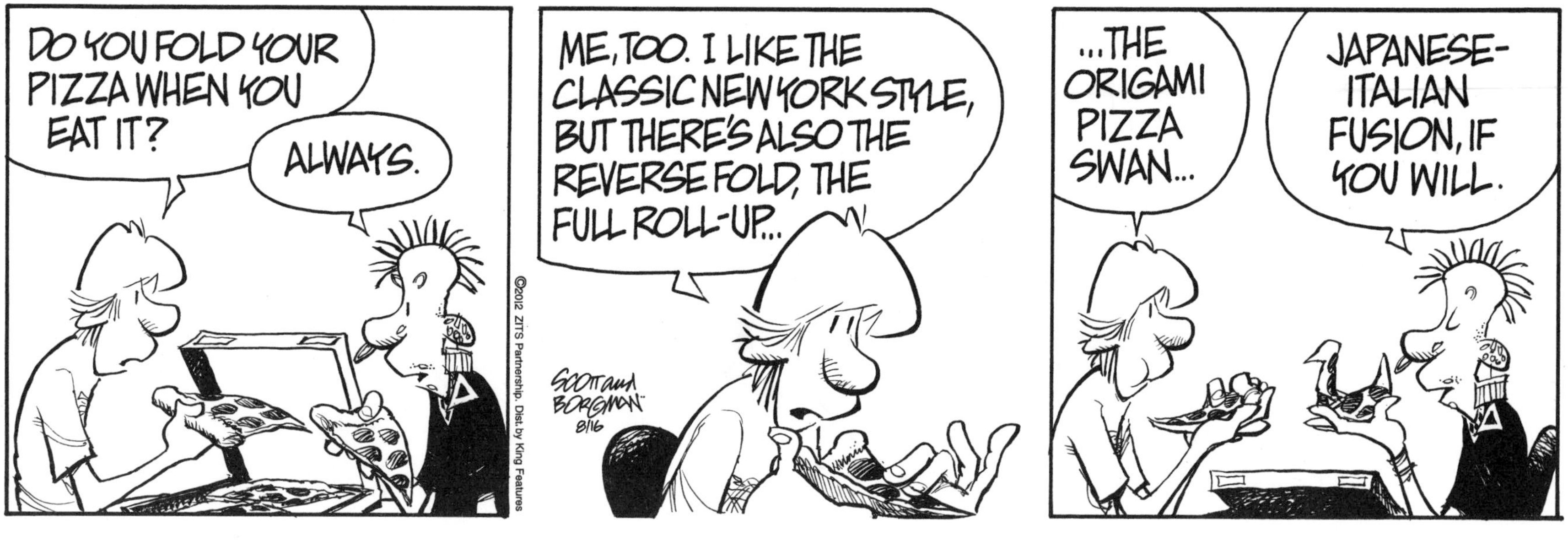
DO YOU FOLD YOUR PIZZA WHEN YOU EAT IT?
ALWAYS.
©2012 ZITS Partnership. Dist.by King Features
ME, TOO. I LIKE THE CLASSIC NEW YORK STYLE, BUT THERE'S ALSO THE REVERSE FOLD, THE FULL ROLL-UP...
SCOTT and BORGMAN 8/16
...THE ORIGAMI PIZZA SWAN...
JAPANESE-ITALIAN FUSION, IF YOU WILL.

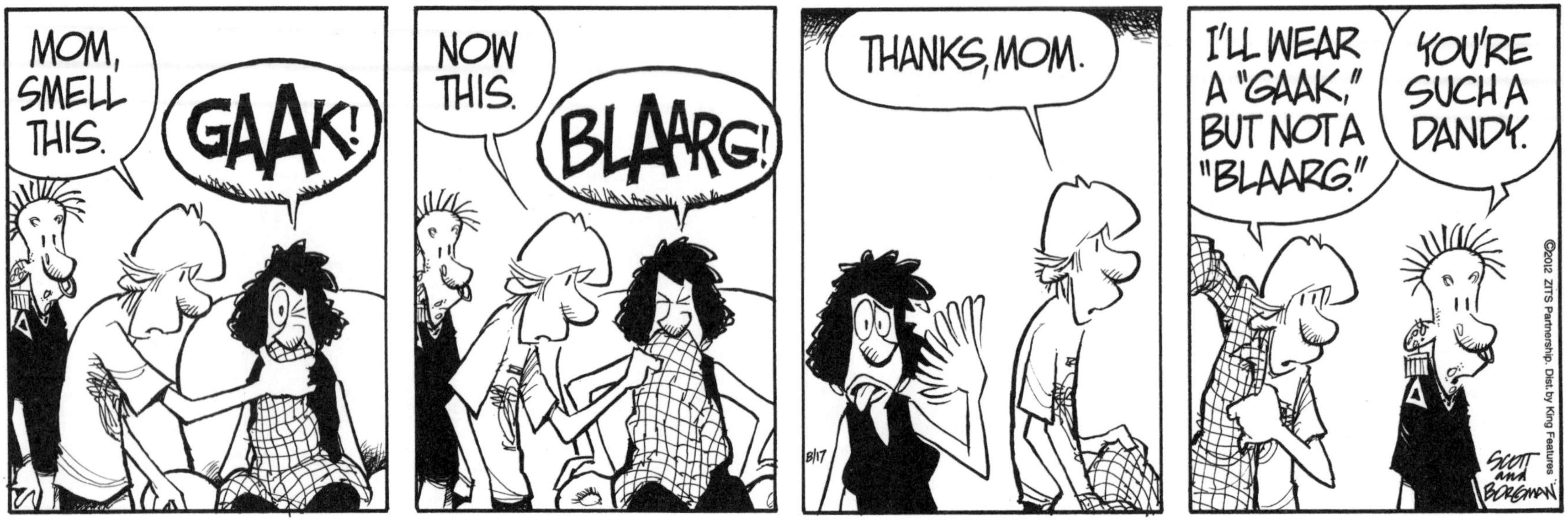
MOM, SMELL THIS.
GAAK!
NOW THIS.
BLAARG!
THANKS, MOM.
8/17
I'LL WEAR A "GAAK," BUT NOT A "BLAARG."
YOU'RE SUCH A DANDY.
©2012 ZITS Partnership. Dist. by King Features
SCOTT and BORGMAN

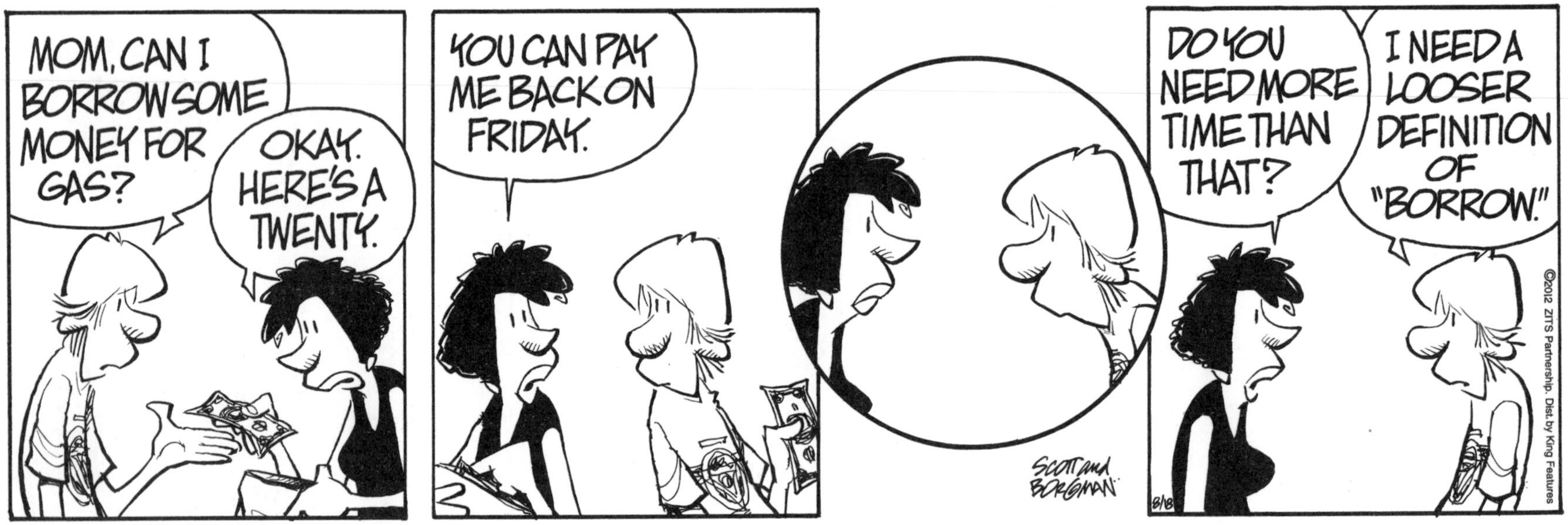
MOM, CAN I BORROW SOME MONEY FOR GAS?
OKAY. HERE'S A TWENTY.
YOU CAN PAY ME BACK ON FRIDAY.
SCOTT AND BORGMAN
8/18
DO YOU NEED MORE TIME THAN THAT?
I NEED A LOOSER DEFINITION OF "BORROW."
©2012 ZITS Partnership. Dist. by King Features

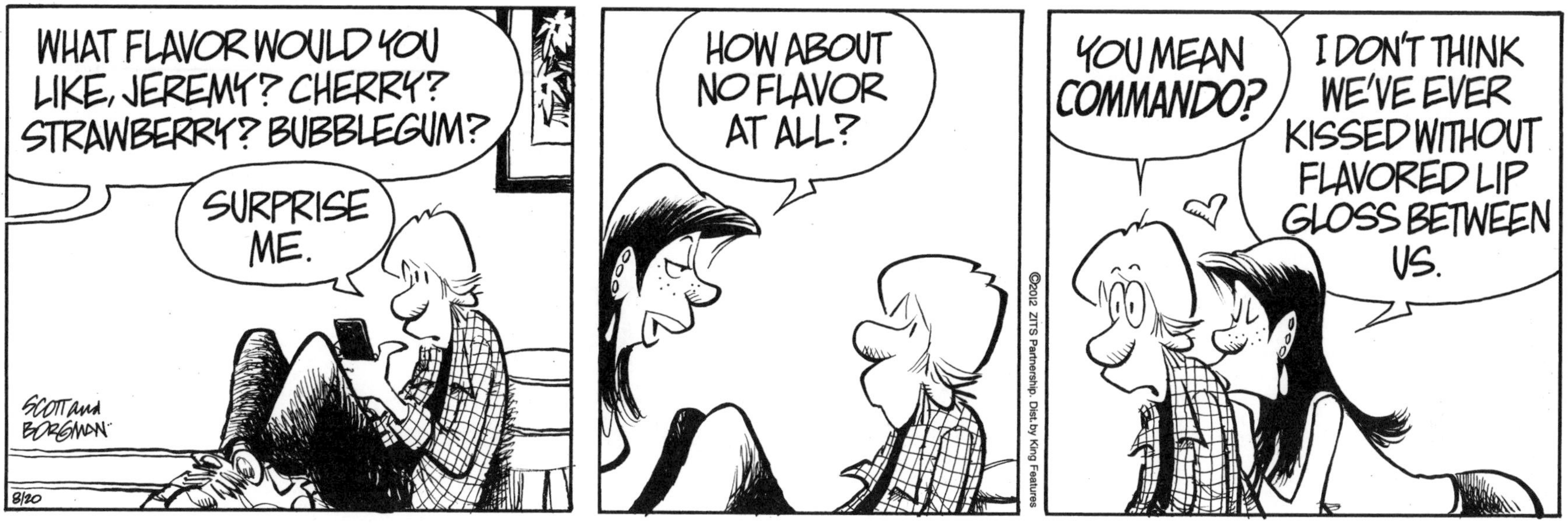
WHAT FLAVOR WOULD YOU LIKE, JEREMY? CHERRY? STRAWBERRY? BUBBLEGUM?
SURPRISE ME.
SCOTT and BORGMAN
8/20
HOW ABOUT NO FLAVOR AT ALL?
©2012 ZITS Partnership. Dist. by King Features
YOU MEAN COMMANDO?
I DON'T THINK WE'VE EVER KISSED WITHOUT FLAVORED LIP GLOSS BETWEEN US.

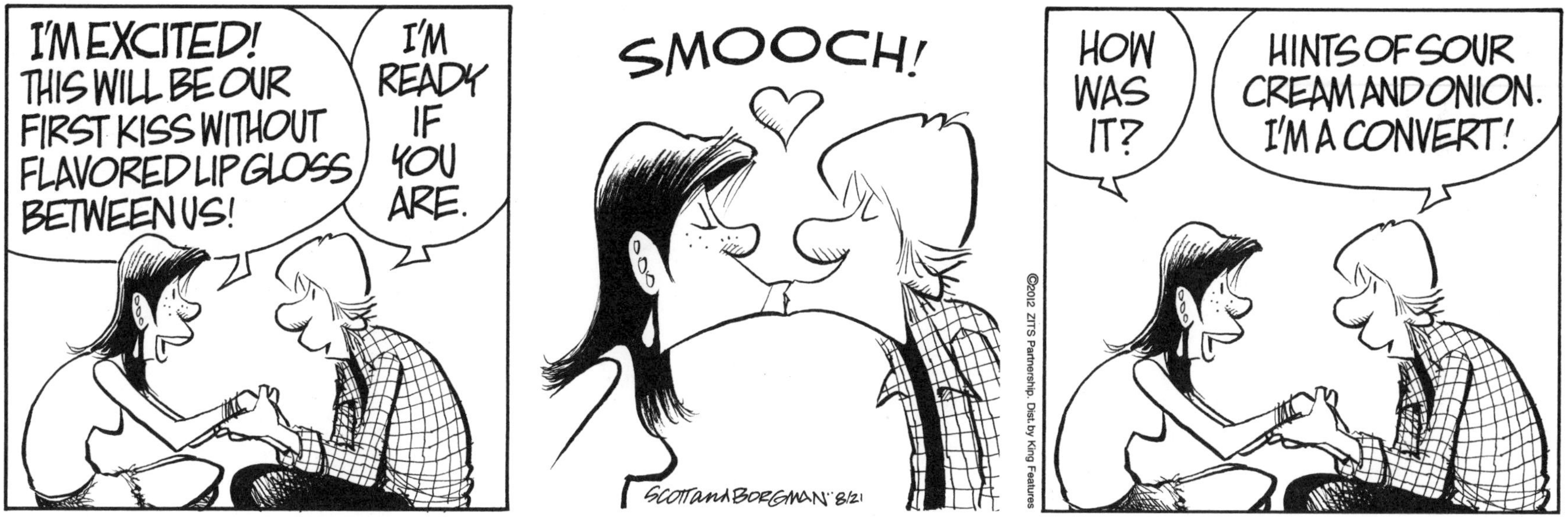
I'M EXCITED! THIS WILL BE OUR FIRST KISS WITHOUT FLAVORED LIP GLOSS BETWEEN US!
I'M READY IF YOU ARE.
SMOOCH!
SCOTT and BORGMAN 8/21
©2012 ZITS Partnership. Dist. by King Features
HOW WAS IT?
HINTS OF SOUR CREAM AND ONION. I'M A CONVERT!

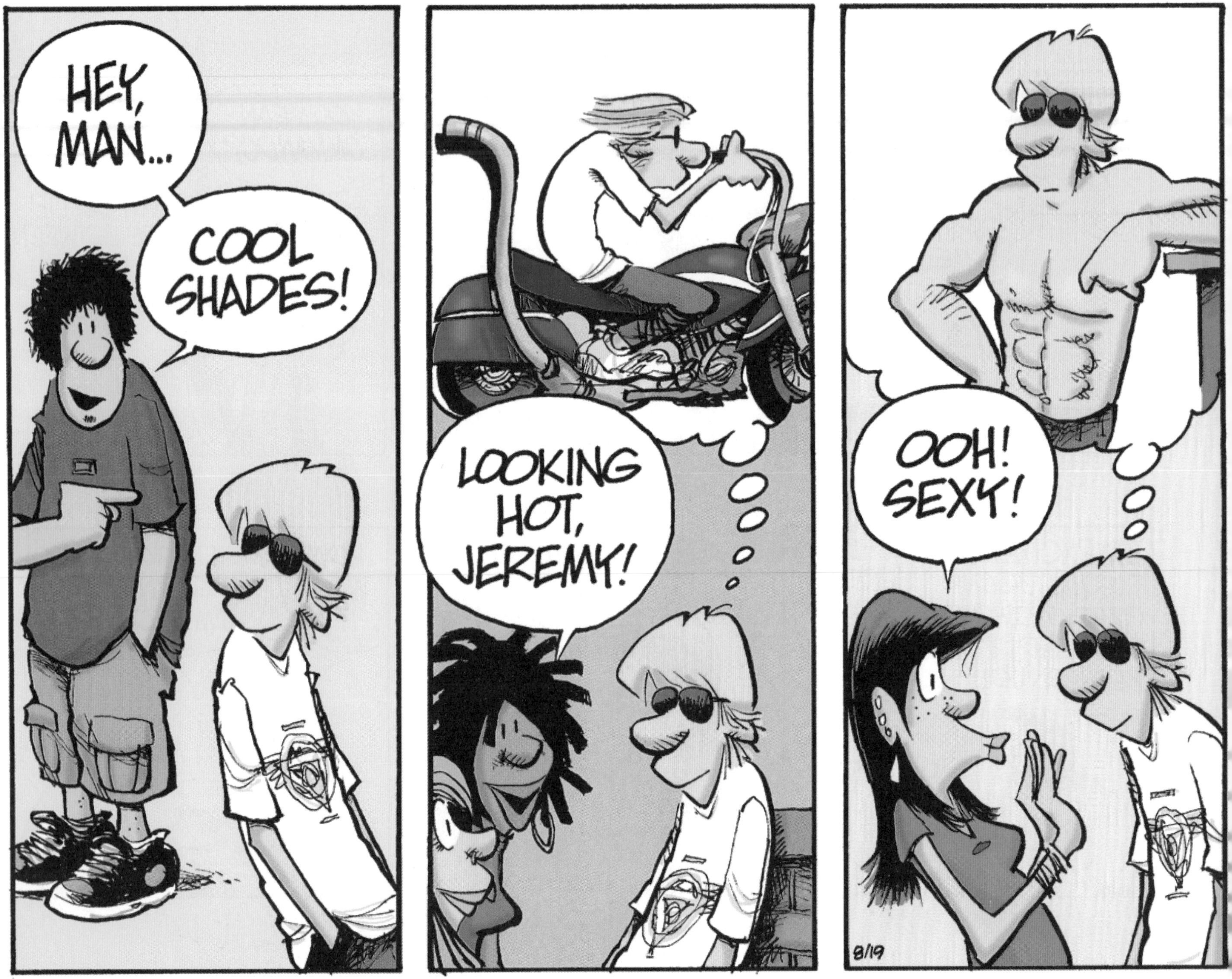
HEY, MAN...
COOL SHADES!
LOOKING HOT, JEREMY!
OOH! SEXY!
8/19

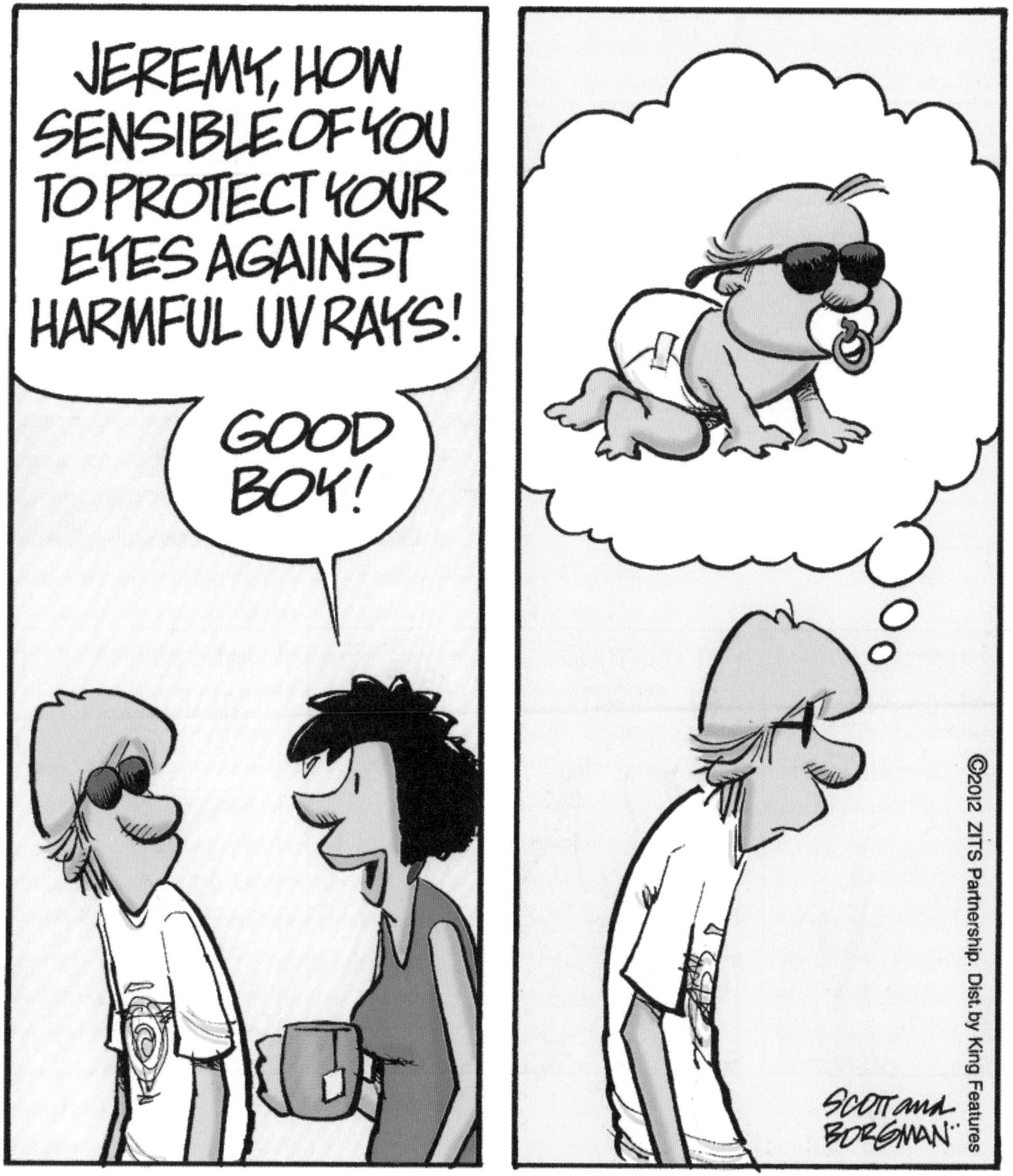
JEREMY, HOW SENSIBLE OF YOU TO PROTECT YOUR EYES AGAINST HARMFUL UV RAYS!
GOOD BOY!
SCOTT and BORGMAN
©2012 ZITS Partnership. Dist. by King Features

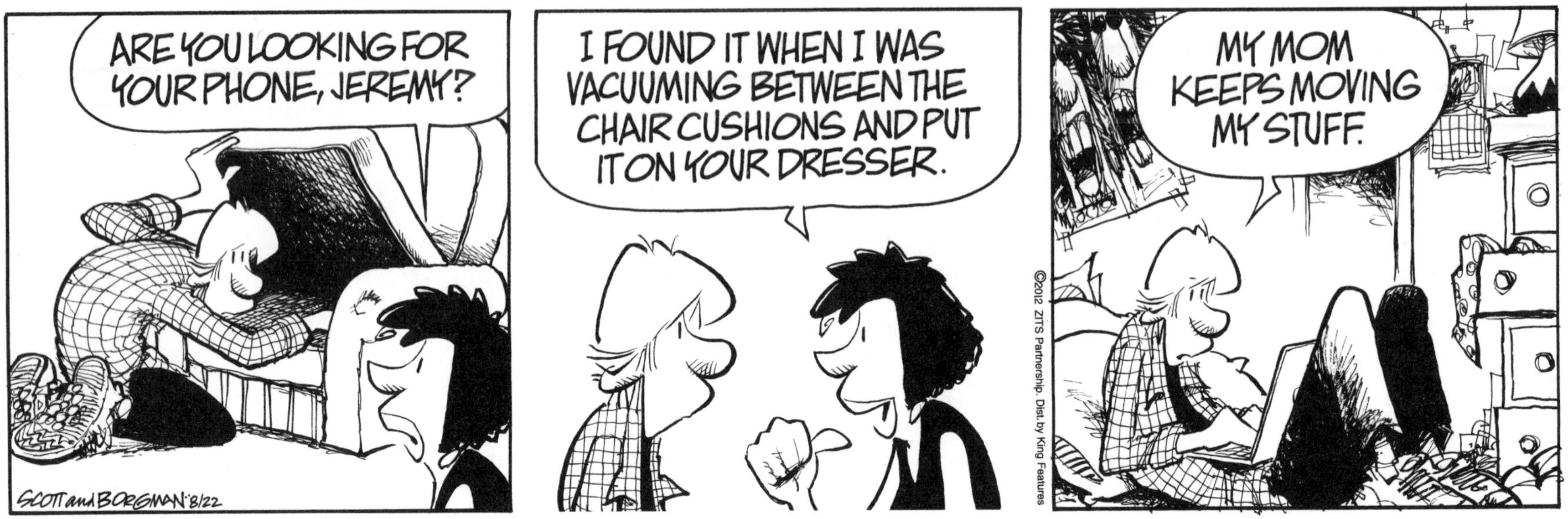
ARE YOU LOOKING FOR YOUR PHONE, JEREMY?
SCOTT and BORGMAN 8/22
I FOUND IT WHEN I WAS VACUUMING BETWEEN THE CHAIR CUSHIONS AND PUT IT ON YOUR DRESSER.
©2012 ZITS Partnership. Dist. by King Features
MY MOM KEEPS MOVING MY STUFF.

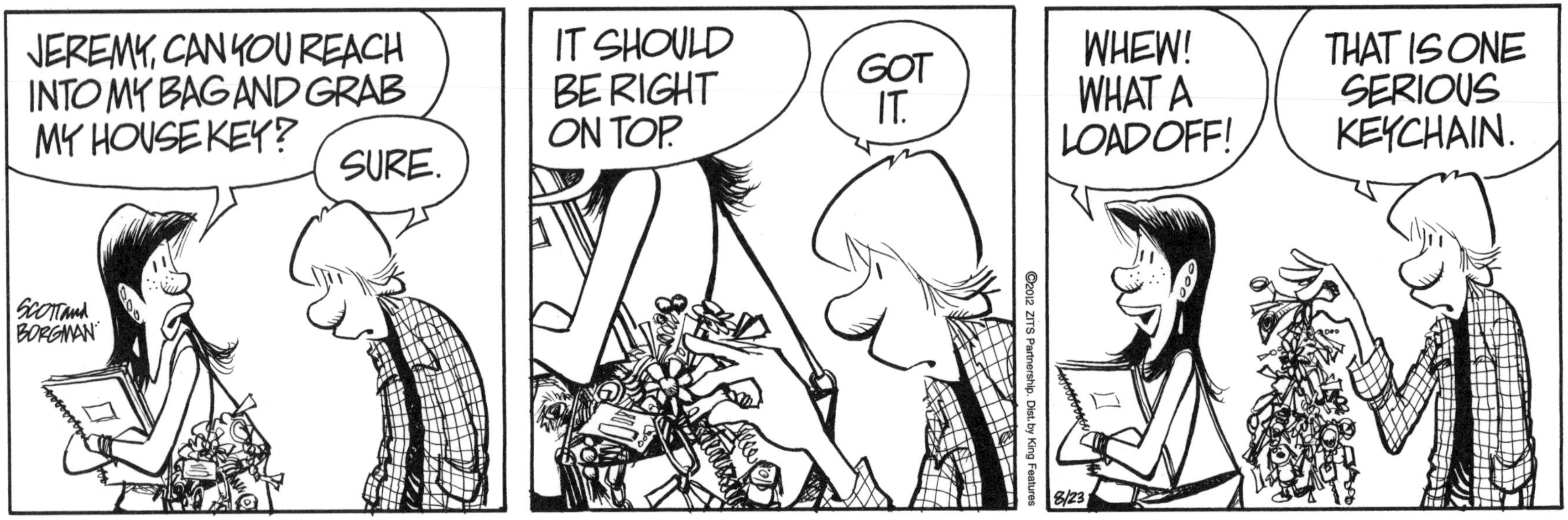
JEREMY, CAN YOU REACH INTO MY BAG AND GRAB MY HOUSE KEY?
SURE.
SCOTT and BORGMAN
IT SHOULD BE RIGHT ON TOP.
GOT IT.
©2012 ZITS Partnership. Dist. by King Features
WHEW! WHAT A LOAD OFF!
THAT IS ONE SERIOUS KEYCHAIN.
8/23

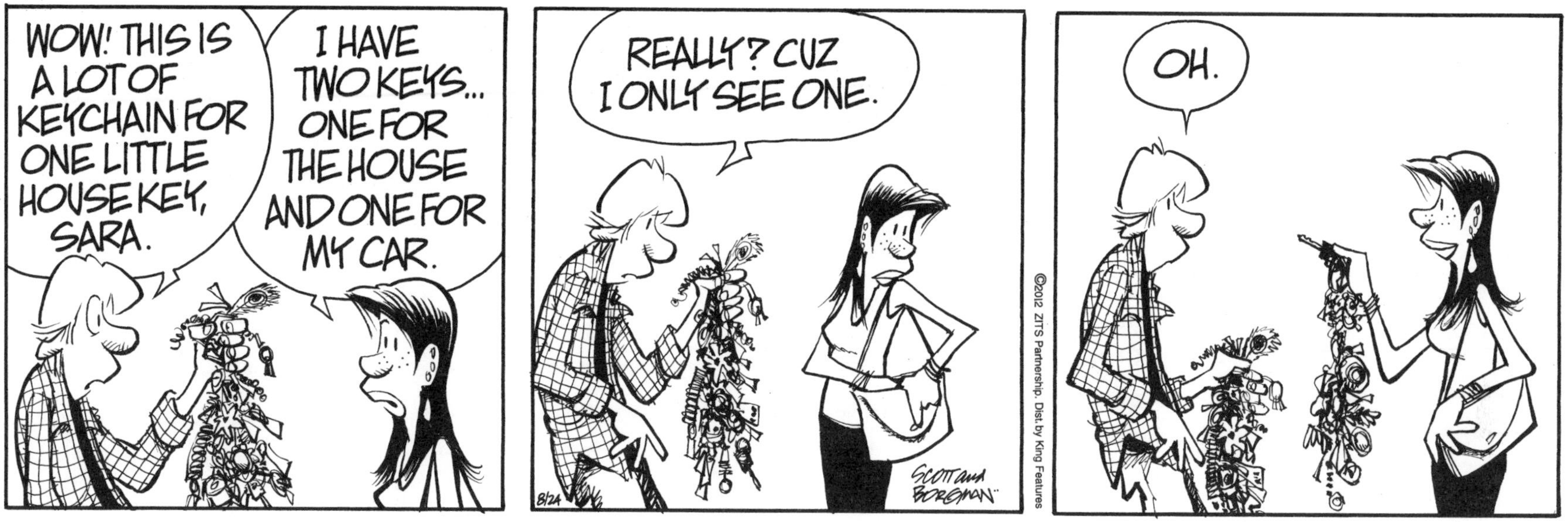
WOW! THIS IS A LOT OF KEYCHAIN FOR ONE LITTLE HOUSE KEY, SARA.
I HAVE TWO KEYS... ONE FOR THE HOUSE AND ONE FOR MY CAR.
REALLY? CUZ I ONLY SEE ONE.
8/24
SCOTT and BORGMAN
©2012 ZITS Partnership. Dist. by King Features
OH.

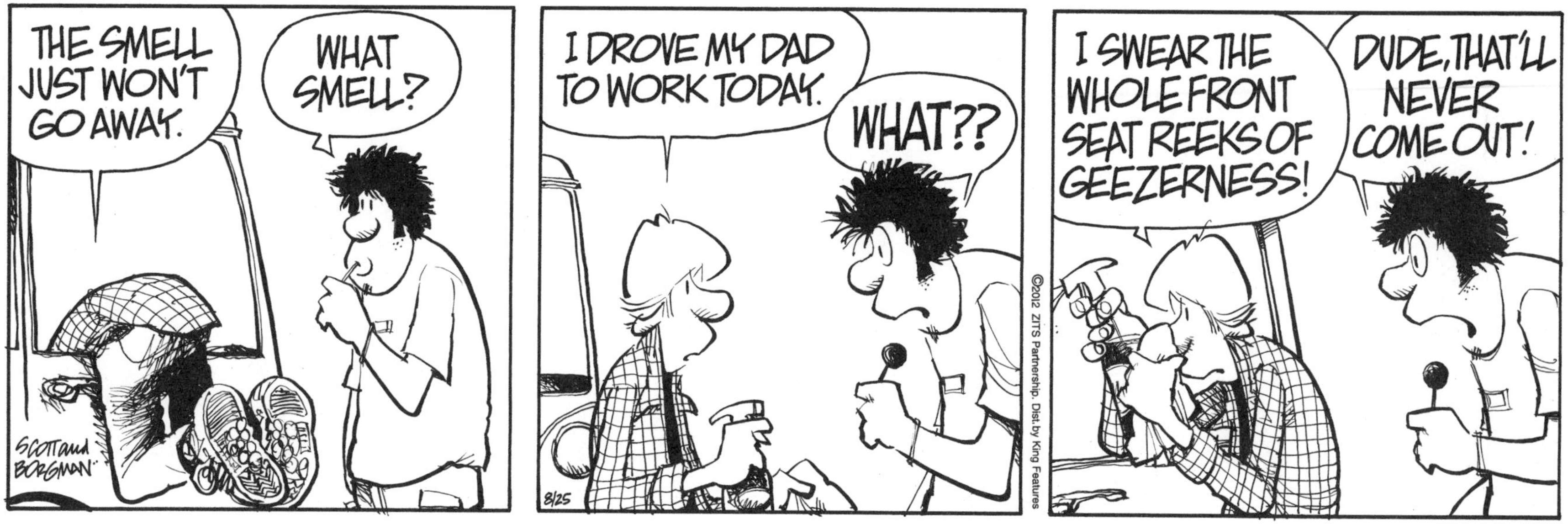
THE SMELL JUST WON'T GO AWAY.
WHAT SMELL?
SCOTT and BORGMAN
I DROVE MY DAD TO WORK TODAY.
WHAT??
8/25
©2012 ZITS Partnership. Dist. by King Features
I SWEAR THE WHOLE FRONT SEAT REEKS OF GEEZERNESS!
DUDE, THAT'LL NEVER COME OUT!

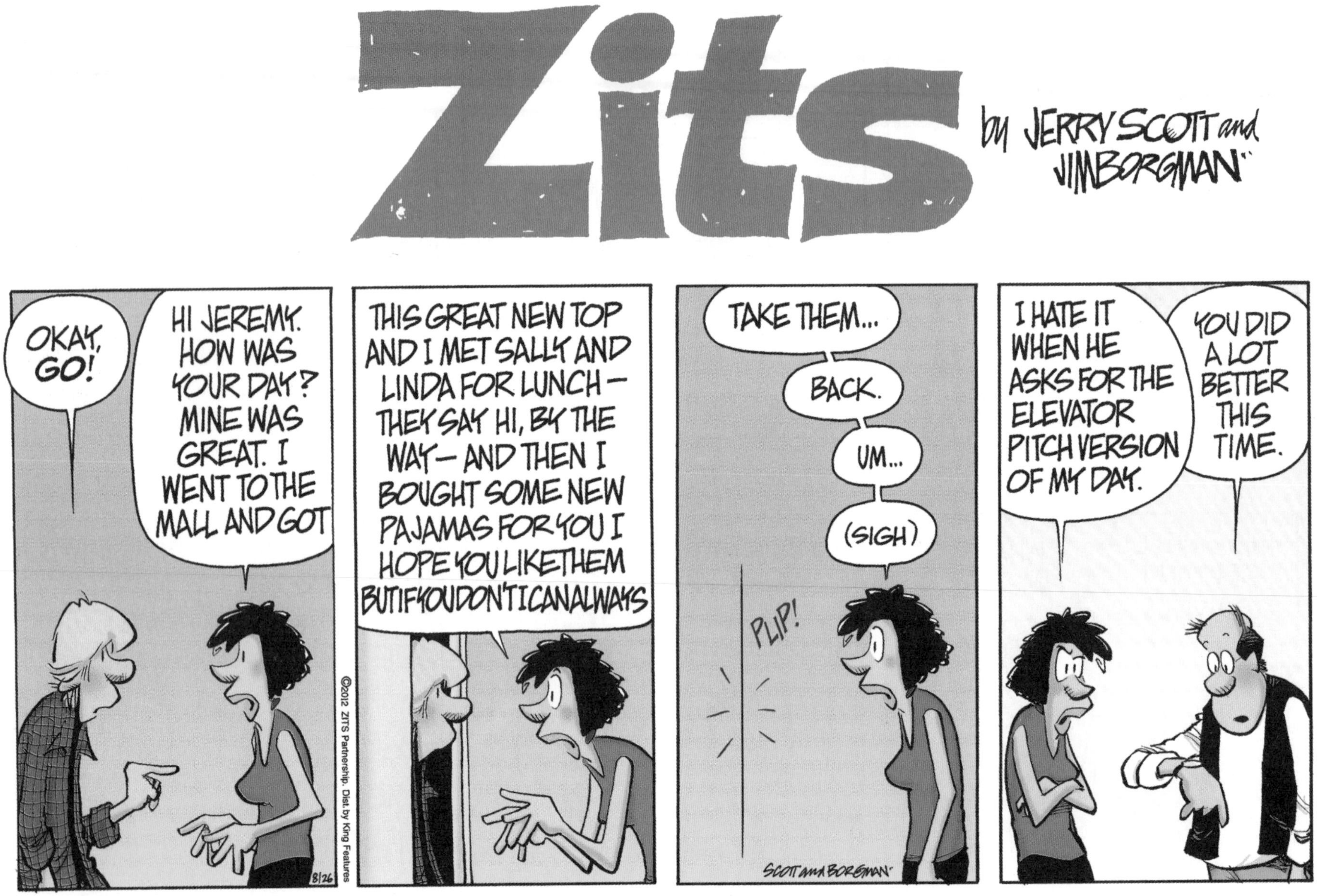
ZITS
by JERRY SCOTT and JIM BORGMAN
OKAY, GO!
HI JEREMY. HOW WAS YOUR DAY? MINE WAS GREAT. I WENT TO THE MALL AND GOT
©2012 ZITS Partnership. Dist. by King Features
8/26
THIS GREAT NEW TOP AND I MET SALLY AND LINDA FOR LUNCH — THEY SAY HI, BY THE WAY — AND THEN I BOUGHT SOME NEW PAJAMAS FOR YOU I HOPE YOU LIKE THEM BUT IF YOU DON'T I CAN ALWAYS
TAKE THEM...
BACK.
UM...
(SIGH)
PLIP!
SCOTT AND BORGMAN
I HATE IT WHEN HE ASKS FOR THE ELEVATOR PITCH VERSION OF MY DAY.
YOU DID A LOT BETTER THIS TIME.

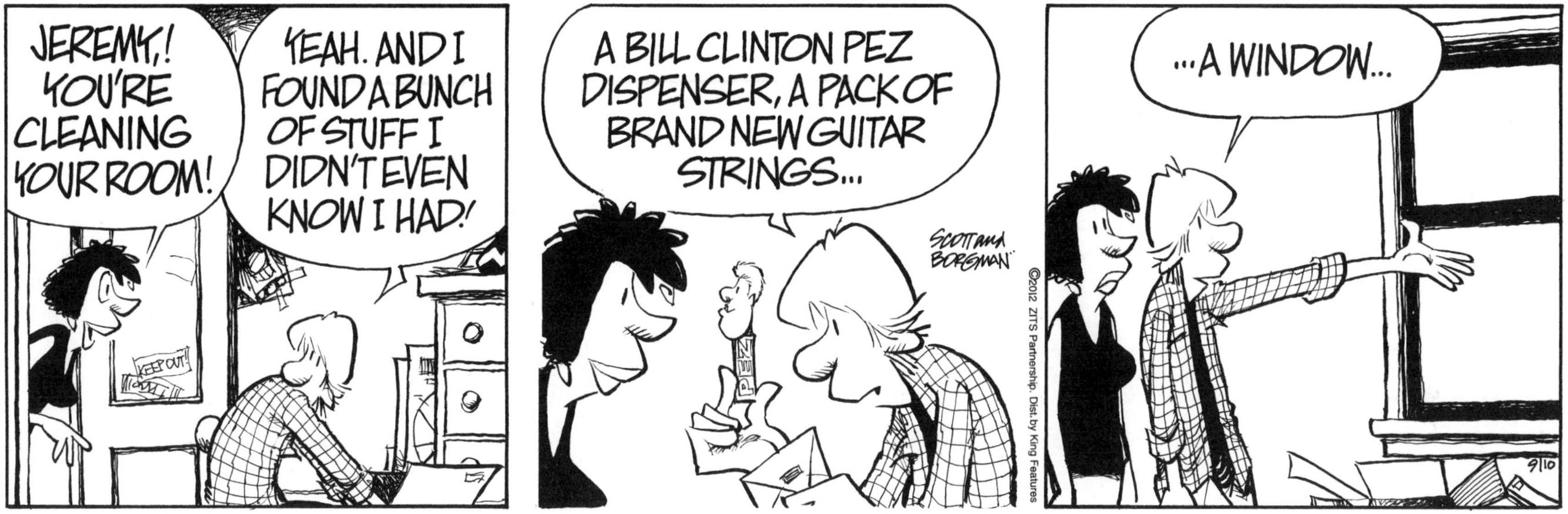
JEREMY! YOU'RE CLEANING YOUR ROOM!
YEAH. AND I FOUND A BUNCH OF STUFF I DIDN'T EVEN KNOW I HAD!
KEEP OUT!
A BILL CLINTON PEZ DISPENSER, A PACK OF BRAND NEW GUITAR STRINGS...
PEZ
SCOTT and BORGMAN
©2012 ZITS Partnership. Dist. by King Features
...A WINDOW...
9/10

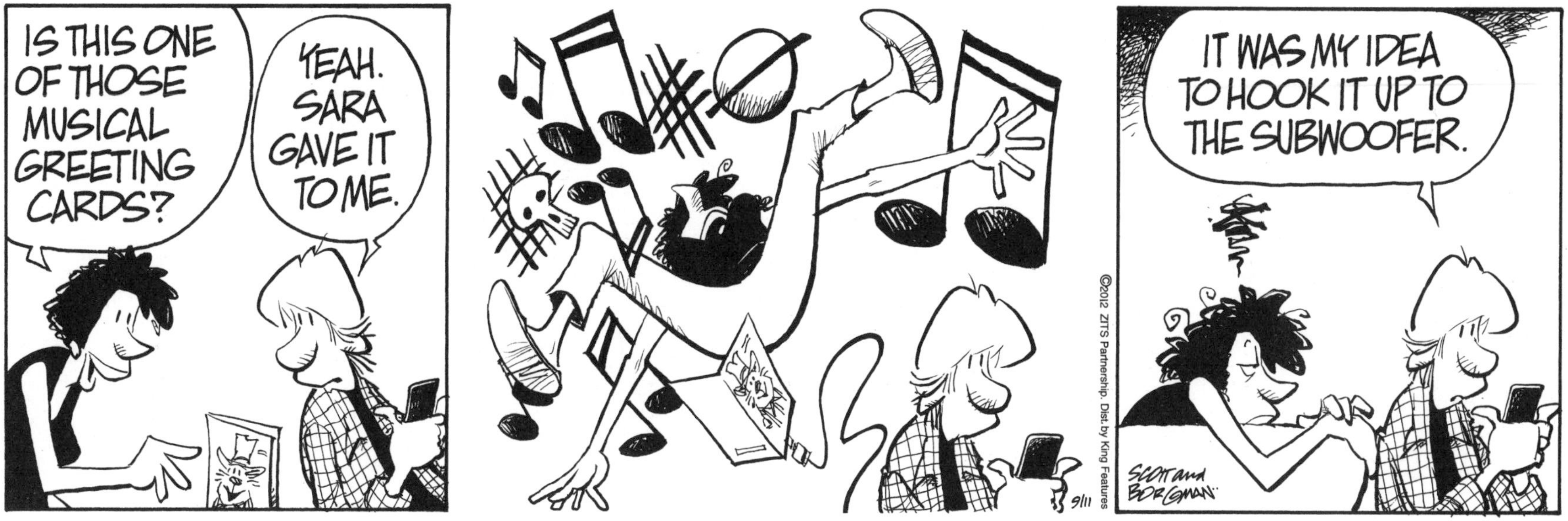
IS THIS ONE OF THOSE MUSICAL GREETING CARDS?
YEAH. SARA GAVE IT TO ME.
9/11
©2012 ZITS Partnership. Dist. by King Features
IT WAS MY IDEA TO HOOK IT UP TO THE SUBWOOFER.
SCOTT and BORGMAN

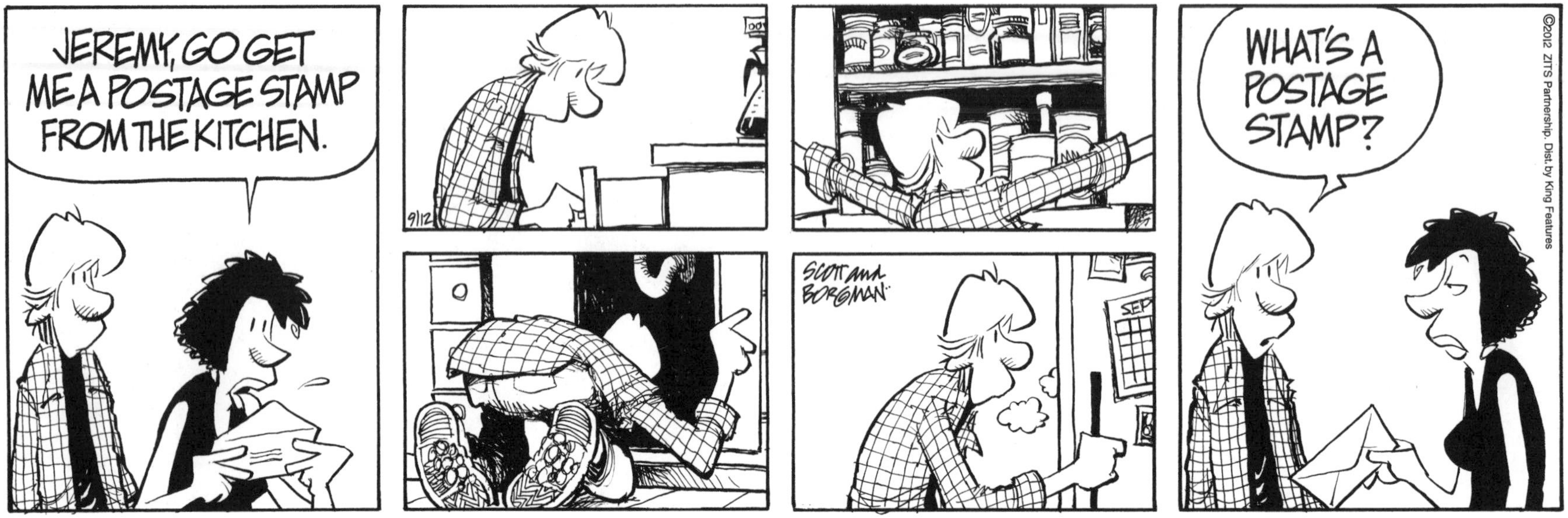
JEREMY, GO GET ME A POSTAGE STAMP FROM THE KITCHEN.
9/12
SCOTT AND BORGMAN
SEP
WHAT'S A POSTAGE STAMP?
©2012 ZITS Partnership. Dist. by King Features

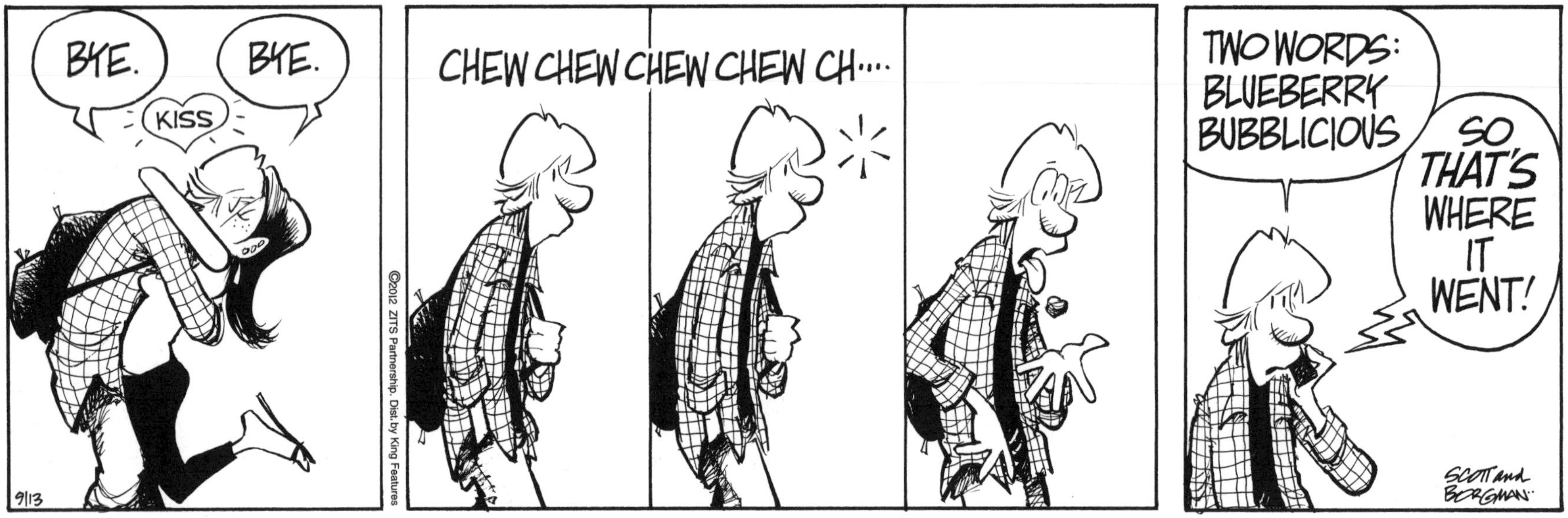
BYE.
KISS
BYE.
9/13
©2012 ZITS Partnership. Dist. by King Features
CHEW CHEW CHEW CHEW CH....
TWO WORDS: BLUEBERRY BUBBLICIOUS
SO THAT'S WHERE IT WENT!
SCOTT AND BORGMAN

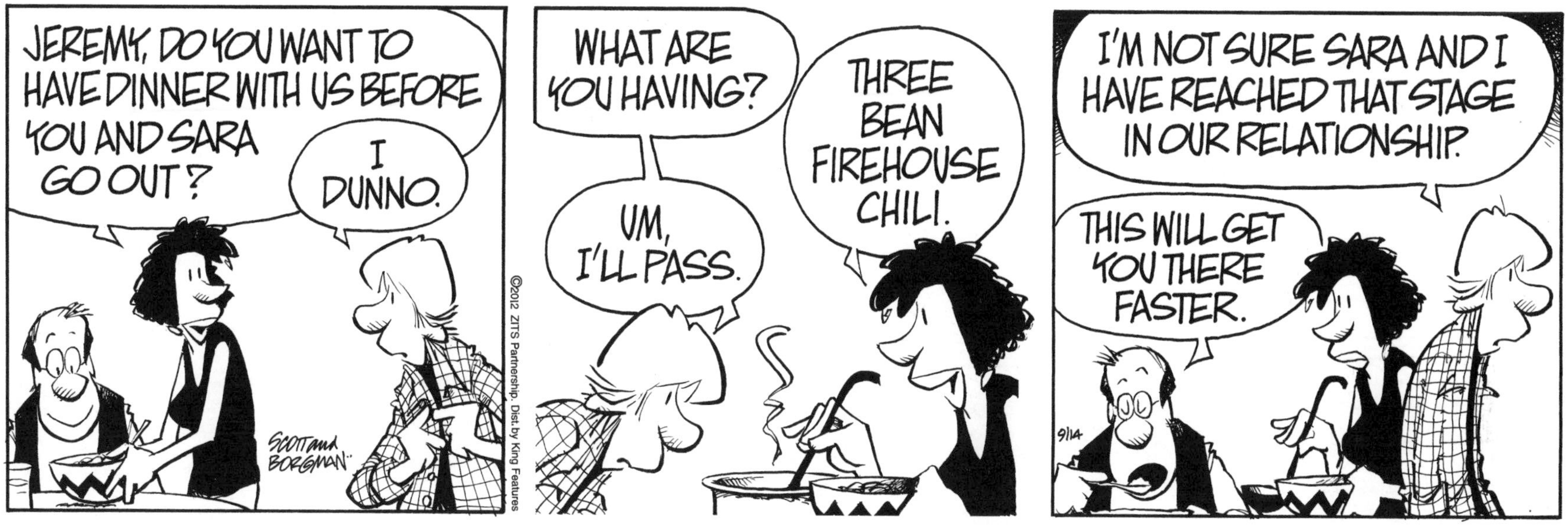
JEREMY, DO YOU WANT TO HAVE DINNER WITH US BEFORE YOU AND SARA GO OUT?
I DUNNO.
SCOTT AND BORGMAN
©2012 ZITS Partnership. Dist. by King Features
WHAT ARE YOU HAVING?
UM, I'LL PASS.
THREE BEAN FIREHOUSE CHILI.
I'M NOT SURE SARA AND I HAVE REACHED THAT STAGE IN OUR RELATIONSHIP.
THIS WILL GET YOU THERE FASTER.
9/14

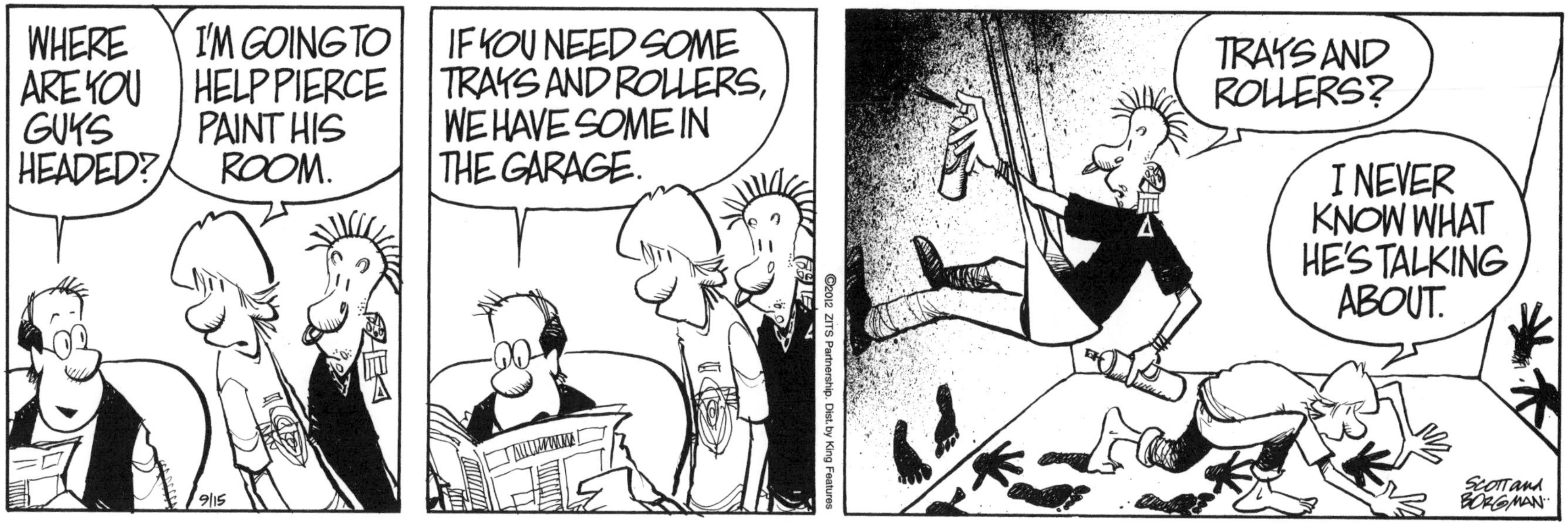
WHERE ARE YOU GUYS HEADED?
I'M GOING TO HELP PIERCE PAINT HIS ROOM.
9/15
IF YOU NEED SOME TRAYS AND ROLLERS, WE HAVE SOME IN THE GARAGE.
©2012 ZITS Partnership. Dist. by King Features
TRAYS AND ROLLERS?
I NEVER KNOW WHAT HE'S TALKING ABOUT.
SCOTT AND BORGMAN

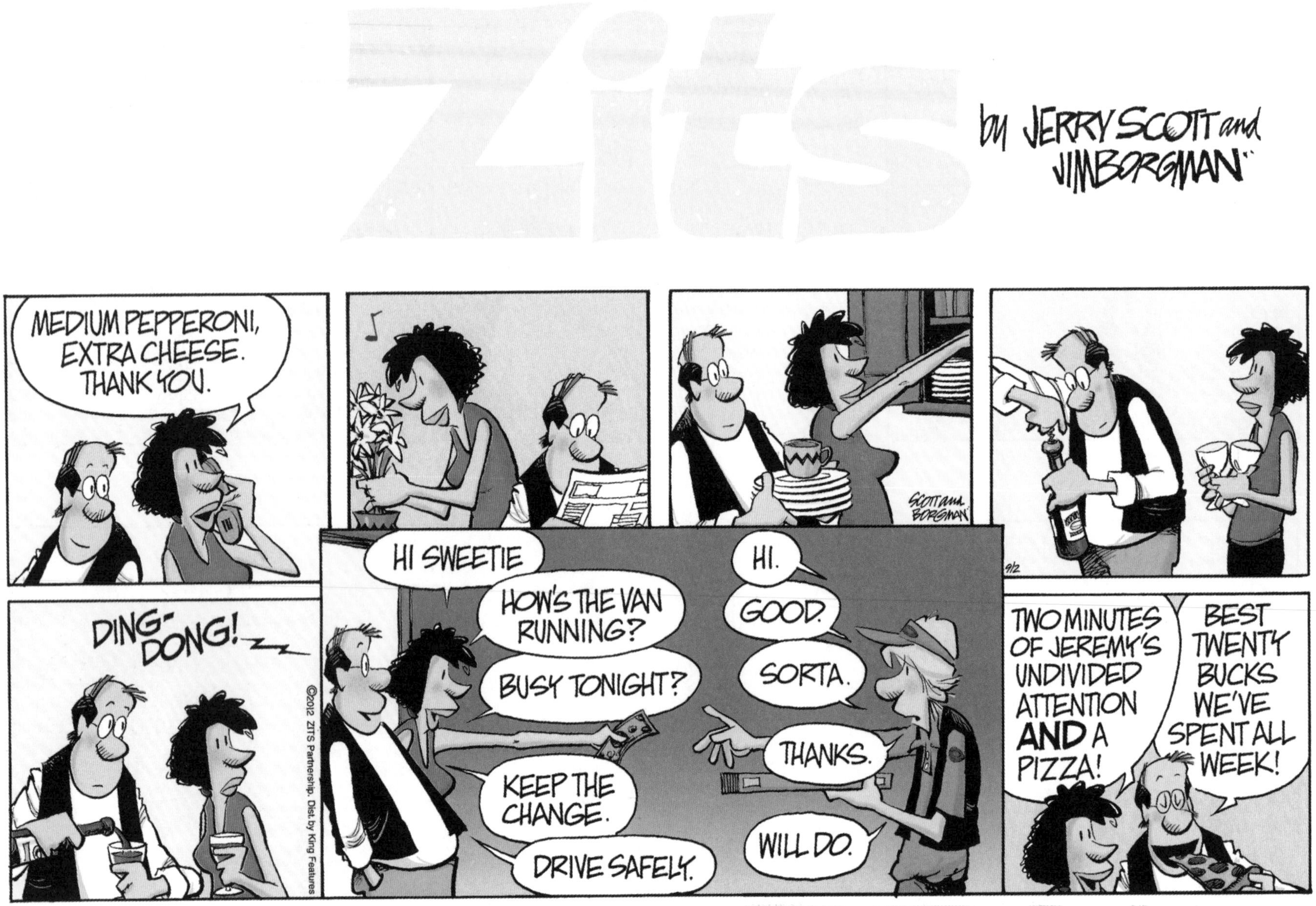
Zits
by JERRY SCOTT and JIM BORGMAN
MEDIUM PEPPERONI, EXTRA CHEESE. THANK YOU.
SCOTT and BORGMAN
DING-DONG!
©2012 ZITS Partnership. Dist. by King Features
HI SWEETIE
HI.
HOW'S THE VAN RUNNING?
GOOD.
BUSY TONIGHT?
SORTA.
THANKS.
KEEP THE CHANGE.
WILL DO.
DRIVE SAFELY.
TWO MINUTES OF JEREMY'S UNDIVIDED ATTENTION **AND** A PIZZA!
BEST TWENTY BUCKS WE'VE SPENT ALL WEEK!

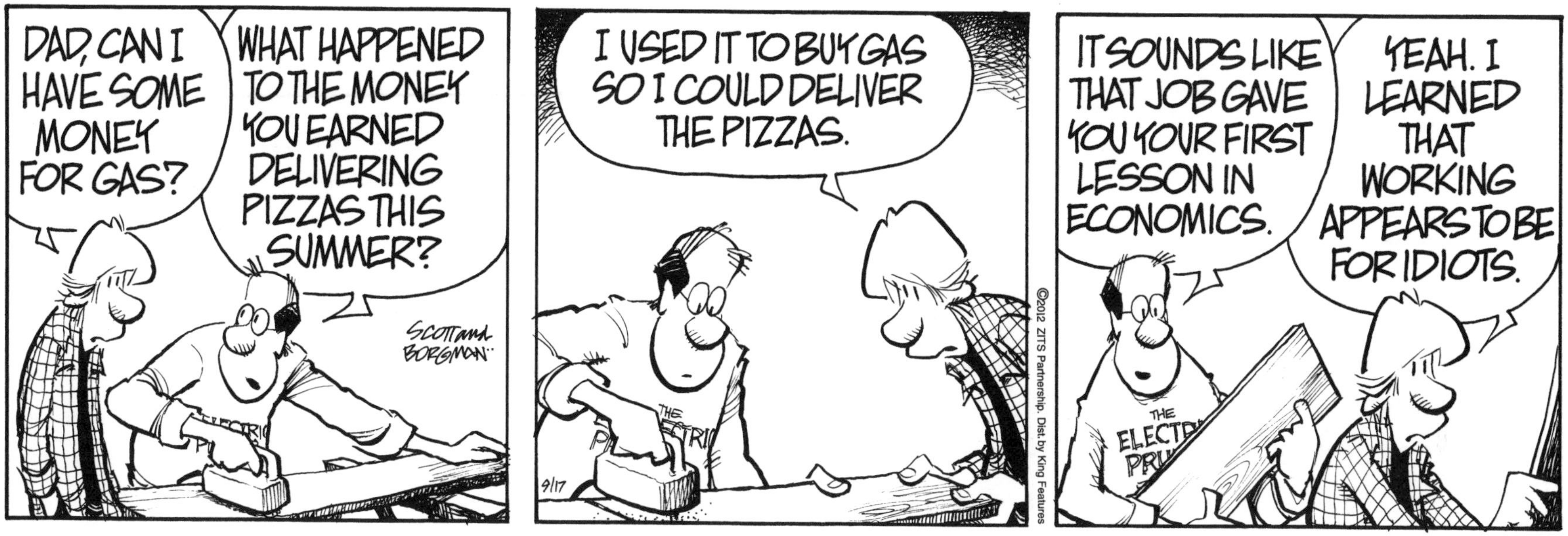
DAD, CAN I HAVE SOME MONEY FOR GAS?
WHAT HAPPENED TO THE MONEY YOU EARNED DELIVERING PIZZAS THIS SUMMER?
SCOTT and BORGMAN
I USED IT TO BUY GAS SO I COULD DELIVER THE PIZZAS.
9/17
©2012 ZITS Partnership. Dist. by King Features
IT SOUNDS LIKE THAT JOB GAVE YOU YOUR FIRST LESSON IN ECONOMICS.
YEAH. I LEARNED THAT WORKING APPEARS TO BE FOR IDIOTS.

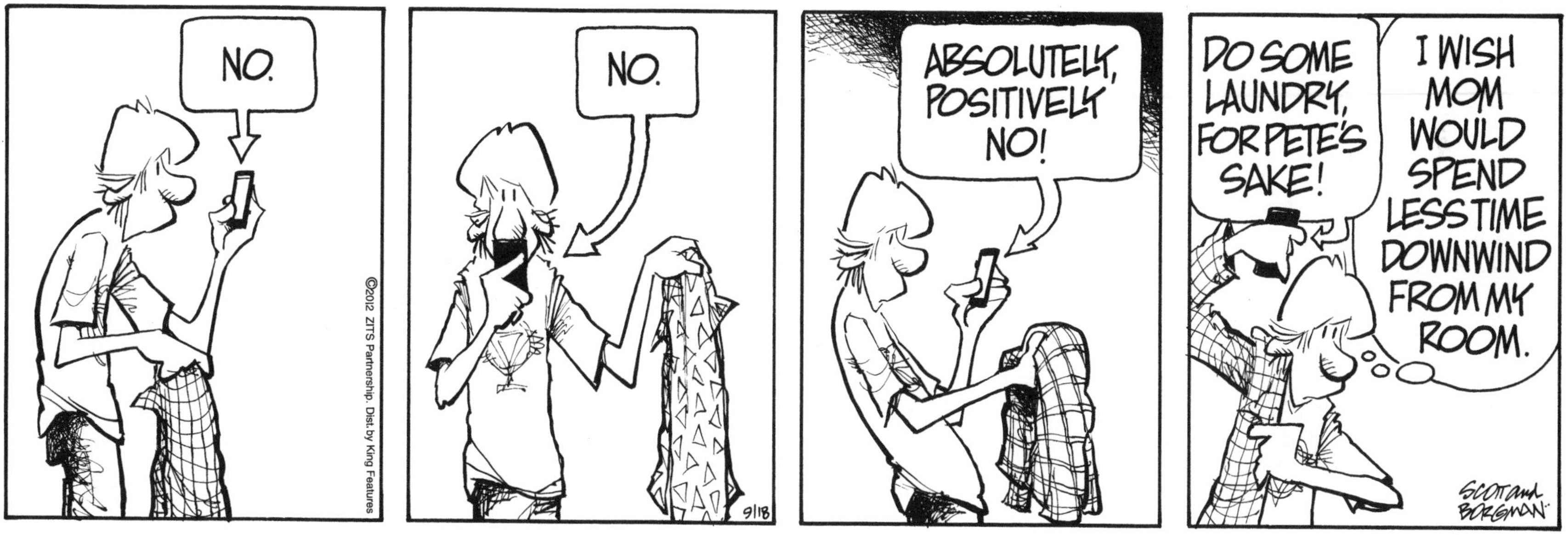
NO.
©2012 ZITS Partnership. Dist. by King Features
NO.
9/18
ABSOLUTELY, POSITIVELY NO!
DO SOME LAUNDRY, FOR PETE'S SAKE!
I WISH MOM WOULD SPEND LESS TIME DOWNWIND FROM MY ROOM.
SCOTT and BORGMAN

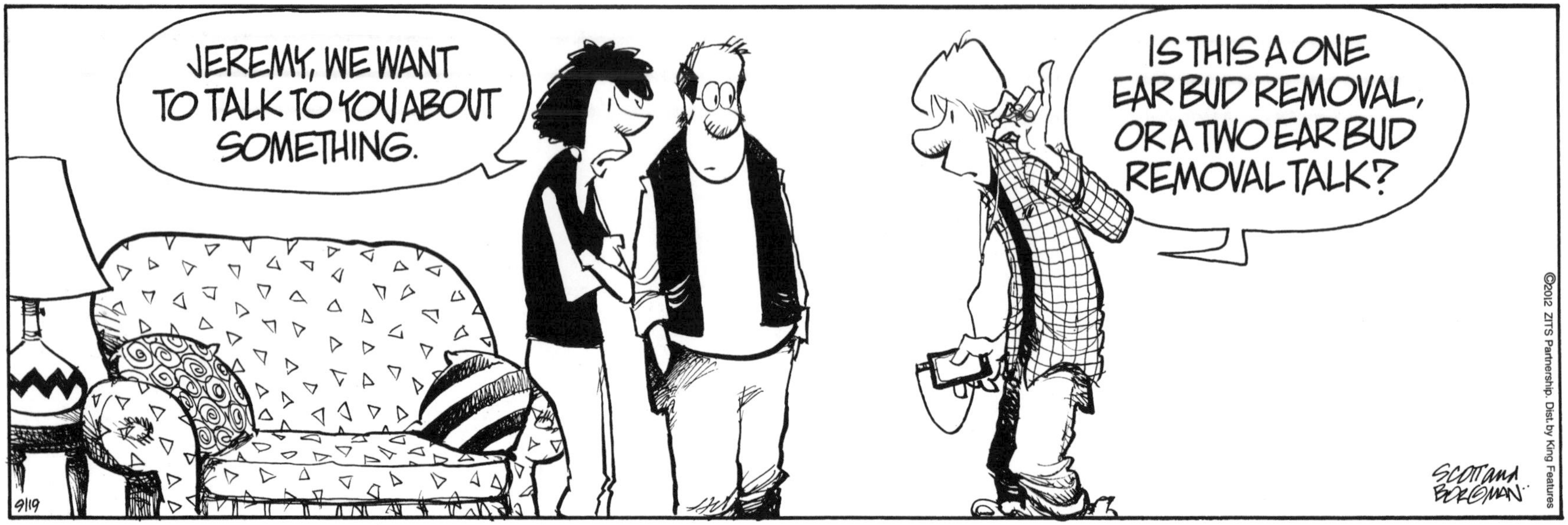
JEREMY, WE WANT TO TALK TO YOU ABOUT SOMETHING.
IS THIS A ONE EAR BUD REMOVAL, OR A TWO EAR BUD REMOVAL TALK?
©2012 ZITS Partnership. Dist. by King Features
SCOTT and BORGMAN
9/19

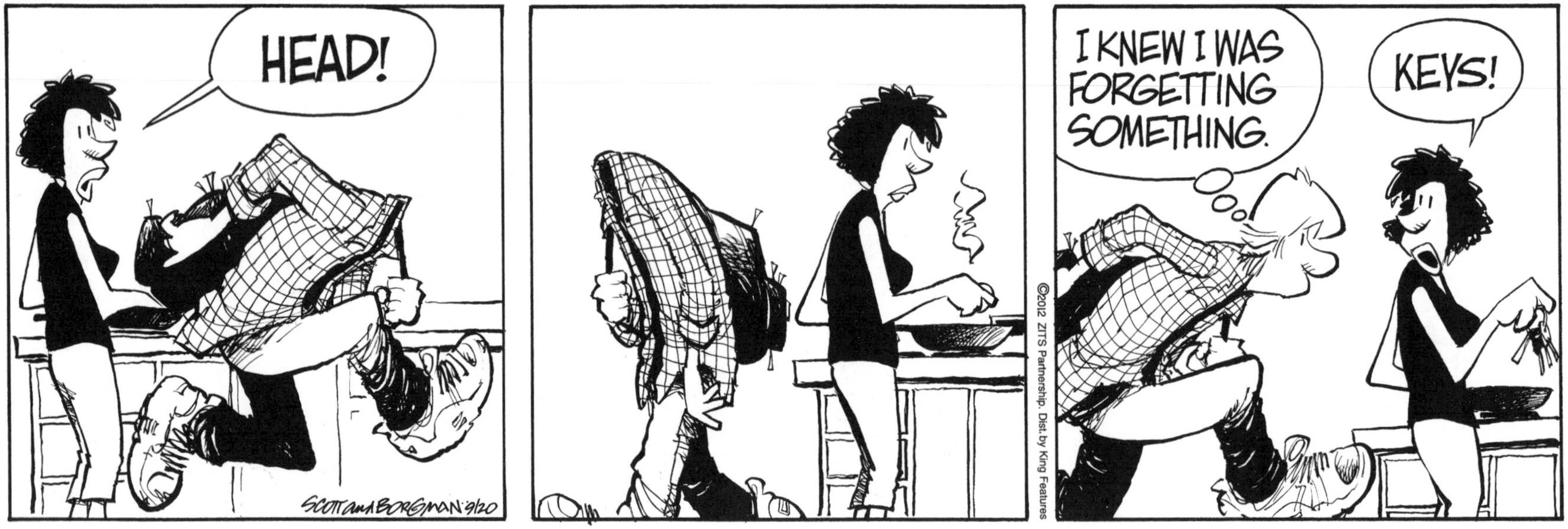
HEAD!
SCOTT and BORGMAN 9/20
©2012 ZITS Partnership. Dist. by King Features
I KNEW I WAS FORGETTING SOMETHING.
KEYS!

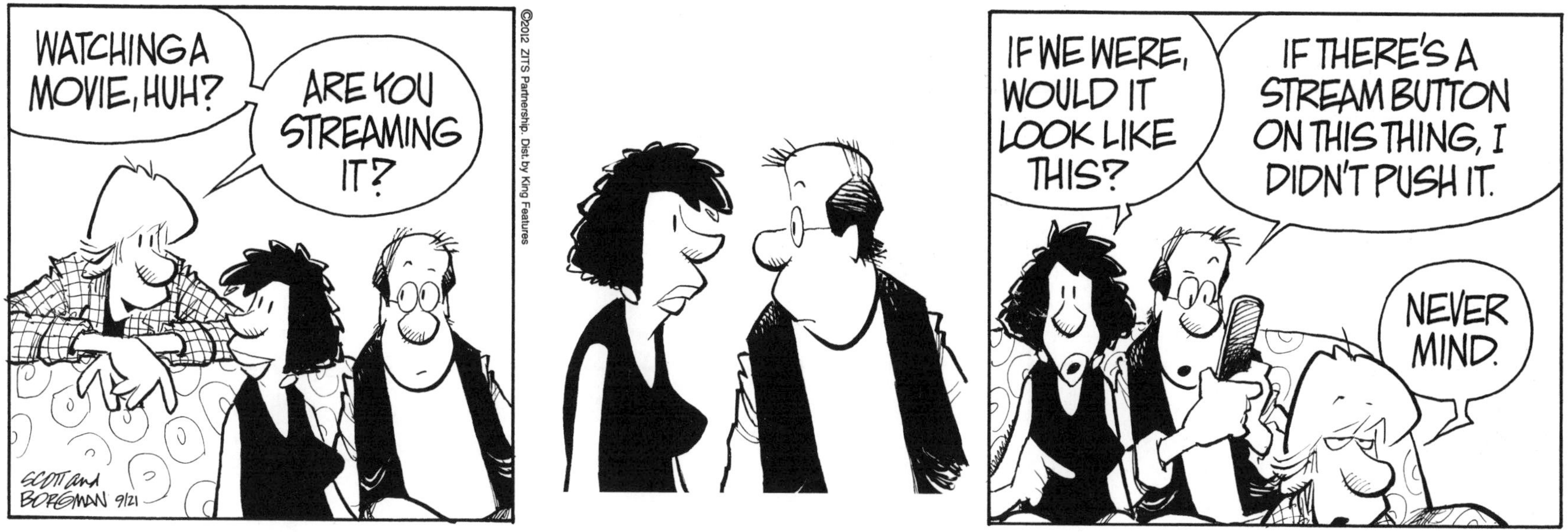
WATCHING A MOVIE, HUH?
ARE YOU STREAMING IT?
SCOTT and BORGMAN 9/21
©2012 ZITS Partnership. Dist. by King Features
IF WE WERE, WOULD IT LOOK LIKE THIS?
IF THERE'S A STREAM BUTTON ON THIS THING, I DIDN'T PUSH IT.
NEVER MIND.

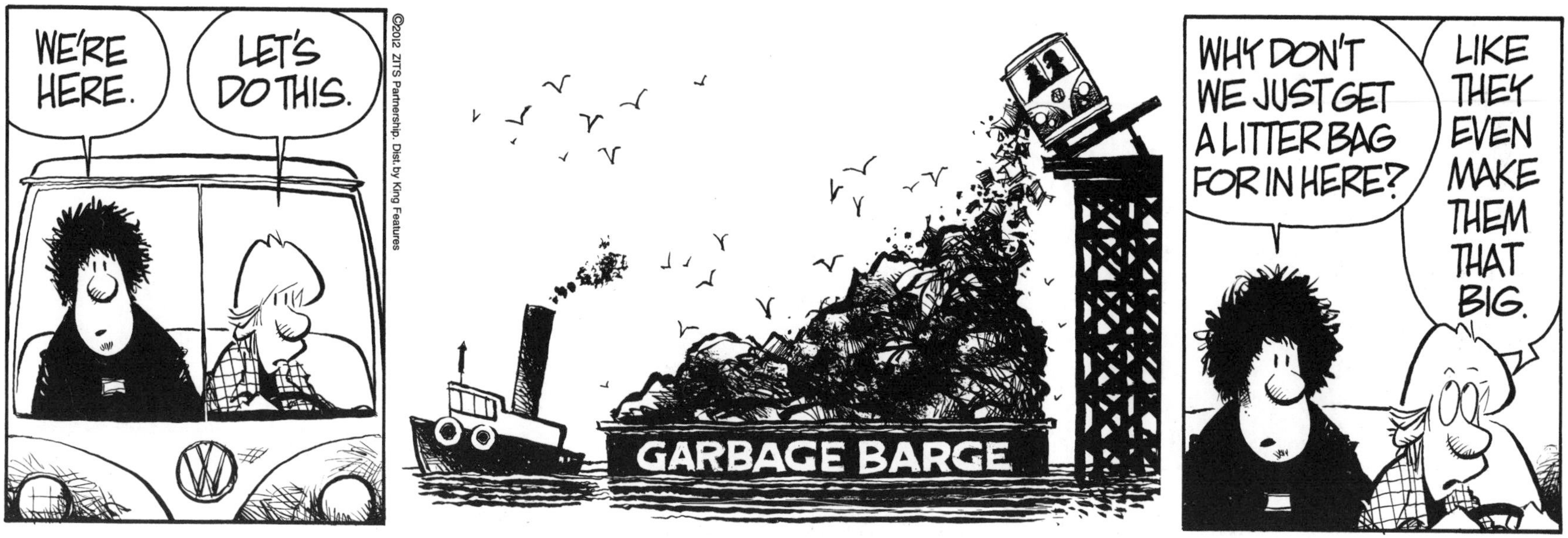
WE'RE HERE.
LET'S DO THIS.
©2012 ZITS Partnership. Dist. by King Features
GARBAGE BARGE
WHY DON'T WE JUST GET A LITTER BAG FOR IN HERE?
LIKE THEY EVEN MAKE THEM THAT BIG.

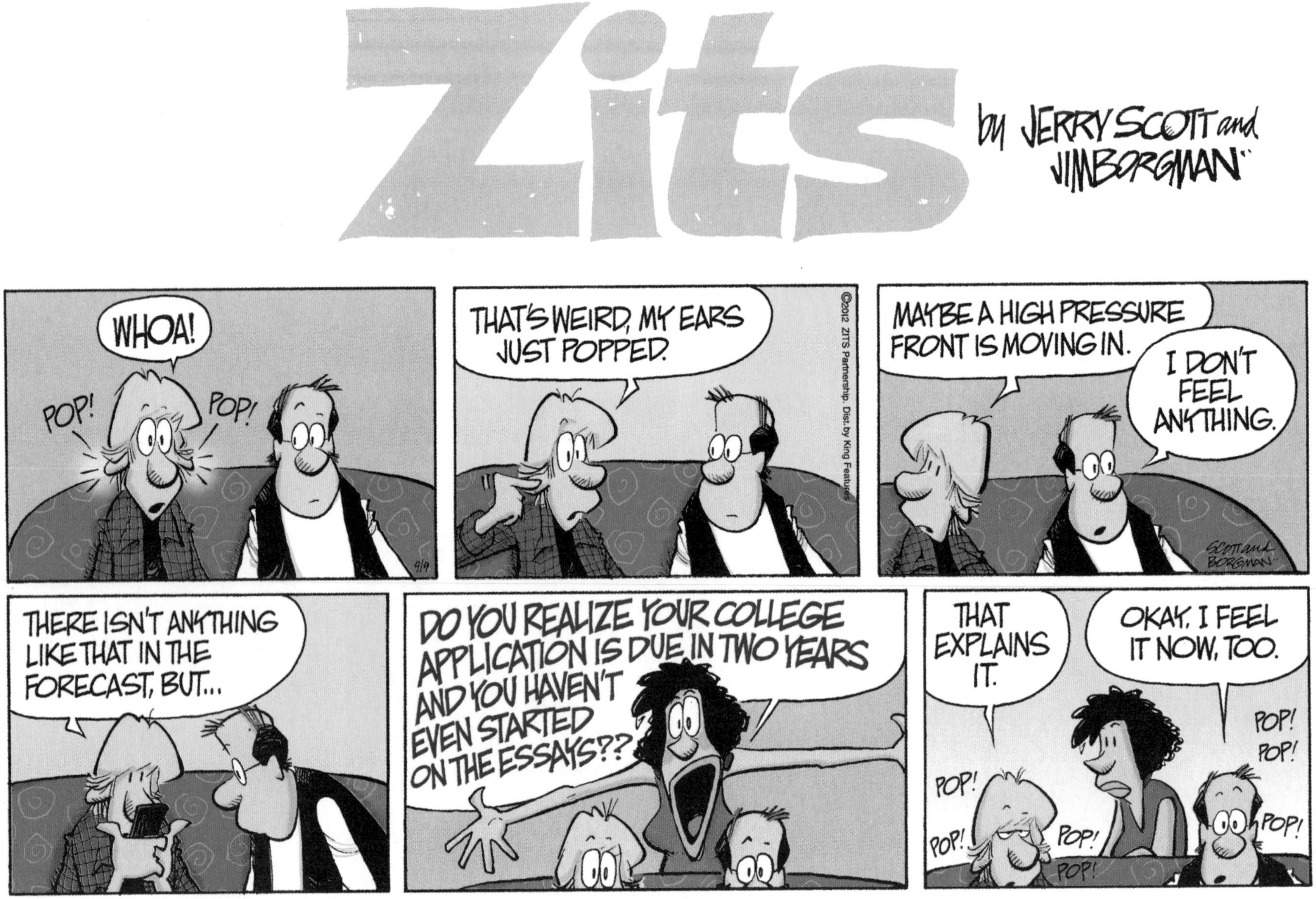
Zits
by JERRY SCOTT and JIM BORGMAN
WHOA!
POP!
POP!
9/9
THAT'S WEIRD, MY EARS JUST POPPED.
©2012 ZITS Partnership. Dist. by King Features
MAYBE A HIGH PRESSURE FRONT IS MOVING IN.
I DON'T FEEL ANYTHING.
SCOTT and BORGMAN
THERE ISN'T ANYTHING LIKE THAT IN THE FORECAST, BUT...
DO YOU REALIZE YOUR COLLEGE APPLICATION IS DUE IN TWO YEARS AND YOU HAVEN'T EVEN STARTED ON THE ESSAYS??
THAT EXPLAINS IT.
OKAY, I FEEL IT NOW, TOO.
POP!
POP!
POP!
POP!
POP!
POP!
POP!

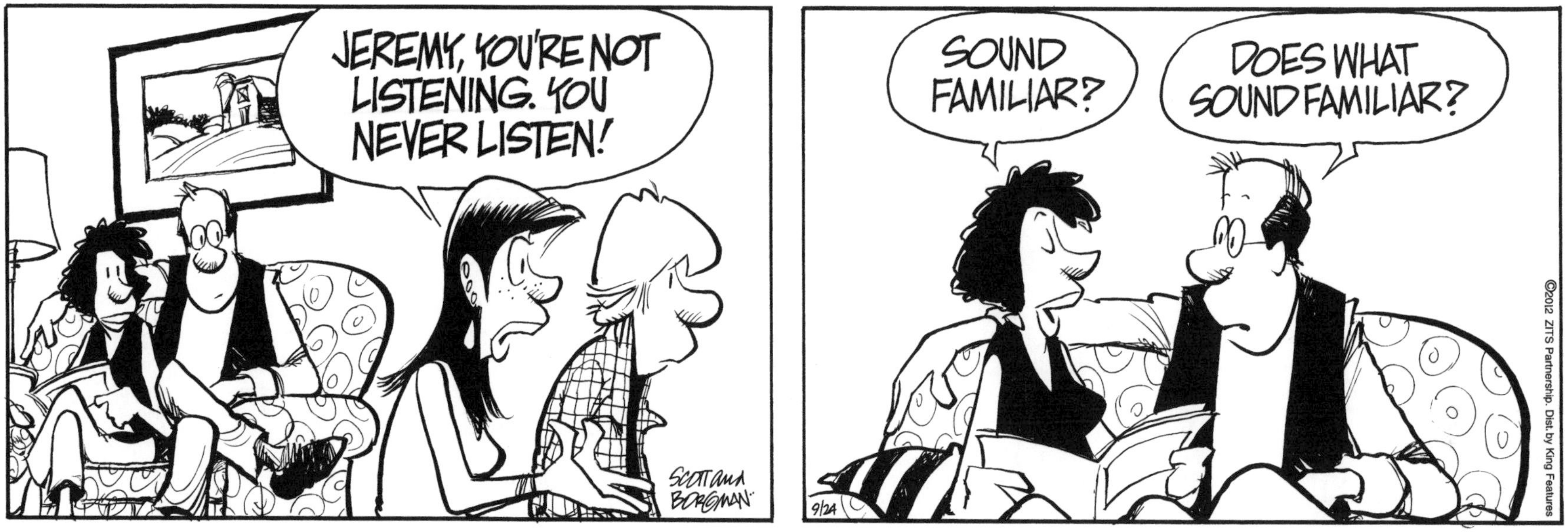
JEREMY, YOU'RE NOT LISTENING. YOU NEVER LISTEN!
SOUND FAMILIAR?
DOES WHAT SOUND FAMILIAR?
SCOTT AND BORGMAN
9/24
©2012 ZITS Partnership. Dist. by King Features

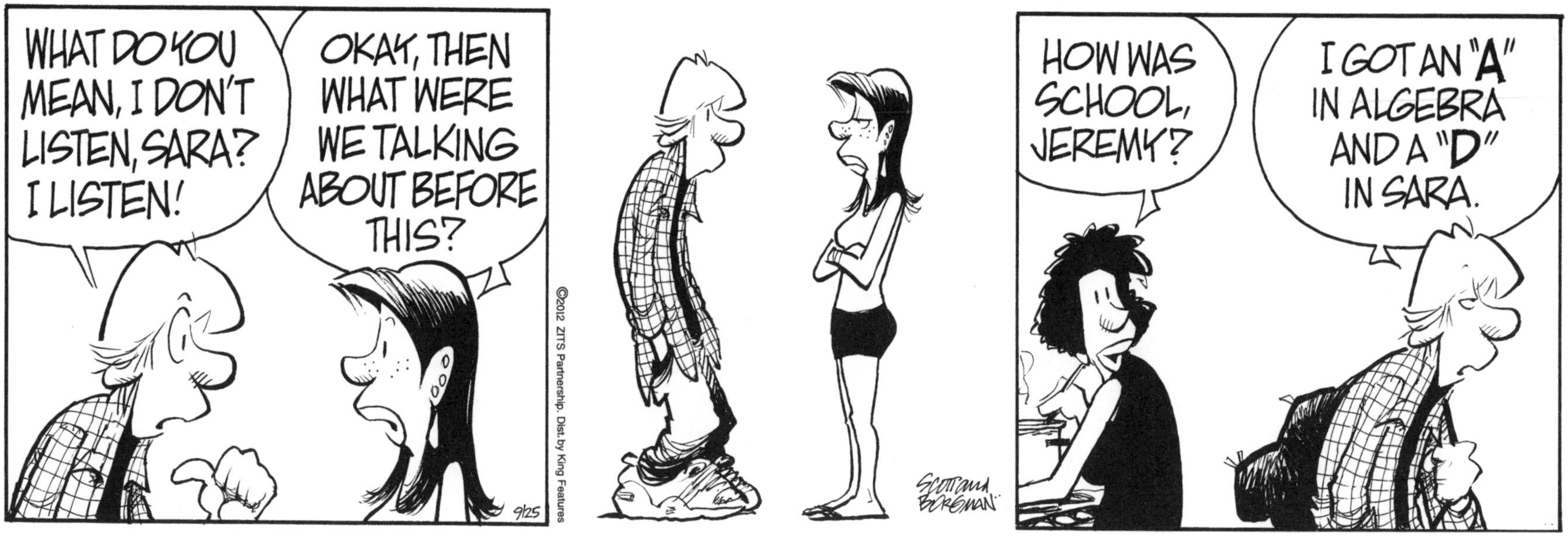
WHAT DO YOU MEAN, I DON'T LISTEN, SARA? I LISTEN!
OKAY, THEN WHAT WERE WE TALKING ABOUT BEFORE THIS?
9/25
©2012 ZITS Partnership. Dist. by King Features
SCOTT AND BORGMAN
HOW WAS SCHOOL, JEREMY?
I GOT AN "A" IN ALGEBRA AND A "D" IN SARA.

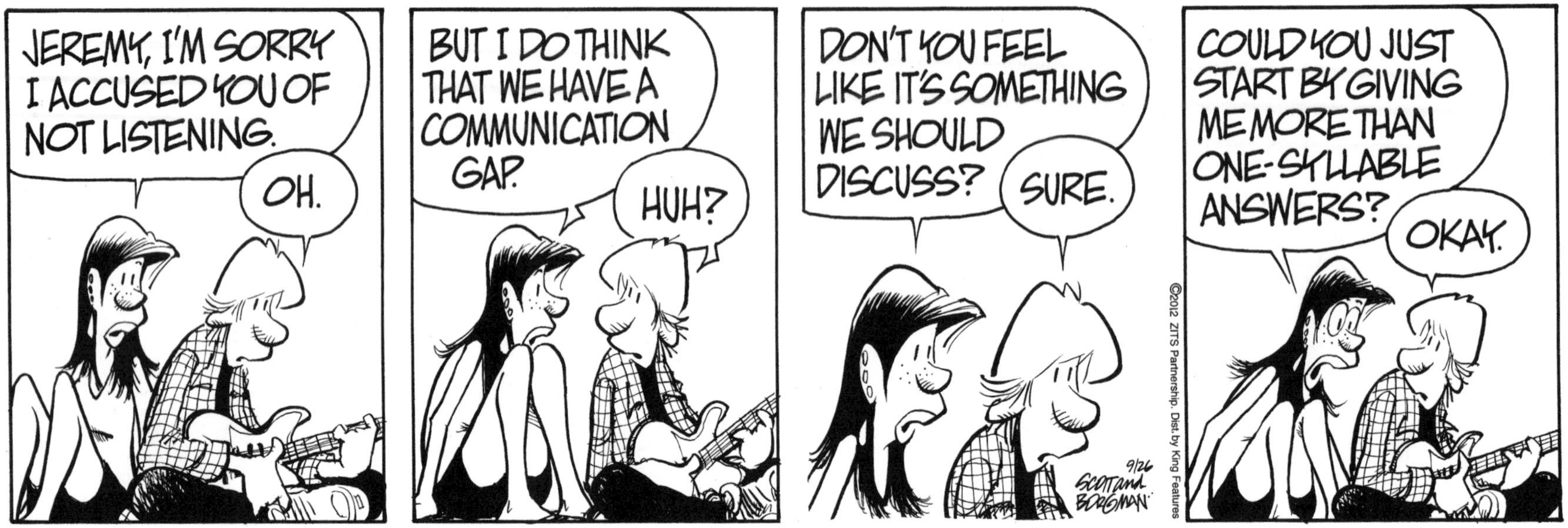
JEREMY, I'M SORRY I ACCUSED YOU OF NOT LISTENING.
OH.
BUT I DO THINK THAT WE HAVE A COMMUNICATION GAP.
HUH?
DON'T YOU FEEL LIKE IT'S SOMETHING WE SHOULD DISCUSS?
SURE.
COULD YOU JUST START BY GIVING ME MORE THAN ONE-SYLLABLE ANSWERS?
OKAY.
9/26 SCOTT and BORGMAN
©2012 ZITS Partnership. Dist. by King Features

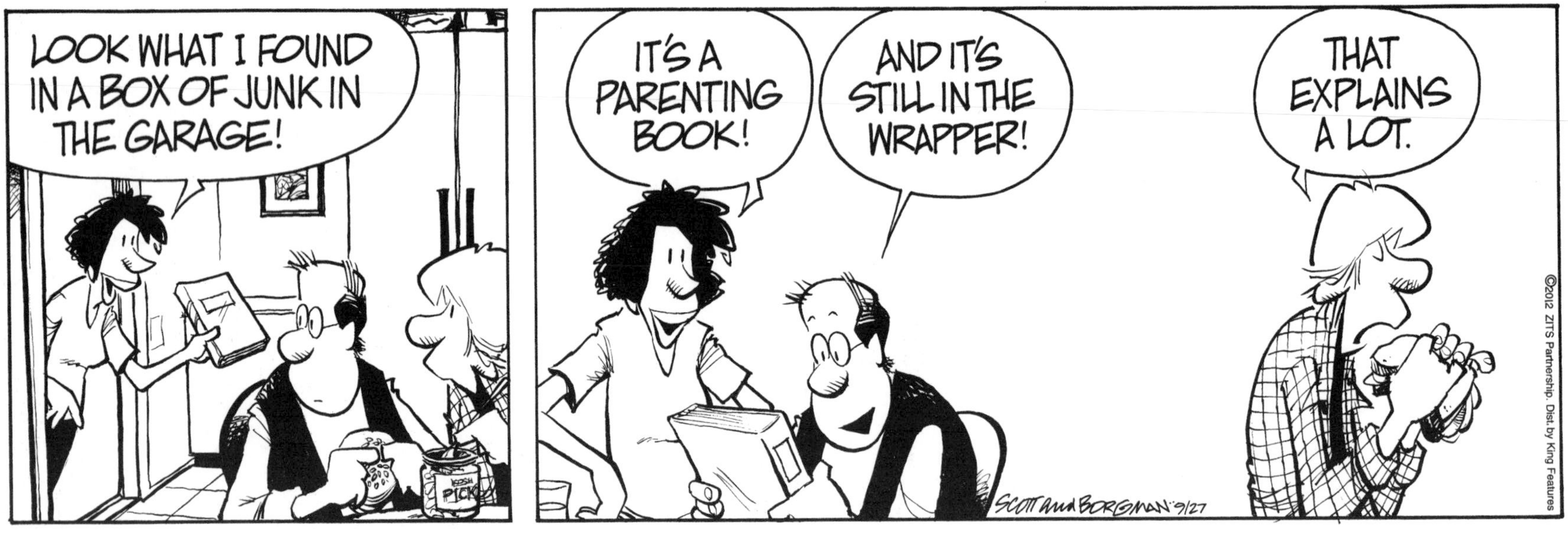
LOOK WHAT I FOUND IN A BOX OF JUNK IN THE GARAGE!
IT'S A PARENTING BOOK!
AND IT'S STILL IN THE WRAPPER!
THAT EXPLAINS A LOT.
SCOTT and BORGMAN 9/27
©2012 ZITS Partnership. Dist. by King Features

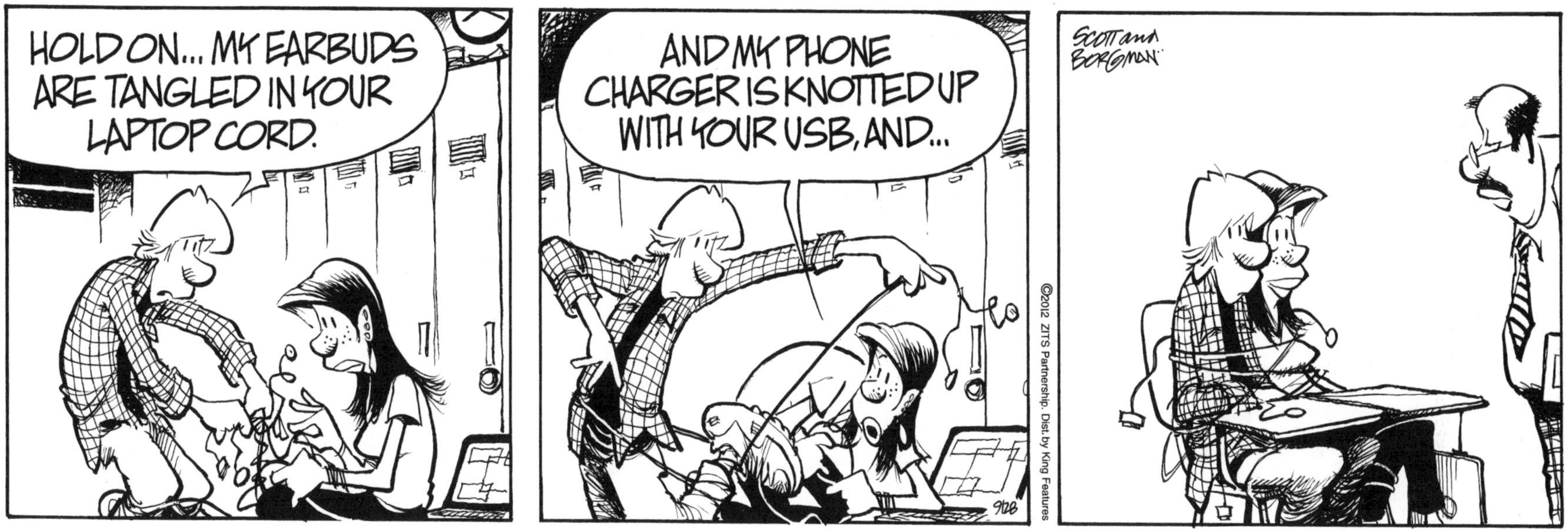
HOLD ON... MY EARBUDS ARE TANGLED IN YOUR LAPTOP CORD.
AND MY PHONE CHARGER IS KNOTTED UP WITH YOUR USB, AND...
©2012 ZITS Partnership. Dist. by King Features
SCOTT and BORGMAN

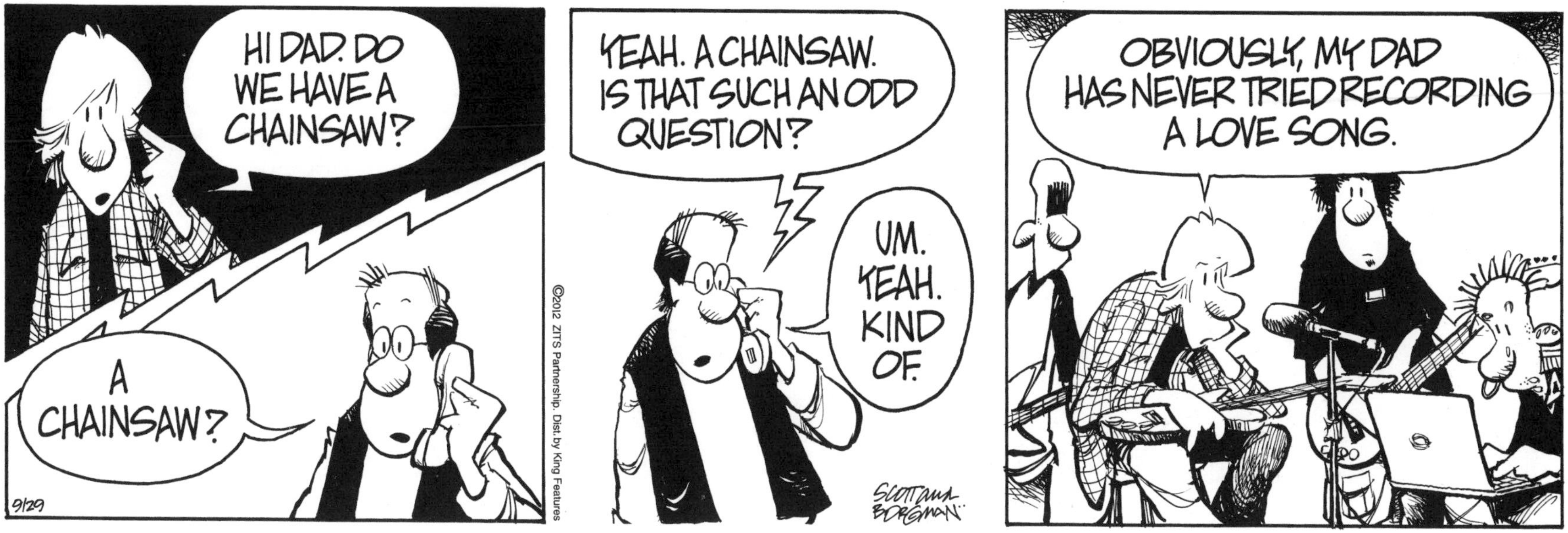
HI DAD. DO WE HAVE A CHAINSAW?
A CHAINSAW?
©2012 ZITS Partnership. Dist. by King Features
YEAH. A CHAINSAW. IS THAT SUCH AN ODD QUESTION?
UM. YEAH. KIND OF.
SCOTT and BORGMAN
OBVIOUSLY, MY DAD HAS NEVER TRIED RECORDING A LOVE SONG.

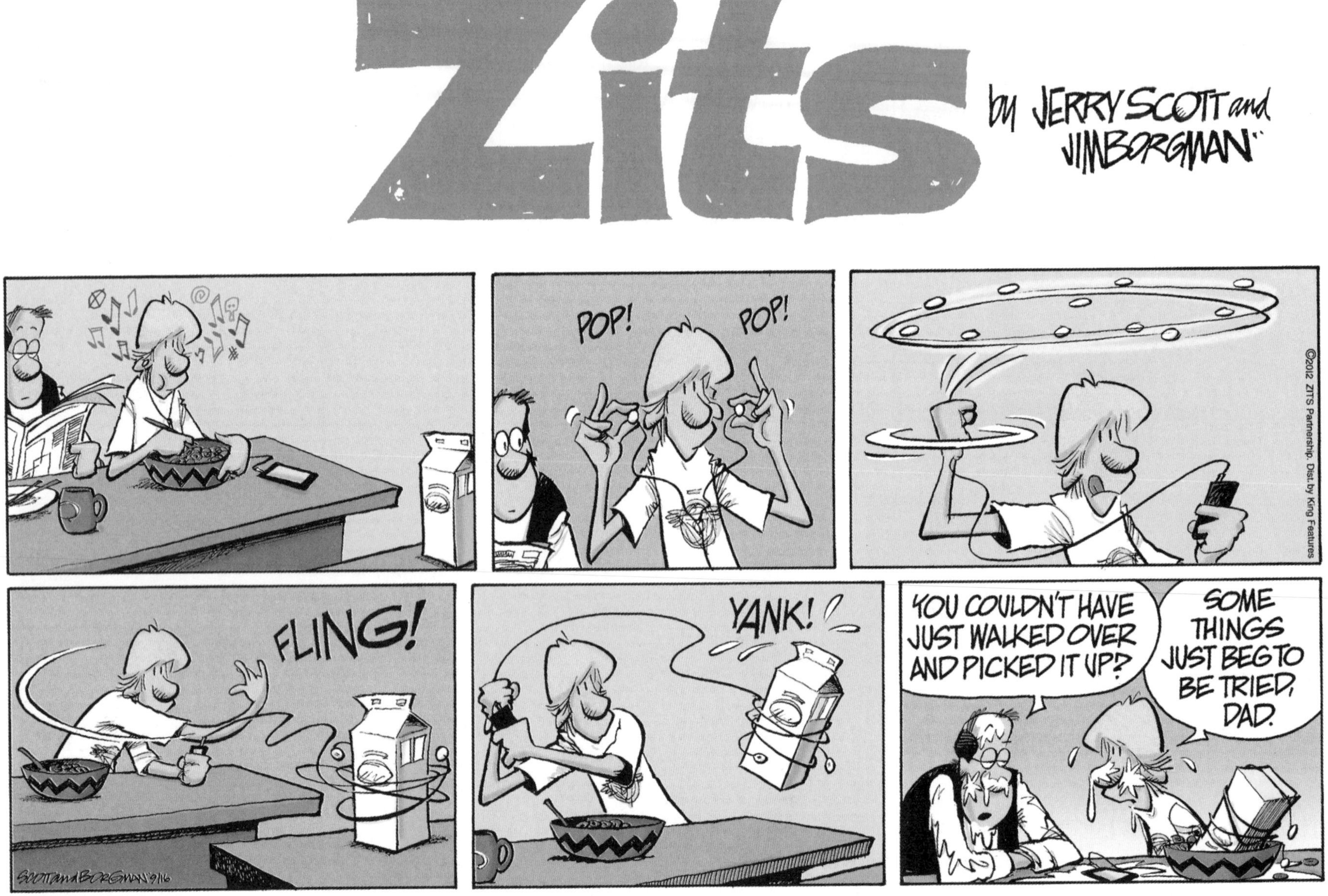
Zits
by JERRY SCOTT and JIM BORGMAN
POP!
POP!
©2012 ZITS Partnership. Dist. by King Features
FLING!
YANK!
YOU COULDN'T HAVE JUST WALKED OVER AND PICKED IT UP?
SOME THINGS JUST BEG TO BE TRIED, DAD.

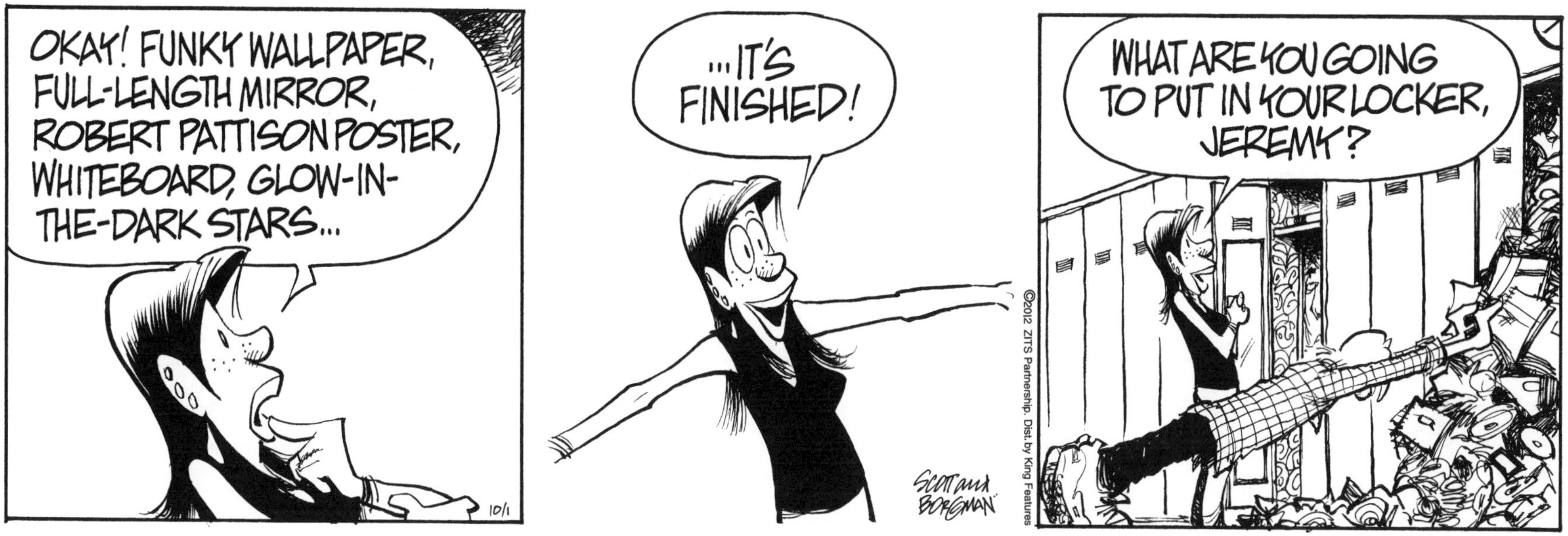
OKAY! FUNKY WALLPAPER, FULL-LENGTH MIRROR, ROBERT PATTISON POSTER, WHITEBOARD, GLOW-IN-THE-DARK STARS...
10/1
...IT'S FINISHED!
SCOTT and BORGMAN
©2012 ZITS Partnership. Dist. by King Features
WHAT ARE YOU GOING TO PUT IN YOUR LOCKER, JEREMY?

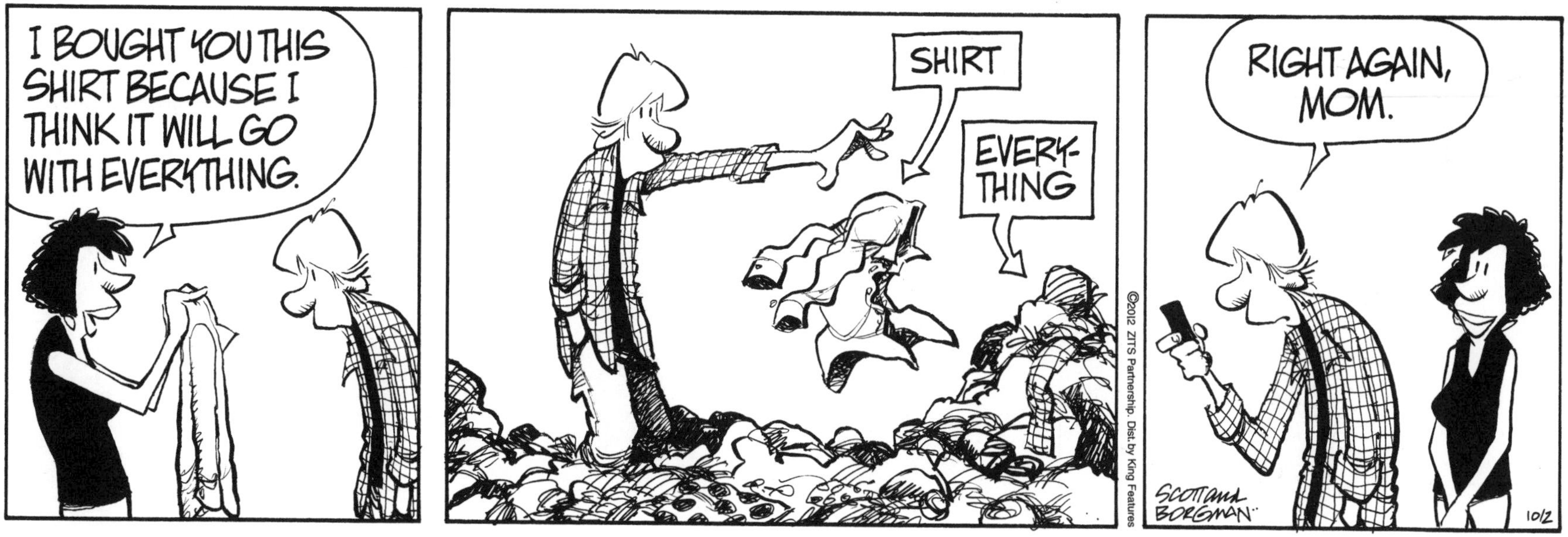
I BOUGHT YOU THIS SHIRT BECAUSE I THINK IT WILL GO WITH EVERYTHING.
SHIRT
EVERY-THING
©2012 ZITS Partnership. Dist. by King Features
RIGHT AGAIN, MOM.
SCOTT and BORGMAN
10/2

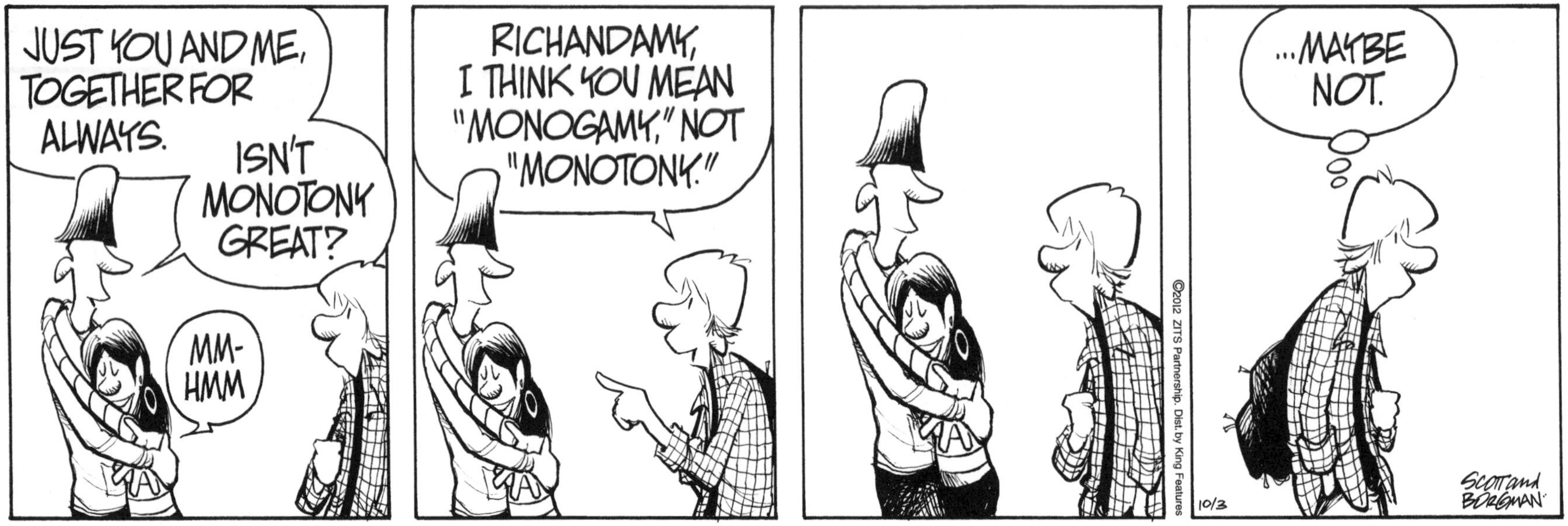
JUST YOU AND ME, TOGETHER FOR ALWAYS.
ISN'T MONOTONY GREAT?
MM-HMM
RICHANDAMY, I THINK YOU MEAN "MONOGAMY," NOT "MONOTONY."
©2012 ZITS Partnership. Dist. by King Features
10/3
...MAYBE NOT.
SCOTT and BORGMAN

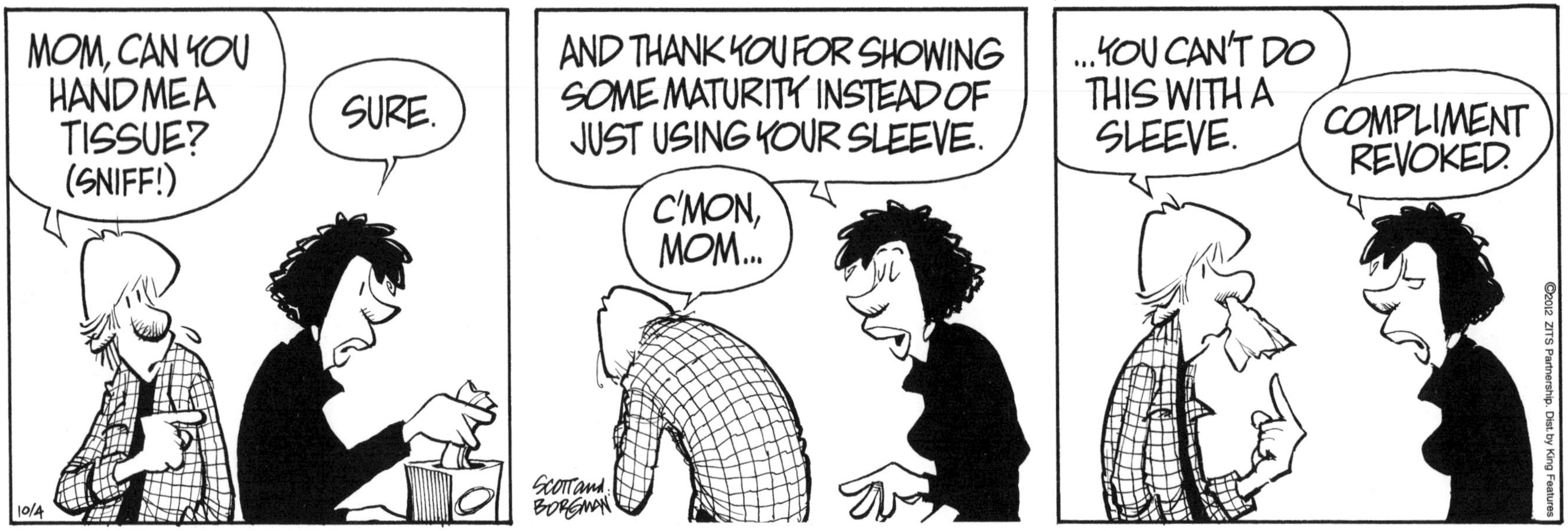
MOM, CAN YOU HAND ME A TISSUE? (SNIFF!)
SURE.
10/4
AND THANK YOU FOR SHOWING SOME MATURITY INSTEAD OF JUST USING YOUR SLEEVE.
C'MON, MOM...
SCOTT and BORGMAN
...YOU CAN'T DO THIS WITH A SLEEVE.
COMPLIMENT REVOKED.
©2012 ZITS Partnership. Dist. by King Features

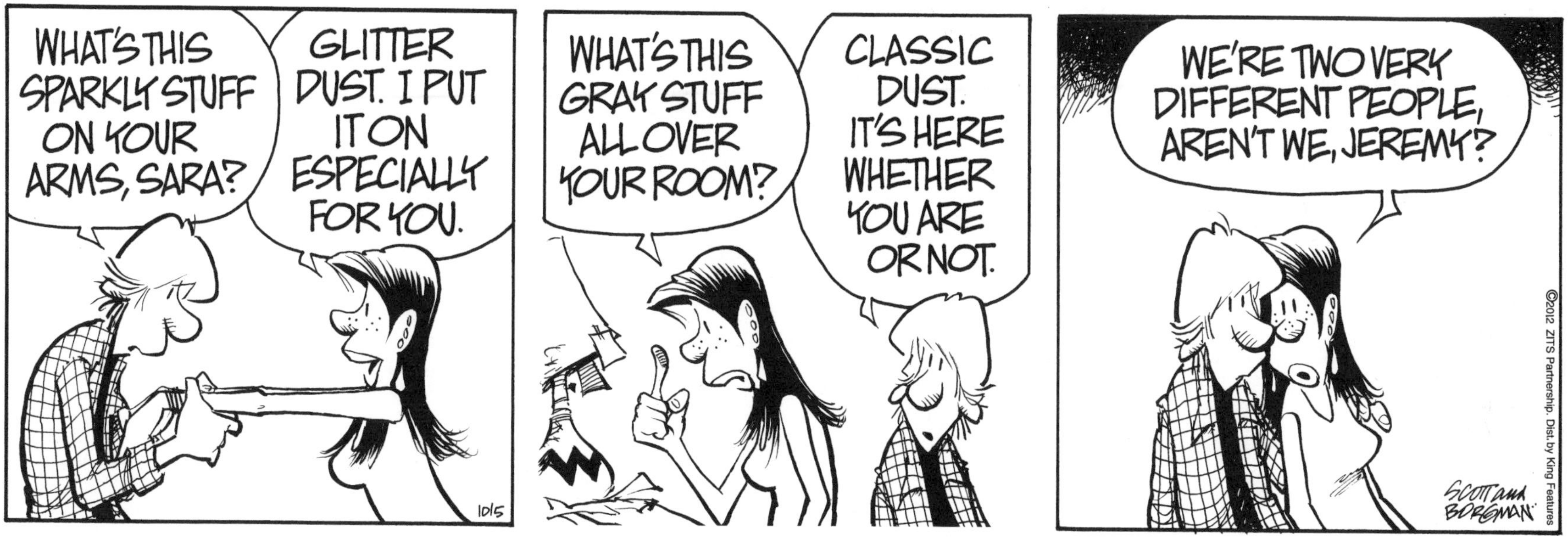
WHAT'S THIS SPARKLY STUFF ON YOUR ARMS, SARA?
GLITTER DUST. I PUT IT ON ESPECIALLY FOR YOU.
10/5
WHAT'S THIS GRAY STUFF ALL OVER YOUR ROOM?
CLASSIC DUST. IT'S HERE WHETHER YOU ARE OR NOT.
WE'RE TWO VERY DIFFERENT PEOPLE, AREN'T WE, JEREMY?
SCOTT and BORGMAN
©2012 ZITS Partnership. Dist. by King Features

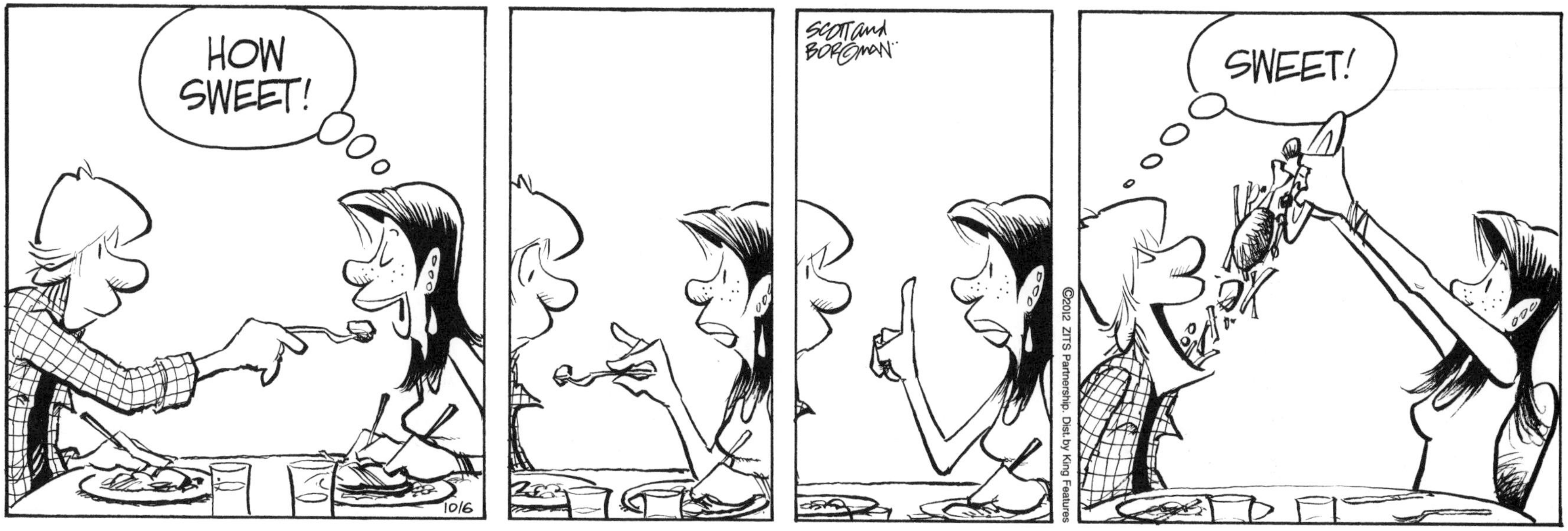
HOW SWEET!
10/6
SCOTT and BORGMAN
©2012 ZITS Partnership. Dist. by King Features
SWEET!

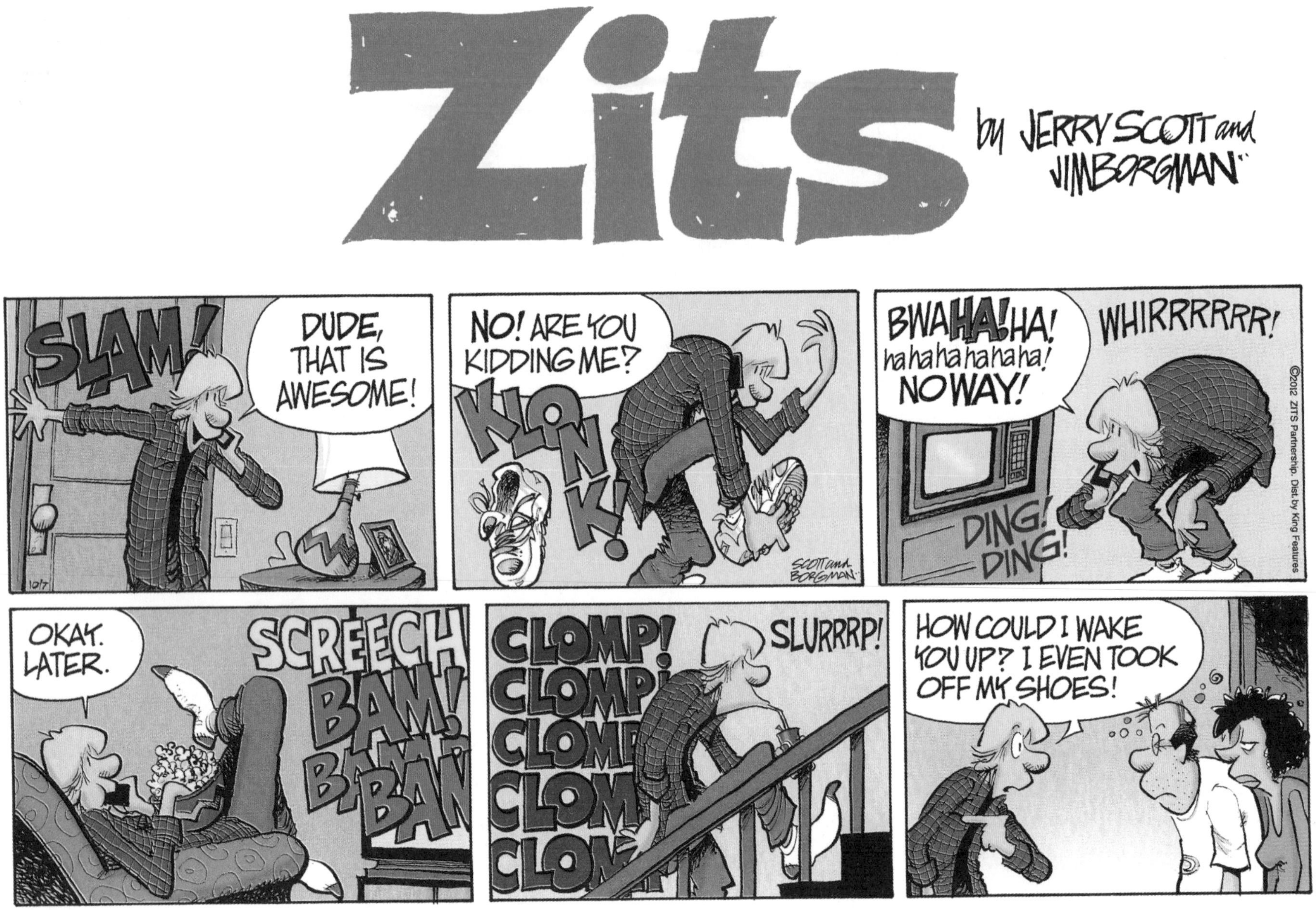
Zits
by JERRY SCOTT and JIM BORGMAN
SLAM!
DUDE, THAT IS AWESOME!
NO! ARE YOU KIDDING ME?
KLONK!
BWAHA! HA! HA! hahahahahaha! NO WAY!
WHIRRRRRR!
DING! DING!
©2012 ZITS Partnership. Dist. by King Features
OKAY. LATER.
SCREECH
BAM!
CLOMP! CLOMP!
SLURRRP!
HOW COULD I WAKE YOU UP? I EVEN TOOK OFF MY SHOES!

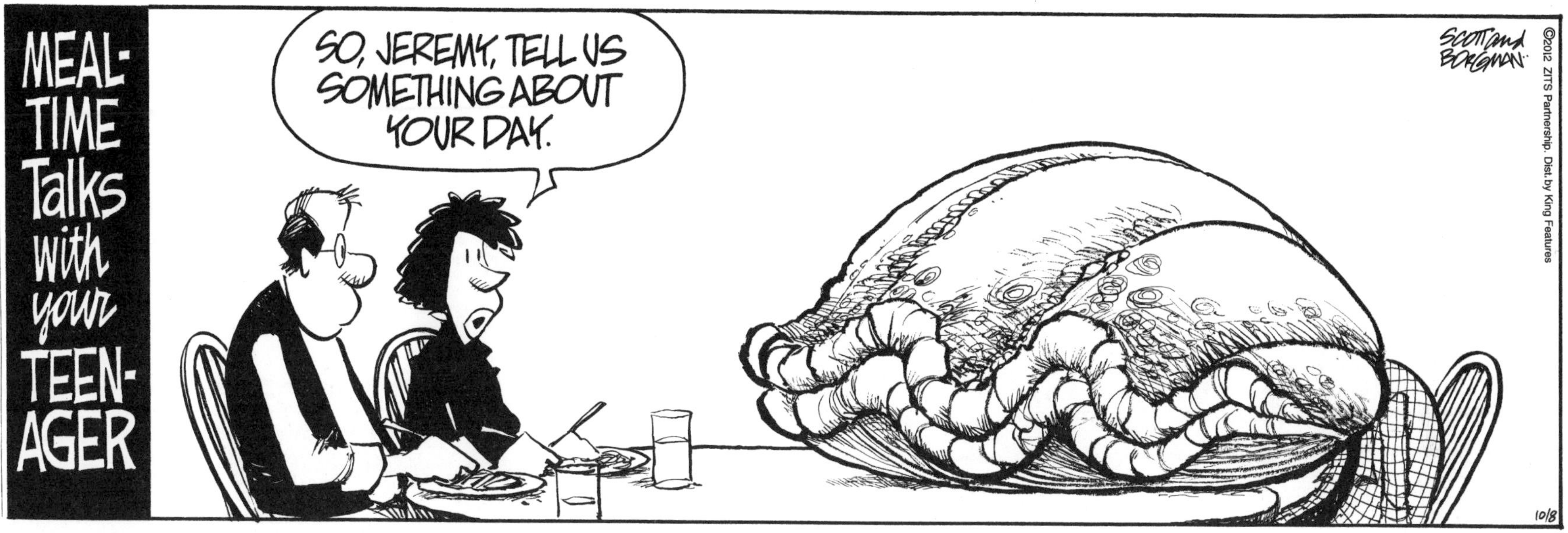
MEAL-TIME Talks with your TEEN-AGER
SO, JEREMY, TELL US SOMETHING ABOUT YOUR DAY.
SCOTT and BORGMAN
©2012 ZITS Partnership. Dist. by King Features
10/8

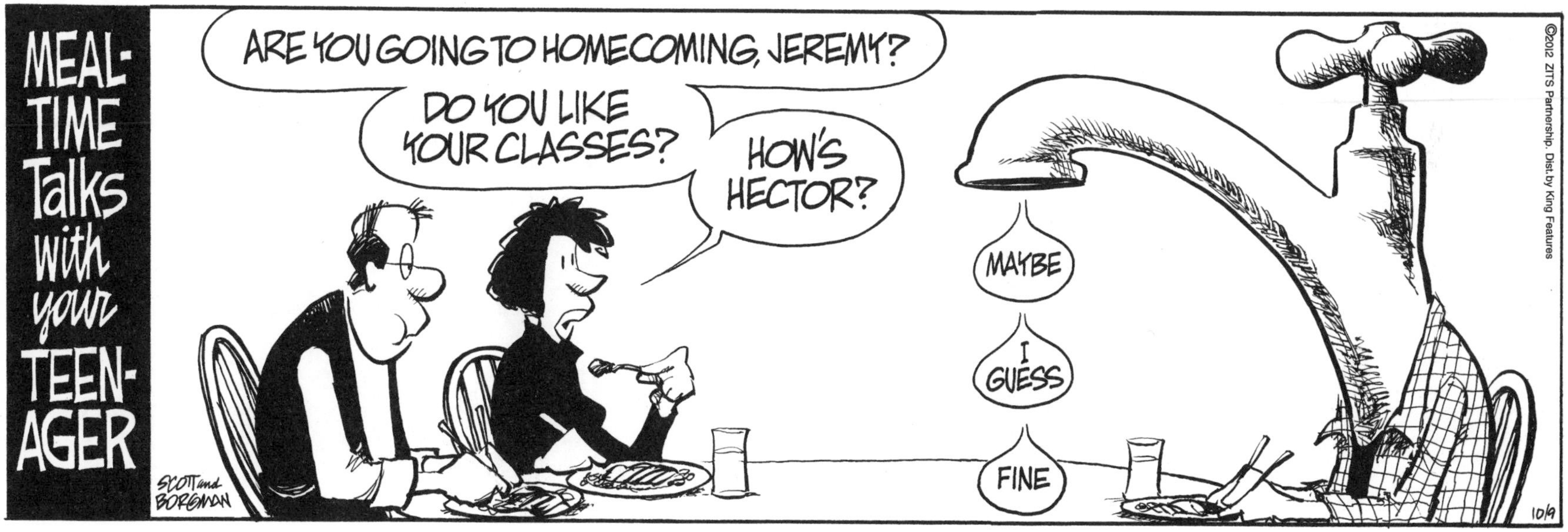
MEAL-TIME Talks with your TEEN-AGER
ARE YOU GOING TO HOMECOMING, JEREMY?
DO YOU LIKE YOUR CLASSES?
HOW'S HECTOR?
MAYBE
I GUESS
FINE
SCOTT and BORGMAN
©2012 ZITS Partnership. Dist. by King Features
10/9

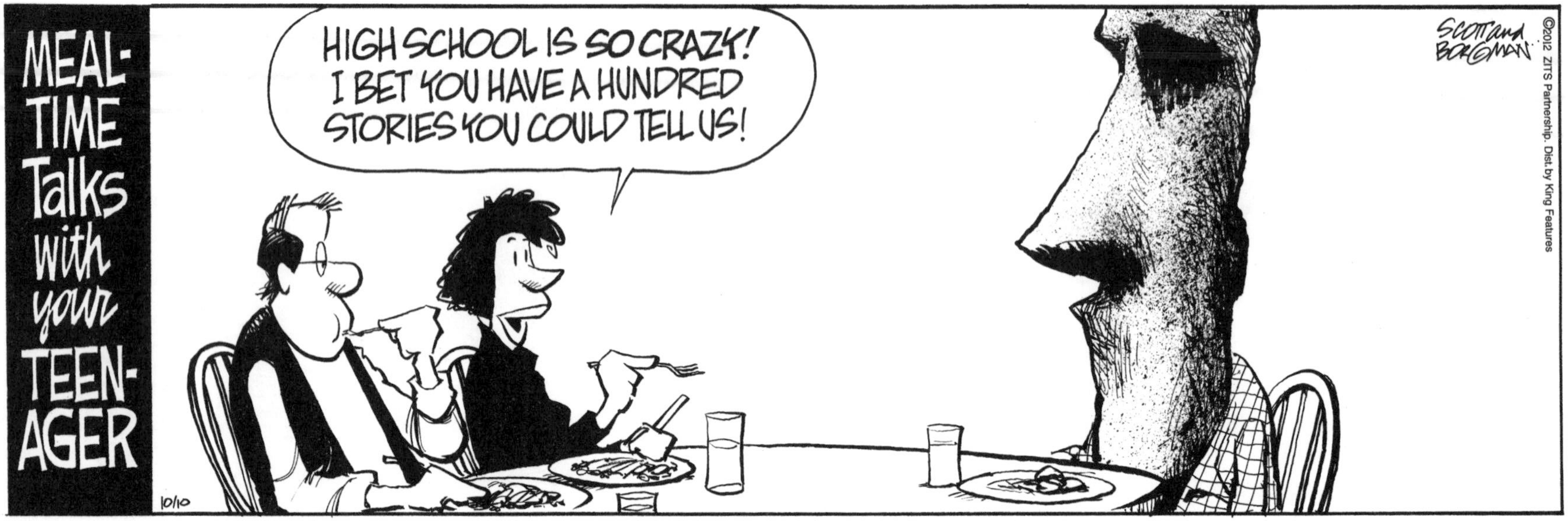
MEAL-TIME Talks with your TEEN-AGER
HIGH SCHOOL IS SO CRAZY! I BET YOU HAVE A HUNDRED STORIES YOU COULD TELL US!
SCOTT and BORGMAN
©2012 ZITS Partnership. Dist. by King Features
10/10

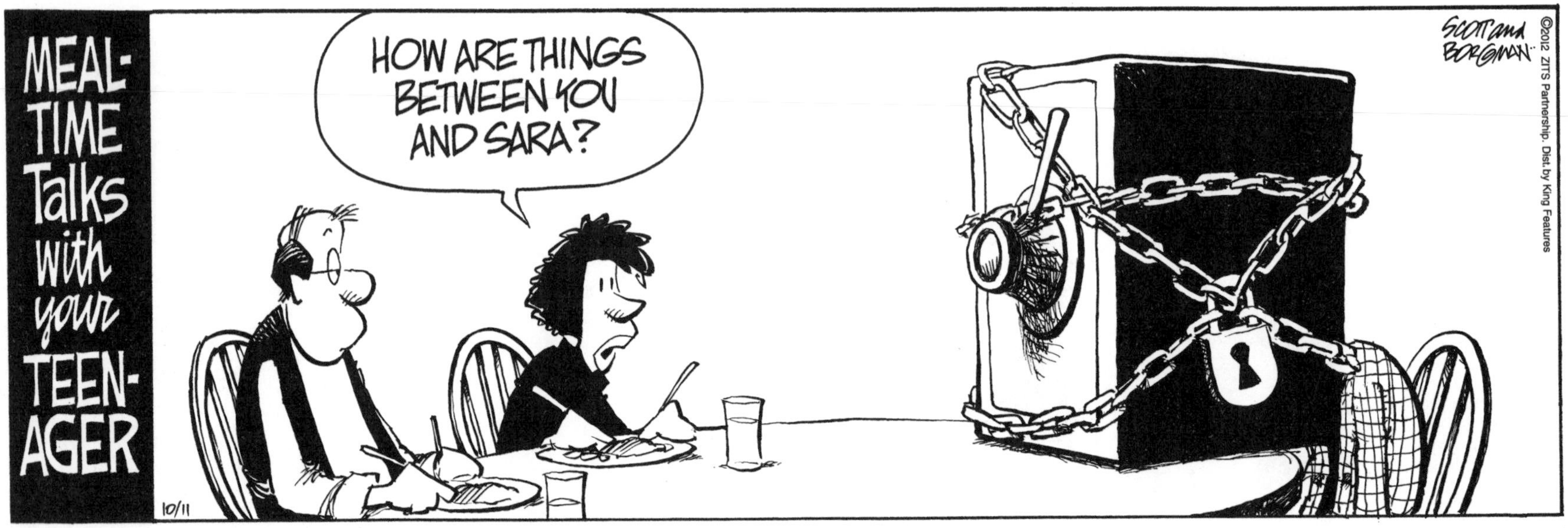
MEAL-TIME Talks with your TEEN-AGER
HOW ARE THINGS BETWEEN YOU AND SARA?
SCOTT and BORGMAN
©2012 ZITS Partnership. Dist. by King Features
10/11

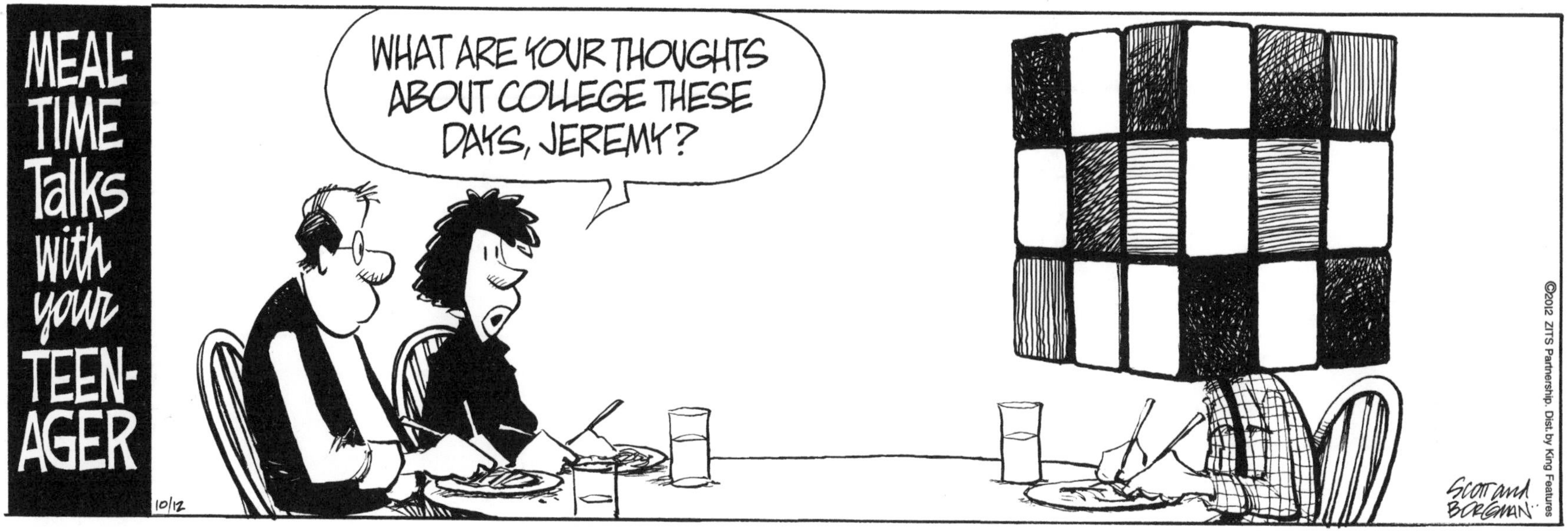
MEAL-TIME Talks with your TEEN-AGER
WHAT ARE YOUR THOUGHTS ABOUT COLLEGE THESE DAYS, JEREMY?
10/12
SCOTT and BORGMAN
©2012 ZITS Partnership. Dist. by King Features

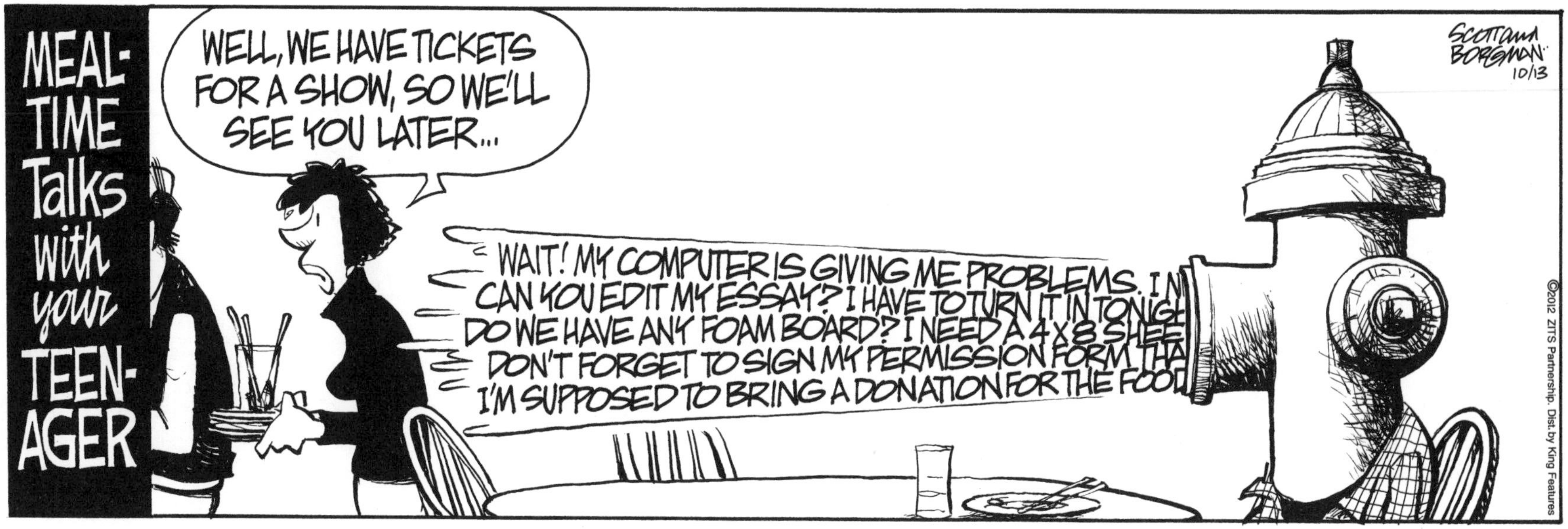
MEAL-TIME Talks with your TEEN-AGER
SCOTT and BORGMAN 10/13
WELL, WE HAVE TICKETS FOR A SHOW, SO WE'LL SEE YOU LATER...
WAIT! MY COMPUTER IS GIVING ME PROBLEMS. I N
CAN YOU EDIT MY ESSAY? I HAVE TO TURN IT IN TONIG
DO WE HAVE ANY FOAM BOARD? I NEED A 4 X 8 SHEE
DON'T FORGET TO SIGN MY PERMISSION FORM THA
I'M SUPPOSED TO BRING A DONATION FOR THE FOO
©2012 ZITS Partnership. Dist. by King Features

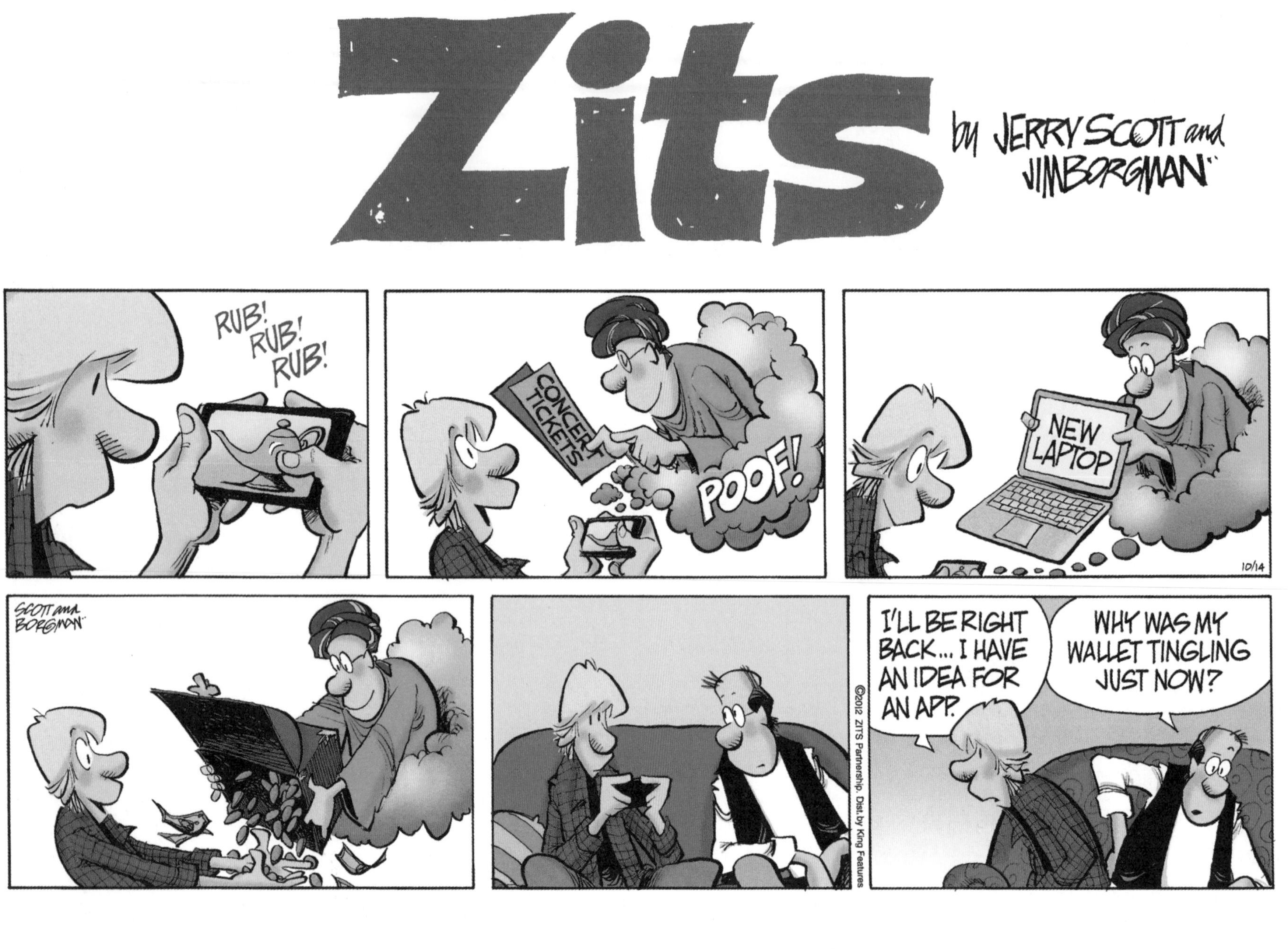
Zits
by JERRY SCOTT and JIM BORGMAN
RUB! RUB! RUB!
CONCERT TICKETS
POOF!
NEW LAPTOP
10/14
SCOTT and BORGMAN
©2012 ZITS Partnership. Dist. by King Features
I'LL BE RIGHT BACK... I HAVE AN IDEA FOR AN APP.
WHY WAS MY WALLET TINGLING JUST NOW?

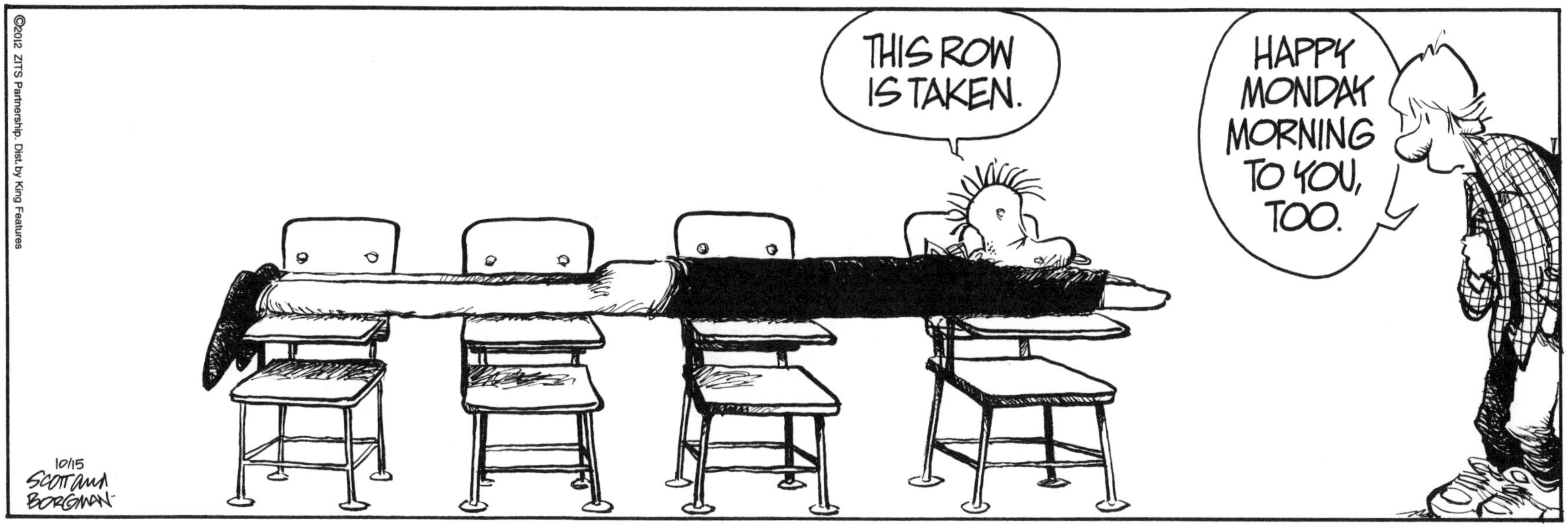
THIS ROW IS TAKEN.
HAPPY MONDAY MORNING TO YOU, TOO.
10/15
SCOTT AND BORGMAN
©2012 ZITS Partnership. Dist. by King Features

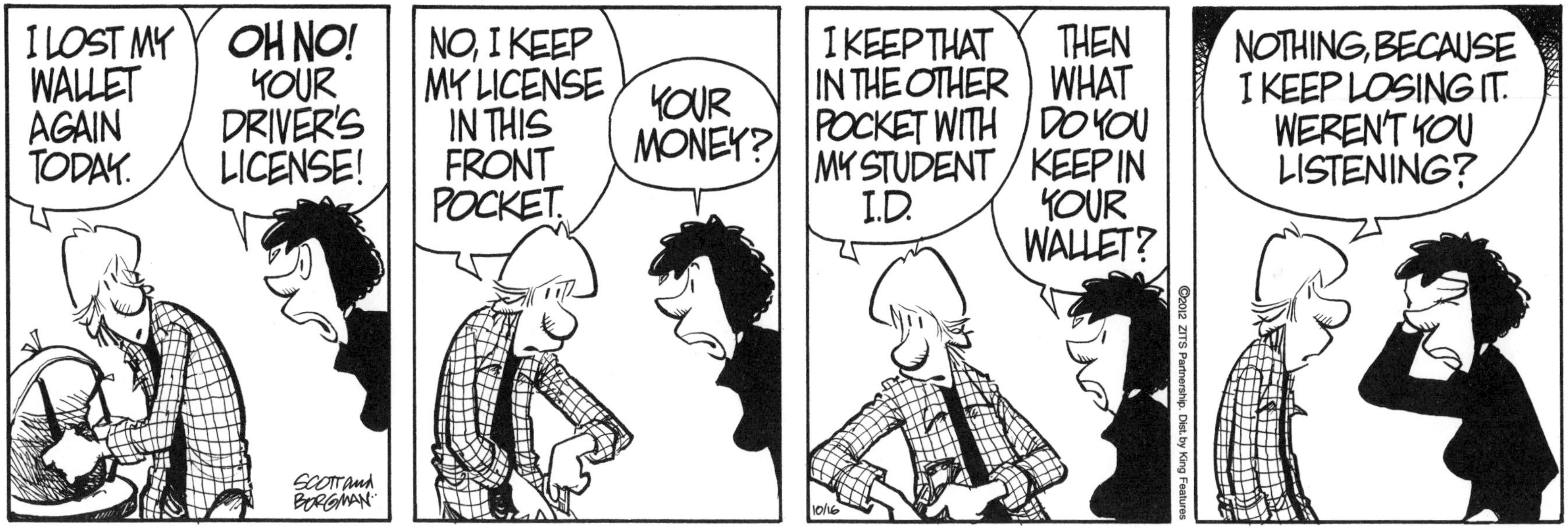
I LOST MY WALLET AGAIN TODAY.
OH NO! YOUR DRIVER'S LICENSE!
SCOTT AND BORGMAN
NO, I KEEP MY LICENSE IN THIS FRONT POCKET.
YOUR MONEY?
I KEEP THAT IN THE OTHER POCKET WITH MY STUDENT I.D.
THEN WHAT DO YOU KEEP IN YOUR WALLET?
10/16
©2012 ZITS Partnership. Dist. by King Features
NOTHING, BECAUSE I KEEP LOSING IT. WEREN'T YOU LISTENING?

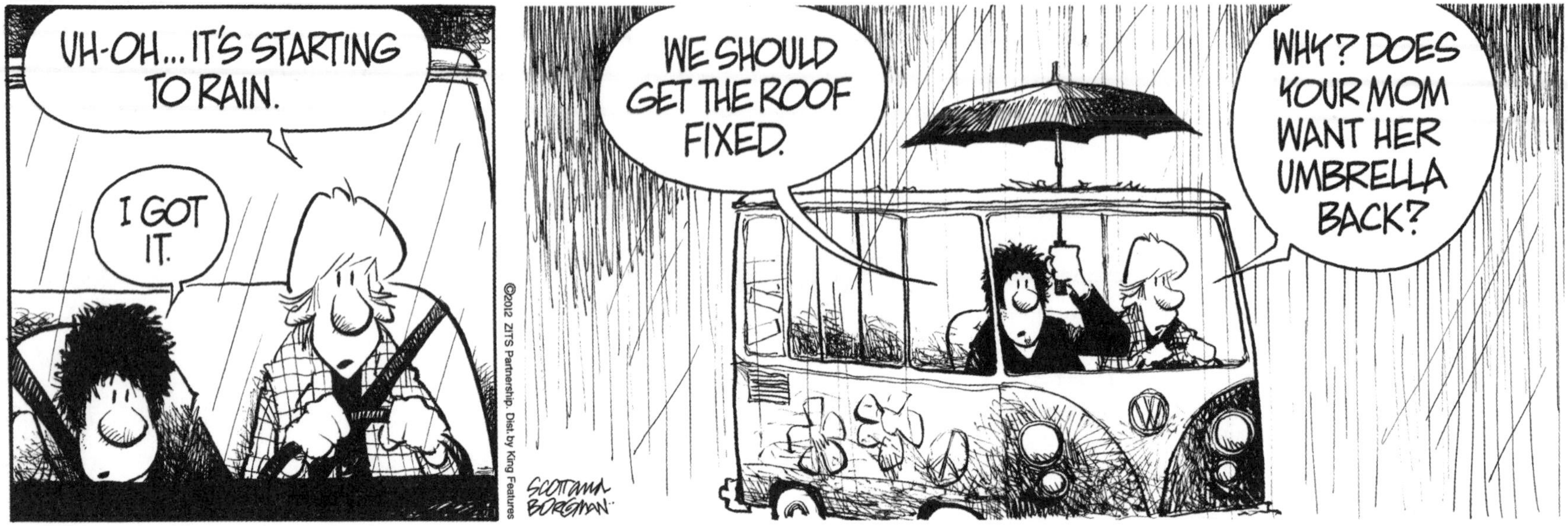
UH-OH... IT'S STARTING TO RAIN.
I GOT IT.
WE SHOULD GET THE ROOF FIXED.
WHY? DOES YOUR MOM WANT HER UMBRELLA BACK?
©2012 ZITS Partnership. Dist. by King Features
SCOTT AND BORGMAN

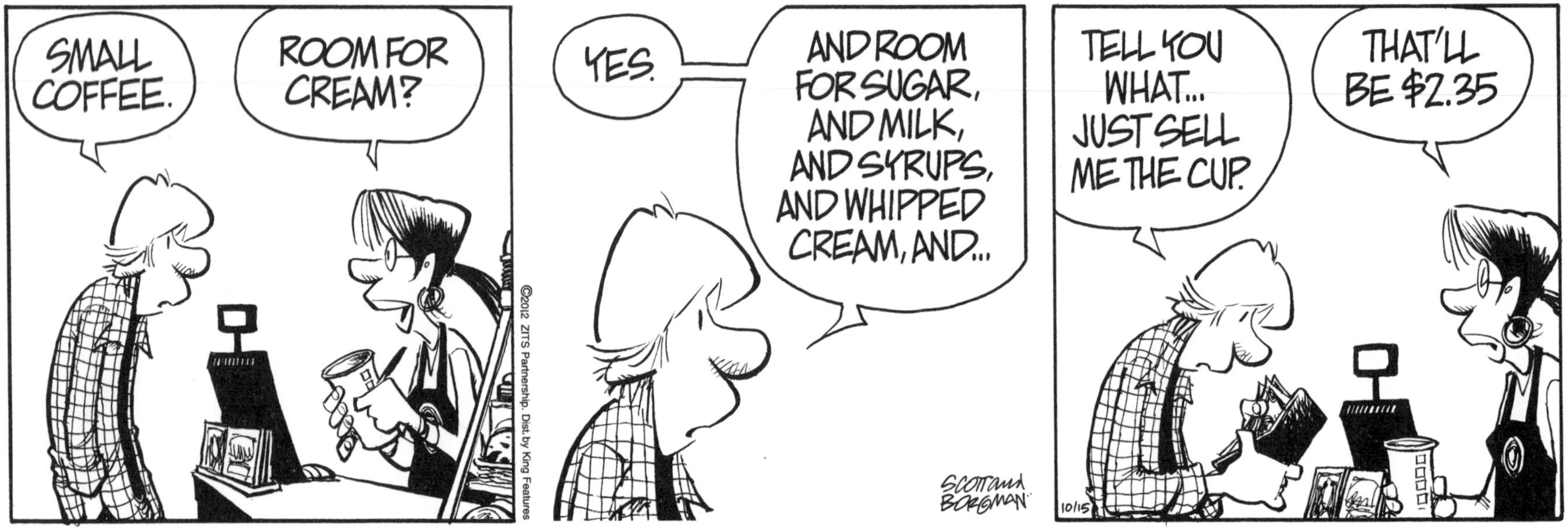
SMALL COFFEE.
ROOM FOR CREAM?
YES.
AND ROOM FOR SUGAR, AND MILK, AND SYRUPS, AND WHIPPED CREAM, AND...
TELL YOU WHAT... JUST SELL ME THE CUP.
THAT'LL BE $2.35
©2012 ZITS Partnership. Dist. by King Features
SCOTT AND BORGMAN
10/15

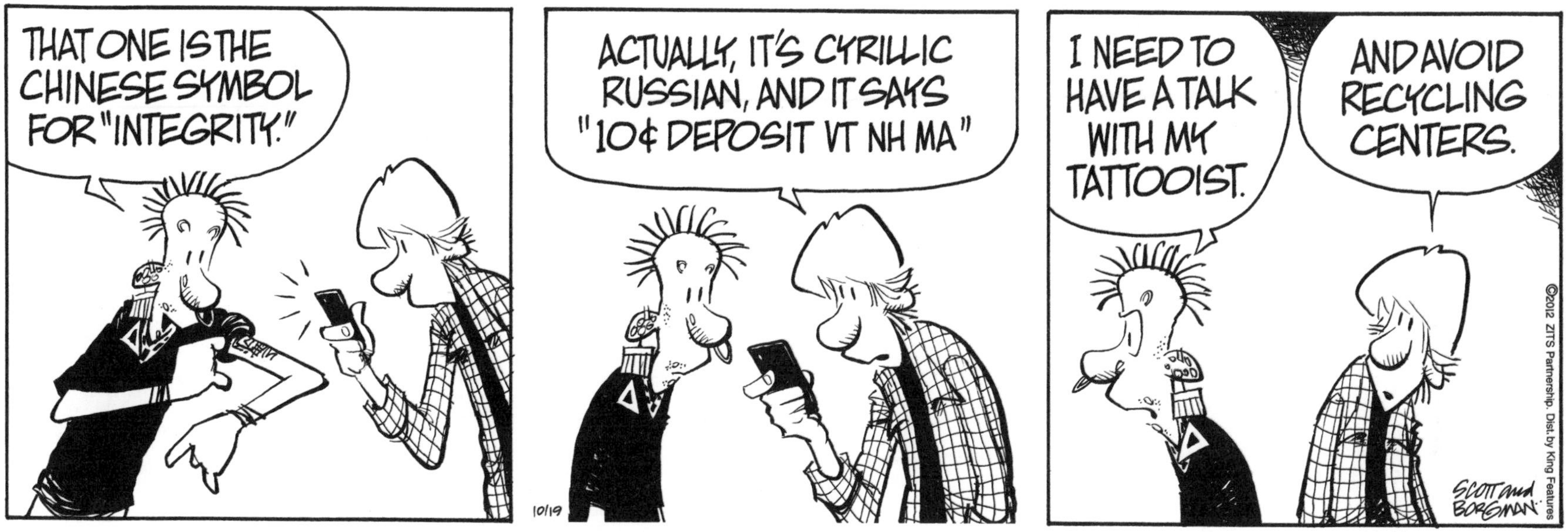
THAT ONE IS THE CHINESE SYMBOL FOR "INTEGRITY."
ACTUALLY, IT'S CYRILLIC RUSSIAN, AND IT SAYS "10¢ DEPOSIT VT NH MA"
10/19
I NEED TO HAVE A TALK WITH MY TATTOOIST.
AND AVOID RECYCLING CENTERS.
©2012 ZITS Partnership. Dist. by King Features
SCOTT and BORGMAN

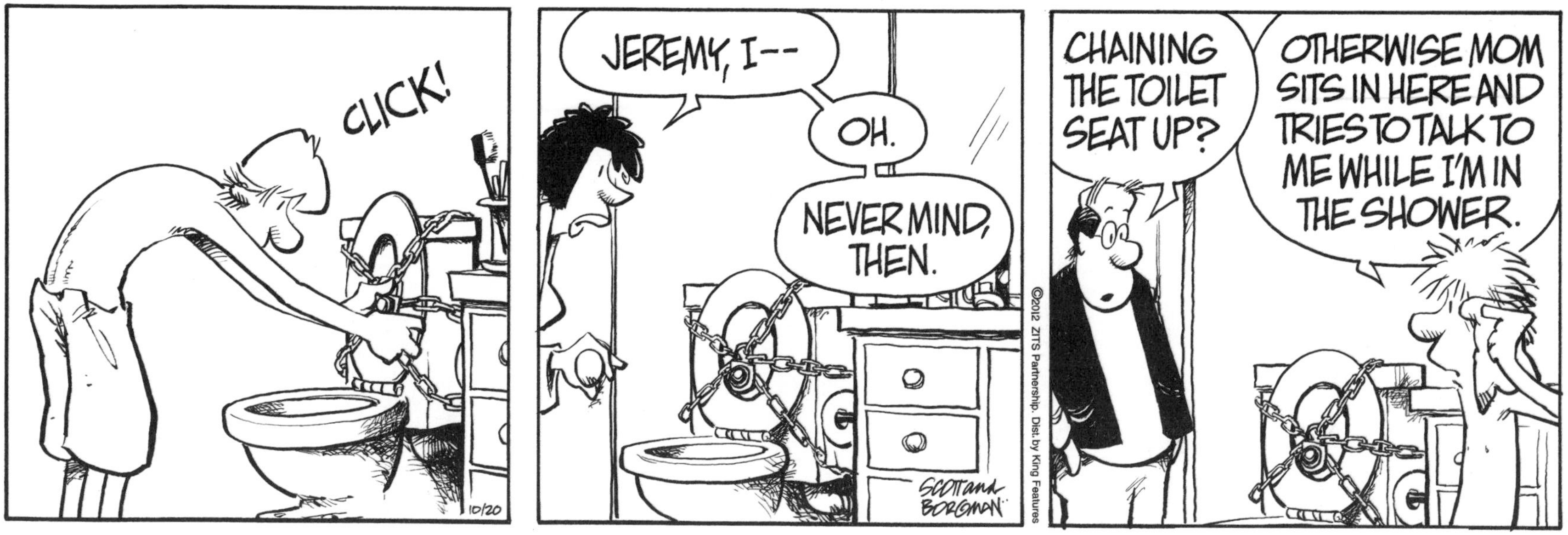
CLICK!
10/20
JEREMY, I--
OH.
NEVER MIND, THEN.
©2012 ZITS Partnership. Dist. by King Features
SCOTT and BORGMAN
CHAINING THE TOILET SEAT UP?
OTHERWISE MOM SITS IN HERE AND TRIES TO TALK TO ME WHILE I'M IN THE SHOWER.

Zits

by JERRY SCOTT and JIM BORGMAN

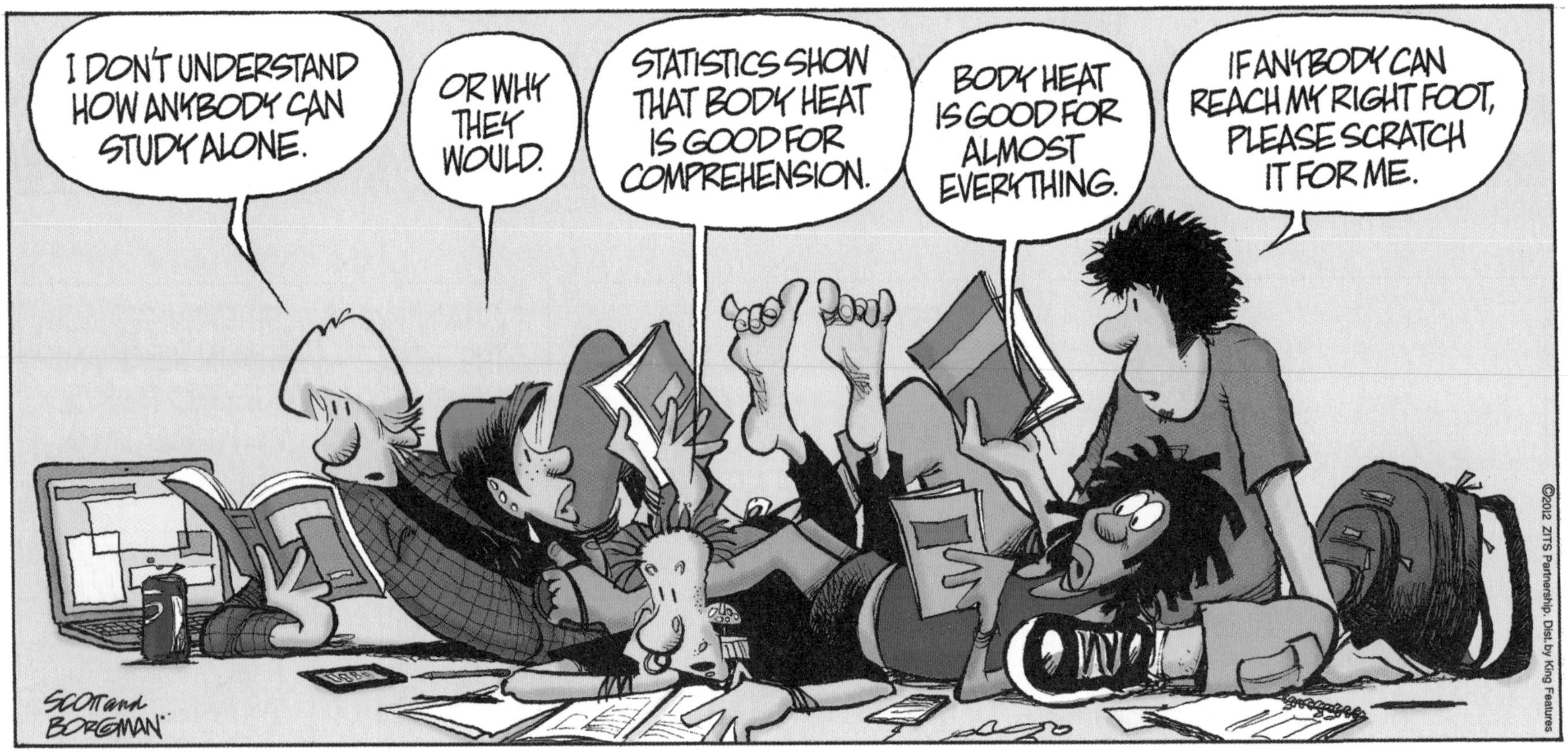
I DON'T UNDERSTAND HOW ANYBODY CAN STUDY ALONE.
OR WHY THEY WOULD.
STATISTICS SHOW THAT BODY HEAT IS GOOD FOR COMPREHENSION.
BODY HEAT IS GOOD FOR ALMOST EVERYTHING.
IF ANYBODY CAN REACH MY RIGHT FOOT, PLEASE SCRATCH IT FOR ME.
SCOTT and BORGMAN
©2012 ZITS Partnership. Dist. by King Features

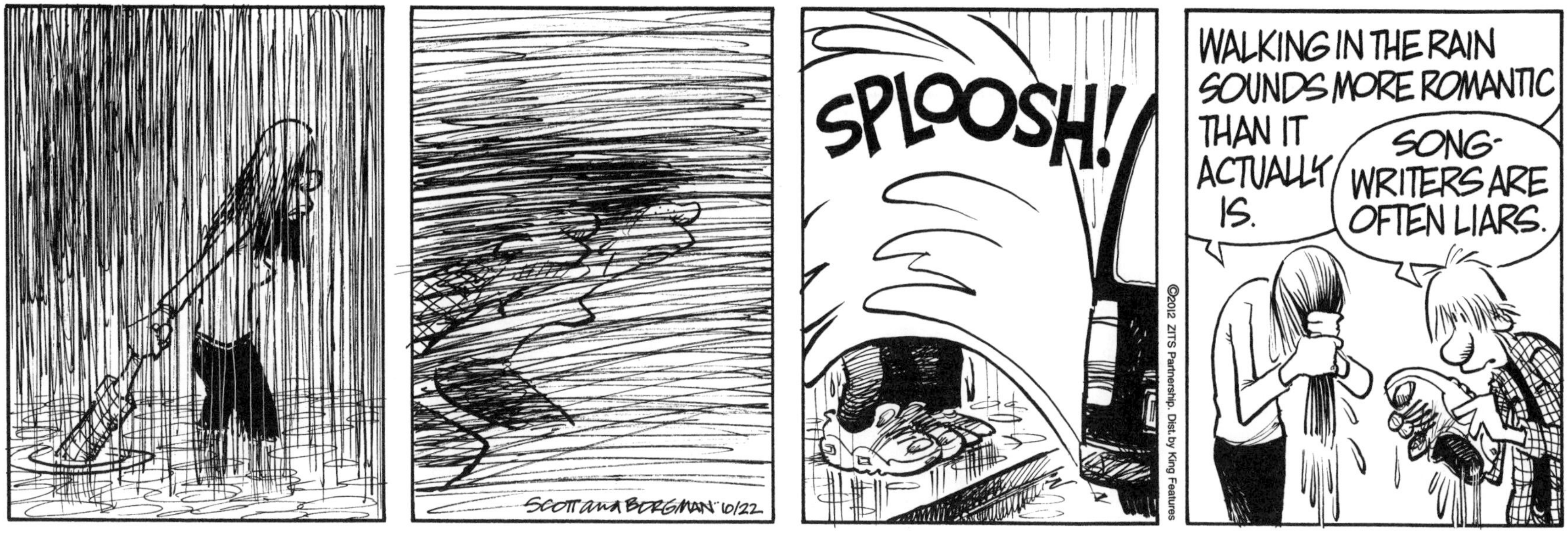
SPLOOSH!
©2012 ZITS Partnership. Dist.by King Features
WALKING IN THE RAIN SOUNDS MORE ROMANTIC THAN IT ACTUALLY IS.
SONG-WRITERS ARE OFTEN LIARS.

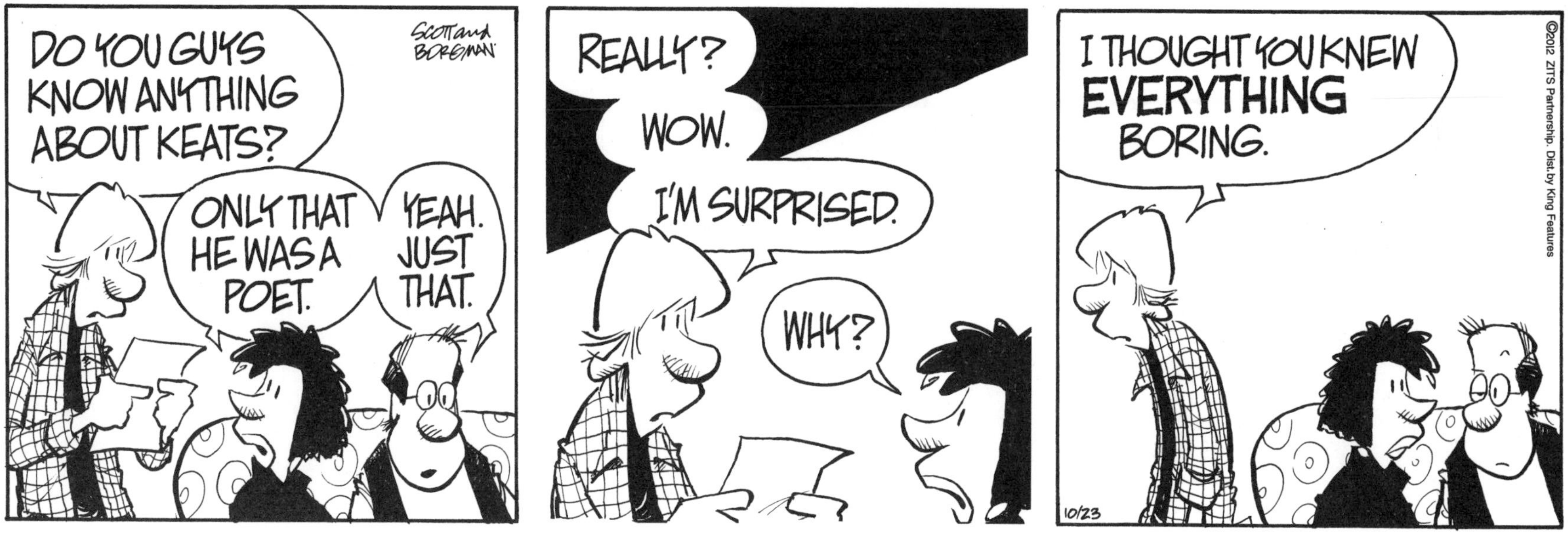
DO YOU GUYS KNOW ANYTHING ABOUT KEATS?
ONLY THAT HE WAS A POET.
YEAH. JUST THAT.
REALLY?
WOW.
I'M SURPRISED.
WHY?
I THOUGHT YOU KNEW EVERYTHING BORING.
©2012 ZITS Partnership. Dist.by King Features

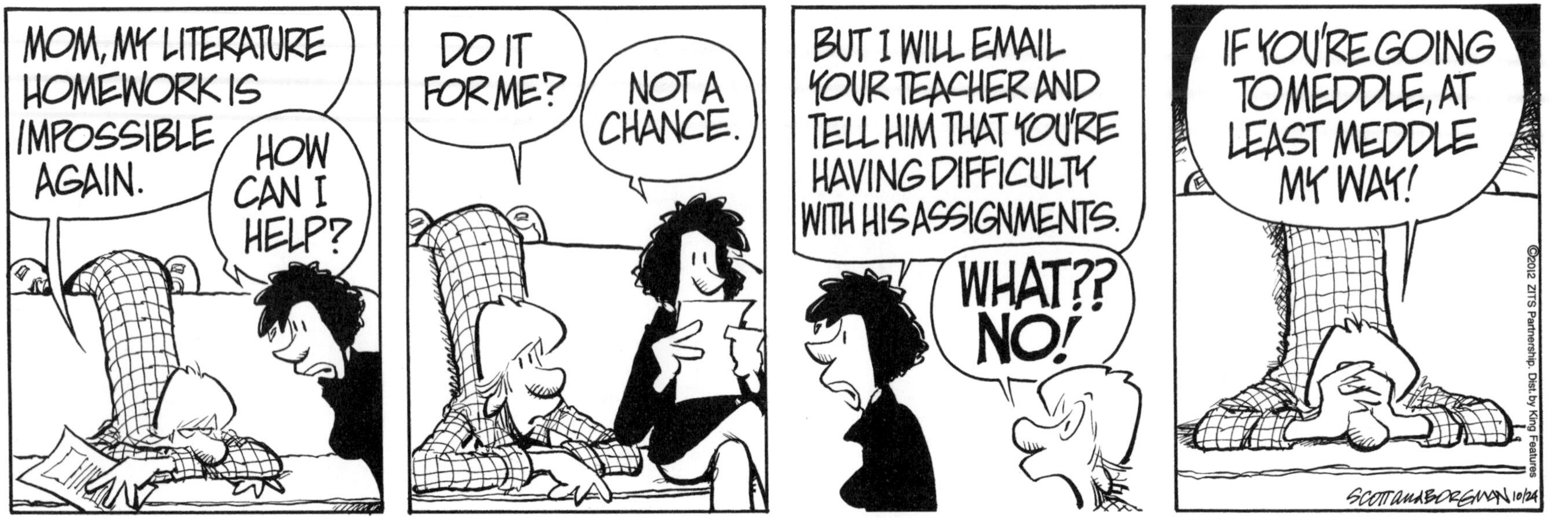
MOM, MY LITERATURE HOMEWORK IS IMPOSSIBLE AGAIN.
HOW CAN I HELP?
DO IT FOR ME?
NOT A CHANCE.
BUT I WILL EMAIL YOUR TEACHER AND TELL HIM THAT YOU'RE HAVING DIFFICULTY WITH HIS ASSIGNMENTS.
WHAT?? NO!
IF YOU'RE GOING TO MEDDLE, AT LEAST MEDDLE MY WAY!
©2012 ZITS Partnership. Dist. by King Features
SCOTT and BORGMAN 10/24

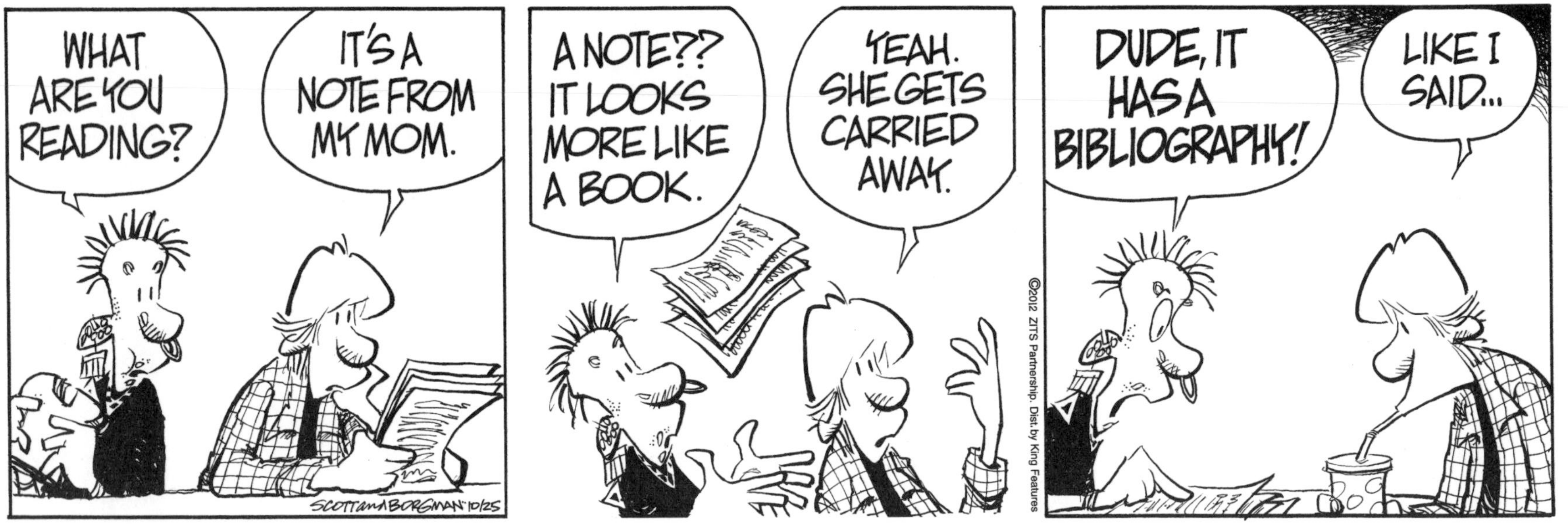
WHAT ARE YOU READING?
IT'S A NOTE FROM MY MOM.
A NOTE?? IT LOOKS MORE LIKE A BOOK.
YEAH. SHE GETS CARRIED AWAY.
DUDE, IT HAS A BIBLIOGRAPHY!
LIKE I SAID...
©2012 ZITS Partnership. Dist. by King Features
SCOTT and BORGMAN 10/25

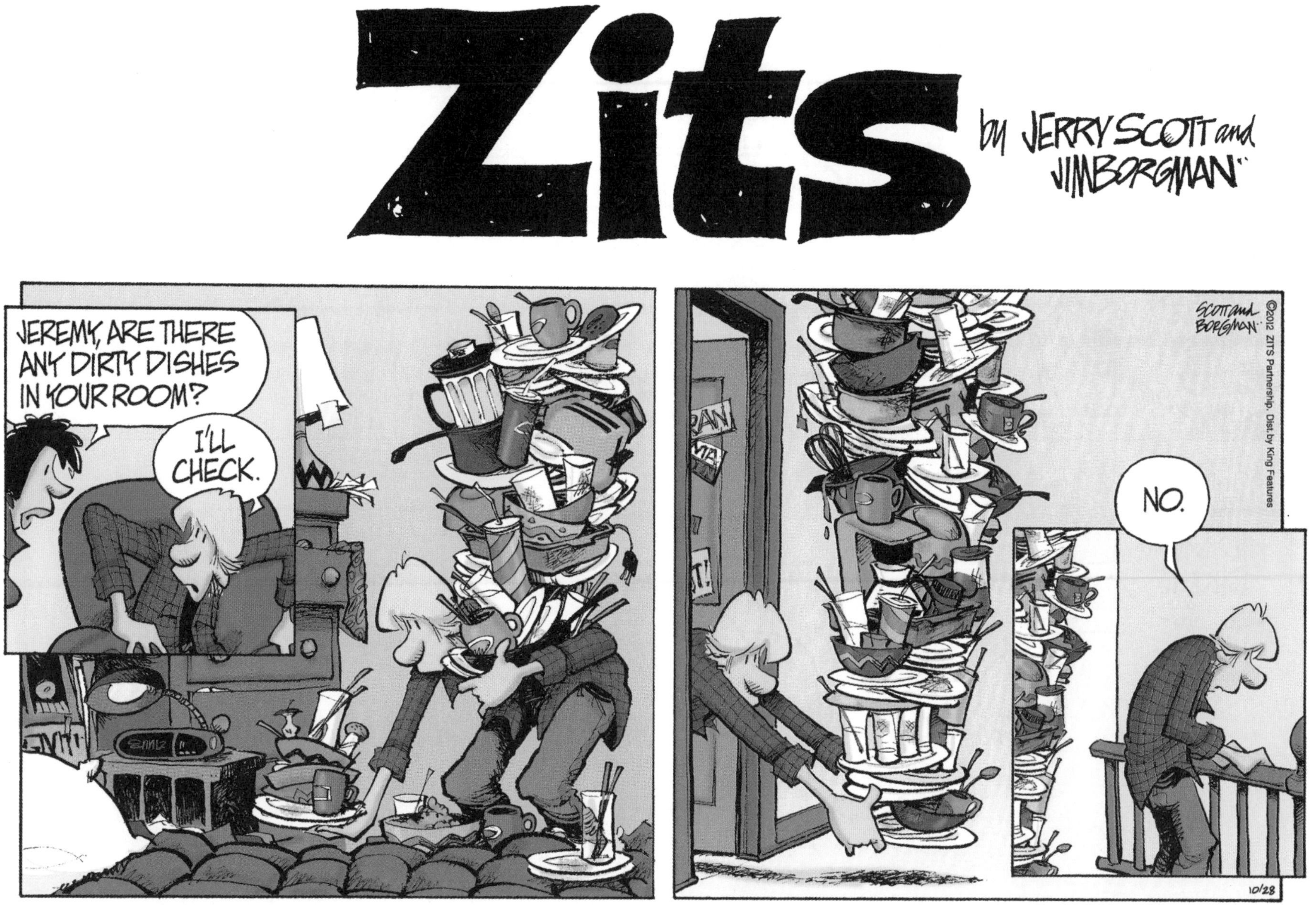
Zits
by JERRY SCOTT and JIM BORGMAN
JEREMY, ARE THERE ANY DIRTY DISHES IN YOUR ROOM?
I'LL CHECK.
SCOTT and BORGMAN
©2012 ZITS Partnership. Dist. by King Features
NO.
10/28

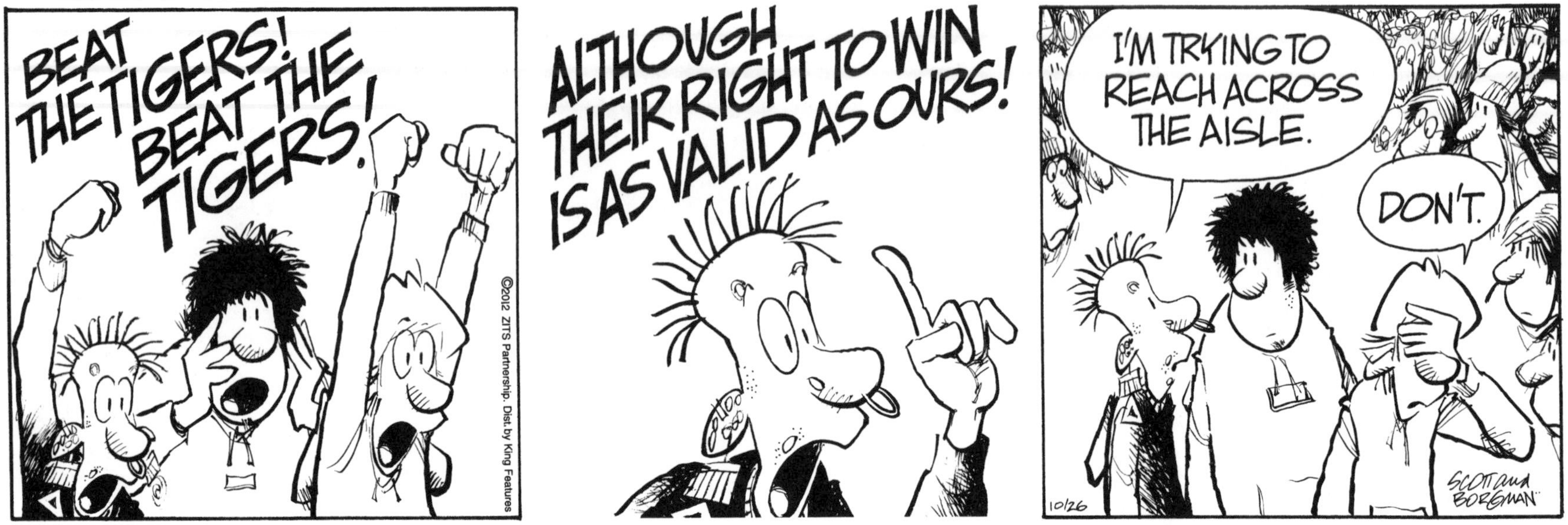
BEAT THE TIGERS! BEAT THE TIGERS!
ALTHOUGH THEIR RIGHT TO WIN IS AS VALID AS OURS!
I'M TRYING TO REACH ACROSS THE AISLE.
DON'T.
©2012 ZITS Partnership. Dist. by King Features
SCOTT and BORGMAN
10/26

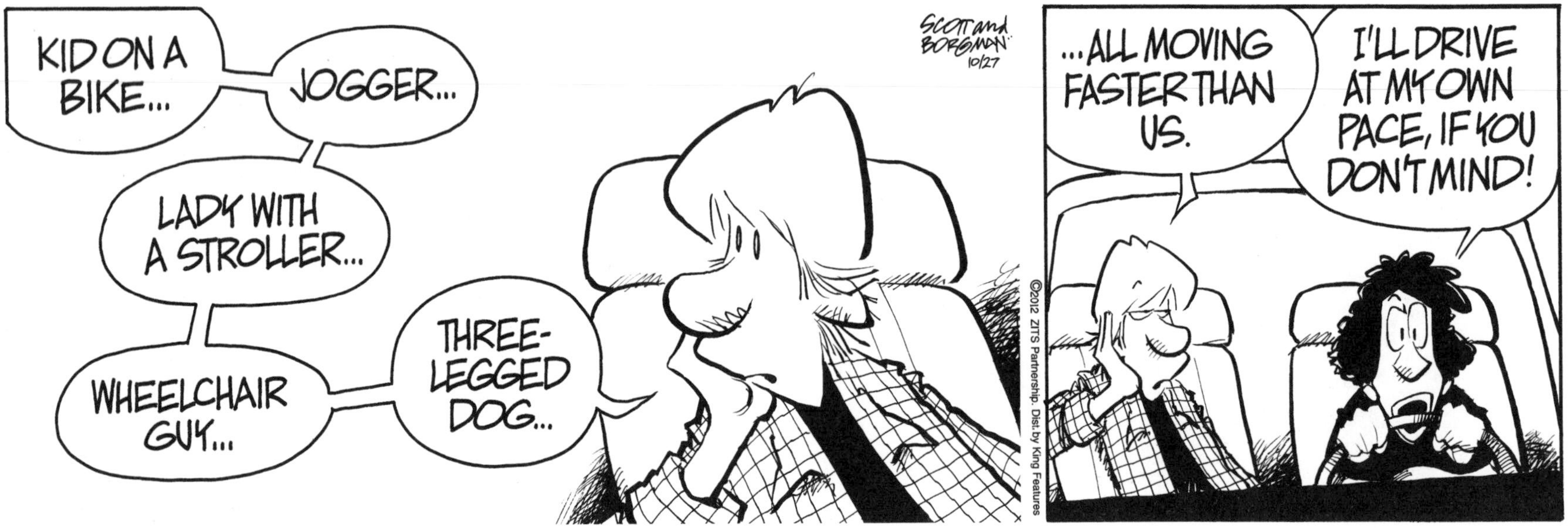
KID ON A BIKE...
JOGGER...
LADY WITH A STROLLER...
WHEELCHAIR GUY...
THREE-LEGGED DOG...
...ALL MOVING FASTER THAN US.
I'LL DRIVE AT MY OWN PACE, IF YOU DON'T MIND!
SCOTT and BORGMAN
10/27
©2012 ZITS Partnership. Dist. by King Features

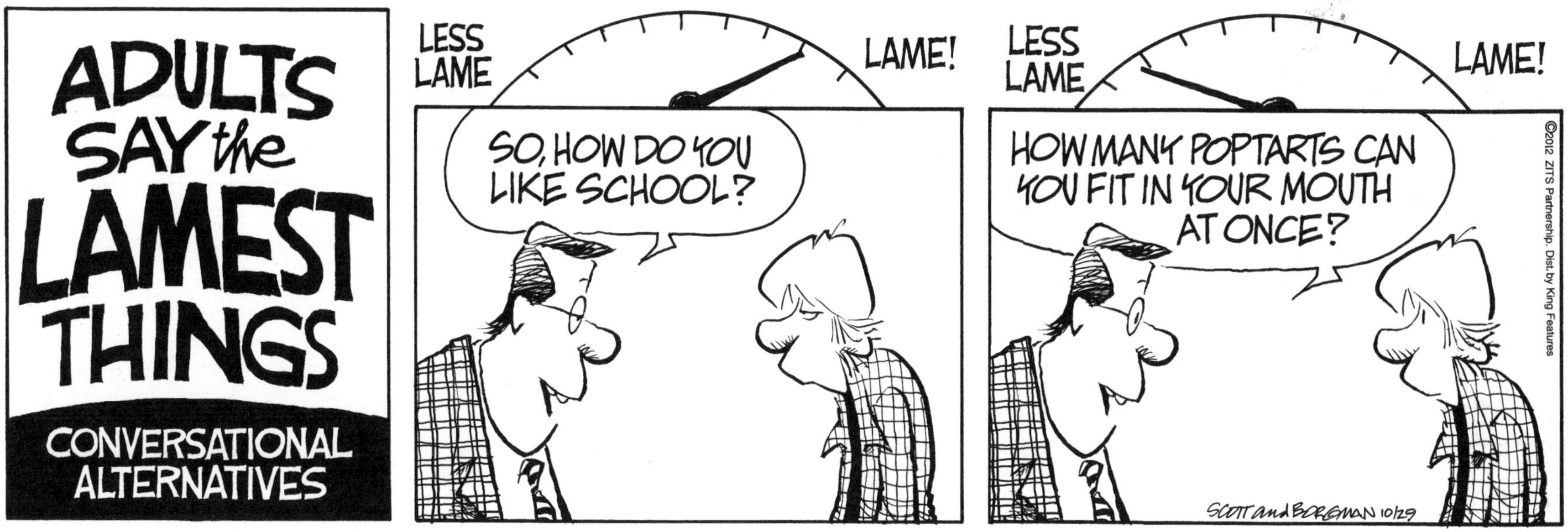
ADULTS SAY the LAMEST THINGS
CONVERSATIONAL ALTERNATIVES
LESS LAME
LAME!
SO, HOW DO YOU LIKE SCHOOL?
LESS LAME
LAME!
HOW MANY POPTARTS CAN YOU FIT IN YOUR MOUTH AT ONCE?
©2012 ZITS Partnership. Dist. by King Features
SCOTT and BORGMAN 10/29

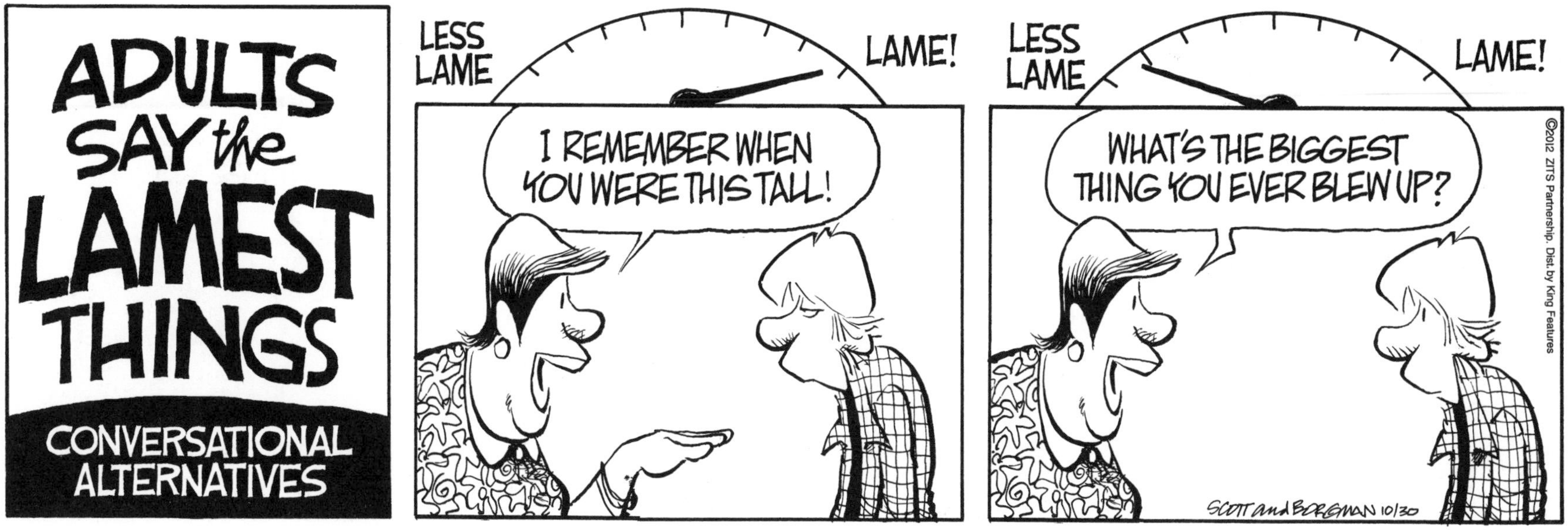
ADULTS SAY the LAMEST THINGS
CONVERSATIONAL ALTERNATIVES
LESS LAME
LAME!
I REMEMBER WHEN YOU WERE THIS TALL!
LESS LAME
LAME!
WHAT'S THE BIGGEST THING YOU EVER BLEW UP?
©2012 ZITS Partnership. Dist. by King Features
SCOTT and BORGMAN 10/30

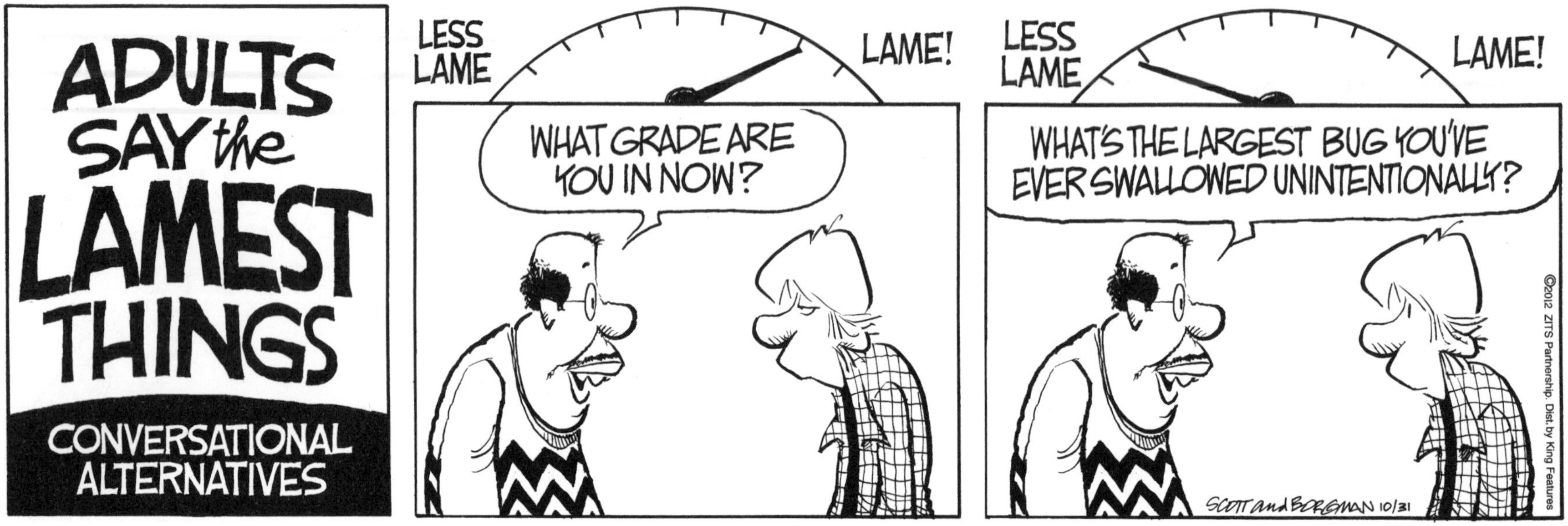
ADULTS SAY the LAMEST THINGS
CONVERSATIONAL ALTERNATIVES
LESS LAME
LAME!
WHAT GRADE ARE YOU IN NOW?
LESS LAME
LAME!
WHAT'S THE LARGEST BUG YOU'VE EVER SWALLOWED UNINTENTIONALLY?
SCOTT and BORGMAN 10/31
©2012 ZITS Partnership. Dist. by King Features

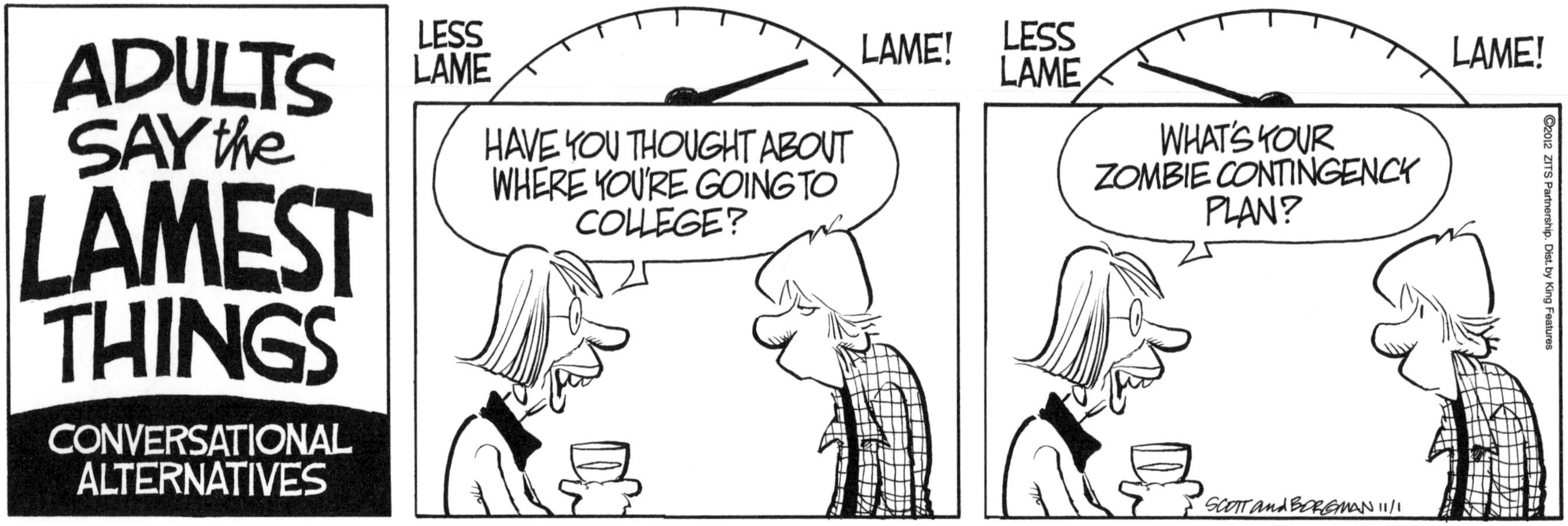
ADULTS SAY the LAMEST THINGS
CONVERSATIONAL ALTERNATIVES
LESS LAME
LAME!
HAVE YOU THOUGHT ABOUT WHERE YOU'RE GOING TO COLLEGE?
LESS LAME
LAME!
WHAT'S YOUR ZOMBIE CONTINGENCY PLAN?
SCOTT and BORGMAN 11/1
©2012 ZITS Partnership. Dist. by King Features

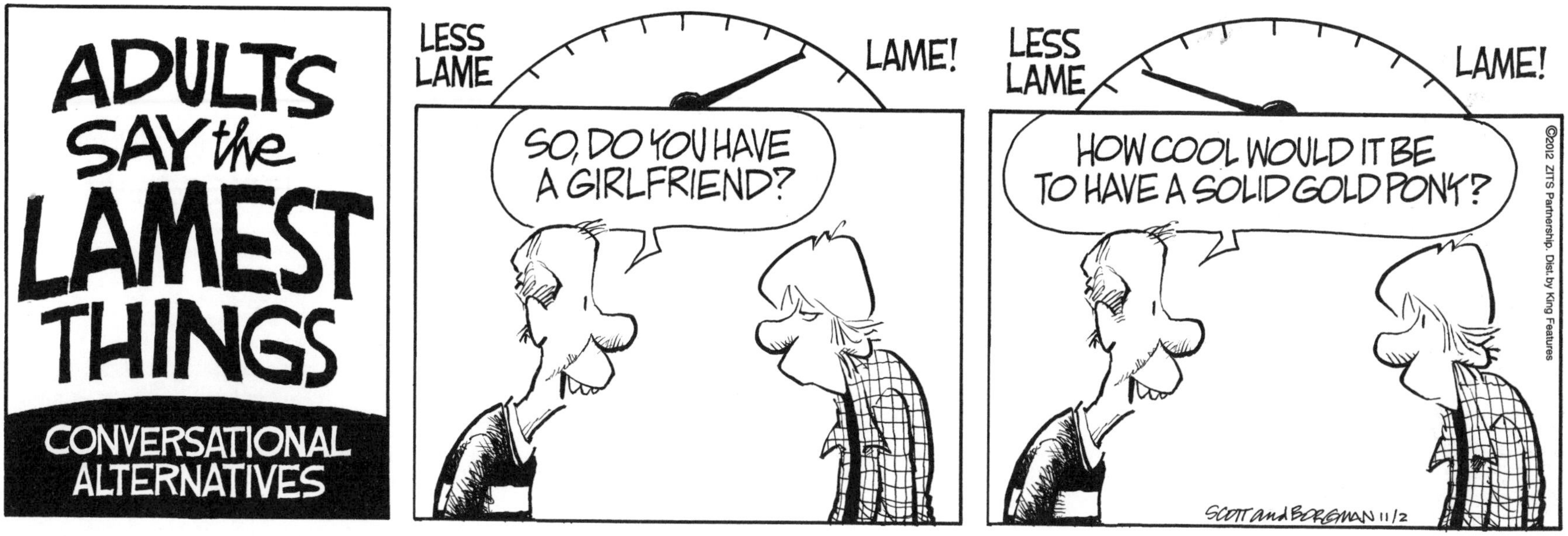
ADULTS SAY the LAMEST THINGS
CONVERSATIONAL ALTERNATIVES
LESS LAME
LAME!
SO, DO YOU HAVE A GIRLFRIEND?
LESS LAME
LAME!
HOW COOL WOULD IT BE TO HAVE A SOLID GOLD PONY?
©2012 ZITS Partnership. Dist. by King Features
SCOTT and BORGMAN 11/2

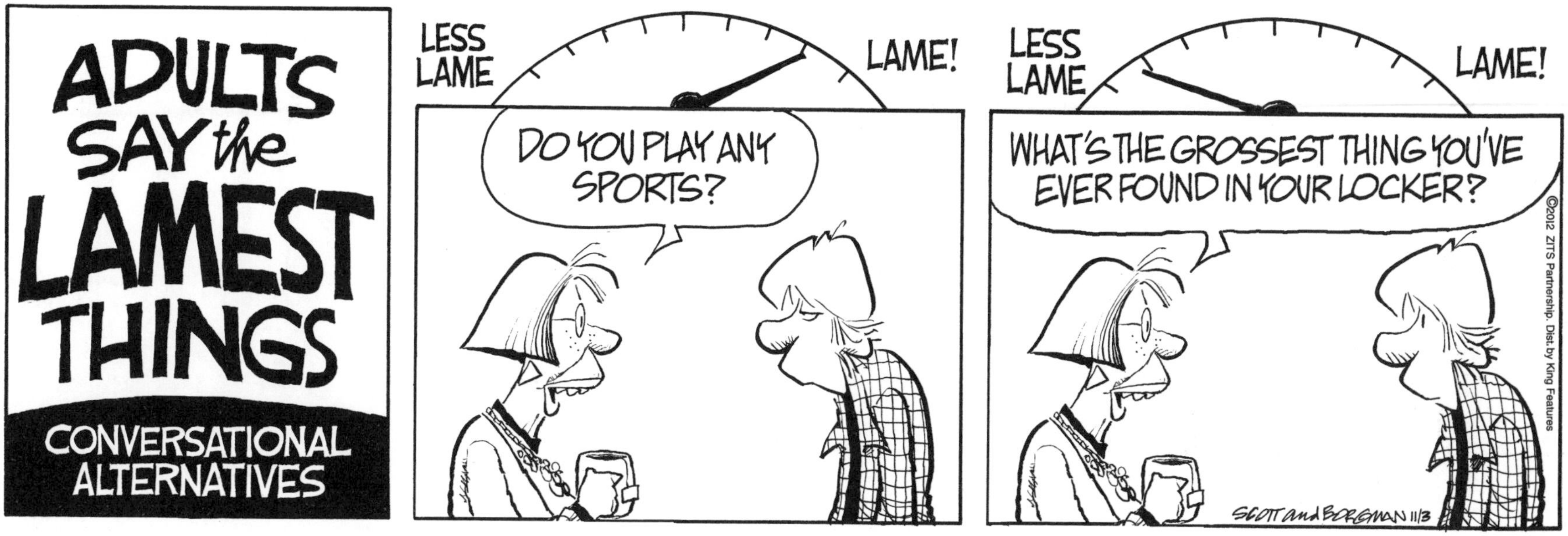
ADULTS SAY the LAMEST THINGS
CONVERSATIONAL ALTERNATIVES
LESS LAME
LAME!
DO YOU PLAY ANY SPORTS?
LESS LAME
LAME!
WHAT'S THE GROSSEST THING YOU'VE EVER FOUND IN YOUR LOCKER?
©2012 ZITS Partnership. Dist. by King Features
SCOTT and BORGMAN 11/3

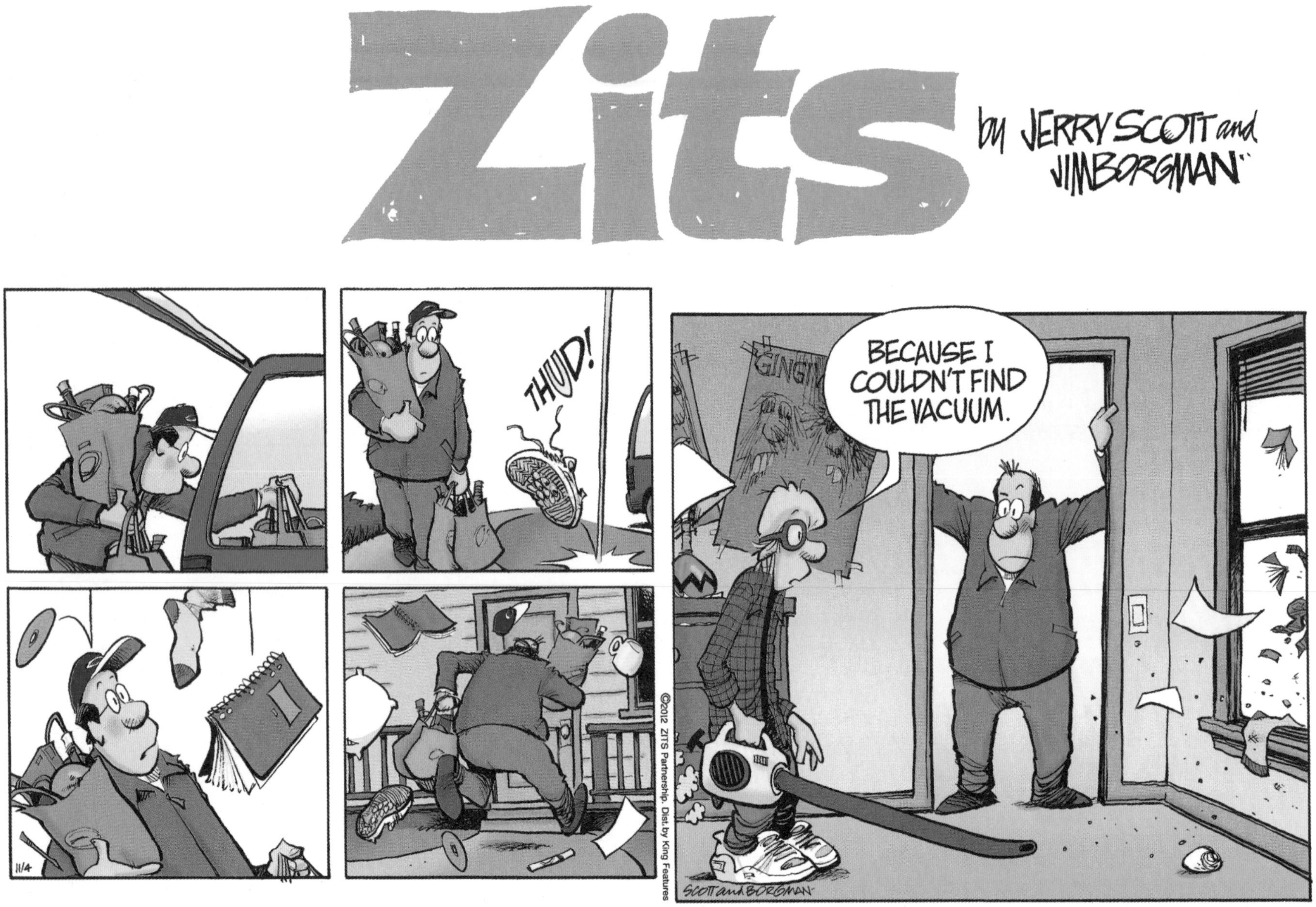
Zits
by JERRY SCOTT and JIM BORGMAN
THUD!
BECAUSE I COULDN'T FIND THE VACUUM.
11/4
©2012 ZITS Partnership. Dist. by King Features
SCOTT and BORGMAN

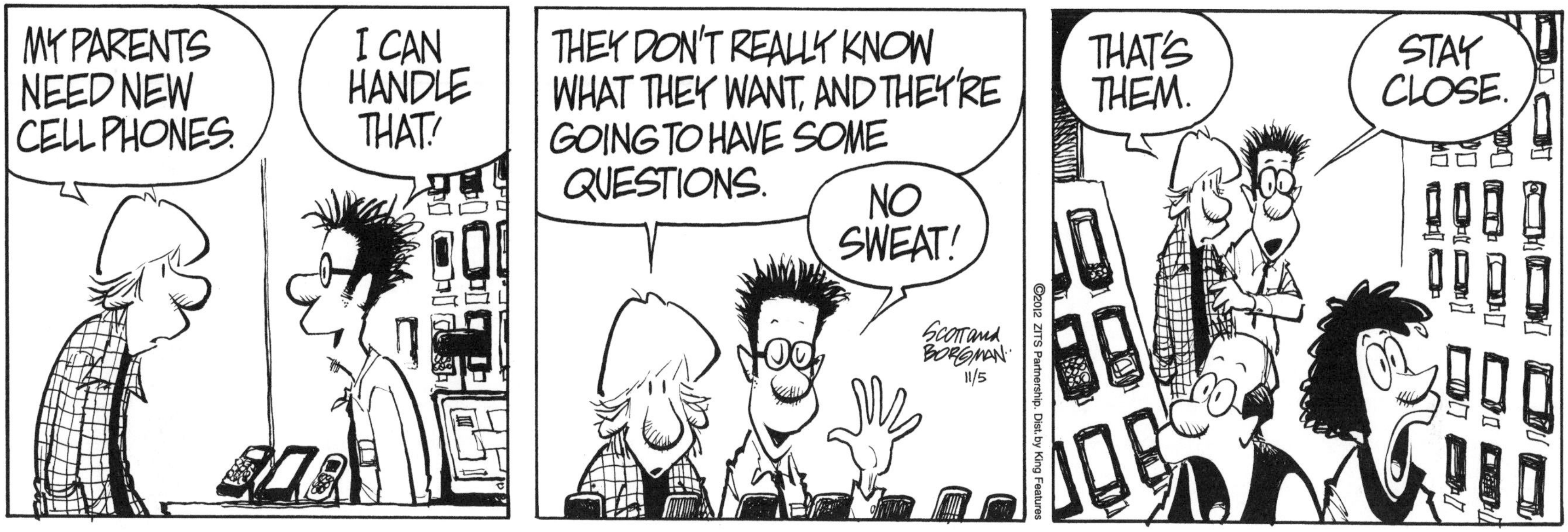
MY PARENTS NEED NEW CELL PHONES.
I CAN HANDLE THAT!
THEY DON'T REALLY KNOW WHAT THEY WANT, AND THEY'RE GOING TO HAVE SOME QUESTIONS.
NO SWEAT!
SCOTT and BORGMAN 11/5
©2012 ZITS Partnership. Dist. by King Features
THAT'S THEM.
STAY CLOSE.

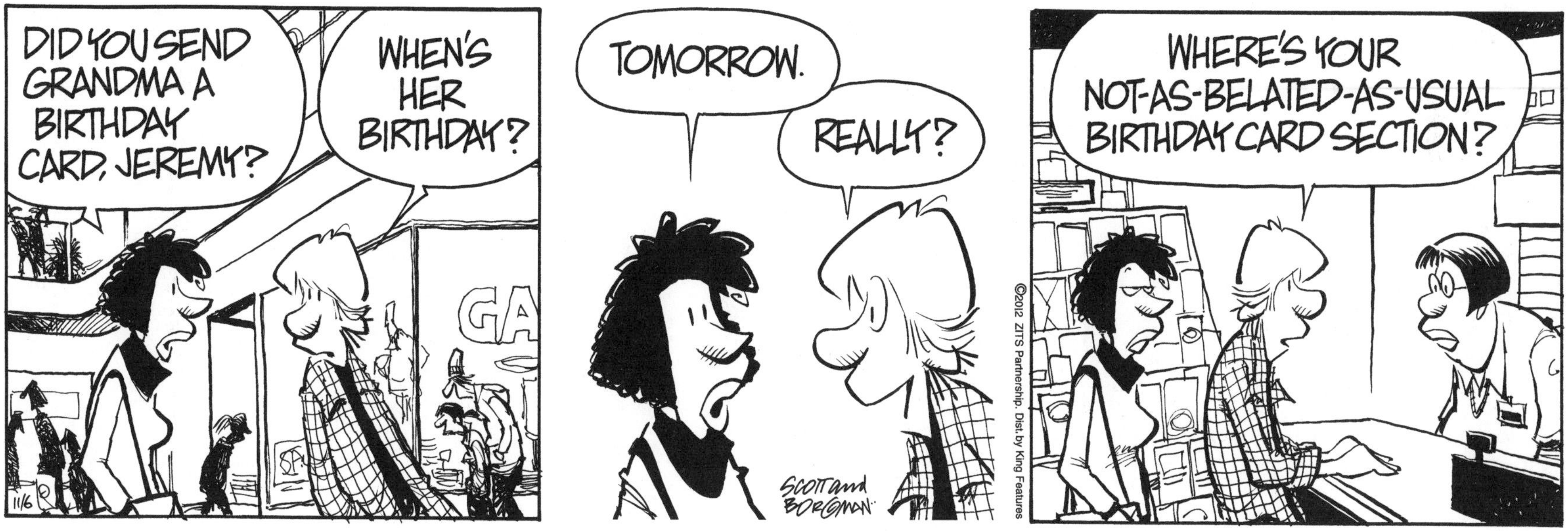
DID YOU SEND GRANDMA A BIRTHDAY CARD, JEREMY?
WHEN'S HER BIRTHDAY?
11/6
TOMORROW.
REALLY?
SCOTT and BORGMAN
©2012 ZITS Partnership. Dist. by King Features
WHERE'S YOUR NOT-AS-BELATED-AS-USUAL BIRTHDAY CARD SECTION?

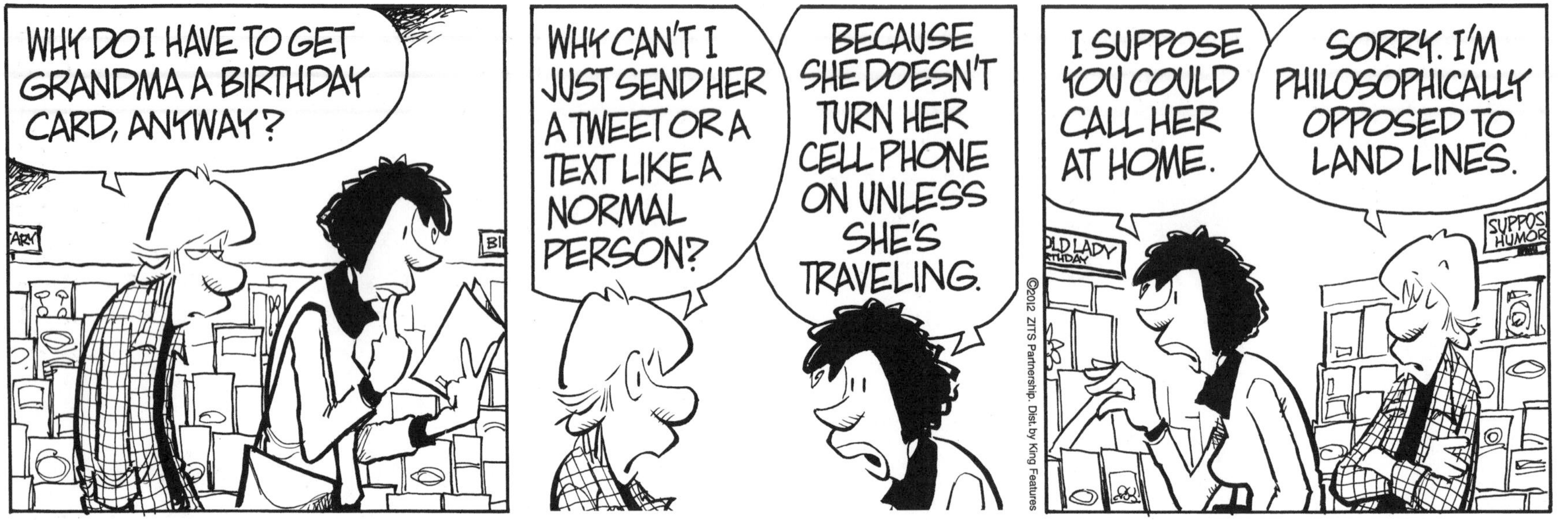
WHY DO I HAVE TO GET GRANDMA A BIRTHDAY CARD, ANYWAY?
WHY CAN'T I JUST SEND HER A TWEET OR A TEXT LIKE A NORMAL PERSON?
BECAUSE SHE DOESN'T TURN HER CELL PHONE ON UNLESS SHE'S TRAVELING.
©2012 ZITS Partnership. Dist. by King Features
I SUPPOSE YOU COULD CALL HER AT HOME.
SORRY. I'M PHILOSOPHICALLY OPPOSED TO LAND LINES.

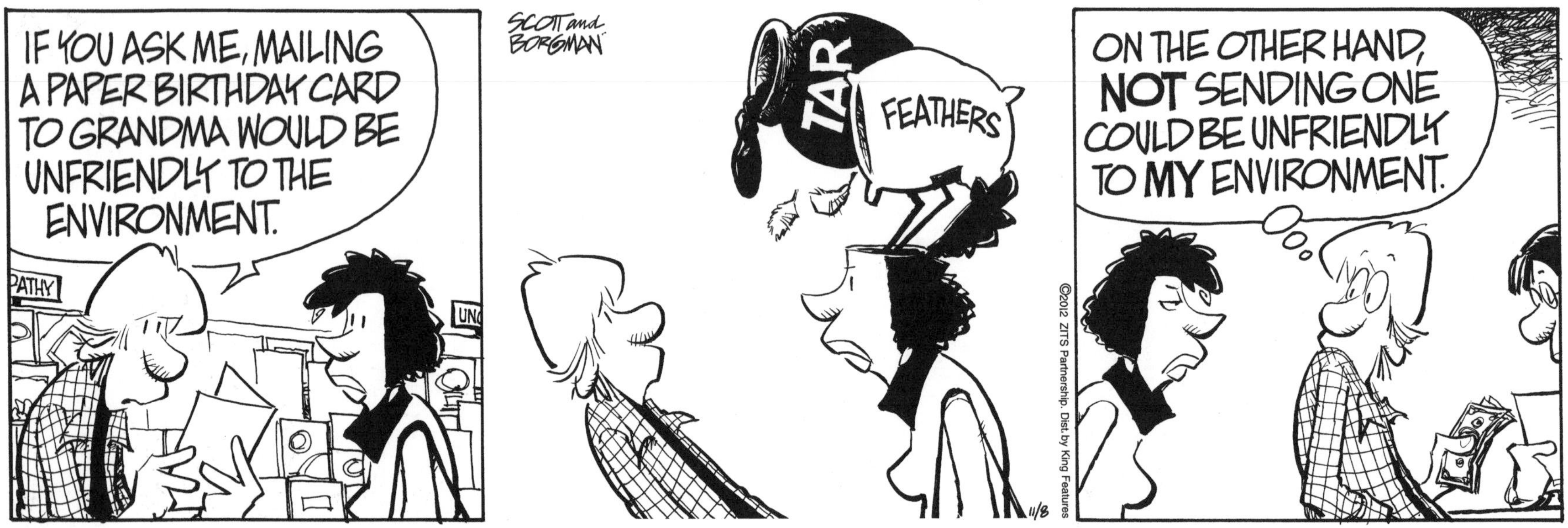
IF YOU ASK ME, MAILING A PAPER BIRTHDAY CARD TO GRANDMA WOULD BE UNFRIENDLY TO THE ENVIRONMENT.
SCOTT and BORGMAN
TAR
FEATHERS
11/8
©2012 ZITS Partnership. Dist. by King Features
ON THE OTHER HAND, NOT SENDING ONE COULD BE UNFRIENDLY TO MY ENVIRONMENT.

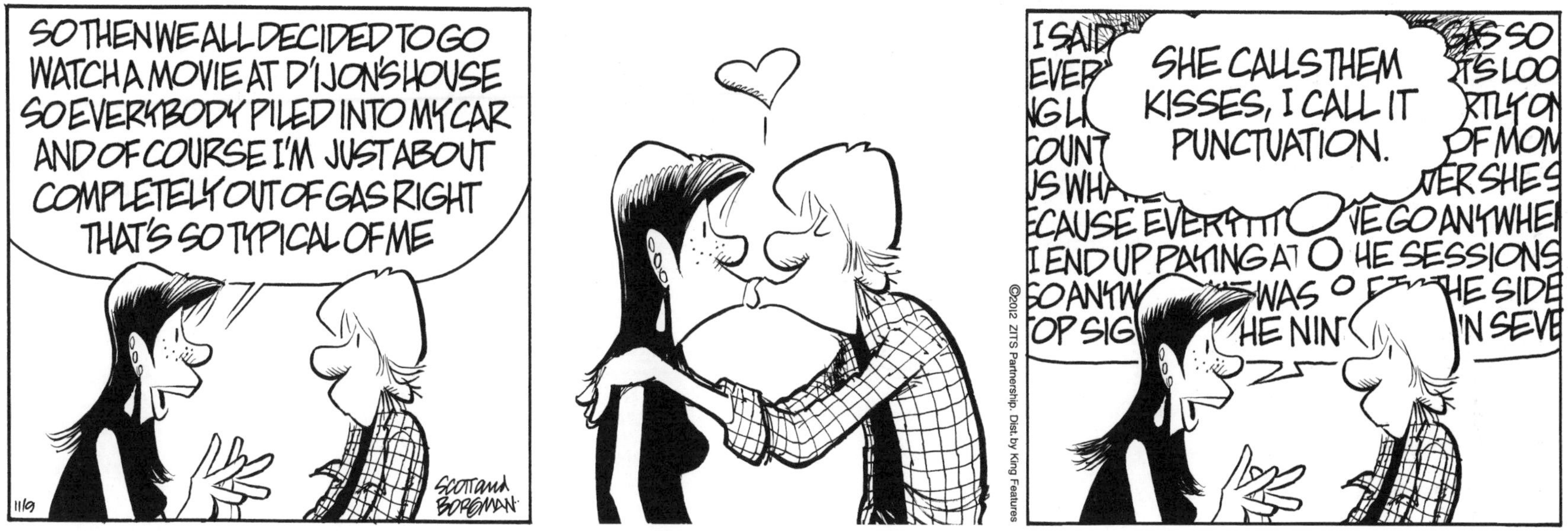
SO THEN WE ALL DECIDED TO GO WATCH A MOVIE AT D'IJON'S HOUSE SO EVERYBODY PILED INTO MY CAR AND OF COURSE I'M JUST ABOUT COMPLETELY OUT OF GAS RIGHT THAT'S SO TYPICAL OF ME
11/9
SCOTT AND BORGMAN
SHE CALLS THEM KISSES, I CALL IT PUNCTUATION.
©2012 ZITS Partnership. Dist. by King Features

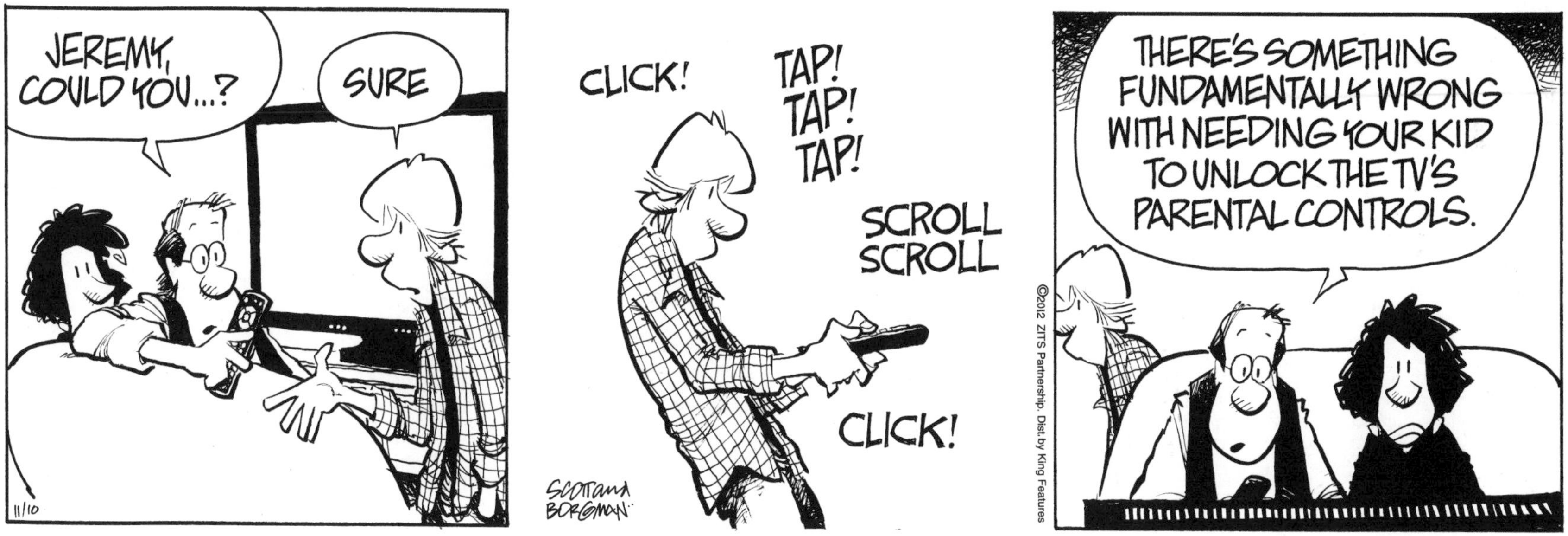
JEREMY, COULD YOU...?
SURE
11/10
CLICK!
TAP! TAP! TAP!
SCROLL SCROLL
CLICK!
SCOTT AND BORGMAN
THERE'S SOMETHING FUNDAMENTALLY WRONG WITH NEEDING YOUR KID TO UNLOCK THE TV'S PARENTAL CONTROLS.
©2012 ZITS Partnership. Dist. by King Features

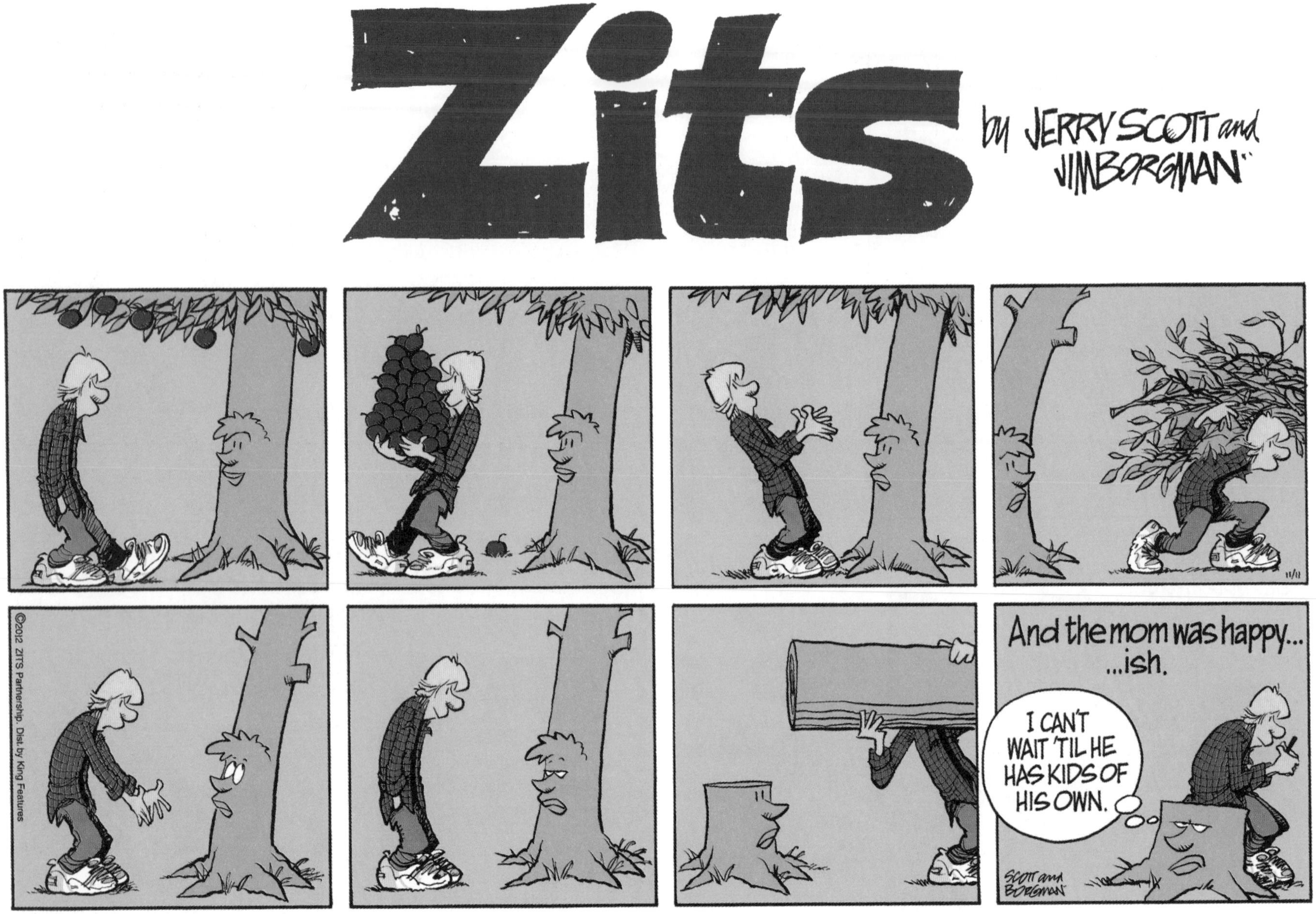
Zits
by JERRY SCOTT and JIM BORGMAN
©2012 ZITS Partnership. Dist. by King Features
And the mom was happy...
...ish.
I CAN'T WAIT 'TIL HE HAS KIDS OF HIS OWN.
SCOTT and BORGMAN

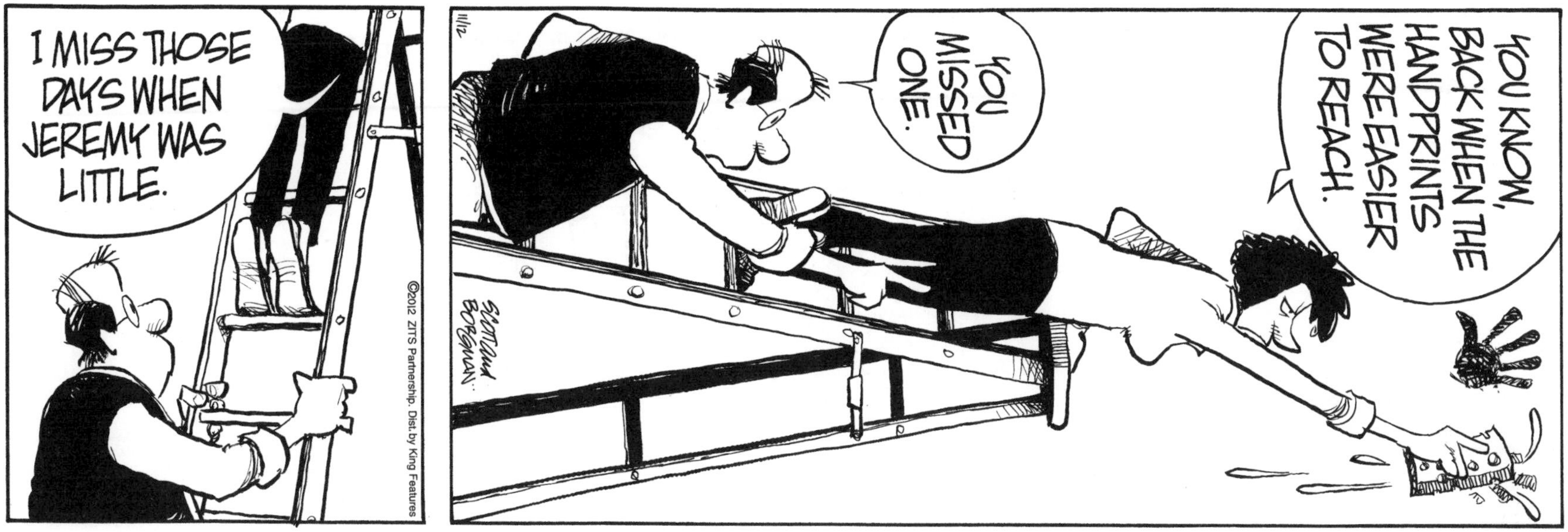
I MISS THOSE DAYS WHEN JEREMY WAS LITTLE.
YOU KNOW, BACK WHEN THE HANDPRINTS WERE EASIER TO REACH.
YOU MISSED ONE.
©2012 ZITS Partnership. Dist. by King Features
SCOTT and BORGMAN
11/12

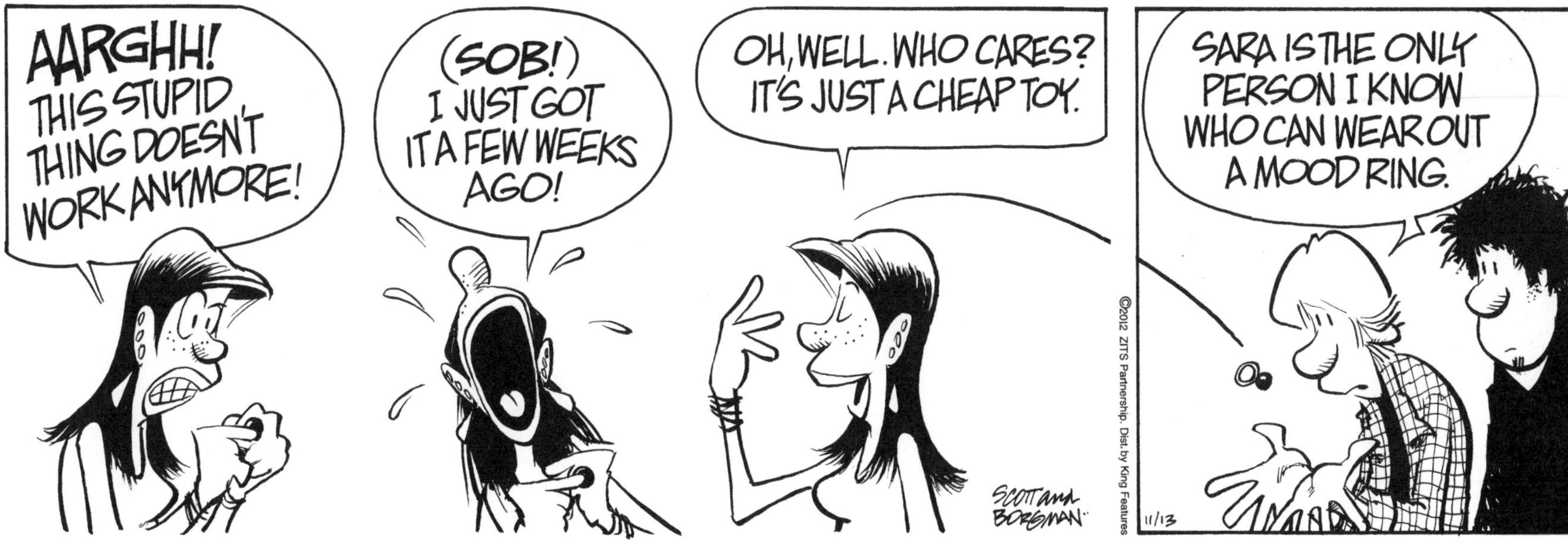
AARGHH! THIS STUPID THING DOESN'T WORK ANYMORE!
(SOB!) I JUST GOT IT A FEW WEEKS AGO!
OH, WELL. WHO CARES? IT'S JUST A CHEAP TOY.
SARA IS THE ONLY PERSON I KNOW WHO CAN WEAR OUT A MOOD RING.
SCOTT and BORGMAN
©2012 ZITS Partnership. Dist. by King Features
11/13

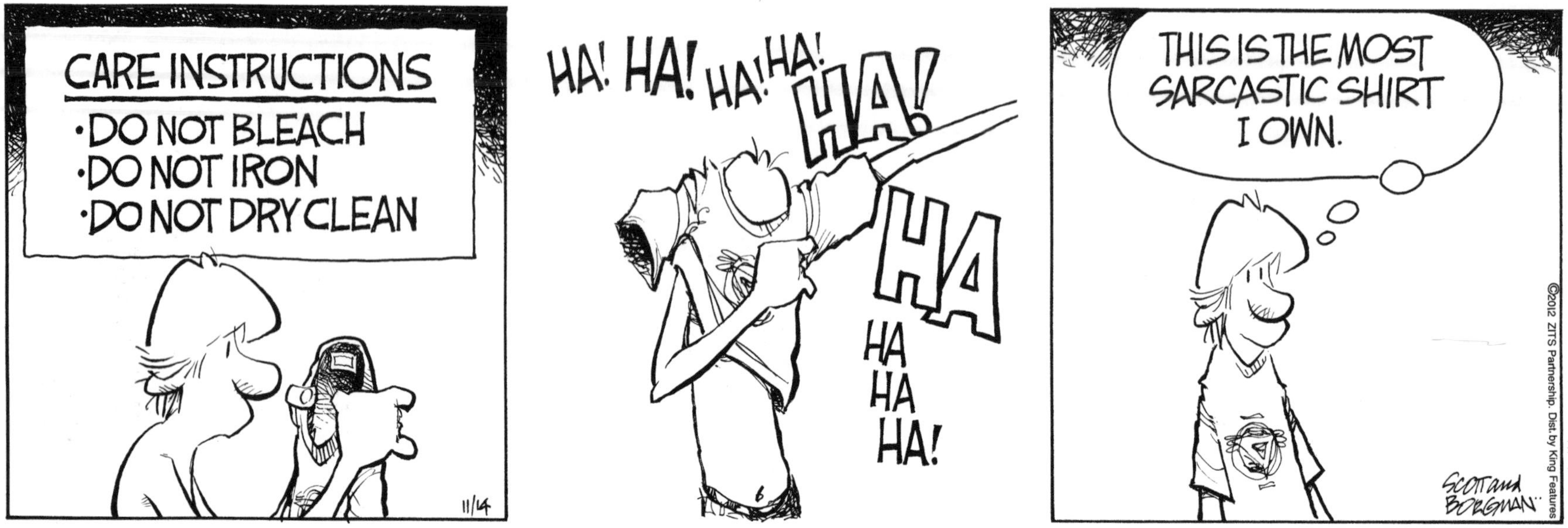
CARE INSTRUCTIONS
•DO NOT BLEACH
•DO NOT IRON
•DO NOT DRY CLEAN
11/14
HA! HA! HA! HA! HA! HA HA HA HA!
THIS IS THE MOST SARCASTIC SHIRT I OWN.
©2012 ZITS Partnership. Dist. by King Features
SCOTT and BORGMAN

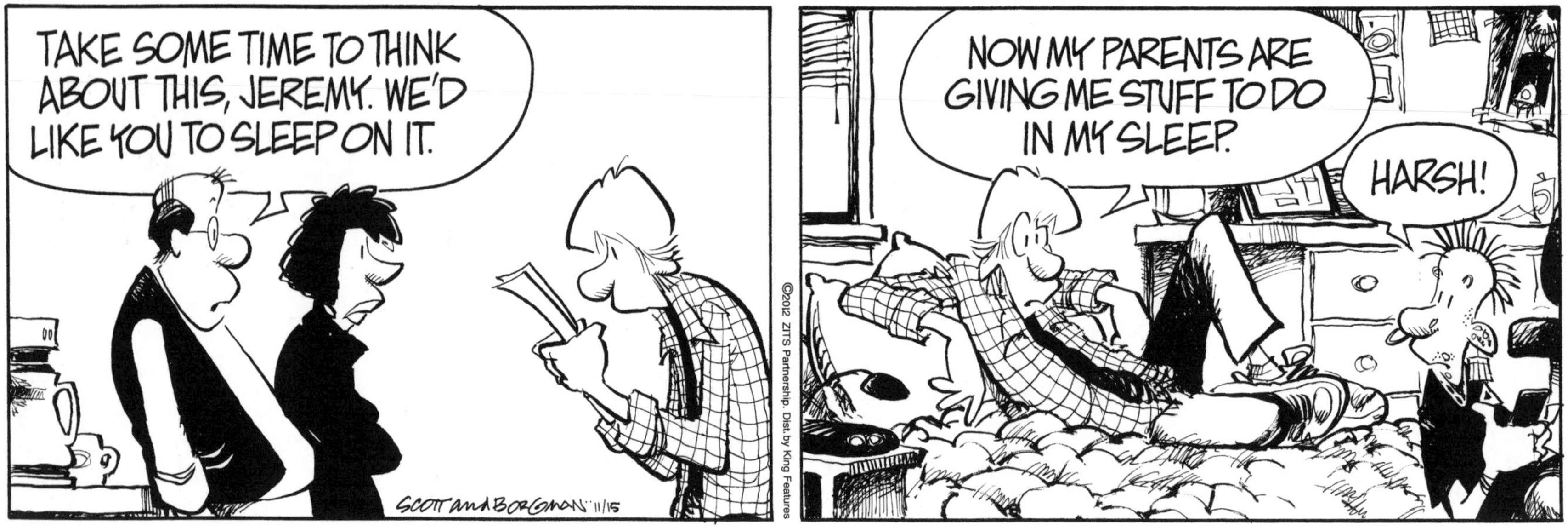
TAKE SOME TIME TO THINK ABOUT THIS, JEREMY. WE'D LIKE YOU TO SLEEP ON IT.
SCOTT and BORGMAN 11/15
©2012 ZITS Partnership. Dist. by King Features
NOW MY PARENTS ARE GIVING ME STUFF TO DO IN MY SLEEP.
HARSH!

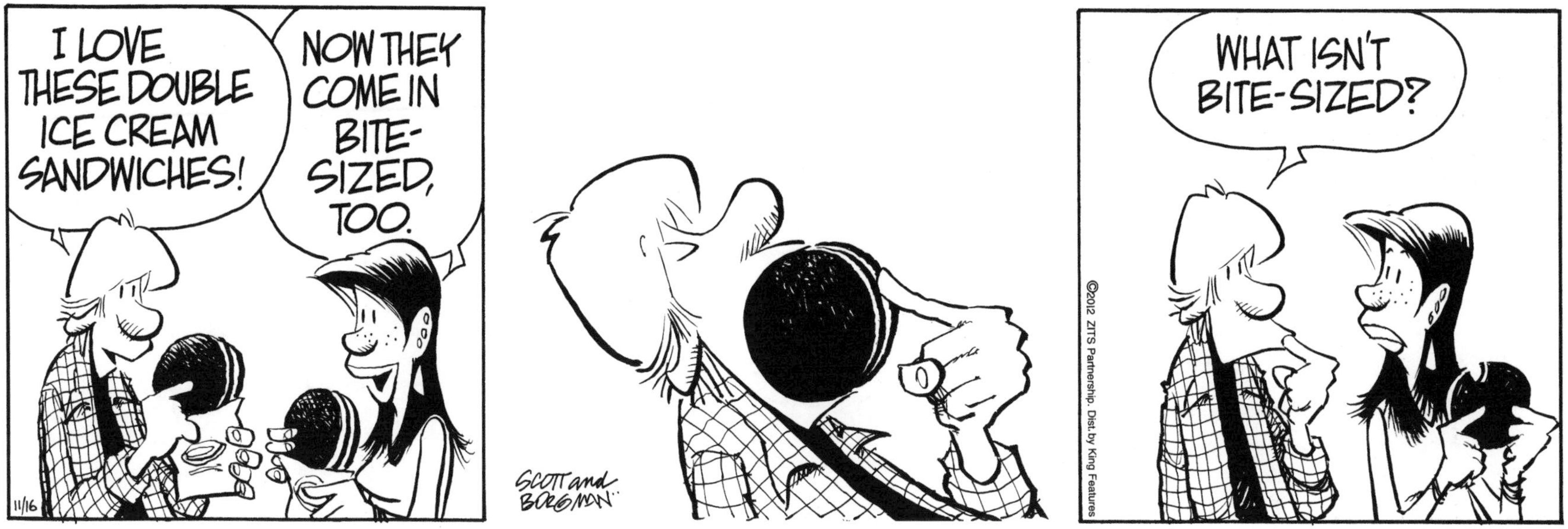
I LOVE THESE DOUBLE ICE CREAM SANDWICHES!
NOW THEY COME IN BITE-SIZED, TOO.
11/16
SCOTT and BORGMAN
WHAT ISN'T BITE-SIZED?
©2012 ZITS Partnership. Dist. by King Features

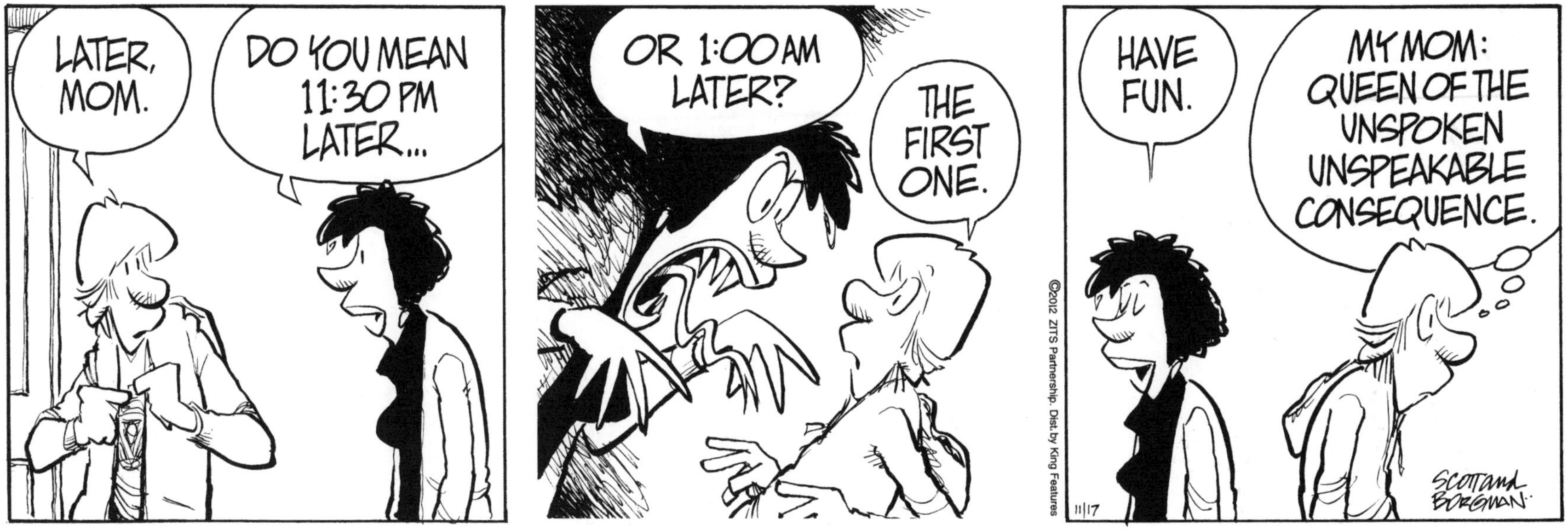
LATER, MOM.
DO YOU MEAN 11:30 PM LATER...
OR 1:00 AM LATER?
THE FIRST ONE.
©2012 ZITS Partnership. Dist. by King Features
HAVE FUN.
MY MOM: QUEEN OF THE UNSPOKEN UNSPEAKABLE CONSEQUENCE.
11/17
SCOTT and BORGMAN

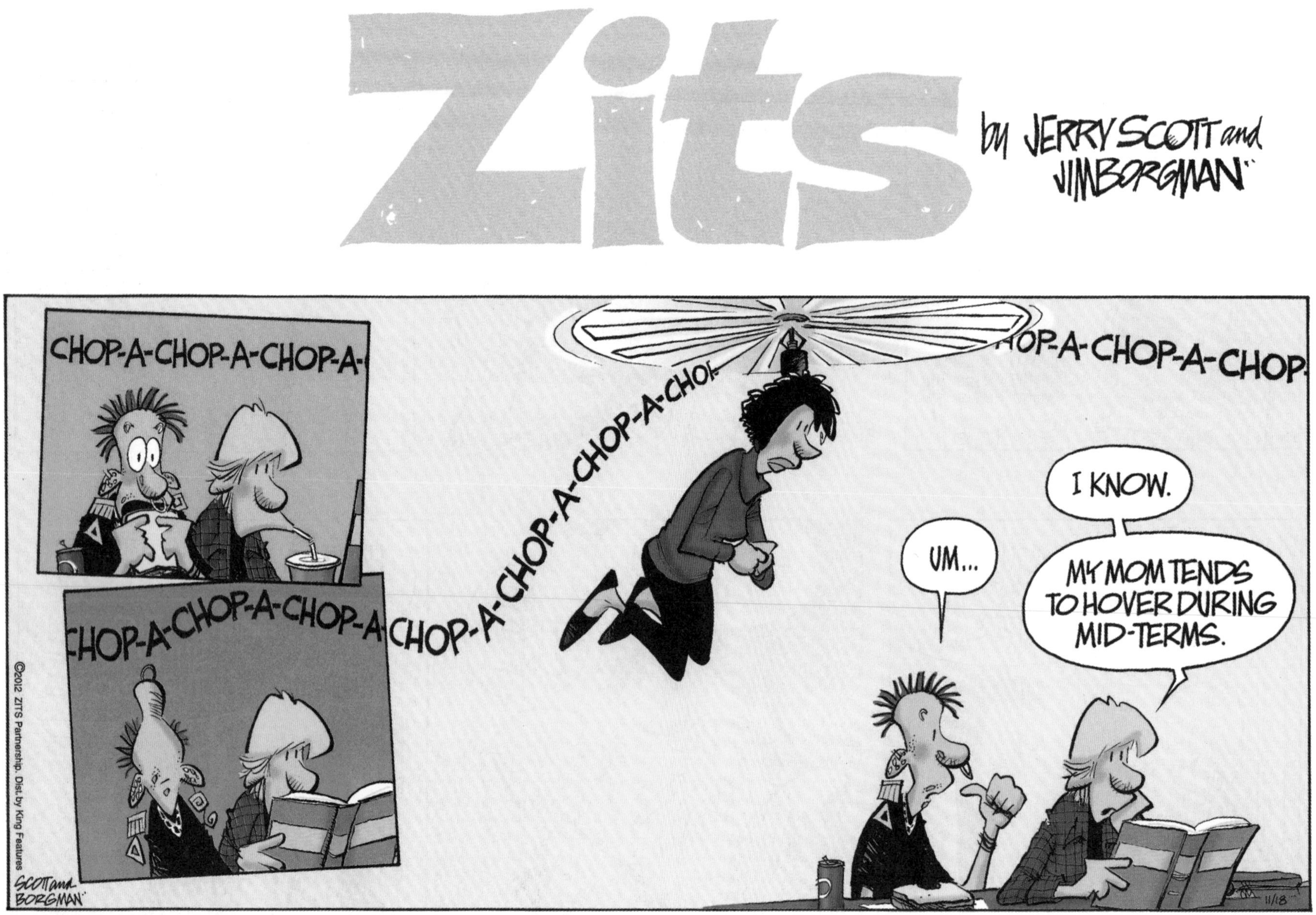
Zits
by JERRY SCOTT and JIM BORGMAN
CHOP-A-CHOP-A-CHOP-A-
CHOP-A-CHOP-A-CHOP-A-CHOP-A-CHOP-A-CHOP-A-CHOP-A-CHO
HOP-A-CHOP-A-CHOP-
UM...
I KNOW.
MY MOM TENDS TO HOVER DURING MID-TERMS.
©2012 ZITS Partnership. Dist. by King Features
SCOTT and BORGMAN

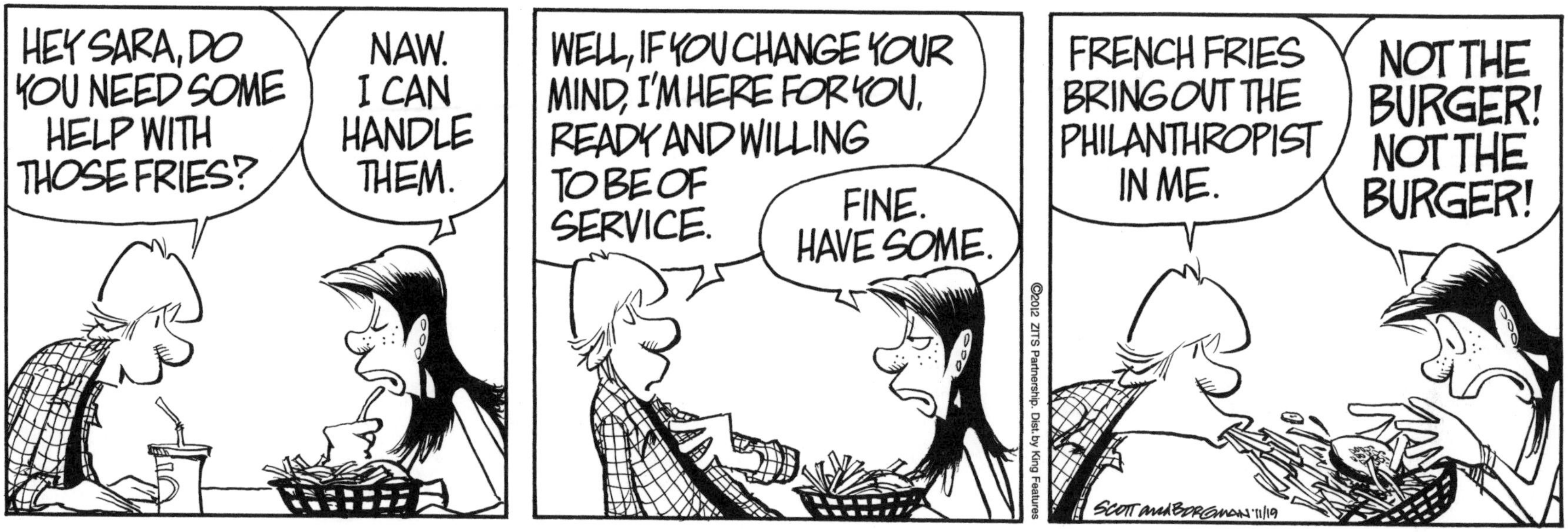
HEY SARA, DO YOU NEED SOME HELP WITH THOSE FRIES?
NAW. I CAN HANDLE THEM.
WELL, IF YOU CHANGE YOUR MIND, I'M HERE FOR YOU, READY AND WILLING TO BE OF SERVICE.
FINE. HAVE SOME.
FRENCH FRIES BRING OUT THE PHILANTHROPIST IN ME.
NOT THE BURGER! NOT THE BURGER!
©2012 ZITS Partnership. Dist. by King Features
SCOTT and BORGMAN 11/19

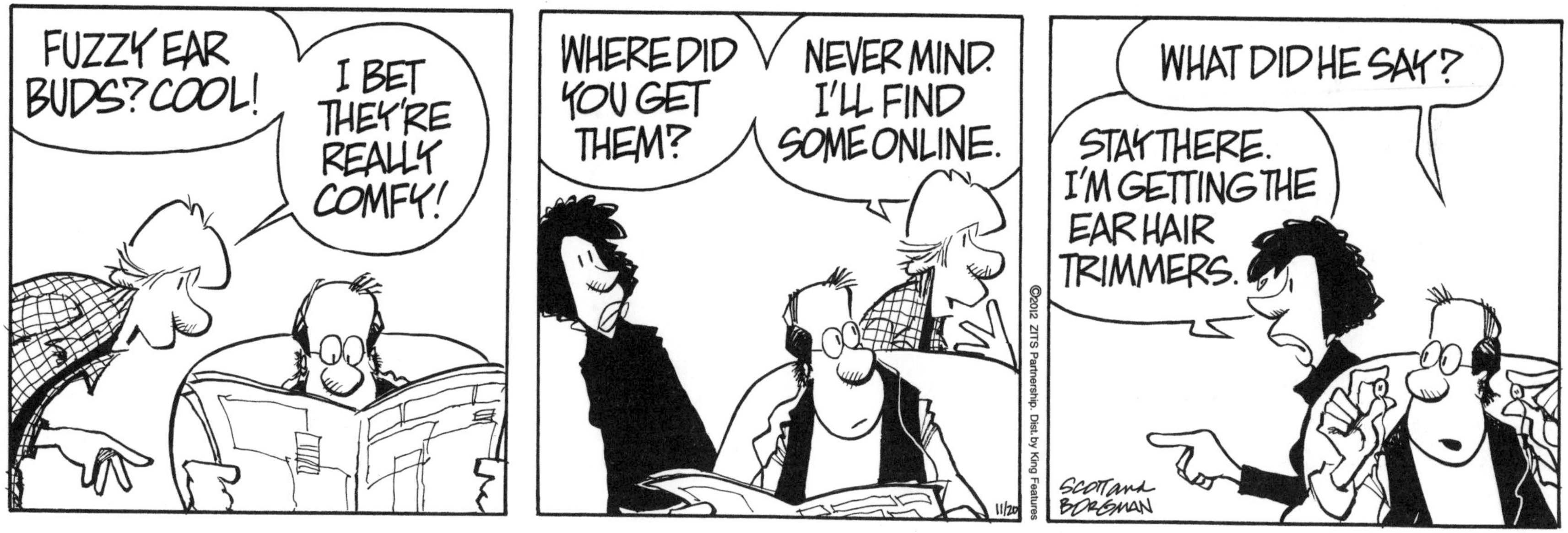
FUZZY EAR BUDS? COOL!
I BET THEY'RE REALLY COMFY!
WHERE DID YOU GET THEM?
NEVER MIND. I'LL FIND SOME ONLINE.
WHAT DID HE SAY?
STAY THERE. I'M GETTING THE EAR HAIR TRIMMERS.
©2012 ZITS Partnership. Dist. by King Features
11/20
SCOTT and BORGMAN

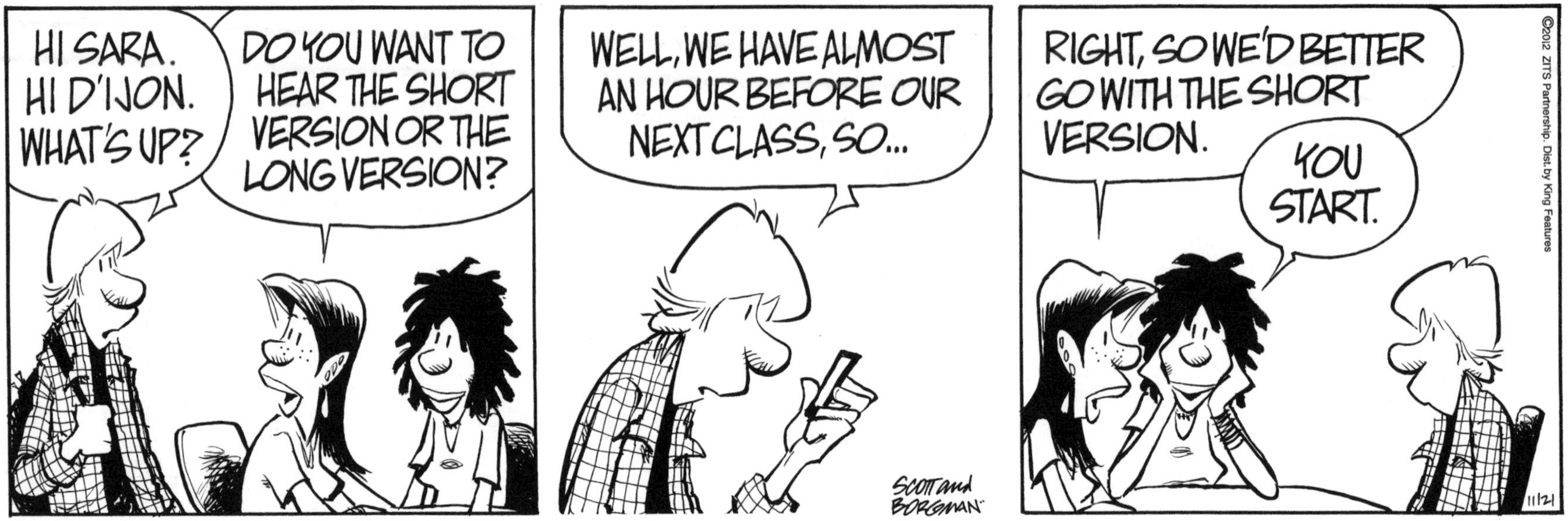
HI SARA. HI D'IJON. WHAT'S UP?
DO YOU WANT TO HEAR THE SHORT VERSION OR THE LONG VERSION?
WELL, WE HAVE ALMOST AN HOUR BEFORE OUR NEXT CLASS, SO...
SCOTT AND BORGMAN
RIGHT, SO WE'D BETTER GO WITH THE SHORT VERSION.
YOU START.
©2012 ZITS Partnership. Dist. by King Features
11/21

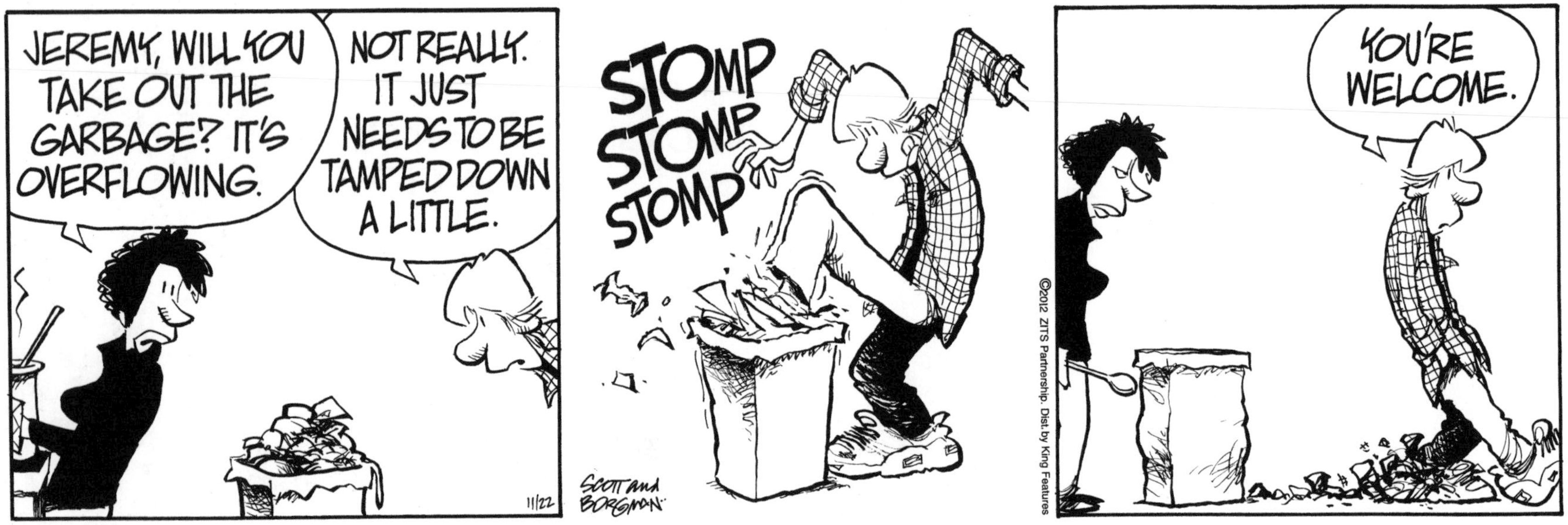
JEREMY, WILL YOU TAKE OUT THE GARBAGE? IT'S OVERFLOWING.
NOT REALLY. IT JUST NEEDS TO BE TAMPED DOWN A LITTLE.
11/22
STOMP STOMP STOMP
SCOTT AND BORGMAN
YOU'RE WELCOME.
©2012 ZITS Partnership. Dist. by King Features

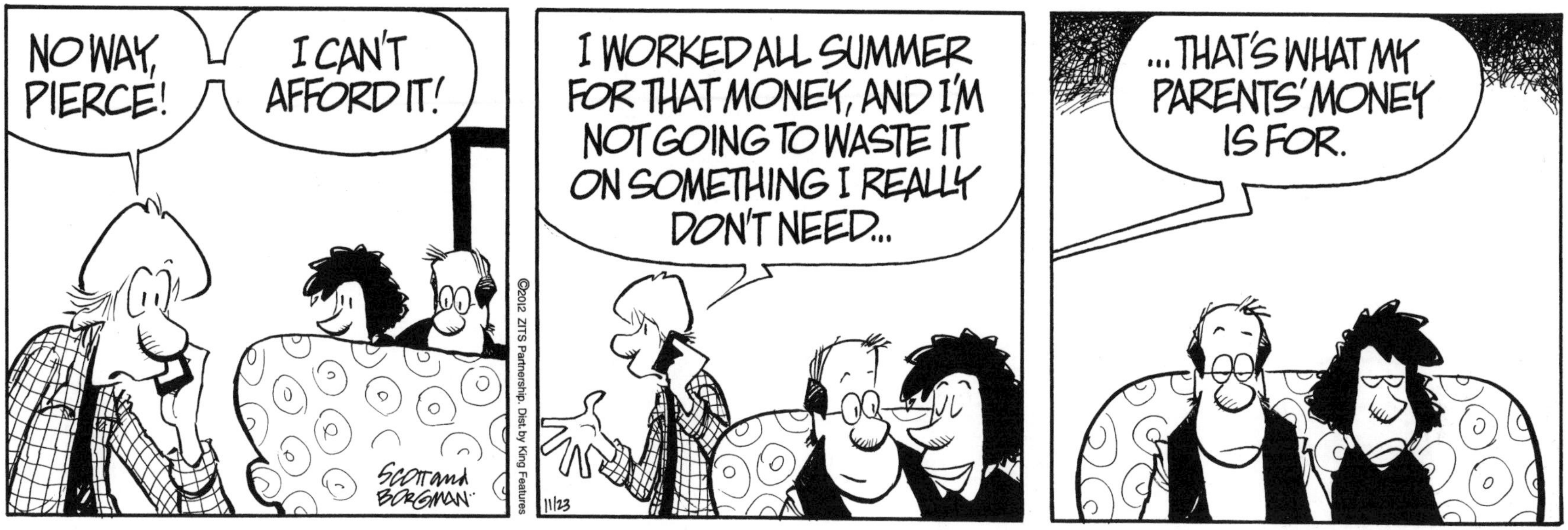
NO WAY, PIERCE!
I CAN'T AFFORD IT!
I WORKED ALL SUMMER FOR THAT MONEY, AND I'M NOT GOING TO WASTE IT ON SOMETHING I REALLY DON'T NEED...
...THAT'S WHAT MY PARENTS' MONEY IS FOR.
SCOTT and BORGMAN
©2012 ZITS Partnership. Dist. by King Features
11/23

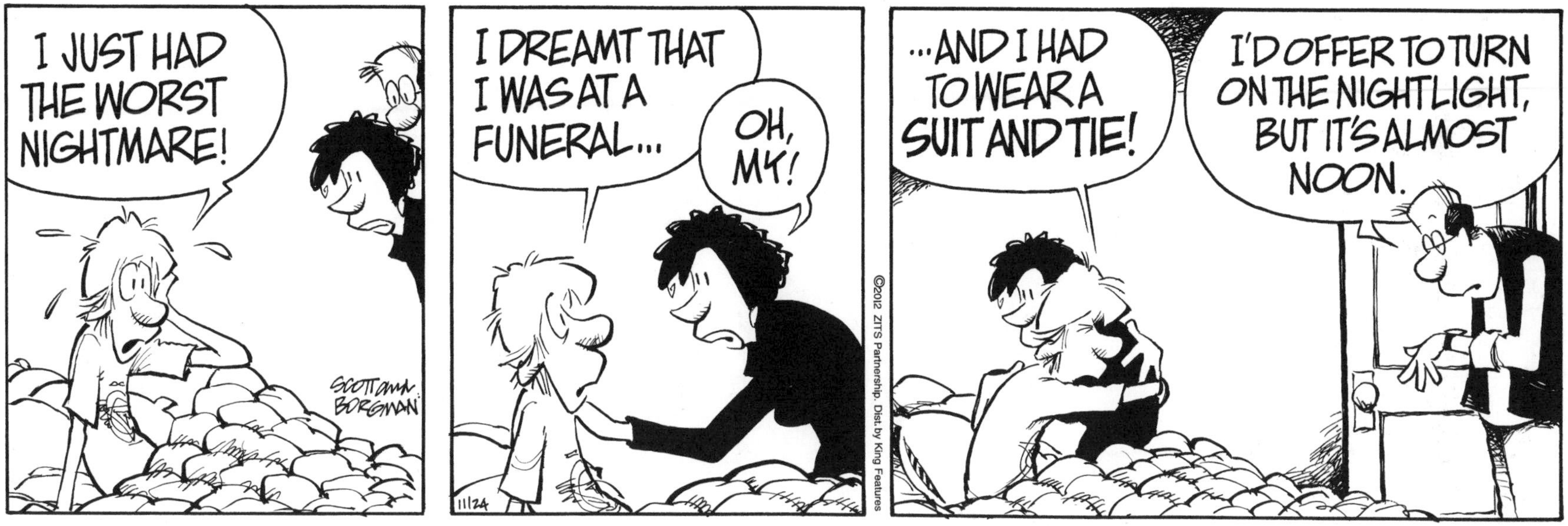
I JUST HAD THE WORST NIGHTMARE!
I DREAMT THAT I WAS AT A FUNERAL...
OH, MY!
...AND I HAD TO WEAR A SUIT AND TIE!
I'D OFFER TO TURN ON THE NIGHTLIGHT, BUT IT'S ALMOST NOON.
SCOTT and BORGMAN
©2012 ZITS Partnership. Dist. by King Features
11/24

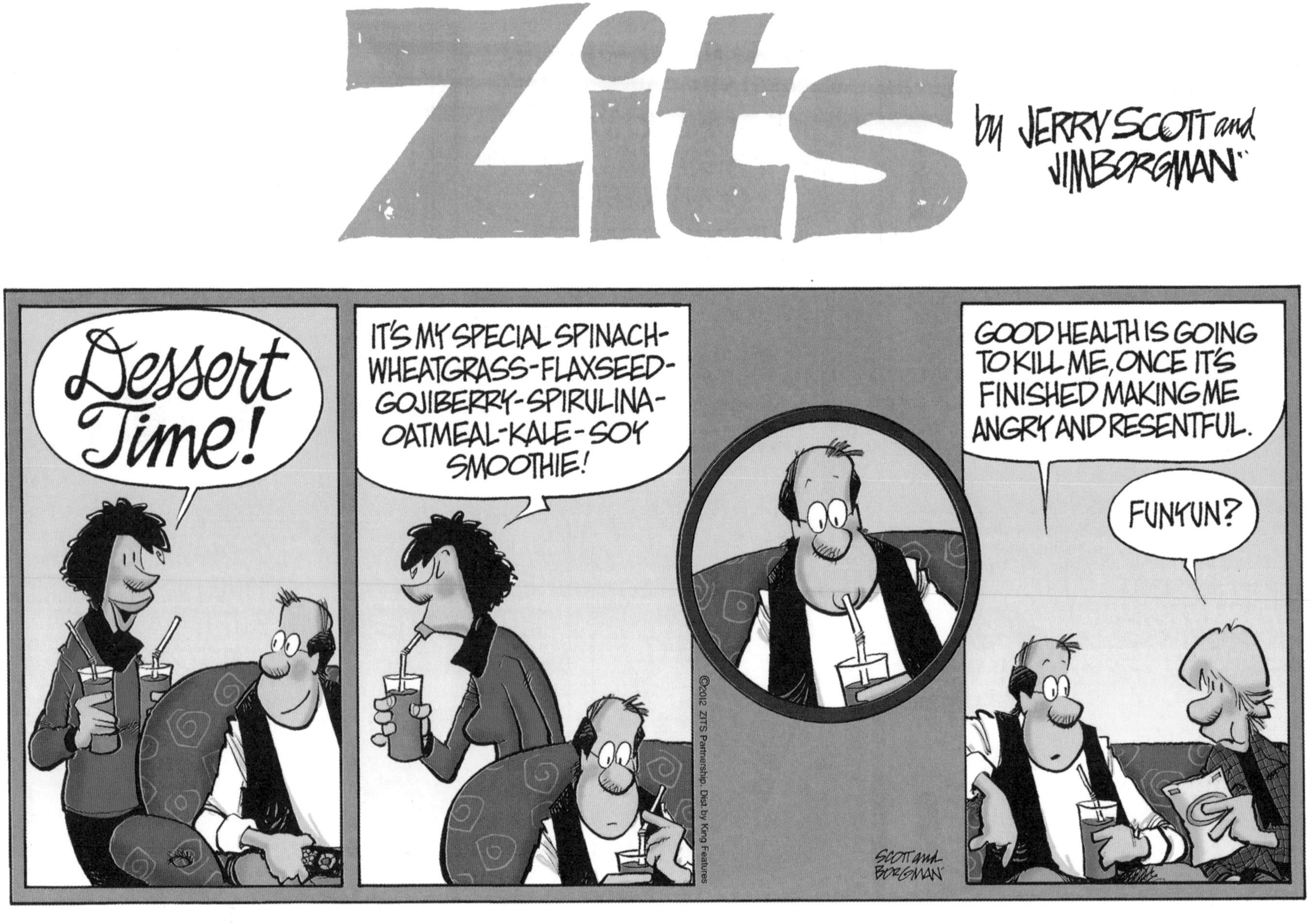
Zits
by JERRY SCOTT and JIM BORGMAN
Dessert Time!
IT'S MY SPECIAL SPINACH-WHEATGRASS-FLAXSEED-GOJIBERRY-SPIRULINA-OATMEAL-KALE-SOY SMOOTHIE!
©2012 ZITS Partnership. Dist. by King Features
GOOD HEALTH IS GOING TO KILL ME, ONCE IT'S FINISHED MAKING ME ANGRY AND RESENTFUL.
FUNYUN?
SCOTT and BORGMAN

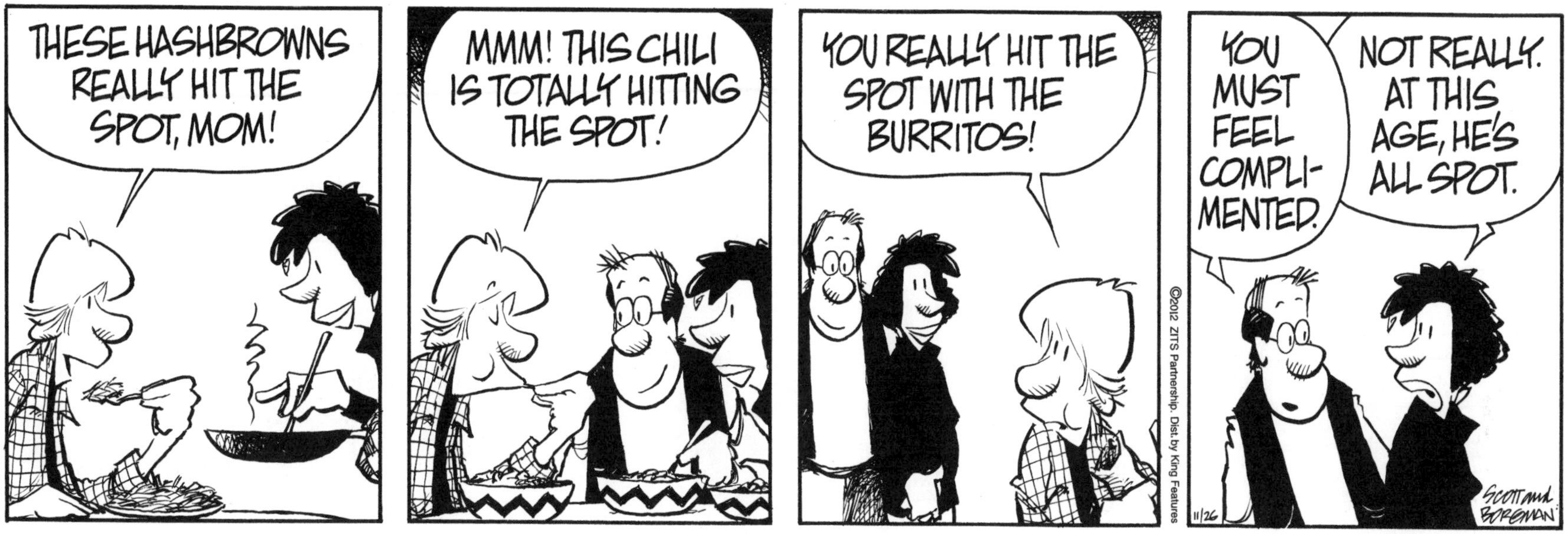
THESE HASHBROWNS REALLY HIT THE SPOT, MOM!
MMM! THIS CHILI IS TOTALLY HITTING THE SPOT!
YOU REALLY HIT THE SPOT WITH THE BURRITOS!
YOU MUST FEEL COMPLI-MENTED.
NOT REALLY. AT THIS AGE, HE'S ALL SPOT.
©2012 ZITS Partnership. Dist. by King Features
SCOTT and BORGMAN
11/26

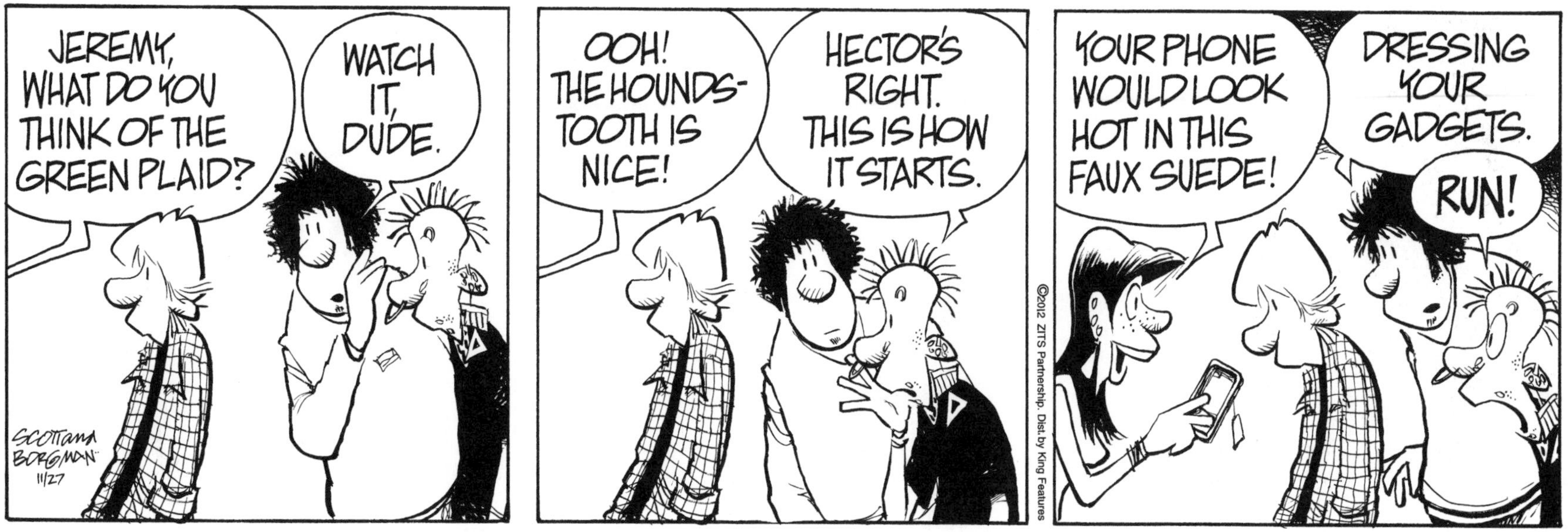
JEREMY, WHAT DO YOU THINK OF THE GREEN PLAID?
WATCH IT, DUDE.
OOH! THE HOUNDS-TOOTH IS NICE!
HECTOR'S RIGHT. THIS IS HOW IT STARTS.
YOUR PHONE WOULD LOOK HOT IN THIS FAUX SUEDE!
DRESSING YOUR GADGETS.
RUN!
©2012 ZITS Partnership. Dist. by King Features
SCOTT and BORGMAN
11/27

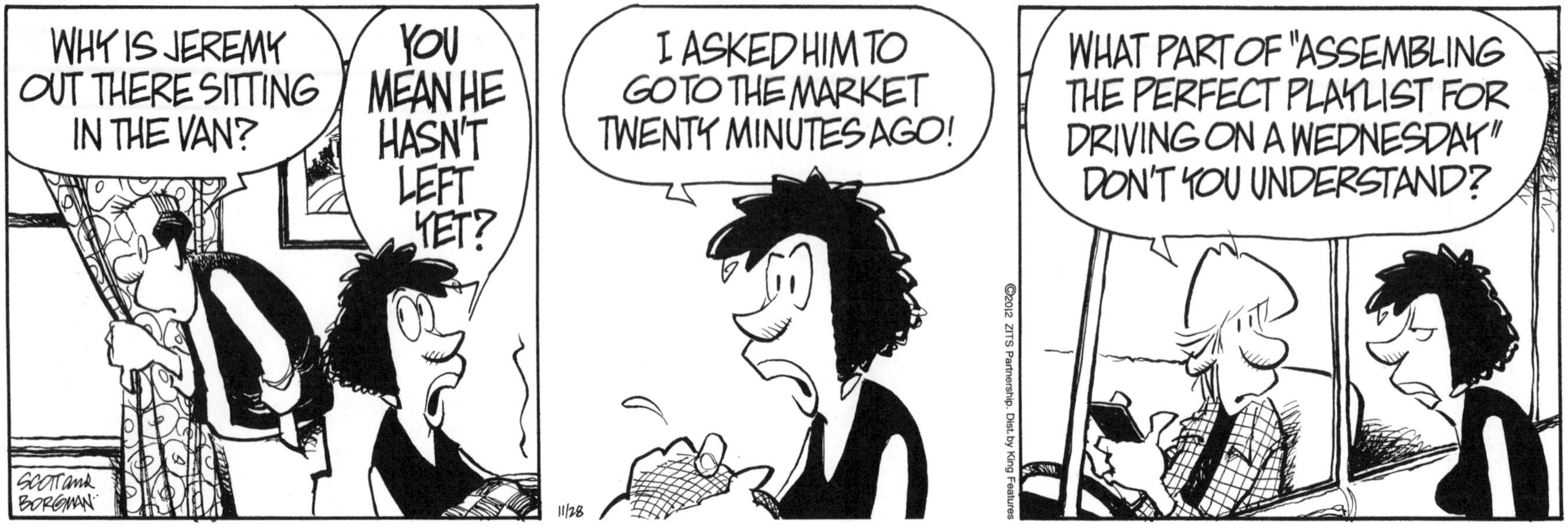
WHY IS JEREMY OUT THERE SITTING IN THE VAN?
YOU MEAN HE HASN'T LEFT YET?
I ASKED HIM TO GO TO THE MARKET TWENTY MINUTES AGO!
WHAT PART OF "ASSEMBLING THE PERFECT PLAYLIST FOR DRIVING ON A WEDNESDAY" DON'T YOU UNDERSTAND?
SCOTT and BORGMAN
11/28
©2012 ZITS Partnership. Dist. by King Features

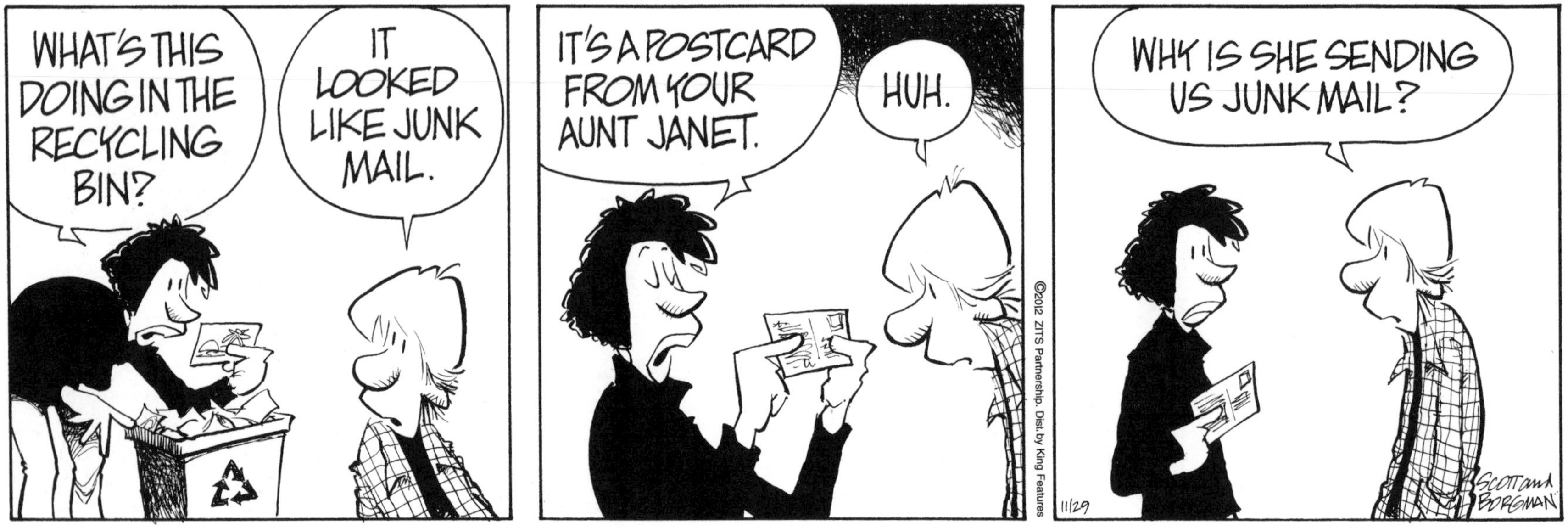
WHAT'S THIS DOING IN THE RECYCLING BIN?
IT LOOKED LIKE JUNK MAIL.
IT'S A POSTCARD FROM YOUR AUNT JANET.
HUH.
WHY IS SHE SENDING US JUNK MAIL?
©2012 ZITS Partnership. Dist. by King Features
11/29
SCOTT and BORGMAN

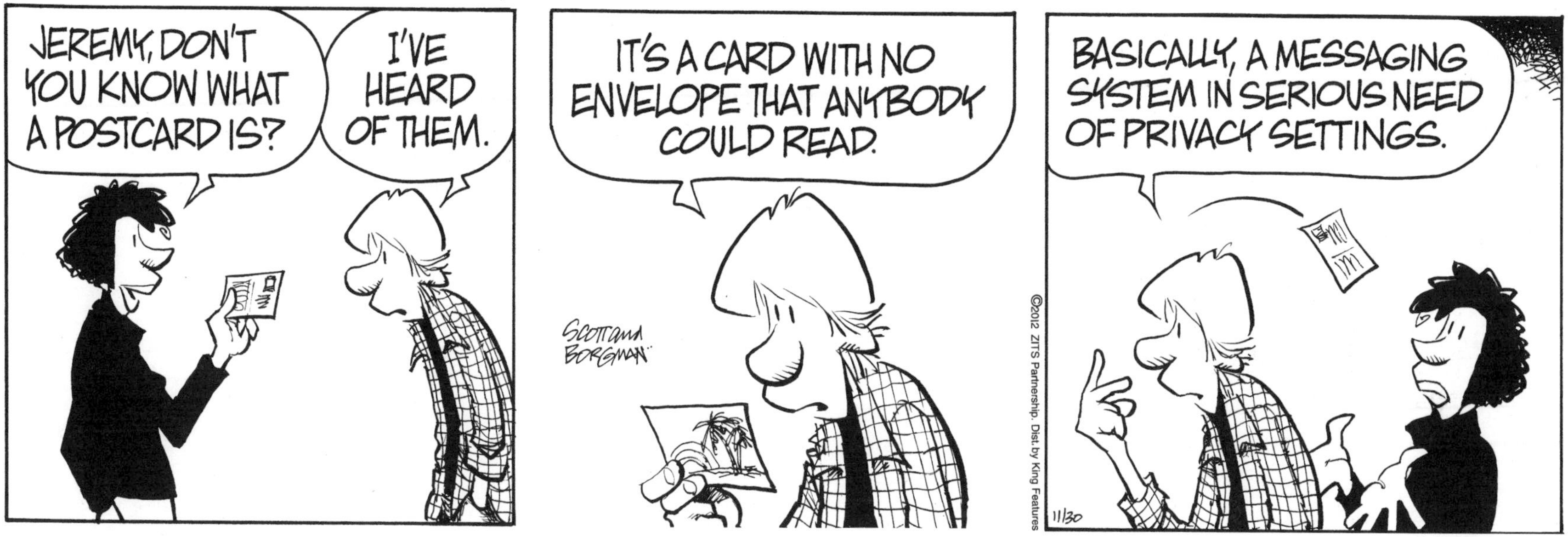
JEREMY, DON'T YOU KNOW WHAT A POSTCARD IS?
I'VE HEARD OF THEM.
IT'S A CARD WITH NO ENVELOPE THAT ANYBODY COULD READ.
BASICALLY, A MESSAGING SYSTEM IN SERIOUS NEED OF PRIVACY SETTINGS.
©2012 ZITS Partnership. Dist.by King Features

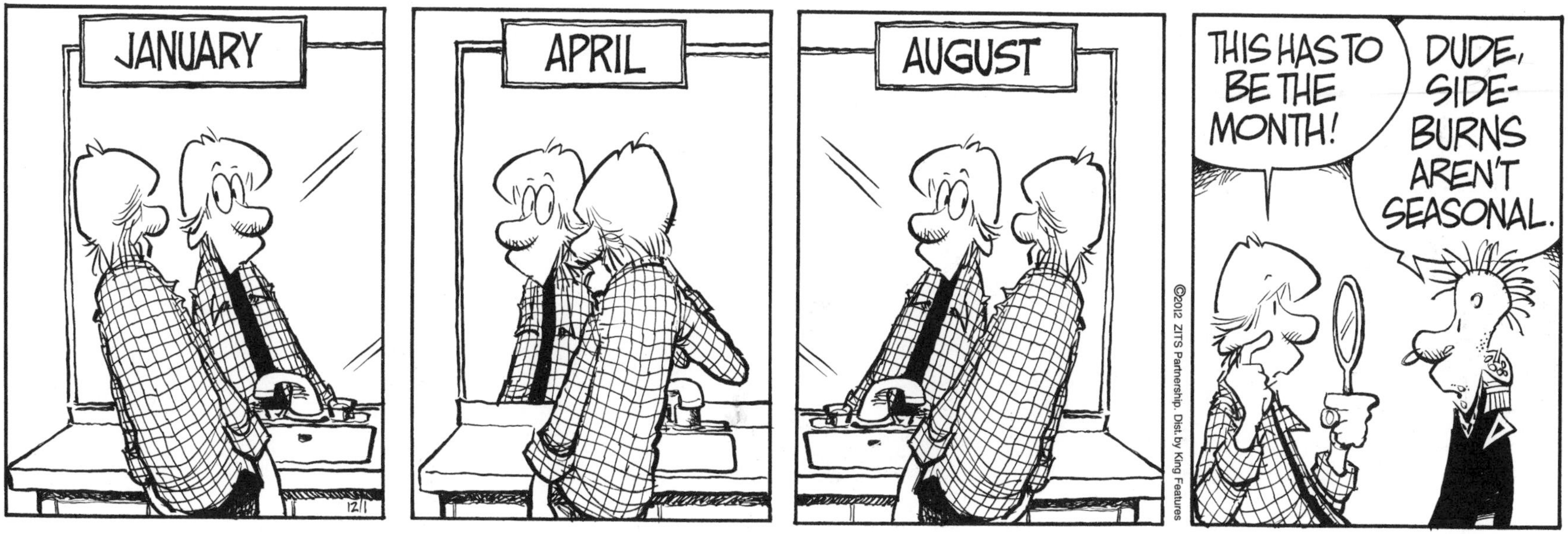
JANUARY
APRIL
AUGUST
THIS HAS TO BE THE MONTH!
DUDE, SIDE-BURNS AREN'T SEASONAL.
©2012 ZITS Partnership. Dist.by King Features

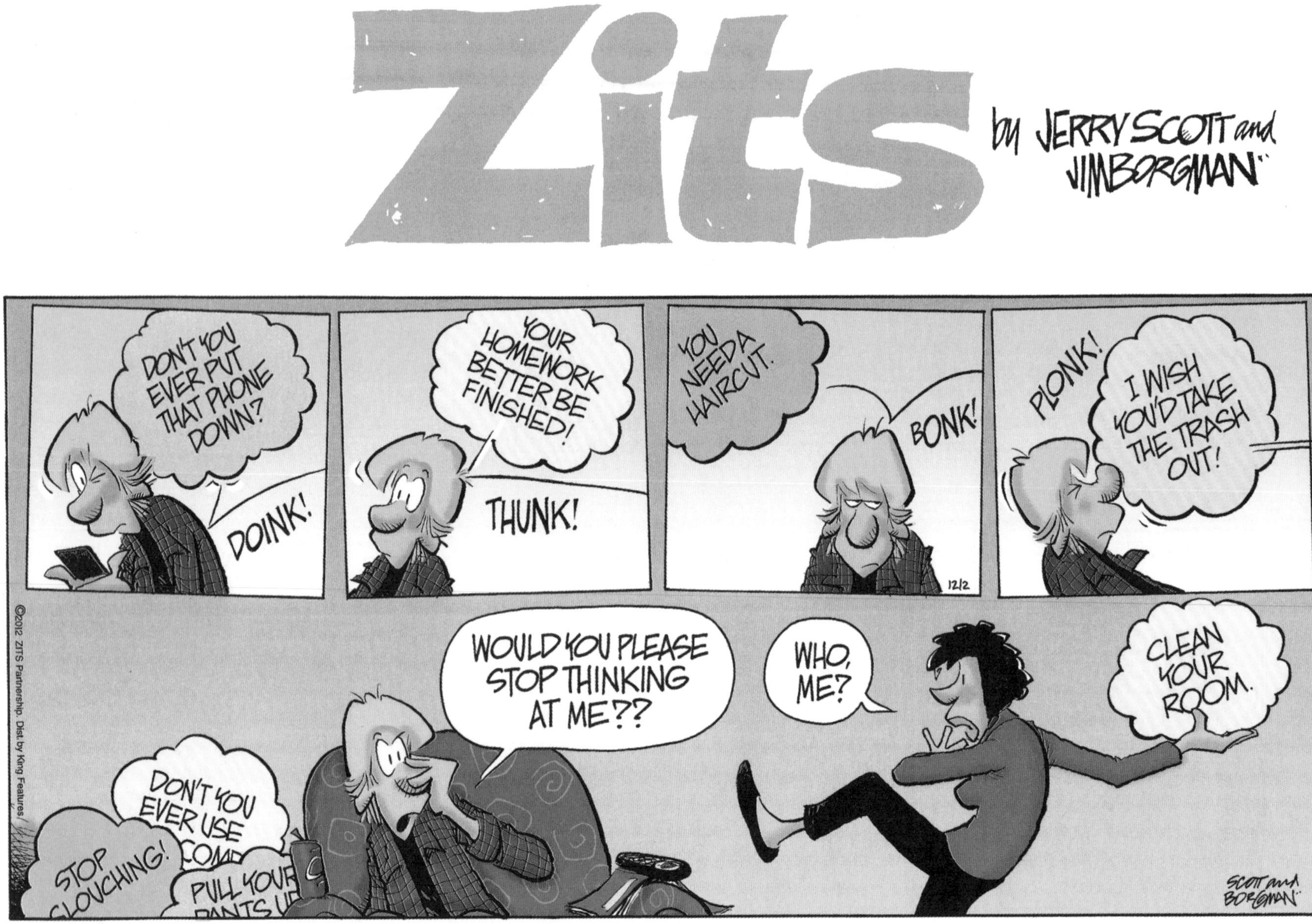
Zits
by JERRY SCOTT and JIM BORGMAN
DON'T YOU EVER PUT THAT PHONE DOWN?
DOINK!
YOUR HOMEWORK BETTER BE FINISHED!
THUNK!
YOU NEED A HAIRCUT.
BONK!
12/2
PLONK!
I WISH YOU'D TAKE THE TRASH OUT!
©2012 ZITS Partnership. Dist. by King Features
STOP SLOUCHING!
DON'T YOU EVER USE
PULL YOUR
WOULD YOU PLEASE STOP THINKING AT ME??
WHO, ME?
CLEAN YOUR ROOM.
SCOTT and BORGMAN

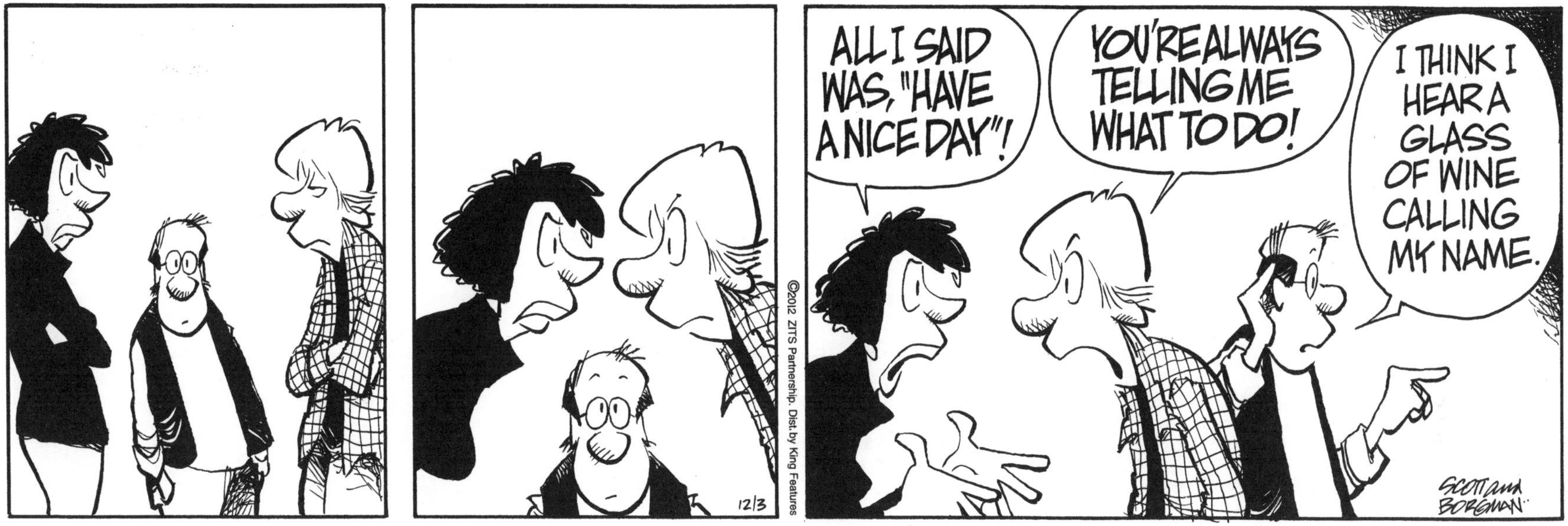
ALL I SAID WAS, "HAVE A NICE DAY"!
YOU'RE ALWAYS TELLING ME WHAT TO DO!
I THINK I HEAR A GLASS OF WINE CALLING MY NAME.
12/3
SCOTT and BORGMAN

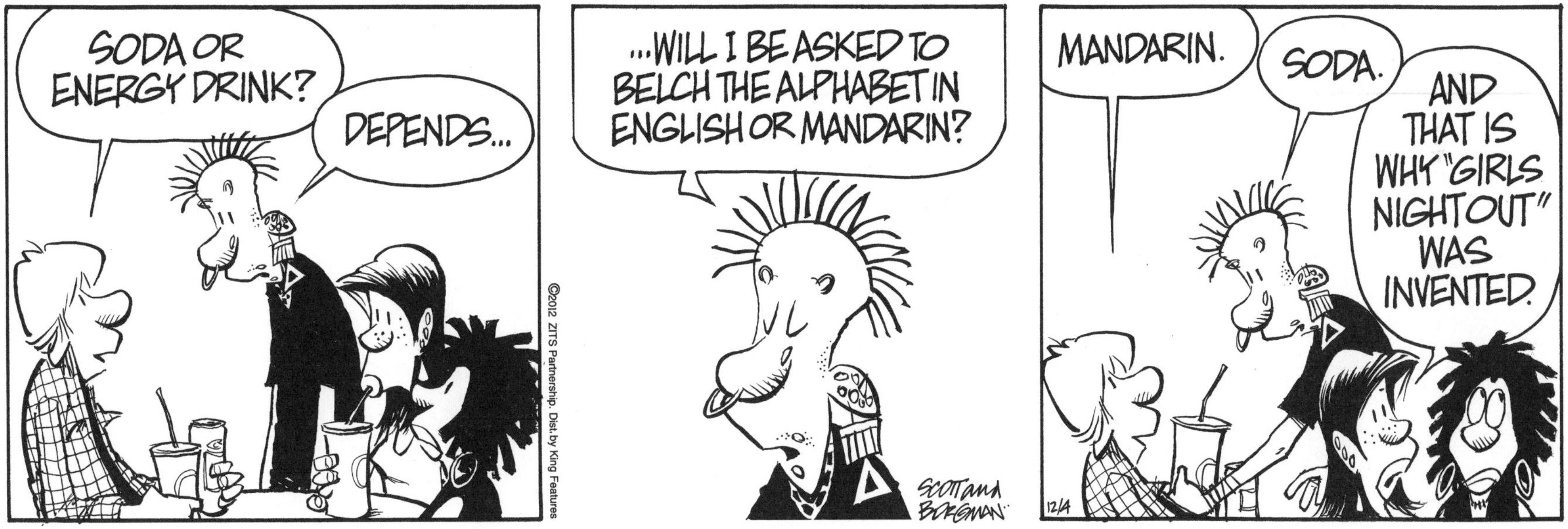
SODA OR ENERGY DRINK?
DEPENDS...
...WILL I BE ASKED TO BELCH THE ALPHABET IN ENGLISH OR MANDARIN?
MANDARIN.
SODA.
AND THAT IS WHY "GIRLS NIGHT OUT" WAS INVENTED.
12/4
SCOTT and BORGMAN

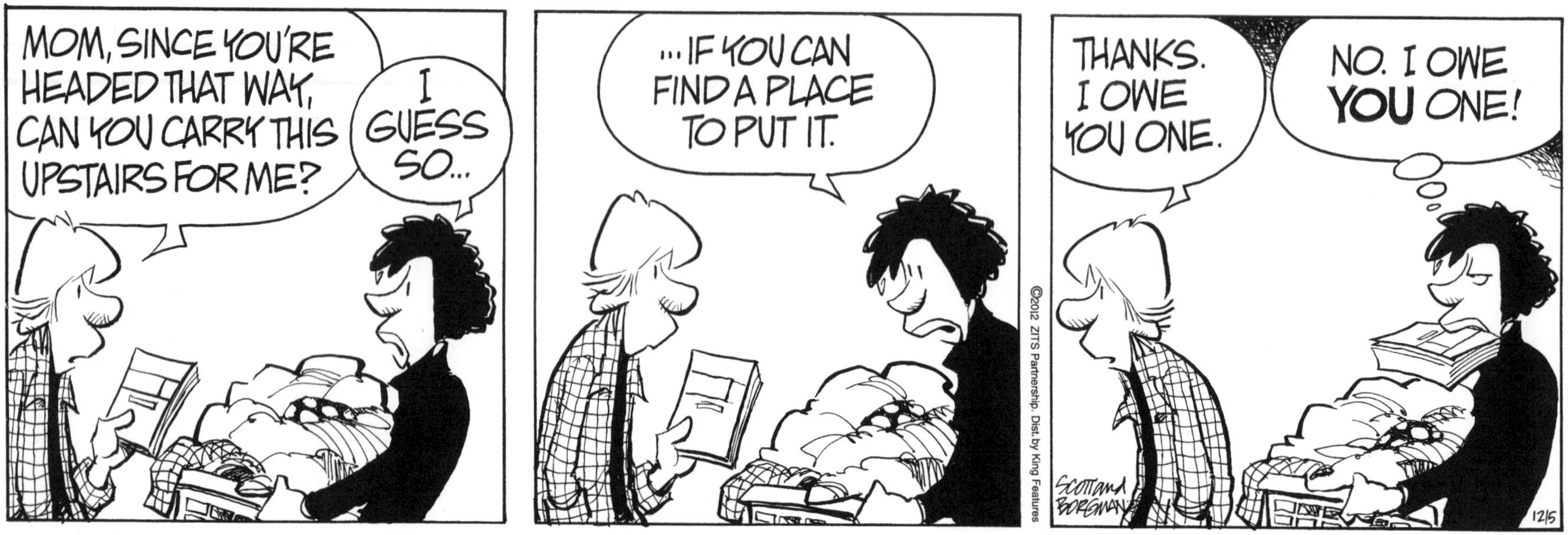
MOM, SINCE YOU'RE HEADED THAT WAY, CAN YOU CARRY THIS UPSTAIRS FOR ME?
I GUESS SO...
...IF YOU CAN FIND A PLACE TO PUT IT.
THANKS. I OWE YOU ONE.
NO. I OWE **YOU** ONE!
©2012 ZITS Partnership. Dist. by King Features
SCOTT and BORGMAN
12/5

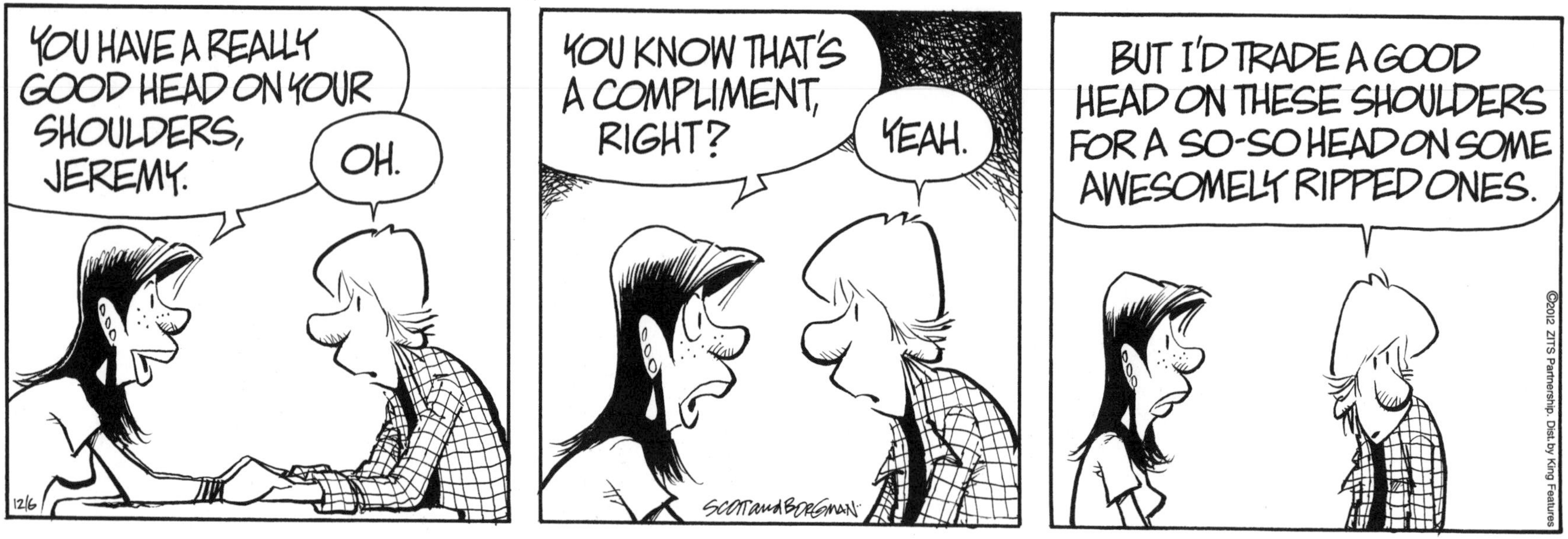
YOU HAVE A REALLY GOOD HEAD ON YOUR SHOULDERS, JEREMY.
OH.
12/6
YOU KNOW THAT'S A COMPLIMENT, RIGHT?
YEAH.
SCOTT and BORGMAN
BUT I'D TRADE A GOOD HEAD ON THESE SHOULDERS FOR A SO-SO HEAD ON SOME AWESOMELY RIPPED ONES.
©2012 ZITS Partnership. Dist. by King Features

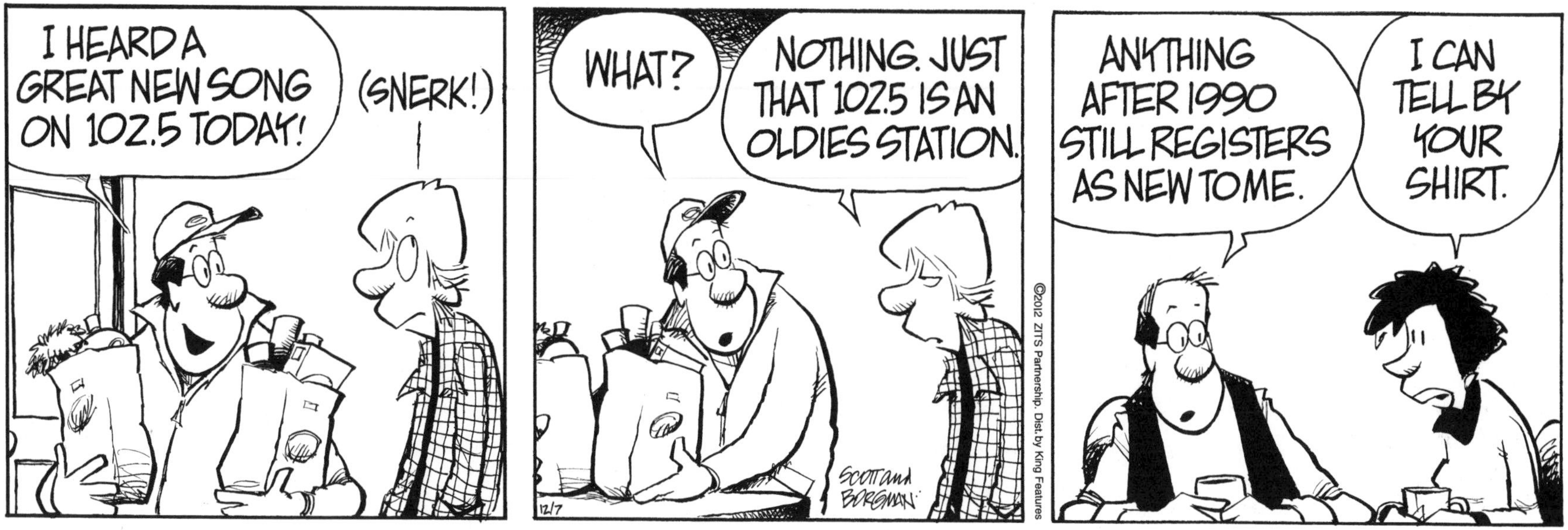
I HEARD A GREAT NEW SONG ON 102.5 TODAY!
(SNERK!)
WHAT?
NOTHING. JUST THAT 102.5 IS AN OLDIES STATION.
ANYTHING AFTER 1990 STILL REGISTERS AS NEW TO ME.
I CAN TELL BY YOUR SHIRT.
12/7
SCOTT and BORGMAN
©2012 ZITS Partnership. Dist. by King Features

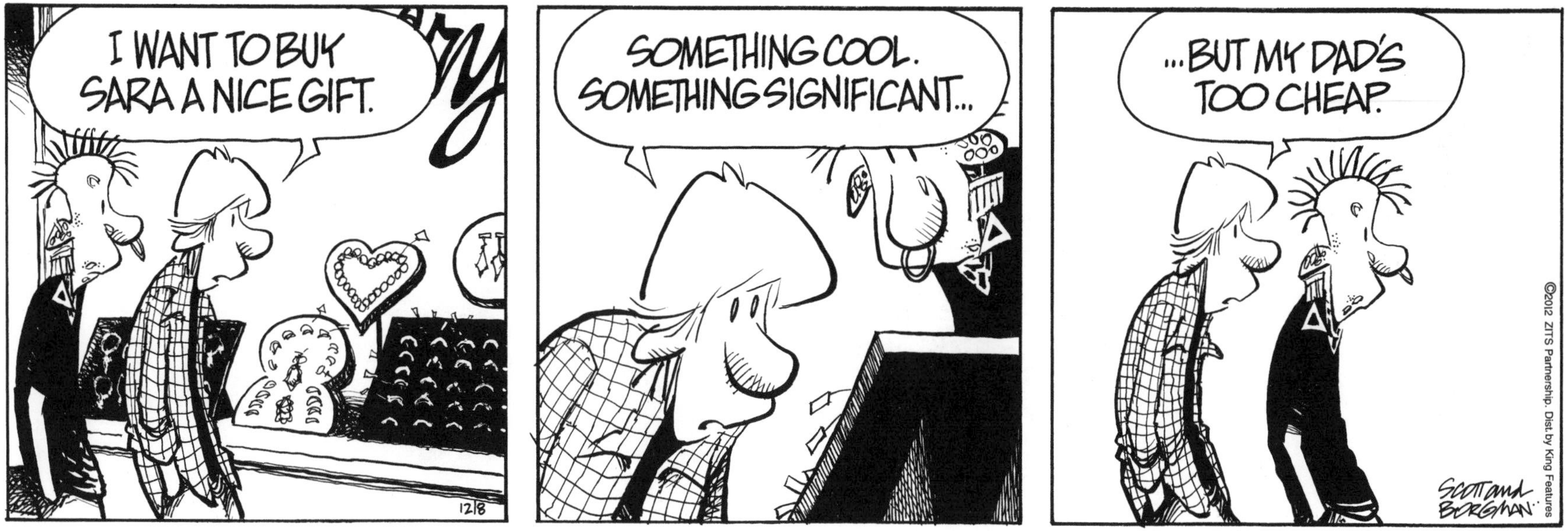
I WANT TO BUY SARA A NICE GIFT.
12/8
SOMETHING COOL. SOMETHING SIGNIFICANT...
...BUT MY DAD'S TOO CHEAP.
SCOTT and BORGMAN
©2012 ZITS Partnership. Dist. by King Features

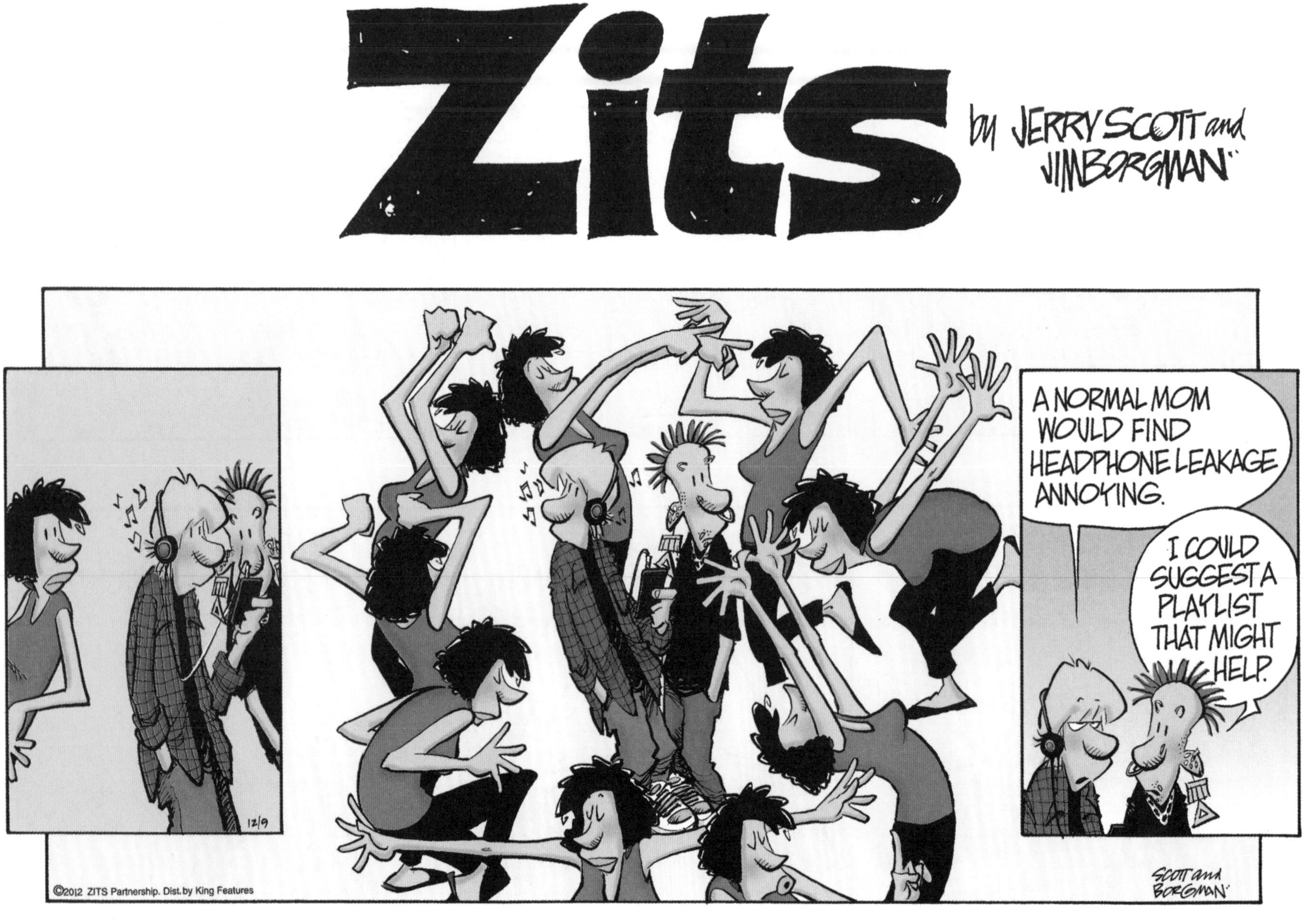
Zits
by JERRY SCOTT and JIM BORGMAN
12/9
A NORMAL MOM WOULD FIND HEADPHONE LEAKAGE ANNOYING.
I COULD SUGGEST A PLAYLIST THAT MIGHT HELP.
©2012 ZITS Partnership. Dist. by King Features
SCOTT and BORGMAN

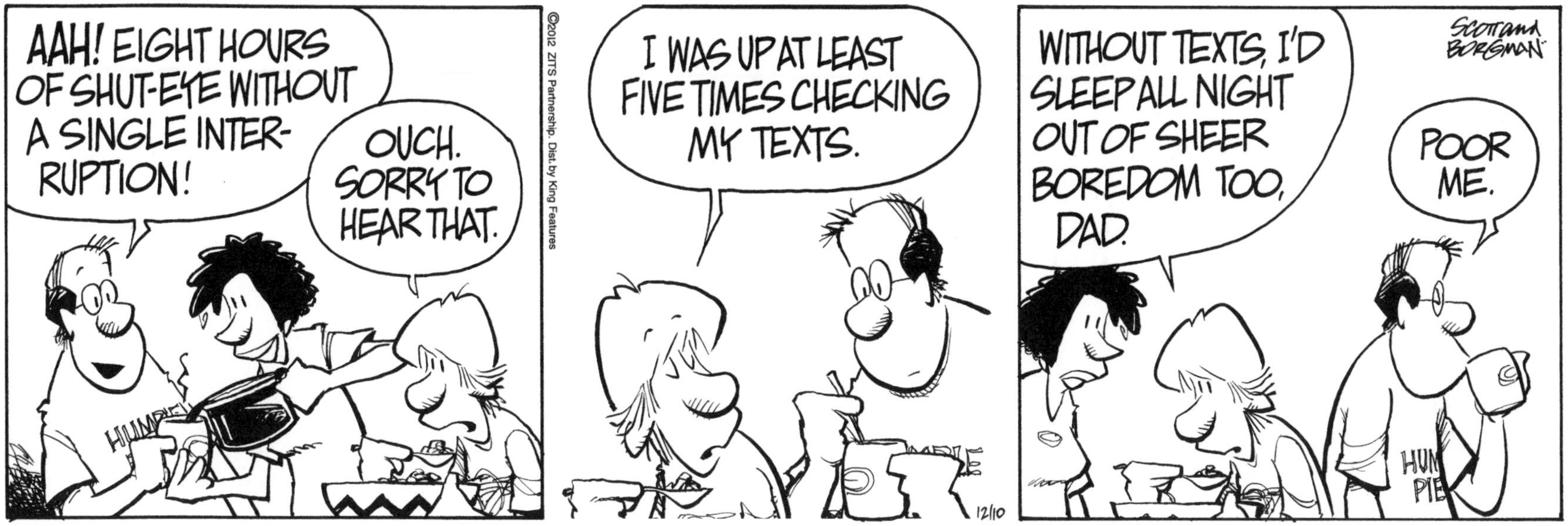
AAH! EIGHT HOURS OF SHUT-EYE WITHOUT A SINGLE INTER-RUPTION!
OUCH. SORRY TO HEAR THAT.
©2012 ZITS Partnership. Dist. by King Features
I WAS UP AT LEAST FIVE TIMES CHECKING MY TEXTS.
12/10
WITHOUT TEXTS, I'D SLEEP ALL NIGHT OUT OF SHEER BOREDOM TOO, DAD.
SCOTT and BORGMAN
POOR ME.

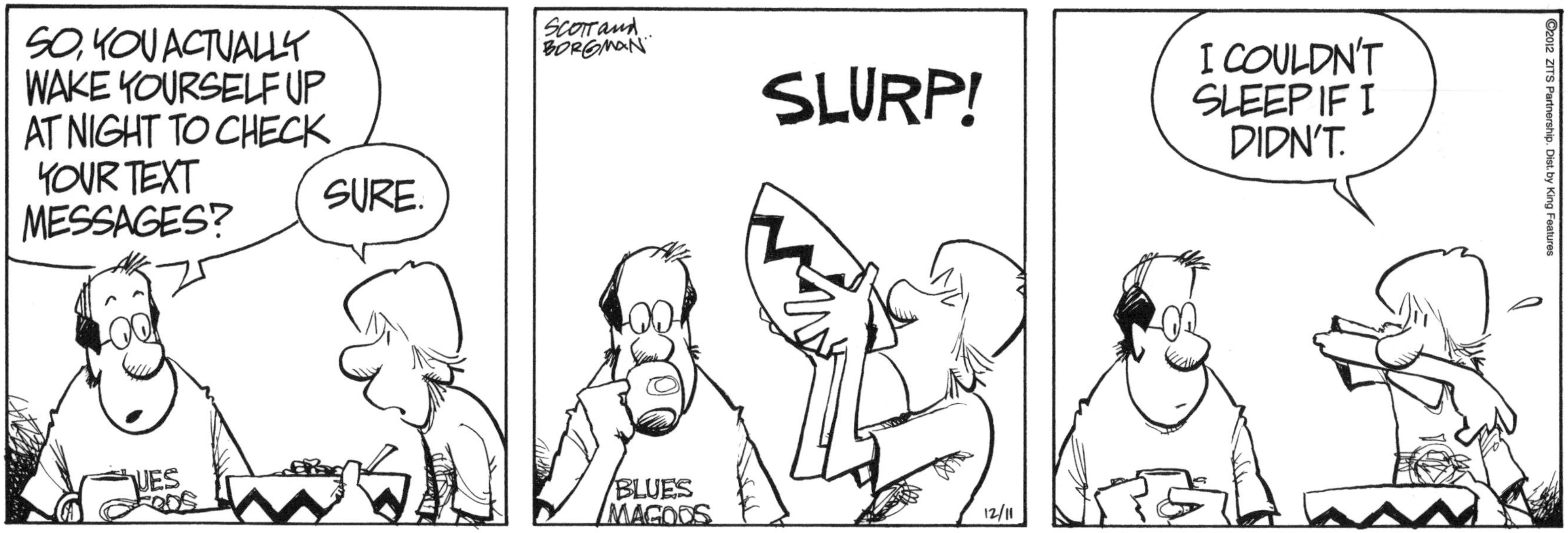
SO, YOU ACTUALLY WAKE YOURSELF UP AT NIGHT TO CHECK YOUR TEXT MESSAGES?
SURE.
SCOTT and BORGMAN
SLURP!
BLUES MAGOODS
12/11
I COULDN'T SLEEP IF I DIDN'T.
©2012 ZITS Partnership. Dist. by King Features

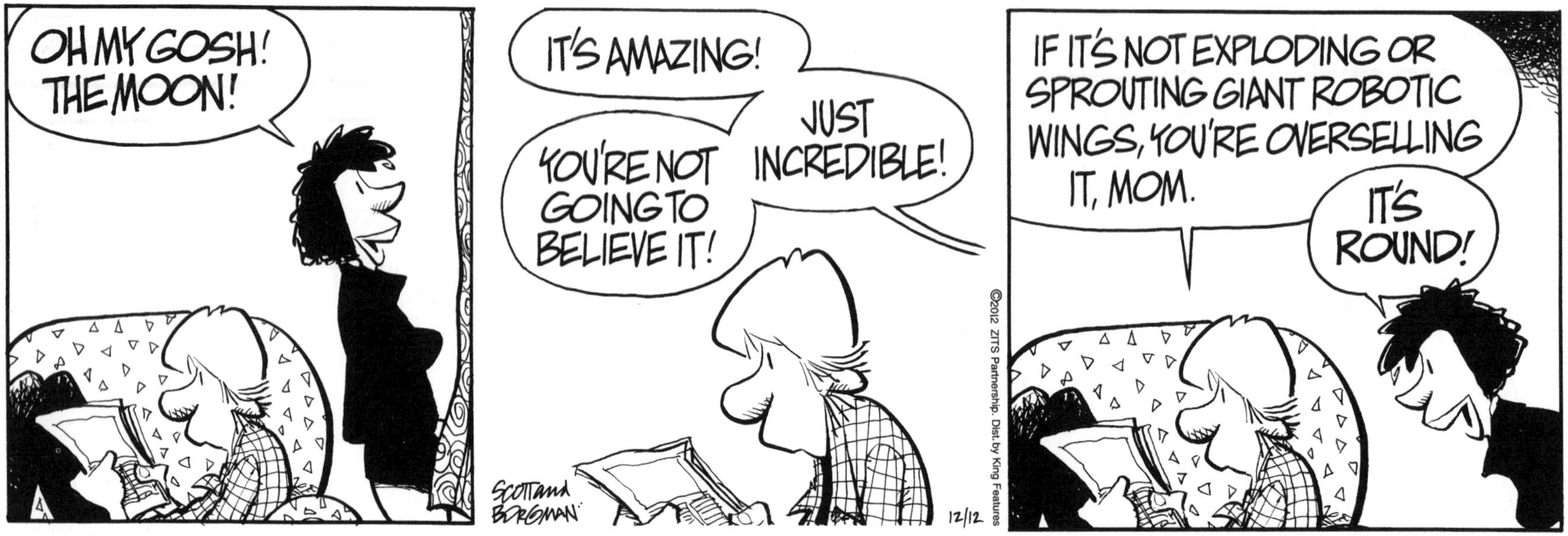
OH MY GOSH! THE MOON!
IT'S AMAZING!
YOU'RE NOT GOING TO BELIEVE IT!
JUST INCREDIBLE!
IF IT'S NOT EXPLODING OR SPROUTING GIANT ROBOTIC WINGS, YOU'RE OVERSELLING IT, MOM.
IT'S ROUND!
SCOTT AND BORGMAN
12/12
©2012 ZITS Partnership. Dist. by King Features

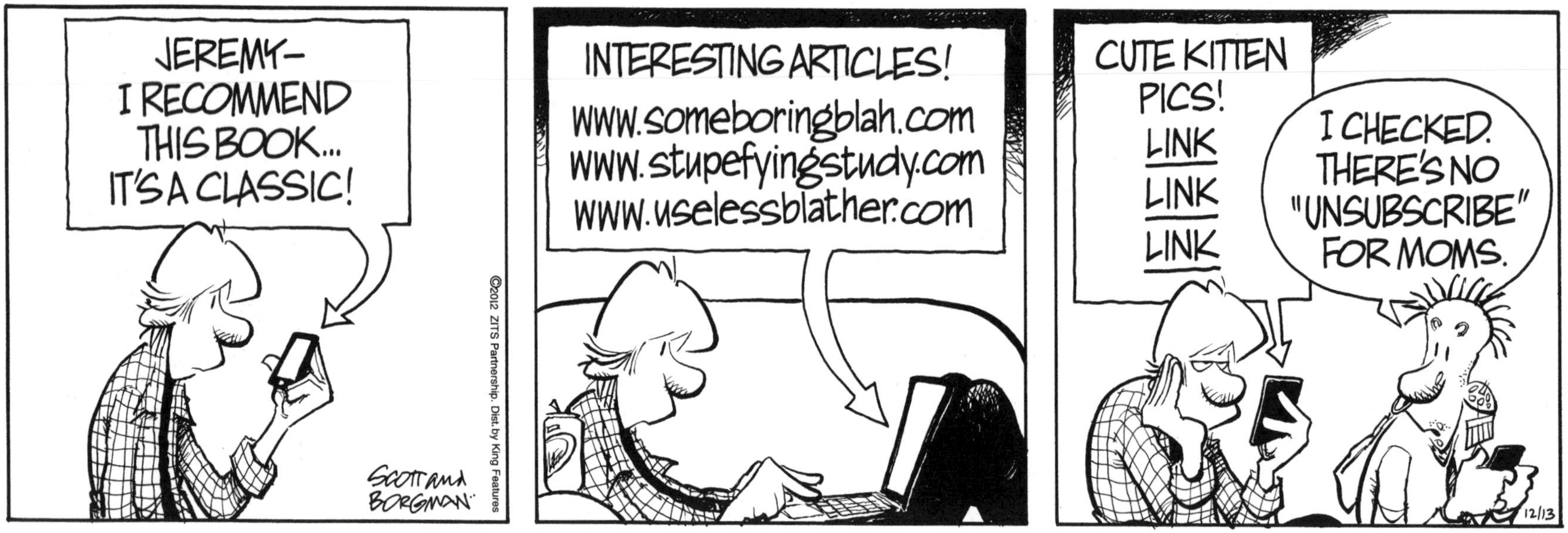
JEREMY— I RECOMMEND THIS BOOK... IT'S A CLASSIC!
INTERESTING ARTICLES!
WWW.SOMEBORINGBLAH.COM
WWW.STUPEFYINGSTUDY.COM
WWW.USELESSBLATHER.COM
CUTE KITTEN PICS!
LINK
LINK
LINK
I CHECKED. THERE'S NO "UNSUBSCRIBE" FOR MOMS.
SCOTT AND BORGMAN
12/13
©2012 ZITS Partnership. Dist. by King Features

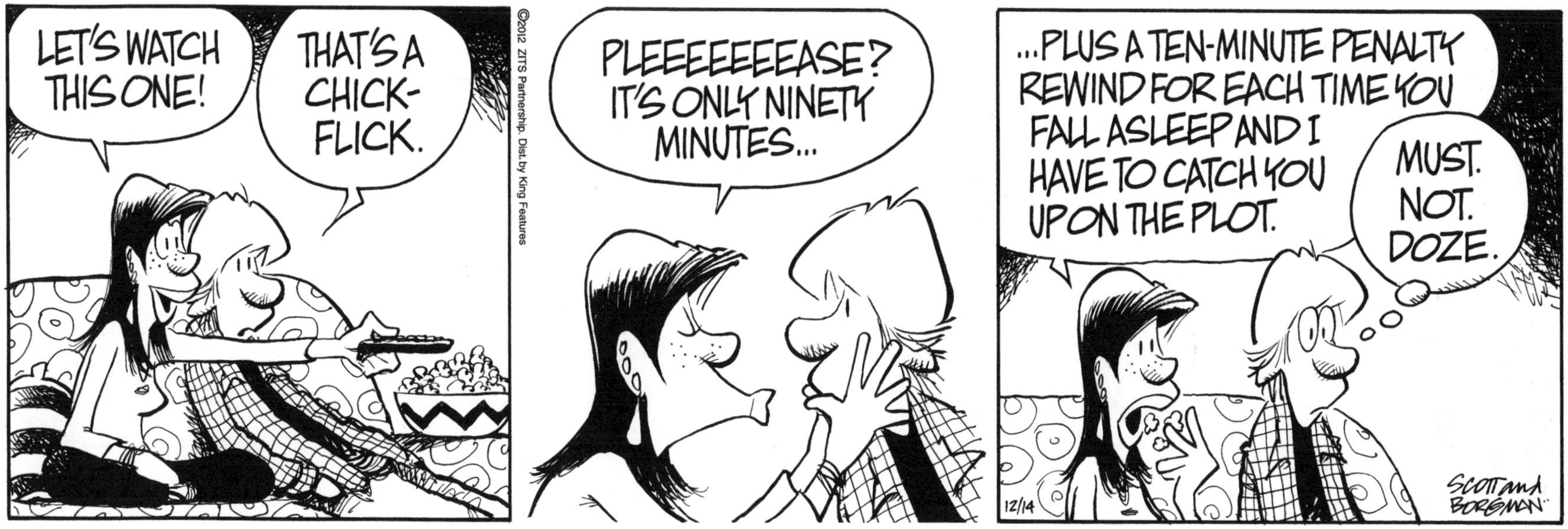
LET'S WATCH THIS ONE!
THAT'S A CHICK-FLICK.
©2012 ZITS Partnership. Dist. by King Features
PLEEEEEEEEASE? IT'S ONLY NINETY MINUTES...
...PLUS A TEN-MINUTE PENALTY REWIND FOR EACH TIME YOU FALL ASLEEP AND I HAVE TO CATCH YOU UP ON THE PLOT.
MUST. NOT. DOZE.
12/14
SCOTT AND BORGMAN

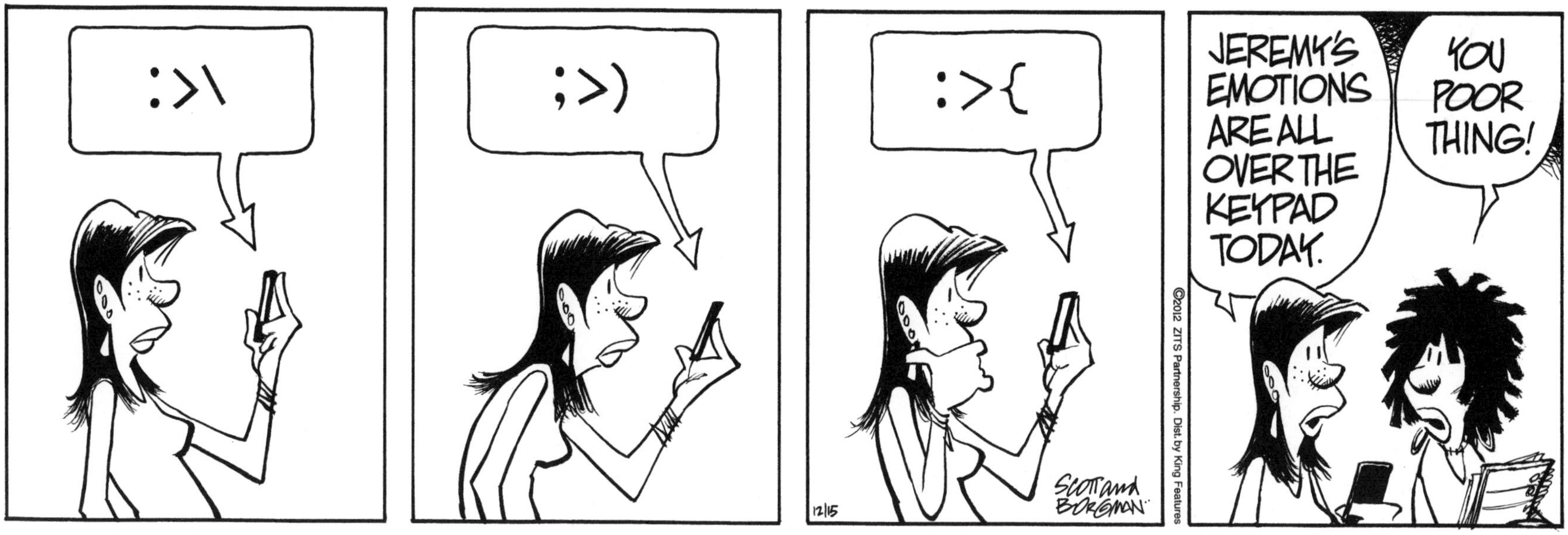
:>\
;>)
:>{
12/15
SCOTT AND BORGMAN
©2012 ZITS Partnership. Dist. by King Features
JEREMY'S EMOTIONS ARE ALL OVER THE KEYPAD TODAY.
YOU POOR THING!

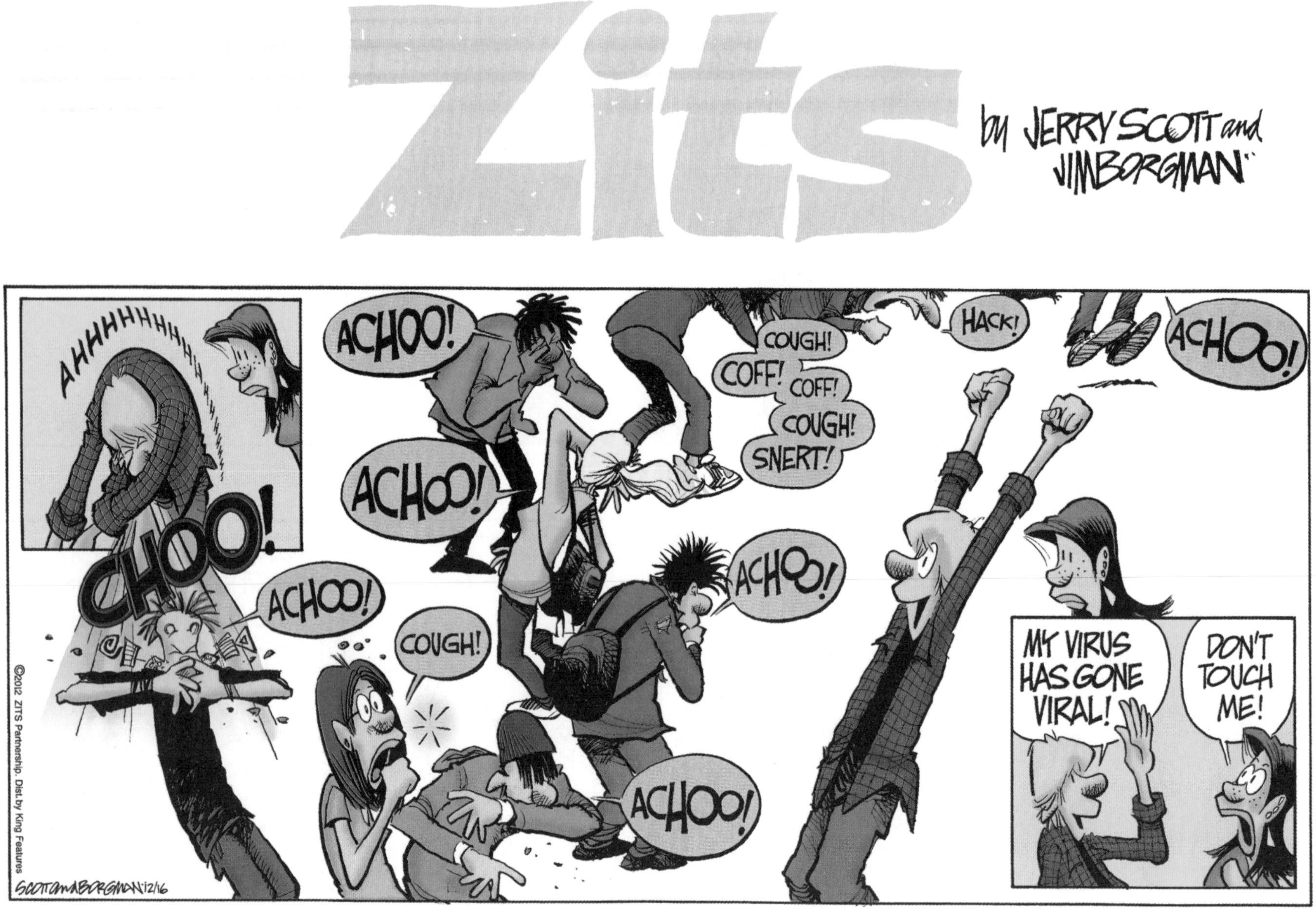

Zits
by JERRY SCOTT and JIM BORGMAN
AHHHHHHHHHHHHHHHHH
CHOO!
ACHOO!
COUGH!
ACHOO!
ACHOO!
COUGH!
COFF!
COFF!
COUGH!
SNERT!
HACK!
ACHOO!
ACHOO!
ACHOO!
MY VIRUS HAS GONE VIRAL!
DON'T TOUCH ME!
©2012 ZITS Partnership. Dist. by King Features
SCOTTandBORGMAN 12/16

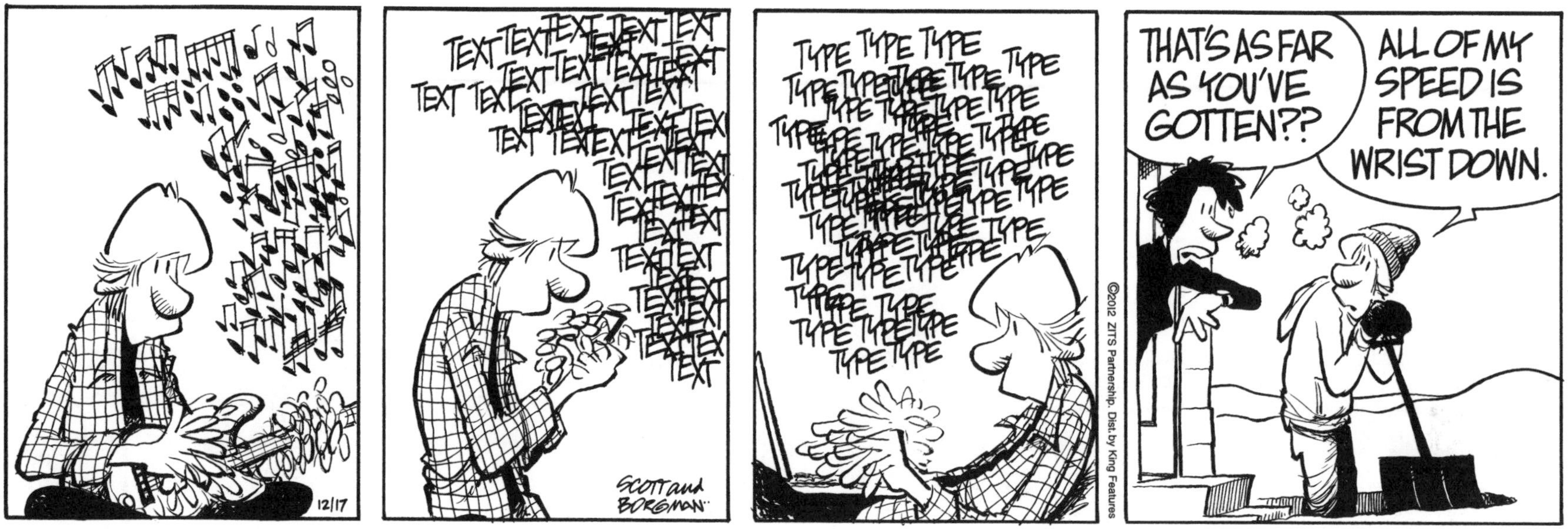
THAT'S AS FAR AS YOU'VE GOTTEN??
ALL OF MY SPEED IS FROM THE WRIST DOWN.

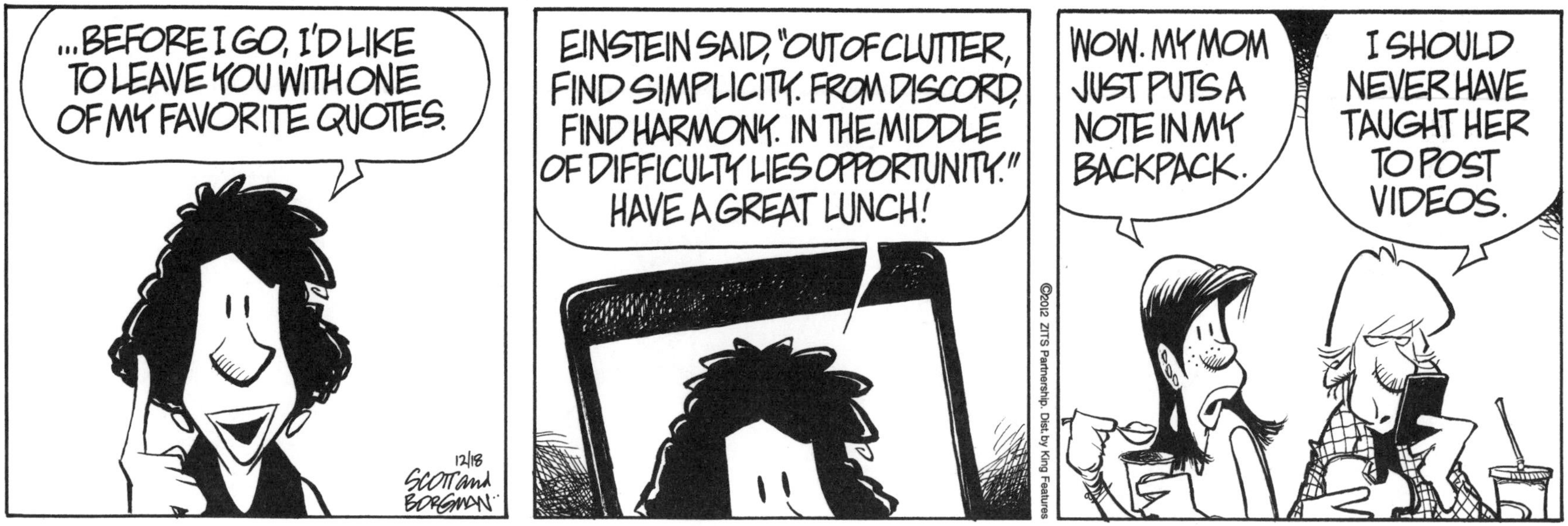
...BEFORE I GO, I'D LIKE TO LEAVE YOU WITH ONE OF MY FAVORITE QUOTES.
EINSTEIN SAID, "OUT OF CLUTTER, FIND SIMPLICITY. FROM DISCORD, FIND HARMONY. IN THE MIDDLE OF DIFFICULTY LIES OPPORTUNITY." HAVE A GREAT LUNCH!
WOW. MY MOM JUST PUTS A NOTE IN MY BACKPACK.
I SHOULD NEVER HAVE TAUGHT HER TO POST VIDEOS.

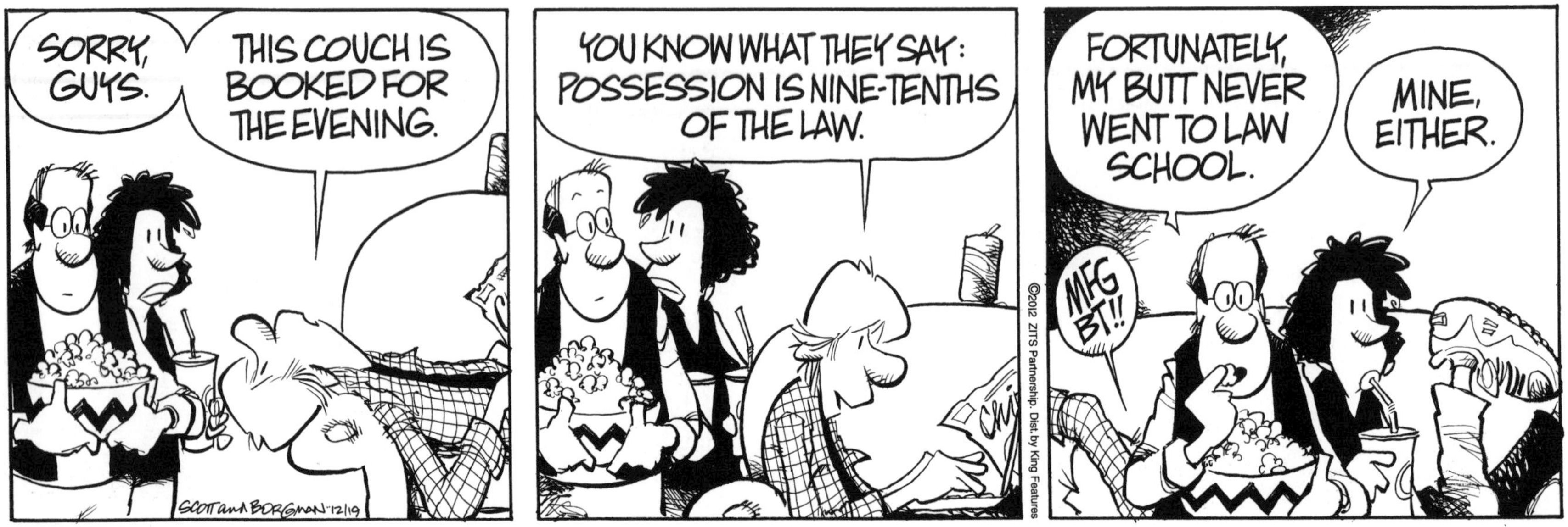
SORRY, GUYS.
THIS COUCH IS BOOKED FOR THE EVENING.
SCOTT and BORGMAN 12/19
YOU KNOW WHAT THEY SAY: POSSESSION IS NINE-TENTHS OF THE LAW.
©2012 ZITS Partnership. Dist. by King Features
FORTUNATELY, MY BUTT NEVER WENT TO LAW SCHOOL.
MFG BT!!
MINE, EITHER.

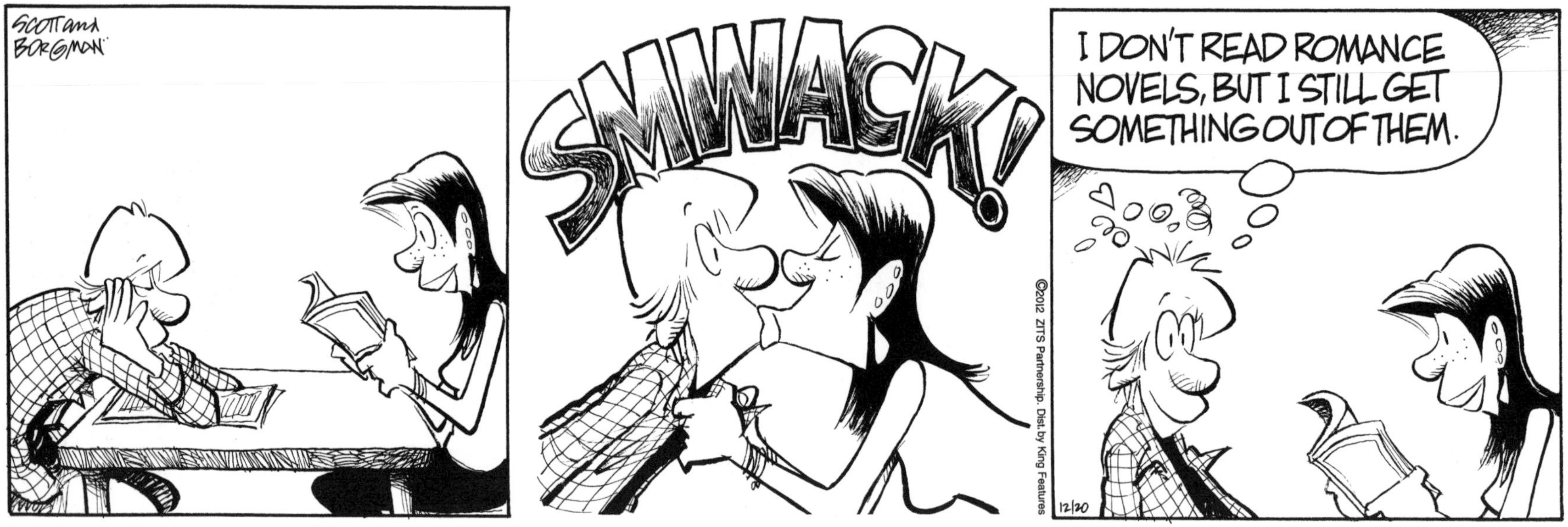
SCOTT and BORGMAN
SMWACK!
©2012 ZITS Partnership. Dist. by King Features
12/20
I DON'T READ ROMANCE NOVELS, BUT I STILL GET SOMETHING OUT OF THEM.

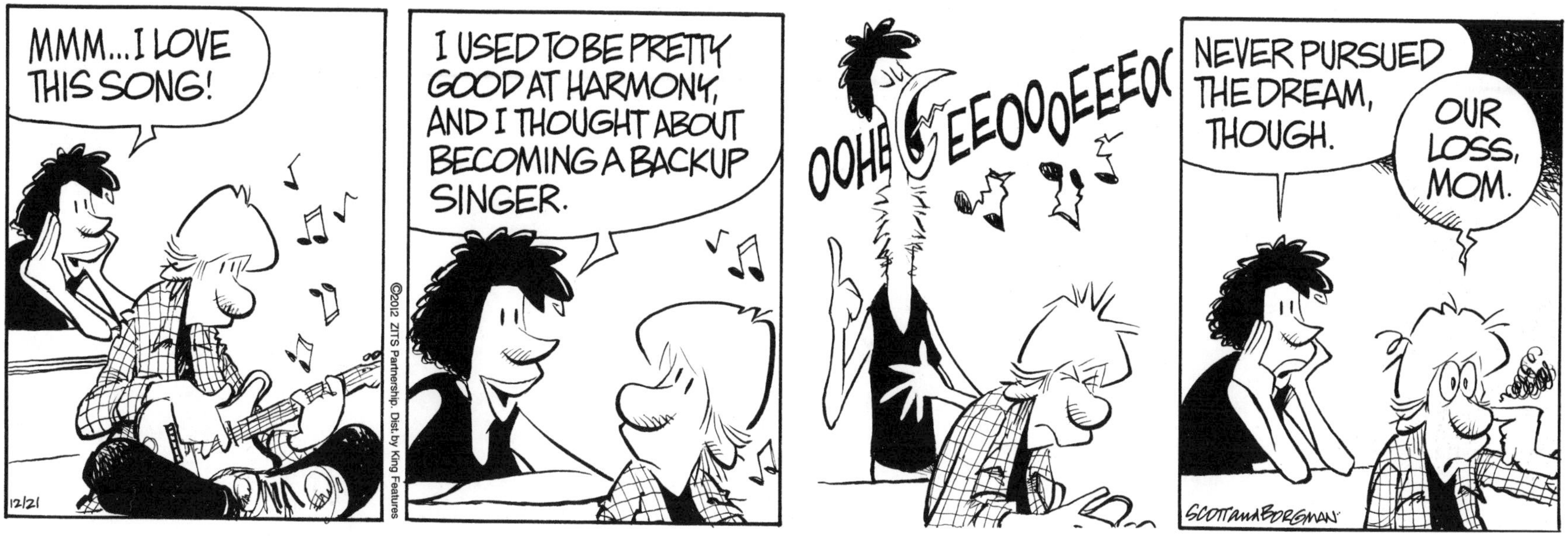
MMM...I LOVE THIS SONG!
I USED TO BE PRETTY GOOD AT HARMONY, AND I THOUGHT ABOUT BECOMING A BACKUP SINGER.
OOHEEEEOOOEEEOO
NEVER PURSUED THE DREAM, THOUGH.
OUR LOSS, MOM.
©2012 ZITS Partnership. Dist. by King Features
12/21
SCOTT and BORGMAN

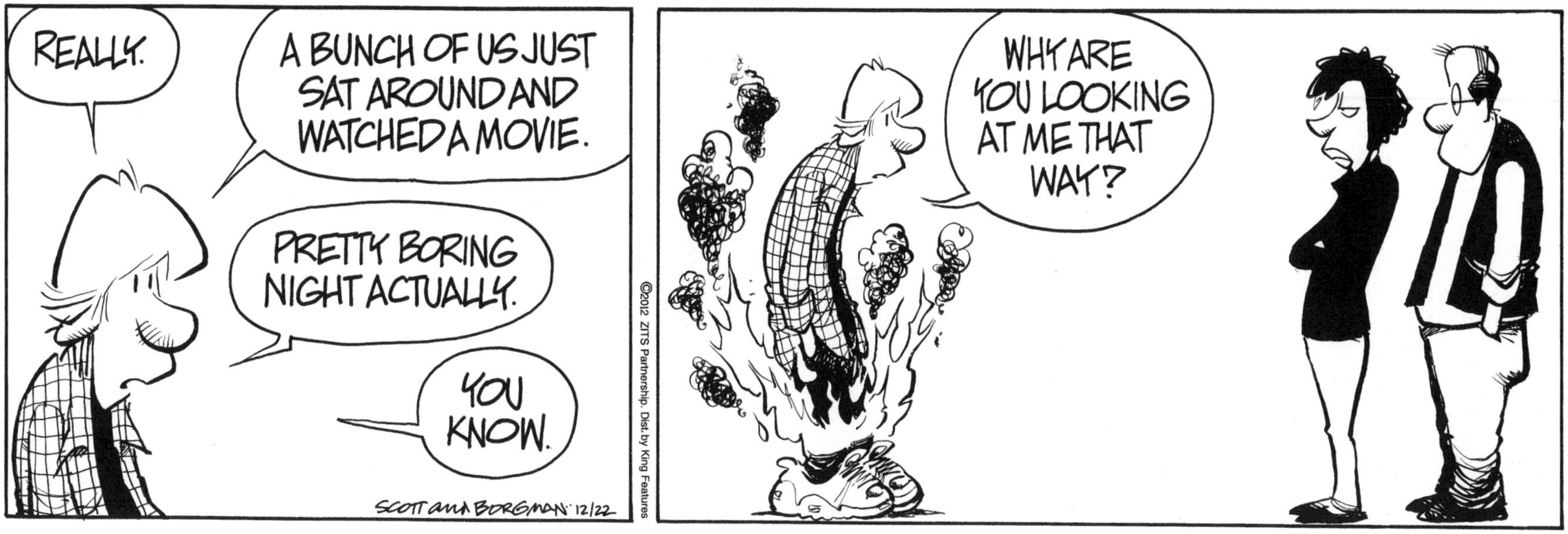
REALLY.
A BUNCH OF US JUST SAT AROUND AND WATCHED A MOVIE.
PRETTY BORING NIGHT ACTUALLY.
YOU KNOW.
SCOTT and BORGMAN 12/22
©2012 ZITS Partnership. Dist. by King Features
WHY ARE YOU LOOKING AT ME THAT WAY?

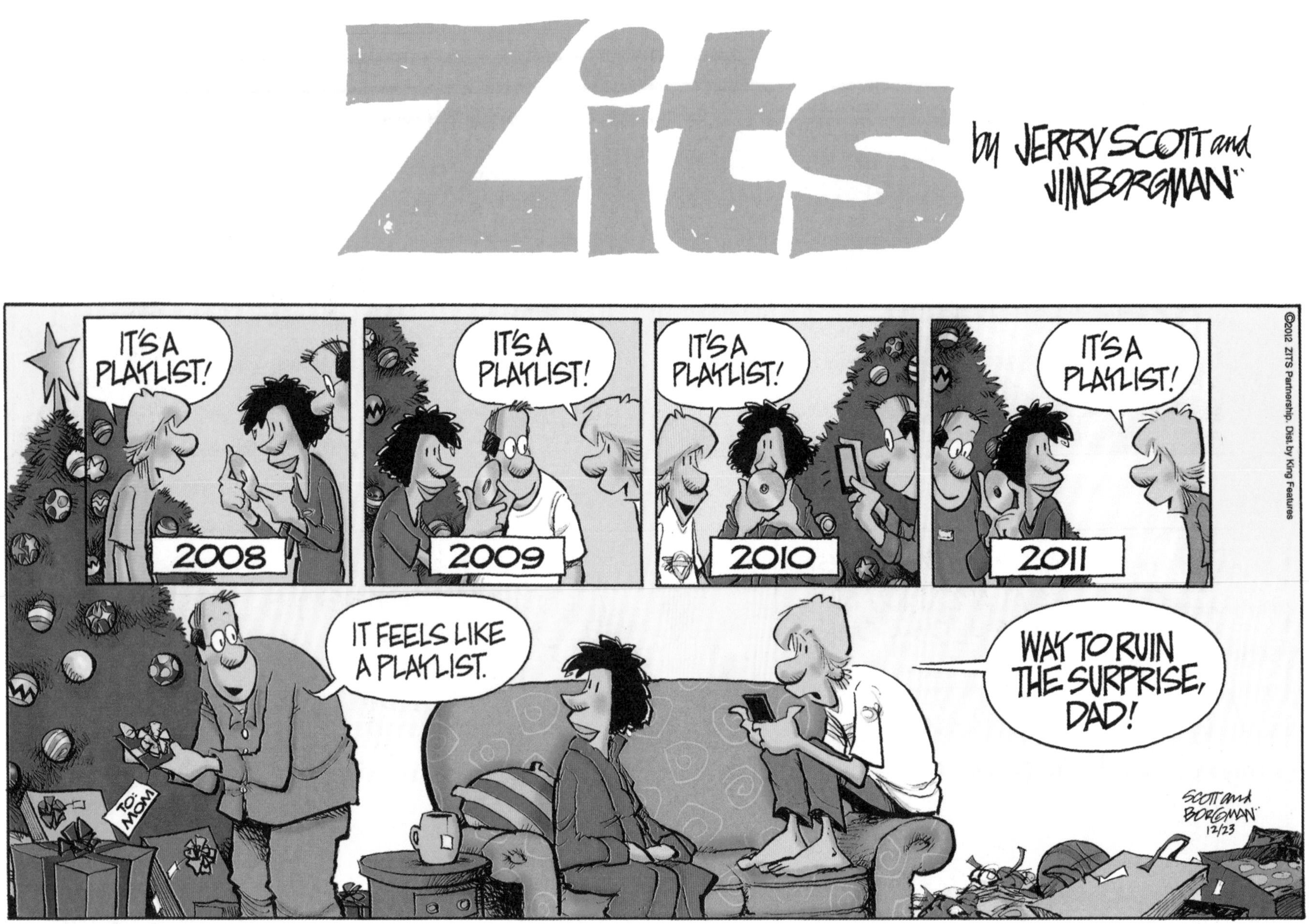
Zits
by JERRY SCOTT and JIM BORGMAN
IT'S A PLAYLIST!
2008
IT'S A PLAYLIST!
2009
IT'S A PLAYLIST!
2010
IT'S A PLAYLIST!
2011
©2012 ZITS Partnership. Dist. by King Features
IT FEELS LIKE A PLAYLIST.
WAY TO RUIN THE SURPRISE, DAD!
TO: MOM
SCOTT and BORGMAN 12/23

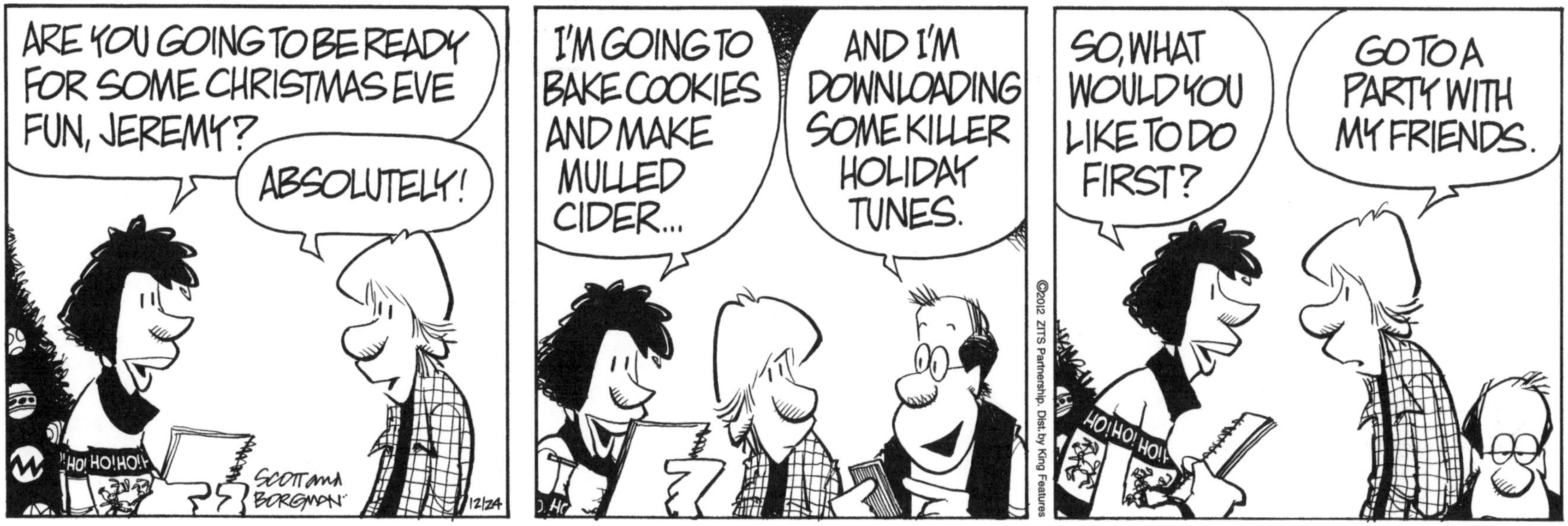
ARE YOU GOING TO BE READY FOR SOME CHRISTMAS EVE FUN, JEREMY?
ABSOLUTELY!
HO! HO! HO!
SCOTT and BORGMAN
12/24
I'M GOING TO BAKE COOKIES AND MAKE MULLED CIDER...
AND I'M DOWNLOADING SOME KILLER HOLIDAY TUNES.
©2012 ZITS Partnership. Dist. by King Features
SO, WHAT WOULD YOU LIKE TO DO FIRST?
GO TO A PARTY WITH MY FRIENDS.
HO! HO! HO!

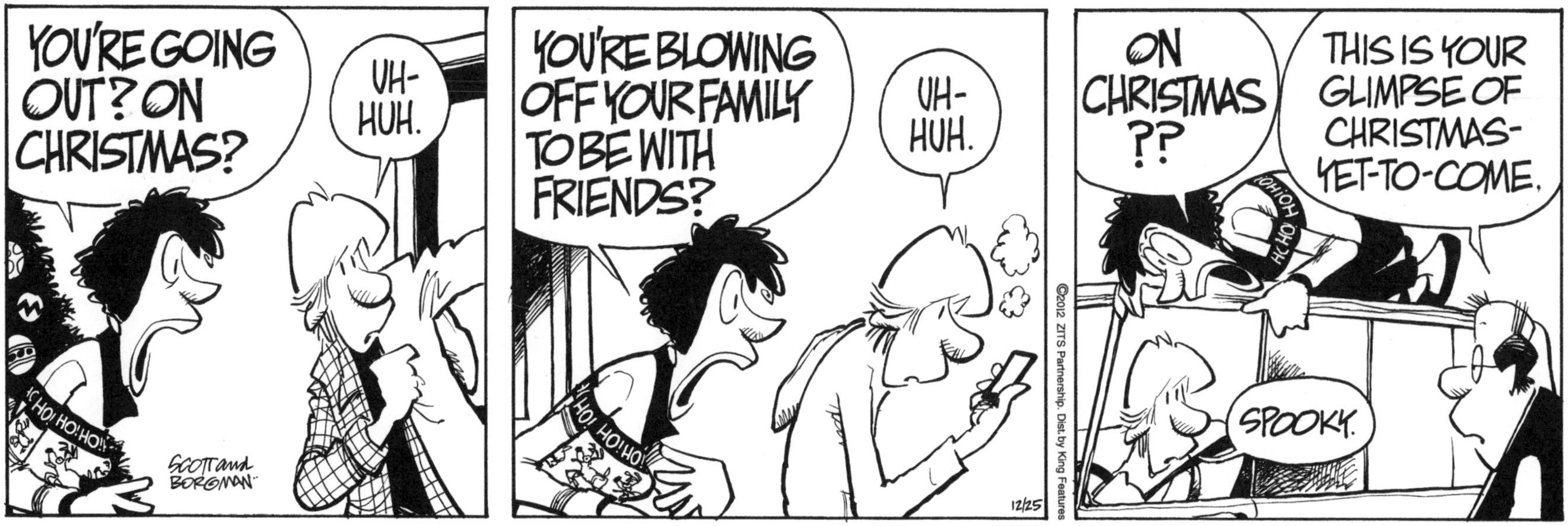
YOU'RE GOING OUT? ON CHRISTMAS?
UH-HUH.
HO! HO! HO!
SCOTT and BORGMAN
YOU'RE BLOWING OFF YOUR FAMILY TO BE WITH FRIENDS?
UH-HUH.
HO! HO! HO!
12/25
©2012 ZITS Partnership. Dist. by King Features
ON CHRISTMAS??
THIS IS YOUR GLIMPSE OF CHRISTMAS-YET-TO-COME.
HO! HO! HO!
SPOOKY.

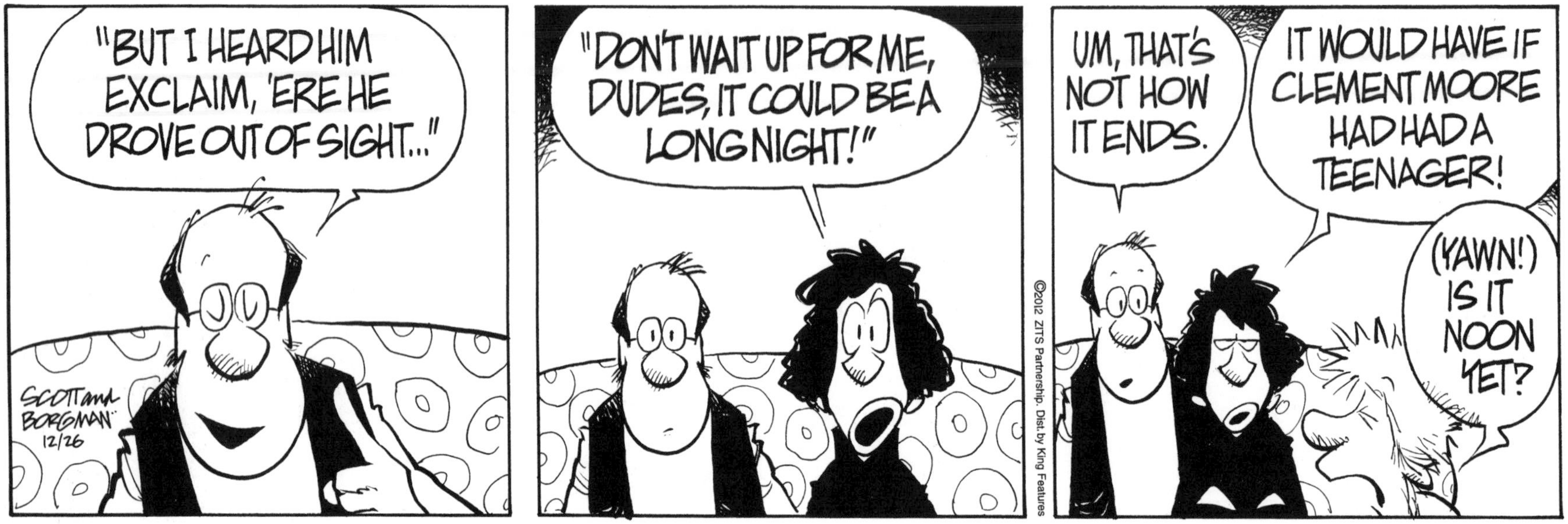
"BUT I HEARD HIM EXCLAIM, 'ERE HE DROVE OUT OF SIGHT..."
SCOTT and BORGMAN 12/26
"DON'T WAIT UP FOR ME, DUDES, IT COULD BE A LONG NIGHT!"
©2012 ZITS Partnership. Dist. by King Features
UM, THAT'S NOT HOW IT ENDS.
IT WOULD HAVE IF CLEMENT MOORE HAD HAD A TEENAGER!
(YAWN!) IS IT NOON YET?

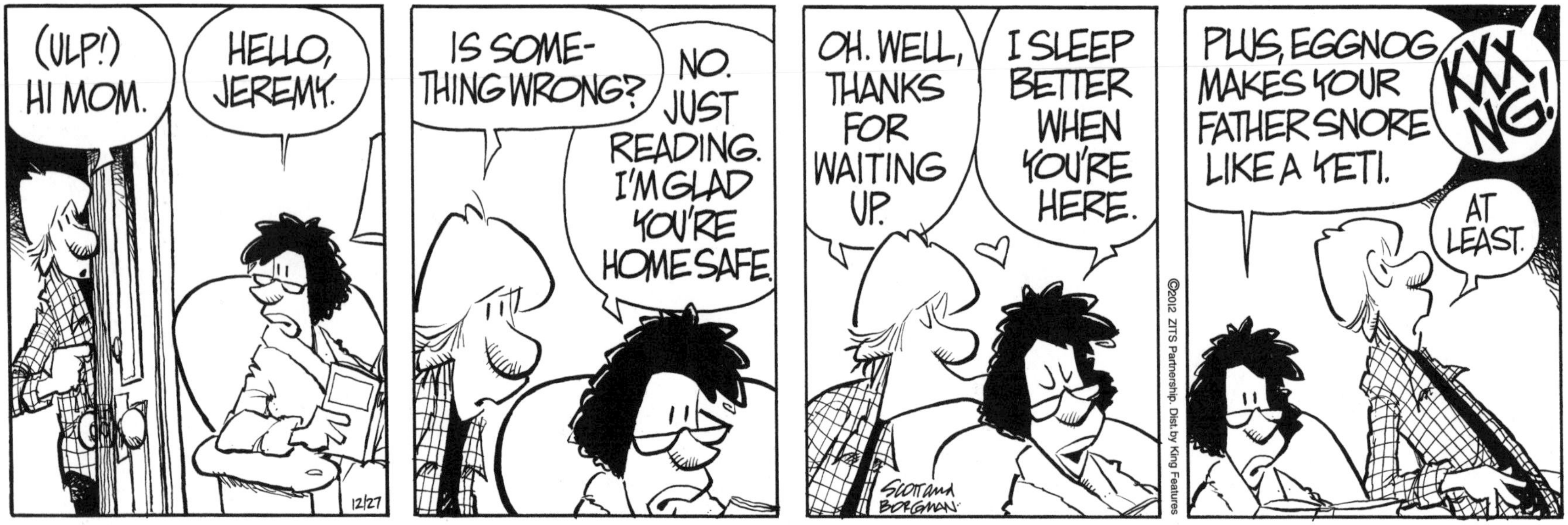
(ULP!) HI MOM.
HELLO, JEREMY.
12/27
IS SOMETHING WRONG?
NO. JUST READING. I'M GLAD YOU'RE HOME SAFE.
OH. WELL, THANKS FOR WAITING UP.
I SLEEP BETTER WHEN YOU'RE HERE.
SCOTT and BORGMAN
©2012 ZITS Partnership. Dist. by King Features
PLUS, EGGNOG MAKES YOUR FATHER SNORE LIKE A YETI.
KXXNG!
AT LEAST.

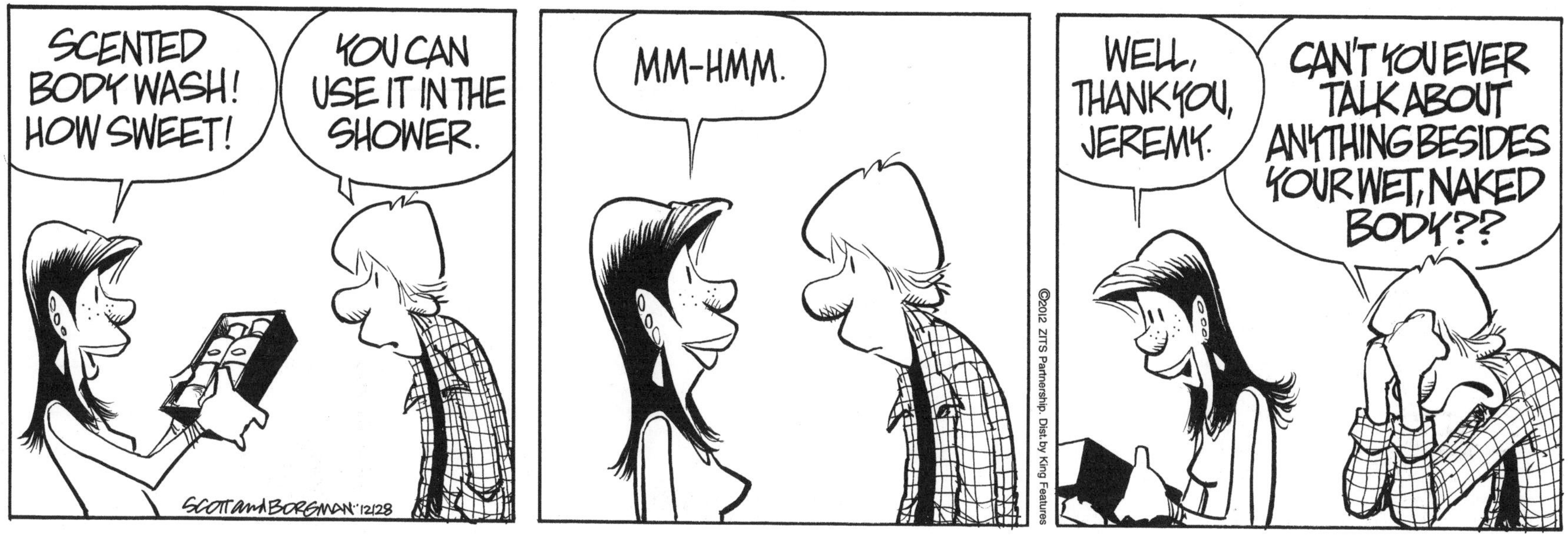
SCENTED BODY WASH! HOW SWEET!
YOU CAN USE IT IN THE SHOWER.
SCOTT and BORGMAN 12/28
MM-HMM.
©2012 ZITS Partnership. Dist. by King Features
WELL, THANK YOU, JEREMY.
CAN'T YOU EVER TALK ABOUT ANYTHING BESIDES YOUR WET, NAKED BODY??

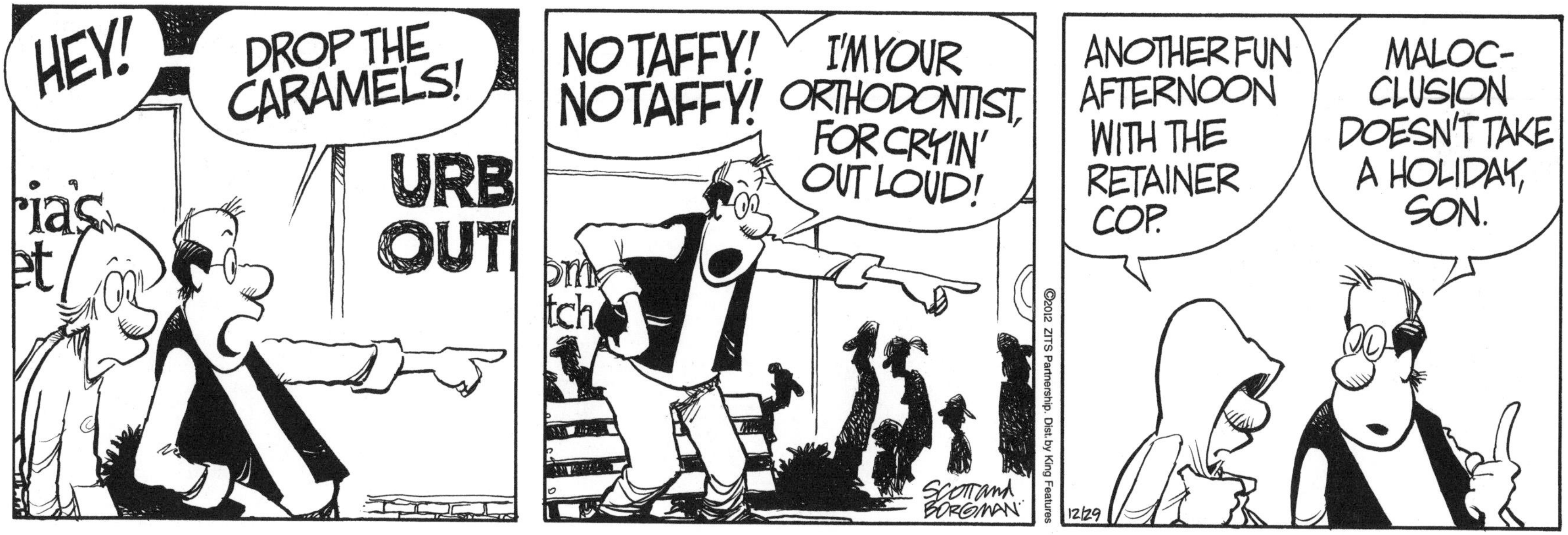
HEY!
DROP THE CARAMELS!
NO TAFFY! NO TAFFY!
I'M YOUR ORTHODONTIST, FOR CRYIN' OUT LOUD!
SCOTT and BORGMAN
©2012 ZITS Partnership. Dist. by King Features
ANOTHER FUN AFTERNOON WITH THE RETAINER COP.
MALOC-CLUSION DOESN'T TAKE A HOLIDAY, SON.
12/29

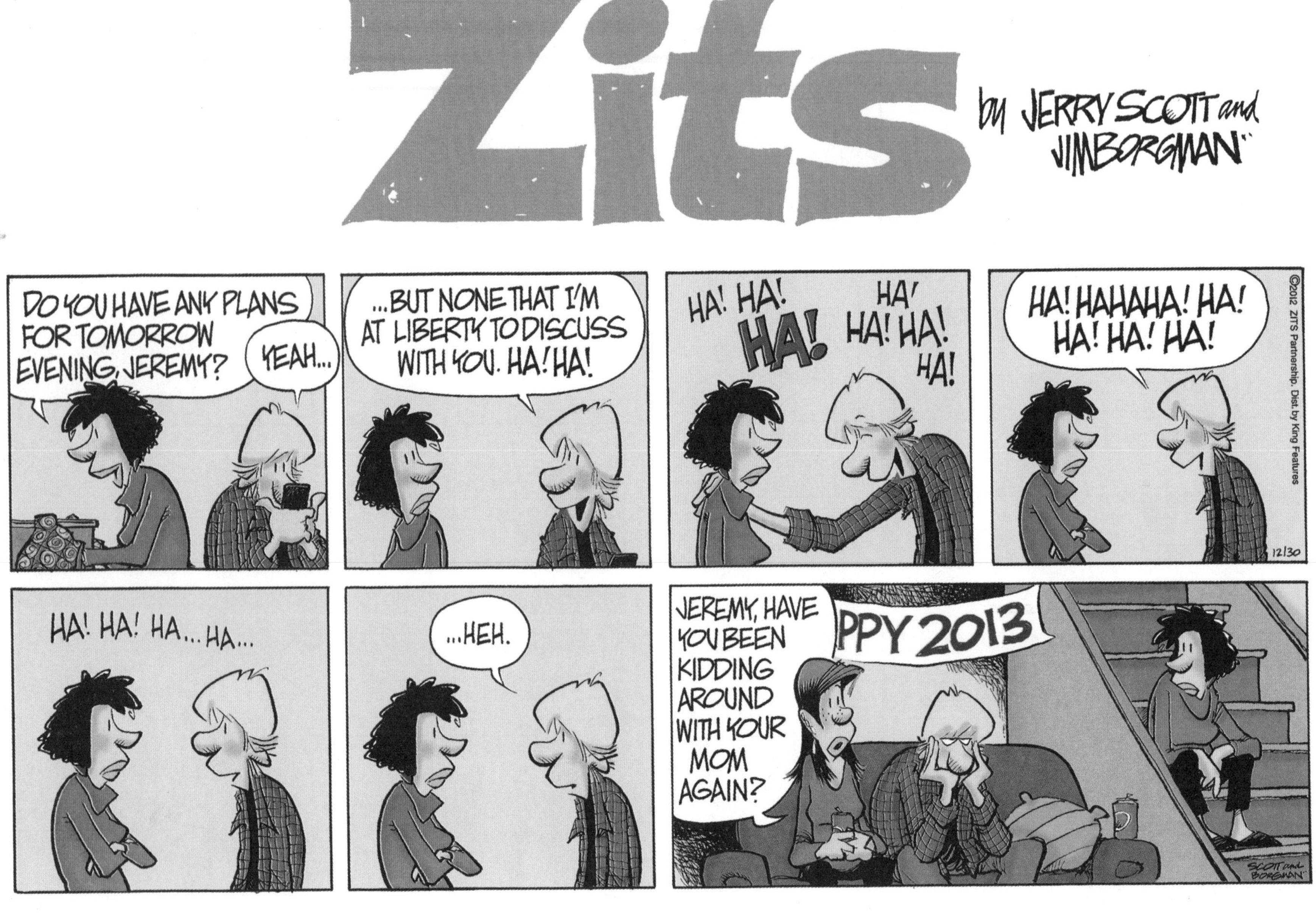
Zits
by JERRY SCOTT and JIM BORGMAN
DO YOU HAVE ANY PLANS FOR TOMORROW EVENING, JEREMY?
YEAH...
...BUT NONE THAT I'M AT LIBERTY TO DISCUSS WITH YOU. HA! HA!
HA! HA!
HA!
HA! HA! HA! HA!
HA! HAHAHA! HA! HA! HA! HA!
©2012 ZITS Partnership. Dist. by King Features
12/30
HA! HA! HA... HA...
...HEH.
JEREMY, HAVE YOU BEEN KIDDING AROUND WITH YOUR MOM AGAIN?
PPY 2013
SCOTT and BORGMAN